nouvelles femmes

MODERN WOMEN of the FRENCH NEW WAVE
and Their Enduring Contribution to Cinema

ERICKA KNUDSON

CHRONICLE CHROMA

To my mother,
To Laurence Schifano,
To Anna Karina,

Women who inspired this book through their strength, style,
intellect, humor, and their joie de vivre.

À ma mère,
À Laurence Schifano,
À Anna Karina,

Des femmes qui, par leur force, leur style, leur intelligence,
leur humour et leur joie de vivre, ont inspiré ce livre.

contents

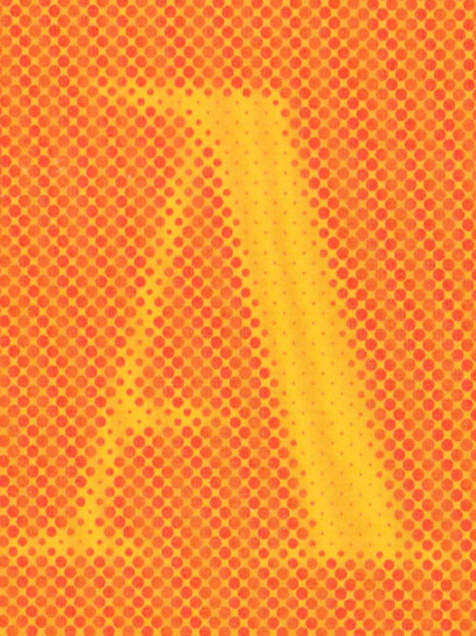

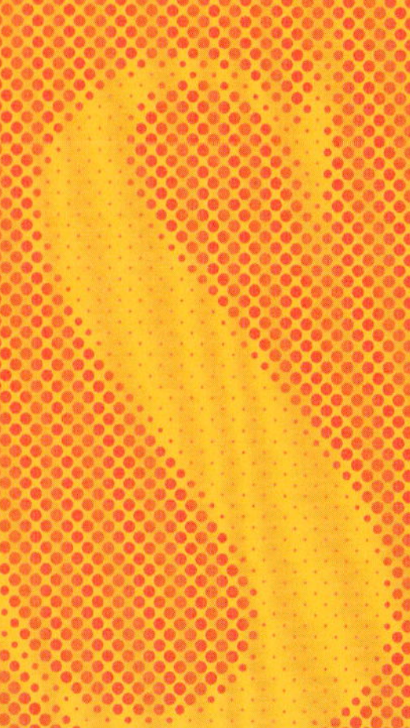
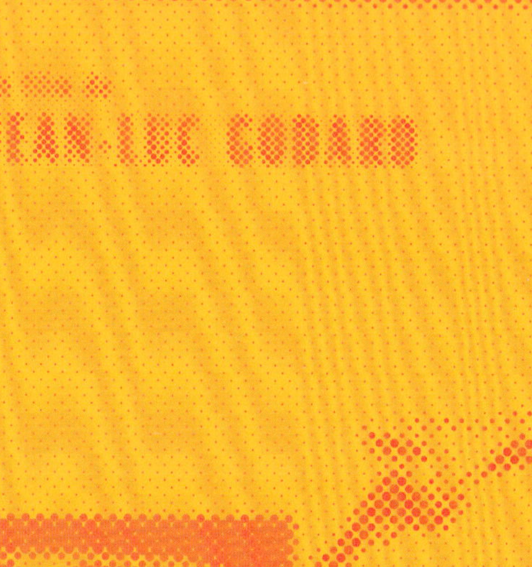
JEAN
SEBERG
JEAN-PAUL
BELMONDO
un film de
JEAN-LUC GODARD
A Bout De Souffle....

introduction

a generational shift in society and cinema

The French New Wave, one of the most influential movements in film history, first arrived on the scene as a foundational shift in French society. A new generation of young people coming of age after World War II began to shake the established order, reshaping values, morals, roles, and relationships between women and men. Their progressive thinking revolutionized the cinematic landscape, guided by young directors whose philosophy and aesthetic celebrated personal style and authenticity. New images of female characters represented a palpable break with the past. Off screen, women were enjoying more freedom while still caught between the conflicting messages of a society grappling with rapid evolution. These new women, these *nouvelles femmes*, suddenly saw their complexities reflected on screen: the roles and the actresses who inhabited them were, in a word, modern.

Jean-Luc Godard's *À bout de souffle* (*Breathless*), 1960, original poster

What lay behind the New Wave phenomenon was a wide-ranging combination of factors, a historical, social, and cinematic context ripe for change. During the years following World War II, France entered a period of economic prosperity that was a welcome relief after years of hardship under German occupation. At the same time, the country was still suffering the war's traumatic repercussions, leaving young people with feelings of despair and despondency that incited them to seek other, freer modes of living. For many, parties, nightlife, and alcohol became the de facto coping mechanisms. Eighteen-year-old literary sensation Françoise Sagan captured this spirit of rebellion in her best-seller, *Bonjour tristesse* (*Hello Sadness*, 1954), through the eyes of an aimless seventeen-year-old named Cécile, a character whom American actress Jean Seberg brought to life in Otto Preminger's 1958 English-language screen adaptation. Seberg's performance attracted the attention of up-and-coming French directors and led to her own entry into the New Wave; she would play another version of the archetype in Jean-Luc Godard's 1960 film *À bout de souffle* (*Breathless*). Sagan's novel even inspired its own term: *Saganism*, a lifestyle in which fast love, fast cars, and Scotch distract from a deeper malaise. The worldview of France's youth was causing a generational rejection of traditional values that struck fear into older members of society. In late 1957, the new generation got a name.

Between 1955 and 1957, acclaimed journalist Françoise Giroud published a series of stories in the weekly news magazine *L'Express* that investigated France's *jeune génération*. She interviewed them on everything from their tastes in music and clothing to their views on love, painting the portrait of a demographic that was disillusioned by war but hungry for freedom and fun. It was Giroud who coined the expression that would come to define an era. "La Nouvelle Vague arrive!" proclaimed her cover story for the October 1957 issue of the magazine. "The New Wave is coming!"

In movie theaters, meanwhile, cinema was prospering financially but stagnating aesthetically. As the old guard of French directors sought to reestablish themselves after the war, they produced films that were artistically stuck in the past: period pieces and socially constrained literary adaptations that young film critics provocatively dubbed *le cinéma de papa* (literally, "daddy's cinema"). A number of these very critics—including François Truffaut, Jean-Luc Godard, Claude Chabrol, Éric Rohmer, and Jacques Rivette, who wrote for the acclaimed film magazine *Cahiers du Cinéma* —would become celebrated New Wave directors, defying convention with their own innovative filmmaking and storytelling techniques. Agnès Varda had already begun that work, taking the camera into the streets and blending fiction and reality years earlier in her first feature, 1955's *La Pointe Courte*. Varda and her contemporaries Alain Resnais and Chris Marker belonged to another camp of New Wave directors, grouped together by default in opposition to the *Cahiers* group on the Rive droite, referring to the right bank of the Seine where the headquarters of the magazine was located. The directors belonging to the Rive gauche, the left bank, an area long associated with intellectuals and artists, approached film with a stylistically experimental lens instead of a critic's eye.

Film critic Pierre Billard was the first to apply the expression *New Wave* to cinema when he used it in the magazine *Cinéma 58*, published in February 1958, to describe the rising class of directors under forty. Many of them had soon-to-be seminal films on the way: Chabrol's *Le Beau Serge* (*Handsome Serge*, 1958) and *Les Cousins* (*The Cousins*, 1959) premiered just months apart; Truffaut's *Les Quatre cents coups* (*The 400 Blows*) debuted at the Cannes Film Festival in 1959; and Godard's *À bout de souffle* followed in 1960. In search of authenticity on screen, these directors embraced director/critic Alexandre Astruc's idea of the *caméra-stylo* ("camera-pen"), which holds that a director can write a personal story with a camera on the same level as an author with a pen. Varda also echoed this notion in what she termed *cinécriture* ("cine-writing"). The directors' choices for the *mise en scène* served the goal of creating fictional narratives that reflected and respected what was real. Directors sometimes interwove aspects of their personal lives into their characters or drew traits directly from their actors. Cinematographers like Raoul Coutard, Nestor Almendros, and Henri Decaë used natural lighting and sensitive film to achieve a realistic look, and they often eschewed constructing sets in favor of shooting in apartments or outdoors in the streets of Paris. Actresses benefited from this commitment to authenticity, too, as natural makeup and casual clothing helped free them from the constrictive standards of the past.

New Wave directors have earned their places in the pantheon of cinema for their profound impact on film history. Their films are recognized not only as monumental works of art but also as markers of style and models of nuanced relationships that explore the dynamics between men and women and, at their core, what it means to be human. Varda deserves a special commendation as one of the era's rare female directors to gain worldwide renown; she's been called the "mother of the French New Wave," having made her first feature years before the movement even had a name. When asked about this unsolicited title in a 1977 interview, she replied provocatively, "Well, yes, we can't all be, like Venus, daughters of the Old Wave, born of the vast sea. So, you do what you can in cinema as elsewhere."[1]

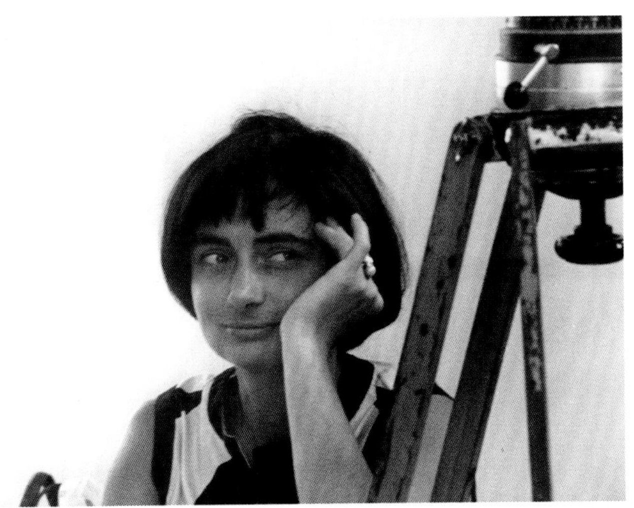

The female faces of the New Wave have become forever etched into our collective memory as well. Anna Karina, Jean Seberg, and Jeanne Moreau—all iconic, all modern, ambitious, and independent women—are now inextricably linked to the movement. But they were much more than just faces: They imbued their roles with modern individuality, playing an integral part in creating multifaceted female characters that both informed and were informed by society's images of women. As male directors pursued authenticity with their camera-pen, it was the women in their lives—both on and off the screen—who helped them achieve it. Some also developed their own art, directing films and writing screenplays or novels, and others promoted humanitarian causes, including women's rights.

Nouvelles Femmes is the story of the French New Wave through the lens of the many women, both iconic and lesser known, at its center—an examination not only of how female characters were portrayed in this unique sociohistorical and aesthetic context but also of how the actresses shaped those portrayals through their voice and vitality, their style, and their efforts behind the scenes. It follows them as they struggle to break out of the idealized fantasies of their on-screen lovers and off-screen directors, building an intricate new blueprint of the modern woman in the process.

Why do these films continue to resonate so strongly in our culture, even as some critics now dismiss them for perpetuating patriarchal dynamics and depictions of women? How did they lay the groundwork for today's actresses and directors, including Léa Seydoux, Adèle Haenel, Marion Cotillard, and Isabelle Huppert; Justine Triet, Céline Sciamma, Mia Hansen-Løve, Catherine Breillat, and Claire Denis (not to mention their American counterparts)? Exploring the women of the New Wave in the context of their own era—in cinema and in society at large—can help us answer these questions.

Agnès Varda on the set of *Le Bonheur* (*Happiness*), 1964

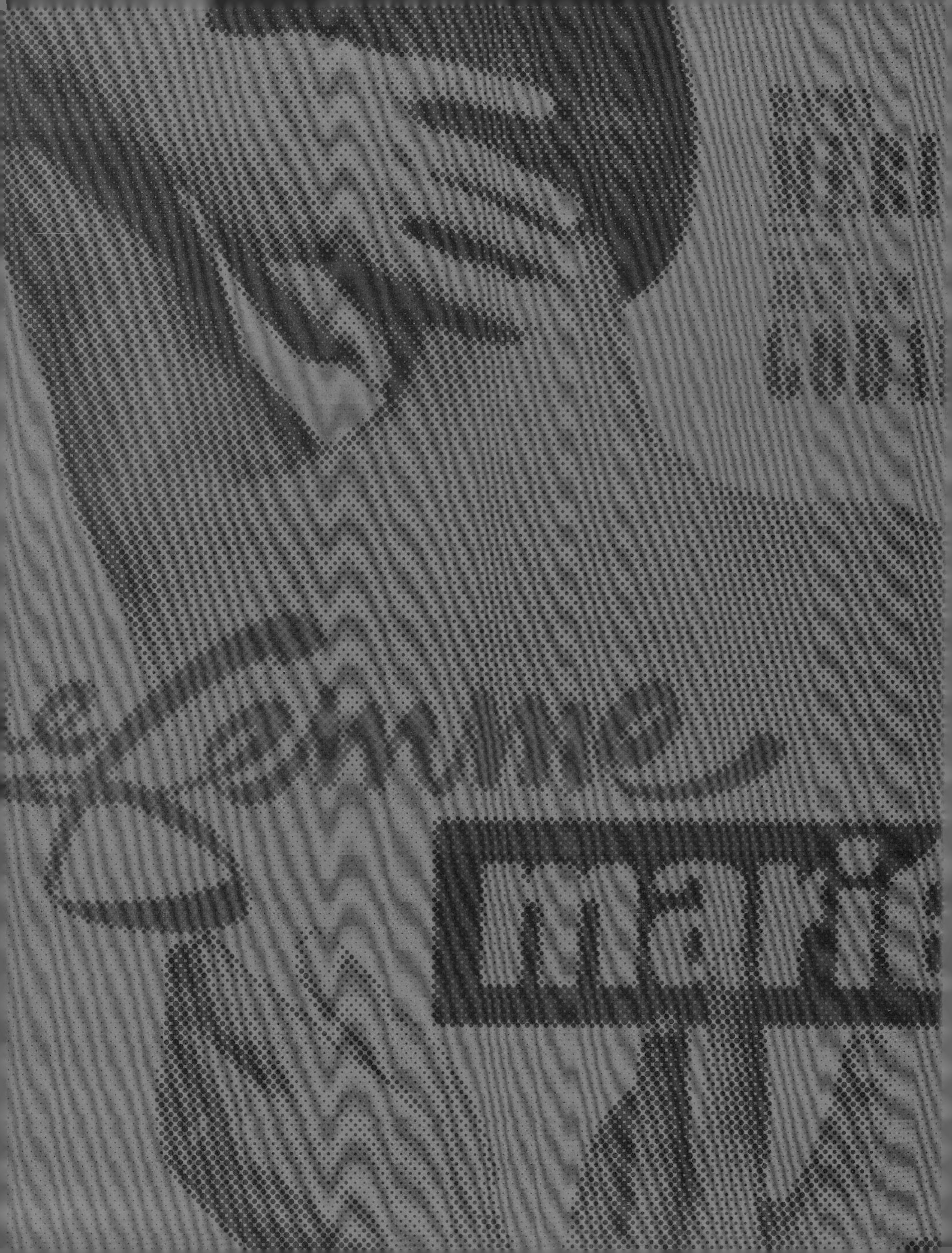

avant la vague

before the wave

THE SEVENTH ART

Since the birth of cinema in 1895 with the Lumière brothers and the first projection of their documentary-style films at the Grand Café on Paris's boulevard des Capucines, France lay claim to its new invention and believed in its possibilities. Georges Méliès celebrated the patron saint of France in *Jeanne d'Arc* (*Joan of Arc*, 1900) in twelve tableaux and initiated the use of special effects with his famous *Le Voyage dans la lune* (*A Trip to the Moon*, 1902). The nation's pride in what became known as the "seventh art" was largely responsible for the aesthetics that earned *le cinéma* such a label. While these pioneers of early cinema continue to be fêted, another, Alice Guy-Blaché, was almost erased entirely from the history books. Overlooked or ignored, only recently has she been recognized for her significant contributions to the industry, including directing some of the first films of narrative fiction, such as *La Fée aux choux* (*The Cabbage Fairy*, 1896). From the beginning of cinema, female voices were articulated but downplayed. Guy-Blaché made the satirical comedy *Les Résultats du féminisme* (*The Consequences of Feminism*), inversing the roles of women and men already in 1906, and she also directed films on social justice. *A Fool and His Money* (1912), for example, is a comical interrogation of poverty featuring an all-Black cast that Guy-Blaché filmed after moving to the United States and cofounding Solax Studios in New York.

By 1910, French cinema dominated world markets, with an estimated 60 to 70 percent of films sold worldwide coming out of Parisian studios. Along with the first newsreels, comedies and adaptations of melodramas and literary works abounded. World War I, however, would devastate the country and put a strain on its film industry, with some studios converted into arms factories. The fallout of the war produced the avant-garde that transformed cinema in the 1920s, one that would be seen as art. New Wave directors would later revere Jean Epstein and Louis Delluc, both avant-garde film theorists, critics, and directors. Delluc made six films with the actress Ève Francis, who became his wife and imprinted his films with her expressive face, like the New Wave directors would do with their actresses—who were often their love interests—forty years later. Delluc also foreshadowed the New Wave's focus on authenticity when he campaigned for a specifically French cinema that would be authentic, freed from theater, and featuring original scripts. Germaine Dulac, one of Delluc's allies, helped realize this vision when she brought to the screen her first script, *La Fête espagnole* (*Spanish Fiesta*, 1920). With her impressionist (and feminist) film *La Souriante Madame Beudet* (*The Smiling Madam Beudet*, 1923), she was applauded for the seriousness of her directing, and more recently, Dulac has gained acclaim for her surrealist experiment *La Coquille et le clergyman* (*The Seashell and the Clergyman*, 1928). While Luis Buñuel and Salvador Dalí's *Un chien andalou* (*An Andalusian Dog*, 1929) remains the ultimate reference of the genre, *La Coquille* has earned its place alongside René Clair's *Entr'acte* (1924) as a skilled representation of cinematic surrealism. Abel Gance was also celebrated for his films during the silent era, such as his epic *Napoléon* (1927). He would be instrumental in the career of writer/director Nelly Kaplan, who became one of the biggest names in feminist cinema almost forty years later.

The year 1927 would transform cinema worldwide with the arrival of talkies, notably Alan Crosland's *The Jazz Singer*, and in France in 1929 when Billancourt Studios became equipped for sound. Clair's first sound films represented a romantic image of Paris, idealizing the working class with its cast of *petit peuple* in an optimistic vision despite the arrival of the Great Depression in France in the early 1930s. A

handful of exceptional films, like *L'Atalante* (1934), written and directed by Jean Vigo, illustrated cinema's capacity for poetry. With its beautiful images of Dita Parlo in her wedding gown boarding a barge set for Paris with her new husband, this cinematic love story exudes hope and dreaminess, hinting at what French cinema might have become had Vigo not suffered a premature death in 1934 at age twenty-nine. The film showcases the respected theater actor Michel Simon as the ship's captain, the same type of scraggly outcast he played in Jean Renoir's films—*Boudu sauvé des eaux* (*Boudu Saved from Drowning*, 1932) being the reference. Renoir's seminal film *Toni* (1935), shot on location in the south of France with nonprofessional actors, would greatly influence Italian neorealism as well as the New Wave.

Along with emerging poetic realism, new faces and new voices populated French cinema in the 1930s, with comedies, literary adaptations, and stories speaking to France's history of colonialism, such as Julien Duvivier's *Pépé le Moko* (1937), featuring the most notable face of the era, that of Jean Gabin. Actors were now at the center of the films that the public followed. The collaboration of director Marcel Carné and poet Jacques Prévert produced films famous for their memorable dialogue delivered by audiences' favorite actors. In *Le Quai des brumes* (*Port of Shadows*, 1938), Michèle Morgan and Gabin's legendary exchange—"T'as d'beaux yeux, tu sais? Embrasse-moi" ("You have beautiful eyes, you know? Kiss me")—endures to this day as one of the most romantic moments in film history. Carné's 1938 *Hôtel du Nord* remains famous for Arletty's unforgettable lines, "Atmosphère, atmosphère!" as well as her outspoken working-class character on the Canal Saint-Martin. Gabin and Arletty appeared together in 1939 in another famous Carné-Prévert collaboration, *Le Jour se lève* (*Daybreak*), a dark love triangle and monumental film, referenced notably by film critic André Bazin. Committed to depicting France's social and political realities of economic difficulties and disillusionment, these films presented stories of everyday life with often tragic outcomes, fate rendering the characters powerless.[1] These somber, defeatist themes of poetic realism were reflected aesthetically in the films' lyrical style and *mise en scène* that used soft focus and chiaroscuro lighting to create a bleak but dreamlike quality.[2] Gabin's characters were filmed in such a way that put him in the spotlight, showcasing his appeal and even his beauty, with his eyes emphasized though glamorous lighting. In the narratives, however, Gabin's heroic characters all die tragically. The darkness of the films reflected the dark era.

The advent of World War II brought about deep shifts in all areas of French life, drastically affecting the cinematic landscape. Production stopped from June to October 1940. France was divided into two zones: one occupied by the Germans who exercised strict administrative control, the other in Vichy under the collaborationist regime of Marshal Pétain. An organizational committee was established for each industrial sector, including cinema, considered an industry. The COIC (Comité d'organisation des industries du cinéma) put into place a number of actions that would affect French cinema for years to come, some for the better: double features were discontinued (and short films could be screened), advances on production were established, and the film school l'IDHEC (L'Institut des hautes études cinématographiques, now the prestigious La Fémis) was founded. Other actions complicated things administratively: A professional card was now required to make films. The Vichy regime also imposed harsh censorship aligned with that of the Germans in the occupied territory and institutionalized antisemitism. Le Statut des Juifs, the Jewish Statute, signed by Pétain on October 3, 1940, banned Jewish people from working in professions associated with the cinema. Many foreign Jewish people who had worked in the industry in France were already incarcerated in French camps or had left the country. After judging the conditions intolerable, many directors fled to the United States: Renoir, Clair, Duvivier, and Max Ophüls were among them, as well as actors Gabin and Morgan.[3]

While English and American films were banned, French cinema had a captive audience of people wishing to escape their own reality at the movies. Gabin and Morgan appeared on screen together again in a tragic love triangle with Madeleine Renaud in a film started before France's defeat, Jean Grémillon's *Remorques* (*Stormy Waters*, 1941), accepted by Vichy censors and released long after its stars had fled to Hollywood. Films like Carné and Prévert's classic *Les Enfants du Paradis* (*Children of Paradise*), a coproduction with Italy that was filmed in Nice in 1943 (completed after the liberation and released in 1945), benefitted from a big budget but was shot under difficult conditions. The plot eluded the political present in a poetic Parisian setting of a theater, showcasing actors Jean-Louis Barrault, Arletty, and Maria Casarès. Other films glorified France's past with adaptations like Christian-Jaque's *La Symphonie fantastique* (*The Fantastic Symphony*, 1942), produced by Continental Films, a German production company that financed French films in France for the French[4] (a collaboration that Carné, for example, refused). Jean Delannoy's *L'Éternel retour* (*The Eternal Return*, 1943), written by Jean Cocteau and starring his muse, Jean Marais, took place in contemporary France but was a retelling of Tristan and Isolde, the love story distancing it enough from the reality of the time that Vichy censors had no issue with its release.

Along with comedies starring popular entertainers like Fernandel, films nourished by theater were part of France's occupied cinema from directors such as Sacha Guitry and Marcel Pagnol. Other innovative directors were on the horizon. Filmed during the war in 1944 under difficult conditions before the liberation of Paris in August, Robert Bresson's *Les Dames du Bois de Boulogne* (*Ladies of the Park*, 1945), inspired by Denis Diderot's eighteenth-century novel *Jacques le fataliste et son maître* (*Jacques the Fatalist and His Master*), showcased Maria Casarès in the role of an imposing, strong woman. Hélène (Casarès) is obsessed with her love interest, Jean (Paul Bernard), who is falling for a young dancer. This love triangle through Bresson's lens was applauded by the future New Wave directors, and Casarès's image remains inseparable from the film.

In late 1945, after the war ended, André Malraux became France's minister of information in charge of cinema. His famous declaration, "Le cinéma est un art; et par ailleurs, c'est aussi une industrie" ("Cinema is an art; and in addition, an industry"), would become a constant reminder of French cinema's double vision (or its ambivalence) as it continues to navigate between the two up to this day. After the liberation, materially, French cinema was in bad shape, having suffered destruction of studios and film stock, and rationing of materials for sets and costumes.[5] Its equipment, sets, and laboratories were either in disrepair or out of date. The question arose of reconstructing it under the control of the State. In 1946, the CNC (Centre national de la cinématographie) was created, a public establishment given financial autonomy under the authority of the minister of information (since 1959, the minister of culture), supplying production and distribution aid through government subsidies.

American competition also became a reality again as France opened its markets to Hollywood films (forbidden during the war). Under the Blum–Byrnes agreement—a provision signed on May 28, 1946,[6] between France's former interim prime minister and then-ambassador Léon Blum and US secretary of state James F. Byrnes to ease France's debt to the United States incurred during the war[7]—French movie theaters were required to show French films for four weeks per quarter.[8] For the remaining nine weeks, they were opened to competition from foreign films, notably American.[9] In order to compete with Hollywood and with pressure to maximize profits in the first week of a film's release so the next film could quickly replace it, the industry became weighed down by commercial themes and styles aimed at attracting moviegoers. In 1948, the French government attempted to ease the financial strain of filmmaking with a law allotting funds to producers proportional to their previous film's box-office performance—which caused them to further fixate on popular topics and familiar aesthetics in an attempt to recreate past successes.[10] Improved upon in 1953, 1955, and 1959, this law lay the foundation of French cinema being a "cultural exception,"[11] but its stylistic repercussions meant directors could take fewer risks.

The period spanning from the end of the war to the birth of the New Wave has been classified as a time of continuity. Censorship also significantly restricted the subjects that films were allowed to address at the time, notably the consequences of World War II, the war in Indochina, as well as the one beginning in Algeria, and decolonization. Rather than risk their films being banned or butchered, directors began self-censoring. This practice kept their films' subject matter far from France's reality.

Cocteau directed a fairy tale, *La Belle et la Bête* (*Beauty and the Beast*, 1946), giving audiences a poetic fantasy world featuring Marais, whose face is revealed in the end to incarnate male beauty. Released in 1946, Renoir's *Partie de campagne* (*A Day in the Country*), made ten years earlier in 1936, stands as a *moment de bonheur*—a moment of happiness—marking a parenthesis of contentment and optimism before the dark years of French cinema. Sylvia Bataille through Renoir's lens prefigures the heroines of Rohmer's cinema in idyllic settings. The contrast is striking when compared to the depiction of actresses in films also released in the late '40s. Micheline Presle in *Le Diable au corps* (*Devil in the Flesh*, 1947), adapted from Raymond Radiguet's eponymous novel, is an unfaithful wife caught in a love triangle with a younger man (played by heartthrob Gérard Philipe, star of stage and screen), while her husband fights on the frontlines during World War I. Simone Signoret starred in films directed by her husband, Yves Allégret, including *Dédée d'Anvers* (*Woman of Antwerp*, 1948), where she played a prostitute. Other films featured actors bringing to life stories from France's illustrious literary heritage. Christian-Jaque's adaptation of Stendhal's *La Chartreuse de Parme* (*The Charterhouse of Parma*), a period piece with elaborate costumes and sets, became a box-office hit in 1948 with Philipe alongside respected stage actresses Renée Faure, "from the Comédie-Française," as the trailer boasts, and Casarès, who worked with Philipe as part of the Théâtre national populaire (TNP). (Incidentally, Agnès Varda's photographs of Casarès and Philipe—as well as of Jeanne Moreau—in her early days as a photographer with the TNP are what brought her into the public eye.)[12] Cécile Aubry as another eighteenth-century heroine in Henri-Georges Clouzot's *Manon* (1949), an adaptation of Abbé Prévost's *Manon Lescaut*, also kept the present at bay but displayed a darkness that reflected Clouzot's earlier work in *Le Corbeau* (*The Raven*, 1943).

Considering the conditions during cinema's reconstruction, with censorship restricting certain topics and rigid administrative rules in place preventing young people from directing, it is no wonder creativity and innovation were stifled. Alexandre Astruc, contributing to major intellectual journals since 1945, wrote on the crisis in contemporary French scriptwriting and argued that cinema should be considered on the same level as painting and the novel "after having been successively a fairground attraction, an amusement analogous to boulevard theater, or a means of preserving images of an era." In his landmark 1948 essay, "Naissance d'une nouvelle avant-garde: la caméra-stylo" ("The Birth of a New Avant-Garde: La Caméra-Stylo"), he asserts that cinema was "gradually becoming a language," a "form in which and by which an artist can express his thoughts . . . translate his obsessions exactly as he does in the contemporary essay or novel"[13] (an idea that would greatly influence the New Wave directors). Subsidized by the French government to glorify France and showcase a rich French literary patrimony, adaptations and costume dramas like the aforementioned *La Chartreuse de Parme*, however, dominated the screen. These big-budget period pieces often did not take any aesthetic risks. Like many of today's blockbusters, they could be considered canned (and would be by the young critics). Claude Autant-Lara's adaptation of Stendhal's *Le Rouge et le noir* (*The Red and the Black*, 1954) was a prime example. Again, it featured Philipe in the lead, playing opposite Danielle Darrieux. Her role in *Le Rouge et le noir* made Darrieux an exemplary representation of the older generation in films that would informally be labeled the *cinéma de papa* by the New Wave. With her theatrical speech, cinched-waist long dresses, and perfect chignon, Darrieux appeared far from the loose, casual, and unbridled sensuality of Brigitte Bardot in *Et Dieu créa la femme* (*And God Created Woman*, 1956) appearing just two years later! The juxtaposition of these two films in the same time frame illustrates the shock effect of Bardot and the films of a new generation. Darrieux was not completely ignored by the New Wave, however. She showed up in Jacques Demy's *Les Demoiselles de Rochefort* (*The Young Girls of Rochefort*, 1967) alongside Catherine Deneuve and Françoise Dorléac. A perfect example of French cinema's transitional phase in the mid-1950s, Darrieux played heroines in films that the future New Wave directors at *Cahiers du cinéma* praised, and others that they condemned.

Truffaut's assault on an artificial type of cinema of the old guard resonated loudly among his fellow critics and young cinephiles. With polemic titles like "Une certaine tendance du cinéma français" ("A Certain Tendency of French Cinema") in the January 1954 issue of *Cahiers du cinéma*,[14] Truf-

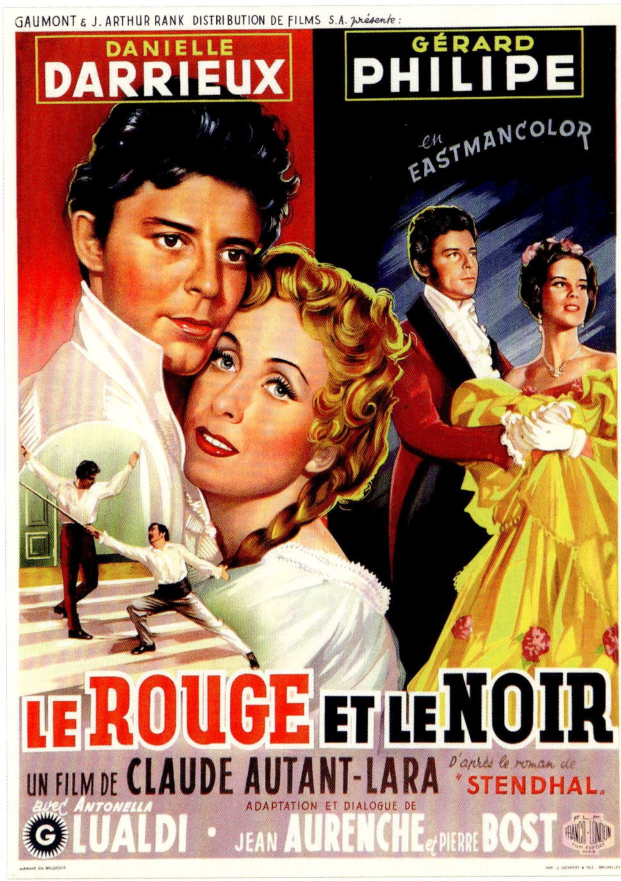

faut specifically attacked films he called "ambitious," ones that routinely won prizes at film festivals and were admired by the foreign press, shot by Delannoy, Autant-Lara, René Clément, and Yves Allégret,[15] for example, those whom he accused of underestimating what cinema could do. "Vous êtes tous témoins dans ce procès: Le cinéma français crève sous les fausses légendes" ("You are all witnesses in this trial: French cinema is dying under false legends") he titled another famous article in 1957.[16] Ironically labeling these types of films "cinéma de la Qualité" (or "cinema of Quality" that he considered the opposite from what the expression implied), Truffaut threw down a gauntlet. He saw this type of cinema—also known as the "Tradition de Qualité" ("Tradition of Quality") and the "Qualité française" ("French Quality"), as well as less formally, the *cinéma de papa*[17]—as not respecting cinema as a language and as an artform. He accused scriptwriters like Jean Aurenche and Pierre Bost, who often worked on adaptions of acclaimed French novels, of searching for "equivalences" between literary techniques and cine-

Claude Autant-Lara's *Le Rouge et le Noir* (*The Red and the Black*), 1954, poster

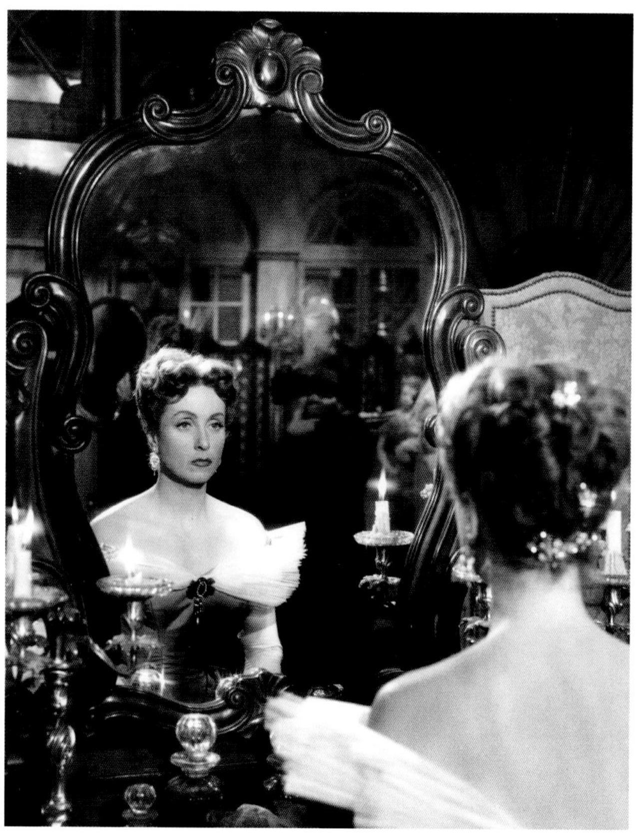

leading actresses played illustrates that it was indeed a time of transition in film. Products of their time, these actresses appeared in costume dramas reflecting the cinéma de la Qualité alongside innovative films that the young directors admired. Darrieux, for example, was perhaps best known for her roles in the films of Max Ophüls, a director revered by the New Wave. In the iconic *Madame de . . .* (*The Earrings of Madame de . . .*, 1953), she appeared as a chic but tragic Parisian heroine. In *Le Plaisir* (*House of Pleasure*, 1952), she played the bubbly Madame Rosa, and in *La Ronde* (1950), an unfaithful married woman alongside Signoret who again played a prostitute. Before World War II, Darrieux also appeared as a remarkably independent and modern woman in Jean Boyer's *Un mauvais garçon* (*Counsel for Romance*, 1936)[19] that prefigured Moreau's transformation in *Jules et Jim* (*Jules and Jim*, 1962), dressed in a similar fashion as a boy in a cap and sweater. Moreau herself was caught in this in-between period as she appeared almost unrecognizable in Jacques Becker's *Touchez pas au grisbi* (*Grisbi*, aka *Honour Among Thieves*, 1954) along with France's prewar hero Gabin before her defining role in Louis Malle's *Ascenseur pour l'échafaud* (*Elevator to the Gallows*, 1958).

matic processes that betrayed the spirit of the original work by changing the locations and content of certain scenes, adding in anarchist or anticlerical themes, and taking dialogue out of context.[18]

By 1958, French cinema was in good financial shape, enjoying commercial success, but was suffering an artistic crisis. Despite the big budgets, there was, in fact, little innovation. Shot inside studios with elaborate costumes and theatrical dialogue, the women in these films also appeared confined, rigid, formal, unnatural, or inauthentic compared to what was happening outside with the arrival of the "new wave" of young people. Though some have been redeemed and others endure today as cult favorites, the films belonging to the cinéma de la Qualité placed their heroines categorically in the realm of the old generation, out of sync with the image of the modern New Wave heroines.

Not all films of that era were condemned by the brassy young critics, however. The variety of roles that some of the

During cinema's protracted metamorphosis, actresses often embodied cinema that was both respected and disdained by the young New Wave critics. Like Darrieux, Casarès appeared in films they adored, such as Bresson's *Les Dames du Bois de Boulogne*, the acclaimed Cocteau films *Orphée* (*Orpheus*, 1950) and *Le Testament d'Orphée* (*Testament of Orpheus*, 1960), as well as the costume drama *La Chartreuse de Parme*.[20] Morgan, getting her big break with Marc Allégret (the director who would go on to discover Brigitte Bardot), won an Oscar for her role in Delannoy's adaptation of André Gide's *La Symphonie pastorale* (*Pastoral Symphony*, 1946) and played an aloof divorcée seduced by Philipe in Clair's classic, *Les Grandes manoeuvres* (*The Grand Maneuver*, 1955), alongside a young Bardot.[21] Well-loved for her role in Becker's *Casque d'or* (*Golden Marie*, 1952), Signoret portrayed villains or femmes fatales in Carné's adaptation of Émile Zola's *Thérèse Raquin* (1953) and in Clouzot's cult classic *Les Diaboliques* (*Diabolique*, 1955).[22] But New Wave directors gave little attention to the erratic career trajectories of these actresses; they were in search of male role

Danielle Darrieux in Max Ophüls's *Madame de . . .* (*The Earrings of Madame de . . .*), 1953

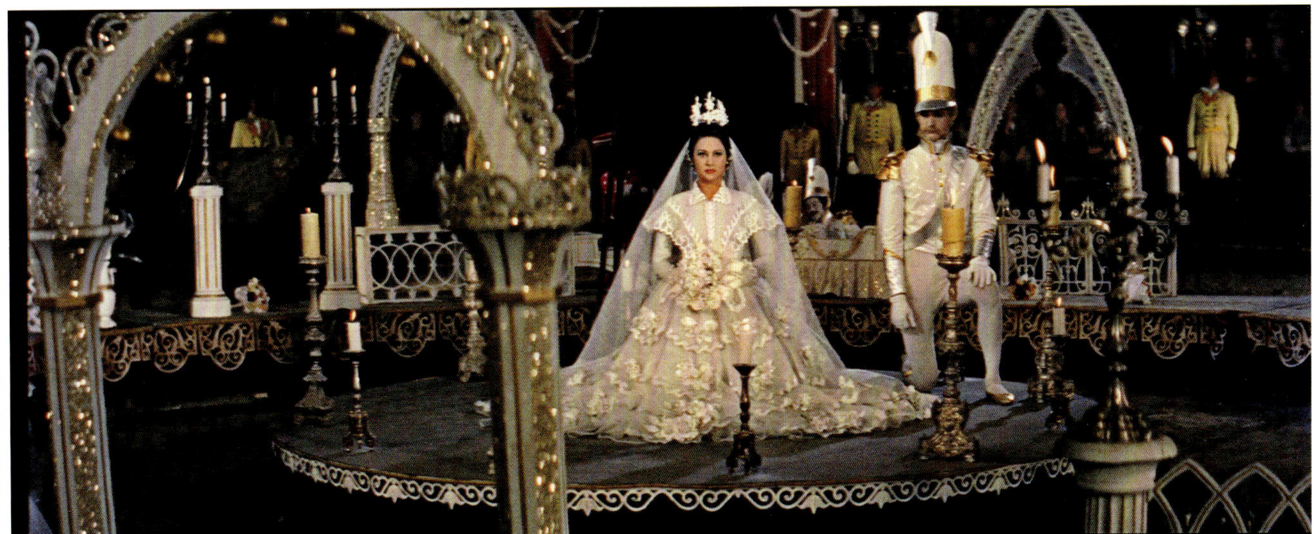

models behind the camera, above all. For them, films were defined by directors (esteemed if the director was considered an auteur), not actors.

This was the case of the actress known as one of the most beautiful women in the world, Martine Carol, a sex symbol during the 1940s and '50s. Considered the French Marilyn Monroe, she often appeared as a blonde seductress. In her most famous role, however, one much revered by the New Wave and the *Cahiers* group in particular, Carol dyed her hair black and played a tragic figure: the titular dancer and courtesan in Ophüls's *Lola Montès* (1955). But it is the director's prowess that is celebrated above all, not the actress's influence. Demy went as far as dedicating his film *Lola* (1961) with Anouk Aimée to Ophüls in the opening credits. By the late 1950s, Carol, though still considered very beautiful and despite her monumental role in *Lola Montès*, was losing out to the more modern Bardot.

Considering these actresses as a group and the roles they portrayed in this pre-New Wave period, certain patterns emerge: unfaithful married women, prostitutes, women controlled by desire, mysterious femmes fatales and apparitions, and ethereal, angelic figures. Though the New Wave directors ardently proclaimed their difference from the *cinéma de papa*, traces appear in the roles they proposed to women in their films as well. The distinction is in how the stories were told, the influence of new, modern actresses,

and *moments de vérité* (moments of authenticity) that constructed their characters. The ways in which filmmakers directed the actresses also influenced the representations of the characters, along with costumes, lighting, and sets. As in the New Wave, the social context placed constraints on women in the period predating it, influencing their roles on screen and off, as did the director's sensibility and relationship to the actress. Women's roles shaped their images, and in turn, these representations shaped how society viewed women.

MEANWHILE IN HOLLYWOOD

Besides French cinema, the future New Wave directors from the *Cahiers* were hugely influenced by the work of directors abroad. When this new generation came of age, for many, cinema was a refuge, a place to escape during the occupation. The phenomenon of *la cinéphilie* (a concept translated literally as "the love of cinema") gained popularity at that time with cinema at the center of young people's universe and *ciné-clubs* all over Paris, facilitated by older cinephiles such as Henri Langlois, director of the Cinémathèque française, founded in 1936 with one of the world's largest collections of films that were screened for the public (a collection almost destroyed during the occupation). Sometimes watching three or four films per day, the young Truffaut, Godard, Chabrol, and Rivette dissected and debated films from all over the world, many times screened without

Martine Carol in Max Ophüls's *Lola Montès*, 1955

subtitles. Scandinavian, Russian, Italian, and, after the Blum–Byrnes agreement after World War II, Hollywood movies—they devoured them all: westerns, gangster films, comedies, musicals, B-movies. This was their film school. Film magazines were also extremely influential, such as *L'Écran français,* in which Astruc's famous article on the *caméra-stylo* appeared in 1948.[23] With the fledgling *Gazette du cinéma*, coming out of the Ciné-club du Quartier Latin, published between May and November 1950 and edited by Rohmer and George Kaplan,[24] young critics like Godard (using the pseudonym Hans Lucas) honed their critical skills and their eye for cinematic detail. Under the influence and guidance of the well-respected theorist André Bazin, who established *Cahiers du cinéma* in 1951, they wrote serious reviews at a young age for the magazine as well as for another important film periodical *Arts*. This is where their ideas solidified about new ways of approaching cinema and soon, about making their own films.

In an attempt to revolutionize film, their philosophy became a type of revolution with a violent overthrowing of the old system (hence the *cinéma de papa*) and a canonizing of those they revered. They emphasized the importance of the director in the quality of a film, making the parallel with an author of a book in terms of the director's own personal style influencing that of a film as a whole. Applauding filmmakers with this quality, Truffaut coined the expression *la politique des auteurs*, an idea that anointed certain directors with the status of auteur (the basis of auteur theory). Roberto Rossellini, Ingmar Bergman, Fritz Lang, Howard Hawks, Orson Welles, and Alfred Hitchcock were among the chosen few. The *Cahiers* group were even sometimes referred to as the "Hitchcocko-Hawksians" for their love of those two Hollywood directors.

It is worth a detour through Hollywood, then, and a closer look at Hitchcock and his heroines for the large influence they had on the New Wave directors. Malle pointed specifically to how Hollywood film impacted his own *mise en scène*: "Like all the other cinephiles of the time, I really loved American film, and I was basically trying to paint a very modern portrait of Paris, for example," *in Ascenseur pour l'echafaud*. "More modern than it really was," added Moreau,

the film's star. Malle stated that he did that on purpose. "It's a Paris as it would be ten years later," he explained. "I was fed up with the atmosphere in French films of old bistros, old-fashioned taxi drivers and their caps, I wanted to move on to something else. This Paris was a bit imaginary in that it didn't really exist yet."[25]

Hollywood films also shed light on how women were seen as well as the expectations placed on them in terms of image and assumed social roles. Hitchcock particularly fascinated many of the New Wave directors. Rohmer and Chabrol wrote one of the first books on him in 1957. Truffaut, with the help of Helen Scott (who worked at the French Film Office in New York and translated the conversations), later conducted in-depth interviews with the master of suspense that were published in 1966 as *Hitchcock/Truffaut*, which became a worldwide success and is still a reference text for all serious film students.

Hitchcock's heroines, like their New Wave successors, have gone down in film history as some of the most beautiful and elegant women of all time, incarnated by some of the most notable actresses of Hollywood: Grace Kelly, Kim Novak, Eva Marie Saint, Tippi Hedren, and Ingrid Bergman, to name a few. Their recognizably sophisticated, polished style, usually consisting of a blonde chignon and tailored high fashion often designed by Edith Head—the iconic costume designer at Paramount and winner of eight Academy Awards—made them conform to a type despite the distinct personality of each actress.

Taking one of the most famous as an example, Grace Kelly in *Rear Window* (1954) has remained influential to this day through her presence and style. Head designed her wardrobe as a way to make Kelly's character appear wealthier than the male protagonist. First seen in the film dressed in a striking black and white cocktail dress with a tulle and chiffon skirt, a pearl necklace, and white gloves, Lisa (Kelly) appears in Jeff's (James Stewart) apartment as an image of polished perfection, one that is sure to win him over. To obtain her goal of a marriage proposal, she must work for it, given his lukewarm interest in her romantically, not to mention his skittish attitude about marriage in general. Dressed

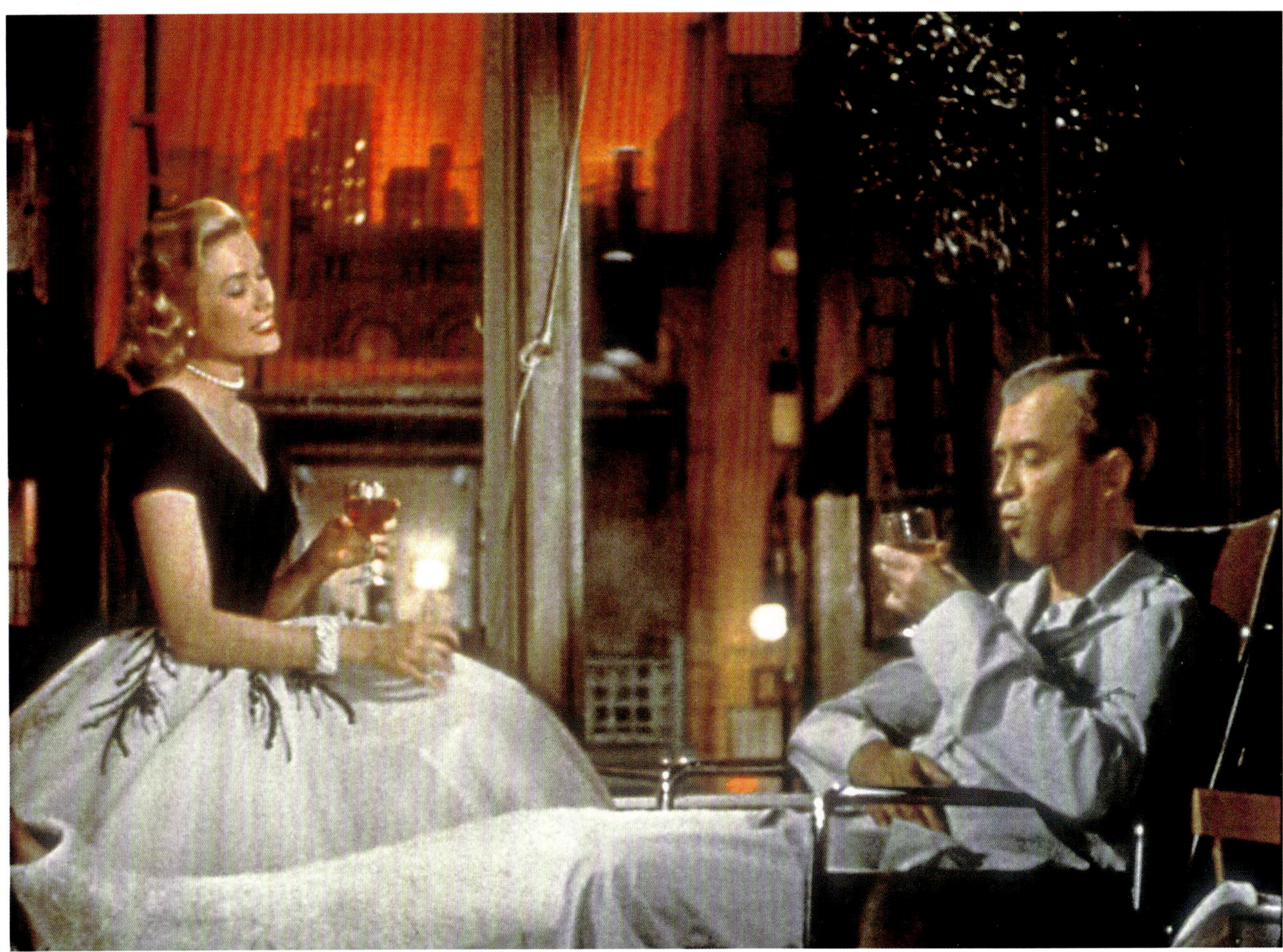

to the nines, she serves him drinks and waits on him in a sort of exhibition of herself in the role of the ideal wife.

Throughout the film, we see a fashion show of her different looks: a sophisticated pistachio-green suit and veiled white pillbox hat, a typical 1950s embroidered floral dress with a flared skirt and cinched waist, and even a more daring silk negligee that Lisa had packed in an overnight bag—this last number giving Jeff a glimpse of what married life would look like with her. Different from this formal attire she has worn so far, Lisa is seen at the end dressed in jeans, a red shirt, and black loafers, this time without pearls or any jewelry, implying that she has reached her goal of finally winning over Jeff. Though it is hard to imagine today, this casual look was almost a sartorial scandal. Ceasing to have to "work" to seduce Jeff through an intricately put-together perfect im-

age also shows that the heroine achieved her aim. Letting him see her in this more casual look, though equally constructed, also illustrates the changing times as women, still locked into societal conventions, started enjoying a bit more freedom in their dress, the very beginning of the ubiquitous "jeans and a T-shirt" style slowly accepted for women that we later see in Seberg's famous look in *À bout de souffle*.[26] Here, though Lisa has let her guard down a bit in terms of fashion, she is still working to correspond to the imagined desire of her love interest in this scene. As Lisa reclines casually on Jeff's divan, she pretends to read a travel book, displaying to him that she shares his interests. As soon as he falls asleep, however, she drops it for a fashion magazine.

In *Rear Window*, we can see clearly, through the narrative and Grace Kelly's clothing, the dynamics at work between

Grace Kelly and James Stewart in Alfred Hitchcock's *Rear Window*, 1954

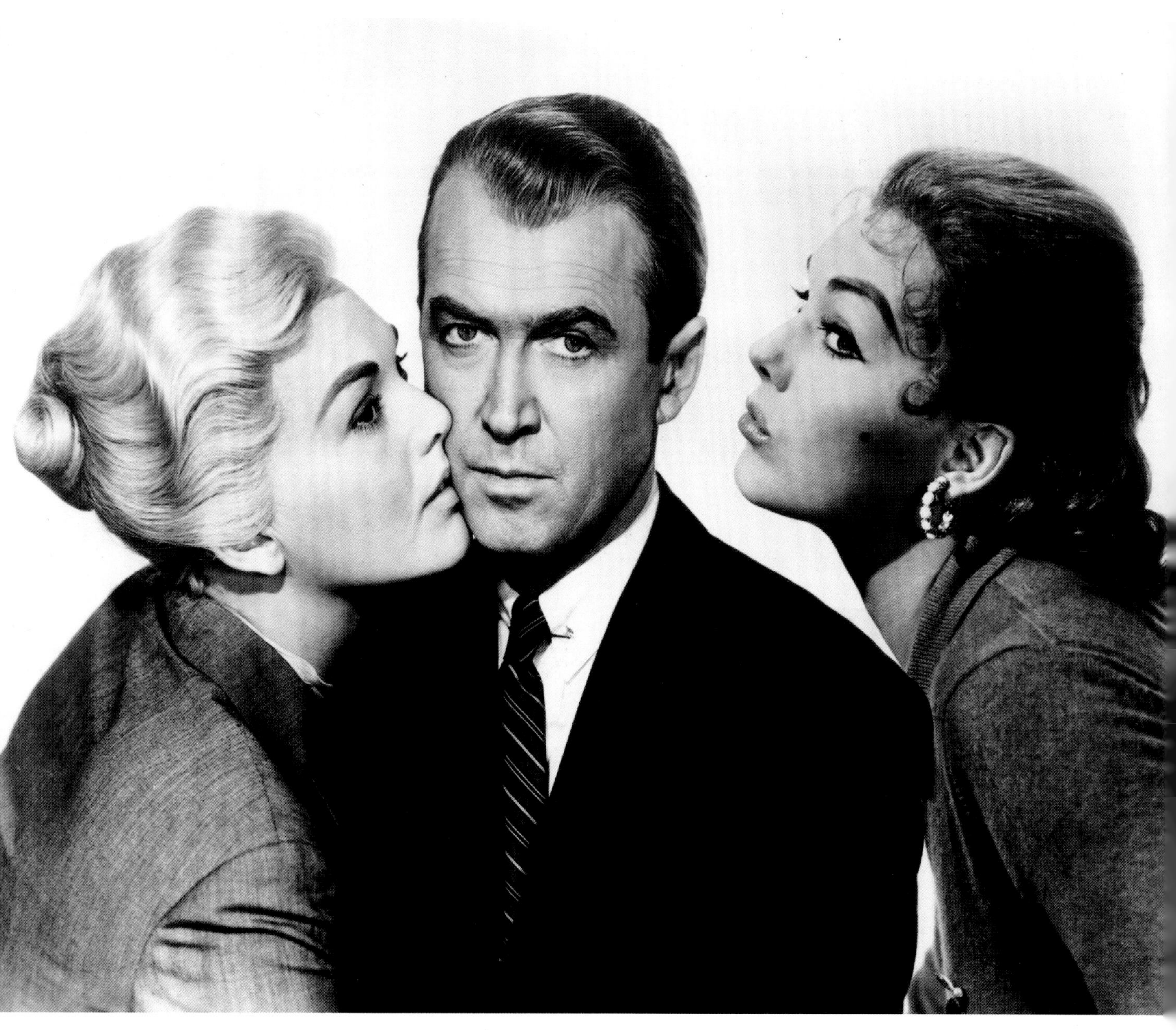

women and men on screen in Hollywood. A decade before the Bechdel test (used to evaluate a work of fiction, usually a film, based on its inclusion and representation of female characters),[27] Laura Mulvey, in her famous 1975 essay "Visual Pleasure and Narrative Cinema,"[28] published in *Screen*,[29] pointed out Hollywood cinema's tendency to characterize women as objects, assigning them a passive role. She placed responsibility on the structure of the gaze in cinema, made up of the audience, the camera, and a film's characters, and suggested that women are typically seen from a male point of view. This so-called "male gaze" implicitly functions to render women passive while men are shown as active, upholding patriarchal dynamics in society.

According to Mulvey's theory, Lisa's finely honed image in *Rear Window* reinforces her passivity and representation of visual perfection. On the other hand, Jeff's profession as a photojournalist illustrates his active stance in the world, but his broken leg renders him a spectator, forcing him into a fantasy position like that of the viewer. Based on the male gaze, according to Mulvey, cinema is a voyeuristic experience, often showing women in fragmented close-up shots of parts of their bodies. She illustrated this idea using the scene in *Rear Window* where Lisa steals into the apartments across the courtyard, entering into Jeff's lens, which ignites his erotic feelings for her (exiting the space next to him in his apartment where he lacks interest). Unconsciously, viewers identify with the active male protagonist, objectifying the woman and reinforcing the idea of the male characters as being in control. Women, identifying with the female characters, internalize the desire to be desired, objectifying themselves, valued for their appearance or desirability alone, as we see in Lisa's motivations. We can still see this dynamic in today's films, and with a distance of seventy years, we can see it clearly at work in *Rear Window*.

As Mulvey suggested, Hitchcock's films epitomized the use of subjective shots (from the male point of view) that established the audience's identification with the protagonist and his voyeuristic position. Hitchcock himself spoke of his "purely cinematic" film, describing "an immobilized man" as one part of the film, "what he sees" as the second, followed by "how he reacts."[30] Likewise, in *Vertigo* (1958), a subjective camera guides the narrative from the male protagonist's point of view. The film tells the story of Scottie, an anxiety-filled retired police detective (again played by James Stewart) who falls in love with a woman he has been hired to spy on but has only seen from a distance. The audience adheres to Scottie's eye, voyeuristically viewing the mysterious blonde, an image of ideal beauty, then witnessing her apparently falling to her death. Kim Novak plays the part of a woman who, herself, plays the part of two women: Madeleine, the blonde, and Judy, a brunette who bears a striking resemblance to Madeleine. When Judy suddenly appears in Scottie's life after the accident, he persuades her to conform to his fantasy image, the idealized woman of his dreams, Madeleine. The makeover process reveals his voyeuristic, active stance, and her passivity in conforming to his desire.

According to Mulvey, *Vertigo* exposes the active (looking) and passive (looked at) split between male and female, as well as the power entrusted to the male hero.[31] Having fallen in love with Scottie, Judy is disappointed when she sees his reaction change from frustration—when her hair does not correspond to the style he requested ("It should be back from your face and pinned at the neck")—to desire after she fixes it to look like his fantasy of Madeleine, sealing his approval with a kiss. At that moment, she realizes that he does not see her but rather the fantasy woman he has imagined. In an interview in 1996, Novak made a parallel with this notion of being reshaped to fit an ideal image to the experience of women in the film industry at that time: "I could really identify with Judy, being pushed and pulled this way and that, being told what dresses to wear, how to walk, how to behave. I think there was a little edge in my performance that I was trying to suggest that I would not allow myself to be pushed beyond a certain point—that I was there, I was me, I insisted on myself."[32]

The disappointment Judy felt finds its parallel in the male protagonist's frustration in her not living up to his dream despite his trying to reshape her to conform to it. This echoes Hitchcock's own obsessive desire for control over his actresses; though Novak allowed that the director gave her "a lot of freedom in creating the character," he was also "very exact in telling [her] exactly what to do." Hitchcock revealed more about their dynamic in his famous interviews with Truffaut:

James Stewart as Scottie with Kim Novak as Madeleine and Judy in Alfred Hitchcock's *Vertigo*, 1958

"Miss Novak arrived on the set with all sorts of preconceived notions that I couldn't possibly go along with. . . . I went to Kim Novak's dressing room and told her about the dresses and hairdos that I had been planning for several months. I also explained that the story was of less importance to me than the overall visual impact on the screen, once the picture is completed." Truffaut's response only reinforces the validity of Novak's complaint: "I can assure you that those who admire *Vertigo* like Kim Novak in it. Very few American actresses are quite as carnal on the screen. When you see Judy walking on the street, the tawny hair and makeup convey an animal-like sensuality. That quality is accentuated, I suppose, by the fact that she wears no brassiere."[33]

Looking back at Hollywood heroines at the time, we see a clear split between fantasy women and girl-next-door types like the cheery Doris Day. With her perpetual smile and bubbly voice, Day often sang of domestic bliss in films like *By the Light of the Silvery Moon* and *Calamity Jane*, both Warner Bros. musicals from 1953. In Hitchcock's *The Man Who Knew Too Much* (1956), with Stewart again in the leading role, Day played a mother who becomes frantic when her son is kidnapped. Reinventing her image, Day starred in the highly successful *Pillow Talk* (1959), highlighting her sex appeal when she played the role of an independent interior decorator in New York City alongside her womanizing neighbor, played by Rock Hudson. With an equally sunny disposition, Debbie Reynolds danced and sang alongside her male counterparts in *Singin' in the Rain* (1952), incidentally one of Chabrol's favorite films. In a darker but equally wholesome version of the archetype, Natalie Wood stood by the troubled James Dean in Nicholas Ray's *Rebel without a Cause* (1955), another favorite of the New Wave.

Alongside these respectable good girls were those with more eccentricity and personality. Upon discovering Audrey Hepburn for his film *Roman Holiday* (1953), William Wyler exclaimed, "She had everything I was looking for: charm, innocence, and talent. She also was very funny. She was absolutely enchanting, and we said, 'That's the girl!'" After her role transforming from a working-class girl to a Parisian sophisticate in Billy Wilder's Cinderella story *Sabrina* (1954),

Hepburn played a nun in Fred Zinnemann's *The Nun's Story* (1959) before portraying the unforgettably eccentric Holly Golightly in Blake Edward's *Breakfast at Tiffany's* (1961). Shirley MacLaine became known for her roles as the quirky but outspoken friend. At just twenty years old, MacLaine also appeared in a Hitchcock black comedy, *The Trouble with Harry* (1955), though her more down-to-earth character was not a typical Hitchcock-style heroine. In Vincente Minnelli's 1958 adaptation of the James Jones novel, *Some Came Running* (later given a nod in *Le Mépris* [*Contempt*, 1963] by Godard), MacLaine's performance was nominated for an Oscar. In it, she plays a wayward but purehearted woman from Chicago who follows the hero, a writer played by Frank Sinatra, to his Midwestern town; and in Wilder's romantic comedy *The Apartment* (1960), regarded as one of the best films ever made, MacLaine played a frank, much-desired elevator girl who becomes the woebegone mistress of the corporation's big boss alongside Jack Lemmon and Fred MacMurray. Though she regarded that role fondly, in New Wave actress Delphine Seyrig's feminist documentary *Sois belle et tais-toi* (*Be Pretty and Shut Up*, made in 1976 and released five years later), MacLaine voiced the fact that women's roles written by men often place women in objectified positions: "The fantasy that they most wanted to see enacted was [women] in the bedroom."

Becoming an icon of this type of fantasy, Marilyn Monroe was a measuring stick by which all other women were judged in terms of desirability. From Jane Russell to Jayne Mansfield,

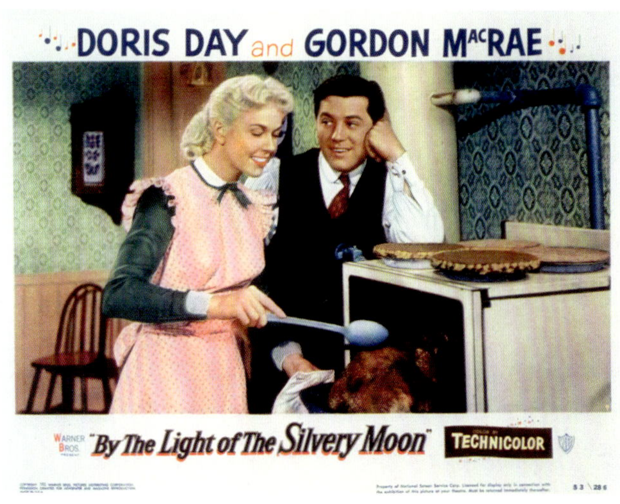

Doris Day and Gordon MacRae in David Butler's *By the Light of the Silvery Moon*, 1953

women as purely visual sex symbols scattered the screen as a balance to the girl-next-door types. Elizabeth Taylor went from playing a wholesome twelve-year-old in *National Velvet* (1944) all the way to the lascivious Maggie the Cat in the 1958 screen adaptation of Tennessee Williams's *Cat on a Hot Tin Roof*. Slinking in front of Paul Newman in her iconic white slip, Taylor lay across a brass bed in a pose anticipating Bardot's equally iconic opening scene in *Le Mépris*.

With these unnamed categories of wholesome domestic ideals, quirky girlfriends, and pure fantasies, Hollywood perpetuated rigid stereotypes, from which it was hard to break. Hitchcock himself voiced the fantasy: "We're after the drawing-room type, the real ladies, who become whores once they're in the bedroom. Poor Marilyn Monroe had sex written all over her face, and Brigitte Bardot isn't very subtle either." "In other words, what intrigues you is the paradox between the inner fire and the cool surface," Truffaut clarified. "Definitely," Hitchcock responded. These Hollywood-manufactured images also influenced the New Wave, especially the Rive droite directors of *Cahiers du cinéma* who obsessively consumed them—but with the help of their starring actresses, they would imbue their characters with something new and more modern.

A CLEAN BREAK FROM A MESSY PAST: WHAT MADE THE NEW WAVE NEW

If many New Wave films still depicted women through the lens of male fantasies, they also brought about freer, more independent images of women with individuality and some amount of agency. In Truffaut's 1957 short *Les Mistons* (*The Mischief Makers*), Bernadette Lafont encapsulated the duality of embodying a pinup in the eyes of the young boys (the young "rascals" or "brats" of the title) spying on her (as well as Truffaut's camera), and, at the same time, a free and free-spirited woman as she rides through town on her bicycle. The film was adapted from Maurice Pons's novel of the same name and foreshadows Truffaut's alter-ego troublemaker Antoine Doinel in *Les Quatre cents coups*. In the south of France, a group of adolescent boys follows Lafont's

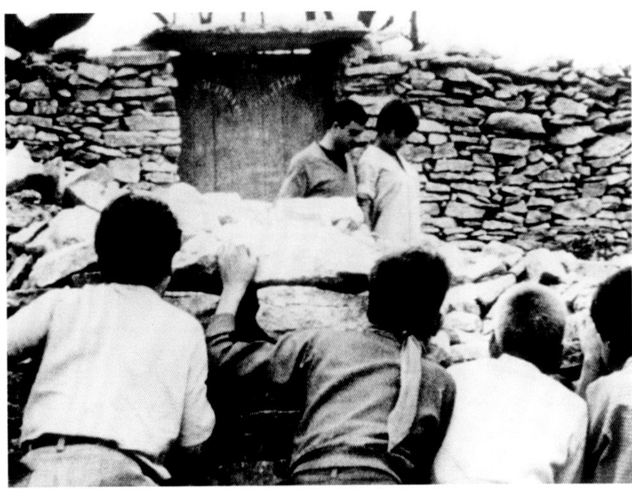

character around, transfixed by her power, fascinated by her body and her relationship with a young French soldier (Gérard Blain) on leave from his military service. Like Bardot in *Et Dieu créa la femme*, Lafont in *Les Mistons* reflects the tension of an emerging feminine agency, translated by the bicycle, in the context of a cinematic and societal tradition of objectifying women through the narrator's gaze, the director's lens. The film opens with a long tracking shot of Lafont riding her bicycle toward the camera before it pans over to reveal the young boys gazing at her from afar as a literary voice-over narrates the story: "Jouve's sister was unbearably beautiful. We couldn't take it. She always rode with her skirt flying, and without a slip. Bernadette led us to discover many of our darkly hidden dreams. She awoke in us the springs of luminous sensuality."

In *Et Dieu créa la femme*, Bardot incarnated this same dichotomy in the extreme, an independent woman riding through Saint-Tropez on her bicycle while moments of pure cinematic spectacle freeze the narrative to focus on her body, gratifying the voyeuristic male gaze. Moreau as Catherine, the strong yet elusive leader of the trio with the titular men of *Jules et Jim*, always has the power over her male counterparts in relationships and otherwise, always in the lead on her bicycle and even beating them both in a whimsical footrace. They fall in love with her, however, for her resemblance to a statue, embodying an absolute, the idea of a woman. Anna Karina as Odile in *Bande à part* (*Band*

Gérard Blain and Bernadette Lafont in François Truffaut's *Les Mistons* (*The Mischief Makers*), 1957

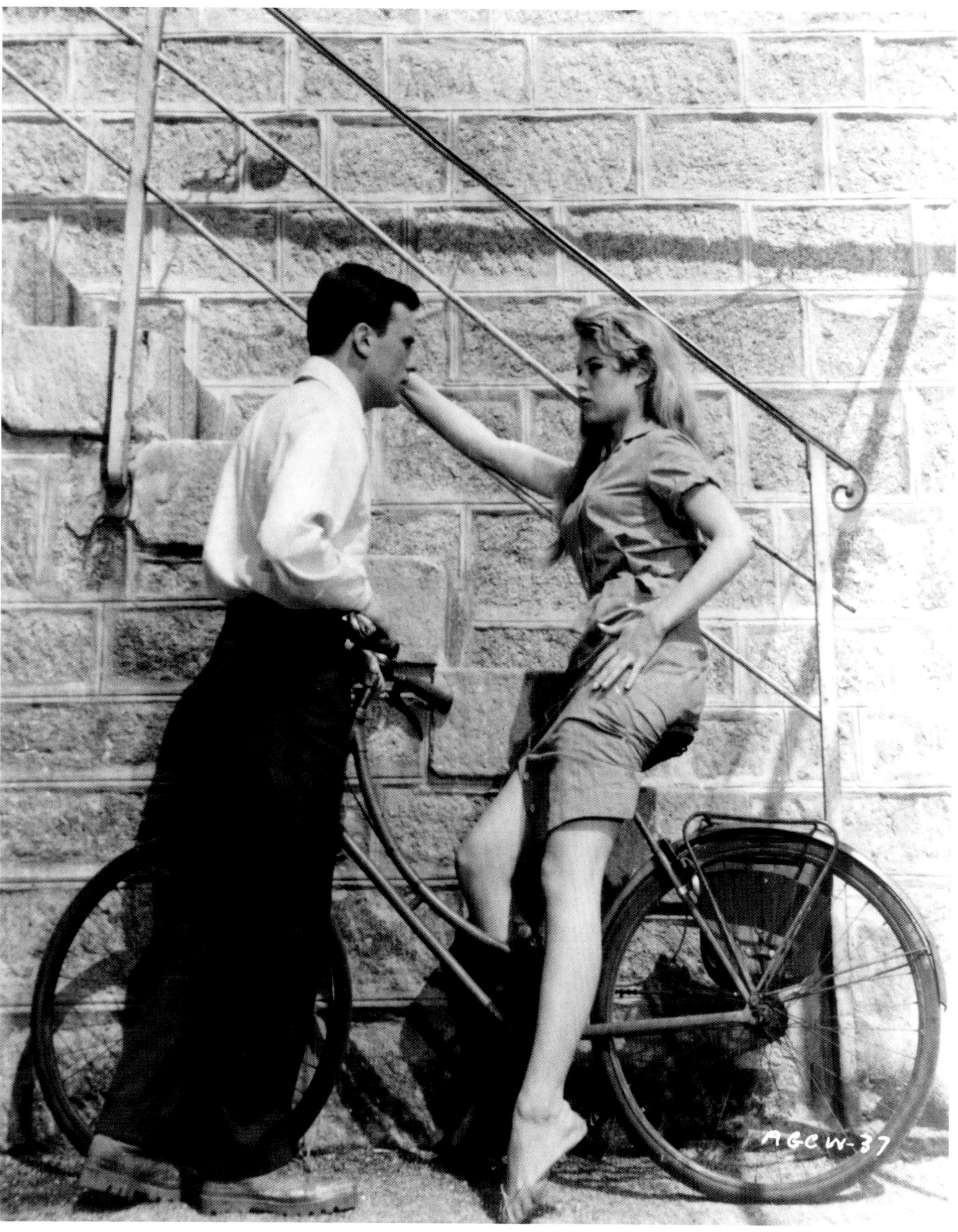
MGEW-37

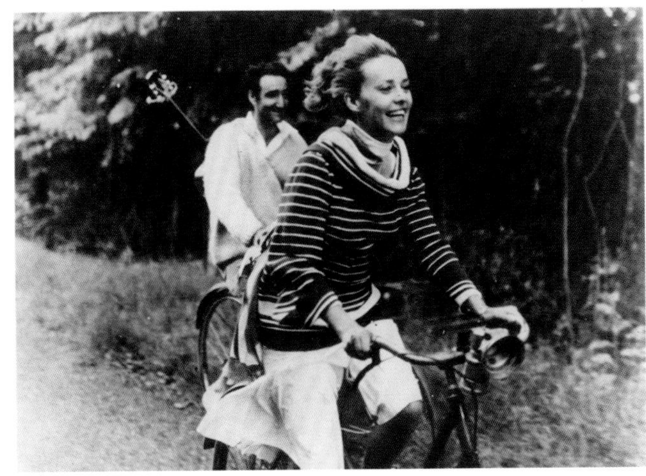

of Outsiders, 1964) also existed as part of a trio, but is portrayed as free-spirited and dressed as a schoolgirl. Though she follows her two shady suitors on a path of crime, unexpected moments of cinematic joy open the narrative, like their run through the Louvre and their dancing the Madison. If these heroines had traces of the old, from French cinema and from Hollywood, they also transcended the confines of old frameworks and touched the soul in new ways.

What made them different? What made them modern? Considering the context, with a confluence of factors coming together, shows what made the New Wave women new.

This generation that had grown up during World War II was disillusioned. The journalist who coined the phrase *Nouvelle Vague*, Françoise Giroud, stated in an interview for French television in 1973[34] that she found them to be "frileux," or fearful when it came to love. At the same time, they had greater moral freedom. With a boom in economic prosperity after a period of financial hardship, they wanted to buy new things that were unavailable to them during the war: refrigerators, vacuum cleaners, cars . . . as described in the Boris Vian song "La Complainte du Progrès" ("Complaint of Progress") in 1956. It was the beginning of consumer society. In the background, another war had been underway since 1954, a war that went unnamed, taboo: The war in Algeria, a French colony seeking independence, lasted until 1962. With extreme violence on both sides, it also left unresolved wounds on both sides.

Describing his first two films as a sort of indictment of society, Malle explained the context of *Ascenseur pour l'échafaud* and *Les Amants* (*The Lovers*, 1958): "[The films] took place in a specific political context—the death throes of the Fourth Republic. France was just coming out of the war in Indochina, which had been very traumatic and was entering the Algerian War, which led to the collapse of the republic and paved the way for de Gaulle's rise to power. In this context, politicians were besieged with accusations. . . . The French no longer believed in their government and the administration kept changing hands."[35] In *Ascenseur*, Malle made the male protagonist a veteran of the war in Indochina who murders a businessman said to be involved in dubious activities. "Don't forget that the French expeditionary force in Indochina suffered more causalities than the American force," Malle explained. "Many French soldiers were killed. So, beneath the crime plot, there were quite specific and very pointed social references." According to Malle, the young male hoodlum (Georges Poujouly) was ahead of his time, belonging to the next generation. He and his girlfriend, in Malle's words, were "a nod to what was coming." As a sort of premonition, *Ascenseur* announced the 1960s where young people became caught in the frenzy of consumer society,[36] while also reverberating with the darkness of the past and shining light on deeper truths. Characters on the fringe of society or those who are trying to break away from the bourgeoisie, like Moreau's character in the film, transmit a feeling of solitude in an authentic *mise en scène* in the street at night.

This duality of lightness and gravity in French society at the time is reflected in many New Wave films. *Adieu Philippine*

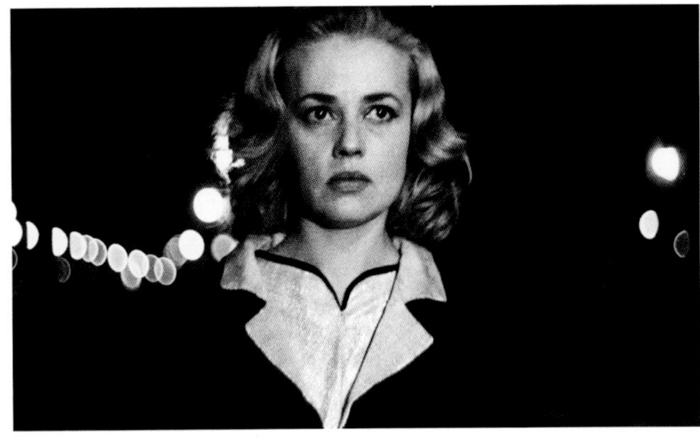

Jeanne Moreau in Louis Malle's *Ascenseur pour l'échafaud* (*Elevator to the Gallows*), 1958

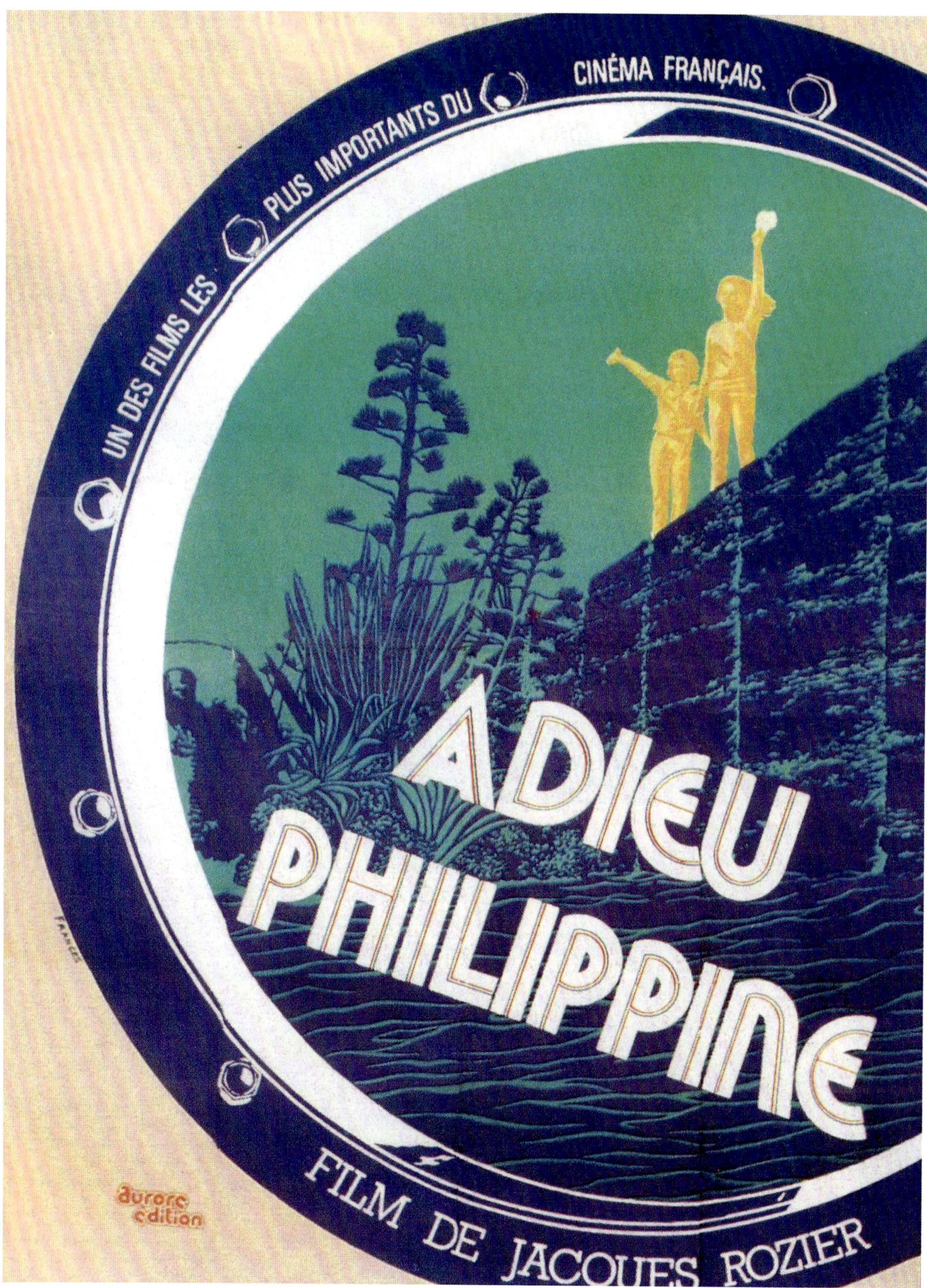

UN DES FILMS LES PLUS IMPORTANTS DU CINÉMA FRANÇAIS.
ADIEU PHILIPPINE
FILM DE JACQUES ROZIER
aurore édition

(filmed in 1960, released in 1963 after the Algerian War), one of the lesser-known of the movement, is perhaps the one that best captures the spirit of the time and its conflicting driving elements: frivolity and seriousness, consumerism and trauma from the wars. Its director, Jacques Rozier, was never included in the canon of names: Godard, Truffaut, Chabrol, Rivette, and Rohmer of the Right Bank, or Varda, Resnais, and Marker of the Left. Rozier was not a critic or part of the *Cahiers* group, nor did he get his start in the arts or in the intellectual scene. Instead, he started off in television after studying at the IDEC (Institut des hautes études cinématographique), then followed the legend of Italian neorealism, Roberto Rossellini, as an assistant director, learning to make films on the spot. In a much more spontaneous way than his Nouvelle Vague cohorts, Rozier's approach to filmmaking perfectly reflected the New Wave philosophy: getting some film and some friends together and going off to make a movie. The process may sound amateurish, but his goal and work ethic were anything but; he spent countless hours in preproduction on *Adieu Philippine* finding his nonprofessional actors through interviews on the street, and after, during the editing process, reading his characters' lips on footage he'd shot without sound to reconstruct the dialogue for dubbing.

Adieu Philippine exuded innocence through the depiction of its characters, a young man not yet called to war and two young women who have not yet left home and still display the joy of adolescence. During a sleepover, they play the game that inspires the film's title, where the first to awaken saying "bonjour Philippine" wins. In moments of complicity as well as adversity, they are filmed in a new way. One memorable sequence suspends the narrative for a moment of pure cinema, capturing the two young women in motion as they walk down the sidewalk, smiling and laughing, over a modern jazz soundtrack, a "moment de grâce," as Rozier later described it.[37] Although they fall into competition over Michel, the French James Dean–type love interest, their rift is resolved with the realization that something more important lurks beneath the puppy-love surface. Michel is going off to war, and they are all left disillusioned in the face of this reality, binding them together in a long farewell to their innocence. In a Q&A after a screening of the film

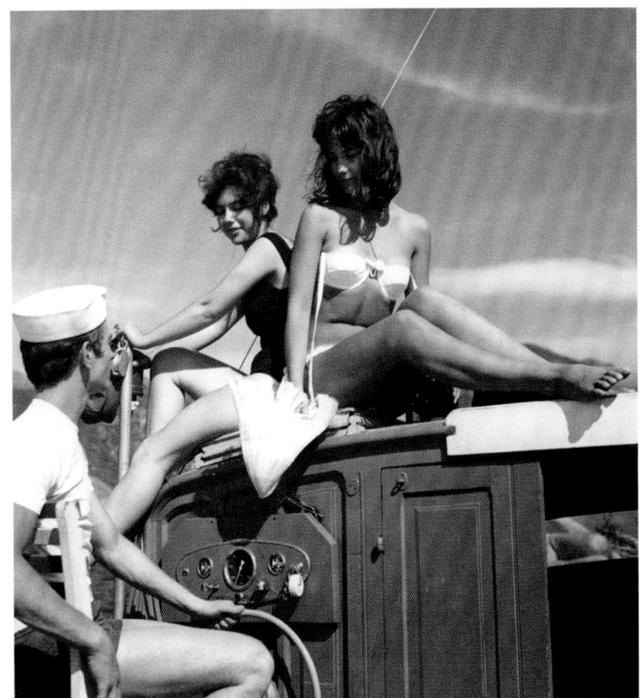

many decades later, Rozier explained that although *Adieu Philippine*'s original poster reflected only the lighter side— showing the two young women side by side in bikinis on a boat, incarnating the free-spirited youth culture—he felt a different image described the film better. At the end of their summer vacation in Corsica, as Michel is leaving to board the ship that would take him to the (unnamed) war in Algeria, he exchanges glances with the two girls. This somber look of knowing translated the gravity of the situation and the characters' loss of innocence, the harsh reality beneath the film's surface.

Besides Rozier, Varda also brought in these two facets. Subtly referencing the Algerian war to avoid censorship, *Cléo de 5 à 7* (*Cléo from 5 to 7*, 1962) shows Cléo and her assistant, Angèle, for example, listening to the news on the radio of a taxi cab that describes the number of those wounded in the war, but the characters do not really pay attention. Cléo is preoccupied at the time with her illness and the potential loss of her superficial identity, built on her appearance. Undergoing a transformative experience, however, through the encounter with a soldier on leave, she gains depth. Towards the end of the film, the soldier confesses: "I don't want to die for the war. I would prefer to die for a woman."

Jacques Rozier's *Adieu Philippine*, 1962, poster

Jean-Claude Aimini (Michel), Stefania Sabatini (Juliette) and Yveline Céry (Liliane) in Jacques Rozier's *Adieu Philippine*, 1962

Along with this complicated social context, affecting the directors' sensibility too was the context in which they grew up during World War II, suffering personal consequences of displacement, like Varda, or seeking refuge from the reality of the occupation in movie theaters, like the *Cahiers* group. Chabrol, Truffaut, Godard, Rivette, and Rohmer were also avid readers of novels, especially those by nineteenth-century Romantic authors such as Honoré de Balzac. Many of this group aspired to be writers themselves; so it follows that they would use the camera as a pen to tell their own stories with their own style.

Technological innovations and new modes of production also influenced the development of the movement. Before the New Wave, the industry in France was locked into a hierarchical process that made it very difficult to make a film. Becoming a director meant going through a series of steps that usually lasted into one's forties before making a first feature, and it also required a big budget for sets and crew. With lighter cameras and the Nagra portable tape recorder, films could now be shot outside, and a big budget was no longer a prerequisite. Taking inspiration from the Italian neorealists, the French took their cameras out into the streets, but instead of filming war, they made films about their own lives. Truffaut argued for this new type of cinema in his famous essay in 1957, calling for authenticity: "The film of tomorrow seems more personal to me than an individual and autobiographical novel, like a confession or a diary," with stories about their lives like their first love, their political awakening, a trip, an illness, their military service, their marriage, or a vacation. People will have to like it, he claimed, because "it will be real and new." Closing the article, Truffaut proclaimed poetically, "The film of tomorrow will be an act of love."[38]

The films of tomorrow would invent a new aesthetic. The directors would tell their own stories in a new cinematic way. Truffaut used entire passages from his childhood diary for *Les Quatre cents coups*. Godard lived out his love story on screen with Anna Karina, starting with *Le Petit soldat* (*The Little Soldier*, 1963). *À bout de souffle*, *La Peau douce* (*The Soft Skin*, 1964), and *Le Coup du berger* (*Fool's Mate*, 1956) took inspiration from *faits divers* (local news stories), but were filmed in the directors' own styles. Unlike the *cinéma de papa*, these films represented the new generation, with young people who looked like them and talked like them, incorporating slang and contemporary fashion. In turn, young people went to the movies more often, making New Wave films profitable. Producers like Georges de Beauregard and Pierre Braunberger supported young talent, financing a record number of first films. With small budgets, directors used new actors and nonprofessionals, their girlfriends and friends, all who were often unpaid. New faces like Jean-Pierre Léaud, Jean-Paul Belmondo, Jean-Claude Brialy, Seberg, Karina, and Lafont revitalized the screens with fresh energy. Their films showed new ways of being that reflected changing morals and more freedom. At times, the content was perceived as scandalous, and the films were restricted for those under sixteen or eighteen years old.

In this context, new stories and new characters emerged that overturned old models. As Malle expressed, evoking his first films, *Ascenseur* and *Les Amants*, "I've always been interested in characters who are breaking with the past. After living a conventional life, they come to a moment of crisis and suddenly they reject the rules of the game. . . . It's an important theme in my early films. Perhaps I had a score to settle with bourgeois society."[39]

For the movement at large, however, that breaking with the past did not happen as one definitive moment of crisis, and we can see elements of the New Wave in innovative films released years before it got its name. Some young directors were addressing new truths about the country's dark history, as Resnais did in *Guernica*, a 1950 short film that examined Picasso's famous anti-war painting, with a text written by Paul Éluard, the great poet of the Resistance. His collaboration with Marker on the postcolonial short *Les Statues meurent aussi* (*Statues Also Die*, 1953) denounces France's destruction of African art; and his monumental documentary *Nuit et brouillard* (*Night and Fog*, 1956), set in a Nazi concentration camp, explores memory with a narration by another poet of the Resistance and Holocaust survivor, Jean Cayrol. In search of authenticity, Varda had already made her first feature set in a real fishing village, and soon after, the young critics at the *Cahiers* were beginning to experiment with short films to show truer, often comical portrayals of relationships. Rohmer and Godard's *Tous les garçons s'appellent Patrick* (*All the Boys Are Called Patrick*, 1957) features a young Brialy, whose character chats up a girl in Luxembourg Gardens, with a constant stream of remarks while she remains silent. "You shouldn't hold [the book] so close. You have very pretty eyes and you'll damage them. I'll loan you my dark glasses. They'll look smashing on you. I'll buy you a drink. Let's go sit under the trees. Will you come?" After their drink, he changes his look and runs into another girl on purpose who is leaving Luxembourg Gardens and who turns out to be the roommate of the first girl. It is one of the earliest depictions of a French *dragueur*, a new type of pick-up artist. In Godard's *Charlotte et son Jules* (*Charlotte and Her Boyfriend*, 1958), a young Belmondo, who later starred in *À bout de souffle*, monopolizes the conversation in the same way Brialy did, delivering a monologue to Charlotte, his soon-to-be-ex-girlfriend (Anne Collette), a tirade that she simply shrugs off while eating her ice cream, but one that betrays the suffering of many of Godard's male protagonists: "I knew you'd come back. I said you would. You can't stay away from me. You're an idiot. You never listen. I know why you're back, Charlotte. You've come to say you're sorry. It's too late. Whatever it is, you'd better not say it, little girl. You should just be quiet."

Of the many facets of New Wave cinema, it may be the dynamics between male and female characters, and indeed the dynamics between the actresses and directors who created these heroines, that continue to fascinate contemporary audiences the most—perhaps in part because they manage to seem both timeless and deeply connected to their own social and cultural landscape. Exploring that landscape from the perspective of the women who lived in it can help us better understand the art they helped create.

MIRROR IMAGES: AGENCY AND OBJECTIFICATION IN THE NEW WAVE AND NOW

"With the nose you have, you'll never be able to act in tragedies." So said a director to Jane Fonda, as she later recounted to Delphine Seyrig in *Sois belle et tais-toi*, implying that she would never be taken seriously because of her appearance.[40] Fonda was advised instead to dye her hair blonde and break her jaw to look more chiseled. Seyrig's documentary centered on women's experiences in the film industry, the title playing off Marc Allégret's 1958 film of the same name. Seyrig provided her fellow actresses a voice that had largely been ignored. Fonda, along with other American and French actresses,[41] went on to describe being scrutinized and judged in ways that were extremely alienating. Too tall, too dark, cheeks too chubby, breasts too small, nose too big—all remarks that women endured, and often internalized, in order to be in the movies. The story of Moreau being deemed unphotogenic by the director of photography in her first film is legendary. These assessments could be seen as a sort of necessary evil in terms of film being an industry, of actors being a commercial product in which investors need to calculate returns as they choose which films or actors to support. However, the mechanisms at work also bleed over into the larger population now just as they did then. In a vicious circle, women are given "role models" in film, literature, and other media that tell them what is valuable, markers that they must hit to feel valuable. Assessing themselves according to what they see on screen, women try to conform to those images, ones that, until recently, were largely imagined by men, and created by a long and complex cultural history.

Since the New Wave era, the women's liberation movement of the 1970s, and more recently with #MeToo, women's agency is now widely promoted, and new role models abound. Today, most are aware of the idea of the male gaze,[42] even if they might not be aware of its origins in Mulvey's 1975 article.[43] Women have taken action against the notion of remaining passive objects, becoming more assertive. They pursue studies in STEM, graduate college at rates outnumbering men,[44] become doctors, pilots, and CEOs, and enjoy financial independence. Self-acceptance through body-positive and age-positive messaging in the media is reinforced by celebrities like Paulina Porizkova, Pamela Anderson, and Alicia Keys, shedding their curated images to embrace their natural, authentic selves. Yet, pressure remains to conform to unachievable standards of beauty and certain roles ingrained in society. With the development of social media, altered images of perfection permeate our lives even more than when fabricated flawlessness only appeared in film or in print. These images extend beyond the purely physical and into the personal, as women strive to project perfection in every sphere of existence: career, family, social life, etc. In this way, social media has both exacerbated the pressure on women to "have it all" and continued the legacy of objectifying them.

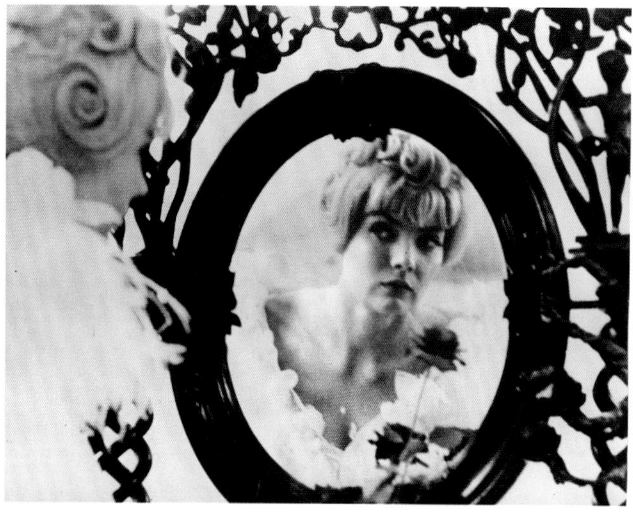

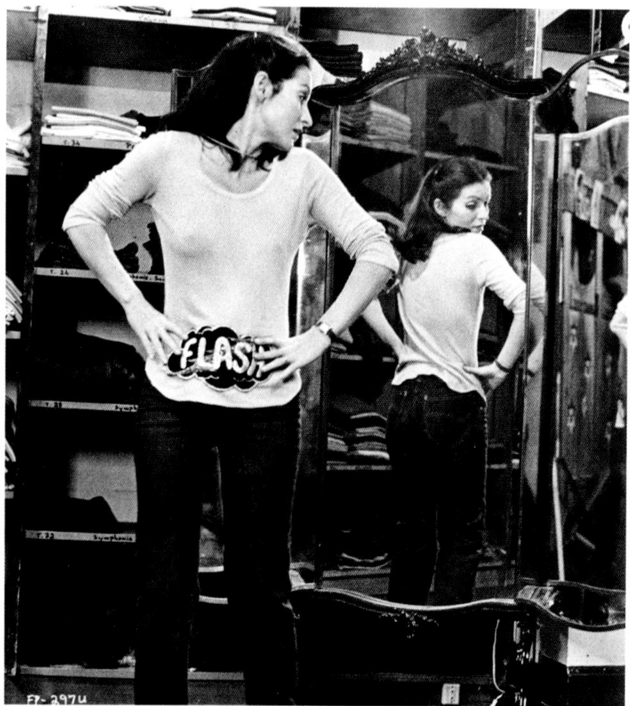

Top: Corinne Marchand in Agnès Varda's *Cléo de 5 à 7* (*Cleo from 5 to 7*), 1962 **Bottom:** Marie-France Pisier in Willard Huyck's *French Postcards*, 1979

It has also subjected them to a troubling new trend. Images of women and their bodies in the media (advertising, magazines, television, film) have historically perpetuated the idea of women as objects, or of assuming certain roles, to sell products. Serving as guideposts, these images and stories are internalized as they seek to define themselves in comparison. With traditional media dealing the cards, it is easy to find a place for blame, but what happens when the person behind the lens is the same one in front of it? With the rise in Instagram culture, women are incited to play an active part in their own objectification from pressure to conform to, or even surpass, the ideal. Lured by societal demands into curating their own images and brands to reach perfection, as defined by unattainable standards, women now objectify themselves in search of approval, abandoning their true selves. As Fonda described it in Seyrig's film, projecting and inhabiting a fabricated image resulted in alienation: her authentic self on one side and the one created for the cinema on the other.

Echoes of Bardot's famous opening scene in Godard's *Le Mépris* reverberate today. "Do you see my feet in the mirror? Do you think they're pretty? And my ankles, do you like them? And do you like my knees, too?" she says, questioning her beauty through her lover's eyes. She doesn't find her shoulders "round enough." Godard's insertion of this scene into the film was a provocative response to the pressure of his producers to include a nude scene of Bardot in order to assure a return on their investment, his acknowledgement of the objectification and commercialization of the female body. In the context of the 1960s, this awareness would seem somewhat new. The pinup, or spectacle of a woman in front of the camera, was taken for granted as the status quo. Before the feminist movements of the 1970s, calling out the process was rare. In today's world, however, the situation is more ambiguous, murkier.

Looking back at the images of women in French cinema, the roots of this phenomenon become clear, with messages conveying that women's worth resided uniquely in their beauty or sex appeal. In Georges Franju's most famous feature, *Les Yeux sans visage* (*Eyes without a Face*, 1960), a father (who happens to be a surgeon) is so obsessed with restoring his daughter's beauty after an accident that he grafts the faces of beautiful women onto hers in a Frankenstein-like story with a clear, implicit message. Many New Wave heroines projected a force below the surface that allowed them to break out of patriarchal cages, but like Bardot's character in *Le Mépris*, there are also examples of insecurity. Karina's character contemplates her body in the mirror in *Bande à part*. Seberg as Patricia tells Michel in *À bout de souffle* that there are many girls in Paris who are prettier than she is. Though the parts were written by men, they convey women's insecurity. Varda places this conflict at the core of *Cléo de 5 à 7* as the heroine reevaluates her power in terms of her beauty when her (artificial) image is shaken after she encounters her own mortality. Portraying her self-doubt and neuroticism, Varda shows her heroine breaking free of this confining image. From a fabricated object, she follows a transformative path to self-realization and authenticity.

In terms of marriage and motherhood, the parallels between today's projection of happiness and perfection are striking in Varda's 1965 feature *Le Bonheur* (*Happiness*). Discussing the film, the director pointed to the contradictions within the *image* of happiness in her characters as a happily married couple, the woman as wife and mother, and the reality underneath. Showing a perfect family on the surface, filmed in beautiful color in an idyllic setting, Varda subtly dismantles this unrealistic (too perfect) image through the narrative. After the angelic wife seemingly accepts her husband's love affair with another woman, she suddenly goes missing and is found dead in a lake. Whether drowning accidentally or on purpose, the wife's death is not resolved. More shockingly, however, the film shows the other woman seamlessly replacing the husband's wife. Slipping into the role of wife from that of lover, the character exposes how the women were interchangeable according to the roles they occupied. "The film provoked a lot of commentary at the time. . . . In a world with all the prefabricated images of happiness in the media, it's worthwhile deconstructing the clichés,"[45] Varda stated in 1977, her words eerily anticipating today's obsession with perfection. Curating images of happiness in our personal lives, we present idealized clichés of perfect families, only instead of being imposed by the media, the images are fabricated by our own hands, our own lenses projecting desired flawlessness.

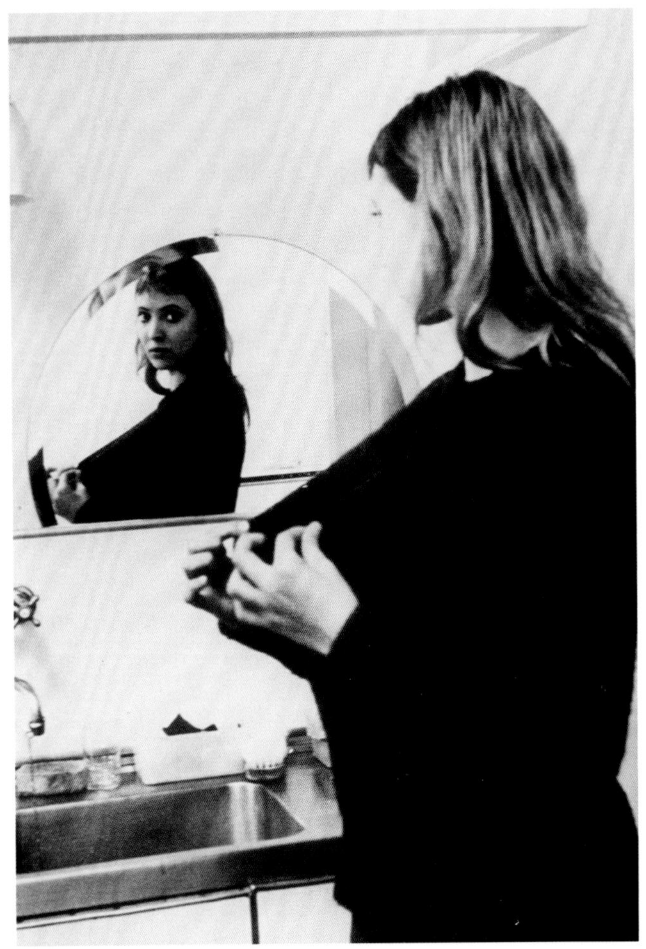

Almost twenty years before Demi Moore's provocative pose on the cover of *Vanity Fair* in 1991, semi-nude and pregnant, and decades before the ubiquitous bare baby-bump images, Varda showcased a very pregnant nude woman dancing and laughing in the television documentary *Réponse de femmes* (*Women Reply*, 1975),[46] the woman declaring, "I feel beautiful, whole/pregnant [a play on words], and desirable." Not meant as a provocation, according to Varda, she included it simply because she found it beautiful. She did not shy away from provocative images, however. Her opening scenes in *L'Opéra-Mouffe* (*Diary of a Pregnant Woman*, 1958) juxtapose a pregnant woman's torso with a close-up of a round squash, cut open violently with a knife at the market to expose its seeds. Pregnant at the time of the shoot, Varda explained that the sequence conveyed her own apprehension and ambivalence at becoming a mother. Her project *Réponse de femmes* poses the question out-

Anna Karina (Odile) in Jean-Luc Godard's *Bande à part* (*Band of Outsiders*), 1964

right: "Do all women want to be mothers?" The film provides different answers through different women. "What is a real woman?" it also asks. "How dare they decide if we're real women or not?" it answers. "How can we be women other than in men's eyes? What is a woman's body if we always must account for our weight and measurements?" Ahead of its time, the film addresses ageism with shots of nude older women who say, "Men deny us the right to age," followed by an insert: "Shot censored by penal code section 283." The next scene implies the content of the missing shot: "If our private parts are a place for pleasure, love and children, how do we inhabit them?"[47] The women then declare, "We don't appear naked in this film just to be seen, nor to be ogled, but to assert our desires. Voluptuousness but not voyeurism, sexuality, not a sex shop, love but not blackmail." The film points out the "enormous contradiction" of living in a woman's body in the 1970s (as well as today): "First, we're told 'hide your private parts.' Then we're told 'expose yourself, you please others, your body sells.' We're told 'be modest, don't show your ass.'" Before vocalizing the contradictions, New Wave women lived them.

In Rohmer's 1967 film *La Collectionneuse* (*The Collector*), the protagonist Haydée mentions to another character that she is "searching." Seberg's Patricia says something similar in *À bout de souffle*. Though what exactly they are searching for remains undefined, they are active in their pursuit, implicitly questioning the expected or pre-assigned roles that society has carved out for them, in search of something more. Many women of the New Wave seemed to be searching, in fact, as if on a mission for deeper meaning in their lives and for agency in the events that shaped them.

Within New Wave films, many female characters portray or articulate challenges for women, voicing concerns of most women in western society in the 1960s. Playing out these tensions in their films, their characters often challenged those conventions and expectations, implicitly raising awareness of socially prescribed confining roles. Some of these same tensions still remain extremely relevant over sixty years later. The search for agency as women in a patriarchal world is still at the center of women's lives today. Con-

cerns about appearance while longing for authenticity still create a seemingly unresolvable conflict for women. New Wave films also articulate concrete questions about the ability to make decisions that direct the path of women's lives, in terms of career, marriage, motherhood, or love.

Starting in the 1960s, an evolution in terms of women's rights began gaining momentum in an era known as the "second wave of feminism." The first wave, dating from the mid-1800s, saw women fighting for the right to an education, for wage equality, and for the right to divorce. With World War I and World War II, women in France made headway in breaking out of women's traditional gender roles and stereotypes, but only obtained the right to vote in 1944. Simone de Beauvoir's revolutionary *Le Deuxième sexe* (*The Second Sex*) in 1949 raised awareness of inequalities and of how women were shaped by society. In turn, the ground started to shift, but female autonomy and broader rights for women were slow to change. The films made during this period house tensions between men and women and conflicts regarding women's roles.

For women, the idea of marriage, for example, represented a defining aspect of their future as well as their identity. For better or worse, women had to weigh their financial well-being against their autonomy in very concrete ways unimaginable today. Anna Karina spoke, for example, about when a woman could not own a bank account or write a check without her husband's approval, also recounting that before she was married, as she was under twenty-one, she was not allowed to sign her own contract to act in her first film with Godard.[48] Women were also not allowed to work without their husband's authorization and would not gain this right until 1965, adding to the challenge of even envisioning a career. In this context, a woman like Varda, with her success as a photographer and then as one of the only women directors in the film industry at the time, is even more admirable. Making her first film in 1954, in her mid-twenties, was almost a miraculous feat.

Many New Wave films address the very real concern for women of conforming to the conventions of married life

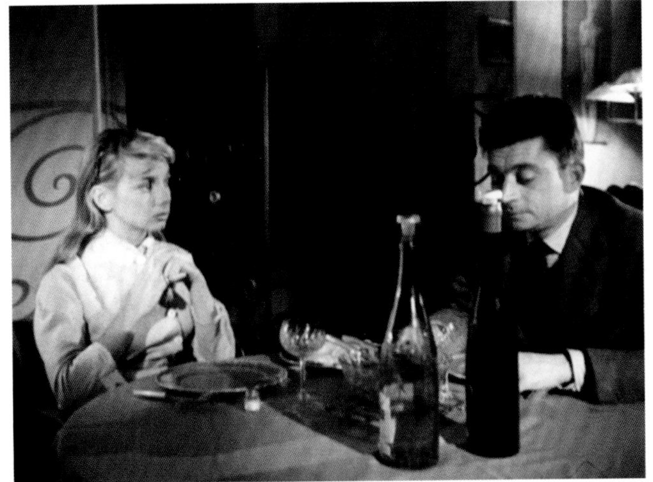

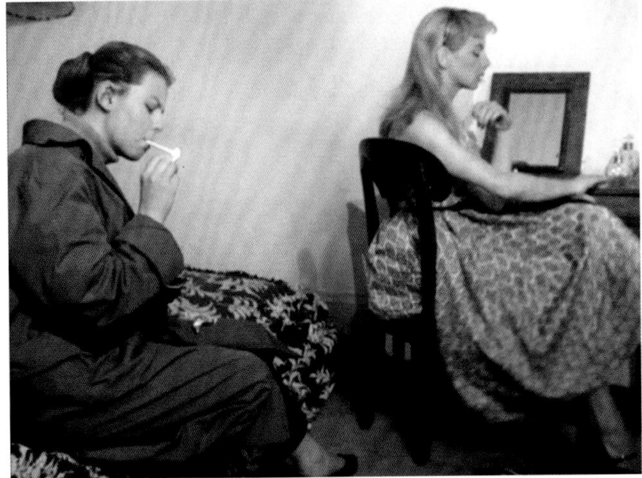

woman, and through her wardrobe of comfortable clothing, juxtaposed with her sister's more formal dress as a bourgeois wife.

Eight years after *Le Coup du berger*, the conflict was still present in society as well as in cinema, and Godard's 1964 film *Une femme mariée* (*A Married Woman*) sheds light on how labels defined the roles of women and men alike. Godard uses the same type of parallel editing as Rivette to show the married woman in similar postures and situations with her husband and with her lover, caught between the two. In doing so, the films both highlight her pursuit of an identity through different statuses as defined by men who are seen as almost interchangeable (like Varda explored in *Le Bonheur*). Macha Méril in the role of the wife in Godard's film seeks to reconcile the idea of being a respectable wife and mother with that of a sensual woman who desires a man outside her marriage (and her socially defined role).

In *Une femme est une femme* (*A Woman Is a Woman*, 1961), Godard showcased Karina playing a newlywed woman who wants to have a baby while aspiring to a career. As Karina's character dances in a cabaret, dreaming of being in a musical, she also dreams of having a child. Off screen, Karina's own dream of becoming a leading actress came true at the same time as she began to contemplate motherhood. Karina, in fact, became pregnant during the shoot. Her character examines herself in the mirror with pillows stuffed under her sweater, projecting what she would look like, recalling Seberg in a similar scene in *À bout de souffle*.

While marriage and motherhood went together at the time, society was evolving. During most of the 1960s, with the Catholic Church still extremely influential in France, however, birth control and abortion were both illegal. This context is important to consider in Godard's later feature, *Une femme mariée*, which addresses birth control, still seen as taboo. Vocalizing a married woman's questions to her doctor on the subject in one of the first times on screen, Charlotte (Méril) evokes desire and motherhood. Addressing France's political hot topic was provocative as the country slowly broke away from Catholicism's stronghold on its cit-

while searching for their identity outside of that construct. In Jacques Rivette's short *Le Coup du berger*, an implicit critique of bourgeois marriage depicts a bored housewife coming up with a plan to create some intrigue in her life. The plot calls to France's theatrical past with a type of marivaudage driving the narrative and illustrates through the metaphor of chess power plays between husband and wife, wife and lover, and between sisters, at a time when women were beginning to gain ground in relationships. Love triangles and adultery were often dedramatized in the New Wave, but they could also hide more serious matters regarding questions of power. The film also brings in a minor character who is more modern: the heroine's sister, who embodies freedom through her status as a young, single

Top: Virginie Vitry (Claire) and Jacques Doniol-Valcroze (Jean, the husband)
Bottom: Anne Doat (Solange) and Virginie Vitry in Jacques Rivette's *Le Coup du berger* (*Fool's Mate*), 1956

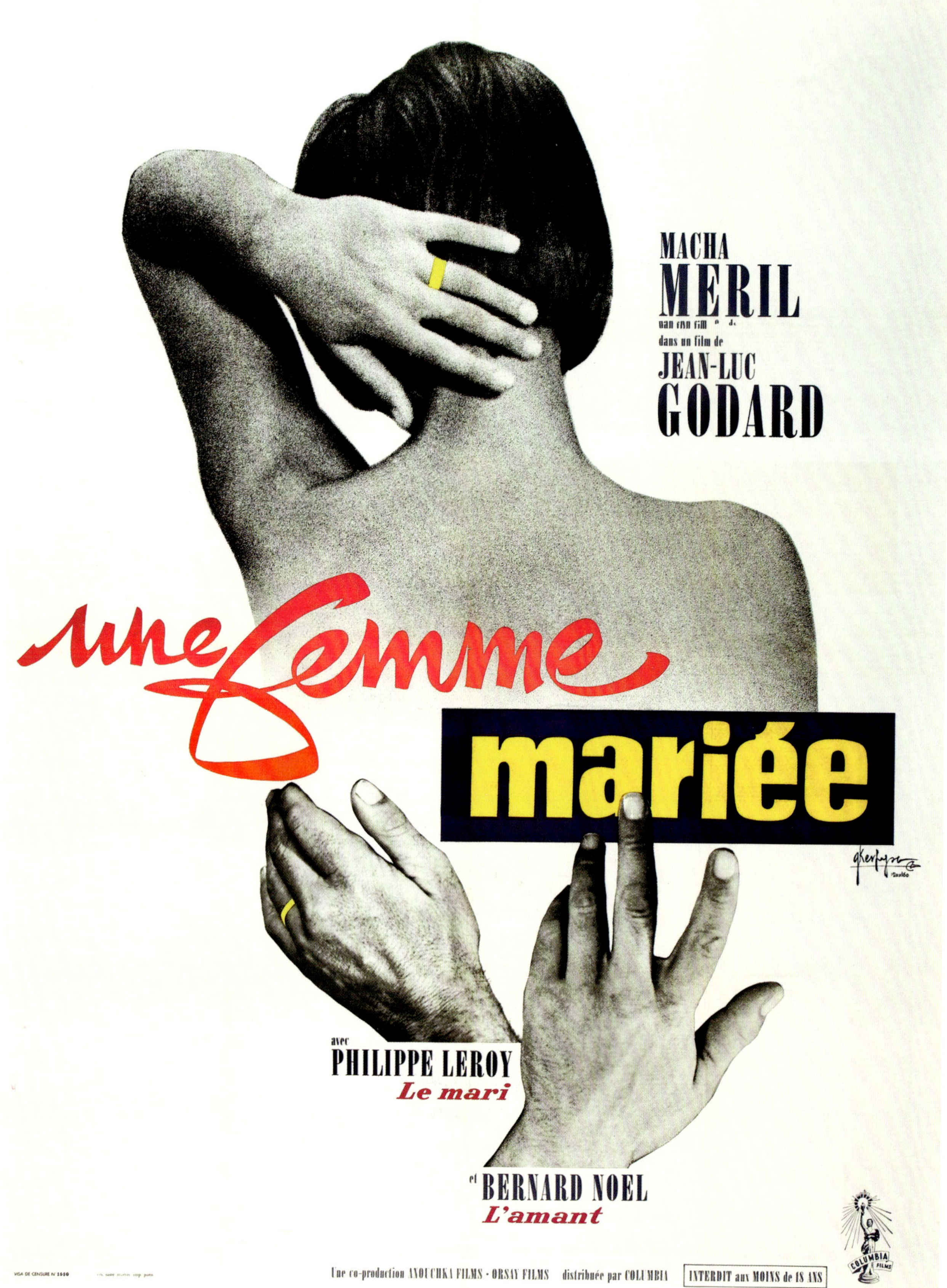

MACHA
MERIL
dans un film de
JEAN-LUC
GODARD
une femme mariée
avec
PHILIPPE LEROY
Le mari
et BERNARD NOEL
L'amant
Une co-production ANOUCHKA FILMS · ORSAY FILMS   distribuée par COLUMBIA   INTERDIT aux MOINS de 18 ANS
COLUMBIA FILMS

izens' freedoms in terms of reproductive rights. Legalized in 1967 under the Neuwirth Act, contraception remained blocked, however, for several years by the conservative government, and it took eight more years for France to legalize abortion in 1975. Chabrol's later feature *Une affaire de femmes* (*Story of Women*, 1988), based on Francis Szpiner's book, tells the true story of Marie-Louise Giraud (played by Isabelle Huppert), who was guillotined in 1943 under Vichy law for having performed twenty-seven abortions to make ends meet in German-occupied France.

In this context, evoking reproductive rights in films, especially abortion, was extremely daring in 1959 and into the 1960s. In Chabrol's *Les Cousins*, for example, a minor character, Geneviève (introduced as *la poule*, "the chick" with whom Paul, the libertine cousin, had enjoyed a summer tryst), appears as a problematic figure, "in trouble" after their fling. Paul is annoyed by the situation, telling Geneviève to "take care of it," doing his part by giving her money to help make the problem go away. Though the scene appears as explicitly misogynistic from today's lens, it is hard to assess Chabrol's level of criticism of Paul, as the character's reaction aligned with how things were often handled at the time. In Godard's *À bout de souffle*, when Patricia shares with Michel that she might be pregnant, he gets angry, telling her "tu aurais dû faire attention"–that *she* should have paid attention, been more careful. The responsibility rested fully on the woman, as did the consequences. Rozier's *Adieu Philippine* shows one of the female protagonists in a similar predicament. Like in *Les Cousins*, the subject of the clandestine abortion goes unnamed but is alluded to by innuendo. Here, a scene at the doctor's office where the scared teenaged girl must carefully ask her family doctor for the procedure (without explicitly naming what she needs) was cut from the final version of the film. Both films articulated (or intended to) this very real concern for women that translated as an unfathomable fear. In *Adieu Philippine*, Rozier showed how greatly the realities of men and women differed, consisting of almost two worlds where men faced the fear of war, and women that of pregnancy.

Alongside the lack of freedom women endured regarding their own bodies, concurrently, the practice of women hiring themselves out to men was largely accepted. Prostitution was depicted as another way a woman had to make a living, though obviously not a respectable one. In the films at the time, prostitute figures were pervasive, appearing as a norm. In a man's life, patronizing *filles de joies* (literally, "girls of joy") was considered a rite of passage or an outside activity in a marriage that was almost expected. Prostitutes occupy center stage in films like Godard's *Vivre sa vie* (*My Life to Live*, 1962), *Deux ou trois choses que je sais d'elle* (*Two or Three Things I Know About Her*, 1967), and Buñuel's *Belle de jour* (1967). They also appear as accessory characters throughout Truffaut's filmography. Along with prostitutes, the figure of the nun appears in Rivette's *La Religieuse* (*The Nun*, 1966), challenging the image of women's historical confinement in another type of cage. The film, taken as an attack on Catholicism, like its eighteenth-century literary source, was banned.

Cinematic depictions of both nun and prostitute at the time ultimately translated a fear of women's sexuality. With a tension between women's agency and objectification, Bardot incarnated the conflict in an exemplary depiction of a strong, sensuous subject-object in Vadim's *Et Dieu créa la femme*. Often, a female character would be depicted as being possessed or overtaken by an invisible force that needed to be resolved by punishing her or showing her on a path to redemption, thereby restoring social order. Similarly, female homosexuality was portrayed as deviant and provocative. *Les Cousins* alludes to the topic by way of the strong yet shady Yvonne (Michèle Méritz), a character that also evokes Parisian corruption. Later, in *Les Biches* (*The Does*, 1968), Chabrol recentered his film on a lesbian relationship to draw audiences to the box office in a story that ends in violence.

As the decade progressed, French society began to shift away from its conservative traditions. Tensions were worked out in many films, vacillating from depictions of women as apparitions or iterations of femmes fatales to those of more autonomous and realistic figures. With the May 1968 period of civil unrest, which featured protests and student movements, women gained more ground. The MLF, le Mouvement de libération des femmes (the French Women's Liberation Movement), came out of this social upheaval. By 1970,

Jean-Luc Godard's *Une femme mariée* (*A Married Woman*), 1964, poster

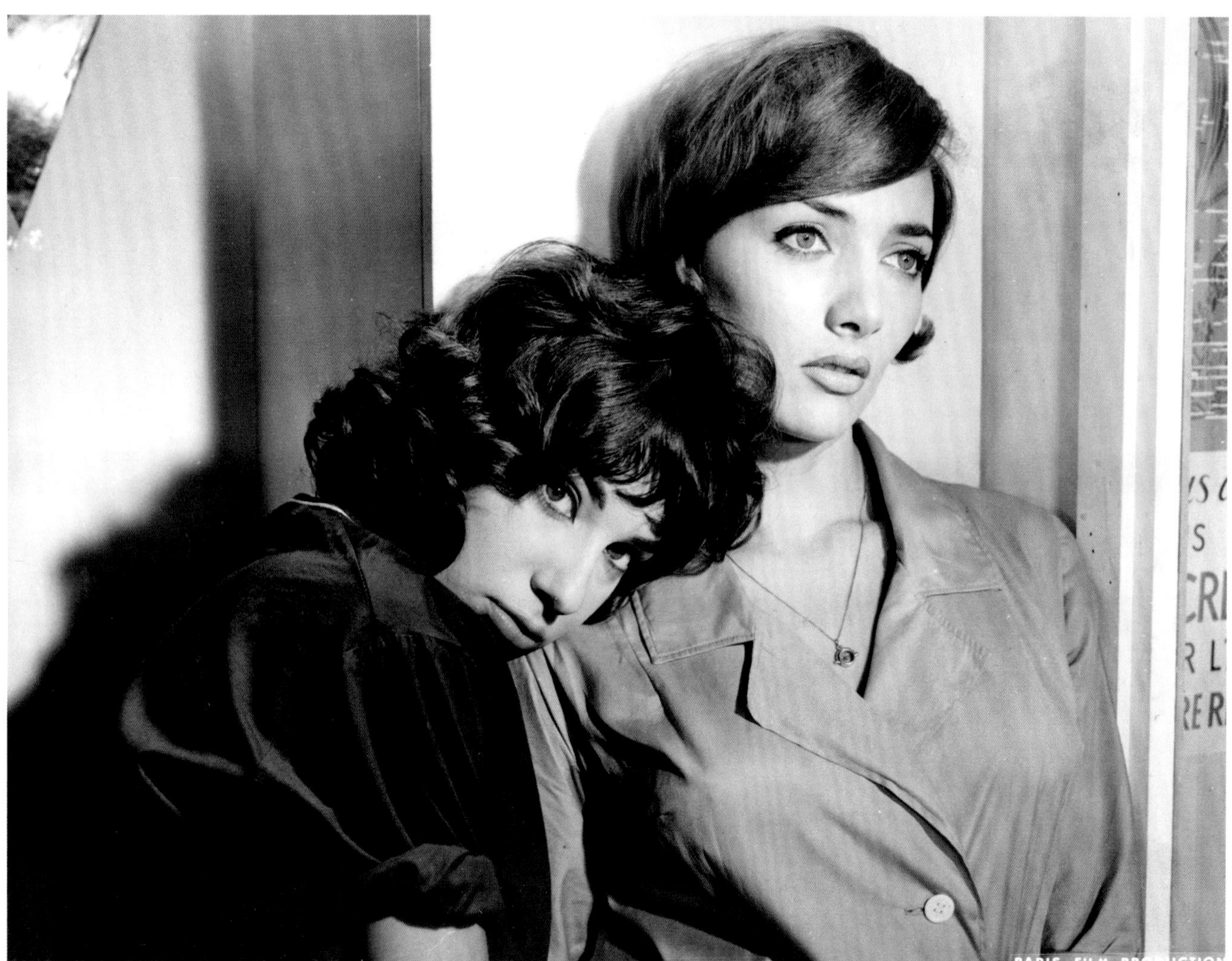

men no longer held authority over the family, and in 1971, women revindicated reproductive rights by signing "Le Manifeste des 343 salopes" ("The Manifesto of 343 Sluts"). This confrontational document, co-written by Gisèle Halimi and Simone de Beauvoir and published in *Le Nouvel observateur*, was a space where women spoke about their illegal abortions, making them vulnerable to serious legal consequences. Thanks in part to the 343 self-proclaimed *salopes* —including many well-known and respected women—who had the courage to sign the manifesto, women's reproductive rights came to the forefront and out of the dark alleys of society. Four years later, in 1975, abortion was legalized after France's minister of health, Simone Veil, drafted the law. This piece of legislation, known as *la loi Veil* (the Veil law), became a landmark moment in French feminism and repre-

sented a break with the Catholic church.[49] Macha Méril (who incarnated the vocal married woman inquiring about reproductive rights in Godard's *Une femme mariée*) spoke in an interview on French radio (RTL) on March 8, 2024, International Women's Day, of the strides made in society since her youth, noting that today's generation was "beginning at a different starting point." She described the founding of the #MeToo movement as *génial* (fantastic), and the expression as "something easy to understand all over the world, quick, international. It's a great idea, very strong." Méril's words speak to the real progress made in France for women since the 1960s.

New Wave films also revealed the tension present for women in the workplace. Opportunities were limited, with

Bernadette Lafont and Stéphane Audran in Claude Chabrol's *Les Bonnes femmes* (*The Good Time Girls*), 1960 secretaries, typists, teachers, nurses, and shopkeepers being some of the only respectable options. But as society changed, some women sought other careers. Seberg's character in *À bout de souffle* is an aspiring journalist. Godard showed not only her ambition but the challenges she faced in a male-dominated, misogynist environment: Parvulesco, the novelist (played by director Jean-Pierre Melville) whom she interviews, answers her questions condescendingly, dismissing her as not a serious reporter. In Chabrol's *Les Bonnes femmes* (*The Good Time Girls*, 1960), Lafont, Stéphane Audran, Lucile Saint-Simon, and Clotilde Joano play bored shopgirls who wish for something bigger while daydreaming of true love in a violent, male-dominated world. Not only does their boss harass them with disdainful remarks and behavior, Lafont's character, after a night out, is raped. Although not shown explicitly, the act is strongly alluded to in Chabrol's sadistic *mise en scène*. Even worse, Joano's idealistic character is punished for naively believing in true love, murdered in a forest after a romantic outing with her love interest—a hopeless message echoing the fate of Giulietta Masina's character in Federico Fellini's *Le notti di Cabiria* (*Nights of Cabiria*, 1957), released a few years earlier.

Seyrig addressed the topic of society's conditioning of women to aspire to love above all else in reference to her character Hélène in Resnais's *Muriel ou le temps d'un retour* (*Muriel, or The Time of Return*, 1963). "I think the career of women is love," she told director Katja Raganelli in 1977.[50] "That's what they're taught, that love is the important thing in life. . . . [T]hey go on believing that love still exists and that they can create it . . . with another person. This is a myth of course and a lot of money is put into this myth to perpetuate it and to cultivate it and to make women believe that it exists, but the people who give the money for this myth of love do not believe in love of course . . . and women buy love and that keeps them from wanting to do anything else."

In *Les Cousins*, the male protagonists illustrate a conflict between romantic love and desire stemming from a shift in values and a new moral freedom, revendicated by the younger generation. With regard to women, their burgeoning liberation is at odds with the pressure to marry. Florence, the

main female character and part of a love triangle with the two cousins, grapples with her desire for true love and stability with the romantic but provincial Charles, and her longing for adventure, freedom, and physical desire with the Parisian libertine, Paul. As illustrated explicitly in Chabrol's *mise en scène*, Florence is confined in this unresolvable predicament, depicted literally behind bars as she sunbathes, adopting a semi-nude Bardot posture on the balcony.

Locked into her incarnation of the elusive ideal for Charles, translated by his gazing up at her through the bars, and her embodiment of pure carnal pleasure for Paul, the lothario, who looms over her in predatory fashion, she is entrapped by both visions. As she searches for agency, there is seemingly no way of reconciling the two as Paul aptly points out in a monologue describing the fastidious monotony she is sure to face with Charles if she adheres to convention and settles down with him. If she chooses freedom with Paul, the libertine, however, she is sure to be punished. She will either be slightly chastised by being labeled a *salope* (a slut), or worse, cast out of bourgeois society, alone, much like the famous libertine Madame de Merteuil in Pierre Choderlos de Laclos's eighteenth-century novel *Les Liaisons dangereuses*.

For actresses, the same types of challenges existed as they were searching for agency in their careers. Often, they were at the mercy of their directors in much the same way that Florence tried to navigate her future through the options defined by her suitors. In her 2024 interview, Méril spoke

Next page: Juliette Mayniel (Florence) and Gérard Blain (Charles) in Claude Chabrol's *Les Cousins* (*The Cousins*), 1959

Above: Jean-Claude Brialy (Paul) and Juliette Mayniel in Chabrol's *Les Cousins*, 1959

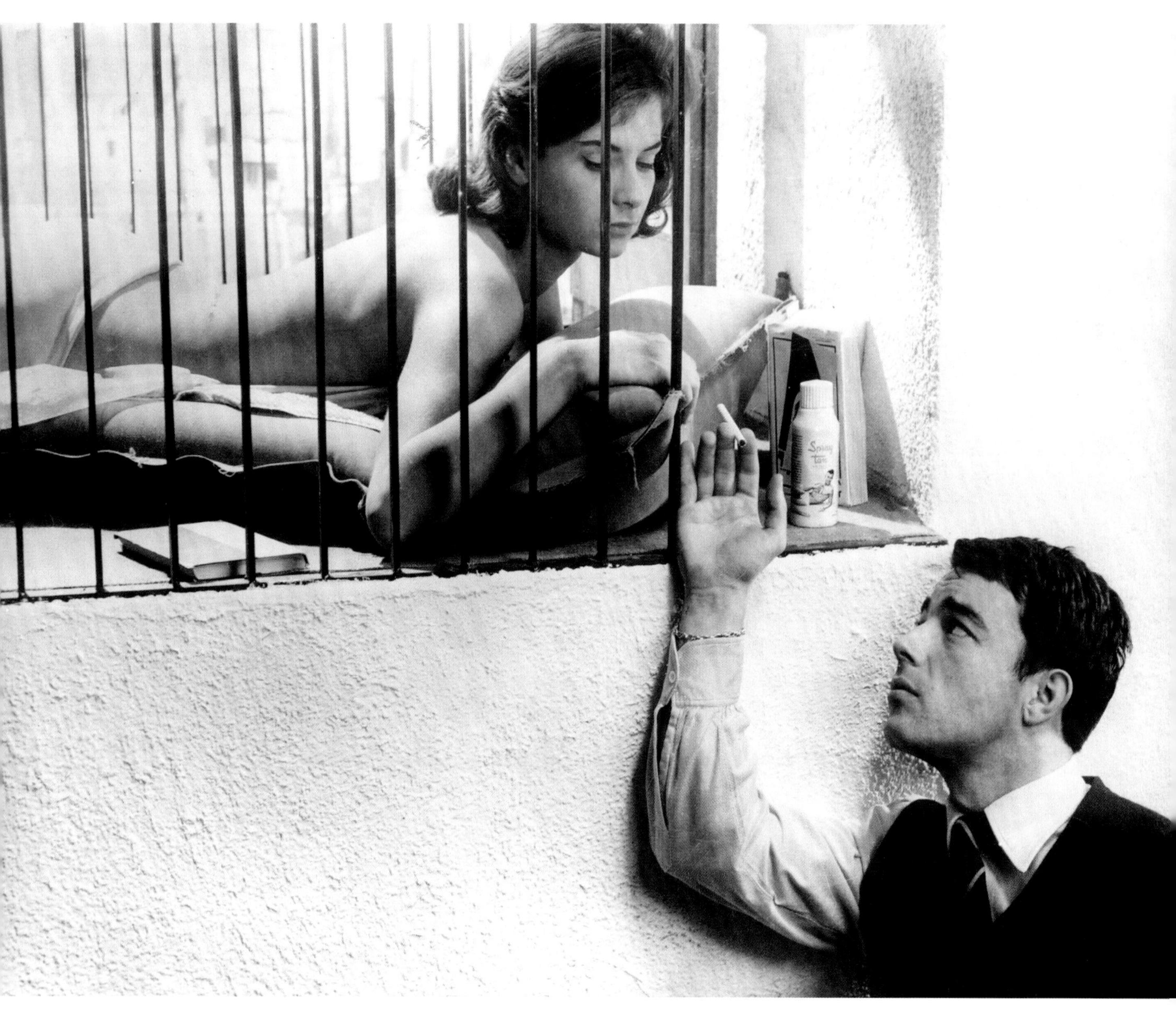

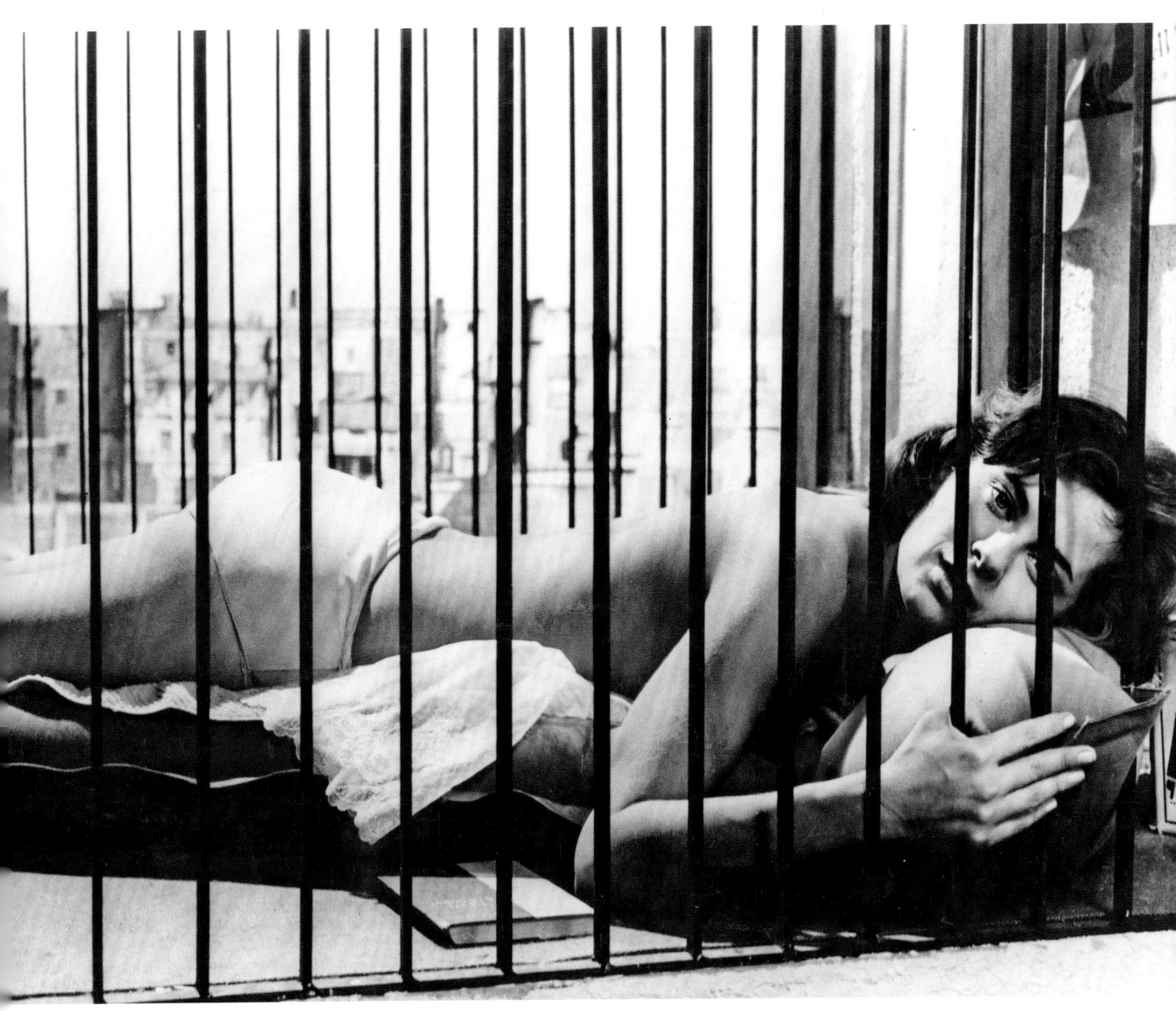

of directors in her day who were "indifferent to [actresses'] pain," describing them as "consuming" women. "It was difficult for many women," she stated. "Look at the fates of Marilyn Monroe, Martine Carol, even of Brigitte Bardot. They are women who only had one way to fight: becoming famous and earning money. There were a few exceptions, and all the rest. I was part of the rest, in fact."[51]

BRIGHT SPARKS: HOW ACTRESS-DIRECTOR ENCOUNTERS GAVE US THE NEW WAVE

"It's not a good screenplay, but he's a good director, and he may make something of it." Kim Novak recalled this remark from Harry Cohn of Columbia Pictures before he loaned her to Universal Studios to make *Vertigo*. While the influence of the director is well-established, with stories like this one as proof, that of the actress, as well-loved and respected as she may be, is somewhat overlooked. The tendency especially holds true for the New Wave, a movement that transfigured the cinematic landscape and still influences many young filmmakers today, in which the directors' names are the ones that are cited and the most applauded. The Godard, Truffaut, Chabrol, Rivette, Rohmer monolith can lead to overlooking the talent and creativity that those without the title of auteur contributed to this collective art. While many of the actresses have reached cult status because of their beauty or iconic roles, their contributions, on screen and off, have not necessarily taken center stage. This is not to condemn the directors, or to lay blame on men. From *Une femme est une femme* and *L'Homme qui aimait les femmes* (*The Man Who Loved Women*, 1977) to *Une femme mariée* and *La Mariée était en noir* (*The Bride Wore Black*, 1968), the importance of the women in these films mostly made by men is visible, as is the impact of the films on women's issues. A trace of the reality of the period lies in the images and sound recorded on film, with deeper truths emerging in the poetry of their cinema. With a movement obsessed with women, little is known about the real women themselves. Reconsidering these works of art through a new lens by reconstructing the context of a time of immense social change and artistic creativity, and reexamining the roles women played in this collective art, corrects the imbalance.

Of the films that have marked the history of cinema, it is the coming together of talent that made them exceptional and gave them their magic. The encounter of actors, cinematographers, scriptwriters, editors, directors, and the many others behind the scenes sets cinema apart as a collective art. Actresses relied on the talent of the directors in the same way that directors relied on that of the actresses. In the 1950s, with a cinema that was not very inventive, Moreau, for example, had difficulty finding her place although she was a well-respected stage actress. Physically, her face did not correspond to the classic beauty of an actress like Michèle Morgan, and her body was not as voluptuous as Bardot's. She was not considered photogenic, and traditional make-up artists tried in vain to modify her features through contouring.[52] Malle, however, found a way past the superficial and with a more natural approach captured a depth that the actress brought to the screen in *Ascenseur* that would change her career. Through the coming together of actress, director, cinematographer, and the music of Miles Davis, the film, like the actress, became modern. The encounter is key.

Although directors usually get most of the credit for a film's success, many contribute to a film's special spark. The convergence of many factors at just the right time in history created the New Wave, a mosaic of voices and encounters contributing to the beauty and soul of the films. In Marguerite Duras's script of *Hiroshima, mon amour* (1959), she described the meeting of her two unnamed protagonists: "The time is summer, 1957—August—at Hiroshima. A French woman, about thirty years old, has come to Hiroshima to play in a film on Peace. . . . The day before her return to France, this French woman, whose name will never be given in the film—this anonymous woman—meets a Japanese (engineer or architect) and has a very brief love affair with him. How they met will not be revealed in the picture. For that is not what really matters. Chance meetings occur everywhere in the world. What is important is what these ordinary meetings lead to."[53]

In the abundance of films appearing between 1957 and the late 1960s, encounters between actresses and directors, who were fascinated by them, produced new, modern roles for women. Historic collaborations like that of Anna Karina with Jean-Luc Godard, Brigitte Bardot with Roger Vadim, and Anouk Aimée with Jacques Demy brought cinema *nouvelles femmes*. In the case of Jeanne Moreau, her creative collaboration with Louis Malle led to a new way of filming that would transform the actress and revolutionize cinema. Their personal relationship influenced their films, integrating Moreau's independent spirit in the roles she played, leading to more authentic and complex portrayals of women. Other encounters would produce equally independent, free-thinking, modern characters. Jean Seberg infused Godard's Patricia in *À bout de souffle* with her American attitude and style, cultivated from her previous roles. Rohmer chose Haydée Politoff to embody the liberated young heroine in *La Collectionneuse*, morphing the character to fit the actress's own modern *façon d'être* (way of being). In *Ma nuit chez Maud* (*My Night at Maud's*, 1969), Rohmer went even further in writing the script with Françoise Fabian in mind specifically for the independent and complex Maud—telling her that if she did not accept the role, he would not make the film. With Alain Resnais, his collaborations with Emmanuelle Riva and Delphine Seyrig produced earlier iterations of independent and mature women, each contributing to their character's complexity. In the case of Agnès Varda, as a director, her philosophy speaks to the value of every person involved in a film's creation: "I think awakening and stimulating each person's creativity is the gift of the director," she declared. "It's also a power, a very gentle power." While the dynamics in these relationships remain complex, with an inherent imbalance of power as the (often male) directors occupy a privileged position, a closer look at the encounter shows just how much influence the actresses had in creating new images of women, showing new perspectives and people and revealing deeper truths.

In *Chronique d'un été* (*Chronicle of a Summer*, 1961), a documentary by the renowned sociologist Edgar Morin in dialogue with the director Jean Rouch, Marceline Loridan-Ivens walks through the streets of Paris, exploring questions of happiness and life in 1960, interviewing passersby on their experiences. With war raging in Algeria and the Congo fighting for its independence at the time of the film, Loridan-Ivens also looks back to reflect on her own experience as a Jewish woman in the wake of World War II. French critic and literary theorist Roland Barthes called *Chronique d'un été* "the first film that made me see others."[54] Much like Varda's whole filmography was defined by her observation and validation of others, through filming their faces and giving the unseen a voice, cinema as a medium and an art form possesses the invaluable quality of projecting other experiences, characters, and perspectives on screen, which can lead to more mutual understanding.

As Moreau expressed near the end of her career: "I think it's really the mirror of the world. A feature film is an allegory. It can be poetry. It's truer than the truth. There is a lovely phrase by Jean Cocteau, 'Ce beau mensonge qui dit la vérité.' This beautiful lie that tells the truth. That is creation, that is art."[55] In a different vein, in her 2024 interview about her Russian film festival in Paris, Méril (of Russian origin) also spoke of the importance of cinema as documenting the truth: "That is why I like cinema. The truth is told to you through film. They show you life in the villages as they are. . . . Cinema brings us truths that no one else tells us, not even journalists or diplomats."[56]

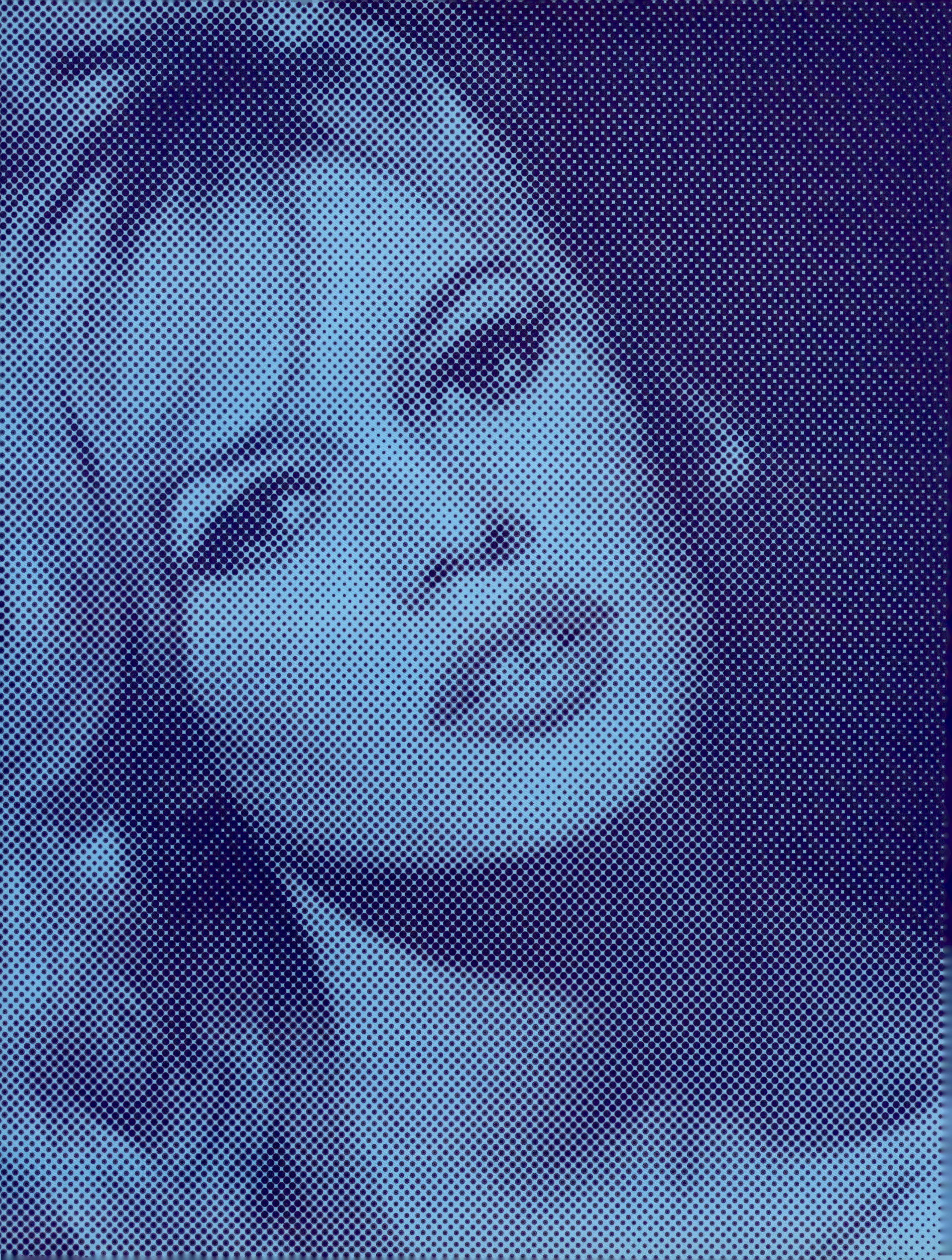

brigitte bardot 2

la femme naturelle | *the natural woman*

BARDOT AND VADIM: A NEW KIND OF STAR IS BORN

Before being known as "the most beautiful woman in the world," before becoming the hottest sex symbol in cinema, long before the "Bardot phenomenon" or being identifiable uniquely by her initials, Brigitte Bardot in 1949 was a French schoolgirl *de bonne famille* who had lived through the difficulties of the war years and, at age fourteen, dreamed of becoming a dancer. While her upbringing in a well-to-do Catholic household would have prepared her for a life as a typical bourgeois wife, given her host of promising eligible bachelors who would have pleased her parents, Bardot, like many of the characters she would go on to portray, sought something different.

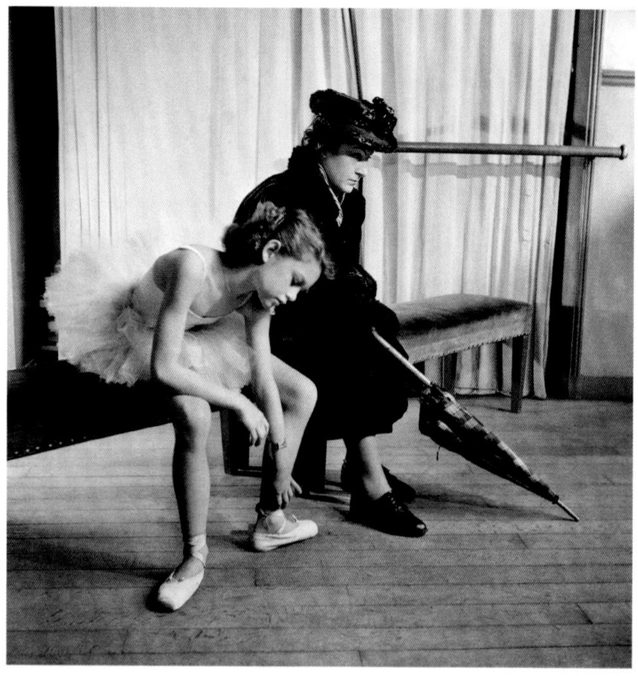

In a twist of fate, that same year, as her prospects for a dance career were unclear, the young Bardot had the chance to do a photo shoot depicting a young modern Frenchwoman for a junior edition of the fashion magazine *Le Jardin des modes* through its editor, Madame de la Villehuchet, a personal friend of Bardot's mother. After she assured Madame Bardot that her daughter would not be considered a "model" since she would "not be paid," preserving her reputation (since modeling was not considered respectable at the time), Bardot was allowed to do the shoot. Then, Hélène Gordon-Lazareff, editor in chief of *Elle* magazine, having seen the cover, wanted Bardot to appear in her magazine. "There'll be no cover girl in this family," her parents protested. But since she would still not be paid, they acquiesced. Arriving in the studio, she was terrified and insecure. "They looked at me, they commented on my teeth, my hair, my nails. No, I didn't have makeup on. I was only fourteen and a half! No, I didn't have a bra. I was only fourteen and a half! No, I didn't know how to pose. I was only fourteen and a half!" Bardot wrote in her memoir. She described being shot in profile for the cover because "it was the only possibility," explaining it through her eyes: "I was ugly."[1] In May 1949, however, Bardot made the cover of *Elle*.[2] As she continued to appear in the magazine, her image began to evolve–though often prim and proper, the spark behind her eyes quietly foretold the explosion to come.

Little did she, or the world, know that the magazine cover would also prompt a meeting that would change not only the face of cinema but also the image of what a woman could be–independent, unconventional, free.[3] Upending stereotypes and constraints that came before her, in real life and on screen, Brigitte Bardot also broke considerable ground in embodying agency for women, even if she was known primarily as a sex symbol. Almost seventy years later, the initials B.B. (as inscribed in musical history by Serge Gainsbourg) still suffice in identifying her, and the world continues to talk about her life and to identify Saint-Tropez with the lifestyle she made famous. In 2023, a six-part series called simply *Bardot* premiered on French television (France 2), depicting her life between those earth-shaking years of 1949 to 1960, a period that would transform France, cinema, and Bardot's own life.

Before the shockwave, Bardot's career mirrored the state of traditional French cinema at the time. A popular director from the older generation (the group that would later be qualified as the *cinéma de papa*), Marc Allégret was known for seeking out young talent[4] and for having discovered a number of stars.[5] He took under his wing the young Roger Vadim, becoming his mentor, friend, and, in Vadim's own words, his "third father."[6] Descended from Russian aristocrats (the Plemiannikovs), Vadim, the son of a Russian diplomat, was born in Paris but grew up in Alexandria, where his father was based, and moved to France after his father's early death. Spending much of World War II in the French Alps, where his stepfather helped smuggle Jewish people and Communists across the Swiss border, he experienced the trauma of the war firsthand. His best friend was burned to death by the Nazi SS.[7]

After the war, Vadim became part of the bohemian crowd of Saint-Germain-des-Prés and acted for three years in theater before tiring of the repetition.[8] Far from the *Cahiers du cinéma* where other New Wave directors would hone their critical eye, Vadim came into film through the old-school approach to movies as Allégret's assistant, and later worked as a journalist for the popular glossy magazine *Paris Match*.[9] The veteran director employed Vadim as his right-hand man, his co-scriptwriter, and eventually his assistant director. After being struck by the image of a girl he saw by chance in *Elle* magazine, Vadim recounted, he brought Bardot to the attention of his boss. Immediately, Allégret saw her potential in front of the camera.

In hopes of bridging the gap with younger audiences, Allégret was planning to film Vadim's screen adaptation of Édouard Dujardin's novel *Les Lauriers sont coupés* (*We'll to the Woods No More*, 1887).[10] The magazine *Cinémonde* had devoted an article to it that showcased Vadim, calling him "the youngest screenwriter in Europe,"[11] anticipating the massive wave of youth in cinema. Allégret was convinced that Bardot was the perfect fit for the film's heroine and asked to meet her for a screen test. Chances were slim that Bardot's conservative parents would agree. She was still only fifteen. Again, they protested, "There'll be no actress in this family,"[12] but Allégret's name held weight. Bardot's mother accompanied her to meet the renowned director. Vadim, who was introduced as the film's screenwriter, welcomed mother and daughter before Allégret spoke to Madame Bardot. Vadim recounted that upon meeting the young Bardot, he was "immediately struck by her posture" and "curved

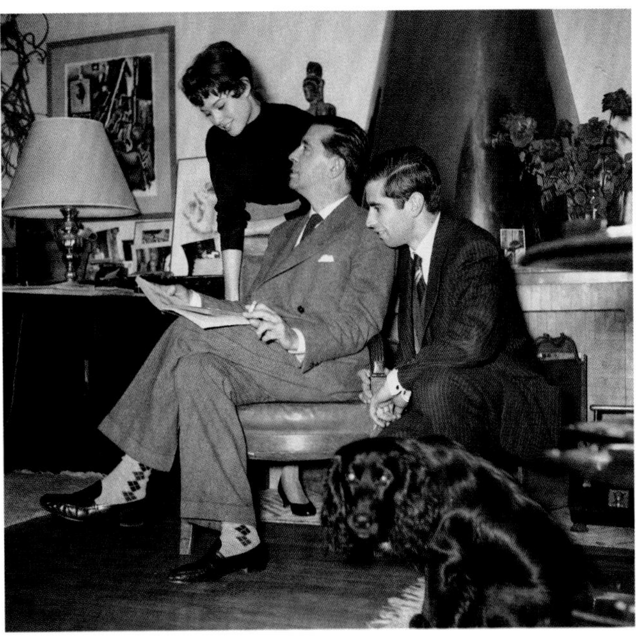

Brigitte Bardot, Marc Allégret, and Roger Vadim at the time of shooting
Futures vedettes (*School of Love*), 1955

waist." Bardot would later confess to being seized by an attack of love at first sight upon meeting Vadim.[13]

Charming Bardot's mother during their meeting, Allégret assured her of his good intentions, and the screen test took place. "I found myself with two centimeters of makeup on my face, my hair pulled back in a bun, dressed in an old rag, and they pushed me out on set. I was awful, unnatural, on the verge of tears," Bardot recounted. Just as she was about to recite her lines, Vadim arrived, in her words, "calm, smiling, kind and handsome, more handsome than I'd ever seen." He would give her her lines. "He took my hand and I held on to him, fascinated," she wrote, and on his suggestion, "they took off my two centimeters of makeup and let my hair be loose and free, and my body too. I felt better." Thanks to his relaxed attitude, she described, "I forgot that I was like a horse on the market whose teeth you look at before you buy." Afterward, Vadim offered to drive Bardot home and ended up staying for dinner. He was different from her regular suitors. "I remember the contrast between this bourgeois, luxurious dinner, with a butler, candles and silverware, and the presence of Vadim, in a worn turtleneck and long hair," the actress recalled, adding that she was "crazy about" his bohemian look.[14]

Bardot won over both Allégret and Vadim with her on-screen presence. "She had no acting experience but she gave the impression that she had been in front of a camera all her life," Vadim noted. The producer was not convinced, however; he "didn't like her teeth" and "thought she opened her mouth too much when she laughed."[15] He failed to see the spark that would make her a star and soon ignite the film industry worldwide. Though she lost the role (and the movie was never made), thanks to this encounter, Vadim and Bardot would go on to make film history. This did not happen immediately, however, as it would in the real-life and cinematic love story of Anna Karina and Jean-Luc Godard. In fact, it was only near the end of their romantic relationship that Vadim directed Bardot. But their personal relationship fueled their work on screen just as ardently.

Bardot, at fifteen, was almost seven years Vadim's junior when they met, so at the beginning of their romance, they kept their meetings hidden from her protective parents. Bardot started skipping school to visit Vadim at his apartment. "I should be in algebra class," Bardot said, according to Vadim, "but I have chosen freedom."[16] When her parents became suspicious, her father started keeping a closer watch on her. One night, upon returning home after "school," he asked her what subjects she studied that day. His daughter responding evasively, he told her that he knew she had been skipping class and that he was sending her to school in England. She would be taking the train the next morning. Under the threat of being separated from Vadim, Bardot attempted suicide that same evening. When her parents and her sister left to see a show, she stayed behind, claiming she had a headache. "I remember turning on the gas in the kitchen, closing tightly the windows and doors; I remember, at sixteen, having put my head in the oven. After, I don't remember anything," she wrote. The show was canceled, and her family came back early and discovered Bardot unconscious with a note. They saved her in the nick of time. The next day, it was decided that Bardot would not see Vadim again until she was of age and that she would be sent to boarding school. After she pleaded with her parents, Monsieur Bardot softened, but said she would only be allowed to marry Vadim when she turned eighteen. His daughter agreed.

The engagement was announced and the wedding set for after Bardot's eighteenth birthday. Because her family insisted they get married in a church, Vadim agreed to attend catechism classes twice a week and present the image of a *bon catholique* so that the priest could marry them. In the meantime, Bardot accompanied Vadim to events around Paris, where she began getting attention and everyone started asking who she was. "In spite of my desire to go unnoticed," she wrote, by the end of the night "the conversation was all about me." Upon meeting Bardot, Colette, the renowned author of *Gigi*, even wanted her to play the character on stage.[17] Bardot began appearing in films, comedies such as *Le Trou normand* (*Crazy for Love,* 1952), primarily for the money, and vowed each time she would never do it again.[18] Behind closed doors, Bardot became pregnant and went to Switzerland to have an abortion, which she hid from her parents.[19] Finally, on December 21, 1952, the couple wed in a civil service and in the Catholic church.

The following year, Bardot took a role on stage In Jean Anouilh's *L'Invitation au château* (*Invitation to the Castle*), a story of Pygmalion, prefiguring her on-screen transformation in front of Vadim's camera. She accepted the theatrical role purely for financial reasons, according to Vadim, not to seek fame or out of ambition to further her career. The Bardot phenomenon had begun germinating, however. Soon, Vadim noticed that his wife was receiving a startling amount of attention, even before she had made many films or was very well known. When she accompanied him to the 1953 Cannes Film Festival on his assignment to photograph Leslie Caron, for example, Vadim saw that she had true star quality from people's reactions to her. In his memoir, Vadim recounted the spectacle of two thousand American Marines applauding her from their aircraft carrier docked in the Bay of Cannes, "jostling each other for a better look" at the bikini-clad beauty who emerged from the sea. Bardot described the incident, saying she found herself aboard the aircraft carrier, saying "Hello, men," with sailors "throwing their caps in the air," while holding her up, shouting, "BRID-GET! BRID-GET! BRID-GET!" "They didn't know who I was

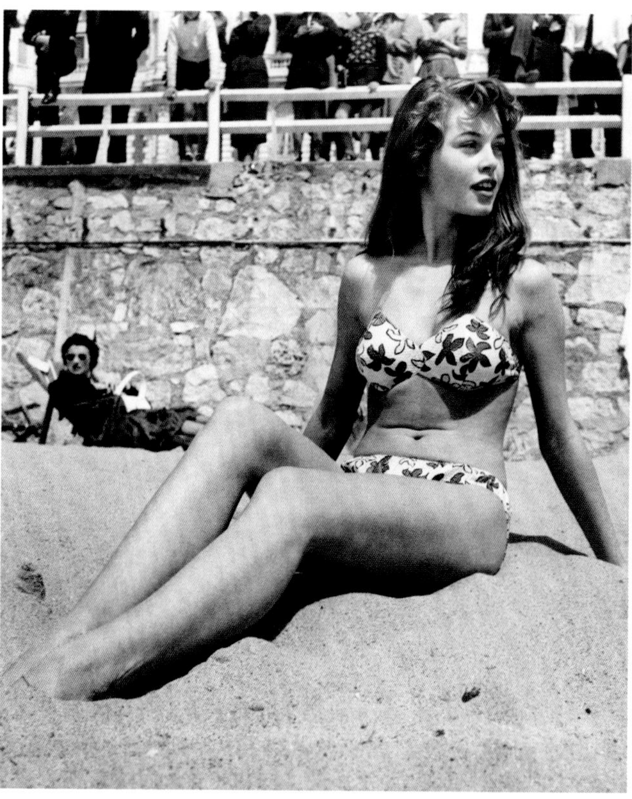

Brigitte Bardot on the beach at the Cannes Film Festival, 1953

at all," she said, "because I was nothing. I didn't know what was happening to me," she wrote, for them to "cheer for the only illustrious unknown in Cannes." Vadim described photographers who "abandoned their usual prey—international stars of both sexes—to pursue Brigitte," dressed in her blue jeans at the Carlton Hotel. With a hint of pride, he relayed the anecdote of Aristotle Onassis inviting her to a reception on his yacht, which she declined, saying she had plans to have dinner with her husband in private.[20] Admitting some professional envy years later, however, Vadim noted that her career began to accelerate just as his appeared to decline.

In the years leading up to their first collaboration, Bardot appeared in other well-known films, such as Sacha Guitry's *Si Versailles m'était conté* (*Royal Affairs in Versailles,* 1954); *Le Fils de Caroline chérie* (*Caroline and the Rebels,* 1955), part of the historical adventure series; and René Clair's *Les Grandes manoeuvres* alongside Michèle Morgan that same year. But the image she is known for today was not yet so apparent in these more conventional roles.

From the beginning, Bardot and Vadim's deep connection, with their life and art influencing each other, blurred the lines between reality and fantasy. The first time she had visited Vadim at his apartment, he told her, "You remind me of Sophie," the heroine in a novel he had written as an adolescent.[21] Like a hall of mirrors, Brigitte was just like the fictional Sophie, "vulnerable and dynamic, romantic, terribly sentimental and very modern in her ideas about sex and her aversion to the rules of middle-class morality," in his words.[22] Vadim claimed his heroine even "talked like Brigitte," her impertinent conversation spiced with crude words, but never vulgar ones. After Bardot read his novel, *Sophie* became her code name. She used it to sign her letters to him.[23] In the 1955 film that Vadim cowrote with Allégret, *Futures vedettes* (*School for Love*, based on a novel by Vicki Baum), Bardot would play Sophie, a dancer, starring opposite Jean Marais. Working again under Allégret, Vadim cowrote the screenplay for *En effeuillant la marguerite* (*Plucking the Daisy*, a.k.a. *Mam'selle Striptease*, 1956), and chose the name *Sophia* as Bardot's character's stage name when she performed a striptease.[24] While filming *Futures vedettes*, Bardot again

became pregnant, "a catastrophe," in her words. "I never in my life wanted to be a mother. . . . I needed to work. I was starting to get small roles. If I stopped, it was over." At the time, "abortion was punishable by prison," she wrote, but she went through with it. After the procedure, performed with no safety or hygiene measures, she had to be rushed to the emergency room and almost died.

On screen, Bardot and Vadim's story played out differently. "Vadim had worked a lot for me and written a script for a funny film in which I was to star, *En effeuillant la marguerite*. I was happy, he gave me a charming character who was a bit sexy, a bit of an ingénue, wreaking havoc along the way,"[25] she described in her memoir. Daniel Gélin, one of Vadim's best friends, appeared as Bardot's love interest, Daniel Roy, a character who also mirrored Vadim's identity as an on-the-move journalist. Bardot's character Agnès was anchored in the expected roles for women at the time: a heroine of the

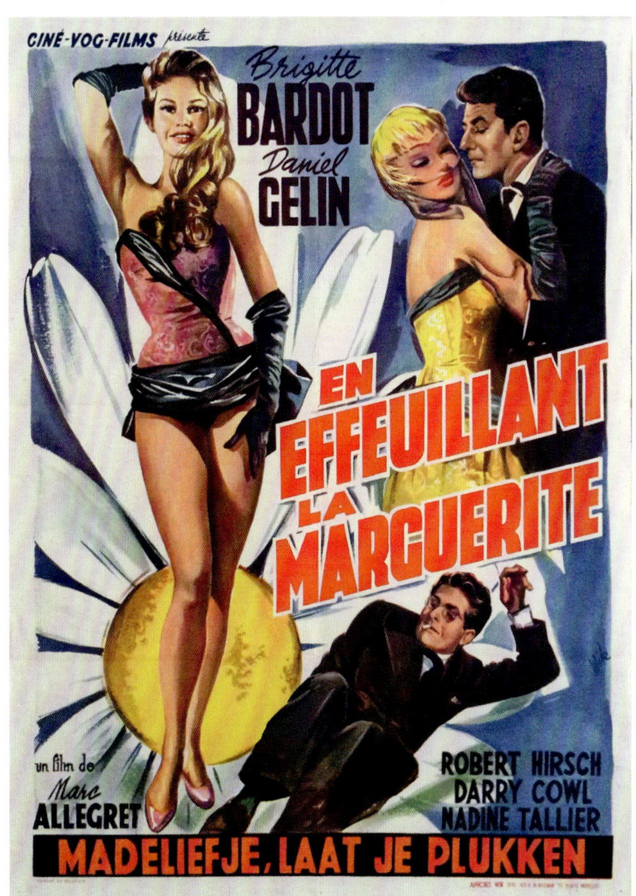

Brigitte Bardot in Marc Allégret's *En effeuillant la marguerite* (*Plucking the Daisy*), 1956, poster

cinéma de papa with a tension between eroticism and moral respectability. With a marriage and happy ending that reestablishes social order, the film promotes good morals and conformity to society's expectations. Its message is clear even as a striptease dance sequence showcases Bardot's ability to seduce.

Some aspects of Bardot's personality and talents can be found in the film, influenced by Vadim cowriting the script, such as in the dance scene. Her character was not as liberated by it on screen, however, as the ones she played later with him directing. Agnès is shown from the beginning as accomplished, independent, and rebellious. The film opens with crowds of people reading the book from which the film gets its name, exposing the dirty laundry of Vichy, where the protagonist's family lives. Later that evening, Agnès confesses to her father, General Dumont, that she had written the book, signing it anonymously in order to protect his name. When her father objects to her plan of being a writer, threatening to kill her or send her to boarding school, she leaves for Paris to join her brother. On the train, she meets Daniel and Roger, introducing herself as a writer. Sneaking into La Maison de Balzac, the museum where her brother works as a guide (instead of as a successful artist like his sister believes), Agnès makes herself at home in the great writer's house, appropriating his slippers and a dressing gown that were on display (and symbolically, therefore, his identity as a writer), and plopping down in his bed. In need of money, she telephones Daniel and Roger, who had offered to help publish her work, and asks for an advance. Though the character up to this point exudes agency, she remains ladylike, rebuffing Roger's advances when she pitches the idea of her novella to him. In a plot twist, Agnès, desperate for money to recover a rare edition of a Balzac novel that she sold to survive, enters a striptease contest that she must win while concealing her good-girl identity behind a mask and the stage name *Sophia*. The dialogue is telling, hinting at a parallel with Bardot, when Agnès asks her colleague what it was like the first time she stripped. The woman replies, "Until you show your breasts, it's not hard. Then, you just try to think of something else. At least striptease is honest. You're paid to show your backside, they pay to see it. No hypocrisy."

Adding to her confusion, Daniel has proposed marriage to Agnès but finds himself in "Sophia's" dressing room, caught in his desire for her. Agnès faces a dilemma, one that recalls Kim Novak's character in *Vertigo* when she realizes Scottie desires her more as his fantasy than for her real self. Finally, when Agnès's friend discloses to Daniel that Sophia and Agnès are the same person, Daniel exclaims, "She really fooled me. I thought she was such an angel." When he confronts Agnès, she condemns her own behavior and tells him, "You're right to judge me harshly." But Daniel assures her that he wants to marry her anyway. In the meantime, her brother has received a telegram from her publisher announcing that they are sending her an advance on royalties for her book, *En effeuillant la marguerite*, the exact sum she needed to buy back the Balzac novel. This fact no longer matters, however, because Agnès is now getting married.

The film's narrative was a familiar one at the time. More independent than was accepted by her parents, Agnès will ultimately conform, a sacrificial lamb as her name implies, to reestablish patriarchal order. Daniel's proposal elevates her status as his wife. There is no more mention of a writing career or of any future pursuits other than getting married. The film's finale shows the couple kissing on a train in Japan on their honeymoon and closes with the animated insert of a family of daisies expanding as the orchestra plays, leaving the audience with a happy end. The written message on the insert reads: "Et ils eurent beaucoup d'enfants," meaning "and they had many children"—the French equivalent of living happily ever after. This trajectory, showing a young woman with too much freedom or ambition coming to her senses, alleviated the threat of social disruption and reassured audiences.

THE BARDOT SHOCKWAVE: *ET DIEU CRÉA LA FEMME*

Though *Et Dieu créa la femme* was released the same year as *En effeuillant la marguerite*, Bardot's explosive image in the former—the first film that Vadim directed—was like nothing that came before it. In 1956, Bardot's body and sensuality in the film produced a shock effect. In the context of the older generations of actresses and roles for women, her image in *Et Dieu créa la femme* was seen as liberating, but in what respect? Breaking with the carefully constructed (and constrained) female characters of 1950s French cinema or the sophisticated Hitchcock heroines, Bardot offered a brand-new image of an uninhibited (or in patriarchal terms, "unbridled") woman. Vadim's *mise en scène*, with many scenes shot on location in Saint-Tropez and his more true-to-life portrayal of younger people, was also groundbreaking. The film inspired future directors of the New Wave to make new kinds of films, ones that resembled their own generation. A transitional film, *Et Dieu créa la femme* ended one era and opened another. This was also true in terms of its models: The film seems to hesitate between a freer type of cinema (natural setting, shot in exteriors, transgressing norms of diction and acting, directness of the love scenes) and the cinema of Hollywood (filmed in color, conventional narrative with the reestablishment of patriarchal order in the end). But from these heterogeneous influences, Vadim contributed

to renewing French cinema with his freer representation of love and youth and his more natural décor. Like the New Wave films to come, Vadim's first feature was also personal. He imagined the story and cowrote and directed it in the spirit of an auteur. His new star was also an in-between character. While Bardot, the actress, first appeared to be modern, a woman free in her body and on screen, Vadim seemed to follow, paradoxically, the process of *creating* a star as it was described in the 1954 Hollywood film *The Barefoot Contessa* (which denounced the corruption of Hollywood) in imagining Bardot's role. Her character conveyed an authentic quality linked to the actress's natural persona. The director also celebrated his wife's spirit (and body), melding events in their life together into the fictional story about a woman and her relationship with three men.

In the film, Bardot, twenty-three at the time, starred as eighteen-year-old Juliette, an orphan whose hunger for freedom and love clashes with the expectations of her strict,

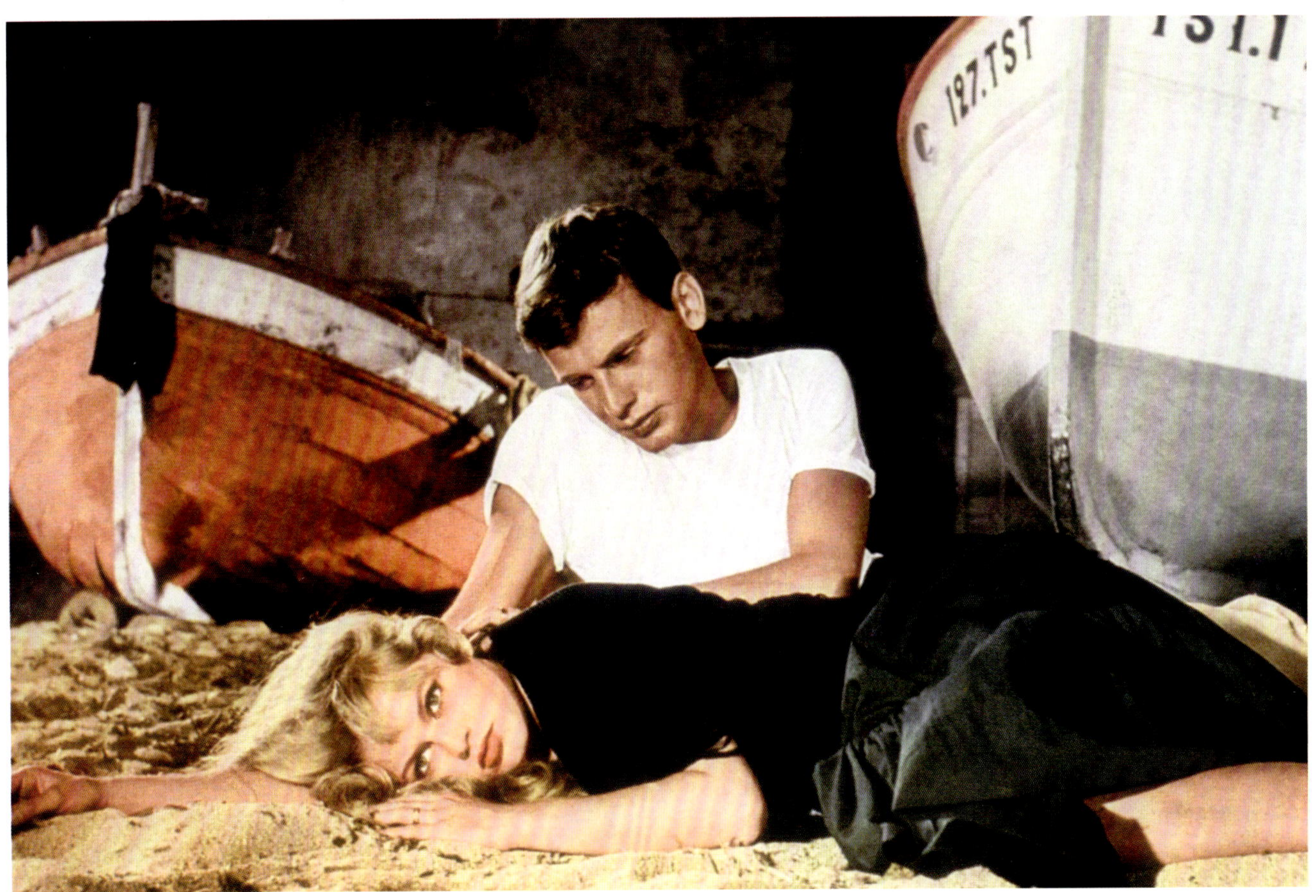

Brigitte Bardot and Jean-Louis Trintignant in Roger Vadim's *Et Dieu créa la femme* (*And God Created Woman*), 1956

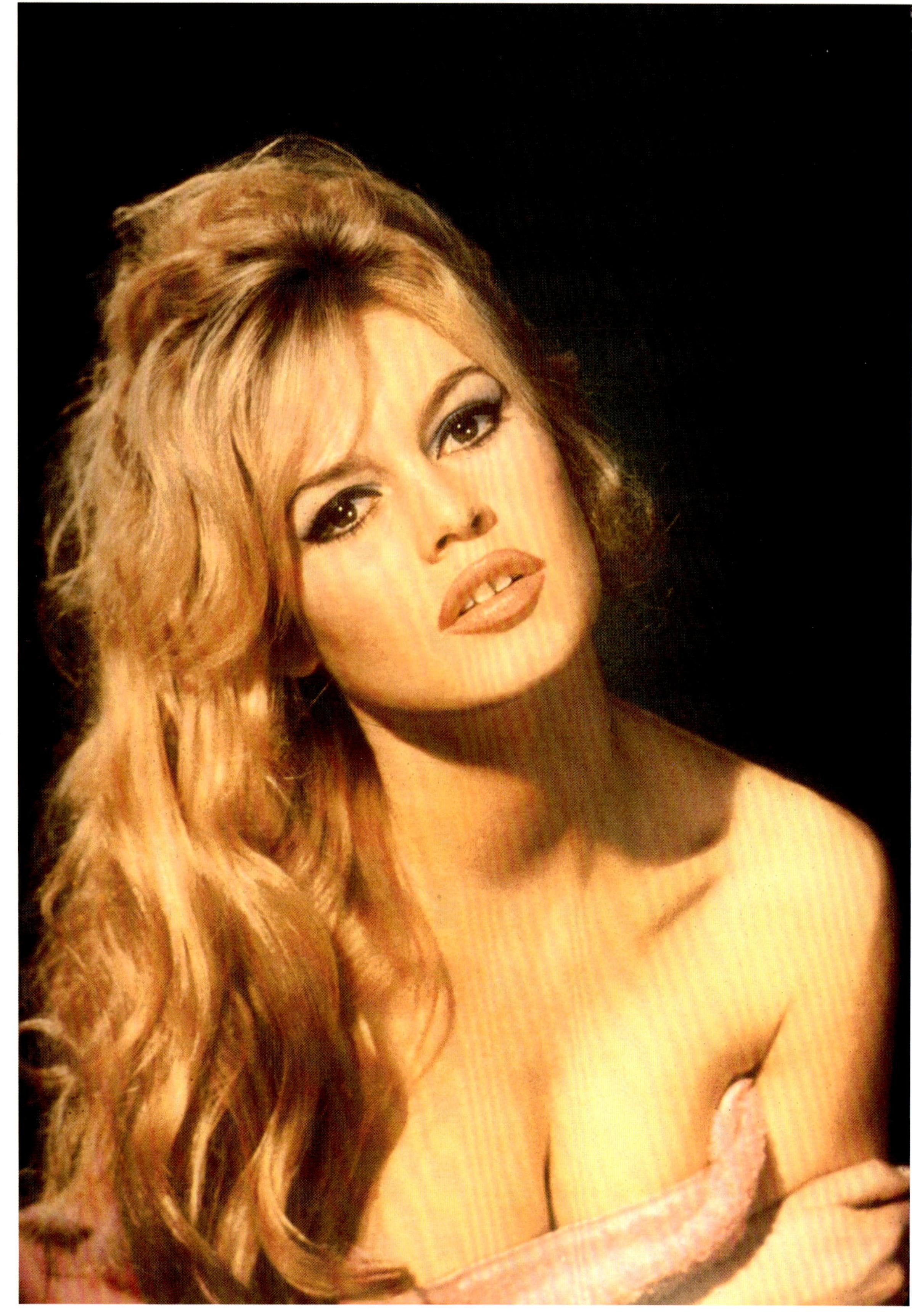

older foster parents. With her beauty and free spirit, she excites men across Saint-Tropez, including a wealthy older man in the opening scene where she is sunbathing nude in her backyard. Though she marries the demure Michel, played by Jean-Louis Trintignant, Juliette is depicted as being controlled by her impulses and becomes entangled in a passionate affair with his brother, Antoine. In the film's climactic dance sequence, Juliette's sensuality is unleashed—and the scene is intolerable for her husband to witness. Off screen, Vadim saw his wife in similar scenarios. Bardot was known to be spontaneous, dancing uninhibited in public, for example, in front of admiring onlookers, while her husband watched.

In the film, though patriarchal order will be restored in the end as a brief addendum, Vadim's script shows Bardot's character as free, sensuous, and independent throughout the narrative, a portrait that shocked audiences unaccustomed to these traits in a female protagonist. When *Et Dieu créa la femme* was released, François Truffaut wrote, "It is on the question of eroticism and of morals that the generations clearly oppose each other."[26] The film contained tensions of a society marked by rapid change and different values embodied by youth. While a certain discourse in the film condemns the transgression of established moral codes (especially that of the older female characters, chastising Juliette for sunbathing nude, for example, and calling her "shameless"), she is not completely condemned by the *mise en scène*. Juliette's freedom is allowed because she is depicted as an innocent character who is close to nature and genuine. Like the heroine in Ingmar Bergman's *Sommaren med Monika* (*Summer with Monika,* 1953), Juliette is associated with nature, water, and the eternal feminine. A sequence by the sea in both films links the two protagonists: Monika is in harmony with nature, often shown nude next to the water; Juliette comes out of the water in wet, transparent clothing, striking a pose on the beach that is somewhere between Monika, a pinup, and the idealized image in Alexandre Cabanel's painting *The Birth of Venus* (1863).

"[*Summer with*] *Monika* was already *Et Dieu créa la femme*,"[27] Godard wrote in a review of the film for *Cahiers du cinéma* in 1958. In Bergman's film, for the first time, a real body was shown on screen: Monika runs naked toward the water, freedom in perfect accord with nature.[28] With its representation of love, the body, nature, and youth, Scandinavian cinema preceded the French by years. The freedom and nudity of Harriet Andersson as Monika influenced the young French directors, and the film would become the very matrix of the New Wave.[29] At the same time, Bergman's films were seen as scandalous by the public, and *Monika* was placed in the "eccentric Nordic" category, not understood as a modern manifesto of new cinematic freedom. Vadim's version three years later was equally scandalous, though his *mise en scène* was more fabricated, less free in its depiction of nudity. *Et Dieu créa la femme* provoked outrage in Europe and was banned in some US states, with morality leagues shouting, "Ban Bardot!" This translated, of course, into huge box-office success, and Bardot would go down in history as one of the biggest French stars of all time.[30]

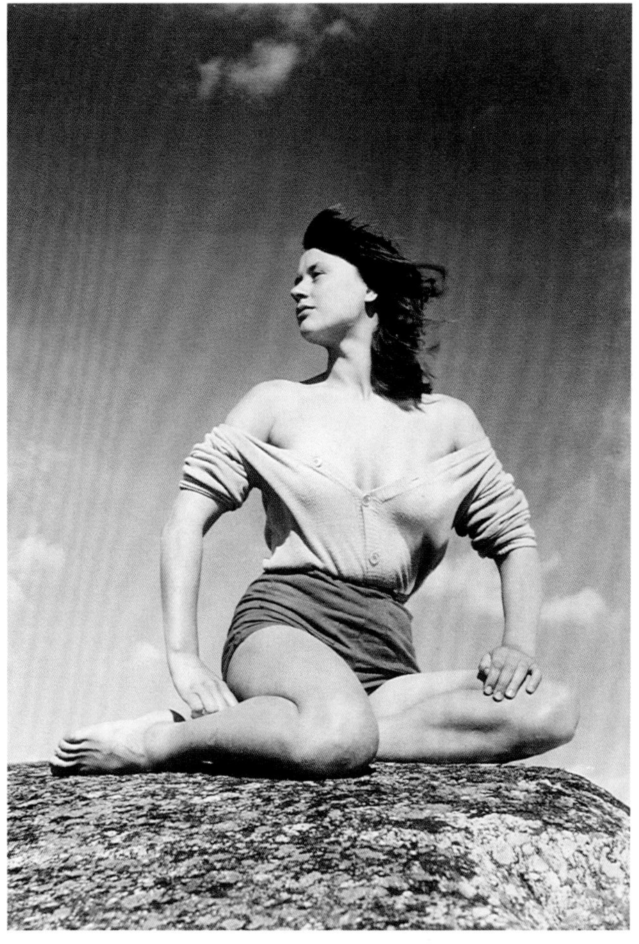

Harriet Andersson in Ingmar Bergman's *Summer with Monika,* 1953

Brigitte Bardot poses for Jean-Luc Godard's *Le Mépris* (*Contempt*), 1963, photograph by Sam Lévin

If we consider certain elements in the film in relation to the norms of the day, with Bardot and Vadim's off-screen relationship in the background, we see clearly why and how their film broke ground in French cinema. Bardot's presence itself shaped her character: Critics would praise her way of seeming completely herself on screen, a wholly natural acting style that liberated Vadim's conception of Juliette from the beginning. During the same time period, with other directors, Bardot played characters that corresponded more to the older generation's traditional image of women in cinema. Her roles in Henri-Georges Clouzot's *La Vérité* (*The Truth,* 1960) and Claude Autant-Lara's *En cas de malheur* (*Love Is My Profession,* 1958), for example, conformed more to this expected image in terms of their clothing, behavior, and acting.

Compared to the norms of the time, Bardot's character in *Et Dieu creá la femme* was striking. In women's fashion in 1950s France, the dominant style was refined and stiff. Women's bodies were rigidly shaped by girdles and bras for form-fitting clothing that accentuated a small waist and high heels that completed the silhouette, showing off the figure and the attire itself. In effect, *la mode* (fashion) was an important part of films in the 1950s that included an array of beautiful evening dresses, worn by the actresses as if for a fashion show. We can see this explicitly in Jacques Becker's *Falbalas* (*Paris Frills,* 1945), predating this era, or in Italy in Michelangelo Antonioni's *Le Amiche* (*The Girlfriends*, 1955), for example. In this context, Bardot's inexpensive and comfortable clothing in *Et Dieu créa la femme* broke with tradition.[31] Her uncorseted cotton dresses, T-shirts with loose skirts, and even her bare feet signified freedom—as did her mode of transportation, the bicycle. Under her own control, the bicycle allowed her to move about without consideration for bus schedules, roads, or any other constraints. Even her hair reflected a freer image and approach to life. Bardot's was long and loose, even wild compared to the sophisticated chignons of Hitchcock's favorite heroines of the era. The image of hair, with its connotations of power, vulnerability, and freedom (or constraint), played a primary role in shaping Bardot's character in Vadim's film as well as the actress's own personal image throughout the years.

Bardot's diction in *Et Dieu créa la femme* was also less theatrical than what can be heard in most films at the time. Though she was criticized by her detractors for her flat intonation that went against the convention of well-articulated dialogue, the future New Wave directors praised her for speaking in a way that seemed "natural," with her own voice. As for her "nonacting," instead of seeking that the actress's behavior conform to a preconceived model, Vadim allowed the role to be shaped by what he saw in Bardot in real life, creating a tailor-made character. This method was largely adopted by the New Wave directors, notably Éric Rohmer in his desire to integrate his actors' own verbal tics into their roles. André Bazin, the venerated father of the *Cahiers du cinéma*, affirmed at the time that "*Et Dieu créa la femme* was made for [Bardot]. She did not say or do anything [in the film] that she wouldn't have known to say or do in real life."[32] He praised Vadim for seeking "to stay as close as possible to her gestures, her expressions, her desires."[33] We can question, however, the culture of the day and how critics downplayed Bardot's contributions, giving credit to the director for channeling her, including her very "desires." Truffaut went as far as saying that "Brigitte Bardot is magnificent, for the first time totally herself," underlining Vadim's role in terms that may seem shocking today: "She is directed *lovingly* like a *little animal*, like Jean Renoir directed Catherine Hessling in *Nana* before her."[34] To his credit, Vadim stated that he "understood immediately that Brigitte was inimitable and that her faults might sometimes be qualities. She needed a gardener more than a professor." Though his metaphors are dated, he did recognize her part in creating the authenticity of the character: "She was the type of flower that one waters but does not cut. It would have been an act of vandalism to train her whimsical voice. She was totally uninterested in discussing a character's psychology or motivation. She understood instinctively or not at all. When she digested the character and made it real through her own emotions, the miracle occurred."[35]

From Bardot's point of view, she recalled being left completely free to improvise the dance scene, for example, but described her "fear" during the shoot. Forced to "forget her girlhood inhibitions" and listen to her body for the scene, she explained that she "let go" for the first time.[36] Attesting to her courage in overcoming her fear, these words also prove her trust in the director. When compared to her work with other filmmakers, it is impossible not to consider how Bardot's intimate personal relationship with Vadim directly influenced her performance. The depth, trust, and emotional charge between them inherently carried over into the director/actor dynamic and inevitably played a part in shaping Bardot's character as well as Vadim's narrative and *mise en scène*. For Bardot, working with Vadim may have reassured her and relieved some of her inhibitions, but it may have also provoked the intensity of the performance. Reciprocally, on the director's end, their relationship necessarily played a part in bringing out aspects of his wife that he knew intimately as well as transposing parts of their personal life onto the screen. The famous mambo scene, for example, takes place near the end of the film in the basement of a bar. Bardot, accompanied by entrancing percussion, shocked audiences with her long, uninhibited performance. An intricate on- and off-screen interplay fuels this scene. It recalls, for instance, the real-life scene Vadim described when, in the midst of their failing marriage, Bardot danced at length voluptuously at a restaurant to the rhythm of a musician playing there. In the film, Trintignant, playing Juliette's husband, is forced to watch the unbearable dance, transfixed, while Vadim looks on from behind the camera. During the shoot, the director remained equally unreactive as his wife began an affair with Trintignant, the lovers going so far as sharing the same apartment as they worked on the film. "Being natural in my love scenes with Jean-Louis Trintignant, my partner in the film, I ended up naturally falling in love with him," Bardot wrote.[37] It is perhaps this interplay with real life that makes the character and performance feel more authentic than or different from the more contrived images of heroines from the *cinéma de papa*. It is also a dynamic we will see play out in many couples working together in films of the New Wave.

FEMALE BODY, MALE LENS: THE CINEMATIC STRIPTEASE

If Vadim played a part in "liberating" Bardot's body in scenes like her performance of the mambo, his *mise en scène* did not reach the level of freedom in Bergman's films. *Monika* may have inspired *Et Dieu créa la femme*, but Vadim's *mise*

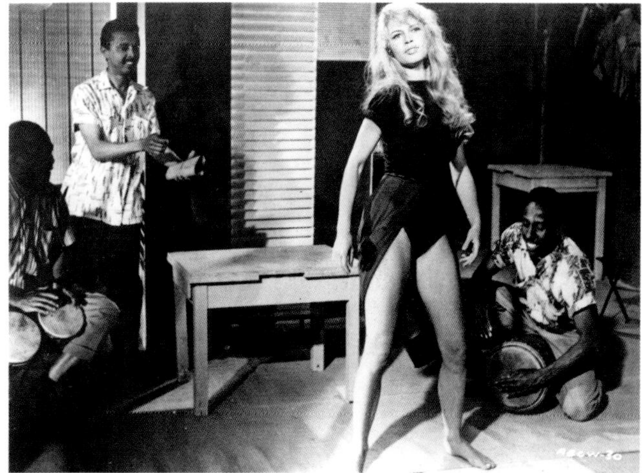

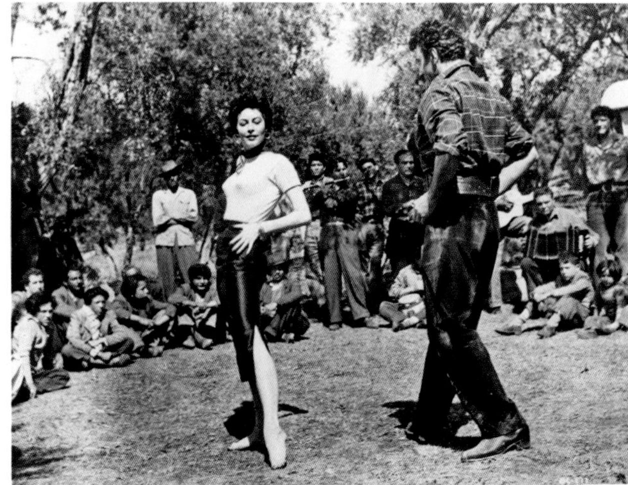

en scène remained closer to Hollywood's depiction of the female body as spectacle. How does the camera shape the viewer's gaze in the eroticization of Bardot's body in the dance scene? Does Vadim's film liberate her, or does it perpetuate the notion of the female body as spectacle?

From the opening sequence in *Et Dieu créa la femme*, the camera focuses on Bardot's body, the film's epicenter, starting at her feet and enacting a kind of striptease for the viewer. Here, Vadim seemed to follow the playbook mapped out in a Hollywood film both in terms of the *mise en scène* as striptease, as well as constructing his "authentic" heroine. In Joseph L. Mankiewicz's *The Barefoot Contessa* (1954), we first see Maria Vargas (Ava Gardner) through the eyes of Humphrey Bogart, who plays a seasoned Hollywood director. Maria is in her dressing room, behind a curtain. Only her

Top: Brigitte Bardot in the famous mambo scene in *Et Dieu créa la femme*, 1956. **Bottom:** Ava Gardner in Joseph L. Mankiewicz's *The Barefoot Contessa*, 1954

bare feet show at the bottom, and they are facing the shoes of a man we assume she is kissing. The scene activates the spectator's desire to see more. Vadim's film opens in a similar way and makes an indirect reference to Mankiewicz's as the rich older businessman Eric Carradine (Curd Jürgens) gazes at Bardot's bare feet peeking out from behind a type of curtain, a white sheet attached to a clothesline. "You have the feet of a marquise," he says as the camera provides the first image of the striptease.

After a series of titillating shots, Bardot's completely nude body is revealed as a shock and spectacle. Seen from the back, she is lying on her stomach in the famous pose that Godard will reference years later in *Le Mépris*, readopting it as a provocation. The spectacle in *Et Dieu créa la femme* is enhanced by Bardot's body being set against the white sheet, reminding us of the movie screen and of our place as cinematic voyeurs.

In Bardot's case, like Gardner's, we see her face and hear her voice only after having seen her body. Each woman evokes first the unknown, a body without identity behind a curtain of suspense. In Vadim's film, the cinematic striptease continues through different scenes: Bardot's clothing hides and reveals, as does his camera through framing—a game that aligns more with old Hollywood films than with a *mise en scène* of modern cinema.

But what is the true aspect of the film that shocked viewers? Are Bardot's nude scenes what created scandal, or is it a game of the *mise en scène* of her body, playing with the viewer like a striptease, that lures us into feeling it is scandalous? In reality, the film shows Bardot's body very little, in very short scenes or with strategic framing that also conceals it. Bardot is, in fact, only nude in the opening scene, lying on her stomach, and in terms of love scenes, it *shows* nothing. Instead, everything is insinuated or portrayed through cinematic illusion. The scenes considered torrid are only suggested and followed by ellipses, such as one of the most intense moments of adulterous love (the label reflecting the morals of the day) on the beach between Juliette and her husband's brother.

Even at its release, for Bazin, the film was pure provocation. He was irritated by the lack of "sincerity" in its eroticism, writing, "I started to think I was a puritan, and in any case, very bourgeois. Was it that it was showing more than usual?" He concluded by saying the love scenes were intolerable because they were not sincerely erotic, that "everything happened as if the erotic feeling was inversely in proportion to the physical. We could go so far as saying the actors actually make love in front of the camera but they are seen as *pretending*, while the problem is actually the contrary, to pretend they are making love in order to inspire it in the viewer's imagination."[38]

What the viewer does see, then, are moments of pure spectacle, the *mise en scène* of the body and of feminine desire. What was found shocking at the time was, more likely, a symptom of its puritanism, as Truffaut suggested: "It is a film typical of our generation, because it is amoral (refusing the current morals and not proposing any others) and puritan (aware of this amorality and worrying about it)."[39] In the end, those puritan impulses won out, as the film closes with Juliette and her husband reunited. But the undercurrent of what Truffaut considered amorality made space for a new type of female protagonist, one shown with much more freedom during the majority of the film, and scenes like her uninhibited dance are the ones we remember. Besides this celebrated freedom, however, could these scenes also reveal something else? Does Bardot's image as the ideal, natural, and free woman reflect her true essence, or is it also a creation of Vadim's *mise en scène*?

Along with her famous dance sequence, other moments of pure spectacle include those where Bardot strikes fixed poses like the one on the beach in a pinup-type posture or the one where she is sunbathing at the beginning of the film. Coming out of this passive model posture through the dance, Bardot frees her character while remaining attached to this trope and to the relationship of artist and model in Vadim filming her. Dancing, the body is free and in motion; its movements are seen as instinctive, and in Bardot's case, almost uncontrollable, while the scene remains a moment of true cinematic spectacle (filmed by a voyeuristic camera).

In this moment, viewers identify with her but also distance her as an object. Roland Barthes, the famed French theorist whose work *Mythologies* (1957) analyzed popular culture at the time, wrote notably about the spectacle of the woman's body and the mechanism of the striptease. According to Barthes, the striptease is a way of domesticating the erotic through rituals and a scene he calls "the spectacle of fear." Because the female body fascinates and frightens, it is as if eroticism is a kind of "delicious terror."[40] The striptease, according to Barthes, is a way of managing a deep fear, revealing what is frightening in order to embrace or exorcise it. In theoretical terms, Barthes claims the bourgeois mentality cannot imagine or assimilate the Other, so it becomes pure object, making it nonthreatening. Put simply, showing the fear-inducing erotic body through the director's gaze tames it. Here is where the myth of Bardot as sex symbol is born: Her body *is* a spectacle, overtaking the "natural" beauty and authentic texture of Bergman's version in *Monika*. Similar dance sequences were pervasive in cinema at the time. *The Barefoot Contessa* features Ava Gardner dancing in a natural setting inside a circle of onlookers, and the Italian classic *Riso amaro* (*Bitter Rice,* 1949) showcases Silvana Mangano doing the same, illustrating a deeper function at play, with a trope going back to Salome.

BORROWING HOLLYWOOD'S PLAYBOOK: THE MYTH OF THE NATURAL WOMAN

"God created woman, but the devil made Bardot," an advertising slogan read at the time of the film's release.[41] Who was really behind this legendary creation? In *The Barefoot Contessa*, Bogart, the director of a film within the film, reveals his plan to create a different kind of star out of his protégée (played by Gardner and rumored to have been based on Rita Hayworth). As the Hollywood director, Bogart's character insists on the originality of maintaining and highlighting the natural quality of his new actress. After viewing her screen test in the film, he decides to create a more relaxed image of her: "Her makeup's too dark and too much. Hair and wardrobe got to be much more simple. No tricks. The less between her and the camera, the better. The voice is good, well placed. I don't want a voice coach within a mile of her." Bogart's character insists on emphasizing her authenticity along with her internal and external beauty. He aims to create a star from a simple woman whose natural allure is apparent (and whose promise of enormous bankability is, too).

Though Vadim claimed Bardot's role was tailor-made for her, inspired by her personality, it is surprising to see how closely he follows this Hollywood idea of "creating" a star. Vadim wrote in his memoir, "I would mess up her hair before each scene and forbid her to add makeup between shots. She felt naked and vulnerable. She was panic-stricken. I knew that no matter how unpleasant this 'psychological striptease' might be, it was indispensable to the success of the film—and to her own success. She had grown used to being a starlet. I was creating a star."[42]

As Bazin noted, "B.B. is a creation of Vadim, but reciprocally . . . Vadim promoted her to the dignity of a star in understanding perfectly how he should use her, that is to say, pushing her to be natural."[43] This idea is not a new one, nor one reserved for French cinema. The producer David O. Selznick, for example, bet on the "natural," unmade-up face of Ingrid Bergman upon her arrival in Hollywood. The actress recalled her conversation with Selznick when they first met in 1939: "I've got an idea that's so simple and yet no one in Hollywood has ever tried it before. Nothing about you is going to be touched. Nothing altered. You remain yourself. You are going to be the first 'natural' actress."[44] We find the same resonances in Italian cinema as well with Silvana Mangano, chosen by Giuseppe De Santis for *Riso amaro*, where the goal was to arrive at an authentic representation, not to create a star. According to screenwriter Carlo Lizzani, they were looking for a very young girl and, if possible, someone not well known. For the casting, they requested girls with minimal experience, such as Gina Lollobrigida and Silvana Pampanini. Lux Film suggested Martine Carol. During the screen tests, Mangano made a good impression but "not more than the other actresses. She arrived with a little too much makeup. . . . She didn't give us what we were looking for," Lizzani stated. Then it rained. De Santis had Mangano come back up with "wet hair, disheveled. She wasn't

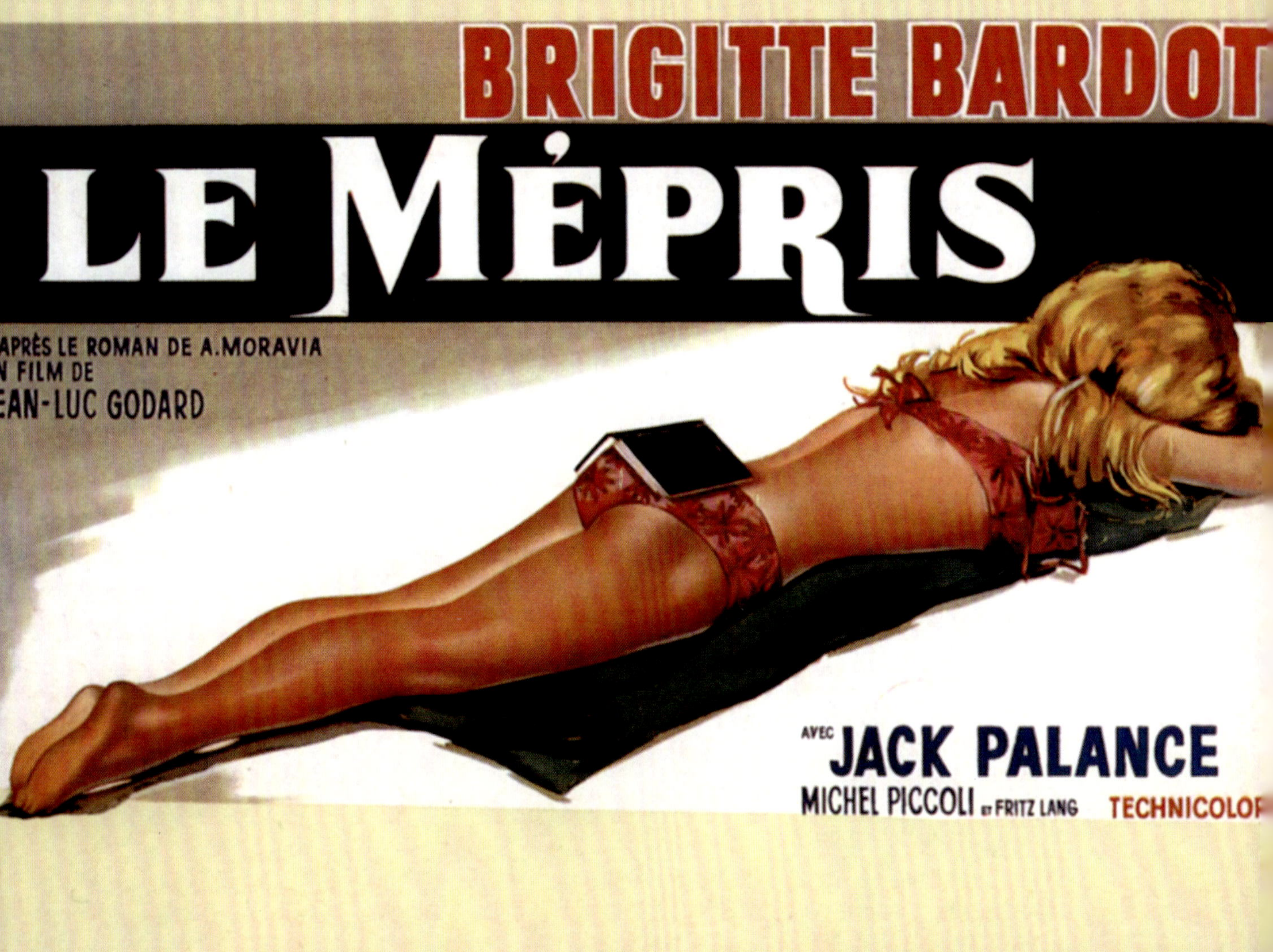

BRIGITTE BARDOT
LE MÉPRIS
D'APRÈS LE ROMAN DE A.MORAVIA
UN FILM DE
JEAN-LUC GODARD
AVEC JACK PALANCE
MICHEL PICCOLI ET FRITZ LANG TECHNICOLOR

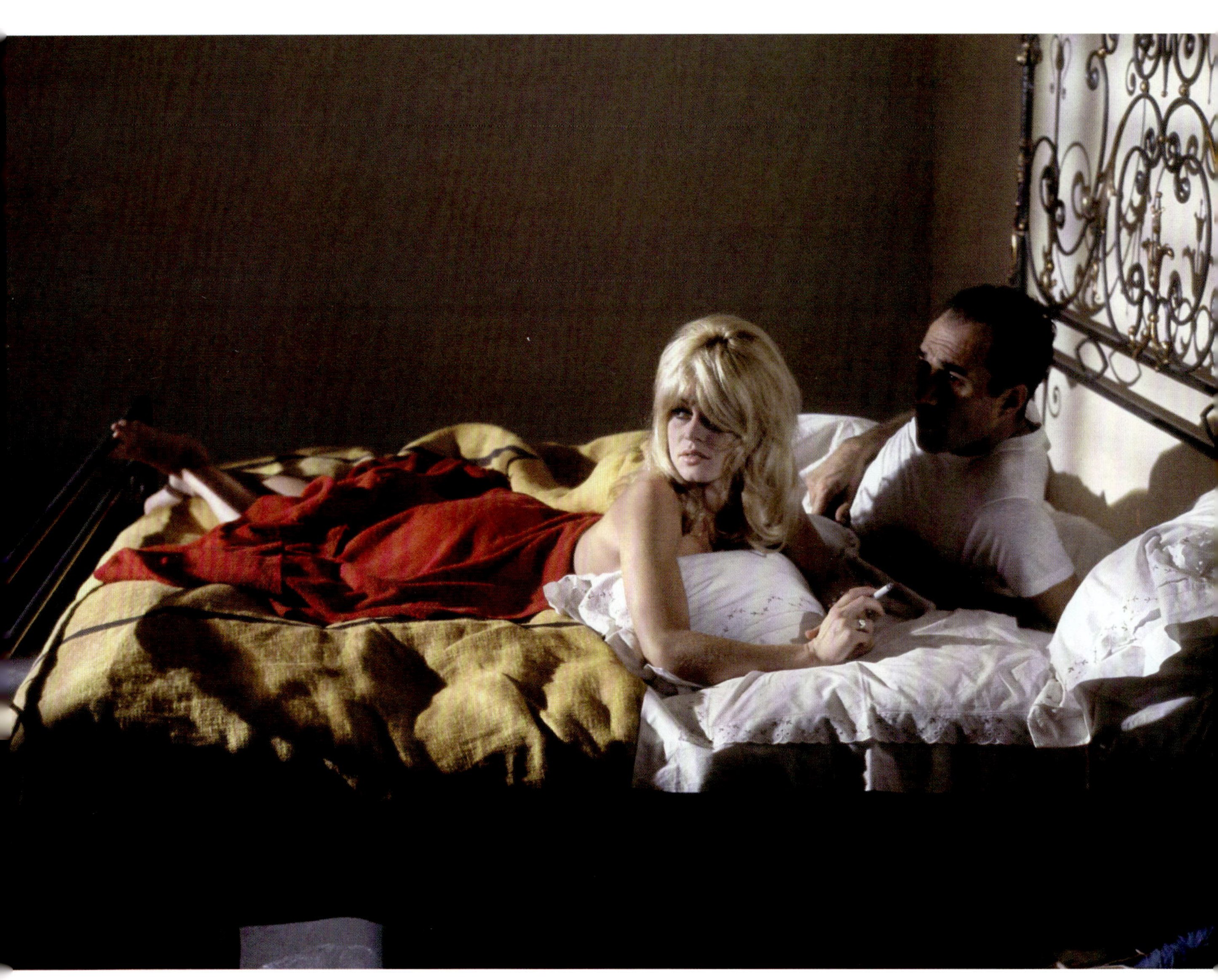

dressed the same as for the screen test. He had the intuition that she was the right, ideal candidate."[45]

Vadim's part in creating a new kind of French star echoes this construction, but we can also look more closely at Bazin's assessment of the process being "reciprocal." Did Vadim exploit Bardot's "natural" presence? Did she play her own role in his *mise en scène*? How did they influence each other, and what are their individual contributions in making this film stand out—and, more broadly, in creating a new image of a modern woman in cinema?

"Accustomed to playing in films that were amusing, erotic and always superficial, she didn't realize that I would demand a type of authenticity and sincerity that she had never had occasion to express on the screen," Vadim wrote in his memoir. "To become Juliette she would have to delve into the depth of her being. Undressing in front of a camera had never embarrassed her. But the thought of baring her soul and revealing her most intimate self terrified her," he claimed.[46] To make her comfortable, Vadim incorporated elements into the film that were close to Bardot. The setting, for example, was significant in that her parents had a summer home in Saint-Tropez where she and Vadim had also spent happy moments together. This choice made her at ease with her surroundings while offering a natural and beautiful backdrop for the film. The director also included different facets of his wife in the character she played. Her love of animals, for example, appears in the film where, in one scene, she sets free a caged bird and rabbit, letting them loose into nature, saying, "Fly away, and watch out for cats! Cities are no place for rabbits, run!" (After her film career, Bardot devoted herself to protecting and saving animals. As her biographer put it, "I don't think there's room in her heart for humans. That space is filled with animals. They love her unconditionally."[47]) This sensitivity manifests throughout the film, at times alluding to Bardot's history of depression. Knowing about Bardot's mental health struggles and her numerous suicide attempts, Vadim filmed her character wandering in the street with a lost and sullen look, walking in front of a car at one point, unfazed.[48] But more than anything, the viewer remembers her strength—playing by her own rules from the opening scene where she is sunbathing, her loose hair and relaxed clothing,

her bicycle, her agency, and her resilience, one that mirrors Bardot's in real life.

AUTHENTICITY AS EMPOWERMENT: HOW BARDOT PAVED THE WAY FOR *NOUVELLES FEMMES*

Besides sensitivity, the real Bardot has always been known for her honesty, for being strong-willed, and for going against rules and conventions. She floated from lover to lover, avoided marriage after her split with Vadim, and was uncomfortable with motherhood. Bardot lived her life on her terms and was even described in a 2021 profile as having lived it "like a man."[49] Though now her behavior could be seen as being true to herself, it was considered scandalous at the time, even if many women secretly aspired to the same freedom.[50] Female protagonists who exhibited the same freedom in films like *Ascenseur pour l'échafaud*, *Les Amants*, and *Une femme mariée* were severely judged or punished. Though some today may question Bardot's true freedom in the film, she nevertheless did break ground in making that first step in creating more modern roles for women. In 1959, Simone de Beauvoir herself recognized this fact in Bardot's choices in real life, applauding her for living her life outside of bourgeois conventions.[51] Freed from social constraints, Bardot, like her character, sought then what we now encourage in not only women and girls but in everyone: empowerment.

Starting with her decision to break with what her parents expected of her, choosing instead to pursue a career and a

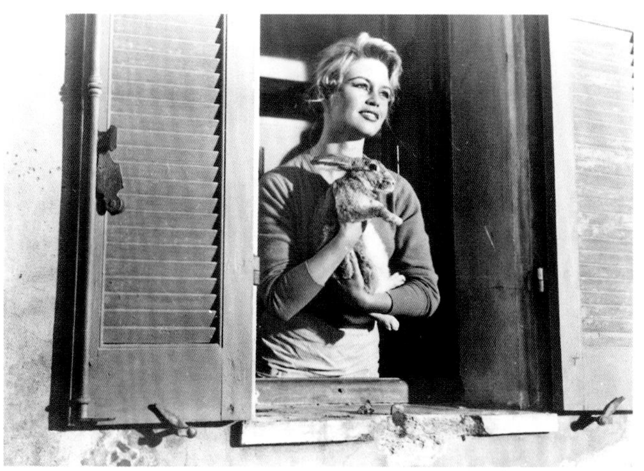

Brigitte Bardot in *Et Dieu créa la femme*, 1956

relationship with the man she loved, Bardot honored her integrity over social conventions. Her collaboration with Vadim contributed to the creation of a new, more empowered character in their film together. The intermingling personal elements at play reveal the behind-the-scenes operation in building a new type of heroine and new type of star. Bazin wrote that if Vadim shined with the film, "it is exactly from the style of the *mise en scène* and especially for his directing of actors that deliberately breaks with dramatic conventions attached to the cinema of genre first and of course with psychological conventions."[52]

Vadim's part in constructing Bardot's image—young, modern, sexy, and natural—may have helped shatter traditional images of femininity and actresses, but it also had repercussions.[53] As Bardot's biographer stated, "[Vadim] taught her how to be Brigitte, the sex symbol," making her an international sensation, but added that she "had never sought fame and was tortured by it."[54] Vadim also seemed to pay a price for his passion. It could be that the very freedom and sensitivity that Bardot possessed and that drew Vadim to her also caused him to suffer. Following their breakup, he left letters for Bardot and his friend Raoul Lévy that were said to have contained his plan to take his own life. After venturing off overnight in the rain and ending up in an alfalfa field, he came to his senses and went to his mother's in Toulon. Years later, he vowed that he had become "immune to the virus" of despair, adding "I never again allowed this unknown demon to take possession of my body and my soul."[55] Though they divorced in 1957, Vadim and Bardot remained on good terms professionally and personally, and still relied on each other.[56] He directed her in three other films, but everything that Vadim became known for in his later career existed in *Et Dieu créa la femme*—including his reputation for casting beautiful women in his films and bringing them into his personal life. From the title of his memoir—*Bardot, Deneuve, Fonda*—it seems that Vadim defined himself vis-à-vis these women in his life, who were all "the most beautiful women in the world" (as he described them in the subtitle of his book), all modeled after Bardot and his love for her. His fascination with them also seemed to be an invitation to creativity as he sought to capture their mystery, exploring and glorifying them all with his camera.

Bardot and Vadim never lost their friendship, and they continued to confide in each other through the years. In Bardot's words, her former husband "knew me by heart and showed me as I was."[57] Perhaps it is the spark and complex relationship between two people along with the timely alchemy of those involved in a film as a collective art that produces such revolutions as *Et Dieu créa la femme*. Through Vadim's relationship with Bardot, he constructed a narrative that celebrated (and idealized) the persona and idiosyncrasies of the woman he loved, and he encouraged her to share those qualities on screen. Through her trust in him, Bardot gave a natural and uninhibited performance, letting what seemed like her authentic self permeate her character. Together, they transformed French cinema, providing a model that would inspire young, soon-to-be directors to make their own first films with the women they admired and loved, making room on screen, one voice and one character at a time, for new roles for modern women. Over fifty years later, however, Bardot spoke of her feelings about the role in *Et Dieu créa la femme* and her career in cinema as a whole, casting doubt on the fact that the camera indeed captured her true self. "All my life," she said in an interview, "during that film, and before and after, I was never what I wanted to be, which was frank, honest, and straightforward. I wasn't scandalous—I didn't want to be. I wanted to be myself. Only myself."[58]

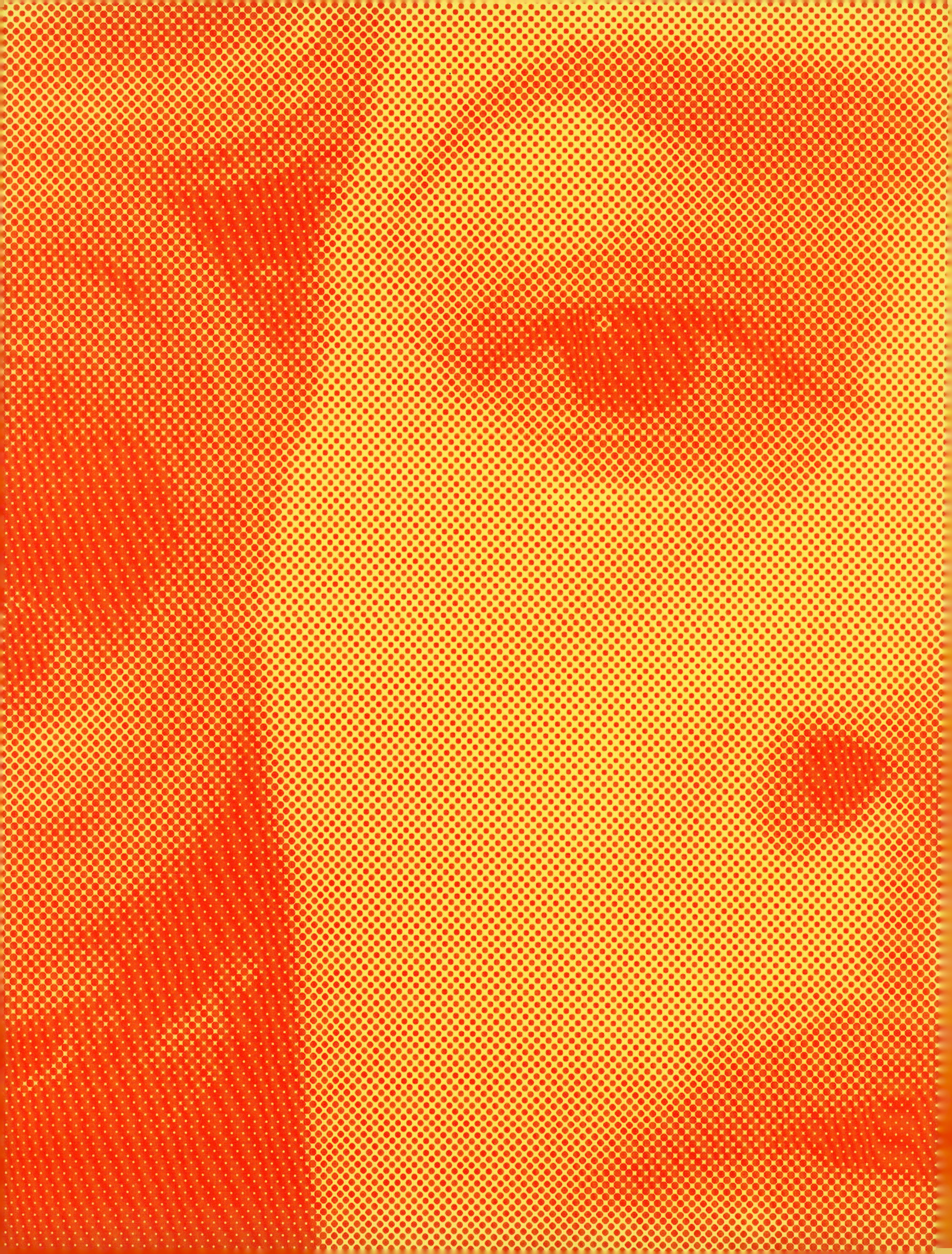

jeanne moreau 3

la femme passionnée | *the passionate woman*

FROM STAGE TO SCREEN: ACTING AS ESCAPE AND REBELLION

Capturing the spirit of the French New Wave, the image of Jeanne Moreau running across the Valmy Bridge in *Jules et Jim* has become emblematic of the movement and of the actress. Dressed as a man, Catherine (Moreau) gives herself a head start against Jules and Jim and wins the race. They all laugh about it, the men having accepted her taking the lead in their harmonious trio. But Moreau, along with most women of her generation, did not have that head start; women struggled just to enter the race. In life as in cinema, customs and hierarchies were well established, and there was no room for women who did not fit the predefined roles. Such was Moreau's case as an actress in the *cinéma de papa* era before she carved out her own place within the New Wave. On screen, she came into her own through encounters with directors who revealed her uniqueness. Off screen, she was a free woman before the women's liberation movement, and a romantic yet transgressive actress in a shifting cinematic context. Disregarding conventions, she intertwined reality and film, always remaining true to herself in both.

Jeanne Moreau in Louis Malle's *Ascenseur pour l'échafaud* (*Elevator to the Gallows*), 1958

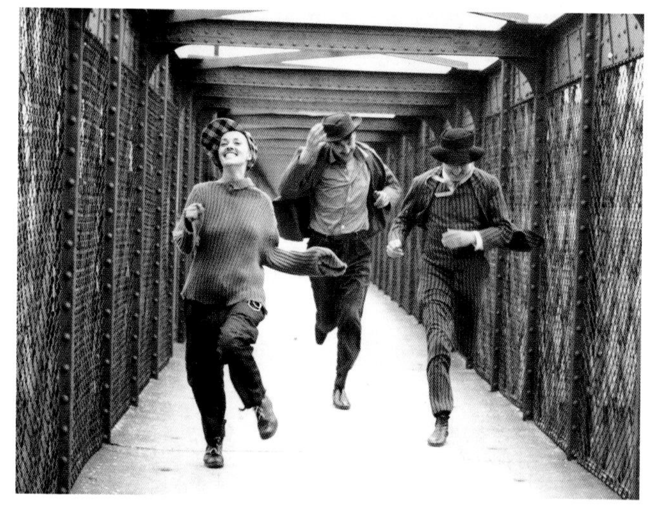

Long before *Jules et Jim*, Moreau, like Bardot, wanted to be a dancer. Then, at age fifteen, she secretly attended a production of Racine's *Phèdre* at the Comédie-Française with the actress Marie Bell—an experience she described as "the shock of my life." It ignited in her an instantaneous desire to become a stage actress, soon reinforced by another play, Jean Anouilh's *Antigone*. "In the limelight, on stage. That's what I wanted, [the surge of love from the audience], but the unseen mysterious audience. The audience can have many faces. It's a fantasy. It's a warm feeling, and it gives you a sense of power," Moreau explained. "I wanted to be in the shoes of those people on stage."[2]

As a young teenager, Moreau found her way to the stage in spite of—but also motivated by—a family life that was difficult financially and emotionally. "When I was a teenager, like all teenagers, I couldn't bear myself in my family in our home," she confessed, describing acting as "an escape from oneself and from others of certain circles." As for her plan to pursue theater, her father "wasn't for it at all," she said. Instead of focusing on school, unbeknownst to him, Moreau spent her time "learning entire Greek tragedies like *Bérénice* or *Andromaque*."[3] Her commitment paid off in July 1947, when she made her stage debut at the Festival d'Avignon as a member of the queen's retinue in Shakespeare's *Richard II*, directed by the renowned Jean Vilar. After joining the Comédie-Française at age twenty, Moreau acted in twenty-two plays over the course of four years, playing "ingénues and young boys."[4] At the same time, she began appearing

in films, starting with Jean Stelli's *Dernier amour* (*Last Love*) in 1949. These early roles were, in her words, "perverse ingénues," and for the better part of a decade, she continued to make commercial films as she tried and failed to secure better roles. Though Moreau auditioned for parts with big-name directors at the time–including Julien Duvivier, René Clair, and Marcel Carné—none hired her.

Despite the respect she earned in the theater for her acting, Moreau's unconventional looks were an obstacle in her early film career: They did not correspond to the beauty standards of 1950s French cinema. "It was the period of Martine Carol, Françoise Arnoul, Dany Robin–blonde girls, big eyes, big tits," she explained.[5] Deemed "unphotogenic"[6] at twenty, according to the actress, for what film professionals saw as irregular features, including a downturned mouth and the beginning of jowls, she also fielded complaints from directors and cameramen about the unforgiving dark circles under her eyes. Moreau disclosed that Duvivier told her agent in front of her, "Sure, she's got everything you want. She's got character, talent, and all that. But physically, zero!" Emphasizing his cruelty, she added, "He said that to my face, as if I were an object." Instead of being defeated, Moreau turned the judgment into a challenge. "It galvanized me," she said, declaring, "I wasn't so into cinema at the time but only because of his remark, I told myself, 'I will make movies.'"[7]

ASCENSEUR POUR L'ÉCHAFAUD: MALLE AND MOREAU'S MODERN EXPERIMENT

"The encounter with Louis Malle was the determining factor in my life," Moreau declared decades later in a 1993 interview where Malle was also present–"my professional life, and since both of them mix together, my personal life was profoundly marked and influenced," she added.[8] Remembering the moment when she broke out of the *cinéma de papa* mold with *Ascenseur pour l'échafaud*, Moreau explained the significance of the role for her as a woman and as an actress. "When I met Louis [Malle], I had been an actress for ten years," Moreau recalled. One evening in 1956, after a stage performance of *Cat on a Hot Tin Roof* at the Théâtre Antoine, two young men asked to see her to

Jeanne Moreau with Henri Serre and Oskar Werner on the Valmy Bridge in François Truffaut's *Jules et Jim*, 1962

"To me, acting is a calling, a way of life more than a career. My life feeds my art, and my art feeds my life. I didn't want the destiny of a regular girl."[1]

—jeanne moreau

talk about a film project. One was a prince descending from Napoleon; the other was a well-known French writer, Roger Nimier. "They took me to a famous place where Hemingway used to go, Harry's Bar," she said. "We went there and had drinks and they started to speak to me about a project, a love story where the lovers never meet." When she asked them who the director was, they replied, "He's just a beginner, very young, twenty-four years old and he made one film." It was a documentary with Jacques Cousteau, they told her, *Le Monde du silence* (*The Silent World*, 1956).[9]

Describing the context, she stated, "Nobody spoke about the New Wave at that time. I knew about the *Cahiers du cinéma*. I knew about a new generation of film directors but they had only made short films, not long feature films." Unlike the big productions of the older generation, Louis Malle's film would have "a very low budget, very small crew," the producer informed her. This new project would also break the mold of production she was used to in her ten years leading up to it. "Hierarchy was very important before that," she explained. "When you were a star, you had to have your driver, your dresser, your stand-in, your makeup, your hairdresser. They said, 'Listen, no driver, maybe somebody to help you get dressed, no makeup.'" Instead of being put off by the lack of resources, Moreau seized the chance to experiment. About the lack of makeup, she said, "Thank you!"—taking it as an opportunity to reinvent her look on her terms. "Because the makeup they used to put on my face was terrible," she explained, "because I didn't have the usual face or the usual look of the women who were stars at that time. My eyes, my mouth, everything was wrong, so I had thick makeup. Suddenly I was so relieved that I could do it myself."[10]

"It was Jeanne who directed me," Malle expressed in the same interview in front of Moreau, "I didn't have a clue! Up until then, all I'd ever directed were fish!"[11] But Moreau stressed the importance of their collaboration: "With Louis, I never thought he'd never directed an actress or an actor. It was just his relationship with the whole, with the lights, with the weather, with the cold, and the shadows and the sunshine, whatever. There was such intensity—it's true that he helped me and I helped him. We were [gestures with fingers intertwined]."[12]

For *Ascenseur pour l'échafaud*, Malle wanted Moreau for the lead although the script was not yet written and its source material, the 1956 novel of the same name by Noël Calef, had no female role. "It was a role we created from scratch with Roger Nimier and that was in no way necessary for the plot,"[13] Malle explained. Without Moreau's performance, however, he claimed the film would not have had the same impact: "Nobody would be discussing it. I wouldn't be here. But I think what really made the film was Jeanne strolling down the Champs-Élysées, shot with a camera in a baby carriage, lit only by shop windows.[14] These recurrent images of Florence Carala (Moreau), the unhappy wife of a wealthy businessman, wandering the streets of Paris in search of her lover, Julien Tavernier (Maurice Ronet), are what stand out in an otherwise common story. The famous opening scene of Florence in a telephone booth talking to her lover reveals the plot for Julien to murder her husband and make it appear a suicide. Only Julien gets caught in the elevator of the husband's office after the murder, and, for the rest of the film, the lovers are separated in what is depicted as a very modern Paris and a backdrop of alienation.

The film and the actress were revolutionary at the time, on many levels. Although Moreau's filmography before *Ascenseur* was extensive, it was her encounter with Malle that set her apart, creating a character that broke with convention and made her unique. "For me, it was total freedom," Moreau explained, "no makeup artist, no hair stylist, being filmed with a bare face, by a handheld camera. I was used to cameramen complaining about how hard I was to film. They'd frame shots so you couldn't see the circles under my eyes or the asymmetry of my face."[15] "After a few days of shooting," Malle recalled, "people came and told the producer: 'He has no right to film Jeanne Moreau that way!'"

The director chose Henri Decaë as the cinematographer after seeing his work with Jean-Pierre Melville, who also greatly influenced the New Wave with films such as *Le Silence de la mer* (*The Silence of the Sea*, 1949) and *Bob le flambeur* (*Bob the Gambler*, 1956). According to Malle, Decaë was the first to shoot in black and white at night without additional lighting.[16] Moreau also spoke of this new way of filming with "natural light with special film that [Malle] bought in

Next page: Jeanne Moreau in Louis Malle's *Ascenseur pour l'échafaud* (*Elevator to the Gallows*), 1958

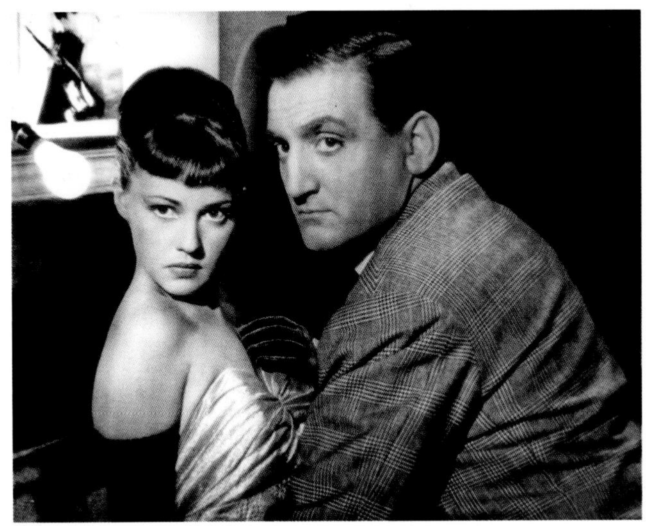

the States," explaining that they could film discreetly without extra lighting and that bystanders would be less likely to notice: "It had never been done before that a cameraman would carry the camera and go around without people turning around." "And even if they turned around to watch this woman," she added, "it didn't matter," as her character "looked so crazy." Malle credited the cinematographer for revealing a more authentic image of Moreau, contrasting it with her earlier films: "They had this way of covering her in makeup and drowning her in light so that it wasn't her in the film. With Decaë, suddenly you could see the real Jeanne."[17]

Not only did Moreau look different in *Ascenseur*, but her experience on set was a marked departure from that of previous films. "I thought it was so boring to be told, 'Okay, now you've finished your sequence. Maybe we need you in about two hours. Go and rest.' [Snarls] I didn't come here to rest, come on!" she said of past productions. For the first time, Moreau was given an active role, a chance to collaborate: "When there was a break, we used to go inside, decide, discuss what we would do . . . all together, ten, twelve people. . . . I like to see what's going on. I like to be part of the creation. I've always been like that."[18]

Moreau was also present during the recording session for the film's now iconic soundtrack with Miles Davis. "With Miles, it started at 7:00 p.m., we watched the film, he improvised with his musicians, . . . stopped the film, started again.

Recorded it all. I stayed for the whole session that lasted until 5:00 a.m.," she recalled.[19] By an extraordinary stroke of luck, according to Malle, Davis had happened to be in Paris, playing at Club Saint-Germain, while Malle was editing the film. With the help of musician Boris Vian, who contacted Davis, Malle convinced him to compose the score, infusing the film with an extra dose of modernity via the subtle and sensual melodies that came to Davis as he screened the images of Moreau's walks through the streets.[20] The photograph of Moreau and Davis captures their playful complicity; as Moreau recalled, "Miles started joking with me, making jokes about the way I walked, all around." The energy the film exudes stems from the coming together of these different elements and people. "There was a general feeling, a flow. Some of these artistic creations, they happen naturally. It works, it's the right timing, the right time, the right day, the right mixture of people," Moreau explained. These fortuitous encounters brought Moreau out of the shadows of traditional cinema and into her own. "I was very happy," she said, "I had the impression that I was really starting to make

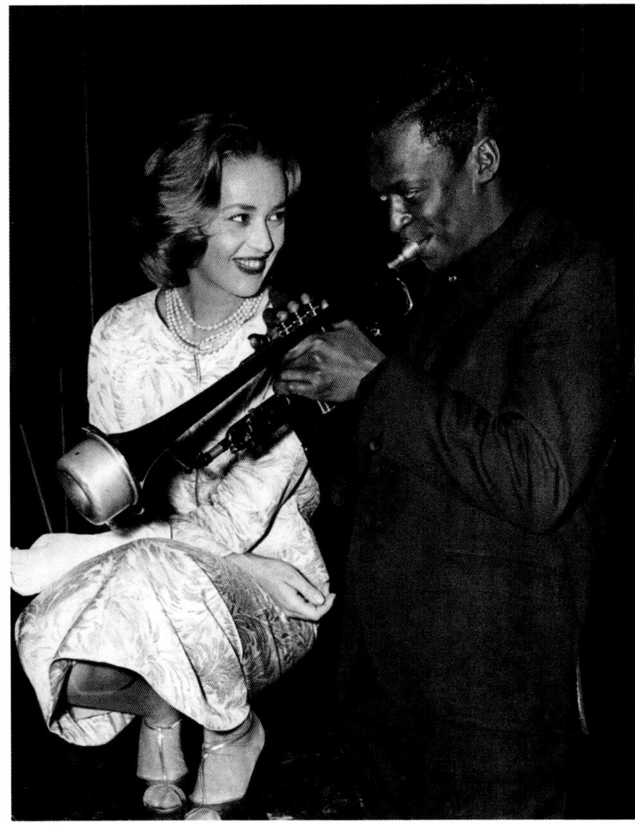

Jeanne Moreau and Miles Davis during the recording of the soundtrack of Malle's *Ascenseur pour l'échafaud*, Dec. 5, 1957

Jeanne Moreau and Lino Ventura in Jacques Becker's *Touchez pas au Grisbi* (*Hands off the Loot!*) 1954

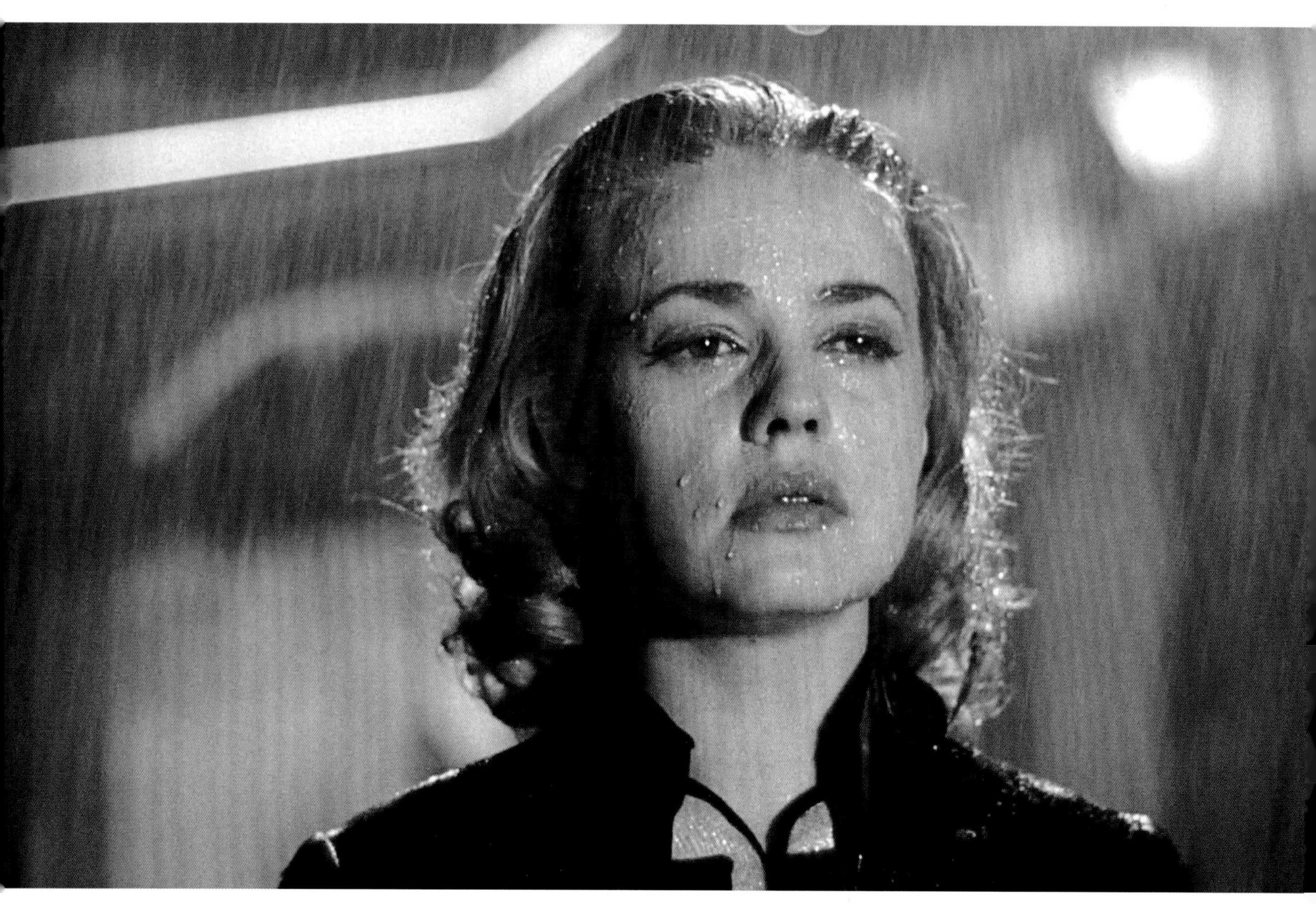

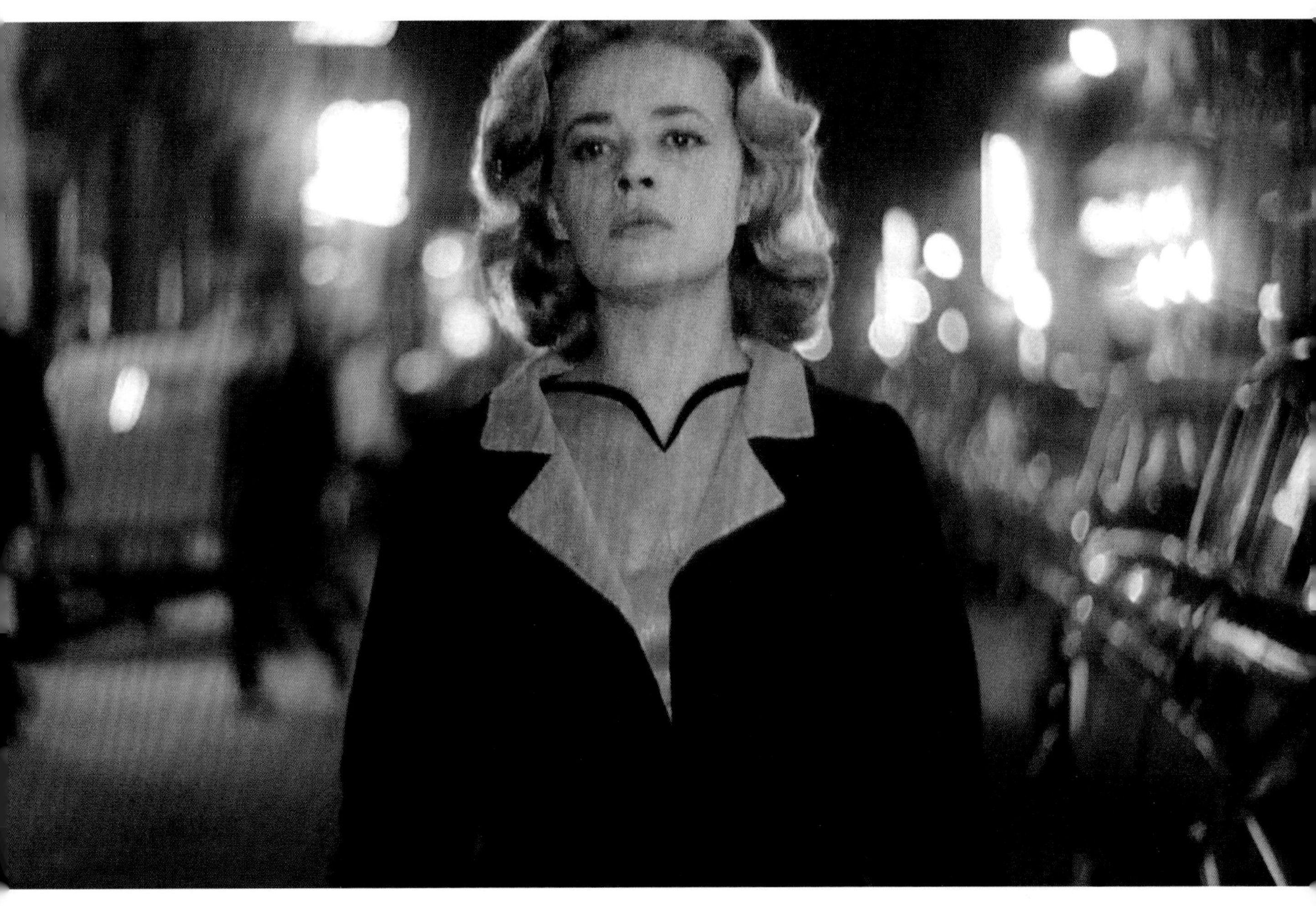

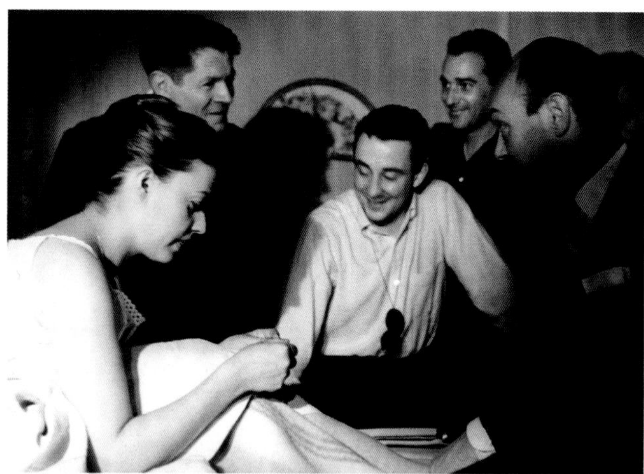

films."[21] In retrospect, the actress measured its importance: "It was a decisive moment for the rest of my life."[22]

Through Malle's style of filming, Moreau discovered "a freedom of physical movement that helped [her] discover an interior freedom," which she described as a "profound change." Again, emphasizing the importance of her encounter with Malle, the actress stated, "He opened doors for me as though I came out of a jail. Through him I discovered the freedom of cinema and exactly what cinema could mean, a modern way of communicating with the world."[23]

In the film, however, Moreau's character, Florence, and her lover, Julien, only communicate by telephone. They never actually meet on screen. Instead, we see their lives in parallel during one long night, as well as their differing perspectives of reality. While Julien is trapped in the elevator, causing him to miss their clandestine rendezvous, Florence imagines her own explanation for his absence as she wanders the streets, desperately searching for a trace of him. By adding her character to the plot, the film also gained another point of view. Moreau described Florence's inner voice—"what goes through her mind and her heart"—as being sometimes so powerful "that while she walks in the street, she looks like a madwoman, even speaking to herself."[24]

The detail is relevant. While we see Moreau as more natural on screen, trying to act independently, she is depicted, nevertheless, as almost insane, trapped by her passion. What's more, the heroine who walks the street alone at night, fol-

lowing her heart, must pay a price for this freedom and for betraying her husband. While Julien is stuck in the elevator, a petty crook absconds with his car, impersonates him, and ends up murdering a German couple. There are photos of the culprit with the couple on Julien's camera, which clear Julien's name of that crime—but the roll of film also harbors images of Julien and Florence, implicating them in the murder of her husband. As she and the police inspector watch the photos of Florence and Julien's happy moments together develop in the lab, Davis's trumpet comes back in, intensifying the sensuality of the images. The inspector says to her bluntly, "You ought to thank me. For the Germans, Tavernier had no alibi. He'd have been sentenced to death. For your husband's murder, he'll probably get ten years. But he'll only do five. But you, Mrs. Carala, I don't think the jury will go easy on you. And quite rightly." Looking straight into the camera, Florence whispers to herself, "Ten years, twenty years. I wasn't indulgent. But I know I still loved you. I wasn't thinking only of myself. I'll be old from now on. But here, we were together. Together again somewhere. You see, they can't keep us apart."

Speaking of this punishment with the distance of almost fifty years, in 2005, Moreau commented on the severity of the heroine's condemnation: "At the end, I was struck by how harsh the judgment is of the police inspector, saying, 'Okay, he's the murderer. He may get ten years, but you are terrible, you are worse, and you'll get more, much more.' And she accepts it at the same time."[25] The severity of the ending illustrates the many obstacles women faced at the end of the 1950s, the era that ushered in the apparent freedom of the New Wave, and it helps relativize the freedom of the characters. Malle, however, gave Moreau the last word even if her dream is only realized in fantasy, in a nonexistent place and time. Moreau's next parts would go even further in questioning women's roles in society as she became a model and an icon of a free woman.

THE LOVE TRIANGLE: SOCIETAL TENSIONS ON DISPLAY

The love triangle at the heart of *Ascenseur* also serves as a base for Malle and Moreau's next collaboration, *Les Amants*. With opposing figures like that of the husband and his wife's lover embodying different values—traditional versus uncon-

Jeanne Moreau, Alain Cuny and Louis Malle on the set of *Les Amants* (*The Lovers*), 1958

ventional, practical versus daring and romantic—the film provides a construct for reflection in which the third character, the wife (Moreau), must navigate the dichotomies and ultimately choose one path. In the context of the New Wave, the triangle of characters, as a product of a society experiencing great tension as it evolves, reveals deeper preoccupations than the surface-level drama playing out on screen.

Love triangles were a favorite source of drama long before the advent of film. From *Tristan and Isolde* to *Madame Bovary*, *The Great Gatsby* to screen classics like *Casablanca* (1942) and *The Philadelphia Story* (1940), to the sultry *Y tu mamá también* (2001) on up to today with Luca Guadagnino's *Challengers* (2024) and Celine Song's *Past Lives* (2023), the fixed roles in this geometric structure provide a framework that lets viewers gauge the distribution of power among the characters within it and track their development as the love story unfolds. Variations on the husband-wife-lover story can also signal broader societal issues, giving us a window into questions that concerned the general population at the time a given film was made. In this way, an investigation of love triangles in New Wave cinema can uncover obstacles that women and men faced with evolving social roles.

During the '60s, French society underwent an extreme transformation in terms of its moral codes. The Catholic Church no longer exercised the same doctrinal authority, and greater moral freedom called into question the role of marriage. Throughout this period, the love triangle was one of cinema's most prevalent subjects, appearing in a number of films covered at length in other chapters of this book, notably Chabrol's *Les Cousins*, Rohmer's *La Boulangère de Monceau* (The Bakery Girl of Monceau, 1963), Truffaut's *La Peau douce*, and Godard's *Une femme mariée,* to name a few.

Though the conventional husband-wife-lover cliché permeated this new cinema, it is symptomatic that the "young Turks," as the *Cahiers du cinéma* group was called for their oppositional attitude toward the old regime of filmmakers, treated adultery in a less dramatic, more ironic way than their predecessors. Its recurrence also reflected the tension of the times. The transformation of French society, coming out of a somewhat puritanical decade and into a new era of moral freedom, brought with it changes in the relationships between men and women, as women started to gain more agency and independence. Examining female characters in love triangles over the course of the New Wave—in how they are treated in films as well as received by the public—reveals how women's newfound agency began to be constructed and how it was viewed by society.

In Rivette's early short *Le Coup du berger*, like in *Ascenseur*, adultery is dedramatized in the love triangle, but the wife is punished in the plot. Malle treats the love triangle more audaciously in *Les Amants*, allowing Moreau's character extreme freedom in her marriage and even the power to leave it—an arc that caused scandal among audiences. As the New Wave developed, the roles within the love triangle transformed. Though they exist largely in the context of marriage, Jeanne Moreau in the trio she forms with Jules and Jim in Truffaut's classic illustrates the representation of women as ideal and destructive, in a long and complex cultural heritage predating cinema. With Truffaut's *La Peau douce*, women start to show up as "real" and attempt to pierce through the fantasies constructed by male protagonists and by the *mise en scène*. In Godard's *Une femme mariée*, Macha Méril's character gives insight into how the arrival of the birth control pill changed dynamics of marital and extramarital relationships.

THE CHEATER'S CHECKMATE: NEW WOMEN, OLD GAMES IN *LE COUP DU BERGER*

Illustrating with a chessboard the power play between husband and wife, Rivette's *Le Coup du berger* deconstructs the image of conventional marriage at a time when women began to gain ground. Neglected by her older husband, who spends his leisure time painting his ideal (nude) woman, Claire (Virginie Vitry), the young wife, is locked in the cage of her bourgeois apartment, counting the seconds of the auspicious tick-tock of the diegetic clock as she waits for a moment to escape to her lover's hideaway.

For this film, predating the official birth of the New Wave, Rivette explained in a 1964 interview[26] that he used the simple plot of a love triangle as a means of experimenting. Still a nascent filmmaker, Rivette made *Le Coup du berger* in an unconventional way, mobilizing his cinephile friends and new actors to participate in it for free. According to the opening credits, the plot was inspired by a news item, but it also harkens back to the works of nineteenth-century author Guy de Maupassant and contains elements of vaudeville and Italian comedy. Claude de Givray, a young critic writing for *Cahiers du cinema* and a friend of Rivette's, outlined the story:

> A young woman imagines a ruse to justify to her husband her wearing a fur coat that her lover gave her. She places it in a suitcase at the train station locker and claims to have found the corresponding ticket in a taxi. At the same time, to lend more credibility to her dupery and to compromise the man she is tricking, she has her husband retrieve the suitcase himself. When she opens the package, the coat has disappeared. In the final sequence of the film, *the young woman understands who played her*.[27]

In 2007, the synopsis of the film on the DVD cover underscored the weaker position of the wife in the equation but also mentioned another interesting character, the wife's sister (who turns out to be the husband's lover):

> When Solange, Claire's sister, arrives that evening for a small impromptu party, she is the one wearing the fur coat. Jean, the husband, seems completely absent before revealing a smarter strategy than his wife . . .[28]

Opening with a close-up of a game of chess, the film announces marriage as a struggle for power. Hands displaying wedding bands hesitate as husband and wife caculate their next moves. The accompanying voice-over foreshadows the film's finale—that the wife will fall into the husband's trap—from the very beginning: "Here is the moral of the story: the best chess player is the one who anticipates a play in advance of the adversary. To take a classic example, the move called 'fool's mate.' Only a beginner can fall for it. It's her turn."

The chessboard appeared frequently in films of that era, also signaling a power struggle in Vadim's *Les Liaisons dangereuses* (*Dangerous Liaisons*, 1959) between Moreau and Gérard Philipe, and in large format in Antonioni's *La notte* (1961), where Monica Vitti and Marcello Mastroianni play out a scene of seduction on the ground in huge black-and-white squares. But *Le Coup du berger* was more than a game between the sexes; it also unveiled the hypocrisy of a certain social class. The classical music used as a backdrop throughout the film implies that the drama will play out among the bourgeoisie, and various other elements of the film suggest a tacit criticism of that class's façades and lack of authenticity.

The characters themselves exist almost as concepts. With theatrical dialogues, contrived diction, and comic repartee, the lovers are aware of their roles, even going so far as to stage themselves in theatrical games. For example, in a scene between Claire and her lover, Claude (Jean-Claude Brialy), the paramour announces in parody, "Curtain!" as he

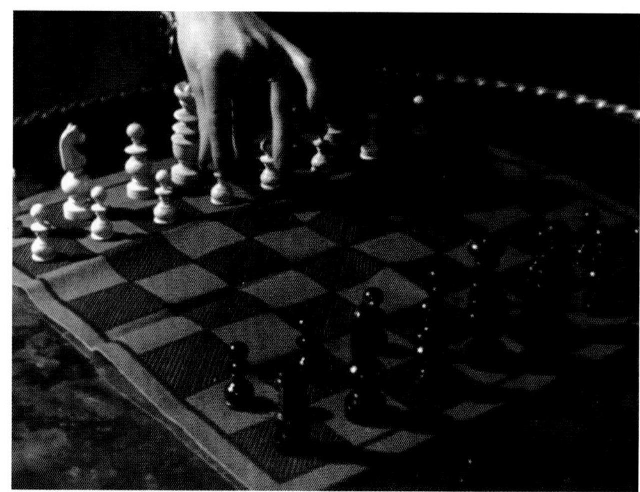

Opening scenes of Jacques Rivette's *Le Coup du berger* (*Fool's Mate*), 1956

draws the curtains in his apartment where their scene will take place. François Couperin's eighteenth-century chamber music signals the characters' entrances and exits in their scenes, showing Claire with her lover and then with her husband. Dramatizing infidelity in such a way, making it explicit, ironically dedramatizes it, giving the story a modern slant. The end, however, reinforces the husband's domination over his wife. Rivette's camera remained objective, refusing to espouse any one character's point of view, a practice he continued more than a decade later in *L'Amour fou* (*Mad Love*, 1969), which also looked at infidelity but through an extremely modern lens.

The geometry of the triangle allows a comparison of stereotypes of women in and outside of marriage. For example, the bourgeois husband Jean (Jacques Doniol-Valcroze) spends his leisure time painting what appears to be an anonymous ideal woman, an image far from the reality he shares with his wife, who is equally bored by their marriage. Claire, meanwhile, invites drama by contriving the plan to wear her ill-gotten fur coat freely, and her mundane but obsessive conversation with Jean about the ticket to the train station locker adds intrigue to a life filled with ennui. The camera follows the unfaithful wife in scenes alternating between her husband and lover, showing them in parallel. The editing presents the two men answering Claire with the same phrases, implying that the two men are alike. Yet Claire is transformed—from a natural, casual, and freer version of herself (dressed in a robe with her hair down) with her lover to a more sophisticated and uptight one in the role of the bourgeois wife (wearing tailored suits and evening gowns, her hair up in a chignon) with her husband, reflecting social constraints.

Interlocked in this love triangle exists yet another triangle that juxtaposes two roles of women: wife and mistress. Claire still occupies that of a married woman, but her sister, Solange (Anne Doat), who is single, supplies the plot twist as she is unveiled as Jean's mistress in the end.

Solange arrives midway through the story in a seemingly insignificant scene. Returning a bracelet she had borrowed from her sister, Solange asks Claire, "Tonight's your little party, right?" Dressed in a loose-fitting trench coat over a bulky turtleneck with black pants, flats, and no makeup, Solange appears more concerned with comfort than fashion—subverting the typical image of a mistress. She sits on Claire's bed and lights a cigarette, giving her an air of rebellion. In direct contrast with Claire, primping in front of the mirror in a tailored dress, Solange seems unburdened by her appearance and conveys the blasé attitude of the new generation. When Claire asks her about the men in her love life, Solange responds, "Which ones?" Claire responds with a smile and asks, "Why? You have several?" Solange repeats back, "Several?" Claire then declares, "I see. It's time for you to get married!" Solange protests, however, "Oh—it's not at all what you think! Everything's going very, *very* well."

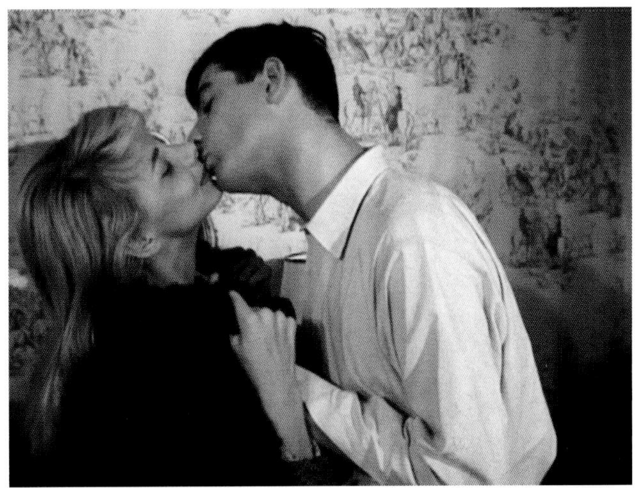

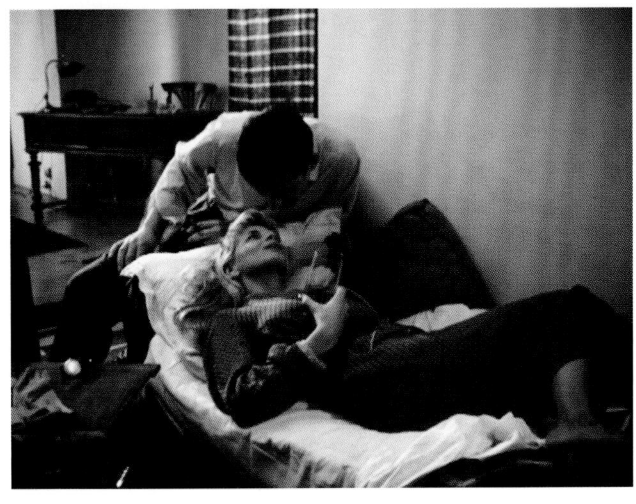

Virginie Vitry (Claire) and Jean-Claude Brialy (her lover) in Jacques Rivette's *Le Coup du berger*, 1956

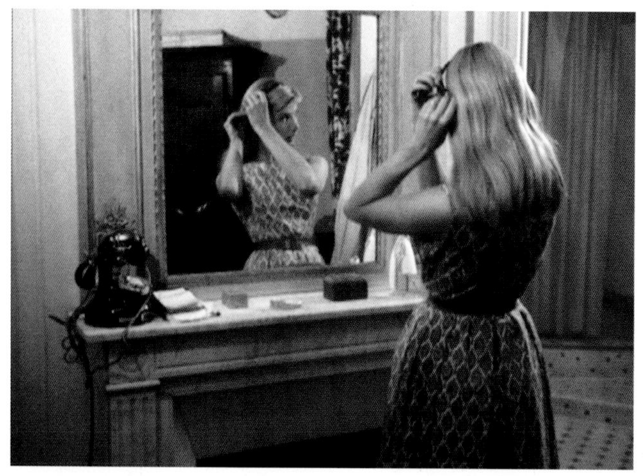

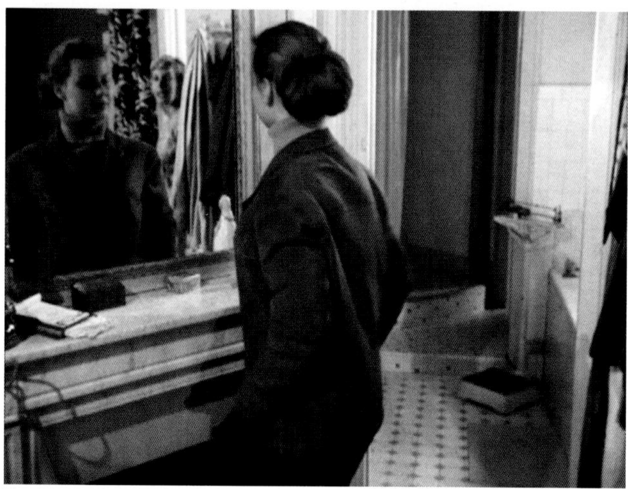

The plot thickens when Solange admires Claire's gray blazer, which Claire lets her try on and then gifts to her. "I don't want to clean you out," Solange answers, inciting Claire's suspicion that her sister is acting strangely. The scene foreshadows the final "fool's mate," when Solange enters the party wearing her sister's coveted fur coat, a move that turns their complicity into rivalry.

The portrait of the unknown ideal woman that Jean had been obsessively painting turns out to be a semi-disguised nude portrait of Solange. While Claire, the bourgeois wife, is ridiculed, Solange, the unconventional, single, and freer sister comes out unpunished as the mistress. She is even rewarded with the coat, but at the expense of her relationship with her sister. The finale therefore reinforces the cliché of feminine rivalry and rewards the husband. Jean played

Top: Virginie Vitry (Claire) **Bottom:** Anne Doat (Solange) in Jacques Rivette's *Le Coup du berger*, 1956

along with Claire's game only to hijack her independence in the end. As the commentary states, "And here is the final blow. Claire understands, too late, who played her." The film ends with a return to patriarchal order where the woman is ridiculed, a turn of events that echoes the outcomes in the *cinéma de papa*. The game and the plot show the wife losing her legitimate power in the marriage. Showing Jean outsmarting his wife, the film also suggests through Solange that a man's affection is the ultimate prize.

LES AMANTS: MALLE AND MOREAU FIND TRUTH IN FICTION

Les Amants, released just months after *Ascenseur*, introduced the public to the new Jeanne Moreau, with Malle's lead actress in the part of a bored bourgeois wife much like the one in *Le Coup du berger*. Unlike Claire, Moreau's character, Jeanne, would achieve freedom on screen—but provoke scandal off it.

Inspired by Vivant Denon's eighteenth-century novella *Point de lendemain* (*No Tomorrow*), *Les Amants* explores power dynamics within a bourgeois marriage. In the novel, a naïve young man falls into the trap of an aristocratic couple's libertine game as he spends a night *sans lendemain* (with no tomorrow) with the wife, while *Les Amants* focuses on the story of (extramarital) romantic love. Malle described it as "the story of a night of passion."[29] Depicting the life of a couple belonging to the haute bourgeoisie in Dijon, the film centers on Jeanne, another wife full of ennui who is neglected by her emotionally distant husband, a newspaper owner. Jeanne fills her days with empty outings and superficial friends, like Maggy and Raoul, Jeanne's clandestine yet conventional polo-playing lover. When Jeanne's car breaks down on the evening Maggy and Raoul are coming to dinner, Bernard—a young, free-spirited archaeologist who has rejected his family money—stops after she flags him down. When he gives her a lift home, their spark is immediate, and when he stays for dinner, their *nuit d'amour* will transform her life.

"I especially like this film because it's the first film that was made for me," Moreau told a journalist in a 2005 interview.[30] When Malle talked to her about making *Les Amants*, she put everything on hold until the film was ready, which meant eight months of

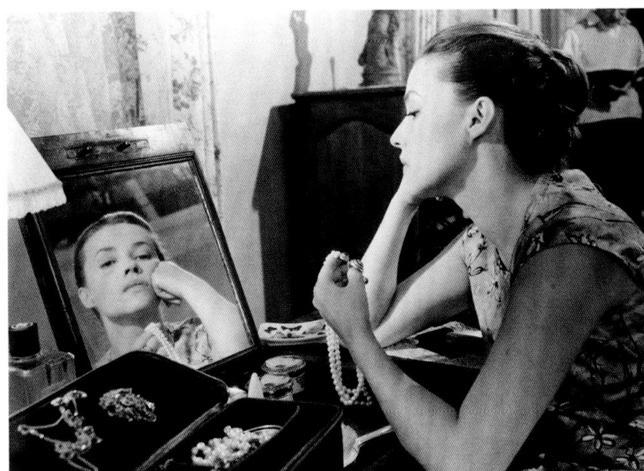

not doing theater or other projects so she could "concentrate solely on this character."[31] According to Moreau, she and Malle became romantically involved on the set of *Ascenseur*,[32] and they also lived together while filming *Les Amants*.

Their own romance helped shape the adaptation of Denon's novella, which served as a perfect pretext for Malle to film the woman he loved. The heroine was not simply transposed to the screen according to Denon's original text, but her portrait became that of Moreau as Malle described Jeanne, the character: "She is barely thirty years old, she is beautiful. Her face is usually seen as [emotionally] moving because it reveals an intelligence and a lucidity beyond her gender. She is also spiritual; she likes to tease, and is intuitive. Men find in her all the qualities they want in a woman, but her clairvoyance and sometimes her cynicism easily disconcerts them."[33]

There are certain undeniable parallels between the characters and their real-life influences. At the time of the filming, Moreau was separated from but still close with her first husband, Jean-Louis Richard, the father of her young son. Bernard, the man Jeanne falls in love with in the film, resembles Malle in his rebellious spirit and his rejection of his haute-bourgeoisie background (though Malle gave his alter ego the audacity to do what he himself could not quite commit to: decline his familial inheritance altogether). They even drive the same car—a Citroën 2CV. When Jeanne's Peugeot 203 breaks down on the side of the road, Bernard picks her up in his "simple 2CV," as he describes it to her, apologizing for it not being fancier. When he introduces himself to

her as Bernard Dubois-Lambert, Jeanne recognizes the last name as being that of a well-to-do family to which she has connections: "I know a Dubois-Lambert who plays golf at Saint-Cloud," she tells him. Bernard answers that the man in question is his cousin whom he "avoids like the plague." As Jeanne describes her husband to Bernard, he pegs him as fitting the image of a typical husband of the haute bourgeoisie, calling him a "brown bear." Arriving at her mansion, she sees her husband fitting Bernard's description and begins laughing uncontrollably. Her view from the car's windshield frames him and their dinner guests waiting in the driveway in fixed poses, transforming them into caricatures, not far from Resnais's rigid characters in *L'Année dernière à Marienbad* (*Last Year at Marienbad*, 1961) or Buñuel's *Le Charme discret de la bourgeoisie* (*The Discreet Charm of the Bourgeoisie*, 1972). Near the end of the film, it is as if Malle speaks through Bernard when he says, "I hate all this. Those footsteps, those voices and all this domestic hubbub. This house, your husband, your friends, your life."

The strongest scenes in the film are the ones where Malle takes the most risks with elements inspired by reality, including, in the intimate and very personal moments with Moreau, some borrowed from the actress herself. At the end of the sequence depicting her night of passion with Bernard, for example, when Jeanne takes a bath, the lines "I always keep my bathtub full, and at night, when it is very hot, I take a bath" were inspired by a letter Moreau sent to Malle before *Ascenseur* in which she explained that the ink had been "diluted" by water falling from her hair as she "took two baths while writing" him because "it was so hot."[34] Details like these give the film authenticity and a modern edge. In an interview many years later, Moreau was asked if she would have done the film if she and Malle had not been lovers. Her reply: "No, not at all. It would not have been possible without him and without me."[35]

Departing from the source material, in which the young libertine Bernard is the main character and narrator, Malle changed perspectives, making Jeanne the heart of his film. A frustrated, bourgeois married woman in the countryside, Jeanne evokes Gustave Flaubert's *Madame Bovary*. Neglected by her husband for his work, Emma Bovary falls in

Jeanne Moreau in Louis Malle's *Les Amants* (*The Lovers*), 1958

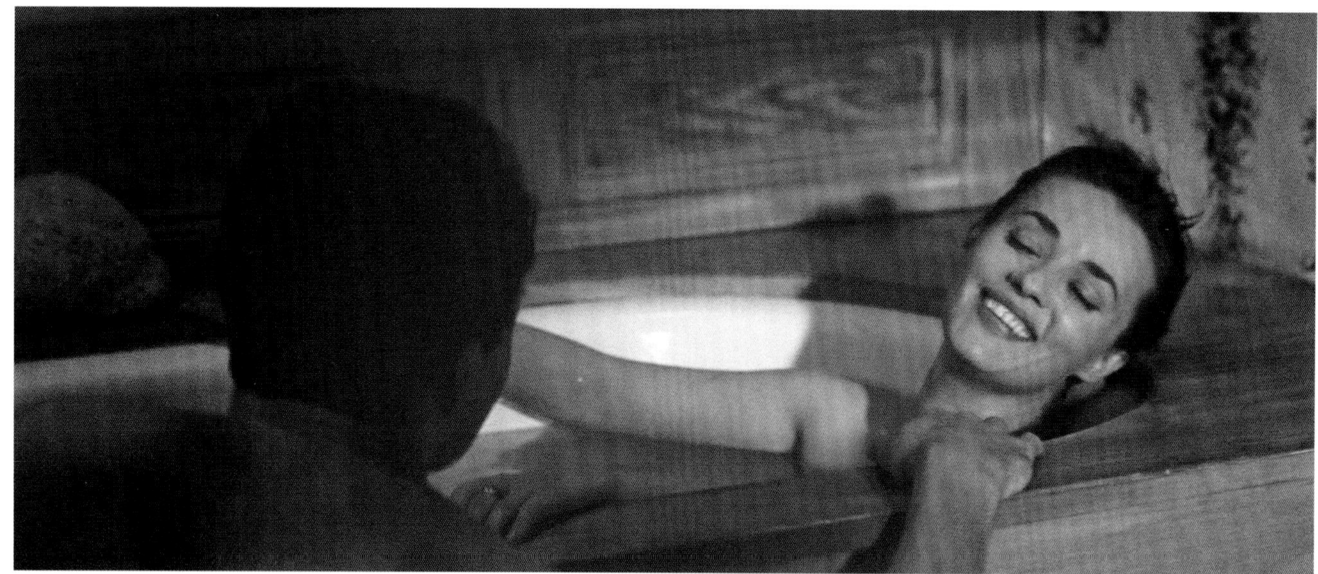

love with the incarnation of her fantasy from the romance novels she reads to distract herself. In Malle's film, however, Jeanne makes her own decisions lucidly regarding Bernard and stands up to her husband. The script illustrates the inequality and power struggle within the marriage through petty disputes. In one scene, Jeanne "goes up to the hi-fi and turns the knob. The music softens, suddenly.... Without letting go of her, [her husband] goes to the hi-fi and turns it up again."[36] Compared to the initial script, however, the version of Jeanne in the film affirms her more, a testament to Moreau's influence and involvement in creating her character. Attempting to define herself outside the conventionally validating role as a "married woman," Jeanne asserts her independence and signals her husband's neglect:

Jeanne: Maggy knows. She thinks that if you're not a great beauty, you need a style.
Henri: But you don't need a style because you have a husband.
Jeanne: A husband who looks at me once in a blue moon.
Henri: If you think I never look at you, then whom do you need a style for?
Jeanne: For no one. For me. To be in style. It's my right.

She also forgoes the Latin lover cliché that is teased at the beginning of the film in the form of Raoul, the polo play-er. Jeanne disrupts expectations and chooses Bernard, who represents the authenticity and the freedom of a new generation on the horizon.

Director Jacques Doniol-Valcroze described the "newness" of the film at the time in *Cahiers du cinéma*, citing its depiction of physical love that goes from the "romanticism" of the scene in the park (where Malle filmed Moreau without makeup and with her hair down, wearing a white flowing nightgown, like an "apparition," in Doniol-Valcroze's words, during the night of passion) to the "realism" of the scene in the bedroom: "the pauses, the phrases that don't mean anything, pillow talk humor, overlooking no detail of intimate traits that make up the intimacy of love, such particular things like the bathtub scene that is one of the most striking by its fresh depiction and its truth."[37] Critics noted the importance of the gestures as well as the ellipses, emphasizing the film's audacity and courage in approaching truth in the love scene between Jeanne and Bernard.

THE OBSCENE UNSEEN: *LES AMANTS'* RADICAL EROTICISM

The love scene that provoked a scandal was actually part of an idyllic whole that consisted of a fairy-tale-like prelude that colored the entire scene with romanticism, echoing back to the Carte du Tendre (a seventeenth-century map of an imaginary

Jeanne Moreau in Louis Malle's *Les Amants* (*The Lovers*), 1958 land leading to love) in the film's opening credits. Jeanne and Bernard drift together in a small boat under the moonlight where she is dressed in a flowing white gown as violins play solemnly Brahms's Sextet No. 1 Op. 18 on the accompanying soundtrack, music that Malle had listened to while writing the script.[38] When the lovers come inside the house, Jeanne stops to kiss her child who is sleeping in the next room, reinforcing her image as a good mother. When Jeanne meets Bernard in the bedroom, like in *Le Coup du berger*, the clock is ticking. She stops it. The next part of the scene exists *hors temps*, out of time. For the more intimate part of the love scene, the absence of scenic indications in the script speaks to Malle's appropriation of the scene from his relations with Moreau. The scene originally provoked a moral question between Malle and Louise de Vilmorin, the script's cowriter. Disapproving of it, de Vilmorin refused to write the scene. The script, therefore, indicated an unwritten sequence, intended to be improvised. Scenes "299 to 330" called for "different shots of Jeanne and Bernard in the bedroom and in the bathroom"[39] during the night of passion, which left Malle and Moreau on their own and free to improvise. According to Moreau, "There were thirty shots without camera movement or dialogue. The scene was shot in a studio the final week of shooting over four days, a close collaboration between Louis Malle, Jean-Marc Bory, and me." She also described her awkward position of playing the scene with another man as Malle directed it: "I knew that if I played the love scenes just as Louis wanted, he would love me as an actress but hate me as a woman. I could not play them without betraying him."[40]

Though no explicit content is shown on screen, the scene proved to be shocking, even obscene, in the true sense of the word. The beginning embraces behind the lace curtains and close-ups of the couple's kiss on the bed were followed by *imagined* scenes, implied through the camera's lingering shots of Moreau's face in close-up accompanied by increasingly louder violins and her repeated calls of "mon amour." The scene ends with a close-up of the lovers' intertwined hands, anticipating the fragmented shots of Godard's lovers in *Une femme mariée*. "Normally, when you film [a love scene], you do a panorama on the window. What *Les Amants* brought in relation to other films before it was that the panorama on the window took place thirty seconds lat-

er,"[41] Malle said, describing the scene. While emphasizing the triple strand of pearls still around her neck, reinforcing her image as a woman of class and her appurtenance in the haute bourgeoisie, Moreau's face is filmed in a way that went against convention. In close-up and without apparent makeup, she looks realistic as she conveys her feelings, her passion. Perhaps adding to this authenticity—and the scandal—was her off-screen romance with Malle. At the end of the sequence, Jeanne caresses Bernard, who is face down on the bed, uttering the words, "I've only known you. I've always known you," before scribbling a private message to him on his back with her finger. "I'm so happy. My whole life would've slipped away." Born from the director's desire to reveal the couple's passion on screen, the film portrays a authentic intimacy between Jeanne and Bernard that was greater than cinema authorized at the time.

When asked by a journalist in 1958 about what he called the "terribly risqué" scene, Moreau defended it: "People gossip about a scandalous scene that lasts an entire night that takes place in the gardens and in the bedroom. And I believe it's a serious misunderstanding because there's not a trace of hypocrisy in this film and that scene wasn't done with a commercial aim to scandalize people and provoke curiosity. It's simply the story of a woman who finds love. It shows in its entirety and with a strong sense of purity this woman's encounter with a young man and her awakening."[42] Moreau is not shy in her portrayal of this awakening. One of the first actresses to appear nude, she explained that she gave herself to the part in the aim of authenticity, not scandal.

JEANNE MOREAU'S NEW *FEMME LIBRE*

The search for authenticity in *Les Amants* extended beyond the erotic; Malle wanted to show a realistic image of desire alongside the poetry of love. In the final sequence, Jeanne leaves her old life behind to embark on a new one with Bernard. When she gets dressed in a simple sweater and skirt and is about to pack her makeup kit, Bernard tells her, "No, don't take anything." When her friend Maggy runs into Jeanne by the stairs as she exits her bedroom with Bernard, she implicitly judges her, saying, "My goodness! I'm speechless." Jeanne tells her, "Shut up, Maggy, and don't try to understand. You never will." As they leave in Bernard's 2CV, faced with the reality of the day, Jeanne is quietly crying, explaining that it is "because of the night." Bernard replies, "I wish it were always night." The long silences and the noise of the car add to this realistic feel. Still softly crying, Jeanne says, "I'm sorry. It's silly, I know but I'm no longer myself." Bernard's reply also illustrates Malle's desire to paint a cinematic portrait of Moreau that is true to her: "But I want you to be yourself. It's you that I want." She looks at herself in the visor mirror and closes her eyes. When Bernard says he wants to kiss her, she begs him, "No, don't look at me!" But suddenly, as a rooster crows, it is as if she wakes up to accept herself as well as the reality of the situation. Looking at Bernard and facing the camera—the dark circles under her eyes at this moment conveying her humanity—Moreau appears authentic, her beauty captured through Malle's lens. Henri Decaë, director of photography, used "raw lighting"

that brings a truth to the story as Jeanne detaches from the stereotype constructed in the first part of the film.

The director specified that the last scene should last a long time and be "filled with a million details, without a return to the past, or an escape to a tomorrow that in fact may not be very different from what their life was before."[43] This last phrase, dedramatizing the outcome of the affair, showed an evolution in relation to the stereotype. The film concentrates on the present moment, without expectations, without thinking of the consequences. At the same time, it is realistic. "They set off on a long journey, aware of its uncertainty, unsure of ever recapturing the happiness of that first night. Already, in the treacherous hours of dawn, Jeanne had her doubts. She was afraid, but she regretted nothing," Jeanne says in voiceover to close the film. Instead of a romantic happy ending or a scene where Jeanne returns to her husband (reestablish-

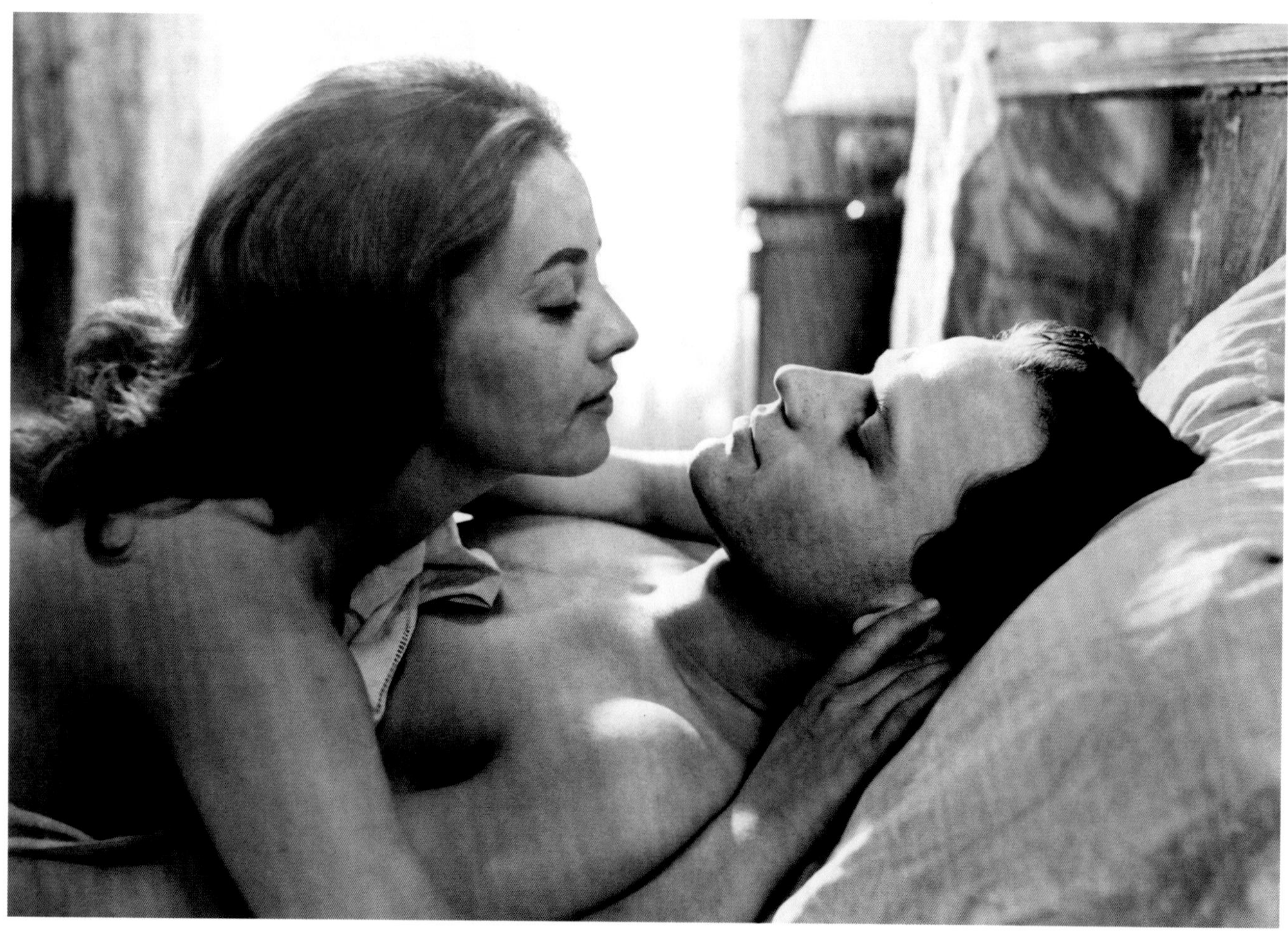

Jeanne Moreau and Jean-Marc Bory in in Louis Malle's *Les Amants* (*The Lovers*) 1958

ing the patriarchal order), the ending here is left open and the heroine without regret. This key choice by Malle made the film modern. "In the original script, Jeanne left Bernard on a square in Dijon and went inside a café where her husband came to get her," explained François Leterrier, Malle's assistant on the film. "This end, that 'brought things full circle' according to the sad convention of most French films, never satisfied Louis Malle," Leterrier stated. "At the time of the shoot, he couldn't bring himself to have Jeanne get out of the car. And he reconstructed this 'open' ending, where the two lovers, still under the charm of their night together, persevered without illusion in their desire to leave together."[44]

The original ending would have mirrored more closely that of the novella, which restores social order by having the wife remain at home while her lover rides away after their brief encounter *sans lendemain*—with no tomorrow—and with no moral to the story. But Malle had realized he did not want to reduce the night of passion to a simple parenthetical moment for Jeanne, locking her into her role as spouse. His rewritten conclusion anticipates unresolved endings like that of *The Graduate* (1967), with the young couple staring into space at the back of the bus, not knowing what lay ahead.

As a transitional film, *Les Amants* broke ground not only in centering the perspective of a woman in the lead role but also in offering a new image of a *femme libre*. The film used the framework of a basic love triangle to deconstruct the rigid cliché of the bored, bourgeois housewife, becoming instead the trajectory of a woman with subjectivity seeking—and then achieving—a more meaningful life. Although Jeanne's step toward liberation was propelled by her love for a man, she nevertheless succeeded in gaining the freedom to follow her own path; together, Moreau and Malle had shaped her character into a rebel against her social class and the status and image of the dutiful wife.[45] Moreau's involvement in that process represented an advancement for women in film, and she, like her character, would go on to rebel in many roles throughout the 1960s as she lived life on her own terms.[46]

Upending the conventional narrative with its hints of realism in the love scenes, autobiographical references that lent authenticity to the story, and the ambiguity in its open ending, *Les Amants* was an early step toward modernizing the cinematic landscape. At the time, however, it was not universally celebrated as such. The frank eroticism depicted in the love scenes disturbed viewers, and the polemic surrounding the film became violent. The popular Catholic newspaper *La Croix* labeled it "indecent," "repugnant," and "immoral" in form and content.[47] France forbade anyone under sixteen years old from seeing it. In Italy, the film provoked riots at the Venice Film Festival and was banned until January 1959, when the censorship commission finally authorized its release after negotiating a few brief cuts with the Italian distributor. In the United States, the affair witnessed unending judicial developments, notably an obscenity conviction brought by the state of Ohio against the theater that screened it there. Though portraying adulterous love, the film's sexual explicitness was in fact confined to a glimpse of Moreau's breast. The case went all the way to the Supreme Court, which reversed the decision,[48] with Justice Potter Stewart famously stating, "I shall not today attempt to further define [obscenity], but I know it when I see it."[49]

The magnitude of the scandal suggests that the film contained extremely shocking material. The reality—that in the most "shocking" love scenes, the viewer sees nothing—suggests that the backlash perhaps also stemmed from the representation of a woman who is not punished after abandoning her husband and child to live freely with her lover. In the '50s, such a plot twist was unimaginable, and indeed, the media (reflecting the moral order) tended to focus on the married woman's betrayal of her husband. After Moreau defended the love scene to a journalist in 1958, he insisted on the film's immorality with a follow-up remark: "But this main character is a woman who cheats on her husband." Moreau, for her part, rejected the notion that this could have contributed to the scandal. "The problem isn't adultery," she stated, "it's the love scene I mentioned . . ."

Despite the media's moral outrage, the film was a success at the box office, and critics celebrated the love scene. Even the scandal in Venice proved useful in a way by helping associate Moreau's image with "eroticism and modernity, intelligence and maturity," according to one critic.[50] Thanks to *Les Amants*, her twenty-second film, Moreau found her niche. With her personal style and individuality, she opened her own door for future endeavors and carved the way for other actresses to assert their own style in the roles they played.[51] Her real-life persona also reinforced her strong on-screen presence, which brought credibility to her characters' liberation from social constraints: She was known as intelligent and an avid reader, and had once said she identified with the rebellious Antigone.

Her pioneering spirit did not protect her from judgment, however. Though her roles projected freedom, they also contained more negative elements that would lead some people to classify them as "perverted" or "depraved," as one journalist put it in a 1972 interview. When he went on to say that Moreau was seen as "sensual,"[52] implying a certain immorality, she replied, "To be very frank, I can border on the indecent or scandalous though I'm very natural and do nothing scandalous. That's why I'm offered roles like that. What drives me to take on those roles is exactly the absence of the notion of good and evil. I can only choose and portray a character if I understand her. It goes beyond like or dislike."

It is Moreau's own absence of judgment, perhaps, that encourages empathy for her characters, engendering acceptance of free women in real life. "I don't judge," the actress stated. "I succeed in finding reasons and motivations that explain why this woman does what she does. The moment I understand her in my mind, I embrace her fully. I don't judge her. I don't find her good or evil. I just become her. At a certain point, there's no distance between us. There's a sort of confusion that's quite troubling and that leaves its mark—like an internal upheaval, as if I'd been inside someone else and at the same time inside myself. It's a real adventure."[53]

MOREAU'S MARRIAGE AND MOTHERHOOD, ON AND OFF SCREEN

Louis Malle left Moreau when she was thirty years old. The relationship between the actress and the characters she played is striking. When asked how she reacted to being left in a relationship, Moreau replied, "I am sad but I accept it—I love my independence too much not to admire it in another person." In *Les Amants*, the actress played a woman who threw aside social norms to follow her own desire to start a new life outside the constraints of bourgeois society, casting aside conventionally defined roles for women in terms of marriage and motherhood. In real life, she did the same.

Moreau became a mother at twenty-one years old, getting married the day before her son was born in 1949. Neither she nor her husband, Jean-Louis Richard, wanted the marriage, she claimed. At the time, contraception and abortion were illegal in France, and Moreau experienced this undesired motherhood as a constraint that pushed her to concessions like her marriage did."[54] Soon, she found herself in a position of being the sole breadwinner in the family when her husband lost his acting job. "I was forced by circumstances to take responsibilities, for me as well as those in my family," she explained. "It's what we call freedom, I think, when it's seen from the outside. It's a freedom that makes you happy, and sometimes we feel fragile and lonely and we cry by ourselves in a corner. We pull out of it, more or less rapidly."[55]

Though the couple divorced, they maintained a close friendship, as the actress attested to in an interview in 1972: "I must admit, I can't live without him. We don't live in the same house but we call each other every morning and every night."[56] Like many of her characters, Moreau's ambivalence created a push-pull in her relationships: "I'm scared of feeling imprisoned. . . . I'm scared of being tied up."[57]

At the dawn of the 1960s, what place did society hold for women who refused to be confined only to the roles of wife or mother? "None," answered Marguerite Duras, whose novel *Moderato cantabile* was adapted to the screen for Moreau.[58] When Peter Brook directed the film in 1960, he said that Moreau was "the only woman in the world who could play the role." Like in *Les Amants*, Moreau's character in *Moderato cantabile* (*Seven Days . . . Seven Nights*) goes against convention, this time a bourgeois wife and mother with an intense attachment to her child and an attraction to a young factory worker incarnated by Jean-Paul Belmondo. During the filming, Moreau's ten-year-old son Jérôme was badly hurt in a car accident with Belmondo at the wheel. Jérôme spent seventeen days in a coma, and Moreau was grief-stricken as she went back to the set after he gained consciousness.

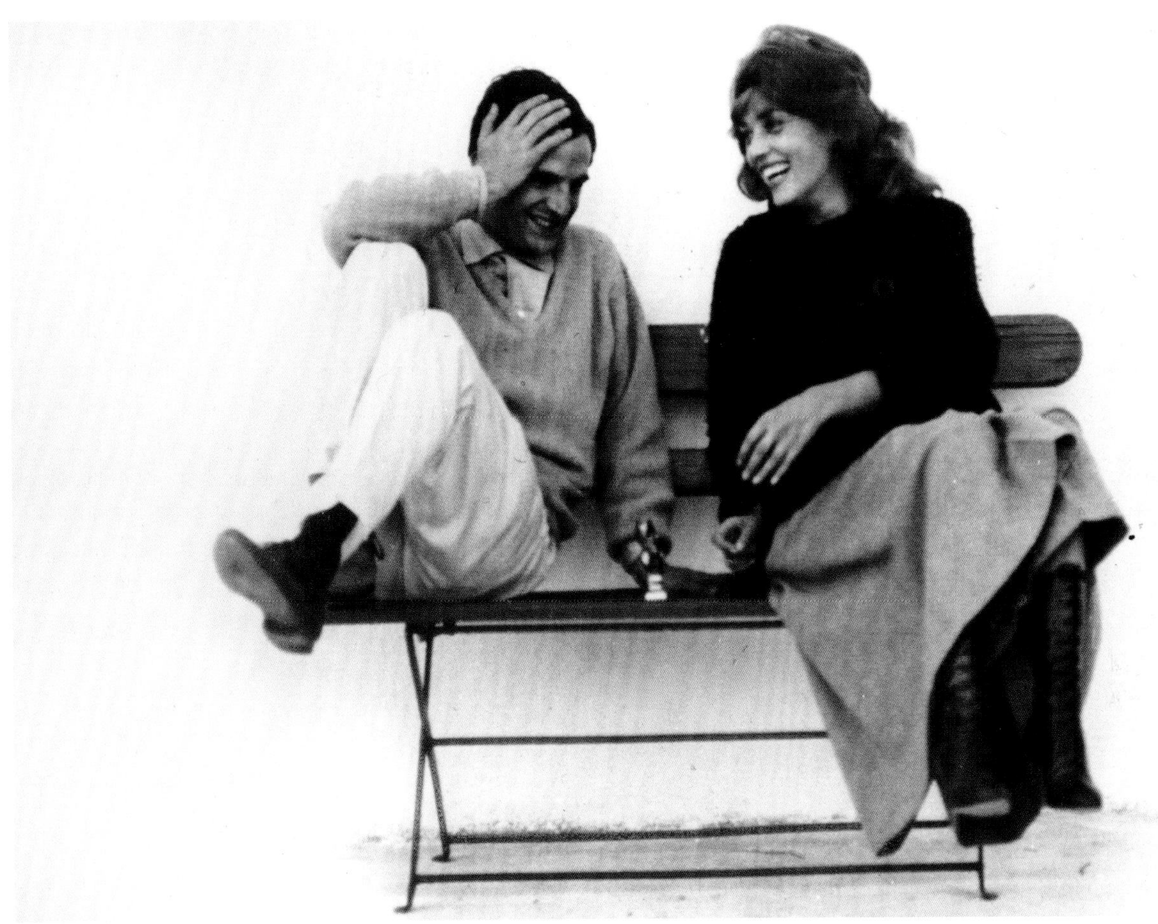

The experience of her son's accident infiltrated Moreau's performance. "I always thought an actress nourished herself from experiences that happened to her every day," she stated, noting the coincidences in life that enhance sensitivity at the right time. In this case, it was in the role of mother.[59] Moreau received letters saying the accident was her punishment for *Les Amants*,[60] but she continued to garner praise and respect from New Wave directors. Godard even enlisted her for a cameo in *Une femme est une femme* the following year; during her scene, Belmondo's character asks her how it's going with *Jules et Jim*, her forthcoming film with Truffaut. "Moderato," she replies, a nod to Brook's film. Her role in *Moderato cantabile* would also earn Moreau her first acting award at the Cannes Film Festival.

MOREAU THROUGH TRUFFAUT: THE WHIRLWIND OF *JULES ET JIM*

It was also in Cannes two years prior that Moreau, there to present *Ascenseur* with Malle, had first met Truffaut. "He was a small young man. Very shy," the actress recalled years later. "He had written terrible reviews about me [about her earlier films]. I was terrorized by him. I imagined him as a judge, somewhat colossal." Shortly after this initial encounter, before he had even made his first film, *Les Quatre cents coups*, Truffaut told her about a book he had read called *Jules et Jim*, saying, "One day, I'll make this movie, and I would like you to play Catherine."[61] The film would become known for its portrayal of one of the most famous love triangles in cinematic history.

After the rupture with Malle and a difficult shoot in Italy working with Antonioni alongside Marcello Mastroianni on *La Notte* in 1961, Moreau decided to make a shift from playing women who were lost, alone, and depressed. "This film allows her to laugh, to smile, to be really alive,"[62] Truf-

François Truffaut and Jeanne Moreau on the set of *Jules et Jim*, 1962, photo by Raymond Cauchetier

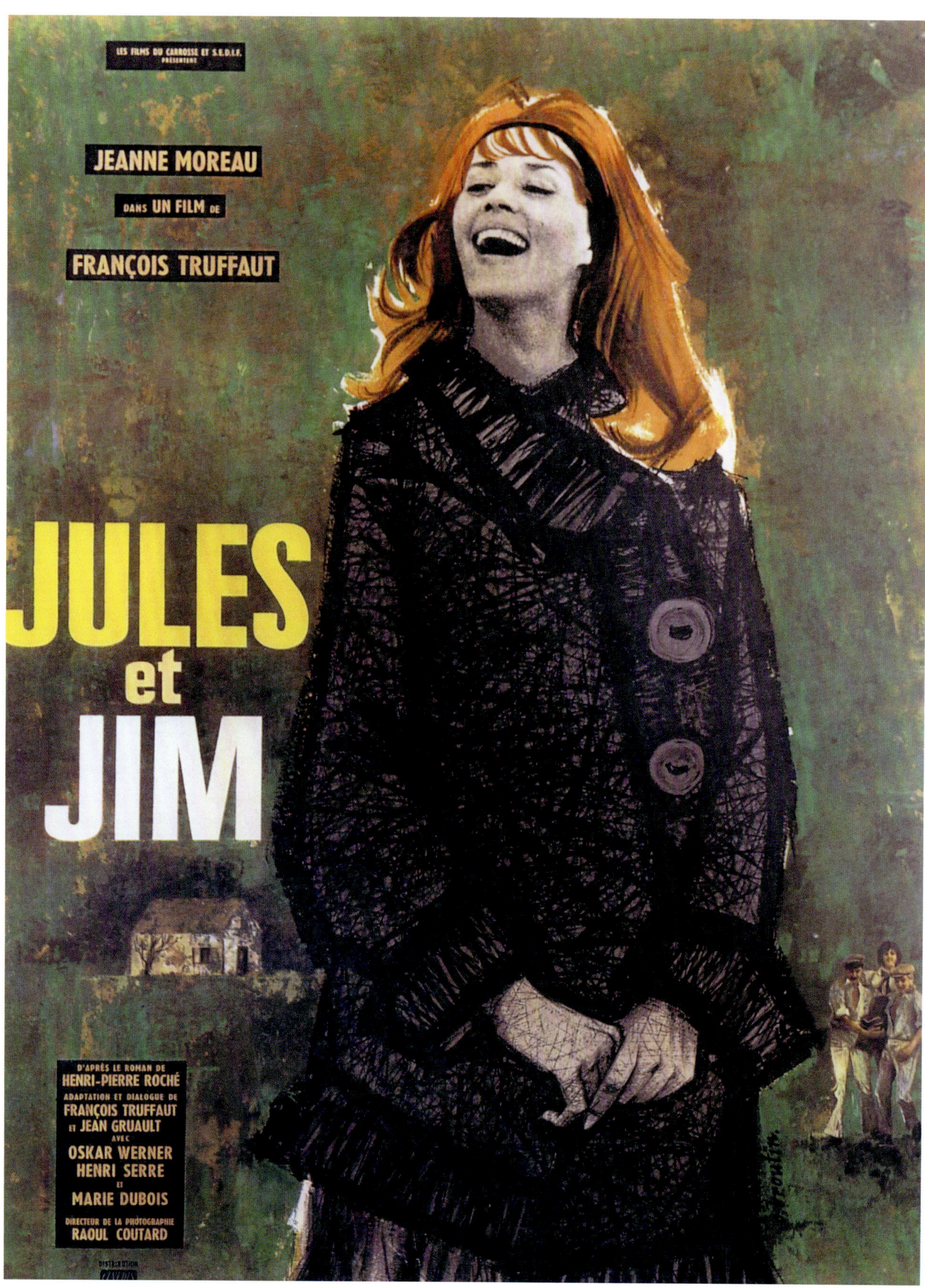
LES FILMS DU CARROSSE ET S.E.D.I.F.
PRÉSENTENT
JEANNE MOREAU
DANS UN FILM DE
FRANÇOIS TRUFFAUT
JULES
et
JIM
D'APRÈS LE ROMAN DE
HENRI-PIERRE ROCHÉ
ADAPTATION ET DIALOGUE DE
FRANÇOIS TRUFFAUT
ET JEAN GRUAULT
AVEC
OSKAR WERNER
HENRI SERRE
ET
MARIE DUBOIS
DIRECTEUR DE LA PHOTOGRAPHIE
RAOUL COUTARD
DISTRIBUTION
CAVOIS

faut stated when their collaboration on *Jules et Jim* finally became a reality. At thirty-four, Moreau incarnated a free woman in the film, leading her life and love life according to her own rules. As "la femme" for Jules and Jim, she was above all an independent woman and the film's driving force. With Truffaut, Moreau incarnated sexual freedom on screen long before the revolution of 1968. But the film's more classic style reflects the director's reluctance to treat the subject matter from Henri-Pierre Roché's novel (or the daring ménage à trois story) in a direct way in terms of the *mise en scène* of love scenes.

From a different perspective, instead of focusing on scandal, we can see how Truffaut shows complicity among the characters in the triangle in the first part of the film and celebrates the deep love and friendship between Jules and Jim. The trust at the beginning of the trio's unconventional relationship allows Catherine to try on the freedom of a man as she puts on a moustache and dresses in men's clothing to test a different identity as they run a race. In imagining how a Hollywood version of the film might focus on the scandal of a ménage à trois, here, we see a cautionary tale of *eros* competing with *agape*, of how, when the triangle splits, passion can ruin a truer type of love found in their harmonious beginnings, leading to destruction.

At the film's center, the song made famous by Moreau, "Le Tourbillon," ("The Whirlwind," selling one million records in 1962),[63] captures the capricious passions between the characters in the love triangle in the film as well as in the actress's life. Written by her friend Serge Rezvani, the words were inspired by Moreau's on-again, off-again relationship with former husband Jean-Louis Richard, to whom she remained close until his death in 2012.

Moreau developed and maintained a close friendship with Truffaut also, sparked by their collaboration on *Jules et Jim* and from the experience they shared of an unhappy childhood. Over a decade later, they still spoke on the phone every day.[64] Truffaut related that *Jules et Jim* was the most luminous episode of his whole filmography thanks to Moreau.[65] Together they produced one of the most iconic female roles of the New Wave.

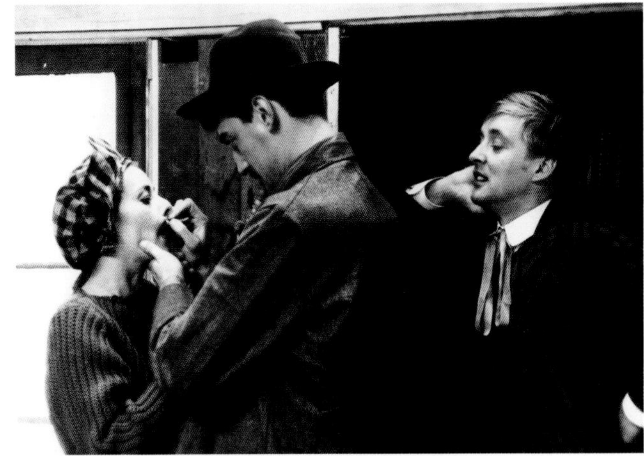

JEANNE MOREAU: THE MALE DIRECTOR'S GUIDE TO WOMEN

Conscious of her unique ability to personify new ideas and roles for women, Moreau spoke of her collaboration with directors where their meeting was key to generating these characters: "Whether with Michelangelo [Antonioni] or Louis Malle, I am very aware that the encounters that I made with the directors, there was a reciprocal attraction even when we didn't know each other, that allowed the men, the directors to discover things about women. I think that there was a marvelous coincidence in what I could represent, what I could provoke and what they were looking to discover."[66]

Moreau's filmography illustrated her choice to work on artistically daring films with directors considered auteurs, from Joseph Losey on *Eva* in 1962 to Buñuel on *Le Journal d'une femme de chambre* (*Diary of a Chambermaid*) in 1964. Moreau also had a special complicity with Orson Welles, meeting him at the Comédie-Française in 1951.[67] She worked with him on *Le Procès* (*The Trial*, 1962), and helped him secure financing by starring in *Falstaff* (also known as *Chimes at Midnight*, 1965) and *Une histoire immortelle* (*The Immortal Story*, 1968).[68] With Demy, she helped produce *La Baie des anges* (*Bay of Angels*) in 1963, accepting the role because she admired his work in *Lola*.[69] With Tony Richardson, she shot an adaptation of Jean Genet's *Mademoiselle* (1966), worked again with Truffaut on 1967's *La Mariée était en noir* and with Jean Renoir on *Le Petit théâtre de Jean Renoir* (*The Little Theatre of Jean Renoir*, 1970).

Left: François Truffaut's *Jules et Jim*, 1962, original poster **Above:** Jeanne Moreau with Henri Serre and Oskar Werner Truffaut's *Jules et Jim*, 1962

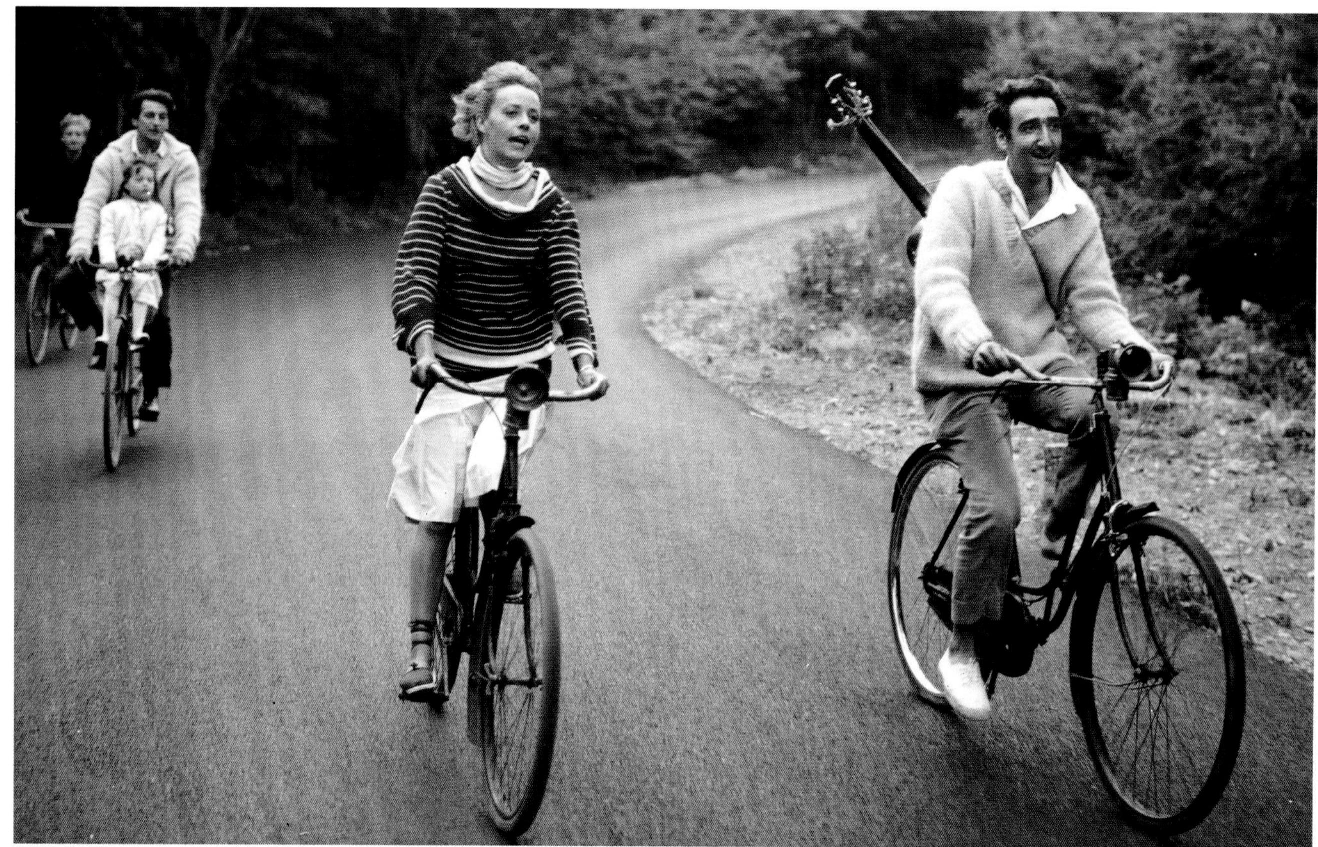

Moreau was famous for having many lovers who remained her friends throughout her life, Malle among them.[70] Of her relationships with directors, Moreau stated, "I didn't mind these people using me. I loved it. Because, using me, allowing them to use me, I knew I was using them at the same time. The relationship between an actress and a director is a relationship of seduction. It's a double relationship. . . . The creative process is very intimate. It goes beyond everything."[71] The actress would work again with Malle alongside Bardot, both incarnating images of modern women, in Mexico on Moreau's forty-first film, *Viva María!* (1965), a costume film. *Life* magazine reported at the time that "to the surprise and vast relief of the company," the two actresses "got along swimmingly," with Bardot commenting, "To me, there are two kinds of women—those who have a wholly feminine character, with all the faults that implies, and those who have the character of a man, completely open and spontaneous. I am the latter kind, and so is Jeanne." Moreau added: "Like me, Brigitte is an animal, but of a very different species. I guess we are both free women—we have that in common."[72]

At the beginning of the 1960s, when women continued to be placed in a position inferior to men, Moreau, like Bardot, presented a freedom that announced women's strides toward liberation during the next decade. Prioritizing her career (with 130 films, fifty plays, and numerous songs[73]) at a time when society demanded that women choose between motherhood and work, Moreau simply refused to abide restrictions on her life—an attitude that sometimes caused her to be judged as amoral in much the same way her heroines were viewed. The courage, in her own life and in the characters she played, however, helped ease rigid attitudes of the day. As Moreau herself remarked, many of the films' narratives centered on women, and her free-spirited intensity allowed directors to approach these roles from new, more interesting angles: "I had the luck to be who I was at that time and though I didn't ask for it, my needs were such that they coincided with the needs of film directors and the preoccupation at that time: Who is a woman? Who is she?"[74]

Jeanne Moreau with Oskar Werner, Henri Serre, Sabine Haudepin and Serge Rezvani in Truffaut's *Jules et Jim*, 1962

"I didn't mind these people using me. I loved it. Because, using me, allowing them to use me, I knew I was using them at the same time. The relationship between an actress and a director is a relationship of seduction. It's a double relationship. . . . The creative process is very intimate. It goes beyond everything."

—jeanne moreau

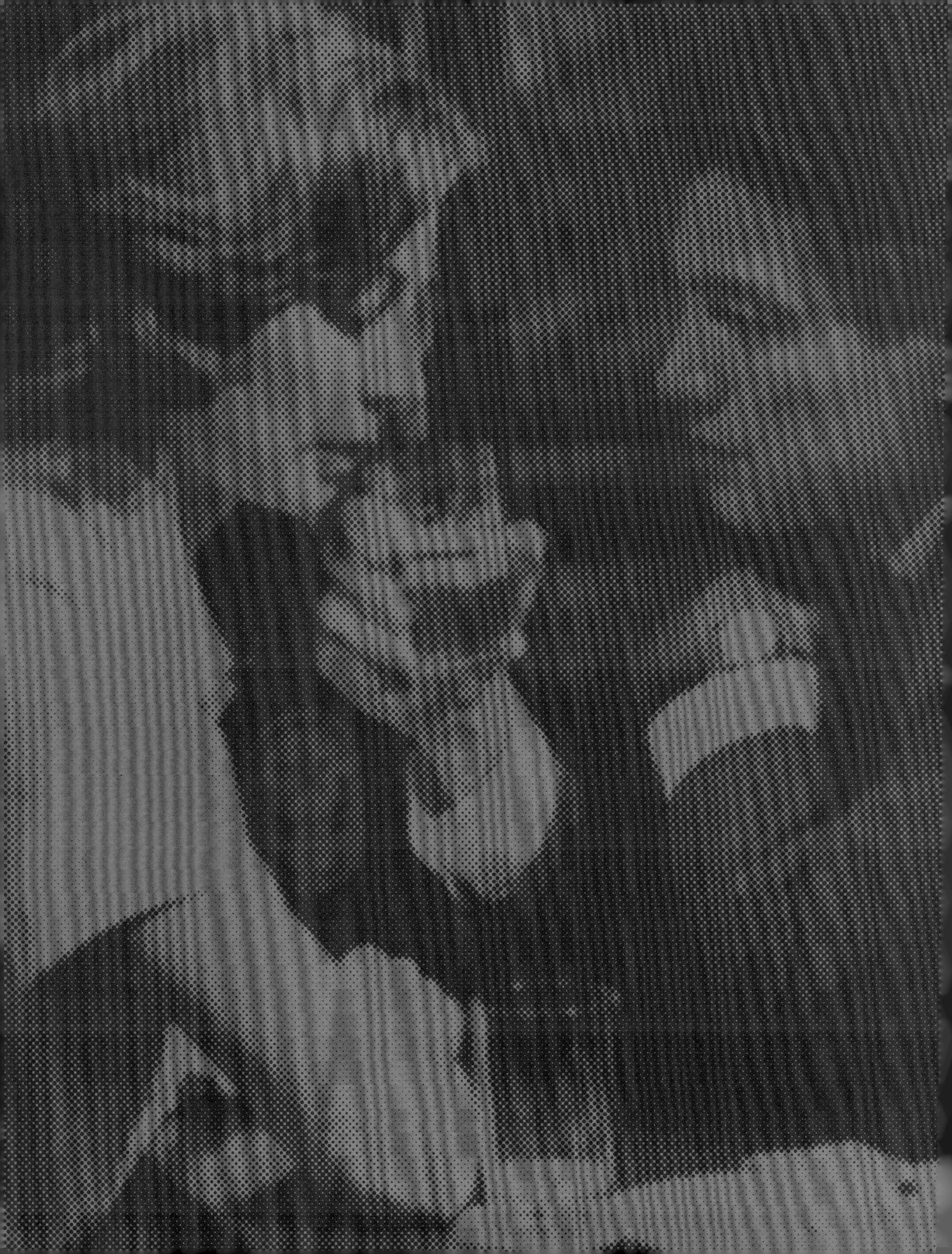

emmanuelle riva 4

la femme mûre | *the mature woman*

RIVA, RESNAIS, DURAS: THE ART OF *HIROSHIMA, MON AMOUR*

"This film was an extraordinary adventure because it was my first film, and I was lucky to meet [Alain] Resnais and Marguerite Duras and to discover Japan and to play a woman's role . . . because in the theater I'm always given the roles of young girls, ingénues [*des rôles d'anges*], it seems to me. They never want to see me play an adulteress. But this time, I'm really an adulteress. I'm an emancipated woman [*une femme libre*]." —Emmanuelle Riva on *Hiroshima, mon amour*, 1959.[1]

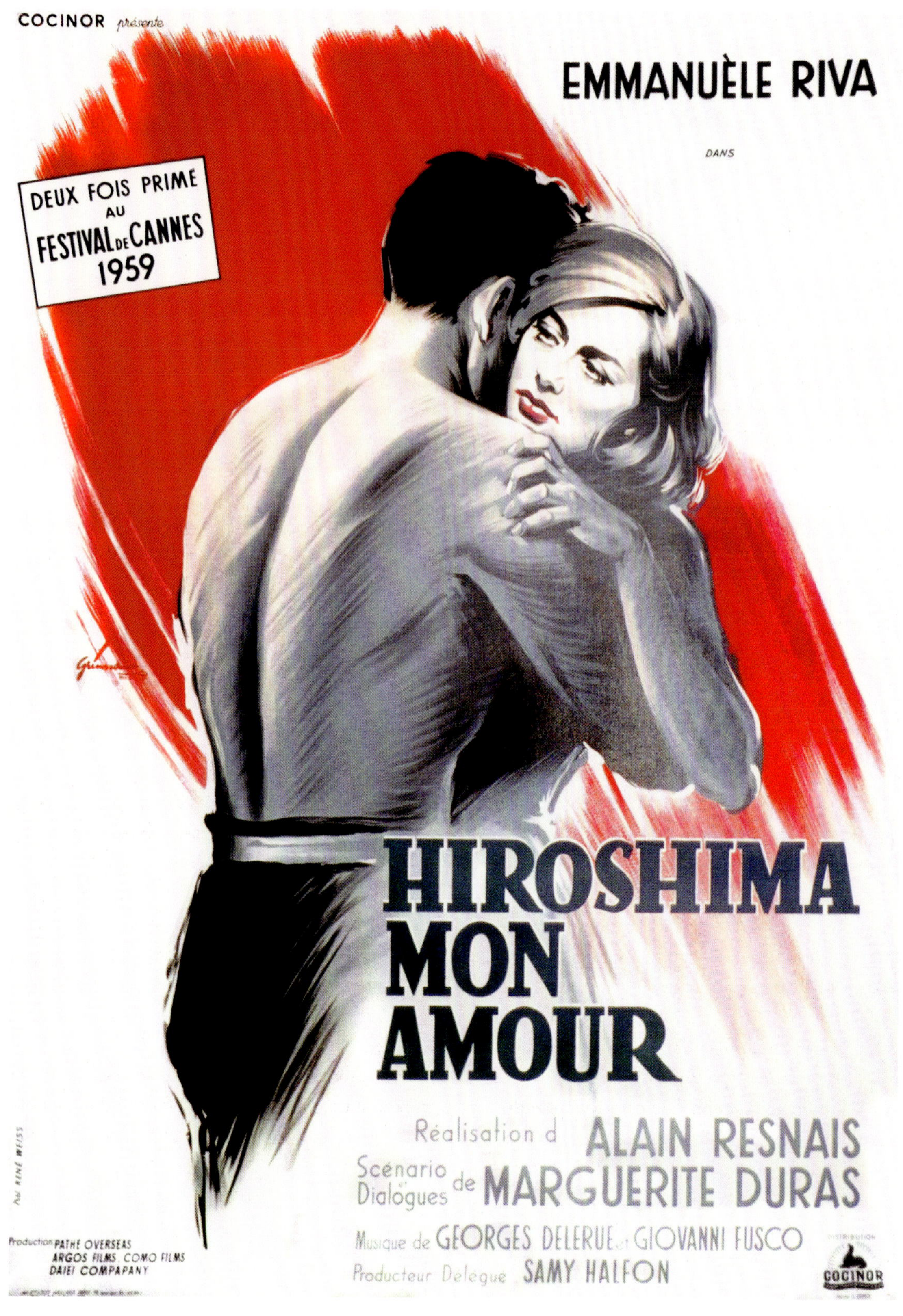

COCINOR présente
EMMANUÈLE RIVA
DANS
DEUX FOIS PRIME
AU
FESTIVAL DE CANNES
1959
HIROSHIMA
MON
AMOUR
Réalisation d ALAIN RESNAIS
Scénario et Dialogues de MARGUERITE DURAS
Musique de GEORGES DELERUE et GIOVANNI FUSCO
Producteur Délégué SAMY HALFON
Production PATHE OVERSEAS
ARGOS FILMS - COMO FILMS
DAIEI COMPAPANY
Par RENÉ WEISS
COCINOR

Unsurprisingly, the films of Alain Resnais, some of the era's most serious and experimental works, present some of the most intriguing, intelligent, and complex women of the New Wave. With Emmanuelle Riva in *Hiroshima, mon amour*, and Delphine Seyrig in *L'Année dernière à Marienbad* and *Muriel ou le temps d'un retour*, Resnais's films contributed a different image of women to French cinema, on the opposite end of the spectrum of young free spirits like Jean Seberg, Anna Karina, and Haydée Politoff. Both Riva and Seyrig projected independence and maturity, intelligence and elegance. Riva's gravitas, minimalist acting, and poise, also found in her voice with her precise articulation, made her characters as strong as they are moving. In every role, she conveyed a deep sense of humanity. In the case of *Hiroshima, mon amour*, Marguerite Duras's screenplay and Riva's performance contributed significantly to creating a multifaceted, sensuous heroine that would mark the history of cinema to this day.

It is also one of the first times a film centers on a mature married woman, who experiences a brief, passionate encounter with another man and is not condemned. The extremely sensual opening scenes already would have shocked audiences in 1959, but the combination of Duras, Riva, and Resnais created a depth and aesthetic allure that steered the *mise en scène* toward art instead of scandal.

In Resnais's first feature, Riva plays the role of a French actress on assignment in Japan to make a film about the aftermath and memory of the bombing of Hiroshima. Riva pointed out that "Resnais wanted to make a film about love set in Hiroshima, the cradle of anxiety where people come to life again, or at least seem to forget. But we haven't forgotten any more than they have."[2] While on location, the heroine meets and falls in love with a Japanese man (played by Eiji Okada). Their encounter plunges her into memories of a lost love, a German soldier she saw clandestinely during the occupation of her hometown, Nevers, but who died before their story could truly begin. In the film, the heroine has no name and her Japanese lover does not either, allowing them to be allegorical stand-ins for France and Japan, Nevers and Hiroshima. The narrative in Japan takes place during the span of one day where the protagonist and her lover

lose themselves in their mutual fascination and deep passion. They fall in love, separate, and find each other again, only to face her departure the next day. In a 1960s interview, Resnais was asked if he had deliberately introduced "transgressive" ideas (of adultery, interracial love, and female sexuality) to condemn France's social norms. "This is not a social problem film, it is a sentimental film," was his answer.[3]

Riva came into cinema by way of theater. Drawn to acting at a young age, she performed in school plays and later for a local theater troupe. "I enjoyed the idea of transforming myself into someone else," she explained.[4] Because her parents objected to her ambition of working as an actress, after graduating from high school, the young Riva first assumed a position that was acceptable for woman at that time: She became a seamstress. An advertisement for auditions in a Paris theater school, however, led her to leave her rural home for the City of Light at twenty-six years old. Reciting lines from Alfred de Musset's play *On ne badine pas avec l'amour* (*No Trifling with Love*), the provincial girl was on her way to fulfilling her dream. After finishing her studies, she appeared in George Bernard Shaw's *Arms and the Man* in 1954, her first role on stage. Just four years later, she would play the lead in *Hiroshima*.[5]

She described the way in which she won the role as a fairy tale. "One day, I got a call from an agent. I didn't have an agent. I was working freelance. [The agent] told me Alain Resnais wanted to see me for a possible part in a movie he was preparing with a script by Marguerite Duras," she said. Resnais had wanted "an unknown actress," so a young agent named Lola Mouloudji had supplied him with photos of potential candidates. "He came across a picture of me, among others, that caught his eye. . . . It's a lovely story because it's a bit like a fairy tale in a way," Riva recalled. "[A]s he was handing [the photos] back, one picture fell to the floor . . . he picked it up, and who was it? It's still Emmanuelle Riva, but a different picture of me. He didn't notice it was the same person." Intrigued, Resnais invited her to meet at his house, where he "gave [her] cues" from *Arms and the Man* and shot footage of her on "a hand-operated camera." "I wasn't the only one in the running. I'm sure he saw two or three others. Then one day he told me, 'You're the one who'll be appearing in *Hiroshima*,'" Riva said. "I was overjoyed. Duras's script was still being written. And that's how I got the part in *Hiroshima, mon amour*."[6]

Resnais was known for using other arts as raw material in his cinematic works, and the producers of *Argos Films* had suggested that he work with writers who could contribute their own style to shape the film. Since he had just read Duras's novel *Moderato cantabile* and admired her work, a meeting between them was arranged. Though others, including Resnais's close collaborator Chris Marker,[7] had refused to work on a story about the atomic bomb, Duras accepted right away based on her high regard for Resnais's 1956 documentary *Nuit et brouillard*. But she later revealed that the subject matter had initially given her pause: "At first *Hiroshima* scared me. And then, on the contrary, it captivated me. Resurrecting a 'subject' from its ashes is third-degree work that deals both with one's self–who forgot–and others–who forgot. Thousands of pages have been written about Hiroshima over fourteen years. What could we do? Thanks to Resnais, I saw that the resurgence of Hiroshima was possible. That we could at least try to do something with this place. He went to great lengths to explain to me that nothing in Hiroshima was a 'given.' That a particular halo had to endow each gesture, each word there with a meaning additional to their literal meaning. That the film's major design was to put an end to the description of horror by horror, because that had been done, accomplished to the end, by the Japanese themselves, but that this horror needed to be brought back from its ashes while retaining its eternal and implacable sense."[8] Duras reportedly told Resnais days after their first meeting about a conversation she had heard between a French woman and a Japanese man in a restaurant, a dialogue that marked the start of the film.[9]

Duras provided a script that was not just a screenplay but a work of art. Different from the clinical geometric structure that writer Alain Robbe-Grillet would later contribute to *Marienbad*, Duras's sensuous presence and the identifiable cadence in her musical phrasing, with repeated words in her dialogue, defined the feel of *Hiroshima*. Hers is not a typical screenplay, devoid of emotion; it is poetry in itself. Her description of the opening scene blends the sensual and horrific, conveying a depth that, though unsaid in the film, Resnais captures in turn with his camera, punctuated with sparse, ambiguous dialogue–Duras's trademark:

As the film opens, two pairs of bare shoulders appear, little by little. All we see are these shoulders–cut off from the body at the height of the head and hips–in an embrace, and as if drenched with ashes, rain, dew, or sweat, whichever is preferred. The main thing is that we get the feeling that this dew, this perspiration, has been deposited by the atomic "mushroom" as it moves away and evaporates. It should produce a violent, conflicting feeling of freshness and desire. The shoulders are of different colors, one dark, one light. Fusco's music accompanies this almost shocking embrace. The difference between the hands is also very marked. The woman's hand lies on the darker shoulder: "lies" is perhaps not the word; "grips" would be closer to it. A man's voice, flat and calm, as if reciting, says:

HE: You saw nothing in Hiroshima. Nothing.

To be used as often as desired. A woman's voice, also substantial, muffled, monotonous, the voice of someone reciting, replies:

SHE: I saw everything. Everything.

Fusco's music, which has faded before this initial exchange, resumes just long enough to accompany the woman's hand tightening on the shoulder again, then letting go, then caressing it. The mark of fingernails on the darker flesh. As if this scratch could give the illusion of being a punishment for: "No. You saw nothing in Hiroshima." Then the woman's voice begins again, still calm, colorless, incantatory:

SHE: The hospital, for instance, I saw it. I'm sure I did. There is a hospital in Hiroshima. How could I help seeing it?

The hospital, hallways, stairs, patients, the camera coldly objective. [We never see her seeing.] Then we come back to the hand gripping—and not letting go of—the darker shoulder.

HE: You did not see the hospital in Hiroshima. You saw nothing in Hiroshima.[10]

BLURRED LINES: RIVA BECOMES HER ROLE

Riva described the relationship between Duras and Resnais and the rest of the team as closely connected. "We were a very close-knit group, on both sides of the camera. We were a family," she explained. "There was a great feeling of harmony. It all unfolded so naturally. It was like a miracle. It's not always like that but it *should* always be like that because it's fantastic. Language wasn't an obstacle. Between Alain Resnais and Marguerite Duras there was constant communication. There were things to be worked out. There always

are. We were always looking for ways to make it believable, more convincing, to do better, to find a better way. . . . We didn't lose sight of each other. We were a team."[11]

The alchemy between Resnais, Duras, and Riva was key in creating an intricate character, one whose persevering nature and past trauma haven't made her cold and closed off. "We all talked together. We discussed a lot of things. We shared our questions," Riva said. "It was all thought out by Duras and Resnais. And then suddenly they'd set us loose and we are the living matter and all we have to do is live. He asked nothing from us but to live. Marvelous, isn't it? It's fabulous. We're set loose. We're free. But within the framework of a rigorous discipline."[12] Riva found herself well suited to this kind of freedom with direction. "I put my complete trust in Alain Resnais," she related. "So, I let myself be guided. The role of a film actress, especially in these conditions, is relatively easy. You do the film in small pieces . . . with the

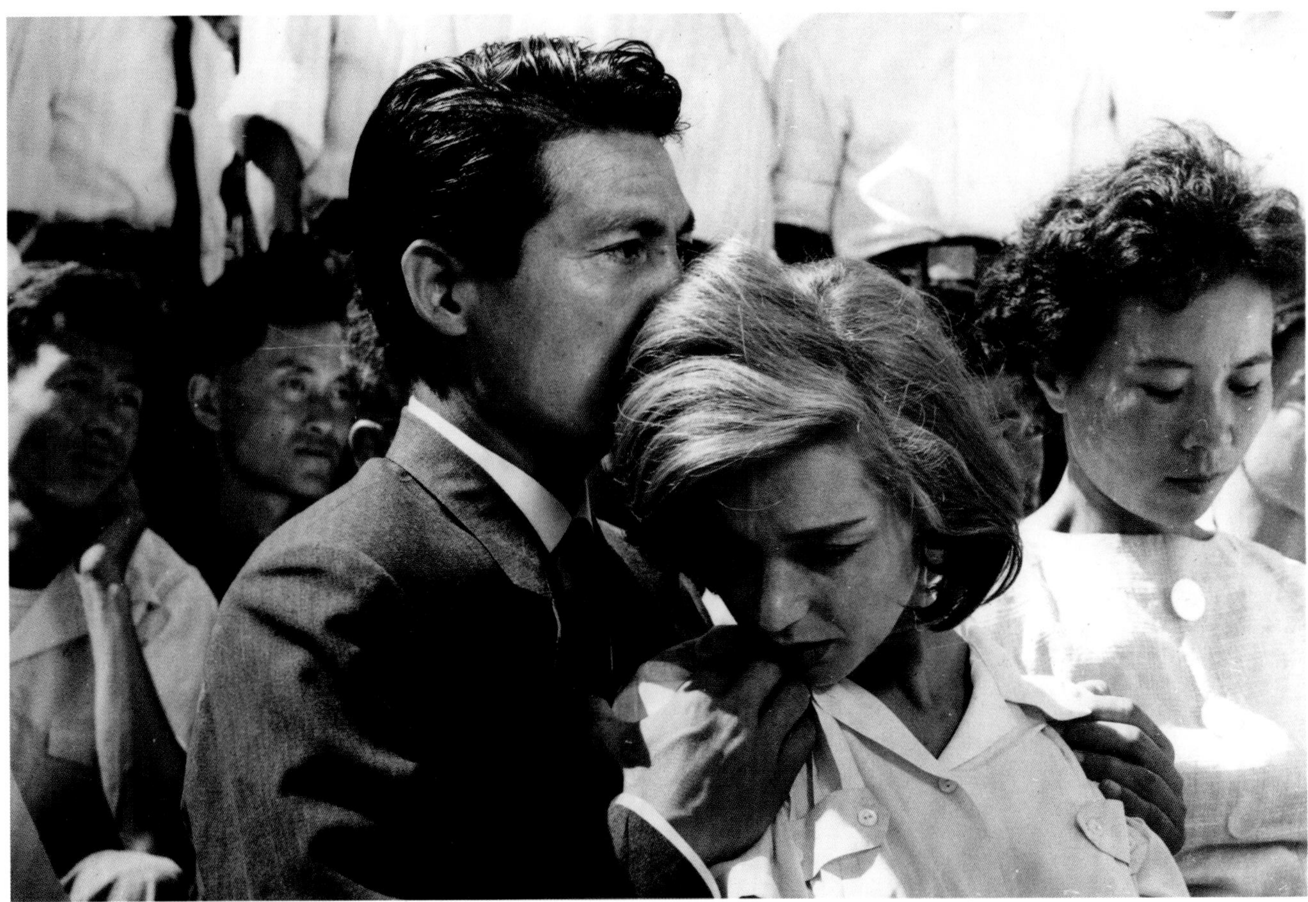

Eiji Okada and Emmanuelle Riva in Alain Resnais's *Hiroshima, mon amour*, 1959

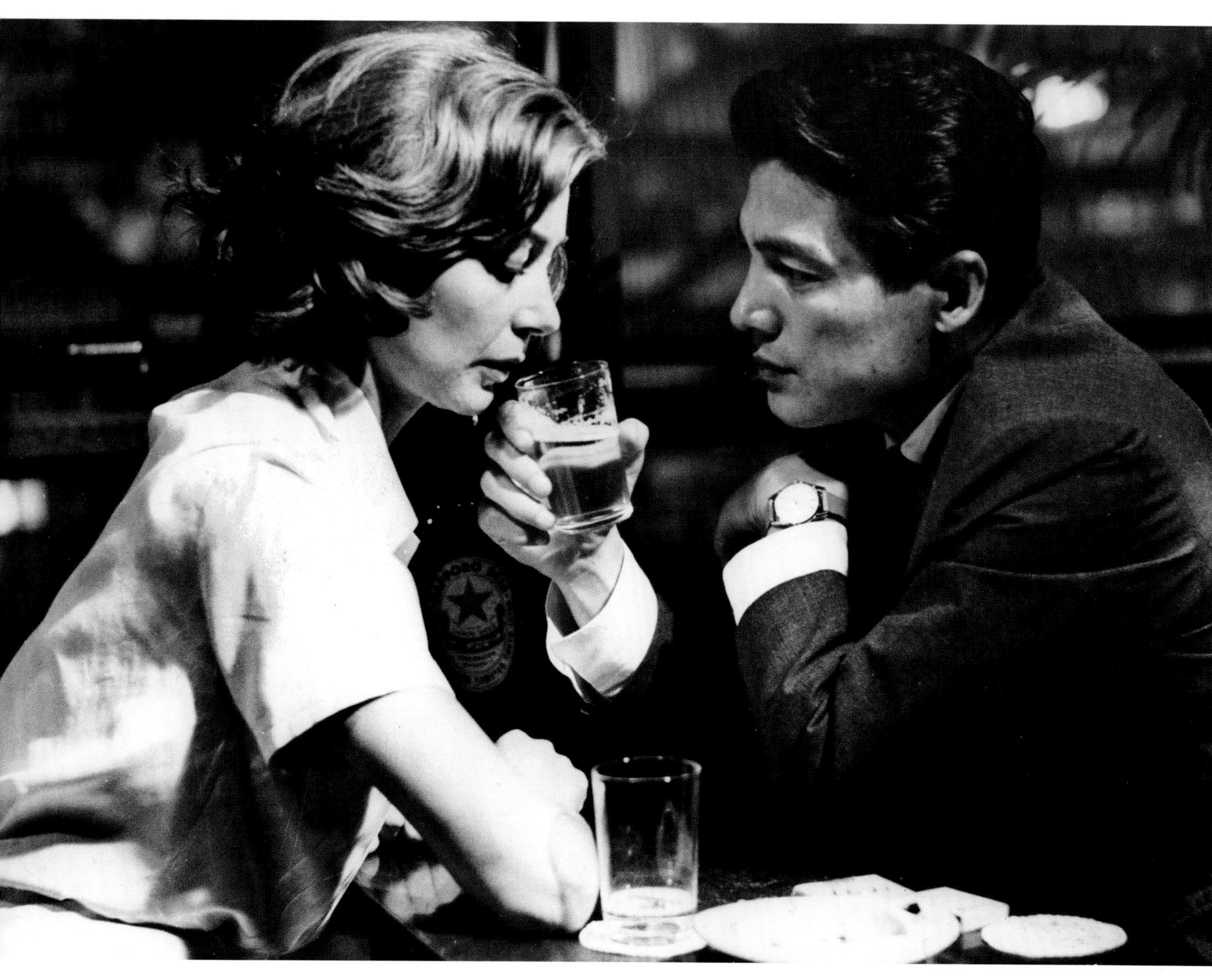

master of the house, in this case the director who tells you the best things to do. I was living in the present."[13]

In an interview in 1958, Duras described Riva in the role:

If one had to speak of Emmanuelle Riva literally, it seems to me this is what one could say: "She could also, in a certain way, be called 'The Look.' Everything about her, from her words to her movement, 'passes through her looking.' This look is forgetful of itself. This woman looks for herself. Her look does not consecrate her behavior, it always reaches beyond it. It's likely that in love all women have beautiful eyes. But this one, love throws her into a disorder of the soul—a deadly disorder (a deliberately Stendhalian choice of words)—a little more so than other women. Because she is more 'in love with love itself' than other women. Through the man she loves, she also loves love. And through love, she is on the lookout, like a celebration, for the chance love represents to lose yourself in it, to the point of never again finding an understanding of a potential compromise between love and life."[14]

In one very Durasian scene, the two lovers drink to oblivion while Riva's character speaks torturously about her first love before her Japanese lover slaps her out of it. The actress later described fully merging with her character, living out the scene as though it were real. "It was my first love, can't you see? He had to slap me, and he wasn't supposed to pretend," Riva recalled. "He would make me drink—I still remember his gesture. We each had a glass of beer. He'd raise his glass and say, 'Drink.' He made me drink, and I, Emmanuelle, drank. I was a little drunk with all this beer. So, I was losing myself in the person in the film. I had lost myself completely. . . . We had to start over several times, and I got slapped each time. It felt like my head was coming off. It hurt and I even cried like a baby."[15]

At the film's release in Cannes, Riva recounted its story in an interview as if it were her own. Emphasizing the resilience of the actress she plays within the film, Riva explained, "In my youth, during the occupation, I fell in love with a German, *un grand amour*. I was supposed to leave for Bavaria, but he died. And I didn't die of a broken heart. So I got married.

Then I became a film actress because being a housewife wasn't quite fulfilling enough for me. And I went to Hiroshima to make a film about peace. There, I met a Japanese man. It was love at first sight, then it becomes a love story. But when I tell this man about my German lover, I remember that this love was an impossible love. And since I once again feel the same love, I decide to go back to France. What's the point of staying?"

This choice of presenting her character in first person, as if she and Riva were one and the same, reflects Riva's relationship with the characters she plays. "I can't talk about characters," she expressed in a 2003 interview. "I'd prefer to talk about the *person* because you merge with the person. What we live through a story, that we're given to live, we make our own. It replaces our life for a moment. It even becomes completely part of our life in its entirety. . . . It's not a matter of saying we identify with the role—it happens on its own if you will. . . . Because when you're filming or doing a play, it takes up such a large part of your day . . . you can't live without it. You can't set it aside. In the theater, it is very consuming. You're no longer master of what you think is your life. That is, you surrender to the other life, which almost becomes your own. In film too, because it fills your entire day, from morning to night . . . It becomes one with your life."[16]

Though Resnais declared at the time that *Hiroshima, mon amour* would "be a film for the Cinémathèque," implying that it would flop with the general public, it turned out to be the exact opposite. A huge success, the film won numerous awards, and Duras's screenplay was nominated for an Oscar. Rohmer called it "the most important film since the war, the first modern film of sound cinema."[17] It made Riva an international star. Her first role on screen, the part brought a sense of pride along with great pressure, reflected in her reply to a journalist asking her about her future roles right after the film: "Thanks to Resnais . . . I might be a disappointment after this, because Resnais pushed me to excel. He made me reach certain heights, I think."[18]

Like Bardot and many others, Riva expressed that stardom was not what drove her to acting: "I've never wanted to be a star, never," she told *The New York Times* in 2013. "I tried

Emmanuelle Riva and Eiji Okada in Alain Resnais's *Hiroshima, mon amour*, 1959

to do things that pleased me. . . . It is dreadful to see actors reproducing the same image constantly."[19] That sentiment had been on her mind since the success of *Hiroshima.* "I know I'm a deeply committed actress, I'd like to play everything from drama to comedy," she said in 1959. "Mostly, I don't want to be typecast. It's awful to be typecast. It's annoying and depressing to play always one type of role."[20] The next three films in her career proved her commitment to this statement.

Though Gillo Pontecorvo's controversial *Kapò* (1960) centered on the equally horrific subject of the Holocaust, Riva's role as Terese, a French Jewish woman in a concentration camp, was unlike her glamorous character in *Hiroshima.* In the final sequence, Terese ends her life by throwing herself against an electric fence—a scene that went down as one of the most notorious in film history. The backlash began with Jacques Rivette's evisceration of the film in his article "De l'abjection," ("Of Abjection"), published in the June 1961 edition of *Cahiers du cinéma.* The director took particular issue with Pontecorvo's choice of a tracking shot to portray suicide in the context of the Holocaust, finding it in extremely poor taste to depict an act of desperation in such a stylized way and for dramatic effect. "The man who decides at this moment to make a forward tracking shot to reframe the dead body—carefully positioning the raised hand in the corner of the final framing—this man is worthy of the most profound contempt," Rivette wrote. His article would become a defining moment for generations of critics who echoed his moral judgment, from Bazin and the notable Serge Daney of *Cahiers du cinéma* in his 1992 article "The Tracking Shot in *Kapò*" to Godard's *Histoire(s) du cinéma* and Gilles Deleuze's *Cinéma.*[21] Riva's next two roles engendered less controversy and radiated passionate intelligence, desire, and a thirst for knowledge and freedom.[22]

LÉON MORIN, PRÊTRE: A WOMAN'S PERSPECTIVE OF WAR AND DESIRE

If, at first glance, we think the most important character in Jean-Pierre Melville's *Léon Morin, prêtre* (*Léon Morin, Priest,* 1961) is the titular one, Riva's performance compels us to reconsider this assessment. In it, she plays Barny, a spirited young widow managing work, motherhood, and burgeoning feelings for a priest—played by Jean-Paul Belmondo, the charismatic lead from *À bout de souffle*—against the backdrop of occupied France. Though Belmondo's priest is undoubtedly central, a closer look at the film reveals that Riva's Barny is just as vital. In fact, *Léon Morin* opens with her in voice-over, and the first shot is of Riva.

Playing the young Barny, Riva projected a different image this time of a *jeune femme* (a young woman), her long hair blowing in the wind as she rides into town on a bicycle. In an open acknowledgement to the ongoing trauma of the war, Barny and two of her friends, all with either Jewish or communist backgrounds, discuss having their children baptized as a way of protecting them. Through her commentary, we learn that the war was also responsible for Barny and other women seeking work at a correspondence school. Barny corrects French assignments in a room full of women who are doing similar jobs or working as secretaries, illustrating the pervasive, unspoken message about what kinds of careers were open to women at the time. In an interesting parallel, Riva's very first (uncredited) appearance in cinema was playing a secretary in Denys de La Patellière's *Les Grandes familles* (*The Possessors,* 1958).

In their first encounter, Barny and Morin occupy equal parts of the frame in Melville's *mise en scène* and are both filmed at eye level. Barny goes to confession as a joke with the aim of shocking the young provincial priest. As Morin opens the curtain between them in the confessional, Barny immediately proclaims, "Religion is the opium of the people," illustrating her rebellious spirit. Without hesitation, the priest replies, unfazed, "Not exactly. It has been diluted by the bourgeoisie in its own interests," to which she replies, "But you let them. You're one and the same now." They go head to head challenging each other with an impressively articulate conversation about faith, Christian morality, collective consciousness, and a number of equally profound topics. A series of different shots echoes their back-and-forth discussion, examining the issues from all sides. Morin finally declares that Barny has just confessed and must ask for forgiveness. When she asks, "To whom?" given the fact that she does not believe in God, the priest replies, "To X," reflecting his open-mindedness. During this exchange, Barny dramatically exits the confessional, deeply affected, opening the curtains abruptly and staggering through the church, then kneeling on the stone floor—the penitence the priest has suggested. When she leaves the church, we hear her thoughts in voice-over: "I walked along cheerfully, feeling buoyant, precious, vulnerable. But I didn't know if my good mood was from the total freedom of my thinking or the absolution I had received." Not only does the sequence show that French society is grappling with Catholicism's authority (that still permeated intellectual thought in the early 1960s), the film conveys the trauma from the war, alluded to in the antisemitic graffiti on the walls of the town, a backdrop where Barny walks.

Barny's conversation with the priest is also an unspoken validation of a woman's voice, an acknowledgement of the importance of a dialogue between genders. Like Riva's next film, *Thérèse Desqueyroux* (1962), *Léon Morin* uses books to indicate the heroine's intellectual curiosity. At the end of her "confession," the priest asks Barny if she would like him to lend her some books. Their first meeting is set up through an intellectual encounter that will lead to many more. Linking desire with knowledge, alongside the verbal exchange, Barny's attraction to the priest develops in the *mise en scène*. When they meet for the first time at the refectory, for example, the camera gives us Barny's point of view of the priest, moving carefully down the buttons of his cassock, conveying her gaze in a subjective shot.

Adapted from the novel *Léon Morin, prêtre* (*The Passionate Heart*) written by Belgian-French writer Béatrix Beck in 1952 as part of the "Barny cycle," the film, like the book, features a very strong female protagonist. Beck was known for writing about active, independent women[23] and received the Prix Goncourt for *Léon Morin*, inspired by her real-life encounter with a priest during World War II. Accordingly, the film's narrative relies on Barny's perspective. As in the opening sequence with her narrative in voice-over, Barny's point of view also serves in constructing Morin and in exploring the tension and desire that develop between them. Though sensuality in the context of the Church was not a new subject in the mid-twentieth century (as we will later see with Diderot's eighteenth-century novel *La Religieuse*), the way

in which Melville's film (in keeping with the spirit of Beck's novel) puts the woman's desire for the priest at the forefront appears fresh and modern. Her desire is also not reserved uniquely for the priest.

Before meeting Morin, Barny is infatuated with her female boss. She describes her desire, painting her portrait in voice-over: "I loved Sabine Levy, the administrative secretary," Barny declares. "Seeing her, I flew through time and space. I thought the beautiful people should lead. I felt a pang of pleasure when my gaze crossed hers, like two duelists, until I could no longer bear it and dropped my eyes, taking delight in her victory." Like Truffaut's male protagonists describing their love objects to their friends, Barny describes Sabine to her female friend: "She reminds me of those beautiful young people in the scriptures with girded loins . . . who are angels. She looks like an Amazon, like Pallas Athena, like a samurai. When she leans over my desk, she's the shade of a palm tree." Curiously, when her interlocuter reacts with "So in a nutshell, you want to sleep with her," Barny replies, "Are you crazy? How horrifying! Sabine fascinates me because she's like a young man, a young man with curious charms, a delicately feminized manliness." But later in voice-over, as Sabine leans sensuously over Barny's desk, she continues, "Everything about her enraptured me: her wide-ranging knowledge, her strange beauty. I felt compelled by her in a way that went beyond the purely physical."

Barny's multifaceted life also exposes the difficulties brought about by the war. Dilemmas about motherhood and about feminine desire are addressed in conversation with her friends, sometimes overlapping with moral questions on wartime complicity. When one friend tells Barny, for example, that "accepting collaboration as a lesser evil doesn't make it a mortal sin," Barny challenges her (with a wider message to the audience): "Yes, it does. It accepts the deporting and killing of innocents. Like Sabine's brother among thousands of others." In another scene, Barny's coworker and friend, Arlette, voices the preoccupation of women about marriage and motherhood. "What I want is to get married. My trousseau will have front-buttoning undergarments for nursing. The awful thing is boys are always following me in the street," Arlette complains. Barny tells her that she would like to introduce her to someone who can help, "a priest who is interested in young people." When she takes Arlette to see Morin, her friend tells her she finds him handsome. Following this remark, Barny describes her attraction to the priest in voice-over: "Now that Arlette had said it, I realized that Morin was indeed handsome. I wondered with a pang of anxiety if it wasn't a sin to take delight in my confessor's physique. But what harm could there be in it? The Gospels imply that Jesus was handsome. Beauty is a gift of God. Thank you, Lord, for having made your servant Morin a refined work of art." In effect, Morin incites crushes in many women as they come to him for guidance. Conveying their desire, through the *mise en scène* and in Barny's voice-over, the film breaks with the traditional depictions of women. Morin goes against expectations (if not convention) as he continues to discuss Christian ideas with Barny, showing himself to be extraordinarily progressive yet firm in his convictions and oath of celibacy when he senses her attraction.

In a later scene, when Morin arrives at Barny's house, she can no longer tolerate the tension and acts on her desire. After subjective shots of the bedroom juxtaposed with Morin reading the Bible, Barny reaches out her hand to him, summoning him: "Come," she pleads. Morin leaps up, as if she were the devil, chastising her. "If only you called to God as you called to a man. That's real prayer," he cries, calling her back to order, then demanding that she come to confession. In the following sequence, Barny confesses to him: "I tried to persuade a priest to break his vows." Riva's performance and Melville's *mise en scène* legitimize voicing feminine desire in this transgressive context. Even if Barny must repent for it to the priest, she is not demonized. Instead, Barny remains a solid, morally intact character, anticipating Françoise Fabian's Maud in Rohmer's critically acclaimed *Ma nuit chez Maud* in 1969, a film that displays the same tension between the morally constrained male protagonist in his relationship with the emancipated heroine.

In this way, Melville, considered a New Wave predecessor, is strikingly modern, showcasing Riva's performance in a groundbreaking depiction of a complex heroine who holds her own intellectually and expresses her own desire, instead of simply existing in relation to that of the protagonist. In an interview at the film's release, Melville explained that he had wanted to film *Léon Morin* for eight years but could never find the right actors until he discovered Riva and then Belmondo. Though the director did not collaborate with Beck to adapt her book—"I think it is a bad system; the author has already said everything," Melville explained—she believed he captured its essence. "In certain scenes it felt like some hidden camera must have been filming over my shoulder as I wrote the novel," Beck told him after seeing the film. [24]

In the final sequence, after Morin tells Barny he is leaving to go to another parish, Barny ascends the stairs for their final meeting. When Morin tells Barny au revoir, she responds, disappointed, "'Until we meet again'; that's a figure of speech." He reassures her, "No, we will meet again, not in this world but in the next." As Barny descends the staircase, devastated, she leaves behind her impossible love just like Riva's character does in *Hiroshima*. In both films, however, it is the woman's experience, desire, and love that drive the narrative. With Duras's screenplay and Beck's novel at the heart of each film, Riva voiced new feminine perspectives that began to echo through modern French cinema.

THÉRÈSE DESQUEYROUX: A PORTRAIT OF FREEDOM THROUGH CULTURE AND KNOWLEDGE

If Riva's fear of being typecast did not happen, like all actors, she carried traces of the characters she previously embodied into her next roles. In Georges Franju's *Thérèse Desqueyroux* (1962), she played another independent, mature woman at the center of a film that showcases her superior intelligence. Again, her character, the titular Thérèse, guides the narrative in voice-over from the opening scenes. Adapted from François Mauriac's 1927 novel of the same name, Franju's film closely adheres to the author's text that is centered on the heroine's struggle in the context of postwar, provincial bourgeois society. From the beginning, Riva's character is framed behind bars as she emerges from the Palais de Justice where she was accused of poisoning her husband. While he is labeled as "a simple man" by other characters, Thérèse is described as strong and intelligent.

"I can't talk about characters. I'd prefer to talk about the *person* because you merge with the person. What we live through a story, that we're given to live, we make our own. It replaces our life for a moment. It even becomes completely part of our life in its entirety. . . . It's not a matter of saying we identify with the role—it happens on its own if you will. . . .

—emmanuelle riva

"Free. What more could I wish for?" Thérèse utters in voice-over as the gates to the courthouse shut. "I never wanted to commit the [crime] I am charged with. I never knew where I would be led by this deranged power inside me and out-side me." With her assigned conventional role as mother and wife to her emotionally absent husband, Thérèse is unfulfilled and suffering great boredom. Unlike Madame Bovary, however, Thérèse is portrayed as keenly intelligent, aware, and highly cultivated. Instead of falling into a fantasy cliché for *a séducteur*, Thérèse, like Riva's character in *Léon Morin*, describes in detail her fascination for her childhood friend, Anne.

Paralleling *Hiroshima*, the film flashes back to Thérèse's provincial youth, showing her riding with Anne on bicycles. Both dressed in white, Thérèse soon distinguishes herself from Anne's pure, angelic image by lighting a cigarette. We learn that Anne was brought up in a convent. As Thérèse's gaze intently focuses on the object of her obsession, she reminisces in voice-over: "Was I ever so happy or honest? I was pure as an angel but an angel full of passion. I didn't need all those ribbons." Thérèse's portrait is painted in the next sequence by Anne's parents, her mother saying, "You can't say Thérèse is pretty but she doesn't seem to care. . . . Too bad she always has a cigarette in her mouth." Anne's father adds to the portrait, saying, "What worries me most about Thérèse is her intelligence." She is, however, well-off, and according to him, that makes up for her lack of beauty.

Thérèse is set to marry a wealthy landowner, Bernard, played by Philippe Noiret, who perfectly incarnates the obtuse *beauf*, or simpleton husband. "The stifling wedding day, it was that morning I first felt lost," Thérèse confesses in voice-over as she enters the church in a dissociated state. The door to the church slams shut loudly. "The wedding night was horrible. No, not that horrible–I played dead," she con-tinues. In direct opposition to her sensuous role in *Hiroshi-ma*, Riva is just as powerful embodying a stifled bourgeoise housewife. Conveying her true thoughts about her role, Thérèse voices the feelings of many women in her position: "In the eyes of the family, only the fruit I bore mattered. . . . I was losing my sense of being as an individual." In a later scene, she continues the commentary: "It was one day after

giving birth that I could no longer tolerate life." Shot from behind the bars of a window, she looks down at the Fête-Dieu (Corpus Christi) procession, Franju's subtle signaling of Catholicism's influence in the town. In the next shot, Thérèse, in black, is juxtaposed with Anne, dressed in white and tak-ing care of Thérèse's baby.

As the story develops, Thérèse transfers her fascination for Anne onto the young man Anne wishes to marry, the culti-vated and curious Jean Azevedo, who just happens to be Jewish. Like *Léon Morin*, Franju's film emphasizes the impor-tance of books and intellectual exchanges in the heroine's life. Sent to try to convince Jean not to marry Anne, Thérèse instead starts to fall for him as he talks with her about phi-losophy, literature, and Anton Chekhov. Citing Chekhov's *Three Sisters*, Jean tells Thérèse of his plan to leave the provinces for his own Moscow: Paris. He in turn reinforces Thérèse's idea that the boring provinces are keeping her from an intellectually and culturally rich Paris, where she be-longs. In direct contrast with her husband, Jean echoes the priest in *Léon Morin* in his place as a stimulating intellectual equal who treats her as such. Both novels, *Léon Morin* and *Thérèse Desqueyroux*, address the war, antisemitism, and the strong presence of the Catholic Church. Thérèse, unlike Barny, does not take issue with Catholicism. Franju instead chose to focus on Thérèse's intellectual curiosity and fight for agency.

A defining element in her character, the importance of the pursuit of knowledge and culture, is reflected through Thérèse's punishment by her husband after it is revealed that she had been increasing the dose of his medication to provoke a fatal attack when she could no longer bear her life with him. Confining her to her room, he takes away her books and records as the ultimate penance. As the isolation causes her to drink and dissociate even more, Thérèse be-comes a shell of herself, which incites her husband to con-cede, bringing her back to life in extremis by allowing her to move to Paris. When they meet later at Paris's Café de la Paix, she realizes that besides culture and freedom, it was human connection that she craved with her husband, something he still refuses to give her. Like in the beginning, we hear Thérèse in voice-over: "Free. What more could I wish for?"

But here, she emphasizes the importance of this humanity: "It's not this town, built of stone, that I cherish, it's this living, struggling forest, hollowed out by passions freer than any thought. The moaning of the pines at Argelouse only moved me so because it sounded almost human." Franju's *mise en scène* thereby centers on Thérèse's humanity, depicting a transgressive but strong and sensitive heroine who, ultimately, is not punished. In an interview at the time of the film's release, a journalist asked Riva if she agreed with her character and excused her for her crime. Riva replied, "Very much. She doesn't need excusing."[25]

Riva went on to win best actress at the 1962 Venice Film Festival. She described being "overjoyed" at being offered the "very rich role" and gave credit to Franju for encouraging her performance: "There's no difficulty in a character from the time we're adopted by a director or author."[26] Interestingly, all three directors, Resnais, Melville, and Franju, focused on giving voice to the heroines of their films. Whether it was motivated by the director's pure curiosity or as an exploration of the Other or of parts of themselves (reflecting Flaubert's famous "Emma Bovary, c'est moi"), these directors explored new facets of female characters in their films. Through the author-director-actress encounter, these films provided new perspectives that enriched French cinema with women in roles defined by their curiosity and maturity, becoming intelligent female role models.

Riva would gain the reputation of refusing roles that did not interest her. She collaborated again with Franju in 1965 on an adaptation of Jean Cocteau's novel *Thomas l'imposteur* (*Thomas the Imposter*, 1965), set during World War I. She continued to work on stage and in television, always drawn to characters who were "boundary breakers, risk takers, women of substance," wrote the *Los Angeles Times* describing her career.[27]

Riva herself was fiercely independent. She never married or had children.[28] As well as several books of poetry, the photographs she had taken during the filming of *Hiroshima, mon amour* were also published in a book fifty years after the film's release.[29] Riva did not travel or watch television, choosing to stay in her apartment, per the *Los Angeles Times*, "surrounding herself instead with art and books. Above her fireplace, she kept a chalkboard full of quotes she heard on the radio about freedom and time and love." At eighty-five years old, she received an Oscar nomination and numerous awards for her performance in Michael Haneke's 2012 film *Amour* that received the Palme d'Or in Cannes. "That Riva was able to break through that particular glass ceiling was remarkable," former *Los Angeles Times* film critic Betsy Sharkey told the paper.[30] About the role, Riva stated simply, "I wasn't playing the part . . . I was being."[31]

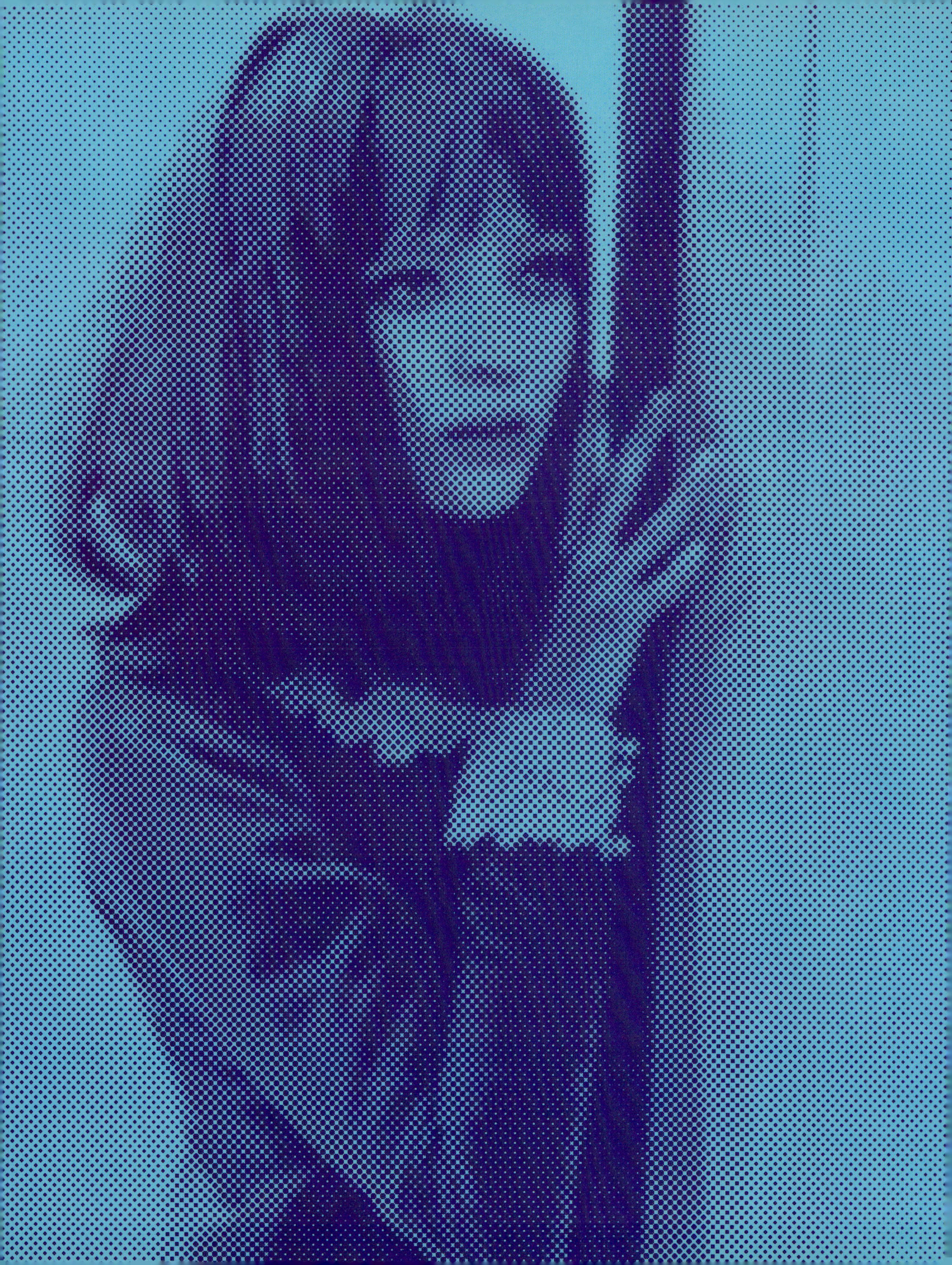

anna karina 5

la femme du portrait ovale | *the woman in the oval portrait*

HANNE KARIN BAYER BECOMES ANNA KARINA

"Je veux vivre, moi!" ("I want to live!")

Near the end of *Pierrot le fou* (*Pierrot the Fool*, 1965), Anna Karina's character, Marianne, voices this desire, staring straight into director Jean-Luc Godard's camera, with the viewer as witness. Defining the actress's spirit, the desire to live seemed to guide Karina's own life from an early age. She fondly told the story of attending a concert by Count Basie, one of her idols, as a little girl in Denmark. When the great jazz musician unexpectedly passed out during the performance, the emcee, trying to manage the situation, asked if there was anyone in the audience who would like to come up and do something while waiting for Basie to recover. Although still a young girl (eight or ten years old, according to Karina), she was already eager to perform. "I shouted, 'Me, me, me, me!'" she recounted almost seventy years later with great enthusiasm. "And I sang a little song called 'I want to be an actress—Jeg vil være et skuespiller en,'" she added in her native Danish. "I didn't imagine that one day, it could really happen to me,"[1] she said, seemingly still surprised that her dream came true, and that she had gone on to appear in over sixty films made all over the world.

Karina would bring the same joy she evoked in that spontaneous performance to the screen, channeling it into the iconic characters she played in the films directed by Jean-Luc Godard, her on- and off-screen partner. Their relationship constituted one of the most emblematic of the New Wave and the point of departure for a new cinematic discourse on love marked by innovative techniques of *mise en scène* and autobiography. "You always end up resembling the roles you play. Or it's the role that ends up resembling you. That's possible too," she declared in an early interview.[2] In effect, Véronica, Angéla, Nana, Odile, Natacha, Marianne—"the women Karina portrayed were beings of instinct, madly engaged with life and who laughed, danced, sang, and fought until their last breath, in praise of freedom,"[3] as critic Yonca Talu put it.

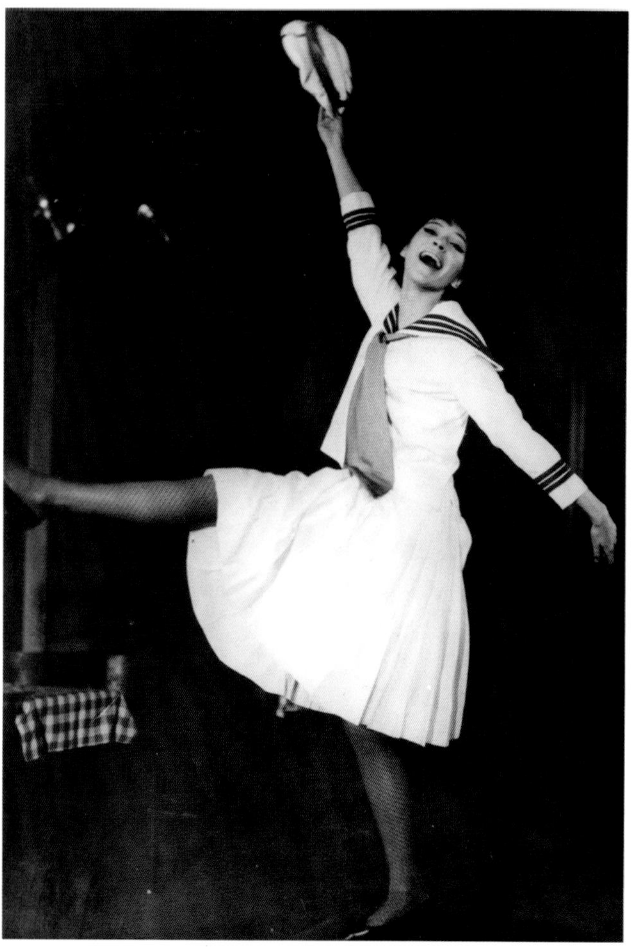

Hanne Karin Bayer was born in Solbjerg, Denmark, in 1940 during the German occupation. Even before her birth, her

Anna Karina in Jean-Luc Godard's *Une femme est une femme* (*A Woman is a Woman*), 1961

life was marked by trauma. Karina's nineteen-year-old mother, after traveling by dogsled while pregnant to pay a surprise visit to her husband, a long-distance ship captain, discovered him with another woman upon boarding the ship stuck in the ice. Devastated, she would never forgive him or let him see their daughter. Adding to the trauma, Karina also recalled, there was that of the war, with bombings, panic, and despair: "We went down into the cellars. There were curfews almost every day." Sent to live with her grandparents, Karina fortunately received love from both of them, and her grandfather in particular shared with her his joie de vivre.

When Karina was four years old, however, she suffered another setback when her grandmother died. Because her grandfather had to work, she was returned to her mother who ran a dress shop and designed costumes for the theater.[4] Considering her a burden, her mother ignored her, told her she was ugly, and left her alone to find ways of feeding herself, prompting the young Karina to run away on multiple occasions. Life in her mother's home began to improve when Karina bonded with her mother's new boyfriend, Benny, over their passion for music. Falling in love with American music, she declared one day, "I'm going to marry Louis Armstrong!" That is why, as a treat from Benny and her mother, Karina wound up getting to see Count Basie in concert.

Besides music, the adolescent Karina also loved the escape of cinema, and, like the future New Wave directors, hundreds of miles away in France, she sought refuge in movie theaters. "I always loved Charlie Chaplin since I was little. At the time, my grandfather was Communist and I passed out a little newspaper when I was eight or ten years old. We were allowed to see Chaplin films. I went to see Bergman films, musical comedies in a little movie theater called Windsor. We could sit in the front row for one crown or twenty cents in Copenhagen, Denmark. I went to see everything, musicals, American movies; there weren't many French films at that time, but I saw them later at the Cinémathèque with Jean-Luc,"[5] she recalled. Enamored by musicals, she watched *Singin' in the Rain* over and over again, and was especially fascinated by Judy Garland in *A Star Is Born*. "I knew all the songs by heart, and I loved everything about musicals," Karina recalled. "I danced and sang all the time."[6] At fourteen, Karina made money with a short-lived gig as an elevator operator and also by drawing and posing for an illustrator. "I made funny faces, the happy girl, the sad girl,"[7] she explained. She even made a Danish short film: *Pigen og skoene* (meaning "the girl and the shoes"), directed by Ib Schmedes, who said he "chose her because she seemed to dance when she walked."[8] The film was released in 1959, several years after it was filmed, and though Karina said it "didn't lead to much because [she] was very young,"[9] she added that it was received well at its premiere in Cannes."[10]

At home, however, the atmosphere had become grim once again when Benny left and her mother's new boyfriend mistreated Karina, often beating her. When she could no longer take the abuse,[11] she left Denmark for good. "I always wanted to leave my country, to go somewhere else,"[12] she expressed. Hitchhiking to Paris at seventeen years old—at a time when such endeavors were by no means the norm, especially for young women— she set out on her own in search of a happier life and with dreams of becoming an actress. From the first time she had visited the city, at age fourteen, Karina knew that was where she wanted to be. "J'adore Paris. C'est pour moi, Paris!'" she declared. "I loved Paris. I was so moved by Paris. . . . I loved the monuments, la Seine, Saint-Germain-des-Prés. And I said to myself, 'One day, I'll go back and live in Paris,' and that's what I did."[13]

Arriving on August 15, 1958[14]—a date she claimed to remember well for the impact it would have on the rest of her life—with almost no money, she possessed, on the other hand, abundant determination, inspired by her grandfather. "He was a simple *ouvrier* [laborer], but he was an extraordinary man. I knew arriving in Paris with nothing that nothing could happen to me because I always had my grandfather in my head and in my heart,"[15] Karina explained.

Although the little money she had upon arrival did not last very long, forcing her to go a long stretch without eating, Karina insisted that she was "lucky." One day, as she walked around the bohemian neighborhood of Saint-Germain-des-Prés in her blue jeans, she happened to stop at the famous

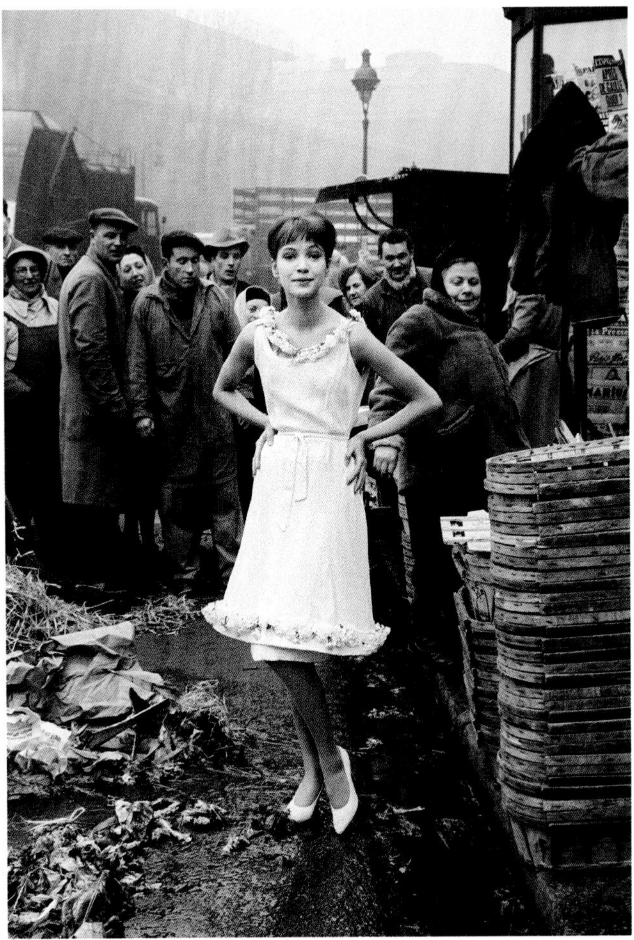

café Les Deux Magots. Despite her self-proclaimed lack of "fashion sense," Karina was spotted there by a young woman who asked her if she wanted to do a photo shoot. Initially wary, Karina recalled that her "grandfather said not to talk to strangers." "But I was the stranger," she later joked. The woman was Catherine Harlé, manager of a famous Parisian modeling agency, who was preparing the photo shoot the very next day for the fashion pages of the magazine *Jours de France*. When Karina realized the offer was serious, she accepted. Although Harlé described her first impression of Karina as a "young, very dirty girl—like today's Beatniks—with a man's dirty raincoat and used shoes,"[16] Harlé excitedly told her, "You're just what I need!"[17]

What drew her to Karina, in Harlé's words, was her "regard extraordinaire," the look in her eyes that "devoured every-

Anna Karina at Les Halles, Paris, for *Jours de France*, 1959, photograph by Frank Horvat

one around her."[18] The inexperienced Karina was suddenly thrust into the world of high fashion when, as she recalled, a whole team of makeup artists and wardrobe people arrived at the shoot.[19] According to Harlé, professional models showed her how to pose.[20]

Though Karina wasn't paid right away—"She owed me nine thousand old francs which wasn't a lot but enough to eat," she said—Harlé gave her addresses for other modeling contacts and sent her to Hélène Gordon-Lazareff,[21] the same director of *Elle* magazine who had photographed the young Brigitte Bardot. "[T]hey cut my hair and dyed it and did my makeup," Karina explained. When one woman asked Karina her name, she replied, "My name is Hanne Karin Bayer, like the aspirin." "'[T]hat doesn't sound good," the woman said. "I heard you tell the makeup artist that you wanted to be an actress. No, you won't call yourself Hanne Karin Bayer, you'll call yourself Anna Karina," Karina recounted. "And it was Coco Chanel. Coco Chanel! I didn't know her, but they told me later, 'She's a grande dame of French haute couture.' I never saw her again, but she gave me my name." When Karina received a copy of her February 1959 cover issue, "it was marked Anna Carina with a *C*. I wanted it to be with a *K*."[22] Swapping the *C* for a *K*, Anna Karina soon made another decisive encounter that shaped not only her own destiny but that of modern cinema.

"No other movie couple was as pivotal to a revolution" in film history as Jean-Luc Godard and Anna Karina, Michael Sragow declared in the 2021 documentary Creative Marriages: Godard & Karina.[23] Before their cinematic partnership in *Le Petit soldat*, Godard had been intrigued by Karina and pursued her intently for his films. After seeing her in a tub of bubbles for a commercial promoting soap, he reached out to Karina about a bit part in *À bout de souffle*. Because the part required seminudity, Karina categorically refused. Recounting the story years later, she laughed about Godard thinking she would accept the role because he had imagined her nude in the commercial. (In reality, she was covered by strategically placed bubbles and also wearing a swimsuit since, as she often expressed, she was very modest.)[24] Although appearing in the film would have meant a break

into cinema, something she desired more than anything, her sense of integrity (and her uneasiness about the man behind Godard's signature dark glasses) guided her decision: "I said, 'I'm not interested in undressing, especially for a small role. That's not my style at all!'" Three months later, Godard had not forgotten her, after seeing a photo of her again at Agnès Varda's home.[25] When he sent Karina a telegram for his second feature, it read, "This time, it's for the leading role." Karina asked her friends, including actor Claude Brasseur, "Who is this Godard?" They reassured her, telling her she *had* to see him—that he'd just made the film everyone was talking about, *À bout de souffle* (that the actress had not yet seen).[26]

Accompanied by her companions, Karina went to meet "Monsieur Godard."[27] When she asked what the film was about, the director replied, "C'est un film politique."[28] Thinking he was crazy, Karina told him she could never deliver a political speech. "You just have to do what we tell you to do," he assured her. "Come tomorrow and sign your contract, it'll be fine." When Karina informed him that she was still a minor (being under twenty-one), he told her to bring her "mother and father." "I don't have a father and my mother is in Copenhagen," she replied. Despite the complications, Karina would appear in the film. She decided to accept the role without knowing much about it ("because he always writes the script at the last minute," she explained),[29] and Godard arranged for her mother to fly from Copenhagen to Paris to sign the contract on her behalf.[30] When asked by an interviewer at the time of *Vivre sa vie* in 1962 (after the couple had wed) if she knew at that first meeting that Godard was going to marry her, Karina was perplexed. "He scared me a bit," she said, describing him as "an odd, timid man with dark glasses." But then she admitted, blushingly, "I really liked him."[31]

From that point on, the couple's relationship evolved and their films went on to become masterpieces of French cinema. Though their marriage lasted only a few years, Godard and Karina made seven films together—or seven and a half, as she liked to say, including the short film Varda made starring the newlyweds, *Les Fiancés du pont Macdonald*

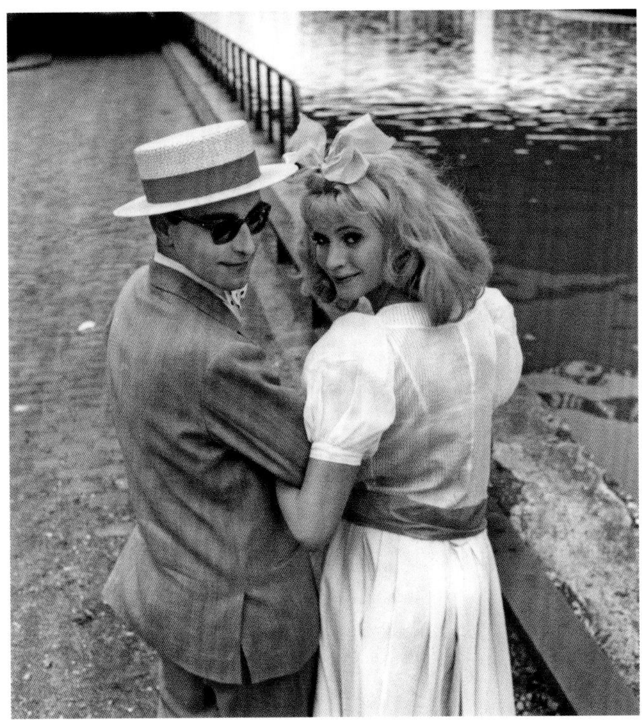

(*The Fiancés of Macdonald Bridge*), which appears in Varda's 1962 film *Cléo de 5 à 7*. *Les années Karina*, the Karina years, as they are commonly labeled within Godard's oeuvre, centered on various portraits of women that the actress brought to life.

Their cinematic love story played out on screen through nuances of their off-screen relationship. With *Le Petit soldat*, Godard and Karina entered the myth of the movement, and as film historian and scholar Antoine de Baecque described, Godard "realizes an absolute cinematic fantasy," joining a long line of legendary actress/director collaborative couples. Godard, in fact, sought this status before he ever met Karina.[32] The ad he placed for his second feature film read that he was looking for "an actress and soul mate," a label that later haunted and troubled Karina, as it led people in the industry to doubt her integrity. During a television reunion with Karina more than twenty years after their separation, Godard reflected on his need to align himself with the directors he so admired: "There was Orson Welles and Rita Hayworth; [Josef von] Sternberg, Marlene Dietrich; [Jean] Renoir, Catherine Hessling; so I told myself, 'Me too.'"[33]

Godard's desire to film the imaginary woman he dreamed of while searching for her in Karina, the real woman, created a confusion that affected their real-life relationship from the beginning.

In the context of renowned artists and directors, it is tempting to view the model or actress as a simple muse, almost relegated to the status of raw material, even if Karina herself insisted that she was honored by this somewhat patronizing and outdated label. She related in numerous interviews that Godard was also her Pygmalion, having met him when she was only eighteen. Having left school at age fourteen in Denmark, "Obviously, I hadn't yet read very much," she related. "Jean-Luc Godard is the one who inspired me to read, write, to be interested in things, painting. He's the one who taught me."[34]

Godard himself later implied that Karina had been a muse or a model (undoubtedly in a blank-slate sense, in line with Robert Bresson's nonprofessional actors that he referred to as "models"): "There is a model, and then, you see afterwards that this model allows you to do certain films, and then, models have a hard time passing over into real life."[35] Through their subjectivity, however, actors escape the reification that would make them just raw material and instead enter into the process of creation. Minimizing Karina's importance would mean overlooking her influence in her relationship with Godard, with real life spilling over into their fiction on screen.

ARTIST MEETS MODEL IN *LE PETIT SOLDAT*

Karina's hold on Godard, as he was falling in love with her, disrupted the original plot of the political film that he was planning to make about torture in the Algerian War, turning it into a hybrid love story. Bruno Forestier (Michel Subor)—a photojournalist and army deserter involved in covert operations by French intelligence in Geneva against pro-FLN (Front de libération nationale, the Algerian nationalist party) agents—becomes infatuated with Véronica (Karina), an FLN sympathizer. The film's politically sensitive plot was

Jean-Luc Godard and Anna Karina in Agnès Varda's *Les Fiancés du point MacDonald* (*The Fiancés of the MacDonald Bridge*), 1961

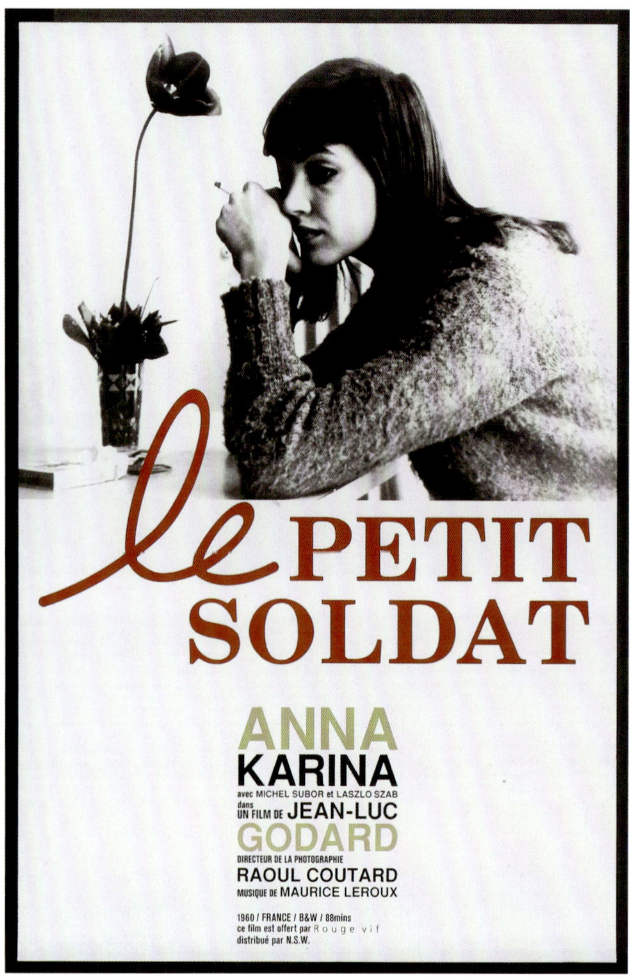

Jean-Luc Godard's *Le Petit soldat* (*The Little Soldier*), 1963, poster

constantly thwarted by the love story as it worked its way into Godard's mind during production. This phenomenon, which transformed the film into a sort of personal diary, also contributed to the film's modern construction.

Moments of distraction imprinted themselves onto the narrative as the couple's off-screen relationship was forming simultaneously in front of the camera. Ruled by his desire, Godard's camera focused on capturing Karina's movements and small gestures. In the now-famous photo-shoot sequence, Bruno follows Véronica with his lens as she dances around the room, echoing Godard's frustration with being unable to control his model, the object of his desire.

The subjectivity and elusive nature of the character and the actress—escaping the protagonist's and the director's con-

trol—feed the frustration and illustrate her power and his powerlessness behind the camera (as well as his desire for her). This recalls the famous mambo scene in *Et Dieu créa la femme*, wherein the spectacle of Bardot's body represents her liberation from the submissive role as a mere object, thus becoming threatening to both protagonist and director. As film theoretician Francis Vanoye put it, "as soon as the model steps out of submission to Art or to the artist, it becomes dangerous."[36] As the artist/director/protagonist tries to capture life by tracking the model's essence, her "truth," he confuses the real woman and his desire for her, encountering his own ambivalence.

Bruno discusses photography's ability to capture life as Véronica, his model, moves about in front of his lens (an idea Godard will further explore in *Vivre sa vie* through Edgar Allen Poe's "The Oval Portrait"). In voice-over, Bruno's thoughts as he photographs Véronica articulate what we can imagine echoed Godard's about cinema and his relationship to Karina, the actress. That internal voice dedramatizes Bruno's feelings and finds fault in Véronica, protecting him while he nevertheless remains fascinated by her: "She had dark circles under her eyes; they were Velásquez gray," or, "She wasn't as beautiful as yesterday afternoon." When asked if Godard told her the lines, "She had the mouth of Leslie Caron; she could have come out of a Giraudoux play," in real life, Karina answered, "He must have thought it since he wrote it."[37] The diegetic double voice of Bruno tries to take control by giving orders to Véronica: "Do what you want while I'm photographing you. Okay, I'm going to ask you questions and you're going to answer. That will be easier." As de Baecque noted, this scene also reenacted the first tests Godard did with Karina in Paris in March 1960 where they rehearsed the "love interrogation" that she would shoot with Subor a month later. In the real-life version, however, things did not go as smoothly as in the scene. When Godard berated Karina with questions, seeking to know more about her, like Véronica in the film, Karina responded, "That's none of your business!"[38]

At the end of the sequence, Véronica stops the record that had been playing—the music of Joseph Haydn—and sits still on the chair. The silence sets the stage for Bruno's (God-

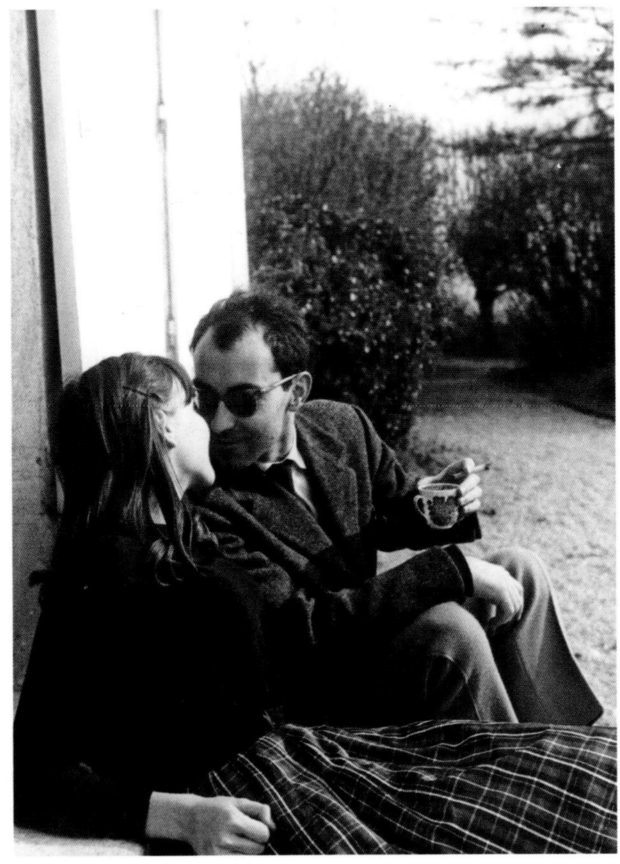

ard's?) discreet declaration of love. When Véronica takes Bruno's drawing test that "reveals a person's personality," she transforms the triangle, square, and circle that he draws for her into a little soldier and a girl and then asks Bruno to play the same game. "I'd like to know your thoughts," she says. Connecting the lines from the geometric shapes, Bruno forms the words "Je vous aime"—I love you. On set, Karina and Godard circulated their own love notes written on movie tickets. Their real-life love story invaded the shoot and caused tension: Godard multiplied and prolonged the takes with Karina, going so far as reshooting a whole scene with her several days after the original shoot.[39] At the end of April 1960, "after a dinner with the team in Lausanne," according to de Baecque, Karina, seated by Godard, "feels his hand under the table as he passes her a little note scribbled on a piece of paper."[40] "I love you. Meet me in Geneva, at Café de la Paix, at midnight," it read, Karina recalled. When she arrived at his table in the café, Godard was reading the newspaper. After a long pause, he lowered it and

told her, "So you're here, let's go," Karina recounted, "and that's it, we left."[41]

Years later, Godard acknowledged that this personal dimension structured his *mise en scène* in the film and created a mix that probably appeared "completely false and sometimes completely authentic,"[42] his typically contradictory way of describing things. From then on, Karina was a presence in his life that shaped their next six films.

GAINING CONFIDENCE AS AN ACTRESS AND AS A WOMAN: *UNE FEMME EST UNE FEMME*

Between *Le Petit soldat* and *Vivre sa vie*, the making of *Une femme est une femme* was one of the happiest moments for Godard and Karina as a couple. After the shoot in Geneva, the couple lived together in Paris, first in a hotel while he edited *Le Petit soldat* and then in a small house, 13 rue Nicolo. The film was banned, however, and the couple received bomb threats in the midst of the Algerian War. With the release delayed (it would eventually debut in 1963), moviegoers would not discover Karina right away. Director Michel Deville, however, after a private screening of the film, wanted Karina for his film, *Ce soir ou jamais* (*Tonight or Never*, 1961). Perhaps out of jealousy, Godard told her she would never be able to do it, to learn the dialogue (as she was still in the process of mastering French).[43] Her successful performance, involving a great deal of physicality and dancing, proved him wrong, and earned her even more of his respect.

Impressed by her capacity to dance and perform, Godard offered her the role in his next film, *Une femme est une femme*, even though multiple actresses had already tried out for it. The move reflected his confidence in Karina, a way of declaring his love for her. The gift of a musical responded to her well-known love of *les comédies musicales*. Inspired by the couple's life together, Godard wrote each scene in a notebook each morning of the shoot that started at noon.[44] Michel Legrand, the film's composer, described the film as "a way to sing everyday life, where everything can become lyrical."[45]

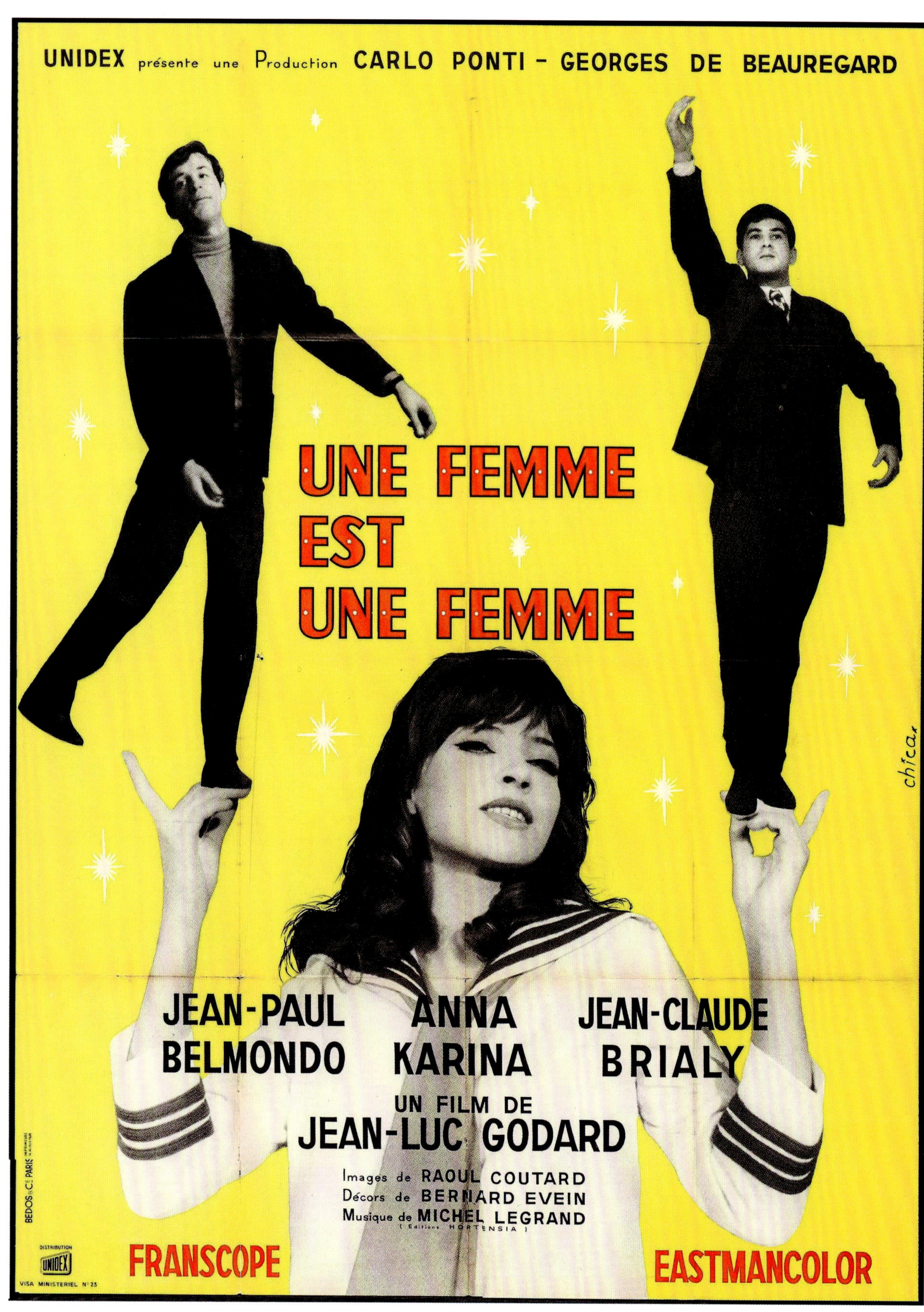

UNIDEX présente une Production CARLO PONTI - GEORGES DE BEAUREGARD

UNE FEMME
EST
UNE FEMME

JEAN-PAUL   ANNA   JEAN-CLAUDE
BELMONDO   KARINA   BRIALY

UN FILM DE
JEAN-LUC GODARD

Images de RAOUL COUTARD
Décors de BERNARD EVEIN
Musique de MICHEL LEGRAND
(Editions HORTENSIA)

FRANSCOPE   EASTMANCOLOR

DISTRIBUTION
UNIDEX
VISA MINISTERIEL N° 23

chica.

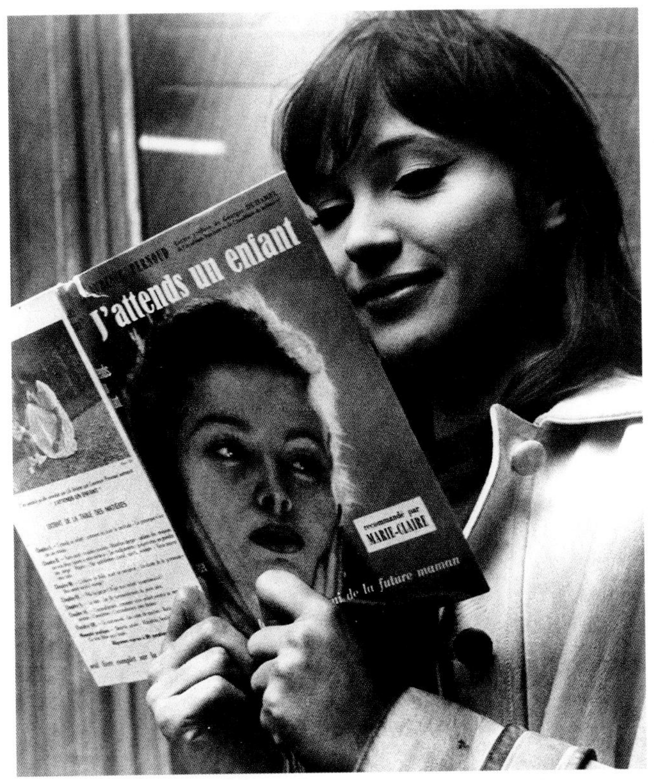

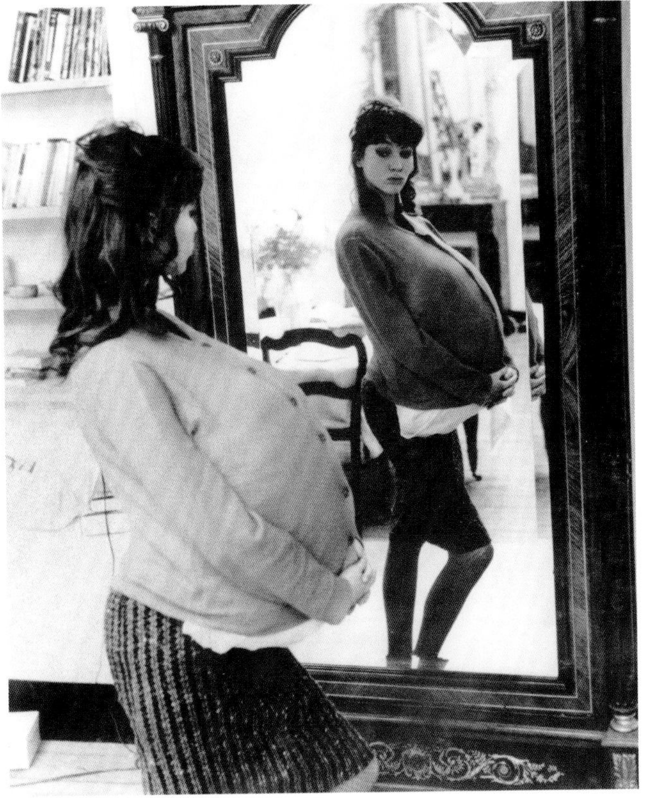

Showcasing Karina's contagious joie de vivre and playful approach to life, the film also reflected her personal style. When Karina was interviewed for French television as a young actress, the journalist told her, "Actresses usually seem all the same, except for the big stars, which we hope you become. They've found their personal style, and you have a style."[46] When asked if Godard told her how to dress, she replied, "Absolutely not."[47] In another interview, she related that for *Une femme est une femme*, "false eyelashes were in style. Everyone wore them, whether you could tell or not. So Jean-Luc came to touch my eyelashes. He wanted to rip them off and I wasn't even wearing any!" Regarding her clothes for the shoot, she said, "He asked me to wear a red sweater against this white wall." The first film Godard shot in color (and in a studio)[48] broke convention since filmmakers, believing pure white and bright red translated poorly on film, generally avoided those hues. "Raoul Coutard was going crazy in the beginning when Godard asked him on the contrary to keep the white and bright red, then he noticed that the result was sublime."[49]

In *Une femme est une femme*, Karina brought light not only to Godard's film but also to his life. In an early interview, she was told that Godard had said that she had influenced him. When asked what she gave him, Karina replied, "He's less timid now—I gave him self-confidence."[50] Her "vivacity and boldness," in Sragow's words, also complemented Godard's "ingenuity and wit."[51]

These traits radiated through Karina's character in *Une femme est une femme*, Angéla. In her scenes with Jean-Claude Brialy as her husband Émile (again Godard's alter ego), they played out scenes of domestic life with great exuberance and fun. Making dinner, brushing their teeth, even arguing—all seem to celebrate the happy life of the newlywed couple. The intensity of the Godard/Karina connection also generated great freedom in cinematic experimentation as the film became the couple's playground. Angéla and Émile interact in scenes of their life together as newlyweds while the camera follows their movements like a choreographed dance. At the dinner table, they sit across from each other and discuss mundane topics before Angéla announces she wants a baby (a posture that Godard

Left: Jean-Luc Godard's *Une femme est une femme* (*A Woman is a Woman*), 1961, original poster. **Above:** Anna Karina (Angéla) in *Une femme est une femme*, 1961 (translation of magazine title: "I'm Expecting a Child")

will later use in *Le Mépris* with Bardot during the couple's disenchantment). Subtitles translate for the spectator each of their motivations and desires, anticipating Woody Allen's transcription of his characters' thoughts in *Annie Hall* (1977). During their equally famous bedtime marital spat, Angéla and Émile circumnavigate their self-imposed silent treatment by communicating their anger silently but humorously through the titles of books they remove from their shelves.

The film also mirrored Karina and Godard's real-life relationship on a highly personal level. Angéla wants a child at all costs, and Karina herself became pregnant in the middle of the shoot. She and Godard married shortly thereafter and soon began their next film. For Godard, as actor Michel Séméniako (who starred in Godard's 1967 film *La Chinoise*) put it, "Cinema is life and life is cinema."[52]

VIVRE SA VIE: KARINA AND GODARD'S OVAL PORTRAIT

For *Vivre sa vie*, Godard gave Jackie Reynal, the film's makeup artist, only one guideline: "Anna is Louise Brooks,"[53] articulating his desire to have her resemble the image of one of the idols of early cinema. Karina, however, also brought her own presence, her own life force, into the role. Though the couple possessed complementary attributes that inspired great creativity from their union, such extreme closeness also complicated matters in their later work. This fusional relationship colored the characters in their films, where Karina often played the role of the masculine protagonist's "double" and, by extension, the double of Godard himself.

While Karina exuded an extreme attachment to life, bringing playfulness and a carefree spirit to her characters, Godard's preoccupation with death permeates the characters in his films. In an interview for *Cahiers du cinéma*, he discussed his views on the relationship between cinema and life, citing Jean Cocteau in *Orphée* who "films death at work," adding, "Painting is immobile; cinema is interesting because it seizes life and the mortal side of life."[54] Similarly, in *Le Petit soldat*, Bruno, while photographing Karina's character, expresses in voice-over, "I had the sensation of photographing death,"

reflecting Godard's own fixation on the idea of capturing or vampirizing a living subject for the sake of creating art.

Edgar Allan Poe's "The Oval Portrait" perfectly illustrates this idea, and Godard was fascinated by the short story. It follows an artist obsessed with creating a lifelike painting of his wife, who endlessly poses for him as he neglects her in pursuit of capturing her essence. Eventually, his neglect kills her. Conscious of the dynamic, or troubled by it, Godard nevertheless actively pursued capturing the essence of Karina on film while neglecting her as a person, his wife.

The idea seemed to haunt Godard. Before *Vivre sa vie*, he envisioned a "faithful but contemporary"[55] adaptation of Poe's "The Oval Portrait" using the same title. His synopsis described two people who cross paths on vacation in Paris and begin dating. When the girl gives her new boyfriend a Super 8 camera on his birthday, he starts filming her incessantly, continuing what becomes an exasperating habit and finally confessing that he no longer loves her because now all he wants to do is film her. Correcting (or contradicting) himself, he then says that he in fact films her *because* he loves her. One day, as they cross the Champs-Élysées, he is filming her when she is suddenly struck by a car, and he continues to shoot as blood pools around her body.[56]

The trajectory of Karina's characters, played out before Godard's camera, mirrors the story in a striking parallel, illustrating a sort of Oval Portrait syndrome, yet Karina, the actress, managed to stay on the side of life even in her darkest moments. Godard and Karina's blissful existence as newlyweds turned tragic after *Une femme est une femme* when Karina lost the baby. She described this painful moment as the start of their difficulties as a couple and the ultimate cause of their separation:

During *Une femme est une femme*, the story of a woman who wants a child, I became pregnant. So we got married. . . . And I had the misfortune of losing this child. I had a very late miscarriage. That is when things started to go badly between us. I became very, very sick; I was traumatized by this story for years, falling into a deep depression and a series of hospitalizations. And Jean-

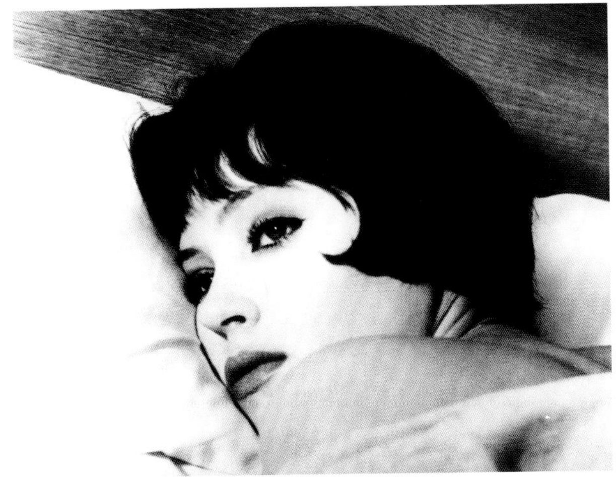

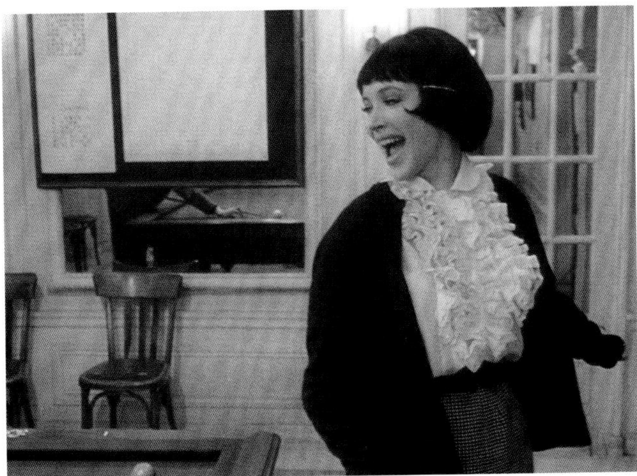

Luc wasn't often there; I think that he also needed to be alone—maybe I took too much space in his life. I was young, I needed him, for him to take care of me, and I didn't understand why he left all the time, even if I was extremely spoiled during the film shoots.

Godard nourished their work with Karina's vitality, giving their films an ineffable and authentic quality that goes beyond a simple artist/model or director/actress relationship. Acknowledging this collaborative component, Godard related, "There was a movement on her part and on mine that gives [our films] something true."[57] Fiction served as the perfect screen for them to express personal conflicts, repressed tensions, and a deep emotional attachment to each other. In *Vivre sa vie*, Godard seemed to use Poe's narrative as a filter, a way of admitting his obsession with cinema and neglect

Anna Karina (Nana) in Jean-Luc Godard's *Vivre sa vie* (*My Life to Live*), 1962

of his wife and even indirectly apologizing to Karina for it. Including Poe's text in a moment of pause in the film's narrative about Nana's trajectory as a prostitute (where she is ultimately killed) represents a digression in the story. It is a way to articulate what is happening between Godard and Karina as artist and model, husband and wife, outside the film.

The deep sadness that emanates from Karina in *Vivre sa vie* undoubtedly reflected a personal dimension. Just after the start of the shoot on February 19, 1962, while struggling with depression after her miscarriage, Karina attempted suicide on March 3. Godard's ambivalence also played out on screen. During the final days of filming, he played hot and cold and mistreated her. In the film, he killed off her character in the end, a scenario that the actress had always refused. The first version of the script was, in fact, less dramatic and ended with Karina's character, Nana, a prostitute, becoming rich and successful. In the final version, however, Godard had her brutally executed in the street from two gunshots fired by rival pimps. The director averred that it was *Vivre sa vie* that marked the beginning of their problems as a couple, but for a different reason from what Karina had described. According to him, she "was furious because she thought we made her ugly, that I did her a considerable harm in making this film; it was the beginning of our breakup."[58]

Despite the dark context, Karina's inner joy and playfulness brighten the screen when she dances around a pool table, playing songs on the jukebox. In her 2016 interview with Karina, Talu described the dance scene as introducing "a breath of youth and cheerfulness into the otherwise somber and rigid film," adding that it is "refreshing to see Nana take charge of her destiny, even for a short while." When asked about the shoot and the choreography, Karina's reply recalls Véronica in *Le Petit soldat* as she is photographed by Bruno: "I totally improvised that and then Godard followed me with the camera. Raoul Coutard is a great cameraman. He could follow anything, he's really a genius."[59]

These types of scenes that populate many of their films reflect Godard's obsession with capturing the *life* of his model/actress/wife. But at other times, his camera tries to contain her, to fix her in his frame with static, flat close-ups of just her head, isolated and cut off at the neck. What lay behind this desire to capture her, instead of giving her freedom, while identifying with her as his double? As the film theoretician Laurence Schifano noted, Karina "does not attain, Godard does not take her, to the sovereign state of freedom, to this freedom of spirit that Cassavetes, Rivette, or Bergman capture in their feminine models (doubles)."[60] Laura Mulvey's work again sheds light on this type of relationship to the double, one that is both "fascinating and terrifying" in that it represents a danger in escaping the other's control.

In the twelfth and final tableau of *Vivre sa vie*, subtitles of the characters' mute dialogue reflect the mundanity of their life as they play out roles as if they are in a silent film:

Nana: What shall we do today?
Young man: I don't know. Should we go to the Luxembourg?
Nana: I think it's going to rain.

The image frames Karina opening their bedroom window. The scene continues with Godard's voice dubbed over footage of the young man (Peter Kassovitz), Nana's new lover, silently reading Edgar Allan Poe's "The Oval Portrait,"[61] intercutting with Karina's head in close-up, telling their story through image and text. Godard first recites excerpts in voice-over from the middle of Poe's tale, wherein the narrator describes a captivating portrait he comes upon at a chateau. He is inextricably taken with this "portrait of a young girl just ripening into womanhood . . . a mere head and shoulders [done in] a vignette manner," which he likens to the work of American painter Thomas Sully. It is not "the execution of the work, nor the immortal beauty of the countenance, which had so suddenly and vehemently moved [him]," but rather "the absolute *life-likeliness* of expression."

Tacked to the white wall behind Karina in close-up is a photo of Elizabeth Taylor, creating a sort of *mise en abyme*—here, a copy of an image within the image—that alludes to the film's story within the story. Nana interrupts the narration to inquire, "Is that your book?" and the voice-over replies, "No, I found it here." She then asks for a cigarette, and the

young man obliges. Again, we hear Godard: "It's our story: a painter who paints a portrait of his wife. Do you want me to continue?" Nana (or Karina) answers yes.

Godard resumes his narration with the end of "The Oval Portrait," in which the narrator reads from a book—layering yet another *mise en abyme*—that reveals how the portrait came to be. In seeking to capture the essence of his wife, the painter became "wild with the ardor of his work, and turned his eyes from the canvas rarely," failing to notice "that the tints which he spread upon the canvas were drawn from the cheeks of her who sat beside him." Finally, when the painter looked upon his completed masterpiece, "he grew tremulous and very pallid, and aghast, and crying with a loud

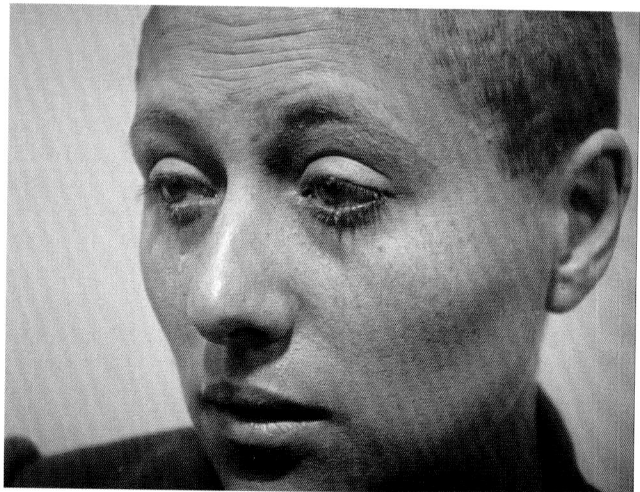

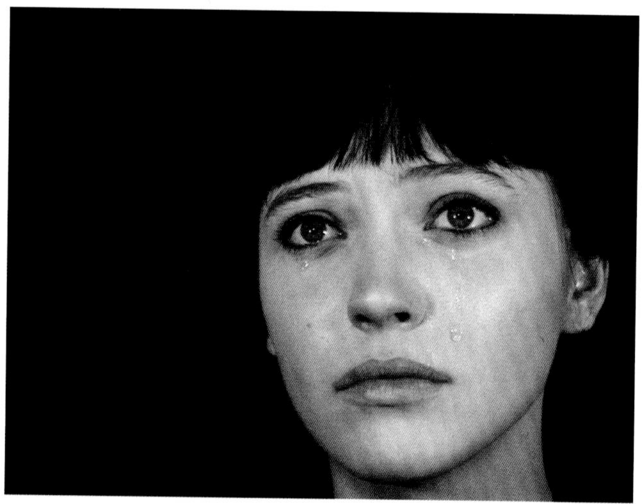

Top: Renée Falconetti in Carl Theodor Dreyer's *The Passion of Joan of Arc*, 1928 (excerpts projected in Godard's *Vivre sa vie*) **Bottom:** Anna Karina (Nana) watching Falconetti in *Vivre sa vie*, (*My Life to Live*), 1962

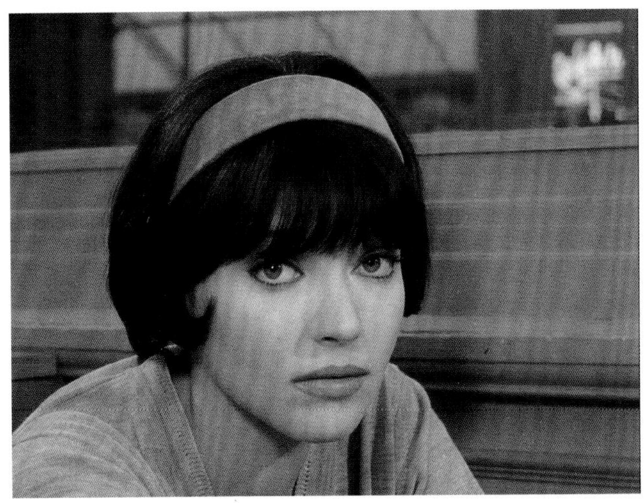

voice 'This is indeed Life itself!' turned suddenly to regard his beloved:–*She was dead*."

Though this scene is far and away the most overt reference to Godard and Karina's struggles in interweaving art and life, the film also addresses it elsewhere, as in the conversation between Nana and the philosopher Brice Parain. As they talk about the difficulty of communication, in finding words that explain thoughts, Karina seems to call out to her husband through her character as she looks to the camera, communicating without words as in silent film. The central place of cinema in the Godard/Karina relationship reinforces the idea of communicating emotion without words (an idea echoed again in *Pierrot le fou*). It appears in another famous scene with close-ups of Nana in the movie theater watching the famous silent film *La Passion de Jeanne d'Arc* (*The Passion of Joan of Arc*, 1928). With tears streaming down her face, Karina mirrors the heroine (Renée Jeanne Falconetti) crying as she is sentenced to death (like Nana herself will be in *Vivre sa vie*). Much admired by Godard, the director, Denmark's Carl Theodor Dreyer, was linked to Karina not only through their nationality: Her mother had worked with him designing costumes for his 1964 film *Gertrud*,[62] and Karina recounted writing articles with his son, Erik Dreyer, at seventeen.[63] Between life and fiction, the camera plays an integral part in the love story of Karina and Godard as it meets the purity of silent film in this scene, portraying pure emotion that both transcends and avoids the difficulty of communication.

Anna Karina (Nana) in conversation with Brice Parain in Godard's *Vivre sa vie*, 1962

When Karina stares straight into the camera in close-up, it also establishes an intimate relationship with viewers, forcing us to act as witnesses to the story playing out on screen (and behind the camera). As Godard stated in the Oval Portrait sequence, "This is our story," but the triangular relationship implies that it is also "our story"–the projected story of the couple on screen, received by us as spectators.

BRIGITTE BARDOT AND THE GHOST OF KARINA IN *LE MÉPRIS*

While the filter of Poe's narrative in *Vivre sa vie* allowed intimate truths to be expressed more freely, in *Le Mépris*, a double filter existed through the source material: Alberto Moravia's 1954 novel *Il disprezzo* (*Contempt*) and another actress in the leading role, Brigitte Bardot. On her relationship with Godard, Bardot related, "He petrified me. I must've terrorized him." Godard simply stated, "I didn't interest her, she didn't interest me."[64]

In Italy for a film shoot, the protagonist Paul (Michel Piccoli), a scriptwriter, and his wife Camille (Bardot) see their marriage begin to falter behind the scenes as the movie is being created. Underneath the adaptation of Moravia's novel and Bardot's incarnation of Camille lie the ghosts of Godard and Karina's relationship–the "anatomy of the failure of a couple," in the words of de Baecque.[65] Karina affirmed this idea: "I found an enormous amount of words and gestures from my everyday life. When Bardot says bad words, that's me, or when she suddenly says, 'I want red velvet curtains.'"[66] Karina often recounted that she recognized literal words from their arguments. The black wig that Bardot wore during those scenes only adds to the intimate authenticity.

Piccoli confirmed that his character functioned as Godard's alter ego: "I quickly saw that I was playing Jean-Luc. When he told me how to dress, I in fact noticed that he was giving me his own clothes and his own hat,"[67] and even his socks! Along with his clothes, Godard also gave Piccoli the "awkwardness of a jealous man,"[68] in de Baecque's words.

In considering the following lines, there is no question that the film was highly autobiographical beneath its guise of adaptation:

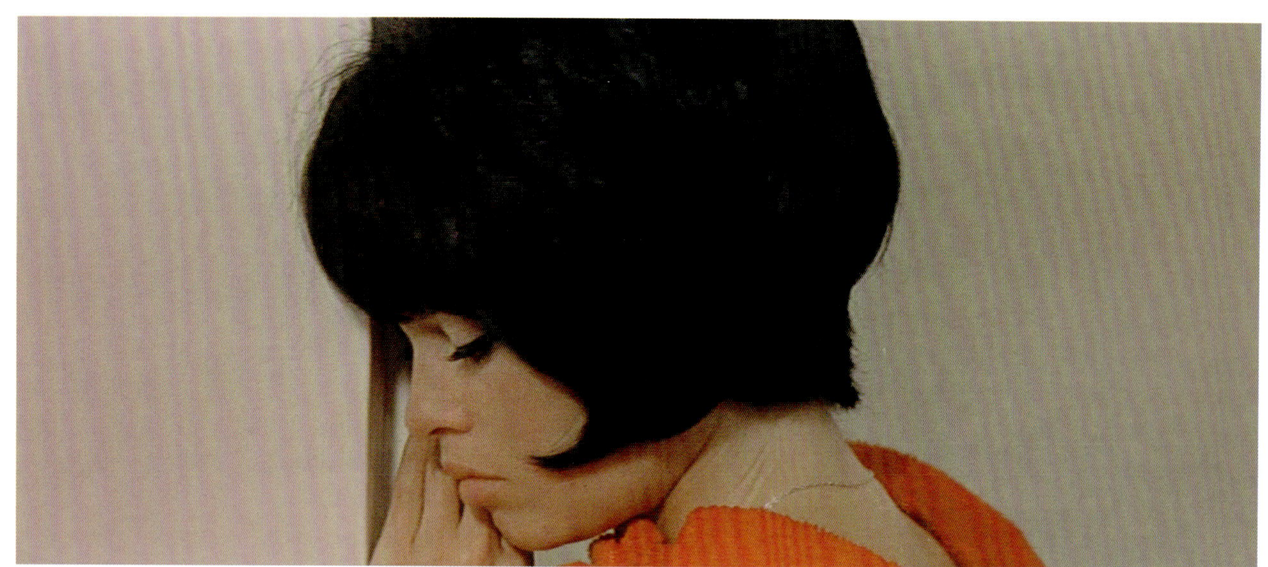

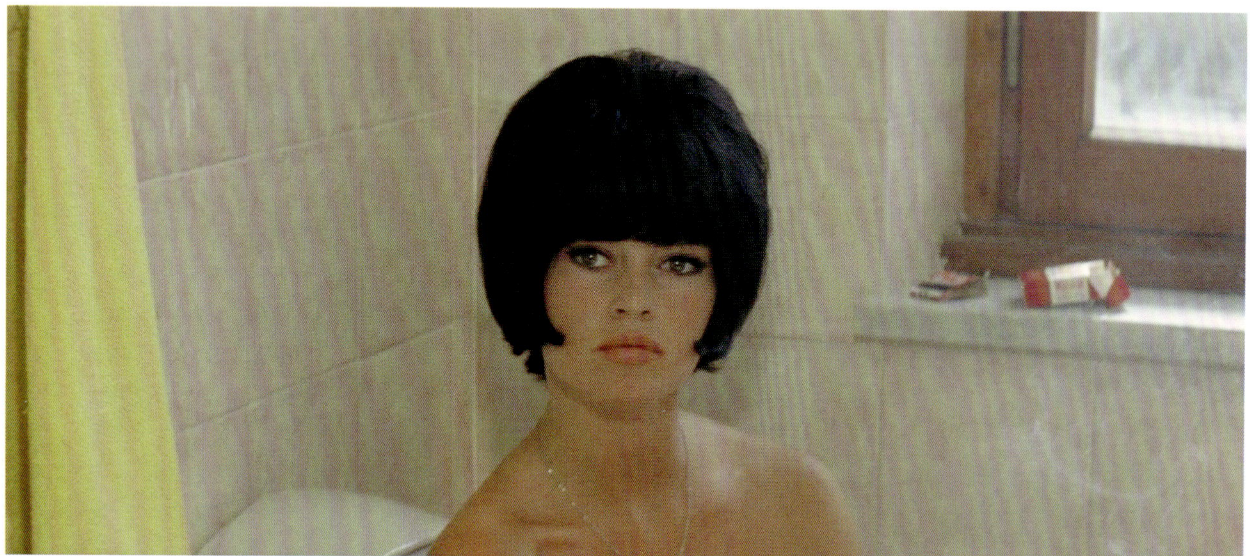

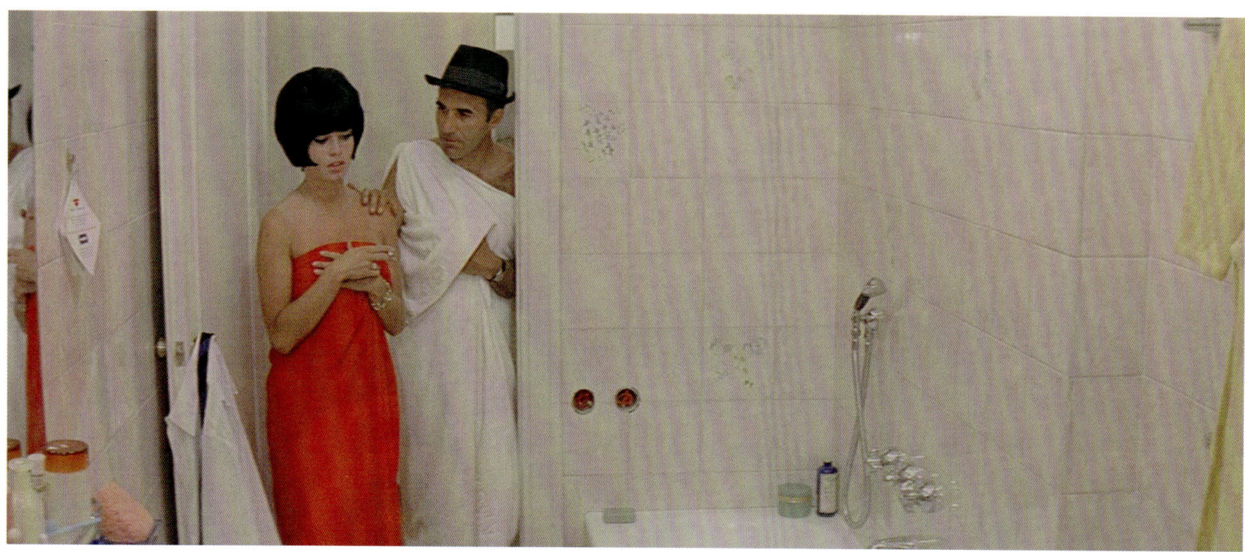

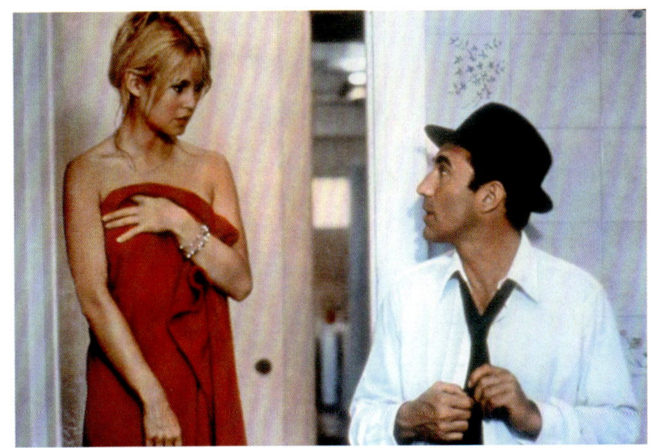

Paul (in voice-over): I'd been thinking, for a while now, that Camille could leave me. I thought of it as a possible disaster. Now the disaster had happened.
Camille (in voice-over): Before, we used to live in a cloud of unawareness, of blissful complicity. Everything happened with a sudden, crazy, enchanted recklessness.

The words accompany nostalgic scenes that represent a parenthetical moment of happiness in the couple's life. They are interspersed with images of Bardot, nude on a white rug, calling back to her role in *Et Dieu créa la femme* (another insert of Bardot's nude body for producers). Within these parentheses, Bardot played herself, in a way, but Godard used the pretext to convey a highly personal moment. In this famous sequence, the on-screen couple voices their unhappiness, echoing Godard's disagreements with Karina (with Bardot in the black wig). As Camille and Paul recount their love story and its degradation, Bardot raises her head and looks straight into the camera. The camera shifts back and forth between the aggrieved spouses, recalling the stance in a playful scene between Angéla and Émile at the dinner table in *Une femme est une femme*. Godard wrote the dialogue for this scene "feverishly each morning," according to de Baecque. It is, in effect, the argument that he and Karina had lived for two years in all its glory. This emotionally charged sequence is reinforced by the haunting soundtrack composed by Georges Delerue. The series of "waves where contempt, bad faith, hatred, anger, and frustration rise in Camille, and the pauses of complicity, remission and even tenderness and sexual reconciliation are those of the cou-

ple on rue Nicolo" (the couple's Paris address), de Baecque wrote. It is clear that Karina's influence remained strong even in her absence. Again, the heroine, Camille (and the ghost of Karina), is killed in the end while the movie that is under construction in the film (in reality, Godard's *Le Mépris*) is being born.

BANDE À PART TO PIERROT LE FOU: MOURNING, CREATION, AND ESCAPING THE OVAL PORTRAIT

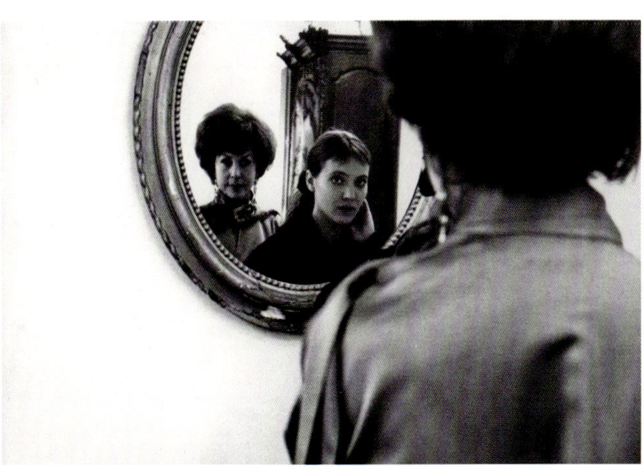

After *Vivre sa vie,* Karina traversed another challenging moment in her life, as she described in a 2016 interview: "I had difficulties at that time to live my life. It was pretty difficult between Jean-Luc and me. I was in the hospital, and not a very good one."[69] In another interview the same year, Karina shed light on the context of her depression: "We got married because, you know, I was pregnant. But then I lost the baby. Ups and downs. And then when *Bande à Part* came along, I was in really bad shape. I didn't want to be alive anymore. I had tried to commit suicide." At a time when society was unaware of how to handle women with depression, Karina was institutionalized for mental illness. "And I wasn't crazy at all," she explained. "But it was a bad situation at that time for women—you could be there forever. But an analyst helped to get me out."[70] Immediately after, Godard arrived, announcing they would be making a new film. "And Jean-Luc came, took me out, and said, 'We are shooting the day after tomorrow,' and I said, 'Okay.' And that's how *Bande à part* came about."[71] In 1964, a somber ambiance haunted

Left: Brigitte Bardot (Camille) in Jean-Luc Godard's *Le Mépris* (*Contempt*), 1963 **Above:** Bardot and Michel Piccoli (Paul) in *Le Mépris*

Louisa Colpeyn (Madame Victoria) with Anna Karina (Odile) in Jean-Luc Godard's *Bande à part* (*Band of Outsiders*) 1964

Godard's "crime movie, heist movie," as Karina described it,[72] with Karina back in the lead. *Bande à part* was filmed in the dead of winter after Karina's hospitalization for depression, and the film can be seen as reanimating her, helping her live again. Karina agreed when Talu described the film as "the story of a woman who fights with all her strength to live."[73] Yet Karina described what it was like to embody this role while living the part of Godard's wife during the shoot:

> When Jean-Luc came to get me for *Bande à part*, everything was spinning; the noise around us, boulevard Saint-Germain, terrified me. I'd just come out of several weeks of calm, and there, what he announced to me, traffic, the city, was a mix of excitement and anxiety. I don't know if he didn't love me enough or if he loved me too much. But when a shoot was on the horizon, he loved me again very deeply. That day, however, I had the impression that he loved me like a marionette. He was the genius, and I the puppet. I didn't know if I should laugh or cry.

The ambiguity in their relationship also appears in the film as Godard continued his trend of nourishing his work with details from all areas of his personal life (here, for example, he gave Karina's character his mother's name, Odile). His mercurial treatment of Karina during production revived illusions for her that things would work out while suffering from the indecipherable mixed messaging in his treatment of her on the set versus behind the scenes.

In *Bande à part*, like in their other films, the short bits of improvisation, digressions, or short parentheses often showcased Karina's spirit, allowing her freedom to express her exuberant life force. "Godard never said you have to do this like this because in a way, it was all in the action, you see, in the dialogue," Karina explained. "He didn't have to explain it. Even with the cameraman, Raoul Coutard, they never really spoke to each other. They just knew what they had to do."[74] These digressions were born in *Bande à part*, according to Suzanne Schiffman, the script supervisor (referred to as a "script girl" at the time) on the film, from the "constant fear of [the film] being too short."[75] These scenes, outside the film's narrative, in fact, turned out to be some

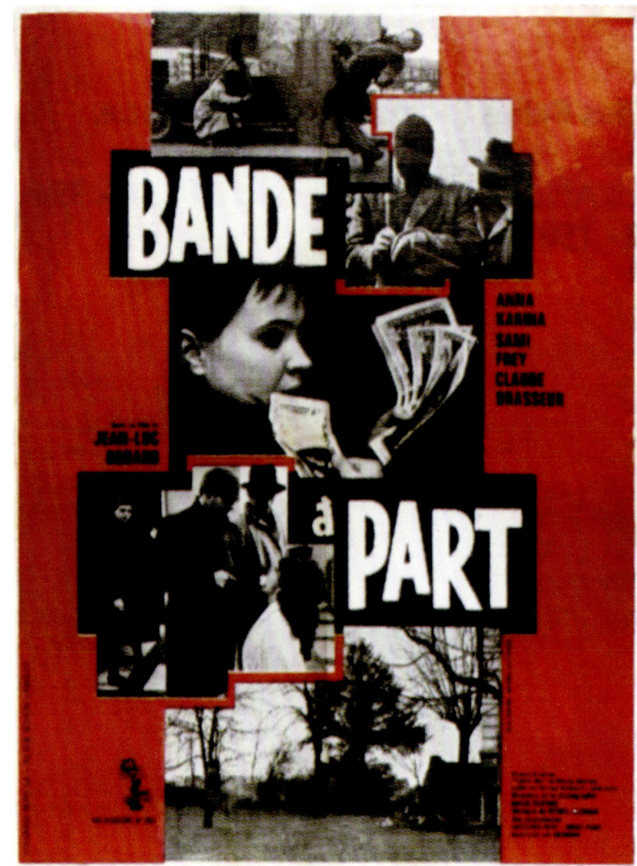

of the most memorable. "Few actors have shown the avid physicality that Karina does" in the film, noted Sragow.[76] The two emblematic digression scenes illustrate Karina's exuberance: the visit to the Louvre, where the three main characters run through the whole museum in "under nine minutes, forty-five seconds"; and Karina dancing the Madison with her two male protagonists, a scene, unlike the others, that was rehearsed at length. "Okay, the Madison, *that* we rehearsed for about three weeks in a nightclub every night after the shoot from 7 to 8 and sometimes from 8 to 9, because the nightclubs never opened before midnight," Karina stated. "So we went there with professional dancers and did the hand clapping and finger snapping. We had to do rehearsals because the two guys, Sami Frey and Claude Brasseur, didn't know how to dance."[77] Even fifty years later, Karina's enthusiasm for this free-spirited scene celebrating life is apparent. Drawing on her own attachment to life through art, Karina latched onto the film to create, pulling herself back toward vitality: "I didn't want to live any-

Jean-Luc Godard's *Bande à part* (*Band of Outsiders*), 1964, original poster

more; everything was going badly. It's true: The film saved my life."[78]

Immediately following *Bande à part*, Godard shot a film centered on a married woman and her infidelity, *Une femme mariée*, with Macha Méril. Again, the ghost of Karina was omnipresent as Godard attempted to decipher the married woman by dissecting her body in the *mise en scène*. Karina, meanwhile, worked on Jean Aurel's *De l'amour* (*All About Loving*, 1964), an episodic film about love featuring a panoply of women. After their respective films made apart, the couple came back together for *Alphaville* (1965), "an operation of mourning," in the words of film scholar and Godard expert Alain Bergala.

Made after their separation, it is a film where feelings are forgotten, where all emotions are forbidden, and where Karina's character (Natacha von Braun) no longer knows the word *love*. The goal driving the plot was to bring that word—

and everything associated with it—back into consciousness. Natacha von Braun is led by Lemmy Caution (Eddie Constantine) on a quest and brought back from emptiness where she finally remembers the words *I love you*. Shot without light, again by Coutard, *Alphaville* fittingly reflects what Bergala called "the darkest moment of mourning" for the couple. This dismal period surrounding the production, in his opinion, allowed them to bounce back to reconquer life in the sunny south of France in their next film.

In *Pierrot le fou*, Ferdinand (Jean-Paul Belmondo), known as Pierrot, and Marianne (Karina) meet each other by chance at the beginning of the film and find themselves together four years after an undefined but presumably romantic encounter. As *Le Petit soldat* marked the beginning of Karina and Godard's real-life love story, *Pierrot le fou* marked the end, or almost the end. In it, the viewer sees and *feels* what is unsaid. What lies outside the film, the personal story that the couple

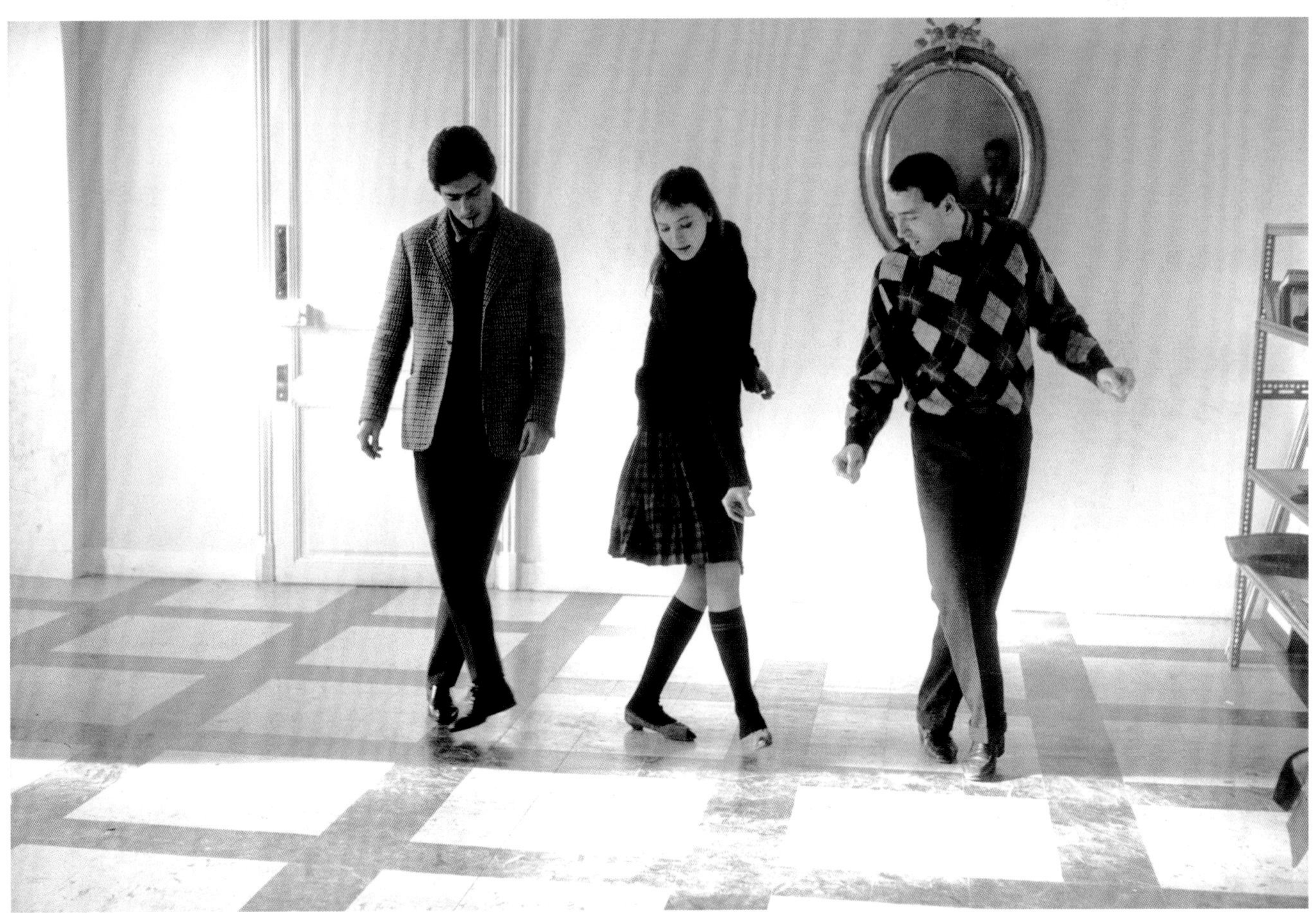

Sami Frey (Franz), Anna Karina (Odile), and Claude Brasseur (Arthur) dancing the Madison in Godard's *Bande à part*, 1964

went through together, etched itself within it: despair and disillusionment along with nostalgia for lost love. Cinematic traces of the couple blend with autobiographical ones. *Le Petit soldat*, *Bande à part*, and *Alphaville* mix with *À bout de souffle*, *Le Mépris*, and even Bergman's *Summer with Monika* and other films whose influence is implicit and explicit through the film's citations. Karina and Belmondo were not intended for the leading roles. Godard had originally considered Richard Burton and Sylvie Vartan after Karina made *Le Voleur du Tibidabo* (*The Thief of Tibidabo*, 1965) and reportedly had an affair with its director, Maurice Ronet.[79] The presence of Godard's veteran actors, however, gives a texture that is both reflexive (in relation to their other characters in Godard's films) and personal. At the heart of the film is Karina's presence intertwined with love and cinema. Their films, in the end, were inseparable from their lives together, their love story inextricable from their fiction on screen.

Starting with the opening credits of *Pierrot le fou*, there is an attempt to recuperate what is missing. As letters of the alphabet appear on the black screen in an initially nonsensical configuration, little by little more letters start to fill in the blanks, spelling out the names of the actors and the director. The first letter to appear, *A*, the beginning of the alphabet, is also the one that begins the word at the center of Godard's cinematic discourse: *Anna*. Karina's voice is also now more present in the narrative. Different from the couple in *Le Mépris*, dominated by the male protagonist's voice-over, in *Pierrot le fou* the voices of the man and woman function together. Buried in sand, Ferdinand and Marianne recite parts of "Life in a Love," the poem by Robert Browning ("a poet named revolver," as Ferdinand puts it, playing on the connection of the poet's surname and the line of firearms) that underlines the idea of ambivalence and destiny:

Ferdinand: a poet named revolver
Marianne: Robert Browning.
Ferdinand: Escape me?
Marianne: Never–
Ferdinand: Beloved!
Marianne: While I am I,
Ferdinand: and you are you,
Marianne: So long as the world contains us both,

Ferdinand: Me the loving
Marianne: and you the loth,
Ferdinand: While the one eludes[80]
Marianne: It seems too much like a fate

Karina recalled that Godard gave them straws to breathe from as she and Belmondo waited, buried in sand, to start shooting the scene.[81] (Yet another attempt at burying their relationship?)

The themes of life and death traversed *Pierrot* through art also. Poetry, song, and painting serve as filters, echoing different moments of Karina and Godard's life and cinematic invention. *Pierrot* was a film made of fragments and collage, considered one of the most modern of its time. The exchange between Marianne and Ferdinand in the car–filmed through the windshield as primary-colored lights intermittently illuminate their faces and a simple melody plays in the background–is a prime example of the intermingling of art and echoes of Karina and Godard's life, creating a profoundly moving scene. Like in *Vivre sa vie* and many of their other films, it is hard not to hear a plea from Godard to Karina in their dialogue:

Ferdinand: You just have to want to.
Marianne: I want to. I'll do anything you'd like.
Ferdinand: Moi aussi, Marianne. [Me too, Marianne.]
Marianne: I'll put my hand on your knee.
Ferdinand: Moi aussi, Marianne.
Marianne: I'll kiss you all over.
Ferdinand: Moi aussi, Marianne.

As Godard's camera contemplates Karina's face, juxtaposed with the little girl's in a Renoir painting (*Petite fille à la gerbe*, 1888), the words of a song, "C'que t'es belle, ma pépée / c'que t'es belle / c'que t'es belle" ("How beautiful you are, my girl . . . ") resonate with the impressionist and cinematic artwork. Celebrating Karina's image with his camera that is imbued with all the emotion from their history together, Godard revived the beauty of the on- and off-screen relationship between actress and director from the days of *Le Petit soldat*, at peace in their work of art.

Next page: Anna Karina (Natacha) in Jean-Luc Godard's *Alphaville*, 1965

"When Jean-Luc came to get me for *Bande à part*, everything was spinning; the noise around us, boulevard Saint-Germain, terrified me. I'd just come out of several weeks of calm, and there, what he announced to me, traffic, the city, was a mix of excitement and anxiety. I don't know if he didn't love me enough or if he loved me too much. But when a shoot was on the horizon, he loved me again very deeply. That day, however, I had the impression that he loved me like a marionette. He was the genius, and I the puppet. I didn't know if I should laugh or cry."

—anna karina

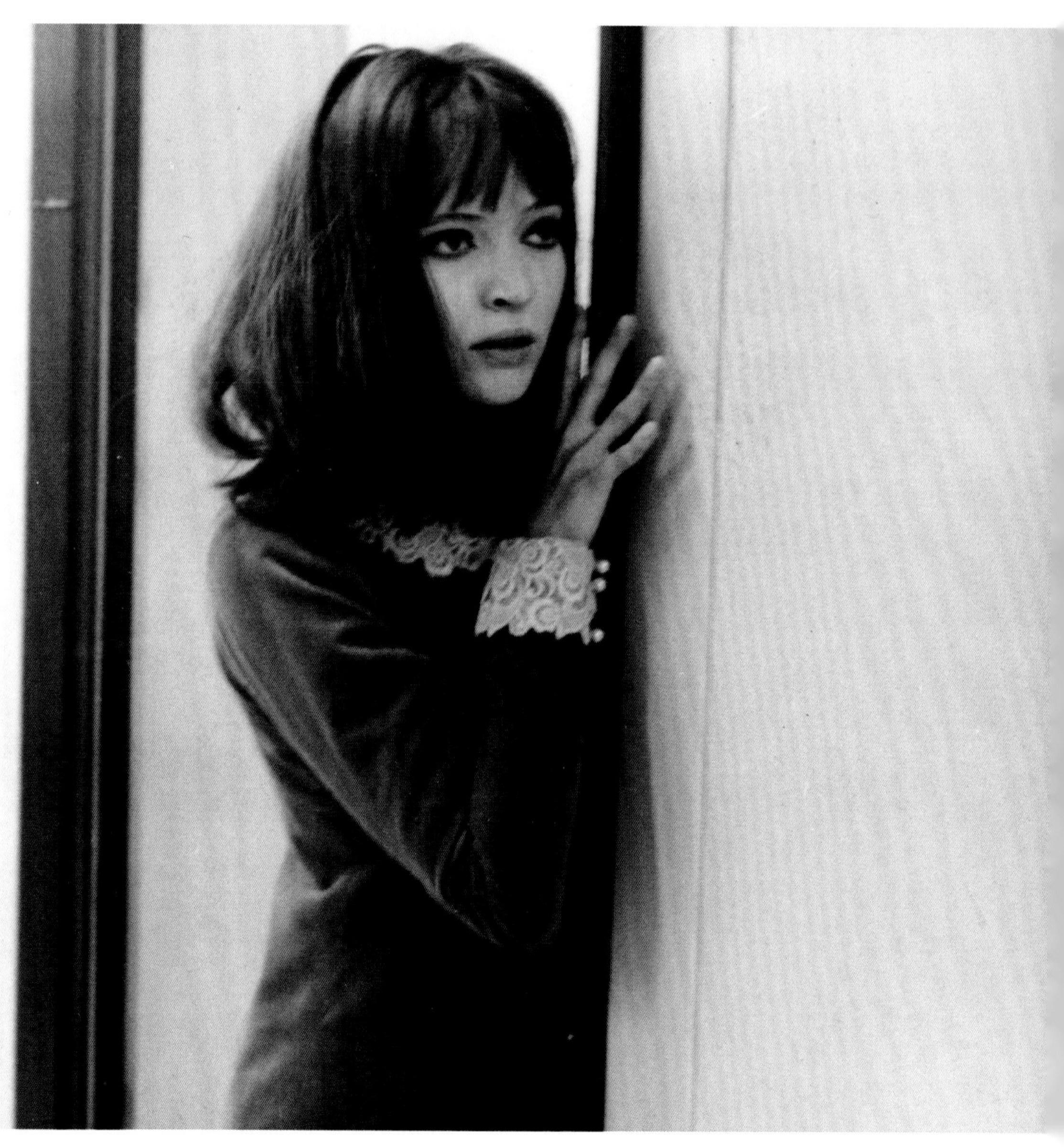

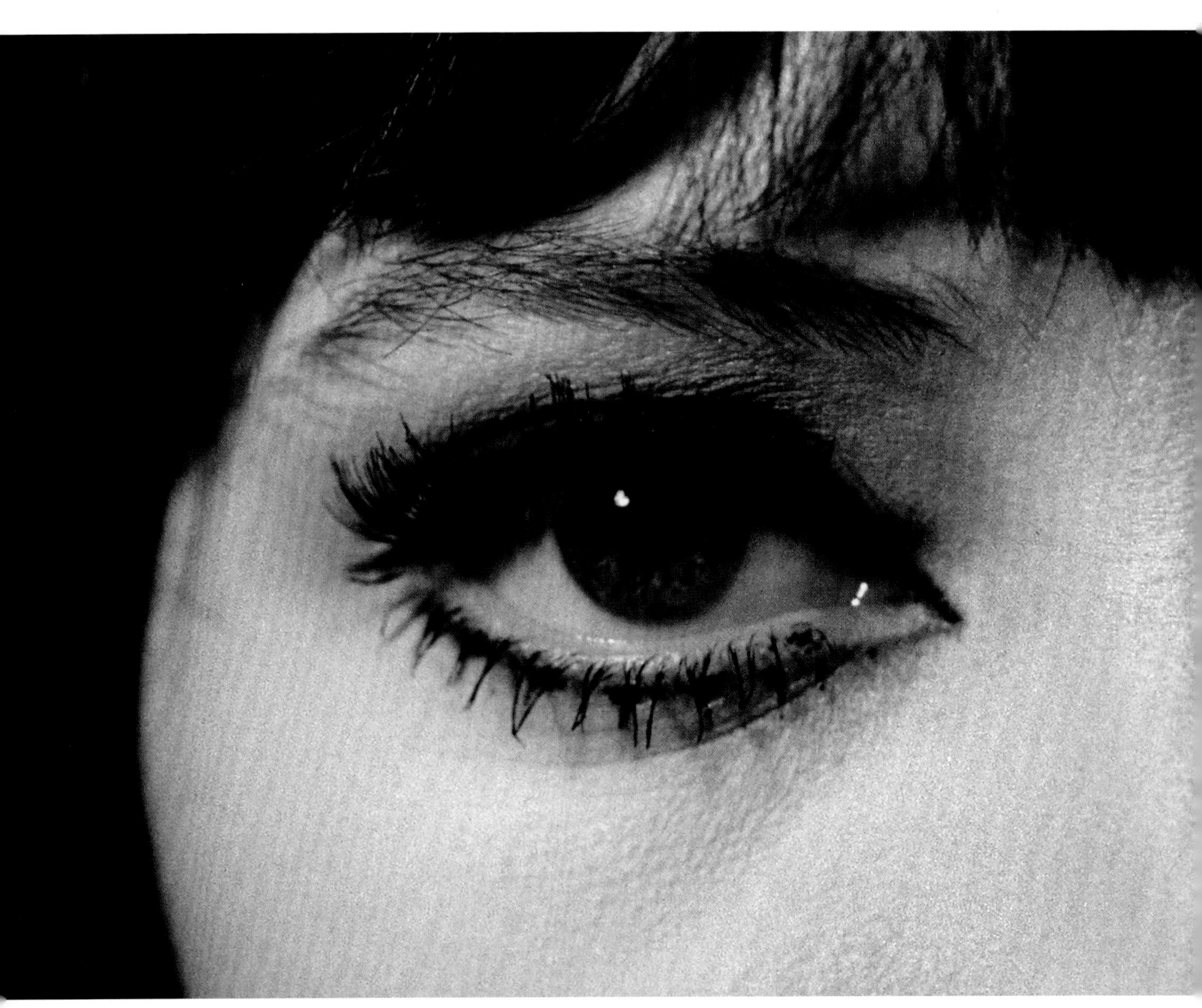

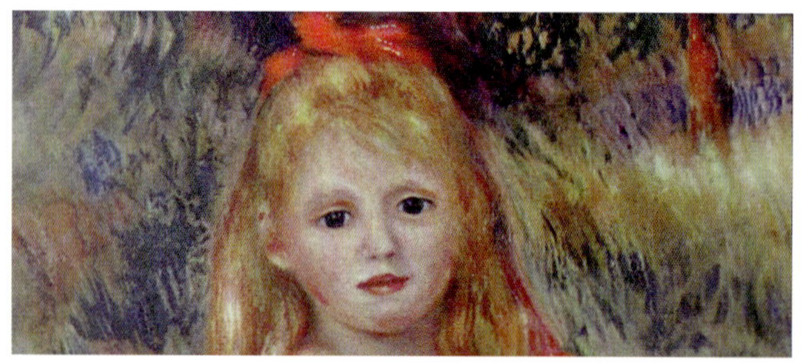

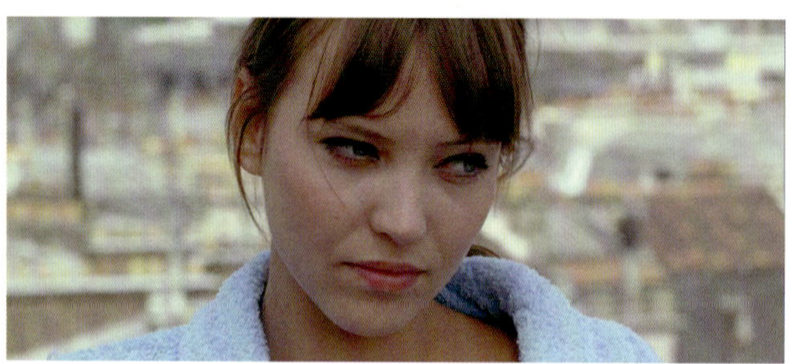

Never would I have believed that you would please me
forever
Oh my love
Never we would have thought we could live together
without getting tired of each other

. . .

Let's hang onto the feeling that our love, from day to day,

That our love is a love with no tomorrow

Belmondo's face in the scene communicates anxiety and re-gret but also the vestiges of love that Marianne's lyrics, sung by Karina, could provoke in Godard. Marianne ambiguously comments after the song, "As for me, I know I love you, but as for you, I'm not so sure. I'm not sure." Ferdinand responds by saying, "Yes, Marianne, yes, I do!"

Karina looks to the camera many times (an implicit reference to Harriet Andersson's famous close-up in *Summer with Monika*), as if questioning Godard (and the viewer). We are made to feel her side of the story, and the misunderstand-ings and disappointments in their relationship, captured by Godard's camera.

Throughout the film, this attempt to recuperate the couple's idyllic love appears along with their disillusionment and frustration. The scene on the island where they live out a *Robinson Crusoe*-style story is at once an echo of the cou-ple in *Monika* and a reconstruction of the camaraderie that characterized Karina and Godard's early relationship. Here, Marianne walks freely along the beach, runs through the for-est, and sings, reflecting Karina's own lighthearted vivacity—and the opposite of the static shots that imprisoned her in *Vivre sa vie*. But soon Ferdinand is lost, immersed in the *idea* of beauty and happiness in his books, mirroring Godard's own tendencies. While Godard was extremely active, he was also consumed by books and ideas; Karina liked perform-ing and engaging with the world. In this scene, Marianne embodies the truth of their relationship, siding with reality against Ferdinand's fiction, the two also illustrating the ten-sion between a life of contemplation (Godard) and a life of action (Karina), as Godard described it.[83]

In the following scene, Marianne descends from the realm of art to the posture of everyday life. Dressed in a blue bathrobe (echoing Bardot's red one in *Le Mépris*), Marianne sings of their failed relationship. Unplanned, the song was inserted in the film as another interlude, reflecting the freedom in which the film was made, evoking the digressions in *Bande à part*. The composer Serge Rezvani (who also composed the famous "Le Tourbillon" for *Jules et Jim*) and his wife happened to be living near the site of the shoot. Open to spontaneity and these chance encounters, Godard integrated two of Rezvani's songs, "Jamais je n'ai dit que je t'aimerai toujours," (meaning, "never did I tell you that I would love you forever"; sometimes called "Sans lendemain," "no tomorrow"), and "Ma Ligne de chance" (meaning, "my line of luck"), into the film.[82]

In the first, Karina sings about the couple's everyday life as she did in *Une femme est une femme*, but the words of the song tell a different story here, one of the realities of a pas-sionate, erratic, and doomed relationship:

Never, I never told you that I would love you forever
Oh my love
Never, you never promised to adore me all my live
Never, we never exchanged such vows, knowing me,
knowing you

. . .

Above: Pierre-Auguste Renoir's *Petite fille à la gerbe*, 1888, and Anna Karina (Marianne) in Jean-Luc Godard's *Pierrot le fou*, 1965

Right: Anna Karina (Marianne) and Jean-Paul Belmondo (Pierrot/Ferdinand) during the sequence of "Jamais je n'ai dit que je t'aimerai toujours" in Godard's *Pierrot le fou*, 1965

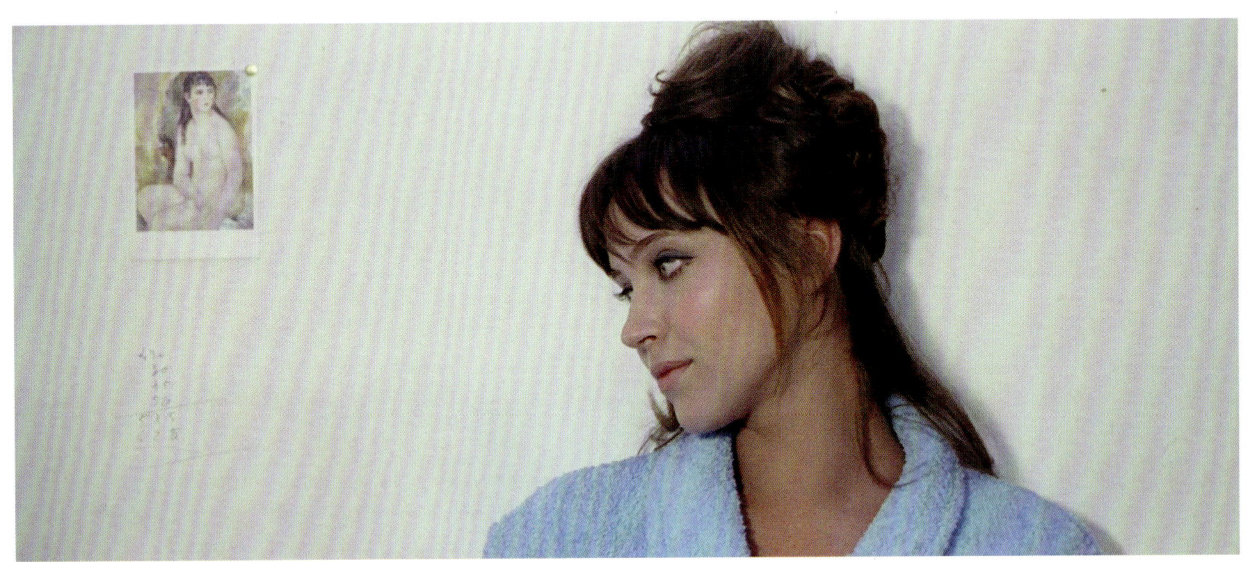

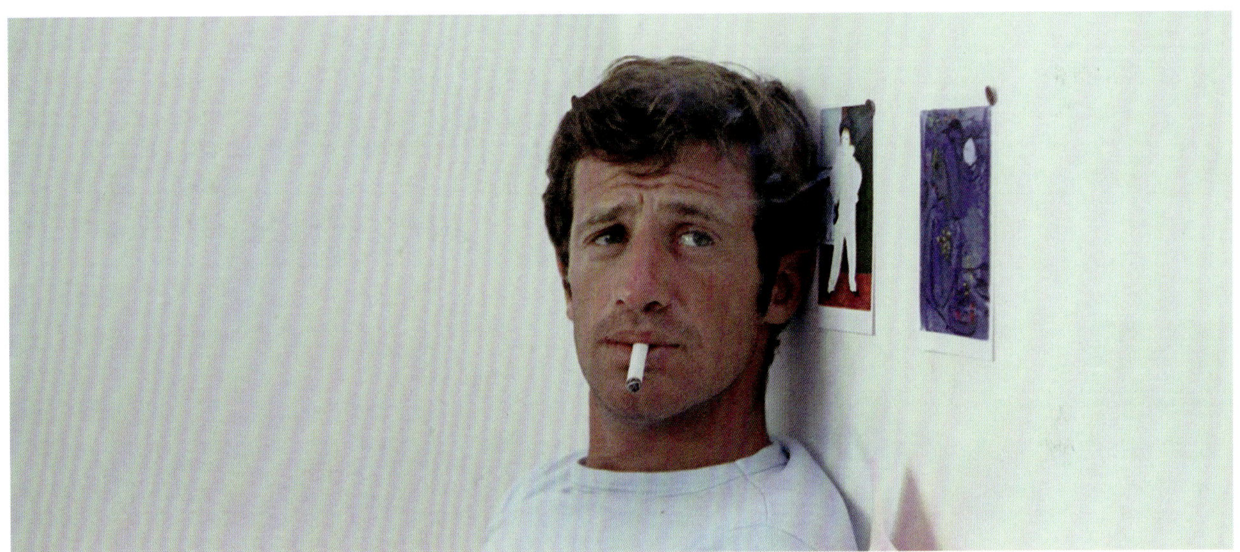

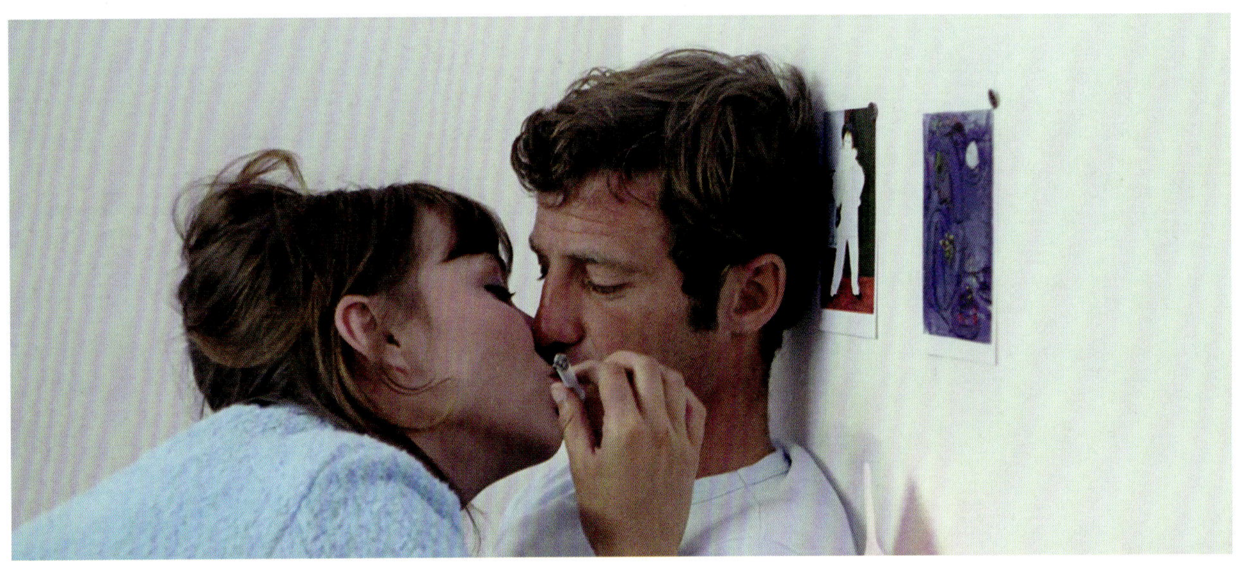

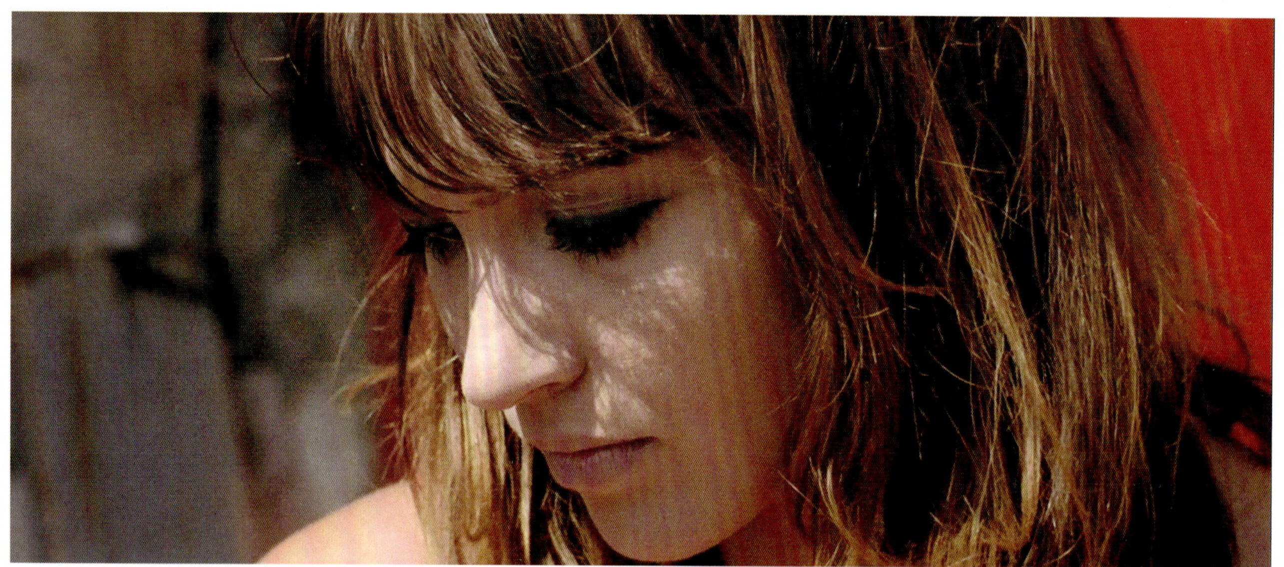

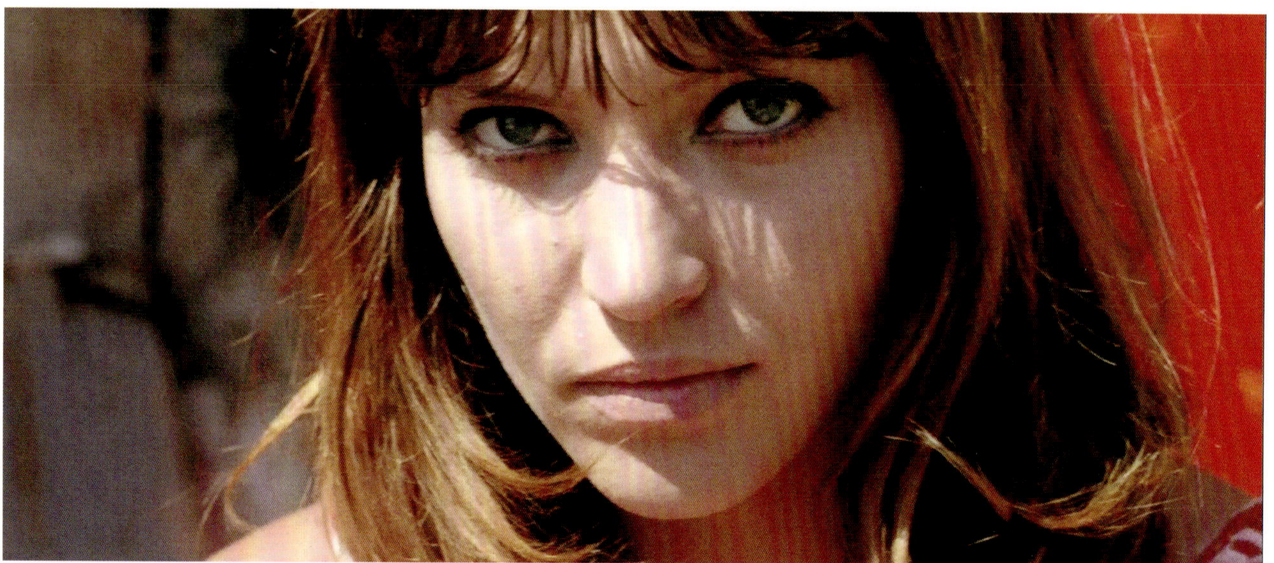

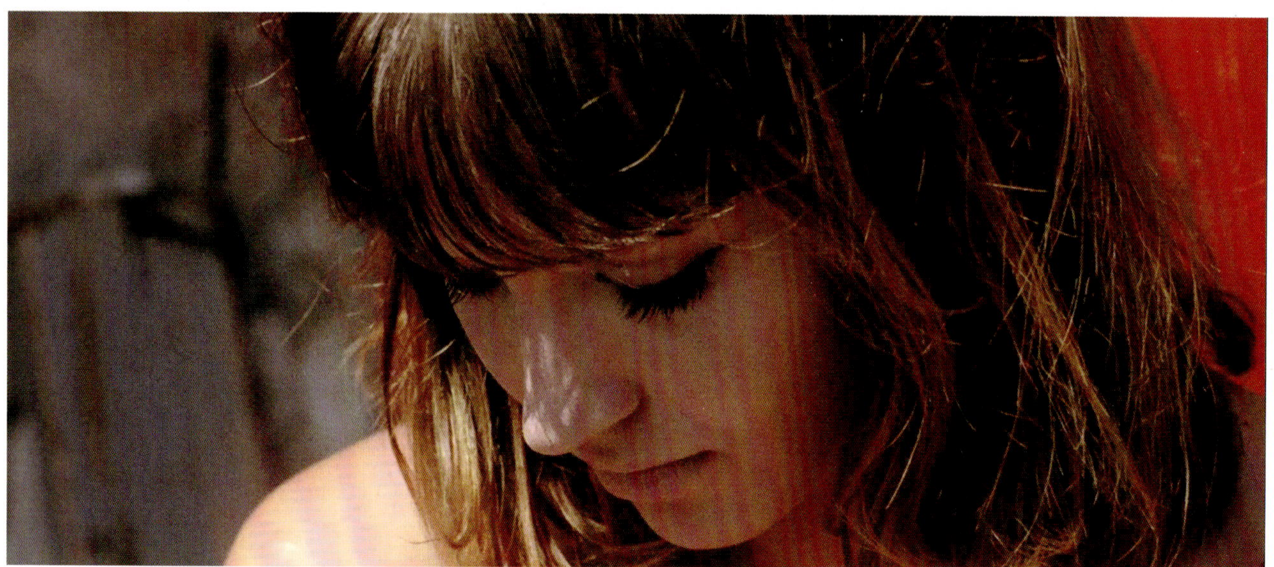

"You speak to me with words, but I look at you with feelings," Marianne tells Ferdinand, a line that Karina recognized as a parallel to their private life—and perhaps also an acknowledgement that Godard knew his own words hardly sufficed to make up for his caprices. "He would write me beautiful letters but then I wouldn't see him for three weeks because he would go out to buy cigarettes and never come back. It was very strange. He would suddenly leave, and then I would be sitting there in front of the telephone, waiting," Karina said. "He always came back with a present," she remembered, along with documents written in languages that helped her deduce where he had been. Swedish suggested a visit with Bergman in London or Sweden; Italian meant a trip to see Roberto Rossellini in Italy; and English implied time in New York with William Faulkner.[84] These spontaneous absences affected Karina on more than just an emotional level. "As a woman, you didn't have any checkbooks, you didn't have any money," Karina explained. "So he was off seeing Ingmar Bergman in Sweden or William Faulkner in America. And I was sitting around the apartment without any food."[85]

Here again, we can feel the unspoken autobiographical echoes as Marianne takes Ferdinand's book and enumerates a list of broken promises: China, Tibet, the Sunda Islands, "marvelous and magical plants—where is all that? Sham sham sham ra ta tam, I took him at his lies." Oblivious, Ferdinand asks, "Will you never leave me?" to which she equivocates, "Of course not. Yes, of course," an ambiguous response given in a series of shots where she looks straight into the camera (at Godard, and at us as viewers), adding more confusion and doubt to the answer she has just given. Behind the shots of Marianne are the traces of Bergman's Monika, who betrays her husband and looks into the director's camera defiantly. Unlike Bergman, Godard punishes Marianne, as Ferdinand targets her with his bow and arrows (as the director does with his camera).

Marianne's lines near the end of the film articulate Karina's will to live, to stay on the side of life: "In the end, I don't care, but he doesn't even understand that. I don't care about anything, books, records; I don't care about anything, even money. Me, what I want is to live, but he will never understand that." After disappointments, broken promises, and

heartache, her character's trajectory mirrors her own, and Marianne's plea to live anticipates Karina's next chapters as she went on to define herself as an artist without Godard.

The life that Karina gave to Godard's films emanated from a deep sensibility and extraordinary presence that, even in her dimmest moments, lit up the screen. But her own hardships in the reality of their relationship also lent a sadness and depth to certain scenes. She functions "as both a life force and a death force" across Godard's films, in Sragow's view, much like how Marianne "awakens Ferdinand's desire and his ambition to create, but she's also a thrill seeker and a killer."[86]

Godard's real-life enactment of the Oval Portrait syndrome traversed his films with Karina violently. A reference to the car accident killing Bardot's Camille at the end of *Le Mépris* appears near the beginning of *Pierrot* in a scene where Marianne and Ferdinand stumble upon a burning car wrecked in a field. Inside the car is a mannequin wearing a black wig, a detail that makes it even more troubling. Near the end, Ferdinand reads Élie Faure's seminal early-twentieth-century book *Histoire de l'art* (*History of Art*) in a movie theater where newsreels roll on Vietnam. Next to him is Jean-Pierre Léaud and on screen Jean Seberg, taking up her role of Patricia in a fragment of the short Godard had made for the episodic film *Les Plus belles escroqueries du monde* (*The World's Most Beautiful Swindlers*, 1964). "Your story ends here," her voice in the film within the film announces. The heroine of *À bout de souffle* now holds a camera (having become a journalist), filming Godard's lens through her own. In voice-over, she suggests the complicated relationship between actor, fictional character, and director (as Belmondo and Léaud look on): "Yes, he turned his back on me, leaving me perplexed," Seberg's character states, a line out of context that can be applied to Godard, as her director. "The care of looking for which moment she [implying herself as Patricia] had abandoned the fictional character to take the real one back. It is in her that he existed"—the idea applies to Seberg's fictional character and Godard, the director. These last words resonate loudly, also calling to mind Karina's many characters and the ways in which Godard combined (or confused?) fiction with reality, confounding the couple's cinematic and real-life story.

Anna Karina (Marianne) in Godard's *Pierrot le fou*, 1965

As Marianne leaves with another man near the end of *Pierrot*, it is as if she is about to realize her dream of "leaving" and "living." Marianne escapes on a boat, alive, but immediately after, she is shot (by a gun and the camera), just like Nana in *Vivre sa vie*. Ferdinand takes her in his arms and carries her to bed while reproaching her, justifying her killing: "You shouldn't have done that." Marianne asks his forgiveness but dies in close-up. Godard punishes her as well as himself.

In the final scene, Ferdinand blows himself up with dynamite in primary colors after failing to realize the idiocy of his act in time. In *Cahiers du cinéma*, Godard pointed to "Marianne Renoir" (Karina) reading a text by Cesare Pavese in the film that says, "You should never ask which came first, words or things, nor what will come next, you feel alive, that's the only important thing." For Godard, this was the true image of cinema reflecting the Oval Portrait: "At the very moment I was sure I had captured life, it escaped me for this reason," he said in 1965.[87] To film, for Godard, was a fatal declaration of love. In his films were the deaths of Karina's characters—in line with the Oval Portrait and Seberg/Patricia's comment describing the confusion between actor and fictional character—also a result of Godard not finding the balance between Karina as an actress and the love of his life, another way of punishing both of them?

It was only in the world of cinema, then, that a truly harmonious encounter for Godard and Karina existed, a creative universe to which they gave their lives. Karina channeled her life force into her characters even when her real life was marked by tragedy, which Godard paid homage to through Marianne. *Pierrot le fou* ends with the hope of eternity reuniting the couple through the realm of poetry and cinema as Ferdinand and Marianne recite Arthur Rimbaud's "L'Éternité" from *Une saison en enfer* ("Eternity" from *A Season in Hell*, 1873): "It's been found again. What? Eternity. It's the sea uniting with the sun," leaving the viewer with a depiction of Godard's eternity in shades of blue, uniting water and sky. Ultimately, Godard would have the final say in Karina's destiny—and theirs as a couple—in *les années Karina* on screen.

The light in *Pierrot le fou* may have finally burned out in *Made in U.S.A.* (1966), the couple's final film together, a sort of postscript. Opening with a close-up of Karina with her eyes closed, the film focuses on the book she holds: *Adieu la vie, adieu l'amour*, the French edition of Horace McCoy's 1948 American novel *Kiss Tomorrow Good-bye*. It announces the final chapter of their story. Karina's character, Paula, looks in the mirror and says, "It's been over for a long time. Yes, it's all been over for a long time." Then, looking *away* from the camera, she says, "He telegraphed me three days ago. I could only come yesterday. We barely saw each other anymore. I don't know if I still love him in the end. But I owed it to him because of this love."

Years after their separation, Godard stated that for him, as an artist, he had exhausted his professional and intellectual relationship with Karina and had lost his desire to film her. Whether truth or fiction, his words again reflected a component of the Oval Portrait syndrome. Claiming that "when the page is turned, it is turned," Godard went on to emphasize, however, the value of their story and work together, adding, "but the book is there." In effect, their cowritten oeuvre of seven chapters stands as one of the most profound and innovative in the history of cinema. Confirming the collaborative aspect of the actor/director relationship, Godard stated, "Just as it is impossible to be solely behind, it is impossible to be uniquely in front of the camera."[88] More than a simple muse, Karina influenced Godard's early and most celebrated films in a way that was unparalleled by any actor in his later work. "I like the earlier ones better," Karina admitted. "The earlier ones are human, the later ones abstract. Like Cubist paintings—not so fun."[89] Film scholar Jean-Pierre Esquenazi affirmed that after *Pierrot le fou*, the female characters in Godard's films became "discouraging." Karina's disappearance from Godard's films marked the end of "a capacity for empathy or an understanding"[90] that appeared intermittently (along with a strong component of machismo) in *Une femme est une femme*, *Le Mépris*, and *Pierrot le fou*.

"The actor for me is someone who wants to express [something]," Godard said years later. "And even between people who like each other in the beginning—Anna Karina and I were in love with each other, despite the faults we could have after, but all you can say is that cinema is what completely separated us."[91]

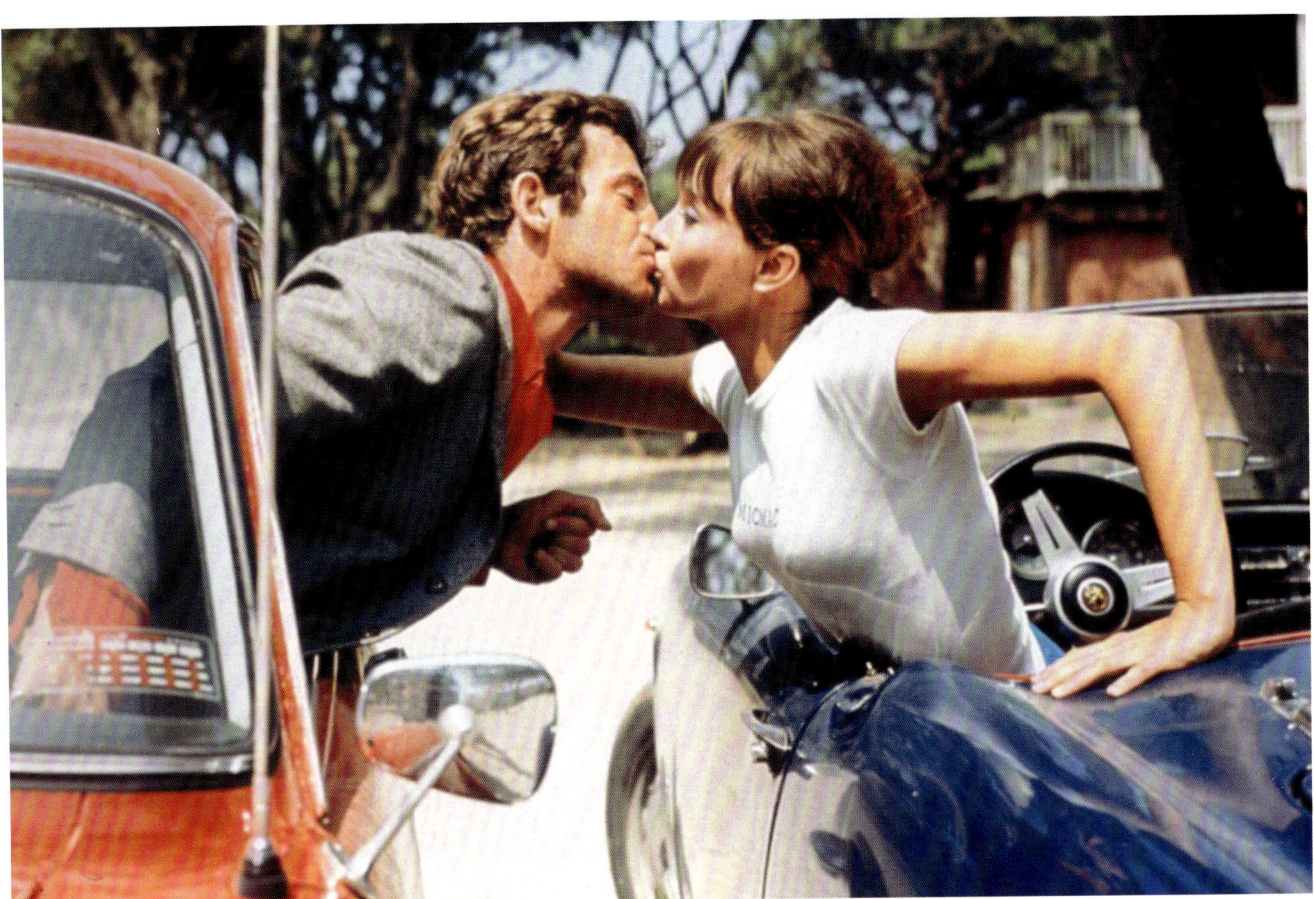

"I think that at that time, I was able to give him my joie de vivre, my happiness,"[92] Karina said. She gave him credit for his profound impact on her—"because he taught me everything . . . in life."[93] To Karina, her experience with Godard served as "a very good school,"[94] and she was an "enthusiastic" student.[95] Late in her career, Karina described their encounter with tenderness and depth: "I found him very fascinating, handsome, with a special kind of strength. Even with his dark glasses, because at first, I didn't really understand this thing with the dark glasses all the time, but when he took them off, he had lovely almond-shaped eyes that were magnificent, and he had something very magnetic. We were both attracted to each other."[96] The actress also reportedly confessed, "He was and will always remain the greatest love of my life."[97]

What is left then is the projection of their history, a fractured story of cinema. It is up to the viewer to unify the fragments of lost love in the films and to let Karina and Godard, and their characters, go their separate ways. In relation to God-

ard's later work, these films allow us to measure the importance of Karina's role, decisive in the modern aspect of her characters and of the *mise en scène*, the stylistic innovations she sparked, the romantic motifs she helped create, and the questions relating to life she revealed. The story of their cinema is also that of a woman breaking away from her initial position as muse or object of desire and gaining the place of subject, creating her characters as well as going on to pursue her own career as an actress, writer, and director. The real relationship between Karina and Godard cannot be reduced to mere biographical points. It opens up into a complex, poetic universe, perhaps joining the "eternity" in Rimbaud's poem that continues to inspire modern cinema to this day.

Jean-Paul Belmondo (Pierrot/Ferdinand) and Anna Karina (Marianne) in Godard's *Pierrot le fou*, 1965

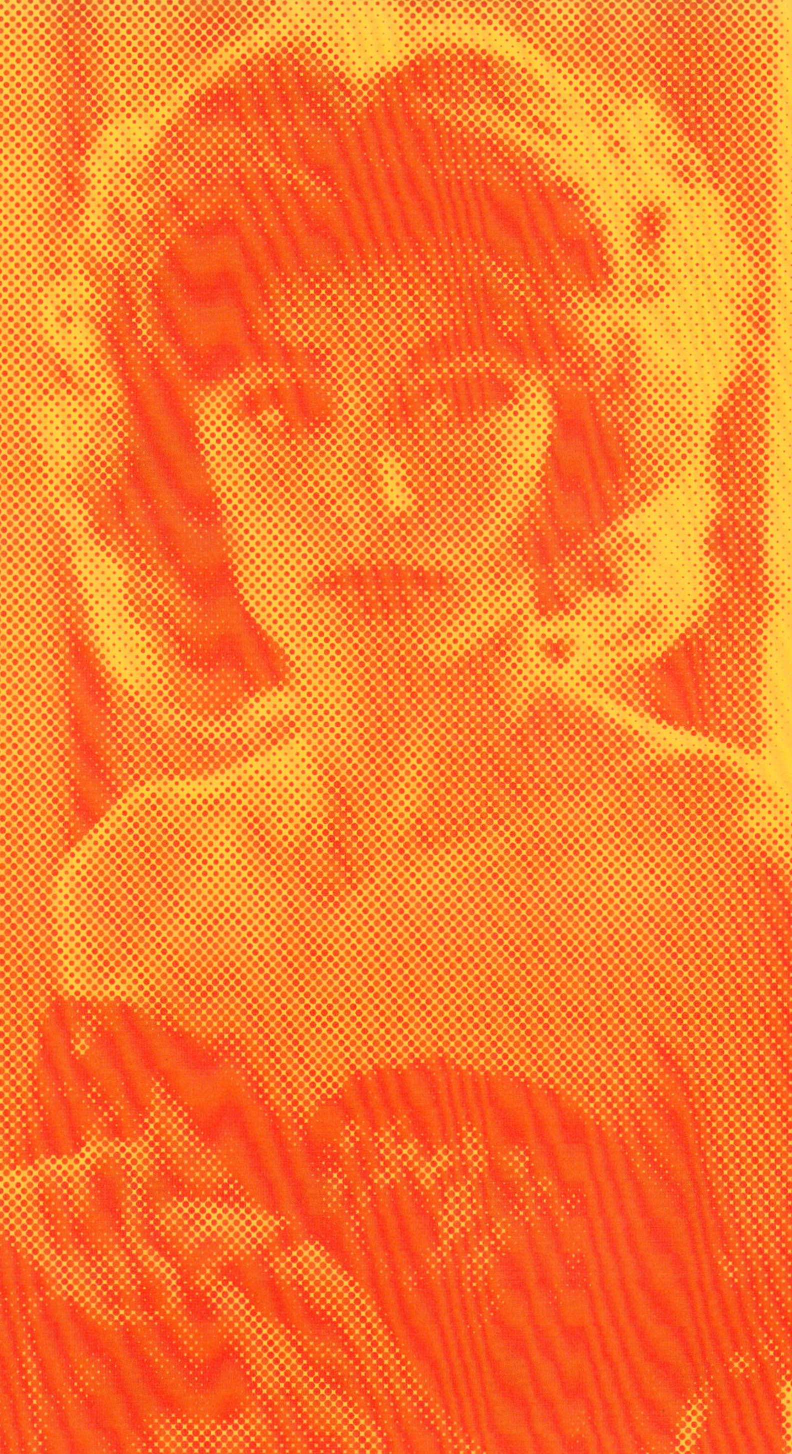

anouk aimée 6

la prostituée romantique | *the romantic prostitute*

PROJECTIONS OF THE PROSTITUTE: ABSENT BODIES, AFFECTIVE SUBSTITUTES

As the Nazi threat loomed in 1940, eight-year-old Nicole Françoise Florence Dreyfus (whose father was Jewish) moved from Paris to Poitou-Charentes with her parents for their safety. As an added precaution, they baptized their daughter Catholic (though she converted to Judaism as an adult). In 1946, the young girl's destiny would take a turn.[1] While walking home from the movies with her mother in Paris, she was approached by the director Henri Calef, who hired her for a small part in his film *La Maison sous la mer* (*The House Under the Sea*, 1947). At age fourteen, she played the role of Anouk and later decided to keep it as her first name. Prévert, who wrote the leading role in André Cayatte's *Les Amants de Vérone* (*The Lovers of Verona*, 1949) specifically for her, coined her surname: *Aimée*, meaning "beloved." In 1952, twenty-year-old Anouk Aimée landed the leading role in *Le Rideau cramoisi* (*The Crimson Curtain*, 1953), a short written and directed by Alexandre Astruc, who applied his ideas of the *caméra-stylo* to the story of Albertine, a *jeune fille sage* (well-behaved girl), daughter of elegant but strict parents belonging to the haute bourgeoisie who find themselves hosting a young soldier during the Napoleonic Wars. In an early illustration of female agency and desire, Astruc shows Aimée rebelling against her imposed constraints by taking the soldier's hand under her parents' dinner table and beginning a passionate affair with him. Though it ends tragically, Aimée opened the cage to expressing desire as a young woman.

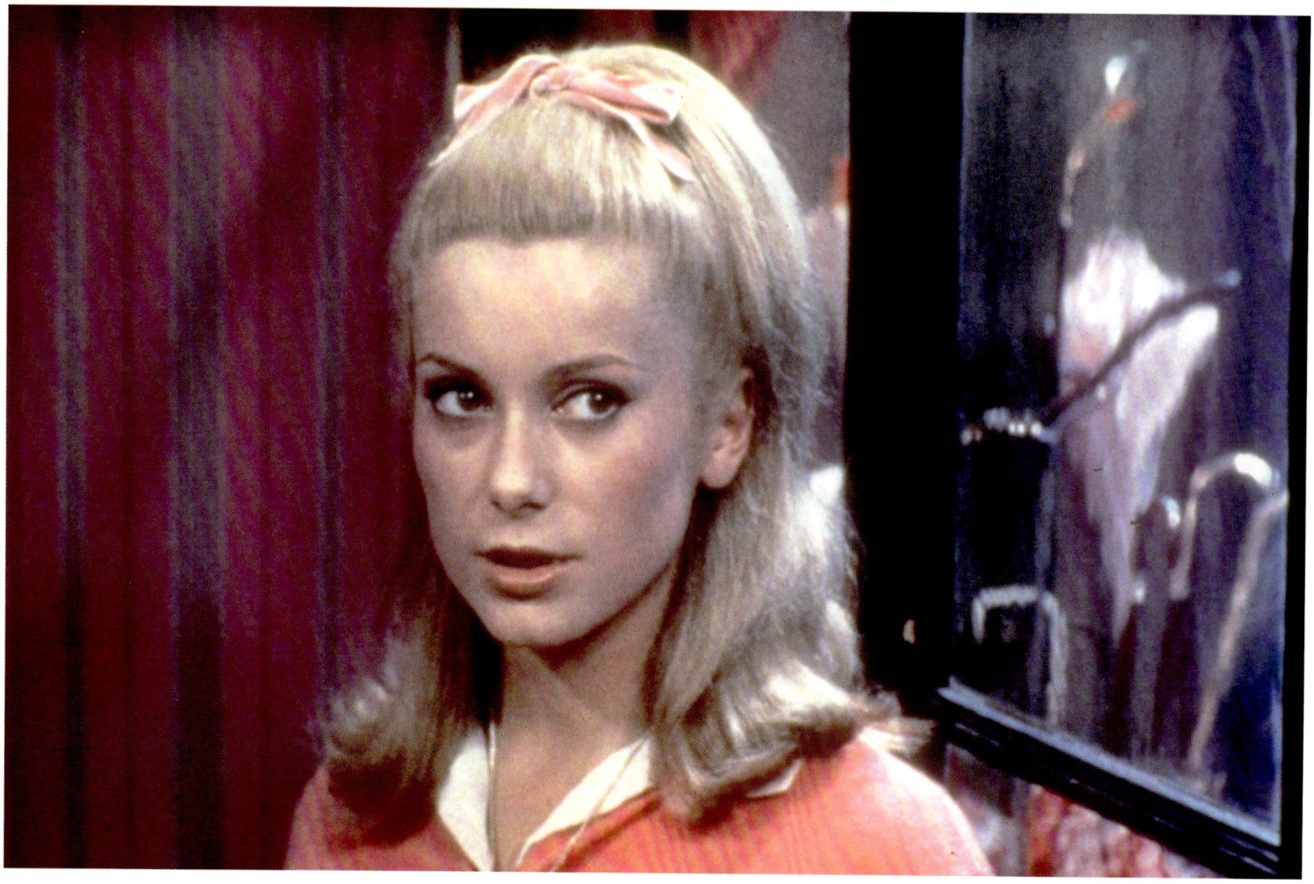

By 1961, Aimée had already acted in many French films and had recently become famous for her role in Federico Fellini's *La dolce vita* (1960). She was not, however, considered a New Wave actress. Her allure in Fellini's film, her elegance and unconventional look, distanced her from the young generation of actresses and placed her especially far from the reality of the prostitute she would play in Jacques Demy's *Lola* (1961).

This was not unlike Catherine Deneuve's unconventional casting in a later film about a prostitute. In Luis Buñuel's *Belle de Jour* (1967), Deneuve in the role of a chic, bourgeois wife turned prostitute was surprising. Not only were the director's surrealist fantasy scenes imagined by the heroine scandalous, but Deneuve in the role–transformed after playing the emotionally fragile and repressed Carol in Roman Polanski's *Repulsion* (1965) and the hopeless romantic Geneviève in Jacques Demy's award-winning musical *Les Parapluies de Cherbourg* (*The Umbrellas of Cherbourg*, 1964)–added an extra element of shock value.

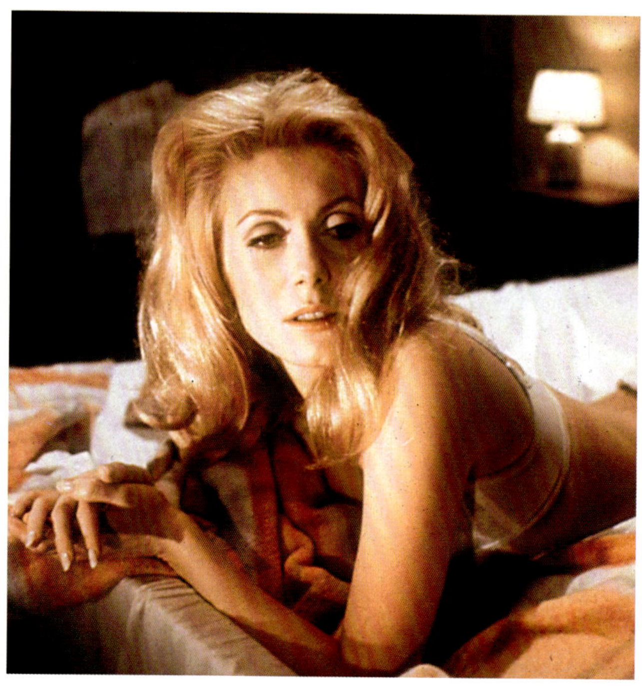

Catherine Deneuve in Jacques Demy's *Les Parapluies de Cherbourg* (*The Umbrellas of Cherbourg*), 1964, and in Luis Buñuel's *Belle de jour*, 1967

In Demy's film, Deneuve's demure girl-next-door character pledges to remain faithful to her true love, Guy (Nino Castelnuovo), before he leaves for the Algerian War. Fate would decide otherwise. After learning she had become pregnant before his departure, she writes to Guy, but his lack of response leads her to believe that he no longer cares for her. Geneviève ends up marrying a wealthy jeweler, and Guy returns wounded from the war, bringing a melancholy ending to the fairy-tale beginning. It is the fairy tale, however, that lingers in the collective memory with Deneuve singing (dubbed by Danielle Licari) Michel Legrand's famous composition, featuring lyrics by Demy, "Je ne pourrai jamais vivre sans toi"—literally, "I will never be able to live without you." (Norman Gimbel's English-language version was simply titled "I Will Wait for You.")

After such a role, Deneuve playing out scenes of sadomasochism on screen was even more transgressive. Like Hitchcock's cinematic predilection for proper women who are seductive behind closed doors, in Buñuel's film, Deneuve plays a prostitute by day (hence her pseudonym, Belle de Jour) and a proper wife by night, Séverine Serizy. Conveying the consequences of the Madonna-whore complex from a female perspective, Buñuel depicts a woman who assumes her role as a perfect bourgeois housewife who resorts to fantasy to express her desire, as she is unable to assume it with her husband whom she loves. Sparked by her curiosity when she learns of a mutual friend who works in a high-class bordello, Séverine enters prostitution almost by chance. As she gains experience, her relationship improves with her husband. However, when she meets Marcel (Pierre Clémenti), a young criminal who fulfills her fantasies through violence and becomes possessive, her double life is under threat of being exposed. Unlike Karina's Nana in *Vivre sa vie*, Deneuve's Belle de Jour gets out alive in the end, also managing to leave prostitution to achieve agency. The male characters, however, do not enjoy this fate. Marcel, becoming jealous of her husband, shoots him, leaving him disabled, and Marcel is mortally wounded by the police. Though Séverine returns to her role as wife in the end, reestablishing the social order, she subtly subverts it by gaining power over her husband (now in a wheelchair) and over her own sexuality. Resolving her dilemma, she informs her husband in the end, "Ever since your accident, I don't dream

anymore," implying that her fantasies have stopped. Resolving also his disability through her (implied) fantasy, in the ambiguous final scene, her husband stands up and leaves his wheelchair to resume their married life together.

The New Wave directors never went as far as Buñuel in their *mise en scène* of prostitution, of love scenes, or in depicting women's agency, even if prostitute figures appeared frequently in their films. Comparing the audacious portrayal of a prostitute in *Belle de Jour* with those of the New Wave shows how they used the figure differently. Instead of using the prostitute as a pretext to justify provocative scenes, New Wave directors left most of their portraits devoid of any scandal at all. Demy filmed Aimée as a prostitute from a sublimated perspective, like Godard did with Karina in *Vivre sa vie*, in which he also addressed prostitution under the angle of documentary, while Truffaut chose pure fantasy or evacuated the tension through humor. These elevated fantasy images of the prostitute seemed to play another role, often filling an affective void for their clients in exchange for money—a relationship that could extend metaphorically to the actresses who sometimes played a similar role for their male directors. What do prostitutes represent in the collective imagination at the time for these directors—often labeled "neoromantics"—and for the women who play them?

France's history regarding prostitution is defined by ambivalence. Considering it a "necessary evil" from the late eighteenth century to the mid-twentieth century, according to a 2018 report on prostitution policies in France, the country implemented requirements for women in prostitution to register at the municipal level and undergo health checks.[2] During the Vichy regime, prostitution was only allowed in brothels—many of which were colluding with the German military—but France banned metropolitan brothels in 1946. As a result, prostitutes no longer had to operate outside of society at large. The greatest stride in permitting prostitution as a private occupation came in 1960, when France ratified the code developed by a 1949 United Nations conference on prostitution and human trafficking—ending registration and health checks, criminalizing prostitution establishments and other third-party business, and more or less validating sex work as self-employment.

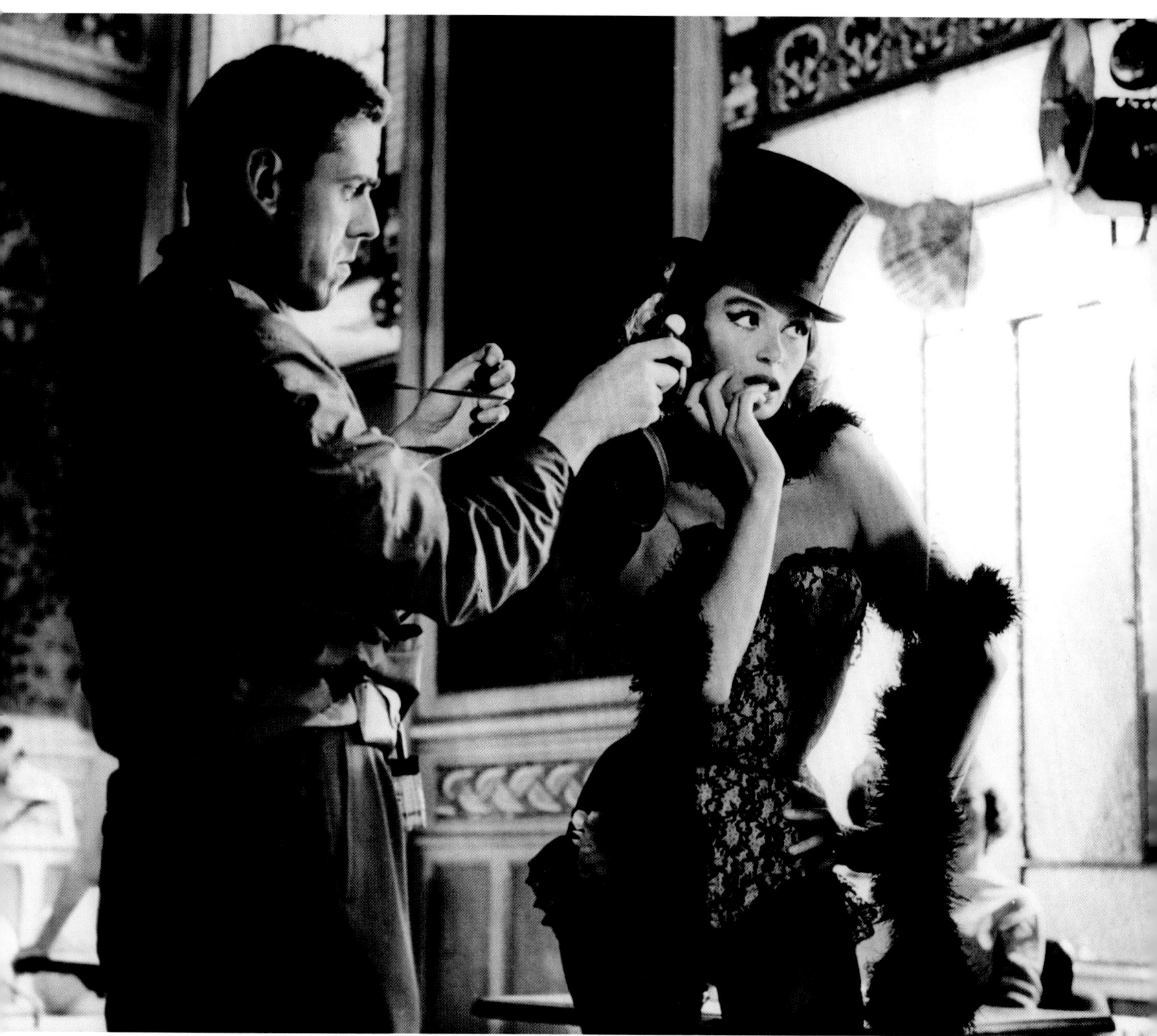

The messaging surrounding this move reflects an incongruity in French policy as well as in French society: Legal writing that accompanied ratification "defined prostitution as a social evil, along with tuberculosis, alcoholism and homosexuality," per the 2018 report, which effectively positioned prostitutes as "socially maladjusted persons who need social work assistance."[3] In other words, though not prohibited, it is implied that prostitution should not exist. These conflicting notions have shaped how society views not only women who become prostitutes but by extension, women in general.

A recurring figure in French literature and cinema, the prostitute has inspired an incalculable number of works, with portraits that are sometimes tender but always ambivalent. One of the most famous is Émile Zola's 1880 novel *Nana*, which inspired Jean Renoir's 1926 film of the same name as well as Karina's Nana in *Vivre sa vie*. Another key depiction of a dangerous woman with a questionable reputation comes from *Manon Lescaut* (1731) by L'Abbé Prévost, whose "man-eating" heroine can be seen on screen in Henri-Georges Clouzot's *Manon* (1949) and Jean Aurel's *Manon 70* (1968). Deneuve, who portrayed Manon in the latter film, would indirectly evoke the character again in Truffaut's *La Sirène du Mississipi* (*Mississippi Mermaid*, 1969). A variation of this type of character is also found in Pierre Louÿs's 1898 novel *La Femme et le pantin* (*The Woman and the Puppet*), adapted for film a handful of times throughout the twentieth century, including Julien Duvivier's 1959 version starring Brigitte Bardot. Adding to this list are *La Dame aux camélias* (*The Lady of the Camellias*, 1848) by Alexandre Dumas fils (son of the author of *The Three Musketeers*) and its 1934 adaptation by Abel Gance; Max Ophüls's 1952 film *Le Plaisir* (*House of Pleasure*), adapted from stories by Guy de Maupassant; and *Casque d'or* by Jacques Becker (1952) with Simone Signoret.[4] How do these literary and cinematic references and the reality of prostitution in France influence the New Wave directors' depiction of prostitutes, and why does the figure appear so often in their films?

LOLA: ANOUK AIMÉE AND JACQUES DEMY'S PURELY CINEMATIC ROMANCE

Raoul Coutard (cinematographer) and Anouk Aimée (Lola) on the set of Jacques Demy's *Lola*, 1961

"When Jacques gave me Lola, it was a marvelous gift. Lola is such a part of me that I can't tell which part is her and which is me. We've grown so close that we mimic each other." – Anouk Aimée in Agnès Varda's *L'Univers de Jacques Demy* (*The World of Jacques Demy*, 1995).

In his homage to Max Ophüls, Jacques Demy in *Lola* (1961) brings to the screen a romantic vision of the title character embodied by Anouk Aimée, almost ignoring her status as a prostitute. In the spirit of Ophüls's *Le Plaisir*, which Demy cites as a reference, prostitution is normalized in the second installment adapted from Maupassant's short story "La Maison Tellier" (1881). "Men went [to the brothel] every night like they would go to a café," the narrator of Ophüls's film recounts, similarly describing Julia Tellier (Madeleine Renaud), the madam, as practicing her trade "just as if she'd been a hatmaker or dressmaker." Incarnating the romantic and maternal Madame Rosa (who works at the brothel), Danielle Darrieux provided a model for Demy's Lola that would come to life in his own film through Aimée.

Like Bardot and Vadim, and Karina and Godard, Anouk Aimée's encounter with Demy produced a character born of the actress's presence and the director's fantasy, brought into the cinematic world through their meeting in front of the camera. Different from these other notable actress/director couples, however, Aimée and Demy were not romantically involved. At the time, Demy had started seeing Varda, whom he first met at a short-film festival in Tours[5] and started living with in 1959. Their romantic encounter intermingled discreetly with their creative one. Varda recalled Demy asking her to read the script for *Lola* as early as 1958,[6] and she later visited the set during the shoot and even wrote the film's theme song. Demy did not have the reputation of being a *séducteur* like Truffaut or a desire to imitate famous director/actress couples like Godard sought with Karina, but Varda compared Lola to Arletty's Garance in 1945's *Les Enfants du Paradis* (written by poet Jacques Prévert): "Like Prévert invented the character of Garance, Jacques created Lola."[7]

Demy would go on to marry Varda, and the couple enjoyed a profound bond and love of cinema lasting beyond his death in 1990 as Varda continued to celebrate his work in her own. (In 2008, she revealed that Demy, who was bisexual, had died of complications from AIDS.)[8]

Demy's encounter with Anouk Aimée sparked a purely cinematic romance. Though their relationship did not include off-screen passion, Demy and Aimée shaped the character of Lola together in much the same way that romantically involved actress-director couples had done before them. Known for their fantasy, color, and dreamlike atmosphere, Demy's films are also tinged with melancholy, not unlike his own life as well as Aimée's, given their pasts during the war. Demy, perhaps seeing something in Aimée that went against type, chose her for the role of Lola against the wishes of producers Georges de Beauregard and Carlo Ponti.

Through Jean-Louis Trintignant—who would costar with her later in Claude Lelouch's *Un homme et une femme* (*A Man and a Woman*, 1966)—Aimée learned that Demy wanted to meet her.[9] During their conversation at Les Deux Magots, the director told her that he had written a story with her in mind. She confessed to loving it right away: "The fact that he'd thought of me for this character who was completely unlike what I'd done before. I'd always played the ingénue, the young girl in love. This character was so original. He fought for me. I know people were suggesting other actresses who were prettier and sexier. And he said, 'No, I want Anouk.' I'll never forget that."[10] Aimée described Lola as "a lovely person. One of those characters Jacques [Prévert] would create who stepped out of one of his poems. She's devoid of any sort of aggressiveness or vulgarity or exhibitionism."[11]

Aimée's description of the character seems to summarize perfectly Demy's approach to Lola, but his approach to life might be better summarized in *Lola's* opening: "Pleure qui peut, rit qui veut" ("Cry who can, laugh who wants to"), quoting the renowned Renaissance essayist Michel de Montaigne. Despite hardships such as the trauma of war that defined the childhood of most New Wave directors and actors, Demy chose to see life through a lens of laughter and joy, a coping strategy that he projected onto Aimée's character in the film. The other characters adopt these same strategies. Disempowered men and financially jeopardized women try to get by the best they can, like Demy, through escapism, either by dreaming of another place or a lost love—or by going to the movies.

Originally titled *Un billet pour Johannesbourg* (*A Ticket for Johannesburg*),[12] the film translates the dream of escaping to a faraway land, one that Roland Cassard, Demy's male alter ego in *Lola*, dreams of, too. It was Godard who recommended Demy to the producer Georges de Beauregard, who made dreams a reality by betting on young, adventurous directors who became the New Wave. Demy had first planned to make a huge musical comedy that would have cost 250 million francs "in color and Scope with lots of dancing and singing and costumes,"[13] as he described—far from the bare-bones New Wave aesthetic. But Beauregard, who had just made *À bout de souffle* for thirty-two million francs, offered Demy only thirty-five million, obliging the director to cut the songs, costumes, and dancers; to reduce the story to five characters; and to shoot with a skeleton crew. "It wasn't much," Demy confirmed. "I shot in five weeks without sets, costumes, or lights. We had film stock, a camera, and actors."[14] Raoul Coutard, whose camerawork was responsible for the modern style of *À bout de souffle*, made a radical choice for the lighting in *Lola*, shooting in very high contrast, which added to its dreamlike quality. Behind the scenes, the film that started out as a technicolor spectacle became the story of one heroine's dream come true, made on a small budget in the true spirit of the New Wave.

As is often the case, constraints can fuel innovation and performances that create magic on screen. The music, for example, was to be written by Quincy Jones. But because Jones was unable to clear his schedule in time, there was no music during production. Though it was common for sound, including dialogue, to be added in postsynchronization after shooting the images, there was no music to guide Aimée's performance. *Lola's* musical moments had to be filmed without sound. The now-legendary composer Michel Legrand, who took Jones's place, found the film "musical in its silence," and Demy himself described it as "a musical without music."[15] For Lola's cabaret number, Varda and Demy suggested to Aimée that she speak the lyrics (which Varda had written) according to a precise rhythm. They recorded it only

Alan Scott (Frankie) and Anouk Aimée (Lola) in Jacques Demy's *Lola*, 1961

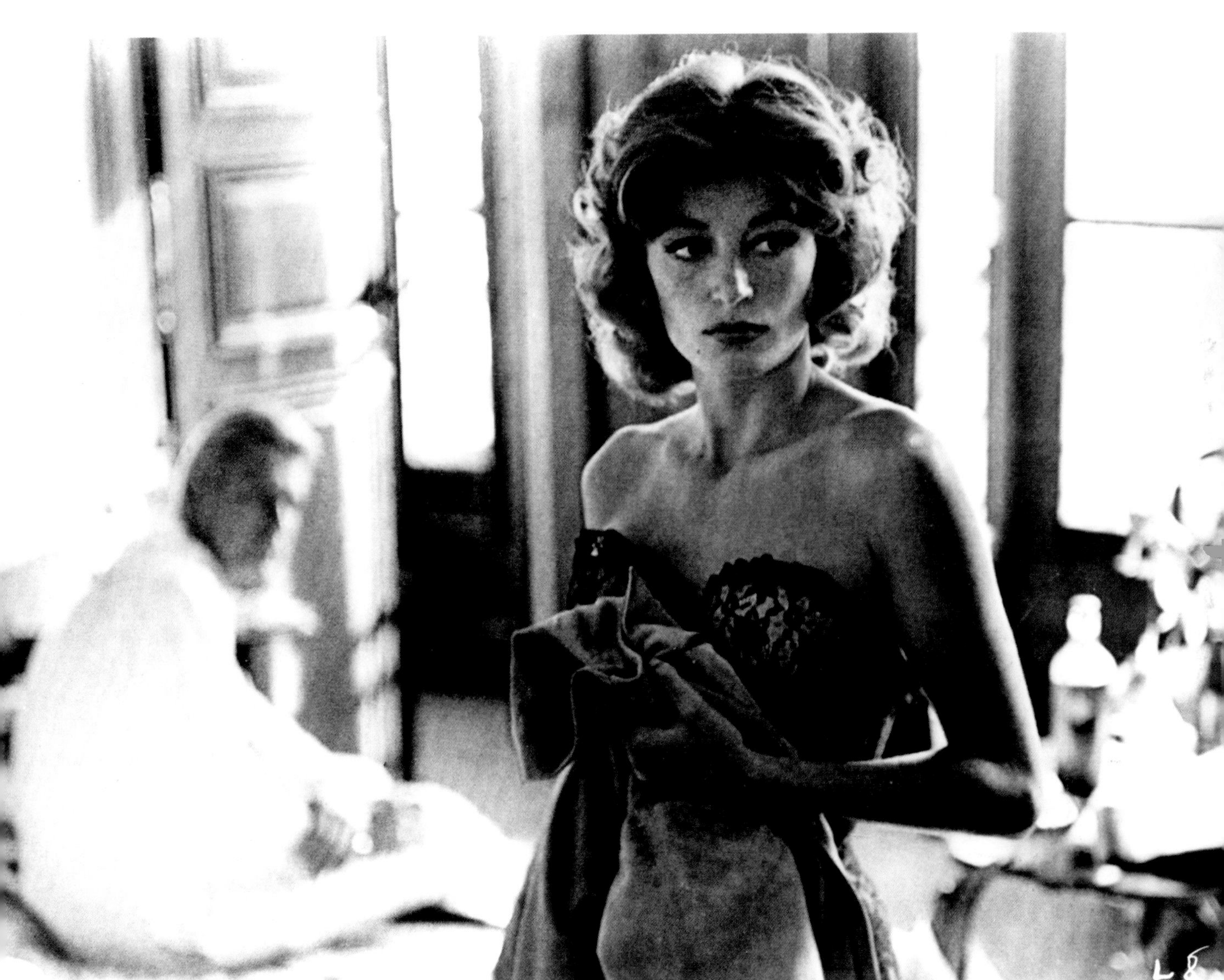

with her voice "like a poetry slam," in Varda's words, with Legrand later creating an accompanying melody. Aimée's performance was a success, and the refrain "C'est moi, c'est Lola" ("It's me, it's Lola") became as emblematic of the film as Aimée's incarnation of Lola, the showgirl fantasy.

LOLA AS BOTH MADONNA AND WHORE

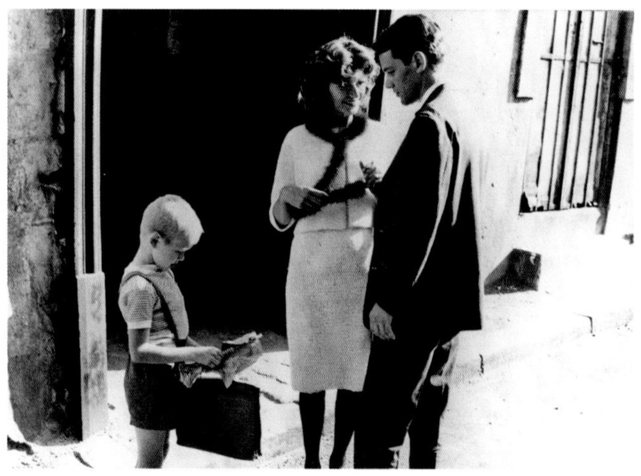

More than a showgirl, Lola is also a mother. We learn that she works in a cabaret in order to make ends meet, as she is raising her son alone, and takes home the clientele in order to make them meet a little more. Although this aspect of her character could provide a perfect pretext for erotic scenes (that were sure to attract moviegoers), there is nothing salacious to be seen here. Lola, instead, exudes a certain purity from the narrative and from the way Demy films her. Who or what, then, is behind the identity of "C'est moi, c'est Lola," the sublimated prostitute?

"Where such men love they have no desire, and where they desire they cannot love," asserted Freud in 1925. The Madonna-whore dichotomy describes the perception and categorization of women as either good and pure (mother figures or Madonnas) or as bad and promiscuous (prostitutes). The complex explains men's anxiety regarding women's sexuality. Splitting them into categories thereby assuages the uncomfortable tension between fear and desire: pure love being reserved for the mother and lust for the whore.[16] Feminist theory suggests, however, that the dichotomy is motivated by a desire to reinforce patriarchy. Related to at-

titudes that not only restrict women's autonomy, it also impairs men's intimate relationships with women,[17] thus producing negative consequences for men as well as women.

Romanticized and inaccessible, Aimée's character embodies the mother while providing a pure image of the desirable whore. She is also simultaneously locked in her own fantasy, that of her (lost) first love, the father of her son. Evolving in a feminine universe equally populated by fantasy figures, Lola works with other showgirls in the cabaret who also make extra money on the side as prostitutes to get by in a man's world. Like Truffaut's collection of prostitutes incarnating stereotyped fantasies in the Antoine Doinel series, Demy's exists in a world of illusion. As in Ophüls's *Lola Montès*, which addresses the question of a woman as spectacle and prisoner of the (viewer's) gaze, Demy's prostitutes are on display in the universe of spectacle, circulating in a space that is apart from the reality outside the doors of the cabaret. None of them fit the description of a risqué showgirl, much less of a prostitute, however. While their profession may be questionable, they are all dreaming of true love with the sensibility of young schoolgirls.

Lola, as imagined by Demy, does not evolve in a typical environment of prostitution but in his dream world, possessing an ethereal quality that distances her from a reality too raw or too ugly to witness. Aimée's presence provides this wistfulness—and Demy incorporated her own idiosyncrasies into the role. From her self-described distracted nature to her speech punctuated by "Ooh" and "Oops," for example, her character can be heard uttering "Oh, I'm lost! Oh, my stocking, oh dear!"[18] Aimée related that the director told her to deliver her lines like Marilyn Monroe, adding an even greater element of fantasy and breathiness to her acting, one that she claimed even influenced her own style.[19] It was also the poetry of the film, she said, that made her act so freely and walk so naturally "only with her nylons on."[20]

Both an ideal vision of femininity and a pure cinematic fabrication, Lola is first seen through the eyes of a group of sailors who pause in front of the Eldorado cabaret to look at her photo on display. When one of them, Frankie, enters to ask if Lola is there, she comes out wearing a black lace corset, clutching

Gérard Delaroche (Yvon, Lola's son), Anouk Aimée (Lola), and Marc Michel (Roland) in Demy's *Lola*, 1961 a cigarette in a long holder. When Frankie tells her that he wants to sleep with her again, she laughs and responds evasively, "I don't." Already, Lola goes against stereotype in her humorous honesty, though she then does leave with Frankie. As they arrive at her apartment building, we discover a little boy playing in the street. It is her son, Yvon, thereby fixing her role as mother as well as prostitute. Leaving her son outside to play, Lola takes Frankie into her apartment, but Demy omits the reality of her profession. Ignoring this unwholesome aspect of her identity in the present, the director chooses to concentrate on the innocence of her past.

As Frankie pulls Lola onto the bed, an abrupt cut to the next sequence shows the young Cécile (a character meant to mirror Lola's past) with her mother outside a bookshop. Instead of showing Lola as a fallen woman, Demy shows how destiny (and war) shapes the paths of the innocent. When Roland (Marc Michel) enters the bookshop and runs into Cécile, he tells her, "I had a childhood friend a long time ago named Cécile, mademoiselle, who looked like you," referring to Lola before she changed her name. "I lost track of her after the war. Your name made me suddenly think of her. You look so much like her that it feels like ten years ago—no, fifteen!" In his memory, Lola still exists with the same innocence as Cécile, who is just about to turn fourteen.

When Roland runs into Lola with her young son by chance shortly after in a covered passageway, he does not recognize her. After she calls his name, he realizes it is the Cécile from his childhood. He tells her about the girl he met who looked like her. "Except you've changed," he adds, since the last time they saw each other before the war. They agree to meet later that night in front of the theater. In the meantime, Roland joins Cécile and her mother for dinner where the young girl tells him she wants to be a dancer, and Lola goes to work in the cabaret.

When they meet that evening on the theater steps, Roland holds the mirror for Lola as she fixes her hair. When they go back to her apartment so she can put Yvon to bed before they go to dinner, again Roland calls her Cécile, reminding her of her innocent past self. "I'm laughing because nobody calls me Cécile anymore," she tells him, explaining that *Lola* is now her *nom de scène*, her stage name. "I'd never recognize you with that hair and makeup," Roland tells her. "Last time I saw you, you were in pigtails," he adds. Now, Lola dresses in black lace, but she changes into a white dress to go out with Roland. When she asks what he has done the past ten years, he lists a number of menial jobs, adding, "I had ambition like everyone. Now, I don't anymore. I'm the quintessential failure. I did nothing but daydream. Now, I'm lost and bored." Lola says that he too has changed and asks about his violin. "I had to give it up during the war," he says, calling it that "putain de guerre" ("damned war," a play on words with the literal translation: "prostitute"). Before, he confesses, he was also in love with her. As in the episode in Roberto Rossellini's *Paisà* (*Paisan*, 1946) depicting innocent girls in Italy becoming prostitutes after the war, the metaphor here is clear. France, like Lola, has lost its innocence because of desperate conditions. Demy's vision of Lola through Roland implies, however, that her integrity is still alive at her core. Through Roland's eyes (and Demy's camera), Lola is still innocent, and she herself still dreams of true love, of her first love coming back, even if seven years have passed. Is Lola a way of reconciling France's dirty past during the occupation? Of rehabilitating its identity of *liberté, égalité, fraternité*?

LOLA: FRANCE'S PAST, PRESENT, AND FUTURE

Lola remains innocent even in the cabaret as she conveys her melancholic, fairy-tale convictions to the other girls: "We love only once and I already have." Her dance number is more sweet than sexy. There is no striptease or metaphor of corruption like in Chabrol's portrayal of the grotesque in *Les Bonnes femmes* (1960) with images of lewd men gawking at women stripping on a stage.

Demy's heroine proclaims unapologetically as she dances, "C'est moi, c'est Lola." Direct and honest, Lola is more a comforting, maternal fantasy than a seductive, erotic one. Nor is she depicted as a corrupt or fallen woman. She fits in with both the dreamy showgirls/prostitutes in the cabaret as well as the other women in the film who are middle-aged maternal figures framing the male protagonist, Roland. From the beginning scenes at the café, these women serve as supports, confidantes, and moral guides to Roland: Claire, who owns

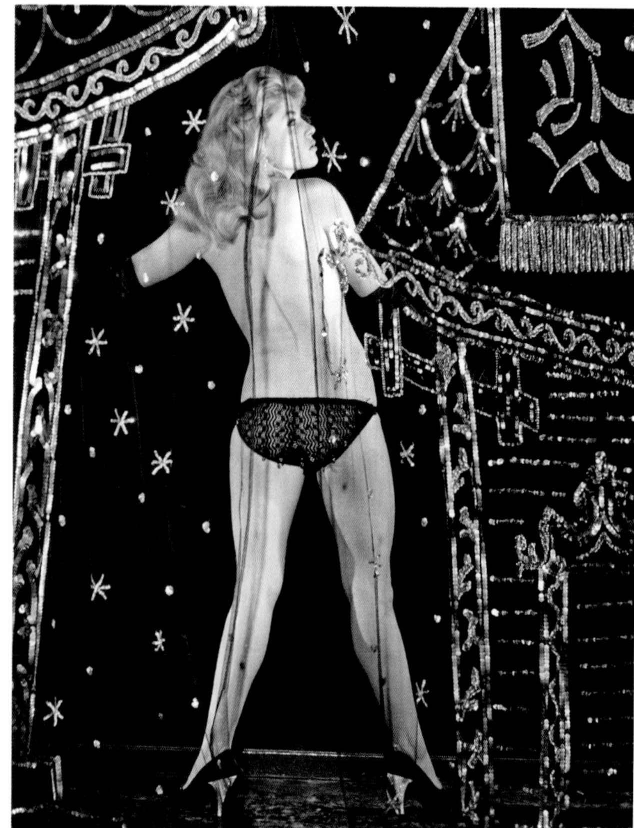

the café; Jeanne, a regular patron and the mother of Lola's elusive Michel; and Cécile's mother, Madame Desnoyers, who hosts him for dinners with the three of them. Madame Desnoyers also articulates the ravages of war, telling Roland, "I lost everything during the war: my mother, my husband."

Lola is the central point where the main characters meet and phases of time intersect. Cécile and her mother encounter reflections of Lola's own past, present, and future through Roland (her past), Frankie (her present), and Michel (her past and future). Even with Frankie, however, Lola remains innocent as sublimated images of her obscure a too harsh reality. Besides the love scenes that never take place, on the last night that Frankie spends with her, Lola informs him that he can sleep there if he promises not to try anything. Lola thus becomes a good friend instead of a *fille de joie*. Michel, Lola's long-lost true love who frames the narrative, reflects her past when she fell in love at fourteen (like Cécile will do), and lost her innocence. He also embodies her fantasy-future. In the opening sequence, Michel first appears driving up the coast

in a white Cadillac, like a male apparition and a Hollywood movie star, hidden behind big sunglasses and a white cowboy hat. In the café, Michel's mother, thinking she had seen him drive by, affirms this characterization by exclaiming that he appeared "right out of a dream, an apparition." In a role reversal, he is the fantasy possessing an aura of the past, the lost (love) object that haunts many love stories. His mysterious presence looms over the rest of the film, creating a nostalgia for true love, be it real or fabricated. When we learn that Lola had been waiting for him to come back for seven years, this narrative turns her into an innocent, hopeless romantic.

The reality is revealed by Jeanne, Michel's mother, who recounts the last words her son told her before leaving town seven years earlier: "Mother, I'm going to be a father any minute now. I'm going to seek my fortune. I'm leaving." She also provides the moral lesson: "You don't abandon your mother and baby. . . . He left a poor girl in need, probably scrubbing floors, slaving away to raise his child." Within the first few minutes, the film, like *Adieu Philippine*, illustrates a difference between the characters' experiences: a man's fear of becoming a father, and a woman's fantasy of true love, that which Lola has created of Michel. Confessing to Roland her girlhood *coup de foudre* (love at first sight) for "a blond man dressed up like an American," as she describes him, Lola explains that the "accident" happened when Michel came back later. Her remarks that follow express her disappointment in not fulfilling her dream of becoming a dancer, while voicing society's validation of her maternal role: "He said he would make me a good dancer. Maybe I'm not a great dancer but I'm a good mother."

With these different encounters, the film provides a key to understanding the divide between women and men in their goals, societal pressures, and experiences. What Lola represents for each character helps articulate deeper concerns. Roland, for example, who longs for the innocent Cécile he once knew in Lola, is a link to her past as well as the country's past before the war. His experience in the present with Lola gives us a picture of his longing for what once was (through Lola), his dissatisfaction with his reality of the present, and his desire to escape it. "What I love most is freedom," Roland confesses in the first part of the film. "People bore me, this town

Lucile Saint-Simon (Rita) in Claude Chabrol's *Les Bonnes femmes* (*The Good Time Girls*), 1960 bores me, the country bores me. I like people sometimes but I get sick of it all—of everything, especially me. I'm hopeless." Roland embodies a man in crisis. Fired from his job for not being punctual, his boss tells him he is "in the clouds." Reflecting Demy's own nature, Roland corrects his boss, saying, "I dream." To escape his reality, also like Demy, Roland goes to the cinema. In *Return to Paradise* (1953), he watches Gary Cooper travel far away, mirroring Roland's desire. Upon returning to the café, Roland announces that he too will leave to get over his ennui, complaining that "here, we don't know how to live." Jeanne reminds him (and us) of how cinema distorts reality: "Au cinéma, c'est toujours plus beau" ("In the movies, it's always more beautiful"). Articulating the societal pressure men like Roland also faced to build a family, Jeanne advises him to have children, because then he "wouldn't be bored." But Roland voices the experience of his generation, disillusioned with their parents' values: "I'm lost and I'm bored."

Roland and Michel also embody the distinction between reality and fantasy. Roland, who is in love with Lola and tied to reality, exists in direct contrast to Michel, a masculine ideal and dream of all the girls, Lola's fantasy. Lola is convinced that he will come back one day, and like in all great fairy tales, he does.

"In the movies, it's always more beautiful," the film reminds us. The New Wave generation is in need of fairy tales. But after the trauma of the war, most of the directors favor tragic or open endings over happy ones. Demy and Aimée's portrayal of Lola is both the exception and the rule. In her song, Lola sings, "The one who says soon, soon, and who laughs behind your back, lost in her thoughts of hope, if you only knew, an enormous crazy hope / The one who opens her arms only to the one she recognizes among a thousand, among a hundred, or three / To whom she'll say you, you, you! C'est moi, c'est Lola." Unlike Chabrol's *Bonnes femmes* or Fellini's *Cabiria*, Demy's film rewards those who believe in true love by letting his heroine realize her dream and her happy ending. In dramatic fashion, Michel enters the café where his mother faints upon seeing him, overcome with joy. Like in all good Hollywood endings, Michel declares, "I've come to get my wife and child. She's been waiting for me." As Lola is leaving the cabaret, Michel appears as if out of a dream, to the relief of Lola's showgirl friends (serving as the audience within the film). They watch and cry as they live their happy ending vicariously through Lola, mirroring our reaction as viewers. Lola tells Michel, "I waited for you." They embrace; the music starts; champagne for everyone! Here, true love wins. Faith is rewarded. The happy end here reconstitutes the family, rehabilitates Lola, restores innocence, and reestablishes the social order, all that is longed for after the trauma of war. Roland, however, is left alone in his sad reality.

LOLA'S LAST LOOK: CASTING DOUBT ON THE HOLLYWOOD HAPPY ENDING

Demy's tendency to make dreams come true in his films, unlike the other New Wave directors, dates back to the stories and first films he created as a boy in his parents' attic in Nantes. Varda in *Jacquot de Nantes* (1991), her film about Demy's childhood, shows the young Demy escaping into his imagination drawing figures by hand—like Méliès at the birth of cinema—on leftover film stock he obtained and salvaged. Like Aimée's family, during World War II, Demy's parents, hoping to keep him safe during the bombings in Nantes, sent him to the countryside, placing him in the care of a wooden shoemaker and his wife. To ease his time there, seeing the young Demy was obsessed with movies, the couple borrowed a projector for him and some short Chaplin films that he showed to his friends. For Demy, as a little boy as well as an established filmmaker, cinema was a refuge, a place to solve inner conflicts and to dream. In his films, it is a world where true love always comes back, and where his characters' dreams come true.

Aimée's childhood, like Demy's, was interrupted and her security jeopardized by being forced to hide during the war. As she escaped into a new identity for her safety, she would later explore new ones through the world of cinema. Her identification with her character in *Lola* appears to have profoundly marked her. Many years later, she related that she did not know where Lola ended and she began: "*Lola* is one of the most important things in my life—in my life, period," she stated. "There's *Lola* and Fellini's films, there's Lelouch and Bellocchio, lots of things, but *Lola* is a part of my life. I owe so much to *Lola*, and therefore to Jacques." In a 2019 profile on French radio, Aimée's agent Dominique

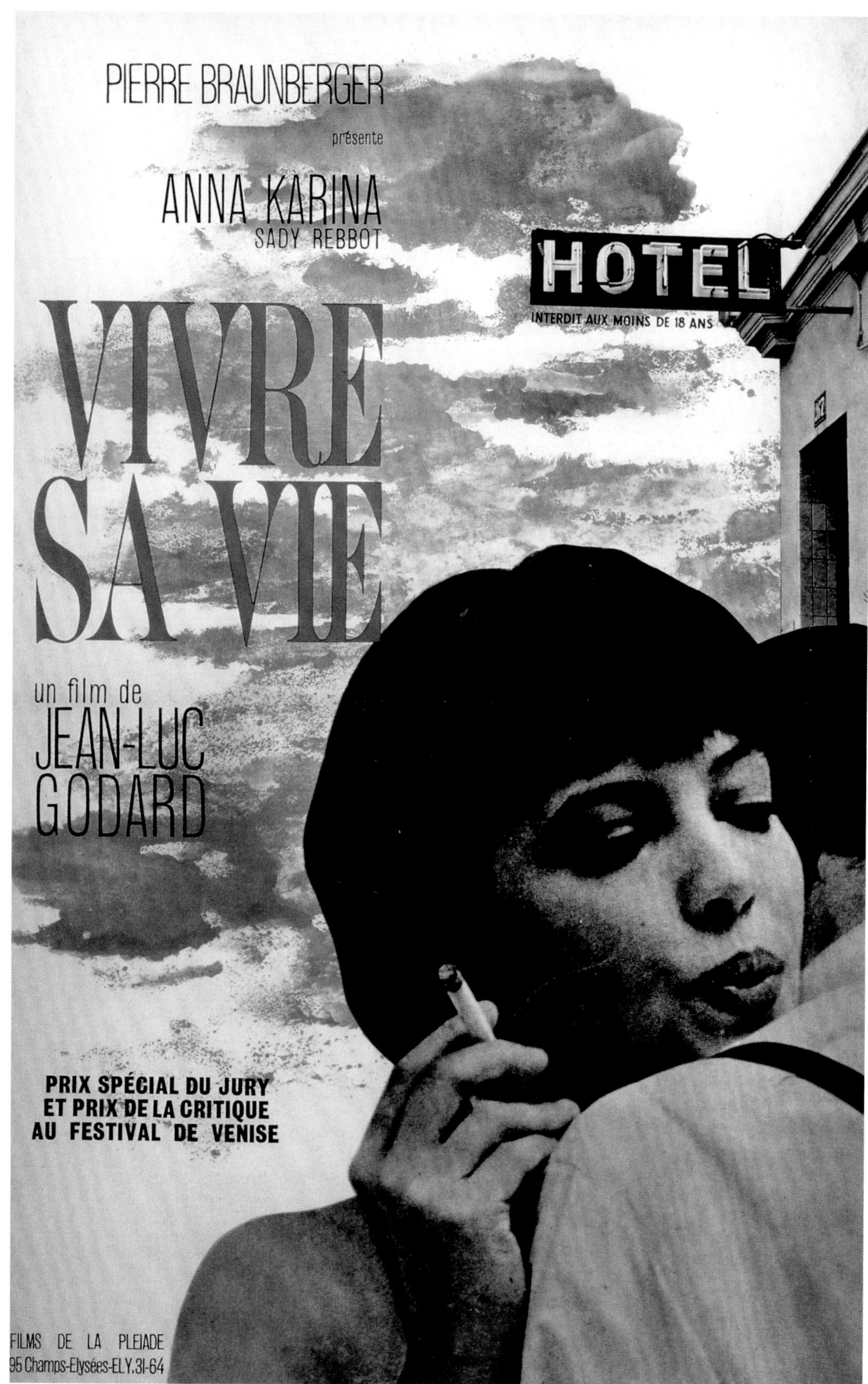
PIERRE BRAUNBERGER
présente
ANNA KARINA
SADY REBBOT
VIVRE SA VIE
un film de
JEAN-LUC GODARD
HOTEL
INTERDIT AUX MOINS DE 18 ANS
PRIX SPÉCIAL DU JURY
ET PRIX DE LA CRITIQUE
AU FESTIVAL DE VENISE
FILMS DE LA PLEIADE
95 Champs-Elysées-ELY. 31-64

Besnehard (who codirected with Muriel Flis-Trèves the 2012 documentary *Anouk Aimée, la beauté du geste*) recounted, "Anouk always seems to me like the incarnation of a feline: both present and independent, too disillusioned to take out her claws, because she fears abandonment and desires to be loved eternally."[21] Upon learning of her death in 2024, he described her as "a nervous dreamer," citing the cause as stemming from her childhood and the war: "She almost got arrested by the Gestapo two times."[22]

Perhaps her sensitivity also mirrored the film's opening quote: "Cry who can, laugh who wants to." Though the film gives the audience the possibility of leaving the movie theater with a feeling of resolve and satisfaction, like the sad ironies of life conveyed in Ophüls's films, Demy suggests in the final scene a more complicated read on contentment. The postscript to this apparently happy ending can in fact deconstruct it, like Lola's reality of prostitution hidden beneath her dreamy veneer. As Lola, her son Yvon, and Michel drive away in his car, they pass Roland, Demy's alter ego, walking alone on the sidewalk. When Lola sees him, Michel notices her expression change. When he asks her what is wrong, she answers, "Nothing." These final moments, though nothing is articulated, pierce the Hollywood ending with a brief flicker of reality, spreading doubt about the fairy tale if we choose to see it. In the end, Lola's humanity (or silent empathy?) breaks the illusion of the dream. Like Montaigne's citation, Demy gives us a choice between two reactions to life. Though Lola's character chooses the dream, Aimée's look conveys a reality that lies beneath the surface, one that is not anticipated but deeply felt in silent recognition. This unspoken truth with a hint of melancholy makes Lola, the woman and the film, modern.

ANNA KARINA AS GODARD'S ACTRESS-PROSTITUTE IN *VIVRE SA VIE*

As Godard stated in a television interview in 1966, "People like prostitutes because to sleep with them you don't have to talk, which is serious, because love, on the contrary, is dialogue."[23] When Godard was forced by producers to include nude shots of Brigitte Bardot in *Le Mépris*, he complied while turning the obligatory images into a romantic love scene, adding dialogue with an intimate exchange between lovers. With

Anna Karina in the role of Nana, a prostitute, he used a similar approach, subverting an expected portrayal by infusing it with depth and romanticism. In *Vivre sa vie*, instead of lascivious love scenes or exhibitions of Karina's body, like Vadim displayed Bardot's, Godard's prostitute shows us something else. Besides the Oval Portrait linking romantic love and art, he uses the figure as a metaphor of a society in decline—like Zola did in *Nana*—and adds a parallel with the movie business.

Zola's narrative addresses the idea of a women being "naturally" corrupted by desire. As scholar Charles Bernheimer put it, "Sexual desire, the generative force of life, is conceived by Zola as potentially the most destructive of deviations from life's wholesome balance. He implies that, once perverted by desire, any woman, whatever her class background, will embrace prostitution as her natural mode and spread the virus of her degenerate infection."[24] This misogynistic view of feminine desire, as ingrained in literary culture as in society, obviously works against women's agency. Godard's narrative, however, does not concentrate on women's desire in that sense. Instead, he exposes their desire to be in the movies at all costs, using prostitution as a metaphor for actresses exploiting themselves. Godard will use this metaphor to explore different ideas, such as the alienation of modern living—architecturally through France's new high-rise apartments—as well as the emptiness of the role of modern housewife in his equally famous *Deux ou trois choses que je sais d'elle* (*Two or Three Things I Know about Her*, 1967) with Marina Vlady portraying another bourgeois mother working secretly as a prostitute by day.

In *Vivre sa vie*, Nana—like Zola's heroine, who reveals a society uniquely preoccupied with pleasure and entertainment—illustrates how the film industry fuels an unhealthy desire to be in the movies. Nana's existential ennui is evoked from the beginning of the film along with her mixing of acting and real life. At a café, she repeats the line, "What do you care?" to her husband, Paul, delivering it in different intonations like an actress. He reminds her that "we're not on stage." While Nana works in a record shop to try to support herself after separating from him, her dreams of becoming an actress elude her, and her reality finds her short on money. Unable to pay her rent, she resorts to prostitution. In real

Jean-Luc Godard's *Vivre sa vie* (*My Life to Live*), 1962, original poster life, Anna Karina refused to undress for a part in *À bout de souffle*, and it cost her the role. Her character in *Vivre sa vie*, on the other hand, will take her clothes off for money.

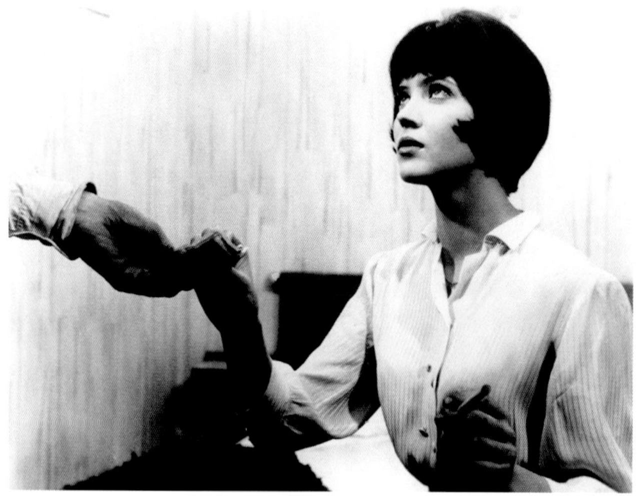

In a sort of mid-twentieth-century prefiguration of #MeToo awareness, Simone de Beauvoir already described in *The Second Sex* the vulnerable power dynamic between actresses and directors as an obstacle to women's agency: "Cinema in particular subjects the star to the director and doesn't allow her to invent or progress in a creative activity. She is exploited for what she is; she does not create a new object. And moreover, it is very rare to become a star."[25] The struggle to gain agency, then, is what links the actress, as described by de Beauvoir, to the prostitute—and by extension, to women in general in 1960s France.

"NOT ON THE MOUTH": AGENCY, PURITANISM, AND VOYEURISM THROUGH THE NEW WAVE'S PROSTITUTES

When Nana resorts to prostituting herself in order to survive, her first experience shows her not knowing her worth. When her client asks her how much, she replies: "I don't know. It's up to you." She accepts his advances but establishes a boundary by refusing his kiss, as he protests, "Why not on the mouth?" Little by little, Nana affirms herself and inquires about prostitution as a profession, writing a letter to a madam. Raoul, a pimp, is puzzled by her ambition, asking, "Why

don't you try to get into the movies? You're a pretty girl." Nana replies that she had already tried, and that two years earlier she had wanted to do theater: "I was in *Pacifico* at Châtelet, and once I was in a film with Eddie Constantine." When it is clear she has made her decision, Nana asks, "When do I start?" Godard then pauses for a parenthetical sort of *reportage* on prostitution, reflecting a certain truth, normalized by the state through statistics, and conveyed in an official tone. Inspired by the 1959 book *Où en est: la prostitution* (in effect, "What is the status of prostitution?") by Marcel Sacotte, a judge,[26] the sequence cites these statistics word for word in a question-and-answer session between Nana and an off-screen, official-sounding voice (presumably that of her pimp). Besides explaining the job to Nana, it describes the situation of prostitution in France at the time while the *mise en scène* turns Nana into a piece of merchandise; we see her slowly transform as she assumes her new profession.[27]

Nana: Is it important to be beautiful?
Voice-over: Beauty is not essential for a prostitute, but it plays an important role in her career, nonetheless. It establishes her place in the hierarchy and, especially, attracts the attention of the pimp since her physical appeal can be a source for them of immense profit.

. . .

Nana: What do I charge?
Voice-over: It can vary greatly. From three hundred to fifteen thousand francs for an encounter lasting from a few minutes to an hour, called a "trick." An "overnight" ranges from five thousand to fifty thousand francs.
Nana: Am I allowed to go anywhere?
Voice-over: Controls have been attempted. In Paris, for instance, a police regulation of August 25, 1958, forbid loitering with intent to solicit during certain hours in the Bois de Boulogne and around the Champs-Élysées.

. . .

Nana: Do I have my own room?
Voice-over: Usually only the towels are changed in between tricks, not the sheets. Some hotels provide only a bottom sheet, not blankets.
Nana: What about the police?
Voice-over: They conduct raids and interrogations. Any woman in violation of regulations can be detained in a

Anna Karina (Nana) in Godard's *Vivre sa vie*, 1962

clinic or hospital as long as necessary for extensive testing.

. . .

Nana: And what if I become pregnant?
Voice-over: One might think a prostitute would seek an abortion at all costs. It is not the case. They do try to avoid pregnancy. They take a drug or practice other means when it appears this is possible. But once pregnancy is confirmed, abortions are rare.
Nana: Do you have to accept everyone?
Voice-over: The prostitute must always be at the client's disposal. She must accept any client who pays.

. . .

Presented as an investigation, the passage gives details on the codification of physical love by the government, explaining how prostitution enters into the system.

From another perspective, certain parallels between actress and director can be drawn from the description. It shows how Nana tries to become a subject in the role of prostitute like that of actress. In the first part of the film, when she is uninformed and unaware of the details, she does not know her value. After her meeting with Raoul, equipped with more knowledge about legal rights and money, she firmly states her worth as a prostitute. When her client, Dmitri, asks how much, she firmly answers, "Three thousand, five thousand to undress." In *Le Petit soldat*, Véronica was bombarded with questions by Bruno (as Karina was in real life upon meeting Godard). In *Vivre sa vie*, as the prostitute, she is the one asking the questions: "Have you already been here? We've already seen each other, haven't we? What's your name? What do you do?" When she learns that one client takes pictures in advertising, she briefly gets her hopes up: "Is it like in the movies?" Settling into the profession, she paradoxically gains confidence and negotiation skills and demands more money for her services. "Are you sentimental?" she asks. "If you give me more, I can stay, you know?" After her dead-end job at the record shop, objectifying and selling herself in this context appears to be the only avenue for her to take control and gain agency. The parallel of an actress selling herself to a director cannot go unnoticed, with both professions objectifying women in terms of their body.

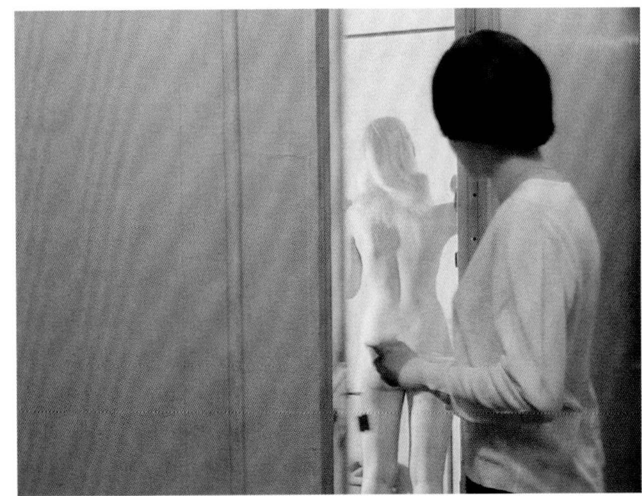

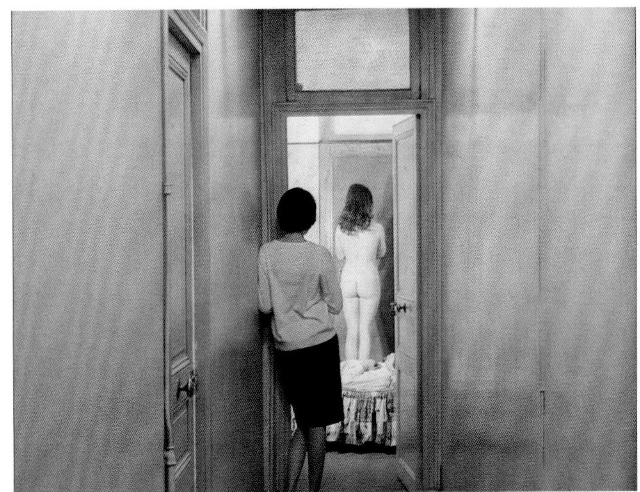

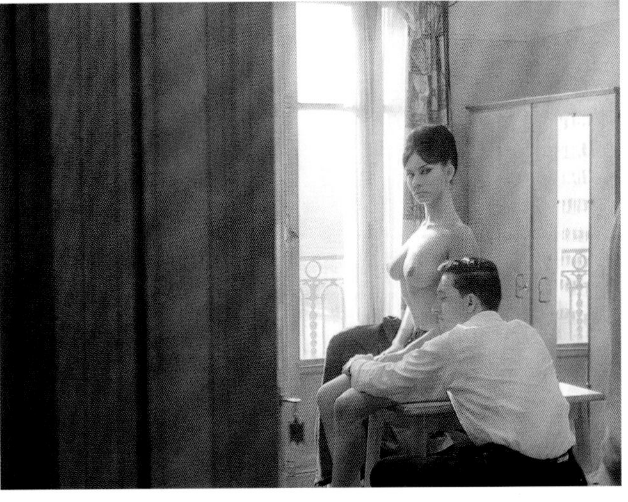

Anna Karina (Nana) looks on at prostitutes in Godard's *Vivre sa vie*, 1962

Like Aimée in *Lola*, however, Karina's body is also hidden, not exposed. When a client asks Nana—who is still fully clothed, wearing an unbuttoned cardigan—for what is implied (in ellipses) to be a second woman, however, the viewer is shown clandestine, voyeuristic shots of prostitutes posing like models. Distanced by a fixed frame, the camera observes them between two doors. These pinup-like scenes force the viewer into the stance of voyeur, creating the sense that the women's nudity is perceived in secret, transgressively. The first are subjective shots, assumed to be from Nana's point of view. In the last, Nana enters the frame from the back, parallel to the nude woman she is looking at, again forcing the viewer into a voyeuristic position in line with Godard's camera. But the spectacle stops there. At the end of the sequence, the client asks for a different woman.

Godard did not expose his wife the way Vadim did Bardot. Nana, like Karina, does not undress. Script supervisor Suzanne Schiffman described Godard's sensibility that guided his self-censorship and led him to avoid vulgarity: "I remember the scene well because the actor says 'yes' at a certain moment. Cinema is strange: This simple 'yes,' that was barely uttered, made the scene vaguely dirty. Godard cut it right away. I don't know anyone more puritanical."[28] The other prostitutes in his *mise en scène* seem absent and detached, dissociating by looking out the window while the men fulfill their fantasies off screen.[29] Godard only shows static shots of them, never in motion.[30]

Far from Bardot's uncontrollable dance, the prostitutes in *Vivre sa vie* remain still, their bodies often depicted in fragmented shots,[31] like Macha Méril's would be in *Une femme mariée*. These dissected bodies are also different from the way in which Éric Rohmer will film Haydée Politoff in *La Collectionneuse*, wherein his camera, though still filming in fragments, seems to focus on the body as artwork. In a similar way that Godard films Bardot at the beginning of *Le Mépris*, in *Vivre sa vie*, he provides an implicit commentary on the female body as merchandise. Whether a reflection of the director's much-cited puritanism or self-censorship, his exploration of prostitution centers on social observation and veers away from the erotic.

Given Godard's admiration for Scandinavian directors like Bergman and Dreyer, we might expect him to employ the

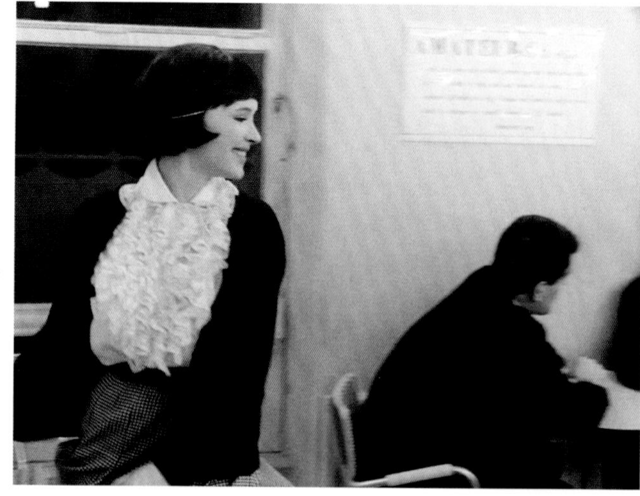

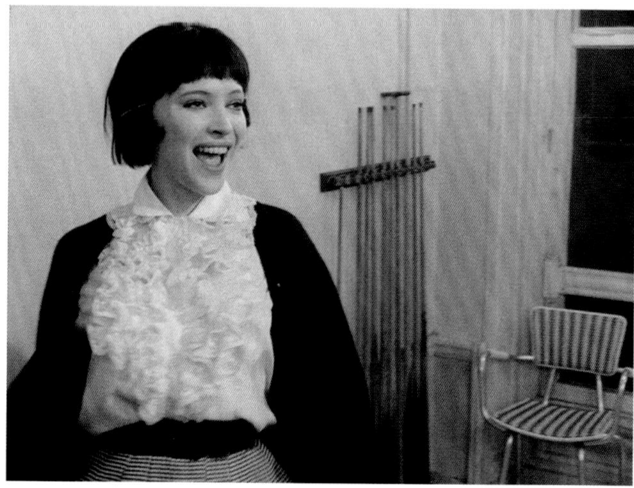

same type of freedom they portray of the physical body on screen, but he does not choose this avenue either. In his portrait of Nana, cinematic echoes of Bergman's *Monika* do in fact resound in Godard's *mise en scène*, with similar shots of Karina reproducing Andersson's famous "look to camera" in particular. But where Monika gains agency, abandoning her lover in the end, Nana falls victim to Godard's choice to annihilate her in the narrative. Monika is shown to be corrupted by society and city life, while Nana is corrupted by ambition and the desire to be an actress. In the Oval Portrait sequence, Nana/Karina remains still in front of a photograph of Elizabeth Taylor while being filmed by Godard's camera, making an implicit reference to her profession of actress and her status as a passive model—or Godard's internal disquiet in filming her as raw material for his work of art, in line with Poe's story.

Anna Karina (Nana) in Godard's *Vivre sa vie*, 1962

When Nana looks into the camera during the sequence of her interview with the philosopher Brice Parain, her expression lacks Monika's defiance, instead implying a plea for understanding. The portrait of Nana here conveys a romantic sensibility that contrasts with the documentary *reportage* about prostitution in the beginning. Nana's death in the crossfire of pimps perhaps translates a society grappling with women's increasing power and Godard's own personal conflicts regarding Karina, as well as his views of hopeful starlets in the movie business.

Godard expressed guilt about the way in which *Vivre sa vie* evoked "relationships with the actress where I was the client and she the prostitute at the same time,"[32] according to de Baecque. The director's desire to film Karina, the real woman who was also his wife, was complicated by his desire to film her as the actress he dreamed of on screen. Godard cited cinema as helping him manage his inner conflicts: "I was especially preoccupied by my problems with women, or with a woman, or with two women, or with three women. Or my problems of going to see prostitutes . . . and sometimes the shame that I could have, given my past or my moralism or things like that. I found cinema useful because you could, if you want, expose it without being uncomfortable."[33] Masked behind the narrator in Poe's Oval Portrait, Godard found the perfect filter to manage this conflict.

The context of this, their third film together, was also particularly painful for the couple as Karina had just lost their baby and attempted suicide shortly before the shoot. Her humanity and strength come through in various scenes: her joyous nature in the jukebox dance sequence, her sincerity in those with the philosopher, and her resilience in playing the role itself with such conviction and depth even after terrible private loss. Karina's portrayal of Nana transcends the morbid script with her will to live—"her life to live," as the title implies—through her immortal performance.

TRUFFAUT'S PROSTITUTES: THE MISGUIDED ROMANTICISM OF ANTOINE DOINEL

In Antoine Doinel's world, as imagined by Truffaut, women are divided into categories: the fantasy and the real. But in the director's *mise en scène*, there is one figure that exists in both, the prostitute. While idealizing and romanticizing the prostitute figure through the eyes of his alter ego, Truffaut also mocks Antoine's naïveté as he shows the women in these roles grounded in reality, breaking the fantasy. Like Demy with his own alter ego Roland in *Lola*, Truffaut portrays masculine figures in crisis, especially with regard to women. Men of authority in the Doinel series appear in blurred, reduced, or degraded images. In *Les Quatre cents coups*, for example, a brief sequence shows Antoine looking at himself in the bathroom mirror. As he wipes away the vapor on the glass, in the background he sees his father, reduced to a blurred, scratched-through image.

In *Baisers volés* (*Stolen Kisses*, 1968), when Antoine works as a detective, he sees himself in the mirror next to his colleague, who has already been defined as weak compared to his take-charge girlfriend. Finally, Antoine's blurred reflection next to his unlikeable and humiliated boss Monsieur Tabard in the mirror as they enter Tabard's apartment reinforces the association Antoine has with weak male role models in his life.

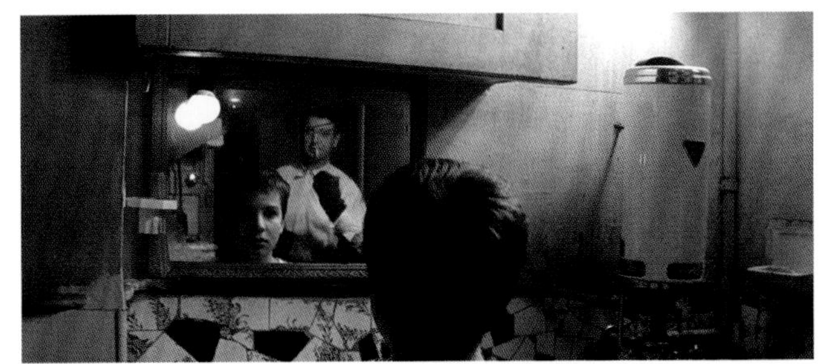

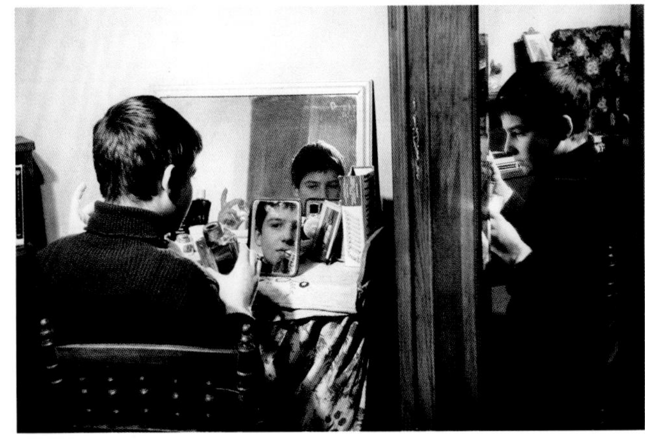

Jean-Pierre Léaud (Antoine Doinel) at his mother's dressing table and with Albert Rémy (his stepfather) in François Truffaut's *Les Quatre cents coups* (*The 400 Blows*), 1959

Do these ill-defined images reflect the poor image Antoine has of himself, his lack of confidence? As a character who is incessantly humiliated by his romantic interests, Antoine is also rejected by prostitutes as he confuses the physical with the romantic in his pursuit of validation and love. His quest for the feminine begins with his mother in *Les Quatre cents coups* as he contemplates his fragmented reflection while seated at her dressing table. His search is never-ending as he then tries to define himself through a series of "exceptional women," in his words, like Fabienne Tabard (Delphine Seyrig), his boss's wife in *Baisers volés*, who fascinates him. The idea of women as mirrors, infinitely reflecting identity, permeates the Doinel series. In search of his own identity and sense of self, Antoine defines himself in relation to a number of strong women: his mother in *Les Quatres cents coups*; Colette in *Antoine et Colette* (*Antoine and Colette*, Truffaut's contribution to the 1962 anthology *L'Amour à vingt ans*, or *Love at Twenty*); and on through Fabienne Tabard among others, including a panoply of prostitute fantasies.

Though Truffaut frequently visited prostitutes throughout his life,[34] he too kept their bodies—and the body in general—at a distance in his *mise en scène*, often filtering depictions of prostitution through comedy. Similar to Godard in his sublimated view of Nana (but without his social commentary), Truffaut projected his romanticism onto Antoine's interactions with prostitutes, signaling the character's desire for love. In *Baisers volés*, a male colleague at the detective agency punctures Antoine's fantasy by harshly describing his own sordid experiences with prostitutes: "They disgust me. They're too filthy. When I was your age, I did dirty girls with their bra attached in the back with a safety pin."

Representing another break with Antoine's romanticism are the women themselves, outspoken and in touch with reality. They articulate the transactional component of the relationship to Antoine when he is searching for love. This contrast is meant as a comedic device (one that humiliates Antoine, and perhaps allows Truffaut to project his own conflicts onto his alter ego). For example, in *Baisers volés*, Antoine comes back from his military service and visits a *maison close* (brothel) multiple times, usually in moments of distress or boredom. In one scene, when Antoine throws himself at a

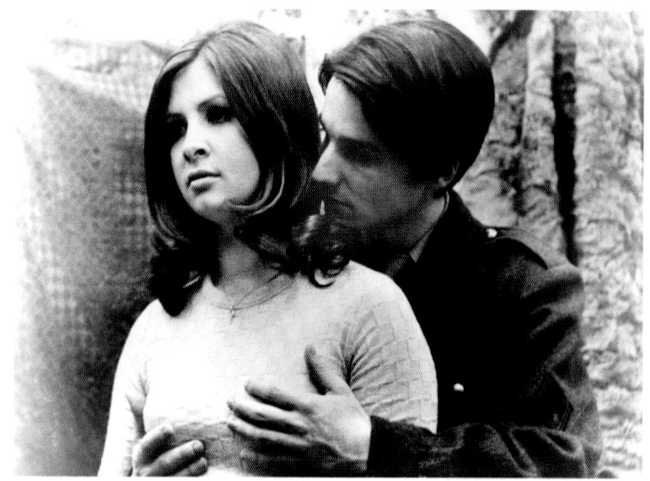

prostitute, trying to kiss her as soon as the door closes, she pushes him back, saying, like Nana in *Vivre sa vie*, "No, no, not on the mouth." Her realism counters Antoine's romantic illusions: "Never with clients!" Truffaut continues the gag of oppositions. Antoine tries to caress her hair: "No, leave my hair alone, I have on hairspray." He tries to take off her sweater: "Oh no, I'm keeping my pullover on, I'm cold, I just had bronchitis." Finally, the door slams. His fantasy is broken. Antoine leaves, but in the hallway of the bordello, he passes another girl and changes his mind. Antoine follows her, looking at her legs in the staircase ("the best part" of an amorous encounter, as Truffaut was known to say). Once again, reality strikes as she says, "You are my first soldier of the day. You're going to bring me luck!" Seen with a distance of over fifty years, and in the context of the #MeToo movement, the scenes lose their comedic value. They are an invaluable window, however, into women's place in society at the time, and reflect, perhaps, the deficit of love certain men were trying to fill through inauthentic or transactional relationships.

At the end of the film, Antoine leaves the funeral of one of his colleagues to find prostitutes waiting along the walls of the cemetery. He chooses one, and when they arrive in the bedroom, she verbalizes the contract—more money for more service, again like Nana in *Vivre sa vie*: "If you give me a little more, I'll undress." Antoine gives her the money but refuses her offer, saying, "Here, I prefer that you keep your clothes on." She insists: "If you want, we can stay together longer." But again Antoine refuses: "No, I don't feel like stay-

Liza Braconnier (Sad Prostitute) with Jean-Pierre Léaud (Antoine Doinel) in François Truffaut's *Baisers volés* (*Stolen Kisses*) 1968

ing longer," rejecting the reality of the situation. The prostitute accepts and puts away her purse.

In *Domicile conjugal* (*Bed and Board*, 1970), the next film in the Doinel series, Antoine arrives at a bordello at night after an argument with his wife. His shadow passes in front of the door to his fantasies, and women appear dressed up as different types, parading in front of him as they descend the staircase and fill the room. Doinel reviews each one, from the woman in leopard print to the secretary-type with glasses, and becomes overwhelmed. Incapable of choosing, he tries to flee the scene, but the maternal madam stops him and convinces him to stay. With an awkward smile, he makes his choice, a young, tall brunette who looks more like a student from the Latin Quarter than a prostitute. Reflecting Antoine's fragmented view of women in general, each prostitute is desired for the unique fantasy she inspires, yet none are irreplaceable—a vision that also drives Truffaut's classic *L'Homme qui aimait les femmes* (*The Man Who Loved Women*, 1977).

Shots of lights and neon signs in Pigalle serve as ellipses for the love scene. Even in this context, the body is totally absent. The scene picks back up when the girl Antoine has chosen, Marie, is putting on her clothes again. Once more, Truffaut diverts the focus away from the physical to give the audience another unexpected moment intended to be comical. As Antoine prepares to leave, Marie discusses politics and the economic situation of the country: "It's rather calm right now. Before, there were clients until the twenty-third of every month. Now, after the fifteenth, everyone is broke. . . . Are you into politics?" She ends the sequence with a moral lesson: "Remember, if you don't care about politics, politics won't care about you, especially at the end of the month!" Antoine responds with a desperate, disappointed, and romantic air, gallantly kissing Marie's hand before leaving. Truffaut emphasizes the difference between them with a wide shot showing Marie towering over Antoine. Though portraying prostitutes in comedic situations, Truffaut does not belittle them, showing them instead as informed subjects who are in touch with reality, even politics. They highlight, however, his protagonist's delusional romantic dreams. Antoine's fantasy is replaced by reality again as he passes his father-in-law in the hallway, reminding him of the banality of these transactional relationships with women, and illustrating the prevalence of prostitution in French society at a time when the tradition of men frequenting bordellos was normalized. For Truffaut, these minor scenes with an array of prostitutes speak more about his alter ego's longing for love rather than physical desire, since these love scenes never actually take place on screen.

Although the viewer intrinsically occupies a voyeuristic position in relation to what is being shown on screen, in the case of the New Wave prostitutes, there is not much to see. As in France's long literary history, the prostitute figure functions as a filter to explore deeper issues. In New Wave films, prostitutes tend to reveal as much about the male protagonists' emotional state as women's changing relationship to power. A symptom of a larger void in French society at the time after years of trauma and war, men are lost as women gain more autonomy over their bodies and their destiny. In the 1960s, fifteen years after World War II, New Wave films struggled to come to terms with the country's painful past along with a rapidly changing society that featured fewer moral constraints and shifting interpersonal roles. Relics of the social, literary, and cinematic past still persisted in directors' internalized, idealized models, creating tension in their films with female sexuality inspiring both fascination and fear. Whether it be a preoedipal fantasy in Demy's *Lola*, a romantic portrait or social commentary in Godard's *Vivre sa vie*, or a lack of (maternal) love in Truffaut's Doinel series, the prostitute is a role that can fill these needs and dreams perhaps because of the inherent transactional nature of the figure as well as its relationship to power. In all these cases, it is also telling that the reality of the profession and the bodies themselves are hidden or absent, illustrating even more that the prostitute's function lies elsewhere. Choosing to turn away from a reality that was too raw, due to their own inhibition, societal taboos, or censorship, directors gravitated toward the fantasy and the ideal. A sublimated eroticism[35] in New Wave cinema translated into idealized visions of romantic prostitutes and the actresses who played them. But glimpses of truth through Anouk Aimée's last look, vitality through Anna Karina's dance, or reality through Truffaut's political prostitute lend a modern perspective to a traditional role.

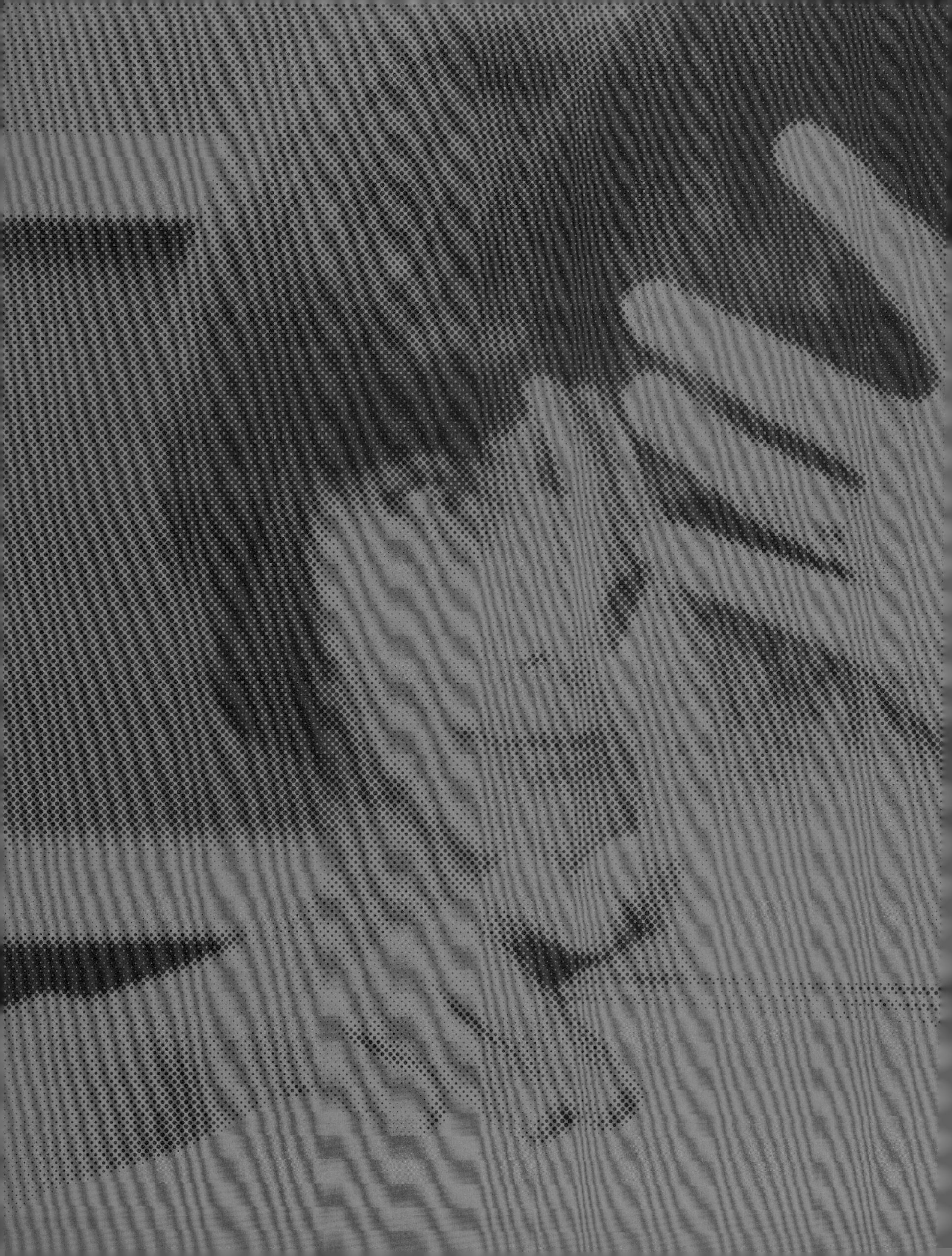

macha méril

la femme censurée | *the censored woman*

DISSECTING THE MARRIED WOMAN IN
UNE FEMME MARIÉE

Despite the progress in early New Wave films, a tension and a double standard persisted when it came to fidelity in marriage in the case of an unfaithful or free woman. The scandalized reaction in 1958 to Jeanne Moreau's portrayal of a married woman in *Les Amants* fleeing with her lover persisted even into 1964 with Jean-Luc Godard's *Une femme mariée* in a society that still seemed unable to tolerate the idea of an unfaithful woman going unpunished. Even the original title, *La Femme mariée*, was offensive to the censors, who had already clashed with Godard over *À bout de souffle, Le Petit soldat,* and *Vivre sa vie.* Changing the title to suggest a specific case study of "a" married woman—rather than a generalized portrait of "the" married woman—eased some of their objections and allowed the film to be shown in France.[1] (Some of those involved in the film, such as Macha Méril and Godard, however, often referred to it by its original title.)

After presenting *Bande à part* at the Cannes Film Festival in May 1964, Godard immediately began working on *Une femme mariée* with a sense of urgency. He started shooting it in July, completing it in a matter of weeks so it would be ready for the Venice Film Festival in early September. The time constraints were doubled by financial ones: Godard had secured $100,000, an extremely small budget at the time, from his deal with Columbia Pictures to make two films in a row. After *Bande à part*, he started *Une femme mariée* in record speed.

"The fact of compressing time affects all the steps in the fabrication of Godard's films," Macha Méril, who played Charlotte, the film's protagonist, explained in an interview in 2010.[2] "I'm thinking about the writing (I think he keeps the concept to himself), then the shoot." According to Méril, they filmed for just two weeks, and the editing was "almost done during the shoot." "I think he knew exactly where his scissors would cut while shooting it," she said. "I think all great directors are like that." Méril recalled shooting "more or less in continuity" through "night and day," without any union to curtail their working hours. "This speed wasn't just in the production . . . but also of expression so that an idea didn't evaporate," she said. "I loved it. It's not neorealism; it's not capturing the real. It's a real invention, Jean-Luc's style, his own music, but that is conceived from elements of truth."[3]

The challenge of this fast pace amused Godard and Raoul Coutard, the director of photography of *À bout de souffle*. With the aim of being a "radar" of his time, Godard became a sociologist, observing everything happening in French society. He wanted to capture the major upheavals and cultural shifts in terms of sexuality as well as the emerging consumer society (the time would become known as Les Trente Glorieuses, the thirty years of economic prosperity following World War II). In a sort of reversal of the story of *Le Petit soldat*, where a political film was invaded by Godard's love story with Karina, this time a film about a woman was haunted by the memory of the atrocities of the Shoah.

Although he addressed the war directly for the first time in his cinema, Godard's main objective was to follow the (mar-ried) woman with his camera, dissecting her in an objective way, like an entomologist. Méril said she felt like she was being tracked, meticulously observed at close range by Godard's camera: "In this film, I was treated like an animal you look at through a magnifying glass," with shots "looking at each part of the body, both the physical and psychological details. I'm in all the shots, and if not, there's a piece of me, a hand, a knee, a piece of my body."[4]

In his typically provocative manner, Godard compared the film to Robert Flaherty's 1922 classic *Nanook of the North*, the controversial "staged" documentary famous for its blending of fiction and fact and for its sociological inquiries. To Godard, *Une femme mariée* examined the married woman as Flaherty's film had examined Inuk life in the Canadian Arctic. Again, Méril agreed: "I was really at the heart of the film and I felt like everyone was coming to get me, pulling me by strings, and everyone needed me—to film me, to be inspired by me, to see if I reacted as a woman, if I was shocked, if I went along with it, if I was happy." With a married woman at its center, *Une femme mariée* is a pop art film that also deconstructs love, marriage, and desire while denouncing consumer society, advertising, and women's designated roles.

It is interesting to remember that 1964 marked an extremely difficult period between Godard and Karina. After making *Bande à part* earlier that year, their marriage hit a turning point, and they both immediately pursued other projects. She sought refuge from the disappointment of her failing marriage with her male costar on another film while still married to Godard. He went on to scrutinize the idea of the married woman who has an affair.

If we imagine Méril standing in for Karina, Godard seemed driven to approach the (married) woman from all angles: from the sociological angle of her status as a married woman and as a consumer, from her motivations in love, and from his desire to find even more intimate answers through inspecting her body in close-up and in parts. "It's a film I wasn't supposed to do," Méril said. "He was looking at young French actresses, for a girl who wasn't an intellectual. . . . He took what he thought was a starlet, and I think, with his director's eye, he especially chose my body, my corpulence. I understood later when we shot the film. He treated me like a statue, like a piece of marble that he would sculpt with this film."

Dissecting Méril's body with his camera, dividing it into close-ups of each part, Godard examined the body, women, and love. In line with his modesty in filming love scenes, his camera conveyed a sort of fascination and fear of the mysterious female body (not unlike Truffaut's protagonist in *La Peau douce*), showing as much as possible but stopping just short of anything truly risqué–perhaps as a way of exorcizing it? Ironically, Godard later wished he had gone further in his *mise en scène* of the body, saying that the film "wants to claim to be a pornographic film and, in fact, it was banned for that reason. All that I regret today is that it wasn't frankly more pornographic. Because we would see more–in the classical sense, like when we see pornographic magazines with asses, hairs, in violent colors that make us have a pretty horrible feeling, like in front of a butcher shop."[5]

SCULPTED NUDITY, SOCIAL COMMENTARY, AND (SELF)-CENSORSHIP

More often than not, the female body remained absent in French New Wave films. As in the not-so-shocking love scenes in *Les Amants*, women appeared more frequently as fantasies or in a romantic light. The rawer, more daring images seen in Swedish films of the time, for example, were not found in their French counterparts–due to censorship, certainly, but perhaps also due to a self-censorship by the directors themselves. Méril found this to be the case with Godard. "Jean-Luc is Swiss, Calvinist–that is to say, he's an extremely modest man. I'd even say prudish, so while he felt he had to show this woman's body, at the same time, it almost shocked him as a viewer himself," she said, adding, "and also there was censorship."

The role of the censors cannot be overlooked. The Commission de contrôle des films cinématographiques[6] (the Film Censorship Commission) was very strict in their assessment of what they considered shocking, and meticulously controlled what could and could not be shown. "The censors said you shouldn't show pubic hair, neither breasts nor hair, so you could only show [the torso]," Méril said, explaining that in one shot, "you only see my naval but it stops at the edge of my pubic hair, and during these nude scenes, I held my arms in front of my chest for the censors."[7]

She also noted two scenes that did not make it past the Commission de contrôle. In one, she said, "I'm in profile and I'm looking at myself in the bathroom mirror, and I'm cutting my bangs and I lower my hands. The camera doesn't follow, it stays on my profile, and we hear the sound of the scissors as if I were cutting my pubic hair–and the sound of the scissors was cut! Maybe it was put back later, but it was considered shocking." She described another scene as being shot especially to provoke the censors: "My hand that turned on the faucet of a bidet. It was too shocking, just water and my hand, but the sound of the bidet, showing, filming a bidet . . . the censors didn't tolerate such things." Yet another sequence meant to infuriate the censors involved bare breasts at the beach–*reportage* footage of the "monokini" shot by Jacques Rozier. This, too, was excised.[8]

Whether from the demands of the censors or the directors' own self-censorship, it is often by allusion that bodies are shown or evoked by the New Wave. At the same time, these films have a real fascination with the female body as an object of investigation. The cameras sought to satisfy a curiosity through close observation, as in the case of Éric Rohmer's early films. In the first sequence with Charlotte and her lover in *Une femme mariée*, there are no extremely revealing or raw images of her body. As described in *L'Avant-scène*, the scene shows Charlotte "still in her underwear, going down the roof staircase, almost dancing while hiding her nude breasts with her arms." Méril described her experience in the nude scenes: "Obviously, we were among the first, and the first women to accept nudity, but in that film, it's such a physical, elegant, and sculpted nudity that it's not *really* nudity."

She went on: "It's the body; it's not the same thing. There's exposing one's intimate parts, and then there's the body, and that's why he put in those shots of the Maillol sculptures that had just been installed in the Tuileries." By entrusting Godard with her body in service of the film, Méril almost allowed the director to sculpt it for the cinematic artwork. He asked her to lose weight in a very short amount of time for the shoot: "five kilos [about eleven pounds] in two weeks, which I did! It showed my desire and my enthusiasm. I had to please him. . . . I gave myself completely. I was completely an object. He could've asked me anything, anything. In fact, I did what he asked me."[9] Méril said she adopted Isabelle Huppert's philosophy about nudity: "When you're an actress, you're an actress. It means you make everything you have available: your hair, your mouth, your voice, and your body."

Later in the first sequence, as the camera lingers on Charlotte getting dressed in extreme close-up, her lingerie and parts of her body are focal points and objects of fantasy. Méril's body was also used for social commentary, illustrating Godard's implicit criticism of using the female body as a means of commercialism. With explicitly fetishizing images, Godard ironically denounced the practice, specifying in the script: "Extreme close-up of Charlotte's hands attaching her stockings to the garter-belt"; "extreme close-up of garter belt; close-up of bra strap, hooked wrong; Charlotte's hands fixing it; close-up of Charlotte's chest from the front covered by the bra; Charlotte buttons her blouse; extreme close-up of Charlotte's hands fastening her skirt."[10]

Cutting up the body in close-up images allows it to be analyzed more closely, and these images are intermingled with advertising and cinematographic, literary, and pictorial icons[11] (such as the image of actor and theater director Louis Jouvet juxtaposed with Charlotte's). This is the spirit that will guide the construction of Godard's epic eight-part video project *Histoire(s) du cinéma* that he undertook over two decades later.

Fragmented images of the female body fetishized in advertising reflected the new consumer society and denounced bourgeois society's artificial appeal to nature, in the spirit of author Roland Barthes's book *Mythologies*, which was influential at the time. Méril pointed to this aspect of *Une femme mariée*, noting years later "how a typical woman is bombarded by advertising." Addressing the power of advertising over women and its evolution today, she added, "How can she manage and think for herself through this bombardment? What would [Godard] say now with advertising the way it is now? At the time, it was the beginning of these big posters, [the] beginning of television also, so [Charlotte] was a woman who was a little lost, confused in front of all these messages crashing in on her."[12]

Critic Henry Chapier described the film in 1964 as a "humanist work," citing Godard's "ferocious satire of this alienation." A prime example is the image of Charlotte walking on the sidewalk, overshadowed by an enormous billboard of a woman's torso in an ad promoting a brassiere. Chapier signaled a "provocative irony" in that, by Godard focusing his camera on the lingerie ads in close-up, he reveals his own fascination with the commercialized female body.[13] Besides showing fetishized images of the body, the film implies how the roles of women (as well as that of the couple) were constructed in society through the written and pictorial messages in advertising. In one scene, Charlotte pages through the glossy images of (and ads aimed at) women in a magazine as she eavesdrops on a conversation at the next table between two high-school girls. This seemingly superficial "girl talk," rarely seen in films at the time, gives insight into their adolescent preoccupation with boys, their bodies, and their insecurities stemming from these idealized and fetishized ads.

As philosopher and filmmaker Guy Debord proposed in his writings defining the era (and influencing Godard), "Spectacle is not an ensemble of images, but a social relationship between people, mediatized by images."[14] In the film, the characters slowly start to repeat fabricated words and ready-made phrases, illustrated in the dinner party scene where Charlotte, her husband, and their guest each recite empty phrases that Godard took from an actual brochure promoting the apartment building in which they were filming. Film scholar Colin MacCabe also cites the influence of Barthes's *Mythologies* in society at the time and thus on the film, a work that explores the "new consumer society, analyzing the ways in which the bourgeois presentation of the world is

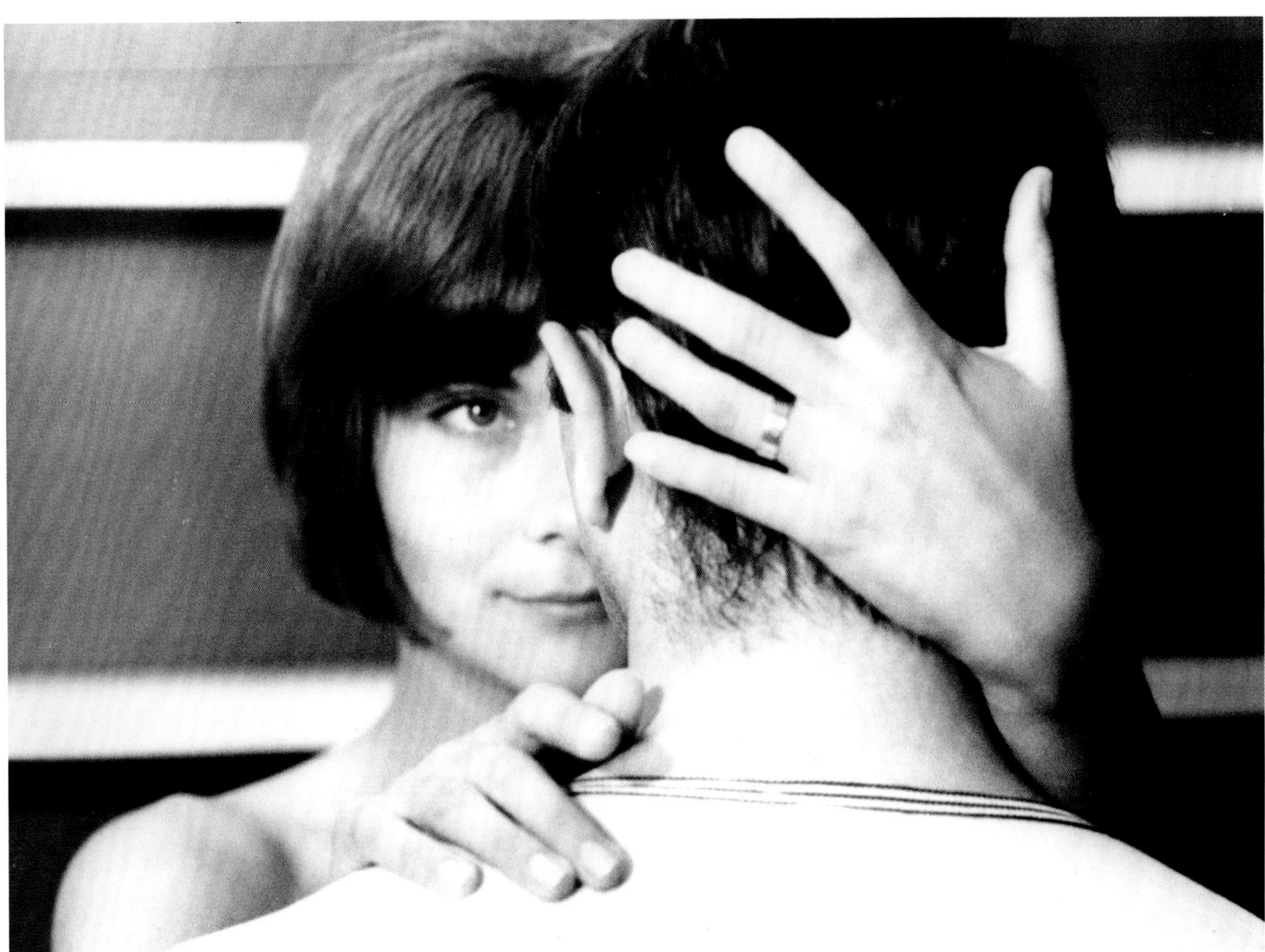

constantly denying history in favour of a totally fake appeal to nature." It is, in MacCabe's words, "this fake appeal to a Paris created from nothing which runs through the advertising texts" of the film.[15] When applied to the female characters, we see that "real" women, in the film as in real life, are now just the shadow of what advertising makes of their image: by synecdoche, the woman is a piece of lingerie.

Translating women's alienation through images, a sequence shows a photo shoot of cover girls and Charlotte on film, reversing the negative and implying that they exist only on celluloid, a social commentary that could easily apply to today's image-obsessed world. Méril also recalled the film's style as inspired by fashion magazines: "[Godard] thought the film should have an aesthetic that corresponded to these glossy magazines, with these big photos. It was also

the '60s, an era of explosive creativity: the beginning of fashion photography. *Elle* is inspired by *Vogue* and *Harper's Bazaar* with these huge photographers who used very bright lights." In fact, Méril herself was previously a Richard Avedon model for *Harper's*.

In the film, her look is more casual, with Godard having chosen her clothes himself at Monoprix, the inexpensive French retail chain. According to Méril, this was in part due to the tight budget and also because Godard considered wardrobe people "superfluous." "He brought me the striped nightgown and something with dots, and there were one or two things that were mine, but since the film was in black and white, he avoided all colors, and already he'd decided that there should be a certain unity in the material and fabrics," Méril recalled. Parisian designer agnès b. praised his

Macha Méril (Charlotte) in Jean-Luc Godard's *Une femme mariee* (*A Married Woman*), 1964

skill at selecting styles and fabrics that were "flattering to the actress." Though his characters tended to have only "two or three outfits per film," they "stood out because they were perfect for the image," she observed.

FOREGROUNDING TABOOS: BRINGING BIRTH CONTROL INTO DIALOGUE

The film also dared to address the reality of women's bodies in brief but key instances, far from the stylized, idealized, and fetishized images that commonly depicted them. With its documentary pretext, it also looked at women's concerns at the time with a focus on the body. While the body in general was usually avoided in New Wave films, the truth of a woman's body—its ability to reproduce, for example—was especially taboo. The subject of birth control was controversial and also avoided. French society in the mid-'60s was divided between conservatives and those with more modern values, and with the upcoming presidential elections of 1965, there were high stakes for both sides. *Une femme mariée* was one of the first French films to evoke "the pill" and birth control.

The question appears first on a billboard advertising contraception, which Charlotte passes on the sidewalk: "How to have children when you want: A doctor reveals what many women ignore." Another shot brings the reality of desire into the context with another billboard reading, "How far can women go in love?" The camera frames each as Charlotte pauses in front of them, emphasizing the reality that women have to navigate between love, physical desire, and childbearing.

Charlotte also visits the doctor to find out the results of a pregnancy test. As she waits, leafing through an anatomy book, she unfolds a sketch of the female body, exposing its organs and muscles in a purely scientific view that the film reveals to viewers in very rapid cutaways. The doctor, played by a real gynecologist Godard hired for the role, announces the results of the test: It is positive. "You're three months pregnant. You're due in May," he says. After seeing Charlotte's reaction, he adds, "This happy event doesn't seem to delight you." The follow-up discussion presents itself as a kind of interview where Charlotte asks direct questions about modern medicine, childbirth, birth control, and physical desire. The doctor's responses reflect the tension surrounding these questions at a time when such topics were taboo.

Charlotte says she is troubled and admits she is afraid. She asks about a new method of childbirth under anesthesia: "Will you let me give birth without pain?" The doctor replies, "Childbirth without pain? That's saying a lot! You need to see it solely as a method . . . whose only goal is preparing the *malade* psychologically to give birth." The word *malade*— meaning "the patient" but also the "ill person"—used to describe a pregnant woman is telling, revealing the doctor's discomfort in evoking the subject or at the very least his attempt to retain a clinical remove from the humanity of sex and motherhood.

"There was a question I always wanted to ask you, doctor," Charlotte continues. "What do you think of contraceptive methods?" A daring question at the time, apparently even for a doctor. He grows ill at ease and answers in a roundabout way. "That is an important question—very important since we are leaning toward these questions in a very important way. In this day and age, when we're about to send rockets to the moon, we conceive on the surface of the Earth as we conceived in the Stone Age." He goes on to talk about plants and animals and "appropriate conditions" for conception, adding that with science, the "human race is going against all this. We must sooner or later manage this conception in one way or another."

Charlotte confesses that she has a problem—that she is hesitating between two men and does not know who the father is. She asks the doctor, "Do you think physical pleasure is evidence?" The doctor disagrees, citing the new example of artificial insemination. "In this case, the *malade* is in a position that is outside the realm of the physical pleasure you are talking about. She only undergoes the procedure." Charlotte asks if physical pleasure and love are the same thing, wondering, "Is physical pleasure bad?" The doctor replies by reinforcing the established conservative view of sexuality: "Physical pleasure is not bad, since it should normally result in the desired conception." Charlotte ends the scene by again saying simply, "I'm afraid."

Contributing to this scene's direct but natural feel, Méril, known to be quite liberated in her own discourse on sexuality,[16] is neither shy nor inhibited as she deals with these taboo subjects. This short sequence offered a much clearer picture of the moral landscape in French society in the '60s: It was yet to be liberated. The actress described the film as "a unique experience that doesn't look completely like cinema because we treated questions spontaneously that were questions that concerned all women and that were at the dawn of the great revolution of '68, which I think sincerely was fomented by cinema."[17]

This moment in the film is only parenthetical. But coming back to the love triangle, the viewer has new insight into Charlotte's difficulty in navigating love. The last sequence shows Charlotte meeting her lover at the cinema at Orly Airport. The curtain in the theater is raised and the film begins. It is Alain Resnais's 1956 Holocaust documentary *Nuit et brouillard*, harking back to the many layers of trauma and the reality of the era. They leave the movie theater after the first scene and enter a hotel room. Knowing that she is pregnant but not knowing who the father is creates tension. In a bold reversal, and adding an almost Hitchcockian suspense to the scene, Charlotte asks her lover if he will marry her and speaks of the possibility of raising a child together:

Charlotte: When I'm divorced, will you marry me?
Robert: Of course.
Charlotte: And if I have a child, will you adopt it even if it's not yours?
Robert: Yes, but it will be mine. Why do you ask me that?

CONSPICUOUS ABSENCE: THE LINGERING INFLUENCE OF ANNA KARINA

Allowing for the comparison and deconstruction of the love triangle stereotypes, fragmented images of the body also correspond to the choice of cinematic form with parallel editing. Similar to Rivette in *Le Coup du berger*, Godard created a triangle with the woman at the center, showing the differences between the two male roles—husband and lover—while highlighting the similarities between the two men

plugged into this formula. In a mix of analogous gestures and words from each man, we see how the roles are in fact mental constructions. Both men, for example, express the

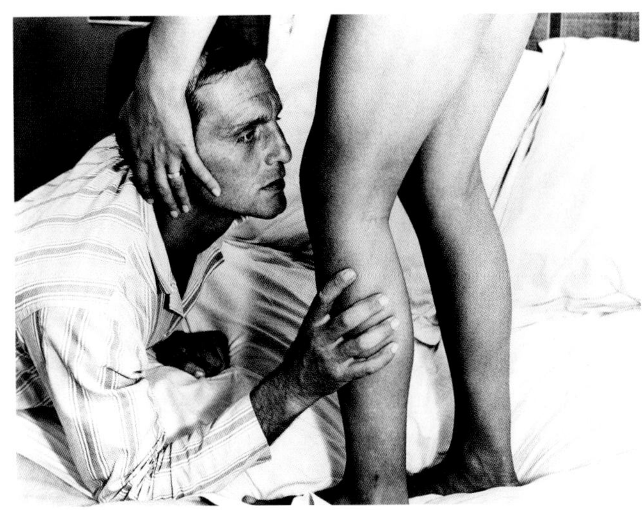

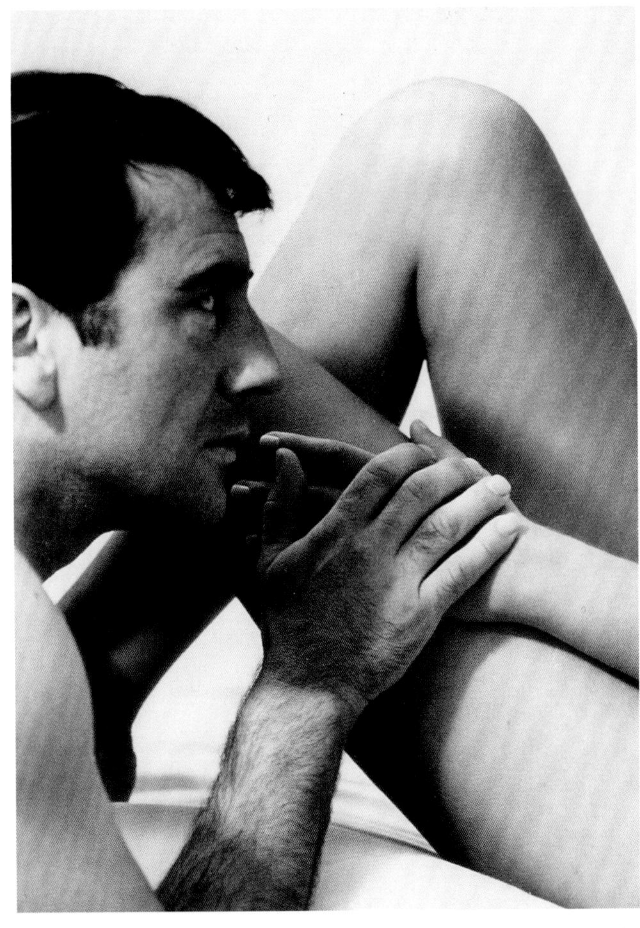

Philippe Leroy (Paul, the Husband) with Macha Méril (Charlotte) and Bernard Noël (Robert, the Lover) with Méril in Jean-Luc Godard's *Une femme mariée (A Married Woman)* 1964

desire to have a child with Charlotte. Her husband asks in an earlier scene:

Pierre: When will we have a child?
Charlotte: You already have one.
Pierre: Yes, but I want one with you.
Charlotte: Have you been thinking about it a long time?
Pierre: Since I met you.

We see the characters in the triangle in the same positions and situations, exchanging the same words, from saying, "I love you," to washing their hands together, whether they are the woman as wife or lover, or the man as lover or husband. They become statues, fixed in poses of love where their body parts are disjointedly framed and their gestures accentuated, eliminating feelings or raw impulses.

This fragmentation and distancing in the editing deconstruct the cliché of the love triangle in that the participants lose their own individuality, appearing on screen as fragments of bodies, an unidentifiable hand, leg, or neck, with each part belonging to an interchangeable person—in this particular love triangle, the men. As they assume identical postures with Charlotte, we see how the different roles (husband, lover, and by extension, wife) are in fact only perceived notions, and the participants are all replaceable.

Far from dated, this social commentary could just as easily apply to today as we search for love in a consumer-driven society that, despite its comforts and overabundance of technology, teaches us only to define ourselves and others through the roles we play. We, like Charlotte, search for love and happiness mediated by an abundance of images. We see Charlotte lost in mixed and confusing messages, and we hear her inner voice expressing alienation as it whispers in voice-over: "Who am I? I never knew exactly. Only one time. It's my fault. I know he loves me. It's difficult. Happiness? I don't know." Godard explained, "They only have physiological reflexes left. Something in them disappeared. It is a film that is missing something. But this something that is missing is also the subject of my film, something that is lost and that must be found again. . . . It is the awareness that they are missing."[18]

It is not surprising that Godard spoke of something missing in this moment in his filmography: What is missing is Anna Karina. Her protagonist in *Alphaville*, having forgotten how to love and even the words to express the feeling, echoes Charlotte's confused inner voice in *Une femme mariée*. *Alphaville*'s male protagonist, Lemmy Caution, is on a mission to help her remember. *Pierrot le fou* also alludes to the notion of something missing in the opening credits, but in the end, Karina's voice announces that "it is found again," reciting Rimbaud's words.

Une femme mariée then is also an investigation into the idea of love, of lost love, and of the feminine mystery, as if Godard is going to the scene of the crime to look for clues. In the first image, a woman's hand crawls up the screen and a man wraps his around her wrist. His whispered dialogue, however, creates distance: "Yes, you kiss someone, you caress them, but in the end, you remain outside. It's like a house that you never enter." Charlotte protests: "But you can meld with someone if you love them." Méril cited this scene when she suggested this was a deeply personal film for Godard:

I think it's Jean-Luc's story. I don't think he really experienced fusion, fusional love with a woman. The maximum he knew was obviously with Anna, who is an extraordinary woman, you know, a very deep, clever, and very rebellious woman. He was troubled because she was like him a bit. They were very similar but I think they were very unhappy. They tortured each other. I'd have to know more about Jean-Luc's childhood and what he experienced, why he's incapable of loving . . . but it's the case with all men, they are afraid of women. We are a vase that you don't know where to start to pick up. A woman is complicated, very complicated.[19]

As the film tries to consolidate the idea of how the same acts and words could be expressed by a woman with a lover and a husband (who was once a lover), the myopic camera analyzes hands, legs, and faces from an objective point of view that excludes sentimentality and eroticism.[20] However, when the husband looks at his wife after sharing an intimate moment together, we see his despair in close-up. Méril again pointed to the resonance with Godard's personal life:

Philippe Leroy (Paul, the Husband) with Macha Méril (Charlotte) in Jean-Luc Godard's *Une femme mariée* (*A Married Woman*) 1964

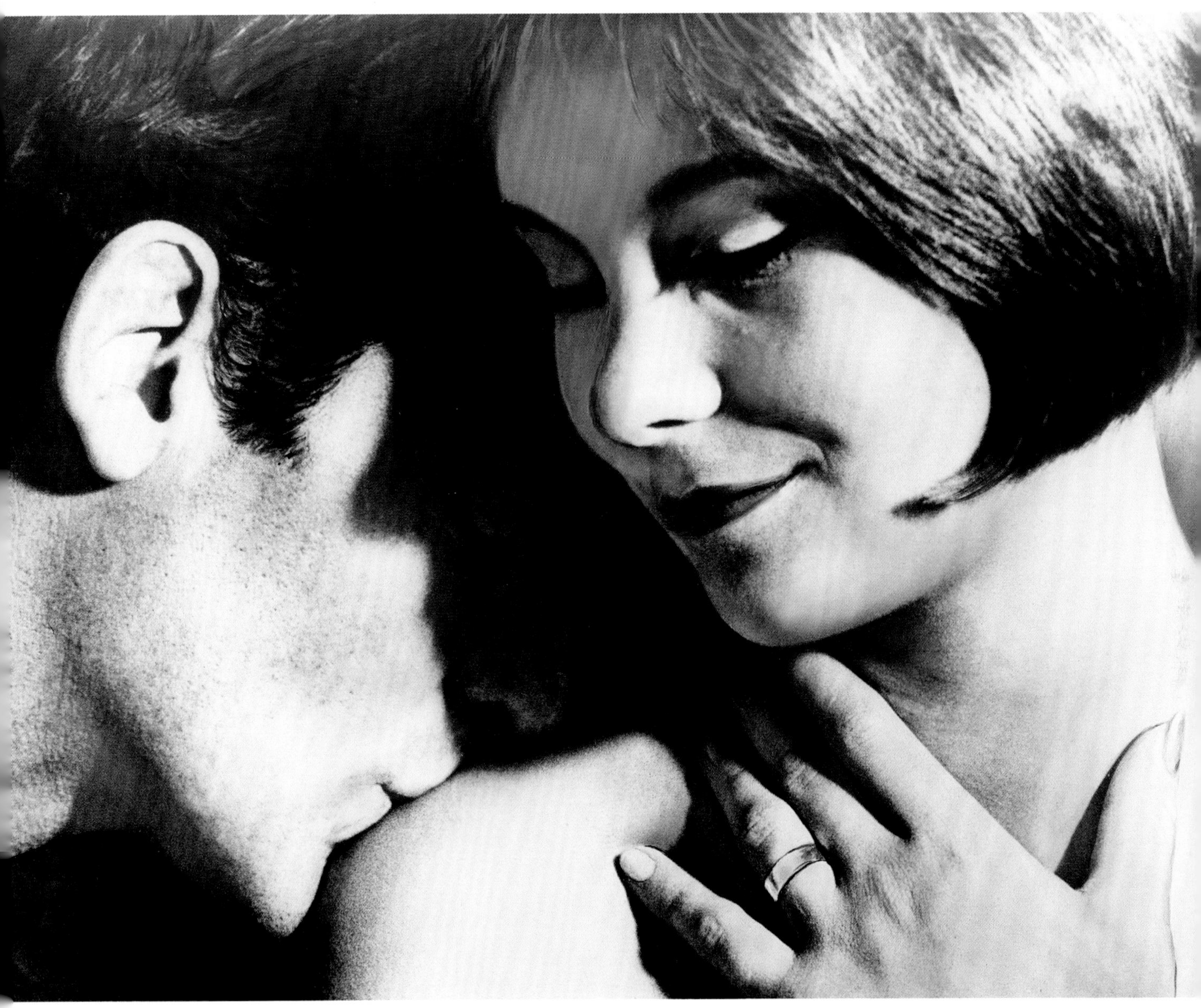

As much as everyone admires *Le Mépris* . . . it's more expressed, he gave more of his despair, his thoughts, his search for purity. . . . He made *Le Mépris* easily, it didn't take much effort. I think that wasn't the case with *La Femme mariée*, a bit because he was suffering in his private life at the time, and also because the film was a bigger commitment, a greater philosophical, political, and cinematic gesture.[21]

Godard explained that he had a "fragmentary and jumbled vision of the world," adding that in the film, he wanted to translate only the most important signs, where the form disappears, leaving space for meaning. "I made *La Femme mariée* to counter *Le Mépris,* which was a long continuous sentence," he stated. An intertitle after the opening credits of *Une femme mariée* reflects that sentiment: "Fragments of a film shot in 1964."

In much the same way Godard inhabited his male protagonists in the films he made with Karina or used Michel Piccoli's character as an alter ego in *Le Mépris, Une femme mariée* also revealed his attempt to understand love—and perhaps the loss of Karina's love—besides his proclaimed mission to denounce women's alienation by advertising. In the scene in the hotel room at Orly Airport, Charlotte presses her lover to answer the question, "What is love for you?" He stumbles in his response, rife with unfinished thoughts and hesitant pauses:

But how do you—I don't know, talking about love, it's talking about relationships in— between two people—You understand, love, is—it's oneself in relation to another— you understand?[22]

He ends by confessing that he doesn't know. "Could you kiss two girls at once and caress them?" Charlotte asks. "I would have to make a choice also," Robert replies. After a few more moments together in the airport hotel room, a voice announces the imminent departure for a flight to Marseille. The couple reads aloud Jean Racine's seventeenth-century play *Bérénice* together in bed, reinforcing the tragic element of their situation. Though she denies she is crying, Charlotte's tears reveal her humanity, just like Kar-

ina's character will awaken in *Alphaville. Une femme mariée* ends with a simple exchange between Charlotte and her lover. "Okay, it's over. I have to go," Robert says. Charlotte confirms this: "Yes, it's over."

Méril commended the film for remaining unresolved, saying, "It's a deeply moving film because there's no answer. The tragedy remains whole." She explained how the film reflected and continues to reflect women's experience in the world as they try to make decisions on multiple levels:

It's interesting to see it again today, because with everything that's happened in women's history and liberation, it seems like a lot of things have progressed—but this pain, it remains, this anxiety about knowing what we're going to become, what we will do with our lives, how are we going to resolve all the questions of happiness. That's the force of art, it's incredible, and this film to me is one of the great films that will remain in posterity among twenty masterpieces of cinema. It was an alarm bell, this film, like all his films. In this way, it's political cinema because it's cinema that alerts, that rings little bells saying, 'Pay attention!'[23]

LA RELIGIEUSE: FROM SUCCESS ON STAGE TO SCANDAL ON SCREEN

After her much celebrated collaboration with Godard, it was for her performance in Rivette's 1966 adaptation of *La Religieuse*—Denis Diderot's eighteenth-century novel about a young girl forced to become a nun—that Anna Karina received recognition as an actress in her own right that was meaningful to her. Rivette himself applauded her work, stating in an interview at the time of the film's release that Karina "just proved she had her place among the best actresses of her generation."[24]

But before the screen adaptation, *La Religieuse* was presented on stage at the Théâtre des Champs-Élysées in May 1963[25] under Rivette's direction. Karina's performance in the leading role earned her new respect for what was acknowledged as a difficult part. She had just finished filming *Vivre sa vie* when Rivette offered her the role of Suzanne Simonin.

"I really worked a lot for *La Religieuse* because, you know, I'm not French. And when I came to Paris, of course I couldn't speak French," Karina recounted. "So I went to the movies to learn French and took lessons and all that. And when Jacques Rivette asked me to do *La Religieuse,* I worked day and night to speak this language Denis Diderot had written centuries ago."[26]

Though Karina's venture on stage was a step toward her independence as an actress, away from her association with Godard, she found out that he had in fact produced the play: "I heard many years later that Jean-Luc produced it. I didn't know, he never told me that! It was like a present."[27] Jean Gruault worked with Rivette to adapt Diderot's novel for the stage, and the production was a huge success. "[Everybody liked it," Karina said. "Even Brigitte Bardot came to the show. She was with Sami Frey at that time, and they saw it on the stage with me and they cried. It was very good, I got good reviews, and even a prize from the radio." She remarked that "there was no scandal at all at the time with the play, to the contrary. . . . It was only afterwards that the film caused a scandal." Karina seemed perplexed, recounting that after making the film three years after the play, "when it was coming out, it was banned by [French minister of culture André] Malraux and the priests and the Catholic Church saying, 'What did you do? *Blasphème*! *Blasphème*!' What did we do?"[28]

In effect, no one seemed to understand the reason behind the scandal, especially considering that when it was banned, the film had not even been screened. The play had not caused any problems, and, on the contrary, was a big hit. Rivette as a film director had a reputation for discretion in his *mise en scene*, and his previous films, *Le Coup du berger* and *Paris nous appartient* (*Paris Belongs to Us*, 1961) were far from salacious.

After the success of the play, and after leaving *Cahiers du cinéma*, Rivette met with producer Georges de Beauregard, who enthusiastically supported the project of bringing Diderot's novel to the screen. In making the cinematic adaptation, however, Rivette was confronted with the very real problem of censorship. The director remarked that "it was an era where censorship still really existed. You had to go before the *précensure* [the censorship commission evaluating a film's content before it was made] for all films that risked having problems." Rivette met several times with the president of the commission, a conservative, fervent Catholic, conveying his good intentions: "I told him that we weren't at all looking to make a scandalous film, that we didn't at all have the intention of 'pulling a Vadim,' like we said at that time."[29]

Yet, the film adaptation of *La Religieuse* provoked one of the biggest scandals in the history of French cinema, echoing that of Buñuel's *L'Âge d'or* (*Age of Gold*, 1930). Were the censors more demanding of cinema than of theater? Or was there something more behind the scandal of the film adaptation? Why was a story from the late eighteenth century seemingly so relevant (so threatening?) in the mid-'60s?

La Religieuse illustrates perhaps better than any other film the idea of an "un-scandalous" scandal with the film's absence of what could be considered provocative or shocking scenes. Certainly, the well-established reputation of Diderot's infamous novel, known for the scandal it provoked in the eighteenth century, laid the groundwork beforehand, feeding the buzz. Written in 1760 and based on the life of Marguerite Delamarre, the novel denounced practices of the Catholic Church that, in the mid-1960s, sent the church and censors into a panic. Shining a light on certain vices of monastic life, and mixing homosexuality and religion, remained taboo even as France approached May '68. Karina brought to light this hypothesis: "It really became a big scandal. Nobody understood why, because of course there's this homosexual thing going on in the story. It was totally forbidden to talk about that at the time but today everybody knows about it! . . . Diderot's book was forbidden for over 150 years in France. Denis Diderot is a big classic, and this book was forbidden in every school for many years."[30] Karina seemed bewildered, however, as she described Diderot's "beautiful novel" with "beautiful language," insisting that she and Rivette did not understand the "big, big scandal."

When the play came to the screen, it was a different time, a different context in France. According to *Le Monde*, under Charles de Gaulle's presidency, during the pre-electoral period, it was not a good idea to offend the Catholic Church, whose moral authority extended to cinema.[31] Karina remembered that Rivette "had a lot of trouble finding a location to shoot," noting that "the nuns wanted to read the script first." The ban was still surprising considering it was a film no one had been able to see. The subject, however, provoked polemical rumors that reached great proportions, illustrating how censorship is often a symptom of a collective panic.[32]

The banning of the film, however, naturally had the opposite effect, creating "an enormous scandal that stayed in the headlines for months," Karina recalled. Malraux decided to send the film to Cannes where it was projected and acclaimed (even if it was banned in France on April 1, 1966). When the film went to Cannes, "everybody started to scream and it was in the papers for six months," noted Karina. She explained that "it couldn't come out because all the priests and all the Catholics in France were so angry and we didn't understand why, and Rivette didn't understand why either." When the film was finally released, she explained, "it was a big success of course because everybody wanted to see the scandalous film that was not really a scandal."[33] As Rivette also confirmed, "We were hurt, sad, we didn't understand. It took more than a year for the film to come out. It was an enormous success."[34] According to *Le Monde*, the scandal lasted from the spring of 1966 into the summer of 1967 after the film waited a year to be officially authorized, but only for those over eighteen years old.[35] It would take twenty years for this age restriction to be lifted.

THE CHURCH, THE PATRIARCHY, AND THE PERILS OF GETTING "TOO CLOSE"

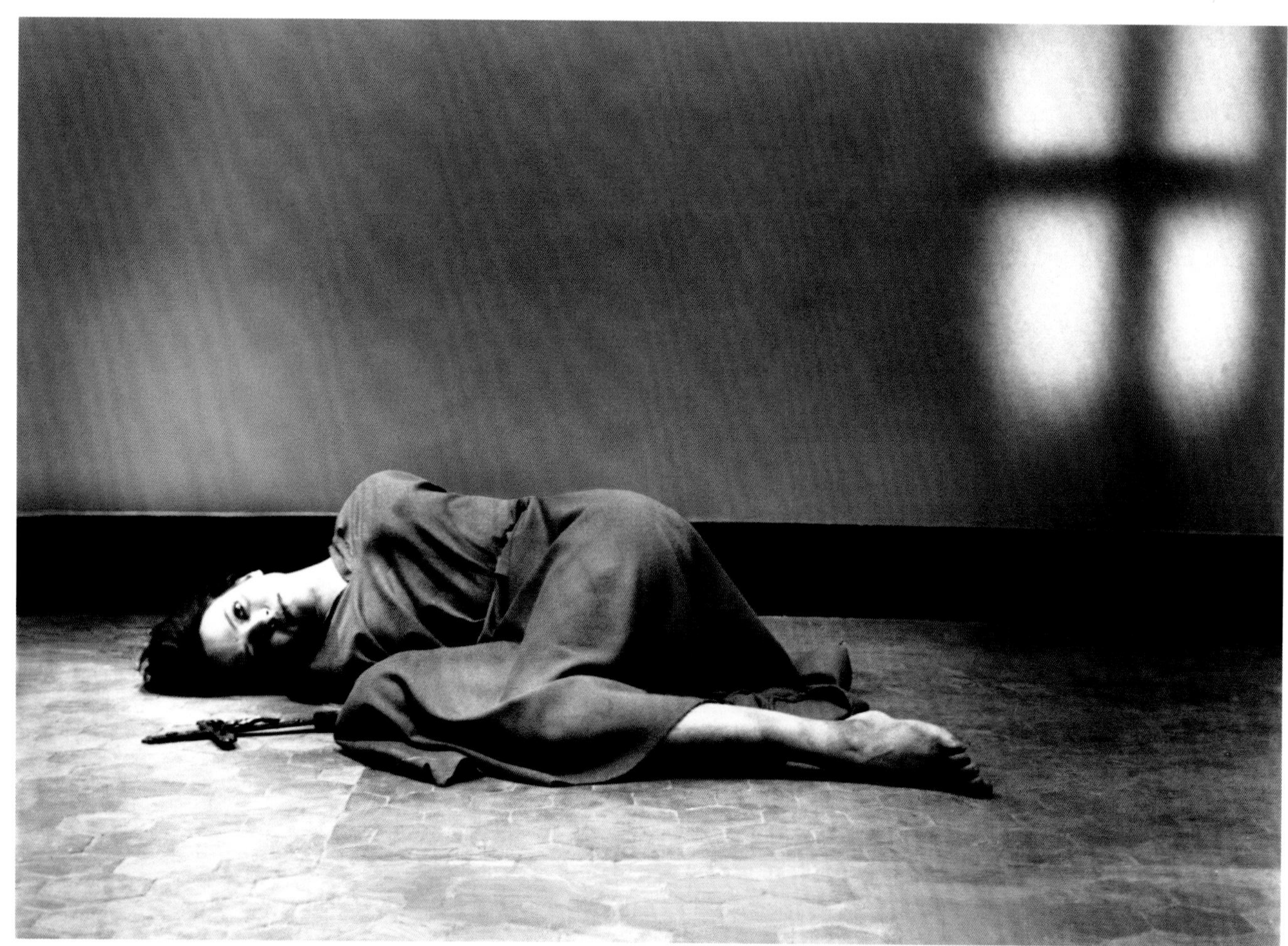

Anna Karina (Suzanne) in Jacques Rivette's *La Religieuse* (*The Nun*), 1966

Why was the film so threatening in 1966, just two years before the societal revolution of May '68? A direct explanation lay in the weakening of the Catholic Church at the time the film was made. Rivette described the story as being "made up of relationships of Suzanne Simonin with her three superiors who each represent a different form of monastic life." He went on to explain that "the film does not attack nuns or religion. It attacks a certain society that is that of the eighteenth century and questions the foundations of monastic life but in noble terms [in relation to] reflection, not satire or basely anticlerical ones."[36] In the novel, Diderot wanted to denounce the isolation of life in the convent, the temptation and sexual vices that stemmed from being confined, and psychological torture. It is obvious to see why the Catholic Church would be against this bad publicity.

In the mid-1960s, Catholicism was undergoing massive change in terms of church attendance and practice. Just a few years prior, Catholics were seen to make up the "ultramajority" in France; in fact, from the late nineteenth century up through the early 1960s, data shows that 98 percent of the population was Roman Catholic.[37] Stemming from cultural changes after World War II, Pope John XXIII announced the need to modernize the Catholic Church (hence the Italian term *aggiornamento*, "bringing up to date") by calling for the creation of the Second Vatican Council in January 1959, which came as a shock to the world.[38] Lasting four sessions, from 1962 to 1965, it sought to update the Church's traditions, from opening Mass to languages besides Latin to encouraging alliances with different faiths,[39] and to renew the Church's global role.[40] Ironically, Mass attendance, confession attendance, and baptisms plummeted in France in 1965—a drop-off that historian Guillaume Cuchet suggests was indirectly caused by Vatican II and its general relaxation of rules and teachings (among other factors), which people may have accepted as a tacit invitation to take religion less seriously.[41]

The jeopardized position of the Catholic Church was certainly one reason for keeping bad publicity to a minimum, but could there be another less direct explanation as well? Like the frequent appearance of the prostitute figure in New Wave films makes us question society's tensions in terms of women's roles, power, representations, and relationships during that era, it is equally telling that the figure of the nun from a centuries-old novel would appear in a *film d'auteur* at the time and cause such a scandal. What might this say about women's growing freedom, about marriage, or about feminine desire? Moreover, why was the film completely banned for a year before its release, and why did it take over twenty years for the restriction for viewers under eighteen to be lifted, for example? Was there something more that disturbed the Establishment?

In his interview at the time, Rivette summarized the film in a way that reveals a possible answer: "It's the story of a girl whose parents force her to enter a convent and become a nun against her will. . . . This isn't because she doesn't have faith, it's because she doesn't want to spend her life in a convent. The book and the film expose why and how she is obliged to accept." Through his commentary, we can see the notions of authoritative parental power at play against the heroine's free will. In the film, Suzanne says simply, "I ask to be free." But she is ultimately coerced into bowing to their demands, escaping in the end only by taking her own life. It is not a far stretch to see the link to patriarchal society of the 1960s in all its power imbalances: As women gained footing to become more independent, they were still weathering powerful societal pressure to conform to traditional norms and standards. In effect, we can see a clear association between the story's young woman locked up against her will in a convent and women forced to live within a patriarchal society at large. Exposing these mechanisms in the eighteenth or twentieth century, then, would be equally threatening to the established order.

Karina's portrayal of Diderot's heroine illustrates the helplessness of a woman desperate for a voice and power over her own life, a prisoner in the thick stone walls of the convent. Showing how this lack of freedom can incite insanity, her story invites the viewer to expand the walls of the convent to encompass society as a whole. In this context of confinement, we can also draw the parallel between the convent and marriage, as depicted in Rivette's *mise en scène* that shows Suzanne behind bars in a white gown and veil, forced to take vows against her will. It is easy to make a correlation with women's lack of power at a time when they were not able to

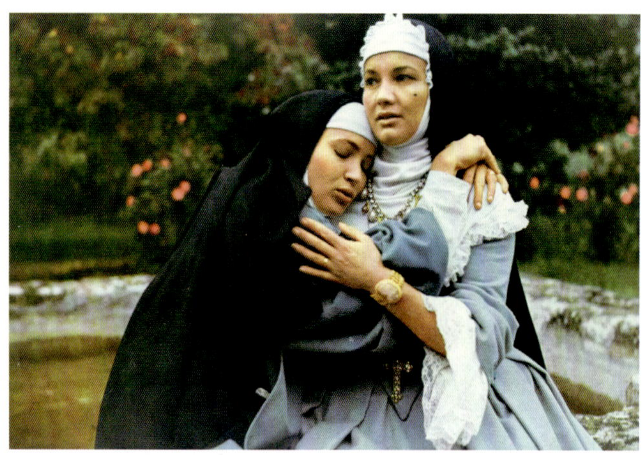

own a bank account, write a check, or work without the authorization of their husbands. Suzanne exclaims, for example, "I took the habit without freedom. I'd like to rip it up!" The lack of freedom under imposed authority and the option to work are also addressed in the film as Suzanne says, "I don't have any vocation. I don't want to obey my parents."

And then there is the question of feminine desire, always an uncomfortable and disturbing subject in the context of patriarchal society. In the film, desire is implied through nonverbal gestures and ambiguous dialogue with mixed messages. One of the superiors tells Suzanne, "God's hand is upon you. It keeps you. It leads you in spite of yourself to your holy spouse, to joy with no end," then begs Suzanne to commit to "chastity, poverty and obedience." In the early morning, the superior visits Suzanne in her bed, embracing her while asking her about her dreams. When the rooster crows, the superior realizes that the others will soon be arriving to dress Suzanne and says she must go: "Being here will distract me. . . . I must have only one thing on my mind." Unable to tolerate the confinement and life in the convent, however, Suzanne breaks down. The sisters label her as possessed and impure, spit on her, and file an exorcism case against her, forcing her to "renounce Satan." In the second part of the film, Rivette shows a different angle of life in the convent, focusing on the superficial distractions the sisters resort to in order to tolerate their existence. Still desiring to leave the convent, Suzanne confides in a superior: "I hate being put away and held back. I feel I am called to something else," adding that the boredom weighs heavily on her.

"Do you feel stirrings within yourself, desires?" the superior asks. "Is it freedom you miss?" When Suzanne responds, "Yes, that [freedom] and perhaps other things," the superior's implied meaning speaks loudly as she asks, "What other things, my friend?" taking Suzanne's hand.

Though feminine desire in the context of the convent is undebatably a scandalous topic, Rivette's camera does not get "too close," choosing instead to portray the nuns' (sometimes violent) reactions to it. The idea remains cerebral and the physical avoided, suppressed. Karina confirmed Rivette's tendency of being discreet as a filmmaker, affirming that he never did "anything perverted—he was so puritanical, he didn't seek to cause a scandal. He can surprise, disturb, maybe, but shock, no." But she also described his meticulous control and habit of not getting too close to his actors with his camera: "It was great to work with Rivette, but sometimes it was a bit tiring because he would rehearse the same scene for five days and it didn't make that much difference," specifying that "in the film, he liked to be far away always to see the whole scene. I think there's only one close-up in the film and I don't even think it's that close."[42] The trait of not getting "too close" is worth considering as it translates the director's discretion, integrity, and commitment to cinema's moral questions of *mise en scène*, but also in what it could reveal about the tendency of New Wave directors to shy away from the body or deep intimacy.

It is hard to put ourselves in the context of France in the mid-1960s when the Catholic Church was undergoing change but still strongly influential in many domains, where prostitution was normalized in a country still rigidly anchored in convention but on the brink of a social revolution that would erupt in 1968. If we examine what was seen as scandalous in that society, however, we get a clearer picture of how courageous and audacious these revolutionary films were in bringing France out of the dark ages to address these changes even through the filter of a literary adaptation.

Daring in their treatment of subject matter with ideas that challenged societal norms, the New Wave directors, like

Anna Karina (Suzanne) and Liselotte Pulver (Mme de Chelles) in Jacques Rivette's *La Religieuse* (*The Nun*) 1966

Rivette, remained influenced by archaic models that kept them from getting "too close" in depicting more audacious scenes of physical desire exposing the body. Looking closely at the *mise en scène*, we see that even in the most scandalous films or passionate love stories, most directors shy away from showing the body or of getting too close to reality, preferring to maintain the women of their dreams as ideas or ideals. It will be the tension created by the women in their lives and the modern actresses in their films that also influences change. In *La Religieuse*, Suzanne's (and Karina's own) valiant attempt at standing up for herself to gain freedom represents a bold step in the right direction.

THE MYTH OF SCANDALOUS CINEMA: WHAT REMAINED TO BE SEEN

For a generation of filmmakers who value authenticity, what is revealed by their tendency of refusing to show a reality that gets too close to women, to the body, and to love scenes? Is it simply a question of imposed censorship at the time, an internalized one, a puritanical trait, or is it something else? It might be surprising to realize this absence of the body, for example, in films where the question of love is so present, almost an obsession. Instead of "free" love scenes like in Bergman's *Monika*–the rare exception in French cinema being Jean Genet's *Un chant d'amour* (A

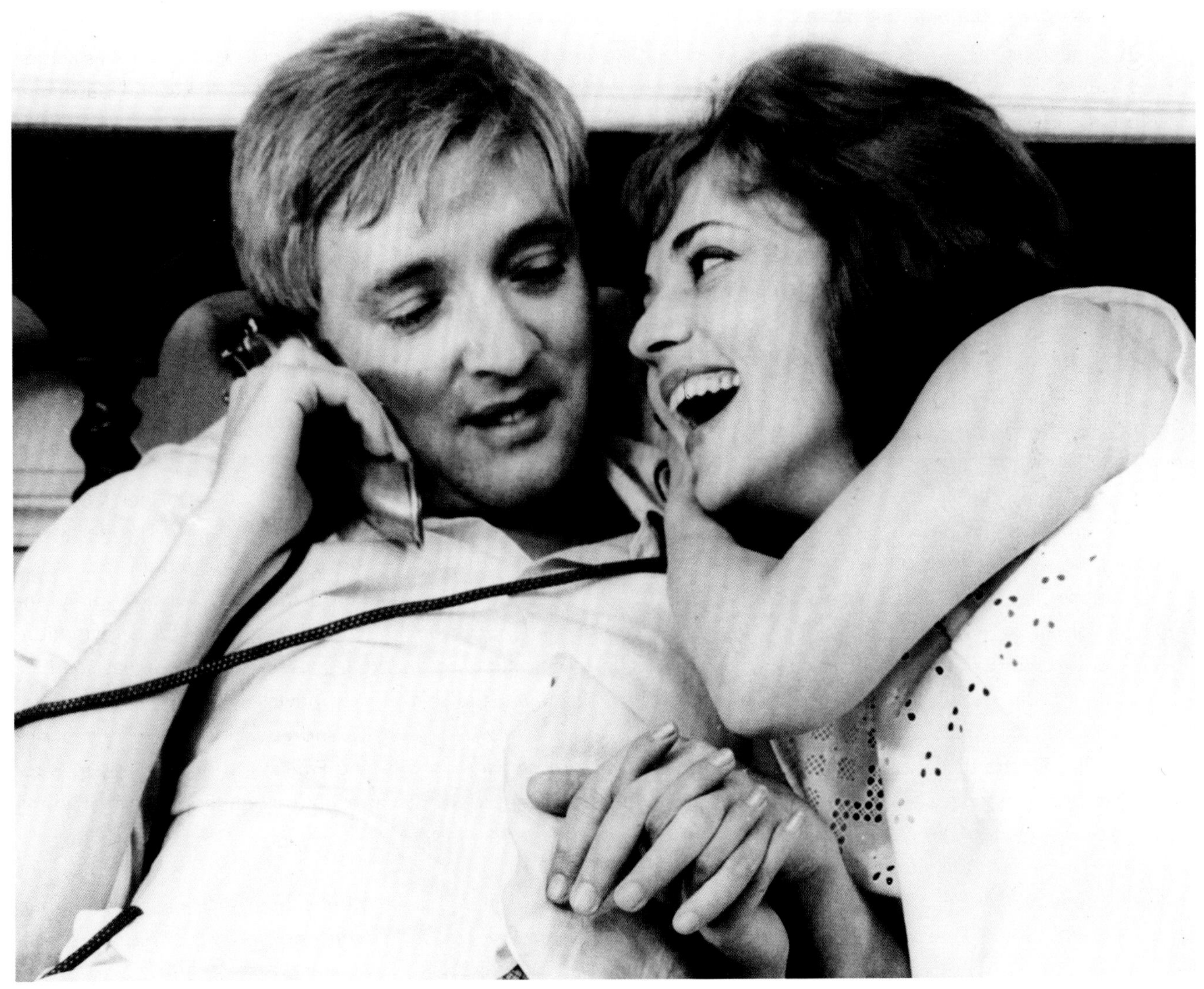

Oskar Werner (Jules) and Jeanne Moreau (Catherine) in François Truffaut's *Jules et Jim*, 1962

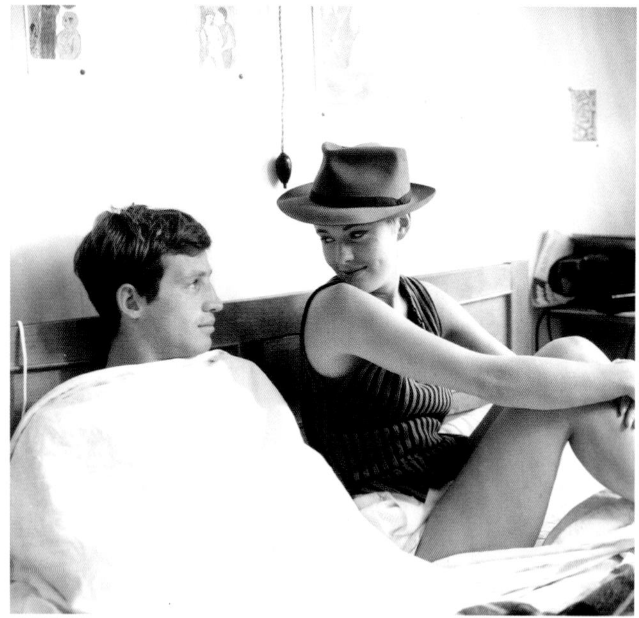

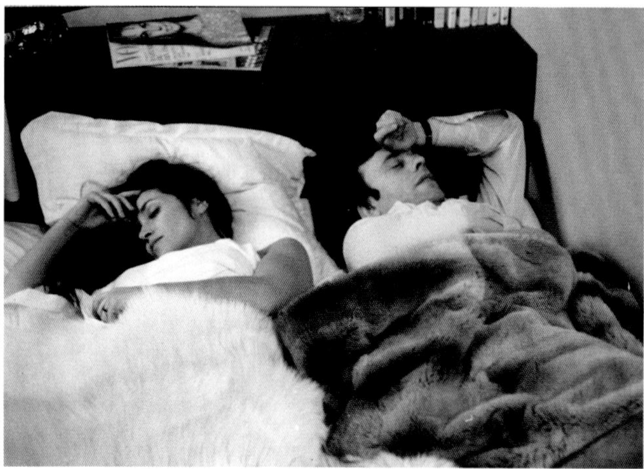

Song of Love, 1950)—the ones evoking the physical concentrate, for the most part, on the actress's face. Even in films considered more daring or scandalous, the love scenes do not go very far, often avoiding, like Rivette, getting too close.

Though Louis Malle's *Les Amants* was seen as scandalous at the time, we saw that there was not much scandal to "see" as the director attempted to capture a passionate love story (and his romance with Jeanne Moreau) on screen. In Anouk Aimée's portrayal of a prostitute in *Lola*, Jacques Demy chose to cut immediately each time there was a hint at her

profession. Godard and Truffaut also remain far away from the reality of prostitution, sidestepping or only alluding to it timidly as they sought to use prostitutes as metaphors, confidants, or maternal-love substitutes.

In *Jules et Jim*, however, Truffaut did not mind tackling one of the most taboo subjects when it comes to storyline. In bringing the story of a ménage à trois to the screen, besides the questions of morals and conventions that would influence the audience's reception of the film, there was the more concrete problem of censorship. In a letter to his *amie américaine*, journalist Helen Scott, before the film came out, Truffaut himself cited his fear of the film being banned for those under eighteen years old, a restriction "that seems almost inevitable for this pure *amour à trois*,"[43] as he called it. Claudine Bouché, the film's editor, remarked, "What seems admissible today, a woman in love with and [the] lover of two men, wasn't easy to show thirty years ago."[44]

Though the story in itself was scandalous, the film focuses on something deeper: the poetry of Henri-Pierre Roché's language in the novel, the beauty of the images, and the complexity of love and friendship. Truffaut focused on this aspect of the film in his letter to Scott, describing it as "an ode to life and to death, a demonstration by joy and sadness of the impossibility of any amorous combination outside the couple."[45] His words again illustrate a certain sensibility (or a symptom of self-censorship) of New Wave directors, choosing to depict love over showing the physical on screen.

In *À bout de souffle*, Godard balances allusions to eroticism, portrayed in a humorous way, with romanticism, creating distance. In the famous long sequence in Patricia's hotel room, the couple (Seberg and Belmondo) discuss their different points of view of the relationship in an attempt to define it. Illustrating with humor the ambiguity between love and sexuality, the dialogue expresses their own incertitude and confusion. Patricia is depicted as contemplative and serious while Michel remains an eternal adolescent. Their different perspectives on love and desire play out in words and images that remain innocent in a new portrayal

Top: Jean-Paul Belmondo (Michel) and Jean Seberg (Patricia) in Jean-Luc Godard's *À bout de souffle* (*Breathless*), 1960. **Bottom:** Françoise Fabian (Maud) and Jean-Louis Trintignant (narrator) in Éric Rohmer's *Ma Nuit chez Maud* (*My Night at Maud's*), 1969

of emerging intimacy between a young couple, even the most unconventional.

Patricia: Leave me alone, I'm thinking.
Michel: About what?
Patricia: The tragedy is that I don't even know. Why did you come back here?
Michel: Because I wanted to sleep with you again.
Patricia: To me, that's not a reason.
Michel: Of course it is; it means I love you.
Patricia: And I don't know yet if I love you.

Godard's *mise en scène* evokes (masculine) desire through Michel's playful dialogue with the images of nudes from the pages of a magazine he is reading. The images in close-up, fantasies of women's bodies, are again subverted by his comedic commentary: "Women never want to do in eight seconds what they are willing to do eight days later. It's the same in the end, eight seconds or eight days, so why not eight centuries?" Patricia's point of view is illustrated with a painting followed by a shot of the couple framed in a similar way, in parallel with the romantic image and Michel's reaction, teasing her. The editing opens the characters' dialogue about gendered stereotypes in describing their desires:

Patricia: I would like it to be like Romeo and Juliet.
Michel: Oh là, là, that's just like a girl, those ideas!
Patricia: You see that that's not what you said last night in the car. Romeo couldn't live without Juliet, but you can.
Michel: No, I can't live without you.
Patricia: Oh là, là, that's just like a boy, those ideas!

The counterpoint between the dialogue and the image here establishes a game of *mise en scène* in the juxtaposition of these perspectives. Even if Godard gives the more grounded point of view to Patricia here—she is the strong one, dealing with the reality of her possible pregnancy—he also shows her as romantic. She assumes her search for meaning as Godard pokes fun at Michel with his adolescent fantasies of women's bodies in the magazine and his clichéd stance of confounding sex and love. In this intimate scene (in a film also forbidden to those under eighteen years old), Godard does not show any scandalous eroticism. Instead, the couple's closeness is depicted through conversation and playfulness, which was applauded by French audiences while perplexing those in the United States. Helen Scott described the reaction to the characters' conversation in a letter to Truffaut about the scenes depicting "Belmondo-Seberg in bed together." She explained that in France, "people very much admired this dialogue that was natural, etc.," but that in the United States, "people complained about the interminable scenes 'where they talk incessantly and you wonder what they're talking about.'"[46] With Godard, then, it is the dialogue that illustrates true intimacy and love, not the body.

Innumerable marks of reserve (or self-censorship) appear with New Wave directors in scenes where nudity might be expected. Rohmer's camera, for example, fixates on Haydée's body on the beach in the prologue of *La Collectionneuse* in statuesque, poetic shots, but shows her in bed, strategically covered, with a collection of young men in very rapid shots. In these seemingly clandestine shots, she is framed between doors like Godard frames the prostitutes in *Vivre sa vie*. With Rohmer, these stolen moments, closer to reality, make the male protagonists ill at ease. In his next film, *Ma nuit chez Maud*, Rohmer's protagonist is horrified to learn that there is no extra bedroom when bad weather obliges him to spend the night with Maud. Although he is visibly attracted to her, the desirable divorcée does not fit the predetermined image of the woman the protagonist wants to marry. When he realizes that he will have to share the bed with Maud that night, he panics. As she gets undressed to go to sleep, in an implicit scene of seduction, Rohmer's prudish protagonist envelopes himself in a blanket to protect himself from feminine desire (or rather, from himself). The expected love scene will not take place. Instead, it will echo iconography from the famous myth of Tristan and Isolde. Maud and the protagonist will also spend a chaste night together like the lovers separated by Tristan's sword. In *L'Amour l'après-midi* (*Love in the Afternoon*, 1972), Rohmer's camera shows another female "temptress," Chloé, in a position where she is nude on a bed in a pictorial pose summoning the protagonist (and the viewer), recalling Manet's *Olympia* (1863). But unlike the painting, here she covers her breasts. Like Maud, Chloé puts the male character in danger of betraying his ideal image of himself (through his own physical desire). Though the underlying sensuality is strong in Rohmer's films, this is as far as he will go. In the years surrounding May '68, and knowing Rohmer's reputation for discretion, we can suppose that the origin of this censorship is the director's own puritanical sensibility.

LOVE STORIES OVER LOVE SCENES: SELF-CENSORSHIP IN *UN HOMME ET UNE FEMME*

In the same year that *La Religieuse* brought Karina both scandal and success, Anouk Aimée found only success in *Un homme et une femme*—though its mainstream style, full of cultural and aesthetic clichés, was a far cry from Rivette's *film d'auteur*. Because of this tendency, Claude Lelouch is not typically considered a New Wave director despite being a contemporary. Lelouch's film offers a point of comparison, however, with the New Wave, depicting a mature woman in a love story, and allowing us to gain insight into the presence of love stories and absence of love scenes, at least ones going very far in representing the body. Unlike the discreet yet rawer images of Malle's story of passion in *Les Amants*, the love scenes in *Un homme et une femme* correspond more to an idea of a G-rated fantasy.

Lelouch's love story about a race car driver (Jean-Louis Trintignant) who lost his wife in an accident and who falls in love with a beautiful young widow (Aimée) opens with a reference to a fairy tale. On the beach, Anne (Aimée) reads the story of Barbe bleue (Bluebeard) to her daughter, and the story that follows, between the two protagonists, is told like a *photo-roman* (a popular genre of novel in the 1950s and '60s that told the story, often a love story, through photos) that allows the viewer to dream. Instead of portraying a passionate affair, Lelouch mixes tragedy with romanticism in the style of Arthur Hiller's *Love Story* (1970) while also reconstructing a family, giving the protagonists' children a central place in the narrative.

By 1966, Aimée had become a much sought-after actress, and her friendship with Trintignant created an on-screen chemistry that translated their off-screen trust. It was Trintignant who introduced her to Lelouch (as he had done with Demy) after the director confided in him that Aimée was his vision of the ideal woman for the part.[47] At thirty, Aimée was an elegant and desirable woman with a maturity that echoed Emmanuelle Riva's character in *Hiroshima, mon amour* and preceded Françoise Fabian in *Ma nuit chez Maud*, but was uncharacteristic of many New Wave roles at the time.

Again, the encounter between actors and directors created an alchemy that added depth to the characters. "When Anouk Aimée arrived in my life, she changed my life," Lelouch confided. "She was the first star with Jean-Louis Trintignant who said yes to me. She made the entire world dream with her voice, her smile, her face . . ."[48] Obtaining his ideal woman for the role of Anne, Lelouch also described this factor when he spoke of his affinity for Trintignant: "I think the relationship between a director and actor is the same relationship as in a love story between two people. One cannot direct an actor if you do not love him or her. And he cannot be good if he or she does not love you in turn."[49] In the case of Aimée and Lelouch, they would call each other "three, four, five times a day" until her death in 2024, the director confided.[50] Both their lives also seemed to revolve around the idea of love: "She was a woman who talked about love her whole life," said Lelouch. "Everything she did in life was to be loved. . . . Every second of her life, she dedicated to the word love, whether it be personally or professionally."[51]

Though the director was open about the importance of love for his actors, directing them in love *scenes* was a different story. Like Demy with Aimée in *Lola*, Lelouch chose to distance his characters from reality, remaining in a fairy tale even for the film's love scenes. He does not show or suggest the body on screen, but instead focuses on the actress's face, centering the scenes in male fantasy. In the film's climactic love scene, at the beginning, there is a (false) impression of documentary-type footage that transmits sensuality in black and white. The images capture the texture of the actors' skin against silences with the absence of music. Rapid cuts, with

close-ups in black and white of Aimée's face, manufacture
an image of authenticity, but it is one made of convention,
illustrating the "myth" or caricature of a love scene.

Like most of the French directors of his generation, Lelouch
revealed his embarrassment at filming love scenes, articulating what others do not readily admit: "I am here to explain what happens up to the moment when the characters
go to bed with each other. . . . Each time that I try to film
nude women, or love scenes, I missed the mark. Because my
camera, at that moment, instead of moving in, moves away."
Describing the shot as almost involuntary (like Rivette's
"not getting too close"), it is as if Lelouch distances himself
from the responsibility, ascribing it, instead, to his camera.
Side-stepping the erotic, the director conveys his pleasure,
however, at filming love *stories*: "On the other hand, I love
explaining in detail why they want to make love. . . . In *Un
homme et une femme*, we see Jean-Louis and Anne make
love, but *in reality, we only see their faces*. In my films, there
are no erotic scenes, because I don't feel the need, and besides, I couldn't film them."[52] In this way, Lelouch suggests
the idea of a "private" (masculine) fantasy that is only imagined while the camera centers on the woman's face. In effect, the director confirms his intentions of depicting fantasy
when he says, "I find that great erotic scenes in cinema are
the ones where we don't see anything at all. . . . In eroticism,
I mean the fact of showing things breaks the dream, breaks
all fantasies, so I think that *Un homme et une femme* suc-
cessfully did that . . . because even when they are in bed,
I film Anouk's face." Lelouch, therefore, invites the viewer
to project this male fantasy onto the female protagonist in
this scene: "Moreover, I film the woman's face because it is
women's faces that speak. When a couple makes love, the
reference is the woman, not the man."[53]

From these words, we can clearly see the motivation of the
director in filming the woman for male visual pleasure, but
in *Un homme et une femme*, Lelouch also gives the viewer
another, unexpected point of view. In the love scene that
lasts over three minutes, there is time for another fairy tale
within this fantasy. As the camera plays with the motif of
the couple's hands in close-up, it alternates with close-ups
of Anne's face also as she remembers the past. The *mise*

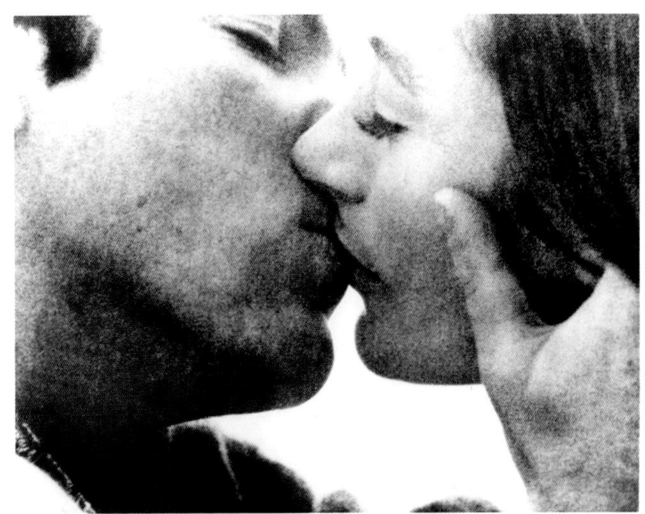

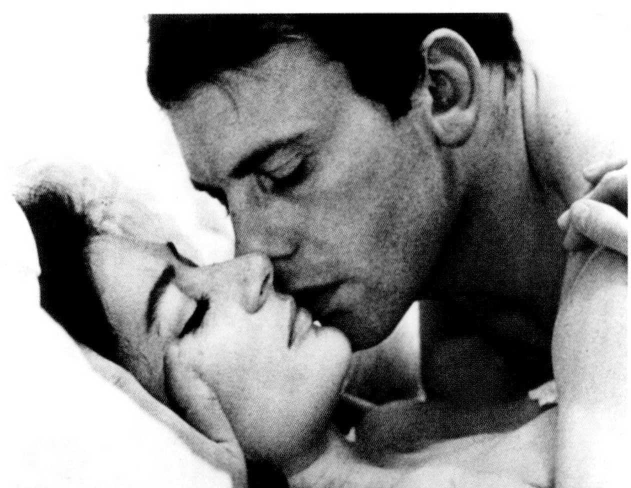

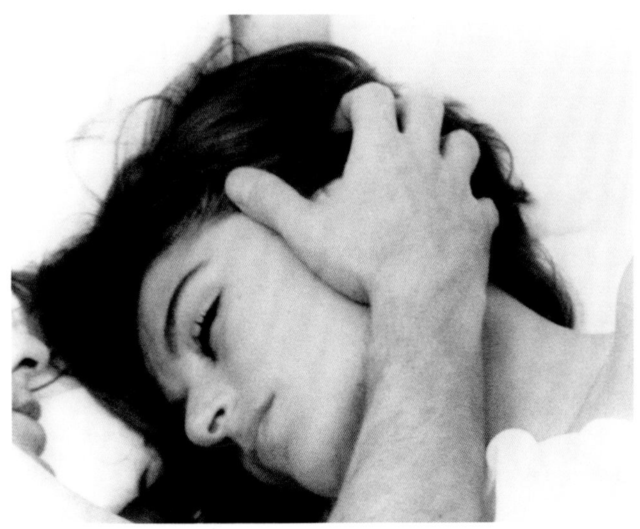

Anouk Aimée (Anne) with Pierre Barouh (Pierre) and Jean-Louis Trintignant
(Jean-Louis) in Claude Lelouch's *Un homme et une femme* (*A Man and a
Woman*), 1966

en scène evokes male fantasy, but it also serves as a screen to depict what the director imagines to be Anne's internal experience. Though this perspective is not often present in New Wave films, we recall the masterfully edited sequence in *Hiroshima, mon amour* where Riva's character remembers her German lover intermingled in her present while in the arms of her new love in Japan. Here, the memory is less subtle, more direct: The black-and-white sequence starts in silence, and Anne's eyes are closed. Against the sound of a heartbeat, close-ups of intertwined hands appear with Anne's displaying a noticeable wedding ring, illustrating her ambivalence in relation to her imaginary fidelity to her late husband. She opens her eyes and her vision is blurred. When she closes them again in silence, she sees her husband in color, in shots resembling a picture book. It is their love story accompanied by a song whose lyrics underline the past that is still present and idealized in her mind: "In the shadow of us / a shadow will remain / nothing more than beauty."

Black-and-white images of her face mix with the haunting memories in color. The words of the song tell the story in her *photo-roman*: "It's the blue of our youth," blending in the nostalgic sensibility of a Truffaut film. The blurred image of Anne's face, appearing in between shots of a castle and folkloric horseback rides with her husband, reinforces the notion of a fairy tale, a dream, and the cliché of idealized lost love.

The last shots resemble each other, alternating between the faces of her husband and Jean-Louis. As she wakes up, the reality of the present becomes clear. The music stops. Jean-Louis realizes that Anne's past still haunts her. The parallel editing that mixes the identities of the two men, past and present, like in *Hiroshima* or *Une femme mariée*, appears here in shot/reverse shot. The couple in profile echoes the image used in a version of the film's poster with Aimée and Trintignant face to face.

Though the scene is far from what could be described as modern, the depiction of Anne's inner experience is a surprising twist in what is often considered a conventional film. While Lelouch focuses on Aimée's face in the love scene, in what he considers a reference for male fantasy, he also portrays her experience instead of objectifying her body.

In the end, the past prevents the new couple from forming as reality returns with this sudden awareness. It is the end of their fairy tale that cannot compete with the one Anne holds in her mind with her late husband. The trauma of losing her husband is stronger than her desire for new love, for the moment. Lelouch in this way does not end the film with the cliché of a happy ending where the characters can forget the past, but he also leaves his characters with hope for the future.

The couple can also serve as a metaphor of a society having trouble rebuilding itself after the trauma of the war, with nostalgia for a simpler, idealized time. We can also question the place that the past holds for Lelouch, who described himself as a "director of the present, of the instant." As he explained, "Memory for me is something crucial. Like culture, it is what remains when we've gone beyond everything. An incredible selection happens through memory. But, I have never been really interested in History with a capital H."[54]

Like Aimée, Lelouch spent difficult years during the war, hiding during the occupation because of his Jewish roots. For the future New Wave directors during that time, cinema was a refuge, but for Lelouch, it was even more than that. "Cinema, for starters, saved my life," he recounted. "My mother hid me in movie theaters when I was little. We were wanted by the Gestapo."[55] As a protective device or coping strategy, cinema was the perfect medium for Lelouch, an escape and a means to create.

Lelouch's history helps explain his preference for fairy tales over history and it might explain why the New Wave directors favor poetry over reality that is "too close," or choose to portray the depth or dream of love stories instead of the superficial in the physical encounter. Demy and Godard in depicting prostitution in a dreamlike way without forcing us to see the reality; Truffaut with his alter ego choosing romanticism against the reality of prostitution. Whether mainstream filmmakers or auteurs, perhaps they all have already seen too much. Growing up under the occupation, their reality is that some of their friends were likely deported, as depicted in Malle's *Au revoir les enfants* (*Goodbye, Children*, 1987). In their entourage, there were likely stories of resistance and hiding as in Truffaut's *Le Dernier Métro* (*The Last Metro*, 1980). And they may have seen or known of women abused by Nazis or who had their heads shaved after falling in love or sleeping with the enemy, as in the scenes from Resnais's *Hiroshima, mon amour* where the heroine remembers her life in Nevers. Happy endings or tragic ones, they all chose to film love stories over stories of war like the Italian neorealists did before them. But even in their love stories, unlike Fellini's women incarnating the wildest male fantasies, the New Wave directors go beyond the erotic to focus on something else. Their love stories all translate experiences that are complex and deeply human as their characters try to navigate the difficulties of relating in a postwar, post-traumatic world. Aimée's character in this mainstream film illustrates strength and independence in her effort to raise a child alone after great loss, and in choosing to remain on her own in the end as she processes it instead of the expected happy end—qualities that also allow us to call her a modern woman.

What made this generation of directors in the 1960s so fascinated by and fearful of women, their bodies, of love, favoring fairy tales or sublimated images over reality? Growing up in the context of the war and in a patriarchal society where women's rights were not a priority, directors were undoubtedly influenced by this environment as well as internalized literary and cinematic models. But journalist Françoise Giroud's observation that the New Wave generation coming out of the war was "frileux," or fearful when it came to love, sheds light on their tendency to avoid getting too close to reality. Whether it is Godard, who zooms in to examine fragments of a woman through his camera-microscope in search of answers for her betrayal or to pierce the mystery of a woman, or Rivette with his distanced but hyper-controlled camera that lingers over Karina in her depiction of a woman enduring the control of society and the Church, or Lelouch in his desire to film a woman in love and maintain the dream while keeping her body at a distance, fear and desire lie at the core. While seemingly more liberated on the surface, the films that kept the "real" hidden behind

fantasy may have had more than taboos and censorship to blame. Perhaps love stories and fairy tales with sublimated images of fallen women or idealized fantasies were a way of approaching love while not getting too close—giving directors a sense of control in their films after an out-of-control childhood, while the women in their films searched to rescue themselves from the fallout.

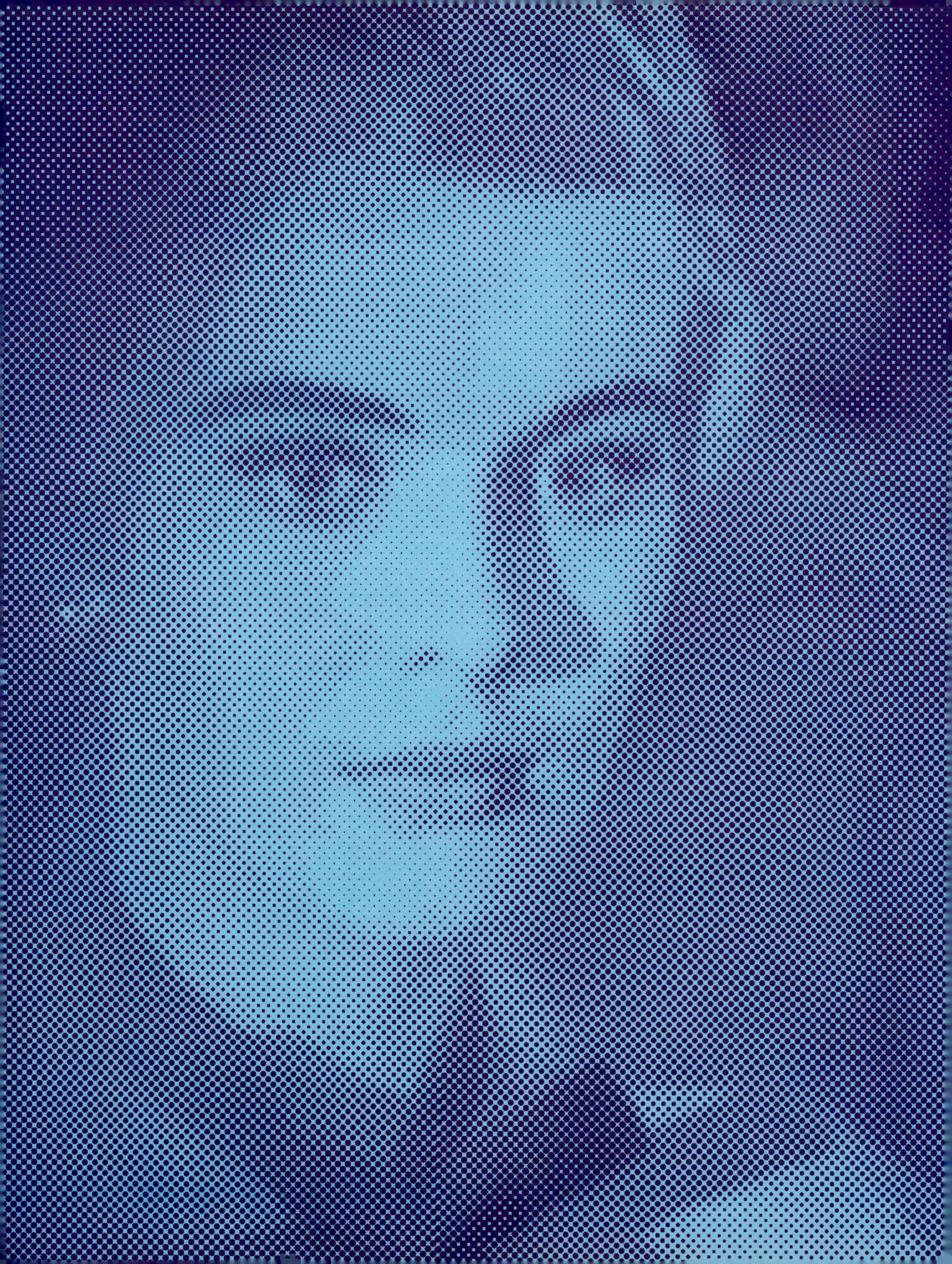

jean seberg

8

l'américaine à paris | *the american in paris*

FROM PREMINGER'S PROMISE TO GODARD'S AMERICAN DREAM

"That girl's going to be a movie star," a member of the audience uttered in 1956 exiting the theater after Jean Seberg's high school performance in *Sabrina Fair*.[1] Many in her hometown of Marshalltown, Iowa, seemed to sense in her that special something that set her apart from the other girls in her class who may have dreamed of stardom but did not necessarily aspire to it. Jeana, as she was known then, must have sensed it too when she told her high school friends she would meet Marlon Brando someday. Whether through her talent, luck, or a combination of both, Seberg beat monumental odds, and only a year later became indeed a household name and Hollywood's most promising new movie star. Though a bright future seemed right around the corner, she would go through agony—even being literally burned at the stake—before arriving at the role that would make her an icon in Godard's *À bout de souffle*.

Jean Seberg, in Otto Preminger's *Bonjour Tristesse*, 1957, photo by Bob Willoughby

Seberg's life had always seemed to be marked by extremes, both light and dark. In high school, she won multiple awards for her acting—her talent confirmed by her very supportive drama teacher, Carol Hollingsworth—and was named most likely to succeed, most sophisticated, and even best dancer. Many also considered her beauty exceptional, and she was known as sensitive and caring, already attached to political causes and the fight against inequality. Seberg was not, however, most popular: Her skills and successes sparked jealousy, leading her schoolmates to criticize her ambition. Her high school friend Dawn Quinn related years later that Seberg told her at the time, "Dawn, I'd trade all of my honors and talent for some true friends and a boy who really loves me."[2]

The summer after high school, in 1956, she won a scholarship to Cape Cod's Priscilla Beach Theatre, where her beauty and poise earned her the nickname "Grace Kelly." She performed the lead in *Picnic*, but it was not this role that so drastically changed her life. On an outing to the movies with her theater friends, Seberg saw a trailer announcing Otto Preminger's search for an actress to star in his forthcoming film about Joan of Arc. Widely distributed and garnering worldwide attention, it also caught the attention of Seberg's theater manager, her high school drama teacher, and two others who all submitted her name for the part. Out of some 18,000 entrants, Seberg was among 3,000 finalists.[3] In September, she auditioned in Chicago, interrupting her first (and last) semester at the University of Iowa.

Like Bardot's parents, who had to be convinced by Allégret to let her do a screen test, Ed and Dorothy Seberg had to be persuaded by Preminger to let their daughter go to New York City for the final round of auditions. "You have a very talented daughter," he told them. That October, she made it to the final four and was asked to cut her hair to conform to the image of Joan of Arc for the screen test. After agreeing, Seberg had her first experience with Preminger's volatile and abusive directing style. "You're nothing but a ham and a phony. You can't act and you will never be able to," he berated her, followed by praise: "Well, you did that almost as well as Rita Hayworth." She got the part. When asked by Ed Sullivan what drew him to Seberg, Preminger replied, "She has an enchanting personality and she captivated me. That's

the best answer: She captivated me." Seberg conveyed her elation during a press conference: "Do I need to tell you that I am the happiest girl in the world?"[4]

Seberg left for London on her eighteenth birthday, November 13, to prepare for her part in *Saint Joan* (1957) before filming began in January. From there, she traveled to France to visit the sites that marked Joan of Arc's life, accompanied by photographer Bob Willoughby and journalist Tom Ryan. In Paris, Ingrid Bergman (who starred in Victor Fleming's *Joan of Arc* in 1948) told Seberg her haircut was "the shortest yet," and the young actress explained that she had it cut every three days.[5] Her excitement turned dark, however, when filming began and Preminger imposed relentless rehearsals.

It was not only the grueling hours that presented a challenge. Richard Widmark, who played the Dauphin (Charles VII) in the film, wrote privately in 1980: "She was working against formidable odds. A talented amateur trying to play an extremely difficult part which taxes the capacities of the most skilled and experienced performer. Preminger treated her very harshly, especially during the two-week rehearsal period. And I admired her tremendously for the way she accepted it, and at least on the outside didn't seem to let it bother her and never lost her cool. . . . Personally, I was under some strain trying to play a part that I never should have attempted, although Preminger and I got along very well. And to see her total confidence impressed me no end."[6] Bob Willoughby, who photographed the set, echoed these remarks: "The pressure on Jean throughout this film was extraordinarily heavy, but this little girl from Iowa had such grit that everyone in the cast and crew could not help but admire her. I was certainly her daily support, for we rode back and forth from London to the set together, and very often ate dinner at night . . . I would see her get a tongue lashing from Preminger, swallow it, go off by herself, and psych herself up. Then she'd come back and do the scene again. She was no quitter under fire. If there were medals for courage, for bravery in the cinema world, Jean would have won them all."[7]

In effect, Seberg persevered despite even the most notoriously traumatic experiences during the shoot. In the film's

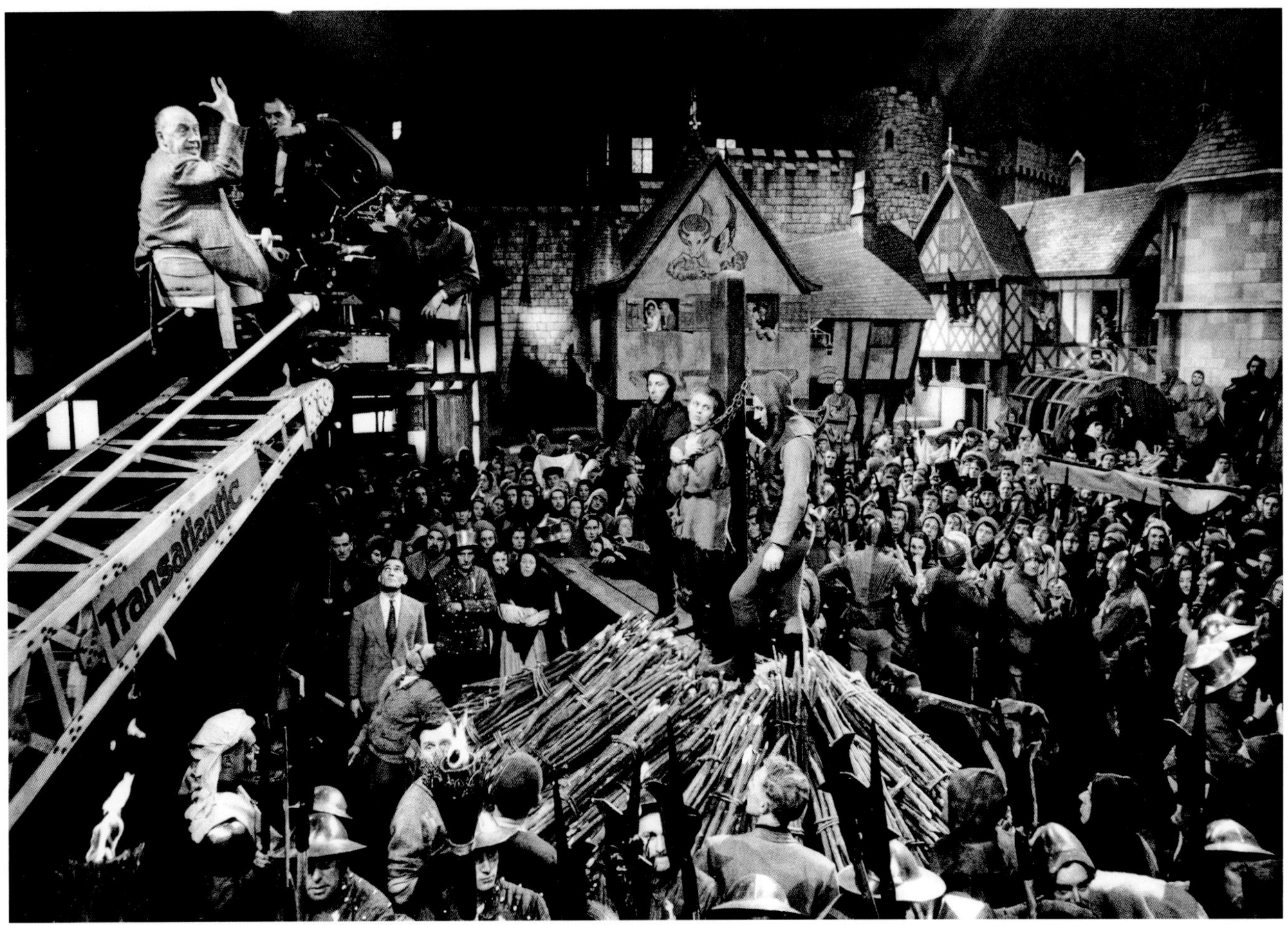

pivotal scene, equipment used to produce flames malfunctioned, putting her life in peril. According to Seberg's biographer Garry McGee, the actress—"chained to the stake with brushwood piled under her feet while extras yelled, 'Burn her, burn her!'"[8]—was herself burned by out-of-control flames. "[B]y some miracle she was able to put her hands up over her face, even though she was chained to the stake," Willoughby recounted.[9] The fire was finally extinguished, but her hands, stomach, and knee were burned; and her hair, singed. As Preminger had invited the press to the set that day, he was accused of using the horrific incident as a publicity stunt.[10]

Despite Seberg's determination, *Saint Joan* was a flop. Many blamed her acting, and because of this, she was not expected to appear in Preminger's next film. Up against Audrey Hepburn, Seberg had little chance of securing the leading

role of Cécile in *Bonjour Tristesse* (1958)—an adaptation of Françoise Sagan's hit novel that captured the young generation's modern mindset. Always in search of publicity, the director arranged a meeting between Seberg and Sagan with seventy-five reporters present. Seberg was surprised when he cast her. "I could have understood if Preminger had decided not to put me in *Bonjour*," she said, "but he showed faith in me no one expected him to show."[11] Again, Preminger's promise seemed bright. Willoughy noticed a difference in Seberg when he was invited back to work on the film: "Gone were the grubby clothes for Jean, now replaced with smart little black dresses from Dior."[12]

But Preminger's cruel treatment of Seberg, still struggling with *Saint Joan*'s failure, continued during the shoot in Nice. The darkness intermingled with light brought by the actress's new romance with saxophonist Paul Desmond, with

Jean Seberg, in Otto Preminger's *Saint Joan,* 1956, photo by Bob Willoughby

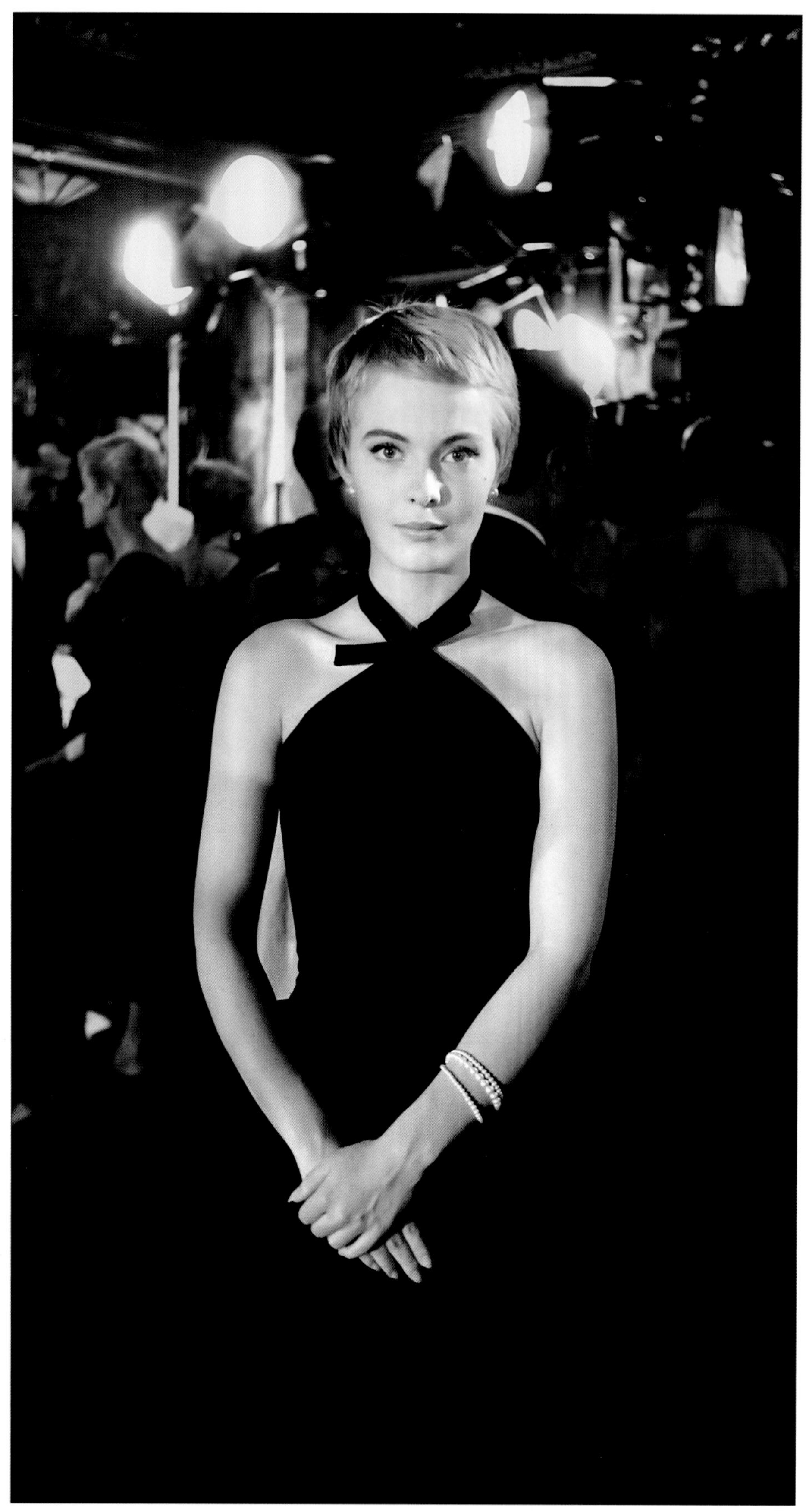

intensity foreshadowing her future. She wrote to a friend that she was "alternating between such mad heights of happiness and depression I think I will die."[13] Unfortunately, this film too was not well received by critics when it opened in the United States, and again Seberg was criticized. "I don't think *Bonjour Tristesse* was quite as bad as it was made out to be," the actress said years later. "Actually, of all the pictures based on Françoise Sagan's stories, I think it came off best. I was still nervous and unsure of myself. My tension is apparent through much of the picture but I was not quite as bad as in *Joan*. As Preminger has said since, he treated me all the wrong ways."[14]

After two flops, many would have given up, but Seberg persisted: "My self-confidence had been ravaged, but I decided I wasn't going to quit. I was determined to give acting the good old college try." In the south of France, she met and later married François Moreuil, a lawyer, and in 1959, the French New Wave began to brighten her career prospects. The magazine *Arts* voted her performance in *Bonjour Tristesse* "Best Feminine Interpretation," and the well-respected *Cahiers du cinéma* called Seberg "the new divine of the cinema," putting her on its February cover.[15]

It was Truffaut who praised her performance, articulating in his review what she brought to the film, a unique style and spark, emphasizing her "sex appeal" but also her newness: "When Jean Seberg is on the screen, which is all the time, you can't look at anything else. Her every movement is graceful, each glance is precise. The shape of her head, her silhouette, her walk, everything is perfect: This kind of sex appeal hasn't been seen on the screen. It is designed, controlled, directed to the nth degree by her director, who is, they say, her fiancé. I wouldn't be surprised, given the kind of love one needs to obtain such perfection. Jean Seberg, short blonde hair on a pharaoh's skull, wide-open blue eyes with a glint of boyish malice, carries the entire weight of this film on her tiny shoulders . . . it is Otto Preminger's love poem to her."[16]

After mixed transatlantic reviews, Seberg sought to better herself as an actress, studying speech for months with acting coach Alice Hermes and taking mime lessons from Éti-

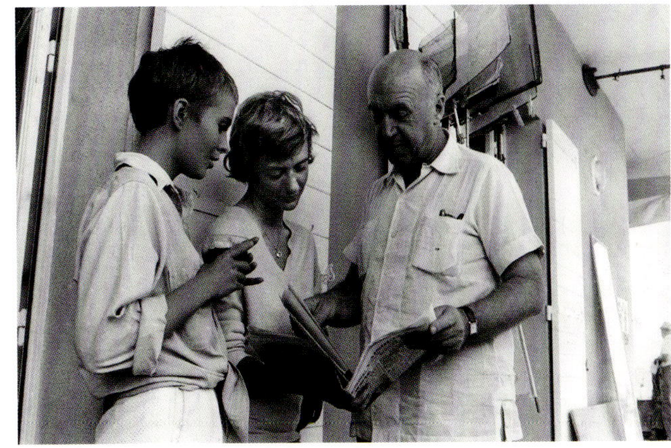

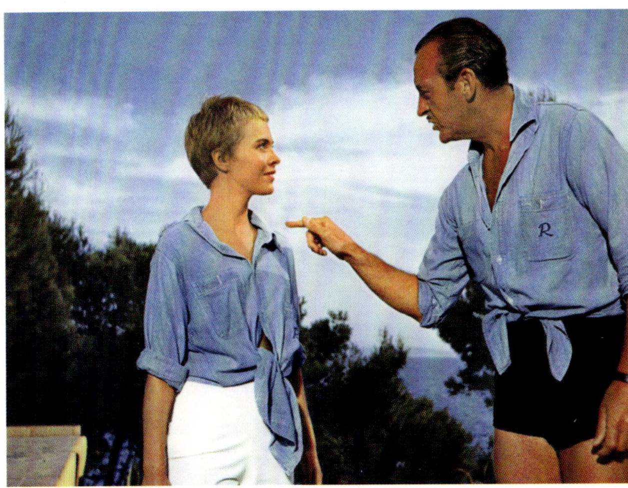

enne Decroux, mentor of Marcel Marceau. She wrote Lee Strasberg in New York City in hopes of studying with him but never received a reply. According to Moreuil, "[s]he wanted to write more than act," and spent most of her time reading and writing, even penning an article in the *New York Herald Tribune*.[17]

Still under contract with Columbia Pictures, Seberg was cast in *The Mouse that Roared* (1959), a small-budget film costarring Peter Sellers, and discovered she had a talent for comedy. In 1959, the studio also set up acting classes in Los Angeles for her with Paton Price, whom she credited with "giving back [her] lost confidence." By the time she returned to Paris in June, the New Wave was hitting the cinema world. Chabrol's *Le Beau Serge* and *Les Cousins* had come out, and Truffaut's *Les Quatre cents coups* had just triumphed in Cannes. Seberg and her husband realized that something important

Left: Jean Seberg, in Otto Preminger's *Bonjour Tristesse*, 1957, photo by Bob Willoughby

Jean Seberg, Françoise Sagan, and Otto Preminger on the set of *Bonjour Tristesse*, 1957.

was happening. Moreuil, who had ambitions to direct, was connected to people in the scene and wanted to be in on it. Later that summer, he found out that Godard—then still an amateur director—was interested in making a film with Seberg. After learning about his credentials, Seberg agreed to meet with him and view his first short, *Charlotte et son Jules* (starring Jean-Paul Belmondo), which she found "very fresh and different."[18] She agreed to meet with Godard again, this time with Truffaut, to discuss the new film.

Close friends with Godard, Truffaut, wanting to help him make his first feature, had given him the outline for a story based on a news item he first saw in the French tabloids: Michel Portail, a petty thief who was living it up with an American girl on the Côte d'Azur, stole a car, shot a policeman, and was turned in by his girlfriend. A synopsis was submitted to the CNC for approval in 1959.[19] In Truffaut's three-page treatment, later published by *L'Avant-scène* in 1968, a car thief named Lucien kills a policeman and hides out with his girlfriend, an American girl in Paris who is still learning French. Like in the news story, she turns him in, but the protagonist escapes, cursing her as he drives away. She does not understand him, however, since her French is still imperfect.

Godard's entire artistic existence was riding on the film. As a cinephile, critic, and short-film director, he was desperate to make his first feature after a "decade's worth of making movies in [his] head."[20] Seberg was adored by the New Wave. Although their films were becoming profitable, Godard still needed to prove himself. Seberg's appearance in the film would serve as insurance, reassuring producer Georges de Beauregard. After two US box-office flops, the actress had virtually nothing left to lose when Godard asked her to appear in his film.

Godard saw Seberg's character, Patricia, as a continuation of her role in *Bonjour Tristesse*. "I could have taken the last shot of Preminger's film and started after dissolving to a title, 'Three Years Later,'" he said. But the project—with its shoestring budget, small crew, and no script—could not have been more different from the Hollywood-style productions Seberg had grown accustomed to with Preminger. She was nervous, wondering how she could learn her lines, and torn knowing that she was the determining factor in Godard getting the film made. She summed up the situation perfectly: "I was Godard's last trump card."[21] She felt compelled to help the young French filmmakers who had embraced her as an actress, returning the favor.

Truffaut, Belmondo, and Moreuil all urged her to accept the role, and Moreuil leveraged his lawyer skills to negotiate with Columbia—which had no other projects scheduled for Seberg—to give her permission to do *À bout de souffle*. The studio accepted $12,000 to loan her for the film (one-sixth of its budget).

À BOUT DE SOUFFLE: THE NEW WAVE MEETS JEAN SEBERG

"Let us show that everything is allowed. What I wanted to do was start from a conventional story and redo, but differently, all cinema that had already been done. I also wanted to give the impression that the ways of making films had just been discovered or felt for the first time,"[22] Godard stated. From Truffaut's original treatment, Godard changed more than just the protagonist's name from Lucien to Michel. The day before the shoot, Godard wrote of his different vision: "Roughly speaking, the subject will be the story of a boy who thinks of death and a girl who doesn't. The adventures of those of a car thief . . . in love with a girl who sells the *New York Herald Tribune* and who takes French civilization courses."[23] Though the main events align with Truffaut's story, the *mise en scène* would illustrate Godard's genius: his inventive cinematic style.

"There are taboos and rules, and the idea was to show that all that had no value,"[24] Godard later explained. Besides cinematic language, this philosophy rang true in terms of Seberg's presence in the film. In much the same way that Jeanne Moreau drew from her more authentic self for her character in *Ascenseur pour l'échafaud*, Seberg was able to relax and let the light and depth of her personality permeate her character in *À bout de souffle*, thanks to Godard's open and experimental way of directing.

Jean-Luc Godard's *À bout de souffle* (*Breathless*), 1960, original poster

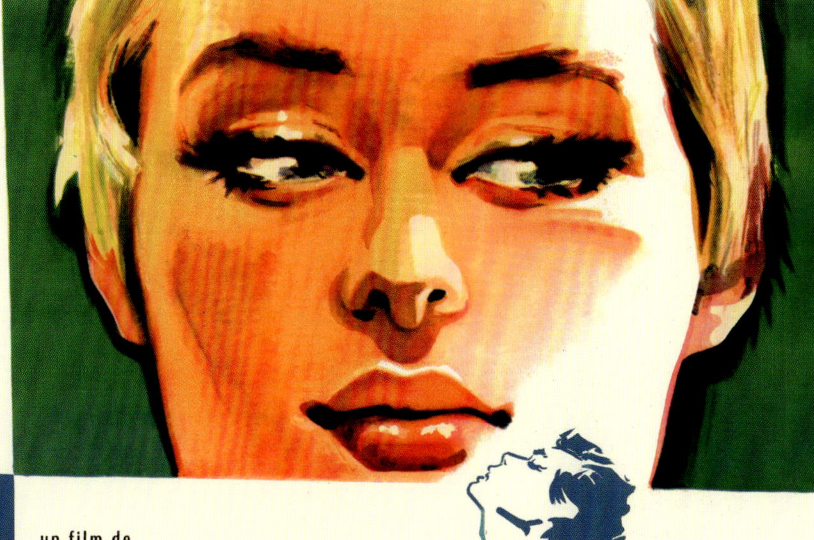

JEAN
SEBERG
JEAN-PAUL
BELMONDO
un film de
JEAN-LUC GODARD
A Bout De Souffle...
Scénario original de FRANÇOIS TRUFFAUT
Conseiller technique CLAUDE CHABROL
Henri-Jacques HUET Liliane DAVID Claude MANSARD VAN DOUDE Daniel BOULANGER
musique de MARTIAL SOLAL éditions Hortensia photographie de Raoul COUTARD
INTERDIT AUX MOINS DE 18 ANS
PRODUCTION GEORGES DE BEAUREGARD

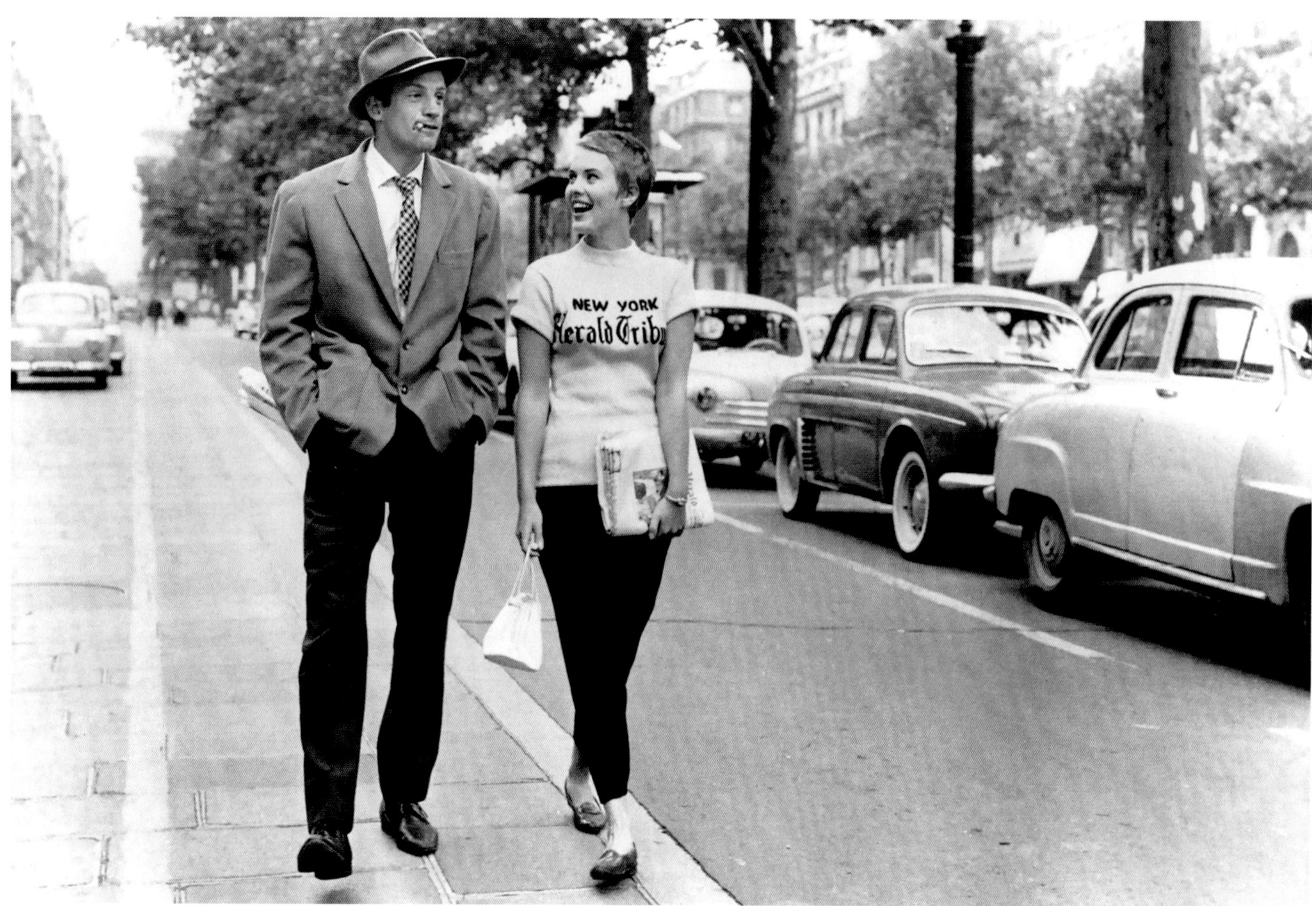

The character of Patricia became fresh and modern. Seberg, with her foreign presence, also contributed to modernizing the film, much like Ingrid Bergman did in Rossellini's Italian neorealist cinema. The actresses' Otherness added a new way of being to the cinematic landscape and an outside eye from which to view the other culture. Seberg also represented the cinema Godard loved and an auteur he admired, Preminger. Her aura from the film transferred to Godard's Patricia, as she took up the character she played in *Bonjour Tristesse*, following Godard's vision. As film scholar Alain Bergala expressed, "Godard didn't try to recreate his own Jean Seberg, he took her practically as he found her in Preminger's film, without any Pygmalion syndrome."[25]

It was said that Godard rarely looked Seberg in the eye when he spoke to her. "Belmondo insists Godard had a mad crush on me," Seberg recalled years later, "but I was unaware of it at the time." But with Seberg, Godard was, above all, in love with the cinema she incarnated, their collaboration differing from the work he would do with Anna Karina, where real life and cinema intertwined. That is not to say there was no conflict between the determined director and his American dream actress. On the first day of the shoot, Seberg almost walked off the set. "Jean-Luc had just emerged from a miserable love affair and was feeling bitter about women," she recalled. "He wanted to make me more terrible-looking than I already was. We agreed to disagree, shook hands, and I left. He followed me, and we made up."[26]

The shoot, running from August to September 1959, was done without authorization and in a way in which Seberg was unaccustomed to working. Without a complete script, at the beginning of each day, Godard gave the actors instructions in a piecemeal manner that destabilized her. "Jean-Luc

Jean-Paul Belmondo (Michel) and Jean Seberg (Patricia) on the Champs-Élysées in Godard's *À bout de souffle* (*Breathless*), 1960

Clothing in the 1960s was also changing. Not long before, it was not considered proper or good taste for women to wear pants (we recall the shock of Grace Kelly in jeans in *Rear Window*). Seberg's gamine haircut, capris, ballerina flats, and *New York Herald Tribune* T-shirt (promoting the newspaper she was selling) presented a new look for a new generation, and also an accessible one.

would arrive every morning with a pocketful of striped yellow notebook pages like students have, filled with what he'd written the night before," Seberg explained. "He was afraid what he was making wouldn't last long enough to be a full-length film."[27] Other times, the actors would repeat the lines that Godard said to them out loud as they shot. Moreuil stated that "she was very disabled because there wasn't a script, and when she would ask him, 'How do you want me to act that?' he'd say, 'How you want to.' It was not the way she was used to acting."[28]

Cinematographer Raoul Coutard described the relationship between director and actress as "tense," stating that "she didn't let herself be pushed around, but she did cooperate. After all, she was an American professional."[29] Though Godard sometimes used childish schoolyard tactics, the tension was nothing like the dictatorial way Preminger had directed her. On the third day, for example, Godard told her, "If you don't behave well, I won't do any close-ups of you." Annoyed, she replied, "Okay, I won't do the film." Despite the numerous, now-famous close-ups, surprisingly—like the cinematographer said about Moreau in her early days on screen—Coutard was not convinced that Seberg would be easy to photograph. "How on earth am I going to film her?" he admitted thinking upon meeting her. Claiming that she did not have good skin, he found that with makeup Seberg was exceptionally photogenic, even in poor lighting.[30]

Coutard, a behind-the-scenes star of the film for his cinematography, brought his experience as a war photographer in Indochina to Godard's experiment. He shot *À bout de souffle* like a documentary using a Caméflex that allowed him to track the actors in small spaces and outside, a real breakthrough that widened the possibilities for the film's locations and aesthetics. Godard pushed a mail-delivery box from which Coutard, unseen by pedestrians, filmed the famous Champs-Élysées sequence where Seberg strolls alongside Belmondo, projecting a modern attitude and style. Clothing in the 1960s was also changing. Not long before, it was not considered proper or good taste for women to wear pants (we recall the shock of Grace Kelly in jeans in *Rear Window*). Seberg's gamine haircut, capris, ballerina flats, and *New York Herald Tribune* T-shirt (promoting the newspaper she

was selling) presented a new look for a new generation, and also an accessible one. The film's budget was reportedly so restricted (roughly $90,000) that Seberg's wardrobe came from the discount store, Prisunic,[31] but her style would soon be copied worldwide.

In the celebrated scene, Patricia and Michel exchange playful banter against a backdrop of the "real Paris"—with random passersby as unwitting extras crossing their path. Like in *Ascenseur*, Paris provided an authentic setting, no longer a fake representation of the city in a studio, that renewed French cinema with a fresh, modern feel in the *mise en scène*. In contrast to Moreau, lost in Malle's Paris by night, Seberg in Godard's Paris exudes light and levity.

Like Moreau's character, Seberg's Patricia is unconventional and embodies freedom. Although it has become more accessible for American college students to travel and study abroad, in 1960, it was still uncommon and a sign of courage and independence. Patricia also possesses a style and ambition that were uncommon in women's roles at the time. A student at the Sorbonne, she is an aspiring journalist who earns her own money selling newspapers.

Choosing to retain Truffaut's original idea of Patricia as an American in Paris, Godard had Seberg speak French with an exaggerated accent, below her foreign-language skills. He asked her to say the lines like an American who was learning French, making mistakes of gender, for example. "It became much more colloquial and much more foreign in a way," Seberg explained. Her foreignness also created a cinematic hybrid, a Franco-American alliance of characters and a mix of genres evoking B-movies, gangster films, and romances.

One of the most memorable (and modern) sequences in the film is a long digression that represents an intimate moment in Patricia and Michel's relationship. In the unconventional love scene, agilely shot by Coutard, the characters spend the afternoon together in Patricia's small hotel room. A mere two short paragraphs in Truffaut's treatment, the sequence takes up almost one-third of Godard's film. Truffaut simply describes the couple making plans for the day, writing that

Patricia still knows nothing about Lucien's identity. For her, he still "plays at being a guy who has money and a nice car." Godard, however, expands the scene and breaks the rules. His characters (and the audience) enjoy a moment of freedom. We spend what feels like twenty minutes of real time with them, although it is punctuated by numerous jump cuts. Filming the intimate, youthful exchange and authentic performances by Seberg and Belmondo, Godard, then afraid of running too long, cut some of the space between shots, editing them to make the now-famous jump cuts. Filmed in close quarters, in room 12 at the Hôtel de Suède on the Rive gauche, "there was hardly anybody else in the room," Seberg remembered, "except for one electrician who'd come in and out to fix up the lights and a girl who tried to keep some kind of a script."[32]

The actors, however, had room to be spontaneous. "We did a lot of improvising," Seberg recalled, "and I believe Belmondo and I often thought we were creating more than we really were. [But] Godard was very much in control of it all." Because they thought nothing would come of the film, according to Belmondo, they decided to "sit back and have fun." Though Seberg had to make do with a café's *toilettes* as her dressing room at times, this way of working allowed her to relax and concentrate on her character. In this different atmosphere, she could be herself and even have fun. "Jean really enjoyed making *Breathless*," Hollingsworth said, adding that "much of it was ad-libbed. It showed what Jean could do when left to her own devices."[33]

PATRICIA AND MICHEL: PHILOSOPHIES IN CONTRAST

Seberg's character was defined by her free spirit and free thinking. Unlike the values of the actress's puritanical upbringing, Patricia's approach to love stemmed from a stereotype of the American girl in Paris. She is seen with different men but is not labeled a debauched woman like Bardot's character in *Et Dieu créa la femme*, thanks to her romantic nature and intellectual pursuits that make her more complex. At the same time, Godard's own modesty stemming from his Swiss Protestant background, mixed with his humor, lent a lighthearted style to the love scenes,

that are only implied by the characters' brief playful moments underneath the white sheets. Seberg also insisted on remaining fully clothed.

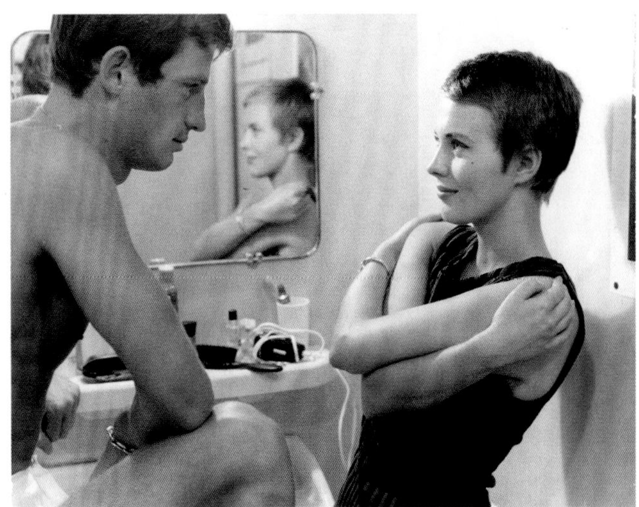

The characters address serious topics in an undramatic, realistic way. Immediately before the hotel room sequence, Patricia catches sight of herself in a mirror behind a store window. Turning to the side, she looks at her stomach in the reflection and counts to herself on her fingers, trying on the image of herself pregnant by sticking out and pulling in her stomach. The scene is brief, just like the discussion between Patricia and Michel when she first arrives to find him waiting for her in her room, unannounced and uninvited. In the midst of their exchange in her bathroom, Patricia offhandedly announces the possibility of her pregnancy to Michel, as discussed earlier.

Patricia: Guess what I wanted to tell you.
Michel: No idea.
Patricia: I'm pregnant, Michel.
Michel: Huh?
Patricia: You heard me.
Michel: Whose is it? Mine?
Patricia: Yes, I think so.

. . .

Michel: You should've been more careful!

The cruelty of Michel's response underlines the gap between his reality and hers, and it speaks to the larger divide

Jean-Paul Belmondo (Michel) and Jean Seberg (Patricia) in Godard's *À bout de souffle* (*Breathless*), 1960

between the separate worlds of men and women at the time. Later in the scene, Michel conveys his anxiety about facing reality when he says, "What a crazy idea to have a child!" He ignores it immediately, however, when he asks her to take off her clothes. The sequence also conveys Patricia's liberated attitude, illustrated by her nonchalant response regarding the identity of the father, but she reveals a deeper anxiety about Michel's feelings and reaction to the possibility. "It's not for sure," she says. "I just wanted to see what you would say."

Through dialogue and juxtaposed images, eroticism and romanticism mix to illustrate, humorously, the ambiguity between love and sexuality and Michel and Patricia's differing points of view:

> Patricia: Leave me alone, I'm thinking.
> Michel: About what?
> Patricia: The tragedy is, I don't even know. . . . Why did you come back here?
> Michel: Because I wanted to sleep with you again.
> Patricia: I don't think that's a good reason
> Michel: Of course it is! It means I love you.
> Patricia: And I don't know yet if I love you.

The images of seminude women in Michel's magazine disguise his romanticism with eroticism while the poster on Patricia's wall of Romeo and Juliet reveals her penchant for romantic love despite the doubts in her commentary. Besides romance, Michel and Patricia talk about their philosophies of life in a discussion in which Godard uses his characters to examine multiple points of view in order to "think" through his characters, a device he will use in many of his future films. Michel says it is pointless to kill one's feelings in order to live longer. Patricia quotes William Faulkner's conclusion to *The Wild Palms*: "Between grief and nothingness, I choose grief," to which Michel responds: "Grief is a compromise. I'd choose nothingness. You've got to have all or nothing."

The counterpoint of dialogue and image conveys different perpectives while also underlining differences in Godard's male and female characters. Michel, for example, talks of death in a bleak monologue and expresses his pessimistic commentary on love, while Patricia searches to define herself through her career and remains lucid about their relationship. In an interview with Dick Cavett in 1980, the talk show host described Godard's male characters as being "full of despair," adding that the female characters seemed to "cope" better. Godard replied that "the girls are more casual, and I think women today are more natural than men." When Cavett also pointed out that critics saw Godard as more sympathetic to women in his films, Godard explained his process of writing dialogue, often attributing his own perspective to his female characters: "I never hesitate in any of my movies. Even in the first one with Jean Seberg, she was an American girl, I gave her my lines. And very often I have a problem with the actor because they are obliged to say my lines—not Shakespeare's lines, not objective lines, but my lines. And very often because [the actor] is a woman, they object, but I think I'm just giving the lines to the actor when I think it's right, whether it is a man or a woman."[34]

Although Godard claimed ownership of the female characters' lines, it is clear that he observed and listened to the women in his life who, in turn, influenced his thoughts and his dialogue. Michel Séméniako of Godard's *La Chinoise* pointed to Godard's keen sense of observation and requests for actors to improvise. When Cavett asked what Godard did "with the actress who says, 'But a woman wouldn't say that,'" Godard replied, "Well, now I think maybe if we have a good relationship, maybe a difficult one, but a good one, maybe I listen a little more and maybe I think that my lines are not so good," adding, "Let's work a little more, let's study it and maybe we'll discover something."[35] Discovering that "something" was a driving force in many of Godard's early films.

Godard seems to have applied this approach with Seberg. When Michel discovers that Patricia has turned him in to the police, his lines reflect a pessimistic, fatalistic view of humankind: "Informers inform, burglars burgle, murderers murder, lovers love." Wanting Patricia to correspond to Michel's philosophy, Godard planned to portray her as a thief to emphasize her betrayal by having her steal Michel's wallet in the final scene. Seberg refused. Her decision left room for ambiguity regarding Patricia's feelings and motivation and added a level of complexity to the character, beyond the one-dimension-al description in Truffaut's treatment and categorical femme fatale in Godard's version. Reflecting on her refusal years later, Seberg stated she was unsure of where it came from—from nervousness, a deeply puritan mentality or something else: "Jean-Luc was grieved. I think there was already between us this misunderstanding of this refusal, a misunderstanding that was, I confess, entirely my fault."[36] Though Seberg stood up for her character, she herself took the blame.

In *Charlotte et son Jules*, Belmondo's character, Jules, works out ambivalent and often conflicting views of women. Godard dubbed his own voice into the postsynchronized soundtrack to berate Charlotte (Godard's own ex-girlfriend, Anne Collette) for leaving him. In a diatribe full of such extreme misogyny that it becomes a parody (Godard's own inside joke?), the *mise en scène* makes fun of Jules (or of his suffering)—perhaps a defense against Godard's own vulnerability to tragic romantic love. His protagonist, in any case, loves Charlotte and hates her at the same time; he hates above all the power she has over him to leave. In this early sketch, Charlotte is also level-headed and grounded. She is not the one suffering, or, as Cavett said, she is able to "cope" better than the protagonist, who tries in vain to save himself from his feelings for Charlotte, revealing his deep despair. Despite the cruel words he pummels her with, Charlotte remains impervious, calm, unaffected—she has *le beau rôle*, the best role.

In *À bout de souffle* also, Patricia is the stronger one and—like Haydée will be in *La Collectionneuse* years later—she is searching. Motivated by ambition as a student and aspiring journalist, Patricia may be searching for a career and a romantic relationship, but she is also searching for something else, something undefinable, deeper. Citing Jean-Paul Sartre, Godard stated that cinema is the medium where "reticence, as it were, is unable to hide its secrets; the most religious of arts, it values man above the essence of things and reveals the soul within the body."[37] It is this soul, this authenticity, that Godard respected in Truffaut's *Les Quatre cents coups* and that comes through in Seberg's character. The actress herself was motivated by the same pursuit, and the role provided her an adventure and a new experience, far from Hollywood.

SEBERG'S REDEMPTION, GODARD'S TRIUMPH

In effect, Godard's low-budget, no-frills, loosely organized but intense pursuit of authenticity and art showed Seberg just how far she had drifted from her start that was so full of promise but so full of hardship just two years earlier. "We knew when we saw the rushes that we were doing something very unusual. Very new in its style," she recalled years later. But when the film wrapped, she was unsure it would even be screened in public. "We didn't know if the film would ever be seen—[or] if the public would ever like it," she confessed.[38] Released in four major theaters in March 1960, it was an immediate success, selling 259,000 tickets in seven weeks.[39] The novelty of the film's style was not made of gimmicks. But this new way of cinematic storytelling, with its now-famous jump cuts and unconventional editing, also disconcerted audiences. Françoise Giroud described *À bout de souffle* as "a real shock, just like Proust's *À la recherche du temps perdu*."[40] The film won several awards in Europe, and Seberg was nominated for Best Foreign Actress by BAFTA (British Academy of Film and Television Arts). Sophia Loren said she was "Fabulous!" A journalist said she was "prettier" and a "better actress" than Brigitte Bardot.[41] Truffaut called her "the best actress in Europe." This was welcome praise for Seberg, who had grown accustomed to being burned at the stake by the press since *Saint Joan*. One of her close friends at the time, Vony Becker, confirmed that the film opened "all doors for her . . . She had character. Her face, her hair, her look—it was new. A little American star here in Paris."[42]

Seberg helped Godard as well. Casting her not only allowed his film to be made at all, it helped it gain US attention. *The New Yorker* labeled it "a masterpiece." The acerbic critic Pauline Kael praised Seberg's performance but also sharply pointed to an aspect of her character that did not sit well with some of middle America. "As Jean Seberg plays her—and that's exquisitely—Patricia is the most terrifyingly simple muse-goddess-bitch of modern movies," she wrote. "Patricia, a naïve, assured, bland and boyish creature, is like a new Daisy Miller—but not quite as envisioned by Henry James. She has the independence, but not the moral qualms or the Puritan conscience or the high aspirations that James saw as

---

Next page: Jean Seberg (Patricia) in Jean-Luc Godard's *Le Grand Escroc* (*The Big Swindler*) segment in *Les Plus Escroqueries du monde* (*The World's Most Beautiful Swindlers*), 1964

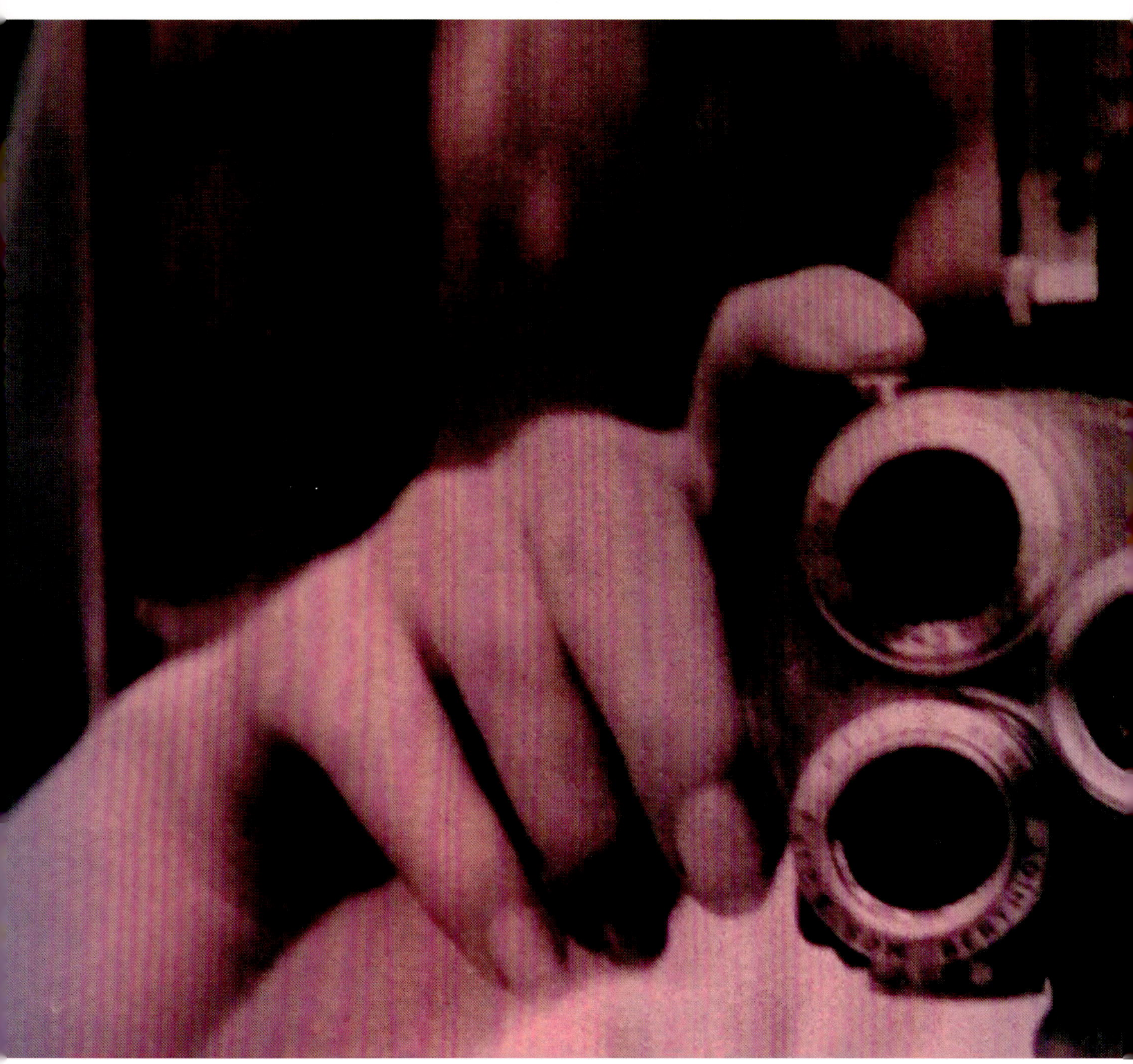

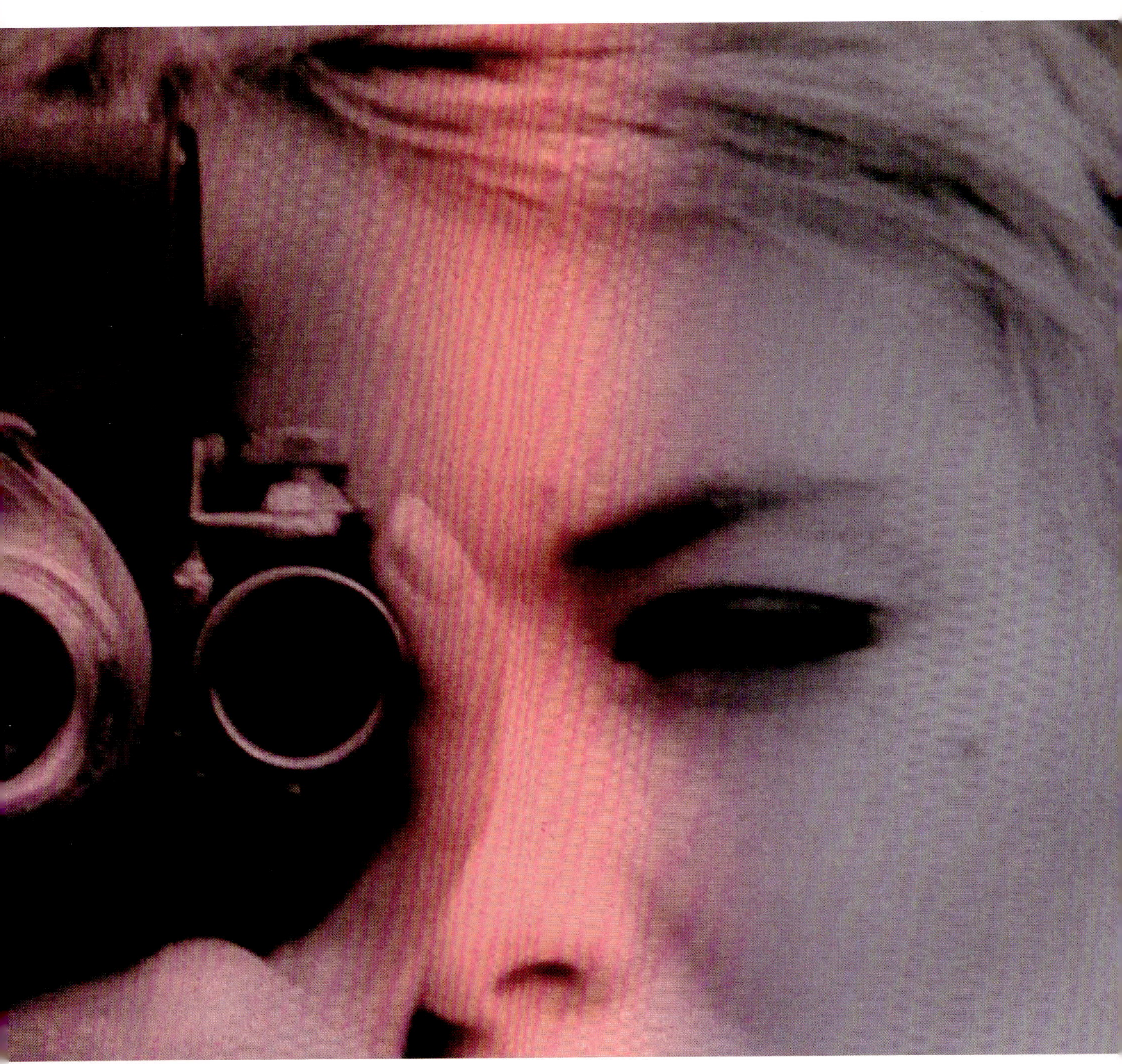

the special qualities of the American girl. . . . [S]he is so free that she has no sense of responsibility or guilt. She seems to be playing at existence, at a career, at 'love'; she's 'trying them on.' But that's all she's capable of in the way of experience. She doesn't want to be bothered; when her lover becomes an inconvenience, she turns him in to the police."[43] Besides being an independent, liberated woman, Seberg was seen by the critic as a modern femme fatale.

Unsurprisingly, her character's morals caused a stir in the actress's Iowa hometown, and Seberg apologized before the film opened there. "Yes, it has some naughty four-letter words, but I don't say any of them, and I expect the English version will be censored," she said. "I'm not sure I'd want my friends here to see it, but if they do, they will have to remember I'm not the type of person portrayed in the movie." In France, the film received a dreaded "interdit aux moins de 18 ans" (forbidden for those under eighteen), and its public reception by the older generation was not quite as glowing as in the press. "I saw *À bout de souffle*, and I think it's gratuitous dirt," one French moviegoer exclaimed as he exited the theater. "It's awful. It's a farce," expressed another older French woman. Their reactions shed light on the generational divide and the atmosphere of the time.[44]

When questioned about her views on censorship, Seberg defended freedom of expression: "The old Hollywood thing of the studio taking von Stroheim films or Welles's and cutting them—I think it's shocking," but she defended the idea of artists' censoring themselves: "The censorship I believe in is self-censorship. Obviously, no censors—or very few—are going to have the taste or discrimination, or the cultural background or sensitivity and delicacy that a great artist in any field will have dealing with his own work. Censorship can be a very dangerous thing."[45] Like in other New Wave films, the lack of scandalous scenes by today's standards might be surprising. However, at the time, the lifestyle and behavior of the characters were considered shocking.

Seberg's own private life would also soon raise eyebrows, but in the meantime, in cinema, she became more in demand and bankable. Only Bardot commanded a higher salary for a film, and Columbia increased Seberg's salary and loan-out fee to $20,000 per film. After filming Columbia's *Let No Man Write My Epitaph* (1960) immediately after Godard's shoot, the actress signed to star in her husband's *La Récréation* (*Love Play*, 1961), then in Jean Valère's *Les Grandes personnes* (*Time Out for Love*, 1961), and Philippe de Broca's comedy *L'Amant de cinq jours* (*Five Day Lover*, 1961), a film that she later claimed was one of her favorites.

When Seberg met Romain Gary, a respected author and France's Consul Général, and then divorced Moreuil in September 1960, her actions were scrutinized. Like the characters she played, "her films and her way of life were considered risqué in the 1960s, but today they would not be blinked at,"[46] Dawn Quinn observed. Though mostly positive, this attention from the public and the media along with her work provoked in her what Moreuil believed to be a mental breakdown. He checked her into the American Hospital of Paris to treat her for exhaustion; then Gary put her in the care of a psychiatrist. Moreuil believed that Gary's action, however, was a way to take control of her.[47] Not long after, Seberg reemerged to appear in the roles for which she had signed that explored new sides of herself and her acting.

Though none would quite capture the ambiance of the Nouvelle Vague, *L'Amant de cinq jours* was a huge success in France. As scandalous as *À bout de souffle*, it also anticipated by three years the controversial aspect of Godard's *Une femme mariée*. "They thought it was really outrageous," Seberg stated. "You would see me one second in the arms of my lover and the next shot would be of me holding my children. It became a bit shocking."

THREE YEARS LATER: PATRICIA BEHIND THE CAMERA

Three years after *À bout de souffle*, Seberg reappeared as Patricia in Godard's short *Le Grand escroc* (meaning "the great swindler"). Intended as part of the episodic film *Les Plus belles escroqueries du monde* (*The World's Most Beautiful Swindlers*, 1964) with other shorts by Chabrol, Roman Polanski, Ugo Gregoretti, and Hiromichi Horikawa, Godard's segment in Marrakech was cut from the lineup without explanation other than that the producers deemed it "weak." The other four shorts, however, were not widely applauded upon their release in 1964. The continuation of Patricia's story makes her one of the most independent women of the New Wave, but the film was not released until the 1967 London Film Festival.[48]

Le Grand escroc was shot in January 1963 again with Coutard, and this time the team was joined by composer Michel Legrand and actors Charles Denner as a thief and *Le Petit soldat*'s László Szabó as a police investigator. While the twenty-minute sketch did not capture the verve and innovation of *À bout de souffle*, the seldom-seen piece was not without merit. Godard's style remained fresh and Seberg's Patricia is more polished and mature. The film explores sociopolitical ideas through the metaphor of thievery, with a more intellectual angle that was less alluring or accessible than Godard's modern romantic gangster hybrid with the witty Belmondo. After Seberg refused to let her character be portrayed as a thief at the end of *À bout de souffle*, here Patricia is investigating one. The once-aspiring journalist is now a full-fledged reporter on assignment in Morocco, covering a story for American television.

The film opens with Patricia alone in a hotel room reading the French translation of Herman Melville's *The Confidence-Man: His Masquerade* (1857), *Le Grand escroc* in French. Godard reads quotes from the book in voice-over, intercut with the words on screen: "La charité ne pense pas le mal. La charité endure toute chose. La charité croit toute chose. La charité n'a jamais de défaillances" ("Charity thinketh no evil. Charity endureth all things. Charity believeth in all things. Charity never faileth"[49]), announcing Godard's underlying subject of contemplation in the film. Patricia is on the phone in the role of reporter, now with power and a voice behind the camera instead of being the object of it: "I think I'll go out; I've got some film left. I'll go to the medina and finish it." She takes her movie camera and points it at the viewer (Godard's camera), like Coutard will do in the opening of *Le Mépris*, a reflexive device that makes us aware that we are watching a film. The reverse shot, the one she is supposedly filming, shows Godard dressed in a djellaba and a

fez, blurring the identities of the director and actress. It is Godard's voice that announces "Moteur!" ("Action!") to start the film that Patricia shoots.

We see close-ups of two Moroccan women, then Patricia stepping out of a convertible in the medina; she is covered with a veil but is wearing high heels. From her perspective behind the camera, we see close-ups of men looking straight into the camera (similar to the passersby on the sidewalk in Varda's *Cléo de 5 à 7*). As Patricia pauses at a market, the police stop her and take her in for questioning. "For three weeks, counterfeit money has been raining on Marrakech," the police inspector (Szabó) says. "So, it's holidays for you here in Marrakech?" he asks. "No, no, it's work," she answers. Patricia is active, lighting his cigarette and later filming him. Godard entrusts Patricia with capturing the "truth" with her camera (with a nod to the concept of the *cinéma-vérité* and filmmaker Jean Rouch). Their exchange, a mix of English and French, explicitly illustrates the confinement inherent in women's preconceived roles, and qualifies Patricia—an independent, active woman with a career—as an aberration:

> Inspector: I thought that in America, pretty women didn't have to work.
> Patricia: Not at all, I'm a reporter for WXYZ in San Francisco, Channel 8.
> Inspector: What is that?
> Patricia: It's a television station. They send me all over the world after reporting jobs.
> [She lights his cigarette.]
> Inspector: I wish you'd explain exactly what means the word *reporting*.
> Patricia: It means shooting. [She films him.] Real things, places, people.
> Inspector: Oh yeah, I understand. You make documentary films like Mr. Rouch.
> Patricia: That's right. It's truth motion picture, *le cinéma-vérité*.
> Inspector: Me too, I'm searching for the truth, but not in the same way. *D'ailleurs, on la trouvera jamais, ni vous, ni moi* [We will never find it, for that matter, neither you nor I].

During her investigation, Patricia interviews a counterfeiter (Denner), who turns out to be a philanthropist in that he gives fake money to the poor. It is not hard to hear Godard's polemic voice behind the counterfeiter's discourse. Traces of Patricia's betrayal of Michel in *À bout de souffle* also color the exchange (in French):

Patricia: Are you making fake bank notes?
Counterfeiter: Are you going to tell the police?
Patricia: No, not at all. I only want to film you.

Traces of *Le Petit soldat*'s photojournalist, Bruno, also appear, mirroring the scene in which he bombards Véronica with questions as he takes photos of her. Here, the roles are reversed. It is Patricia with the camera, asking a barrage of questions to the counterfeiter: "I promise that I won't say anything. So, do you agree that I film you and ask you questions?" The counterfeiter answers with typical Godardian ambiguity: "Charity endureth all things. From evil comes good. Suspicion is a step towards trust."

Again, Godard uses his characters to debate ideas, just as Patricia and Michel philosophized about love and death in *À bout de souffle*. Here, the discourse on forgetting after trauma appears as a monologue delivered by the counterfeiter. In his long diatribe are echoes of the war that France is starting to forget and of Godard's own personal trauma with Karina, as well as hints of a trauma that happened to Patricia's character during her episode with Michel.

Counterfeiter: Tell me, Mademoiselle, didn't you have an accident four years ago? A headwound? Strange things happen from that, not only do we remain unaware of what happens for a certain time immediately following the injury, but another strange thing, we totally forget, irremediably, everything that happened for a certain amount of time immediately before the injury—that is to say a time where the mind was perfectly conscious of what was happening to it and perfectly capable also of recording in its memory what was causing so many effects, but all that in vain because the injury then came to erase everything.

Accompanied by non-diegetic jazz music, Patricia circles around him with her camera, frustrated. "Why don't you want to answer? What is your name? Why do you give the money you make to beggars?" she asks assertively. The counterfeiter replies, again ambiguously, evoking the notion of doubles (that haunts many of Godard's works): "It is not easy to know oneself. Who knows, Mademoiselle, if you did not mistake yourself for another for a certain period. Stranger things have happened." Patricia, here a double of Godard, is also his *porte-parole*, his spokesperson, who articulates his motivation to film, while the counterfeiter provides the opposite viewpoint:

Patricia: People aren't furious when they notice that it's fake money? It's the worst of swindles. It's almost theft.
Counterfeiter: No, charity knoweth no evil. . . . Why do you film me like that?
Patricia: I don't know. Because I am searching for something of—the truth.
Counterfeiter: For what?
Patricia: To show people.
Counterfeiter: So, you steal something from me and you too give it to others.

In line with Godard's answer to Cavett about giving his lines to his characters, here Patricia and the counterfeiter posit their shifting identities as well as film's (in)capacity to convey the truth. With her camera, Patricia, in the place of Godard, seeks to justify his search for the truth through film, while the counterfeiter signals this act as unscrupulous. Patricia has assumed the role of journalist like the protagonist in *Le Petit soldat*, (and her aspired profession in *À bout de souffle*), in search of the truth, but she will betray the man whose trust she was trying to earn. In the next shot, Patricia is in a police truck with the investigator. When he asks her why she is telling him all this now, she replies, "To have a clear conscience." In the final scene, Seberg's ambiguous voice-over blurs the lines of reality and fiction, character and actor: "Yes, he turned his back on me, leaving me perplexed, taking care to find out at what moment he had abandoned the fictive character to take back the real one, assuming there is one." "Yes, assuming there is one," the investigator replies.

Godard will use these particular lines about the confusion between actor and character, and the idea of doubles, in the movie theater scene in *Pierrot le fou*. When Seberg appears on screen and points her camera at Jean-Pierre Léaud and Belmondo in the audience, it reinforces the confusion between actors and the characters that all three of them play as well as the counterfeit notion of truth in film. At the end of *Le Grand escroc*, Godard has the final word. In his own voice-over, the director closes the film with his words and those of Shakespeare, blending life and art, truth and fiction: "And these very common lines came back to the young filmmaker's mind from San Francisco, charged with a very strong meaning while she watched the stranger ride away: 'All the world's a stage, and all the men and women merely players; they have their exits and their entrances; and one man in his time plays many parts.'"

In Seberg's own life, she played many parts, never settling on one. In Moreuil's words, "Jean was ahead of her time. She was a very strong personality. There was something in her that kept her moving from man to man, moving from one country to another country, moving from one part of herself to other parts of herself."[50] In one of her most noteworthy roles after *À bout de souffle*, Seberg left the Franco-American persona she had cultivated with Godard and others to star in the 1964 Robert Rossen adaption of J.R. Salamanca's novel *Lilith* for Columbia. Showcasing her acting range, she played a patient in a psychiatric hospital. The role foreshadowed the actress's own struggles with mental health after a multitude of traumatic experiences, from Preminger's abuse to an FBI smear campaign. During that period, she had also been looking forward to doing more New Wave films, notably working with Truffaut on his adaptation of Ray Bradbury's *Fahrenheit 451*. "I owe a great deal to François Truffaut because he was sort of the spearhead of all of it, and made the most wonderful pronouncements about admiring me and thinking I was a good actress," she said. "At the time it was terribly important for my morale." Though the role went to Julie Christie in Truffaut's 1966 production, Seberg's Patricia appeared in Godard's *Pierrot le fou* in the form of "found footage" from *Le Grand escroc*. Pointing her camera at Godard's, she looks at us, the audience as well as all the iconic characters/actors, bringing us together again in a fragmented postmodern collage transcending time and space and incarnating the idea that all of the characters, all of the actors in the history of cinema, remain immortally embedded in every new film, in every new role.

JEAN SEBERG'S IDEALISTIC ACTIVISM

The McCarthy era shook many lives in the film industry. Perhaps one of the most notorious and tragic was that of Jean Seberg. She may have spent most of her adult life outside her homeland, but the FBI did not let her live her life in total freedom. Like Patricia, Seberg was independent, ambitious, and modern, but she was also extremely sensitive and idealistic, and highly empathetic to those less fortunate. Guided by Midwestern values and earnestness (or naïveté, as some would say), she was driven to stand up for their rights. Like the Saint Joan she portrayed as a teenager, Seberg seemed to have a calling. Despite her good intentions in her fight for social justice, she would pay for this calling with her life.

Growing up the daughter of a small-town pharmacist, the son of Swedish immigrants, Seberg seemed to learn by example. Her father modeled the behavior in his practice, dropping off prescriptions for the elderly and opening the drug store after hours to be of service to the community. Seberg's sister Mary Ann recalled Jean befriending a man on a bus and giving him all the money she had saved up for a vacation because she felt sorry for him. She once won an award as part of a United Way campaign, the Red Feather Kids. According to her best friend at the time, Lynda Haupert, "If it wasn't an animal, it was other things. She always had something she was working toward not only to better herself, but society." Her mother described her as "what the town felt as 'different,'" and added that her daughter lived "a rather lonely life of her own choice in a world of her vivid imagination."[51] At the same time, she was greatly enthusiastic and sincere about every project she was involved in, for better or worse, and this spirit seemed to guide her whole life.

From a young age, her focus was split between acting and civic involvement. According to her sister, "From the time she was tiny, she was acting, she was performing. She was always going to be a movie star. That's all we ever heard." But her awareness of social injustice was equally strong. Seberg recalled reading a book at eight years old about a little Black girl and her mother riding a bus where people looked at her strangely; she stated that the book "revealed a whole new world" about the existence of racism and the issues Black Americans had to confront every day. In ninth grade, she was elected copresident of the student body and applied to be a member of the Des Moines NAACP. Considered shocking in small-town Iowa during McCarthyism, her actions led to gossip among the community and concern from her parents. "[People] will say you're a Communist,"[52] her father warned, not knowing the prescience of his statement.

In the same vein, the idealistic Seberg was impressed with a controversial, outspoken instructor at her high school, Paul Richer, who had taught a course on communism. After her junior year, Seberg became more invested in politics. Chosen to represent her high school at Girls State, a youth forum sponsored by the American Legion, she was sent to Washington, DC, where she met with then–Vice President Richard Nixon. In 1955, she became the first teenage chairperson of the Iowa March of Dimes campaign. In a filmed interview with Iowa's governor, she stated, "We're growing up. Soon it will be our responsibility that you and other people in Iowa and America have. And we want to show you and other Iowa grown-ups that we can do that job. We appreciate our way of life, our health, and our need to know how to assume and carry out responsibility." The extent of her engagement at this young age carried over to the causes she supported later in life, proving they were not just Hollywood PR stunts. Her friends in high school described her as going out of her way to befriend unpopular kids, and as Hollingsworth said, "I'll never forget how she was for the underdog."[53]

After moving to France, Seberg held fast to her political views while she devoted her time to acting. Moreuil recalled this aspect in their relationship, saying, "The only thing we didn't agree upon was politics. I am a Gaullist, and a very determined one, and my mother was to the left and still is. Jean and my mother shared the same political beliefs–radical."[54]

Her views were broad and her engagement wide-ranging. While shooting *Congo vivo* (*Eruption*, 1962) in Léopoldville (now Kinshasa), she observed the inequalities from colonialism. Intuitively describing Pierre Bourdieu's idea of cultural capital regarding the unfair disadvantage of those born without privilege, she spoke out against certain practices of the colonizers. She told reporter Sheilah Graham, "The Belgians bungled things badly in the Congo. . . . [They] built two universities that presumably were open to all. But to get in, you had to know Greek, which automatically kept out [most] Congolese."[55]

Though *À bout de souffle* had helped make Seberg the face of liberated women, she did not embrace the women's liberation movement, per se. "These days women seem to behave in a bizarre fashion," she asserted. "They are so concerned with not being regarded as sex objects that it makes them aggressive and distanced, attempting to dominate men by a lofty rejection. It's a great pity because in this way they deny their own nature and impede its fulfillment. I hope this ridiculous fashion will pass, but I'm afraid men will have to show patience in the next fifteen years." Not without controversy, she hid the news of the birth of her son with Romain Gary, Diego, who was raised for the first two years in Spain by a nanny. But in Marshalltown, she defended herself (and all women) in the roles her fellow Iowans found objectionable, saying, "To label a girl 'good' or 'bad' is silly, stupid, and cruel."[56]

After a meeting with John F. Kennedy and Jacqueline Kennedy, Seberg was upset, according to her sister, that "the men were all invited to go to one room and given cigars, and the women had to go to another room to talk about 'lady things.' She would have much rather preferred being in on the political discussion with the men." It was likely this that drew her to Romain Gary, who provided her with stimulating intellectual exchange. When they married, she mingled in cultivated circles and met high-ranking officials such as Charles de Gaulle. "If Jean hadn't been an actress, she probably would have been a politician–and a very good one. She understood people, their needs, and the problems in society," her sister said. When making a film in Colombia, Seberg was disheartened by the crime and poverty around

SAC, Los Angeles (157-4054)   5/6/70
        EC-52

Director, FBI (100-448006)-1766
        7-11.

COUNTERINTELLIGENCE PROGRAM
BLACK NATIONALIST HATE GROUPS
RACIAL INTELLIGENCE - BLACK PANTHER PARTY

                Reurairtel 4/27/70.

                Reairtel requests Bureau authority to forward a
letter from a fictitious person to Hollywood, California,
gossip columnists to publicize the pregnancy of Jean Seberg,
well-known white movie actress, by ▮▮▮▮▮▮▮▮▮▮ BPP
▮▮▮▮▮▮▮▮▮▮▮▮▮▮▮▮ to possibly cause her embarrassment
and tarnish her image with the general public. Information
from ▮▮▮▮▮▮▮ indicated that Seberg was four months
pregnant by ▮▮▮▮▮▮

                To protect the sensitive source of information
from possible compromise and to insure the success of your
plan, Bureau feels it would be better to wait approximately
two additional months until Seberg's pregnancy would be
obvious to everyone. If deemed warranted, submit your
recommendation at that time.

        1 - San Francisco

        JFM:drl
          (5)

NOTE:

                Jean Seberg has been a financial supporter of the
BPP and should be neutralized. Her current pregnancy by
▮▮▮▮▮▮▮ while still married affords an opportunity for such
effort. The plan suggested by Los Angeles appears to have
merit except for the timing since the sensitive source
might be compromised if implemented prematurely. A copy is
designated to San Francisco since its sensitive source
coverage is involved.

97 MAY 8 1970

COINTELPRO document outlining the FBI's plans to "neutralize" Jean
Seberg for her support of the Black Panther Party, April 1970

her, stating a few years later, "If I had lived in South America, I would have fought with Che."[57]

These convictions are undoubtedly what led to Seberg's involvement with the Black Panthers. In April 1968, while she was in Washington, DC, to shoot George Schaefer's *Pendulum* (1969), Martin Luther King Jr. was assassinated and riots broke out at the capitol. Shooting the film became dangerous, and the cast and crew were confined to their hotel rooms. Witnessing the events firsthand, Seberg wrote to her friend Vony Becker, "The indifference of the white population is almost total." Speaking to writer Margaret Ronan, Seberg conveyed her hands-on attitude in terms of civil action: "We help cause crime if we elect the wrong legislators, or if we don't see that the police have enough manpower to do their job properly. The Supreme Court can't appropriate money for law enforcement, or clean up the slums, or stop drug pushers. We have to do these things, and in too many cases, we're trying to pass the buck." Living in Los Angeles at that time, the actress also became more aware of racial intolerance and the US involvement in Vietnam. She voiced her views as she always had, but their resonance rang louder in this context. She funded diverse progressive causes, all in the aim of overcoming poverty, inequality, and racism. Along with helping an organization establish Black-owned businesses in poor Los Angeles neighborhoods, she donated to riot-torn Watts. In France, she led a campaign to raise the labor standards for Arab workers. In Marshalltown, she organized a scholarship to help male students attend college rather than being forced to go to Vietnam.

When Seberg met Hakim Jamal, who described himself to her as "a part-time member of the Black Panther party," his causes caught the actress's interest. Jamal had formed the Malcolm X Foundation, which served as a cultural center, and founded a Montessori school for disadvantaged Black children. After hearing that a fire had partially destroyed the foundation's headquarters and that Jamal was receiving death threats, Seberg contributed money of her own and also introduced Jamal to her Hollywood friends to aid the Montessori school. Although Seberg soon became disenchanted with Jamal, finding his endeavors ineffective, he eventually managed to convince her to continue support-

ing them. In the meantime, she became more and more involved in the Black Panther Party's causes, such as their free breakfast program for children in poverty, which she donated to under a pseudonym.

"She was not interested in giving cocktail parties for us," Elaine Brown, a member (and eventual head) of the party, said of Seberg's commitment. "She wanted to do something." Speaking of Seberg's idealism, Brown later stated, "Jean had her own ideals. She simply believed what she was taught in Marshalltown, embodied in the words about freedom and equality found in the Declaration of Independence. . . . To me, Jean seemed a free spirit and a true believer." [58]

Some also felt that she was used, especially by Jamal. Fundraisers, for example, were held at Seberg's Los Angeles home at Coldwater Canyon, which also became a hangout for the Black Panthers. Others thought of Seberg as a Jane Fonda type. By 1968, the FBI had infiltrated many Black activist groups through its counterintelligence program, and she was soon targeted. She began to feel as if she was being spied on by both disgruntled or jealous members of the Panthers and the FBI. Later, her FBI files would show that she and Jamal were indeed under surveillance in May of 1969. In June, the FBI official in charge of monitoring extremist groups recommended an "active discreet investigation" of Seberg, who, according to the report, was "providing funds and assistance to black extremists, including leaders in the Black Panther Party."

The covert investigation of Seberg began in 1969 with phone tapping, spying, and eventually plans for a smear campaign. In May 1970, FBI director J. Edgar Hoover authorized agents to disseminate a rumor that Seberg, who was expecting a child with then-husband Gary, had actually become pregnant by a member of the Black Panthers. "Jean Seberg has been a financial supporter of the BPP and should be neutralized. Her current pregnancy by [name deleted], while still married affords an opportunity for such effort. The plan suggested by Los Angeles appears to have merit except for the timing since the sensitive source might be compromised if implemented prematurely," read the memo. "Bureau feels it would be better to wait approximately two additional months until Seberg's pregnancy would be obvious to everyone."[59] The story was leaked to *Los Angeles Times* gossip columnist Joyce Haber, who clearly described Seberg in her column but omitted her name. Over the next few months, high-profile publications like *The Hollywood Reporter* and *Newsweek* published the story with more unverified details, identifying Seberg outright. In August, under considerable stress from the constant persecution, Seberg gave birth prematurely to a daughter who did not survive. Gary blamed the press.

Even in these darkest days, Seberg's commitment to helping those less fortunate appeared to be hard-wired. While in Marshalltown for the baby's funeral, she visited the Meskwaki Nation settlement, which was in the midst of a poverty crisis, to offer assistance; and on the way back, she reportedly tried to help an injured dog on the side of the road. Seen by some as naïve, her good intentions were met with discord that then caused her even more problems. During the same trip to Marshalltown, she bought a house for Black athletes who were attending the community college, causing an uproar in the still largely segregated community. "To understand Jean," wrote Gary, "you have to understand the Midwest. She emerged from it intelligent, talented and beautiful but with the naivety of a child. She has the kind of goodwill that to me is infuriating—persistent, totally unrealistic idealism. It has made her totally defenseless."[60] To the end, she never abandoned her boundless solicitude but could not carry the weight of this degree of sensitivity, the unimaginable loss, or the trauma of the FBI smear campaign. The circumstances surrounding Seberg's death are vague. She disappeared in Paris in the late summer of 1979, and her body was found in her car ten days later. With it was a bottle of barbiturates and a note, and her death was ruled a probable suicide. Seberg was forty years old. "Jean attempted all of her life to be of help and comfort to any who were in need," her father told reporters after her funeral in Marshalltown.

Seberg's meteoric trajectory from Midwestern obscurity to the Parisian silver screen has made her one of the New Wave's most idiosyncratic figures; and her destruction by a rancorous government has made her one of Hollywood's most tragic. But to those who knew her, she was more than her narrative—she was someone with an unyielding, guileless compassion who wanted to give herself to everyone, even at her own expense. "I feel Jean got suckered in by people sometimes," Haupert once said. "But all of these causes Jean supported, from the March of Dimes to the Black Panthers, were to help the downtrodden, to make a difference for the better."[61]

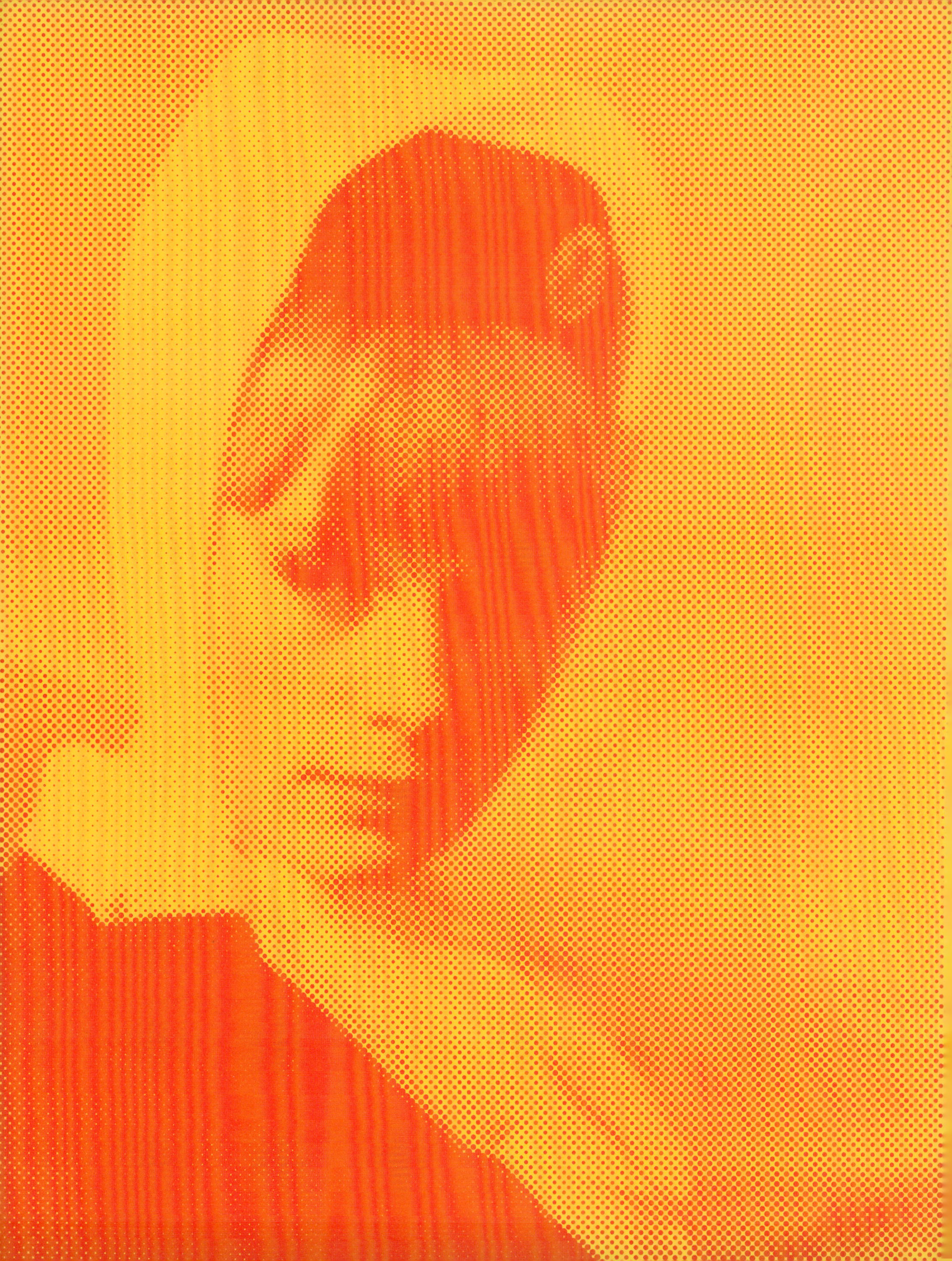

françoise dorléac 9

la femme réelle | *the real woman*

FRANÇOISE DORLÉAC FINDS HER FOOTING

Though Françoise Dorléac may not be synonymous with the Nouvelle Vague, she embodied its spirit as an actress and as a woman, perhaps one of the most modern of her generation. Often remembered as the older sister of the iconic Catherine Deneuve, Dorléac had suffered from the constant comparisons between them since youth. "I was an ugly little girl," she said in 1964. "You know, the kind where they say, 'She has pretty eyes.' And I was flat: At seventeen, I could've gone swimming without a top with no problem; nobody would've even noticed. On the beach like on stage, people only noticed Catherine. Now, it's okay! Except my jawline and my enormous forehead, but my hair hides everything."[1]

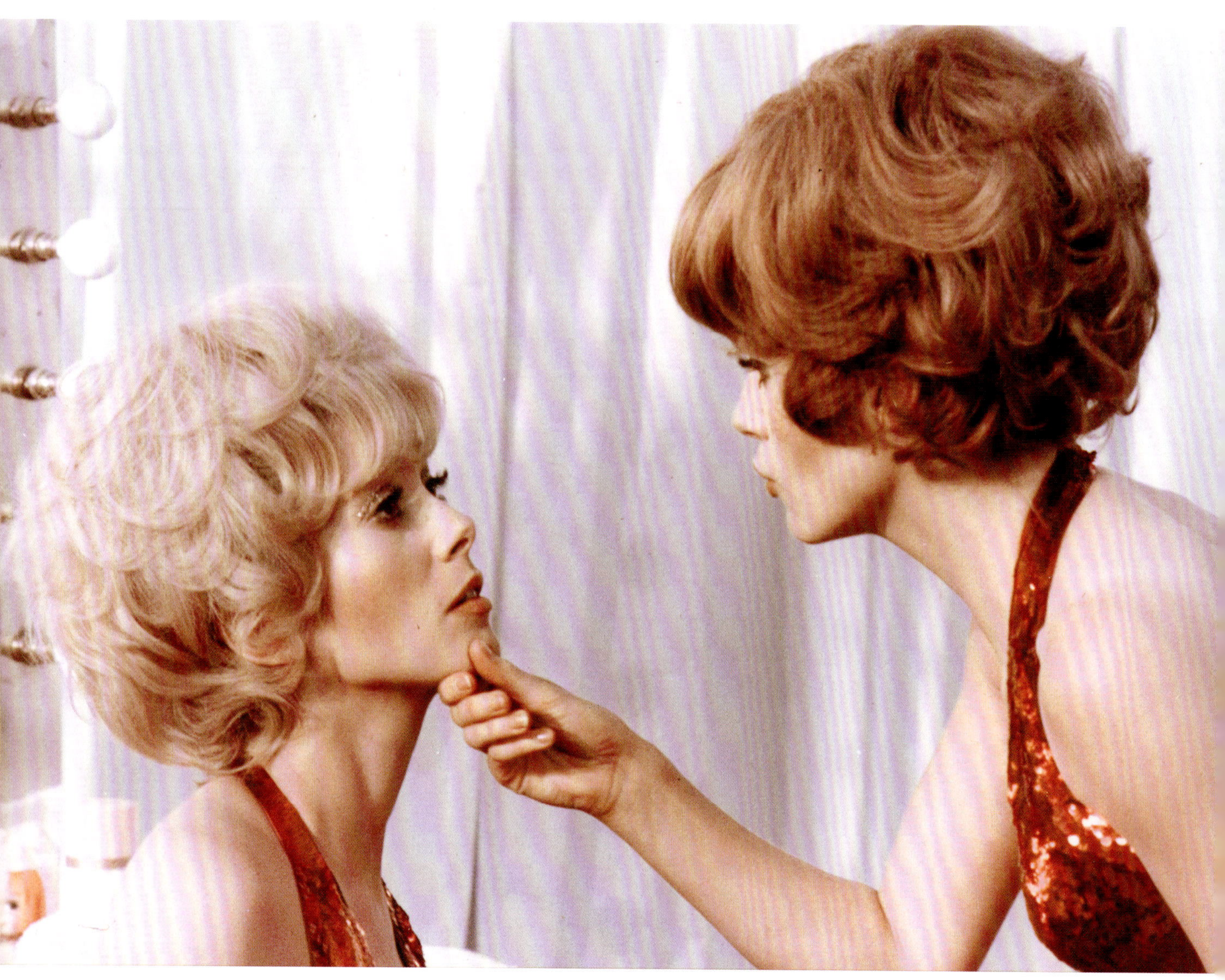

Despite this harsh (and inaccurate) self-assessment, it was Dorléac, not Deneuve, who dreamed of becoming an actress from a young age, voicing her ambition to follow in her parents' footsteps (stage actors who later became famous for their work dubbing foreign films into French). In 1951, she was almost on her way, recommended by a friend of the family, actress Monique Mélinand, for a child's role in Louis Jouvet's stage adaptation of Graham Greene's *The Power and the Glory* (1940). Though the project fell through after Jouvet's sudden death that year, ten-year-old Dorléac landed her first job in the fall of 1952: lending her voice to Elsbeth Sigmund's titular role in the French dub of Luigi Comencini's Swiss German classic, *Heidi* (1952).[2]

At seventeen, Dorléac entered the Conservatoire d'art dramatique in Paris to study acting and made her first appearance in front of the camera in Hervé Bromberger's *Les Loups dans la bergerie* (*The Wolves in the Sheepfold*, 1960). When the script specified that Dorléac appear topless, she complied, a gesture that already illustrated her complex personality. Vacillating between revealing and concealing herself, she sometimes hid behind thick makeup and bangs covering her forehead, while at other times appearing natural or nude—all or nothing. The film earned her attention, and in March 1960, she gained more in the leading role of the successful stage adaptation of Colette's *Gigi*, a character known for her funny face. Though Dorléac's next film, *Les Portes claquent* (*The Door Slams*, 1960) by Michel Fermaud and Jacques Poitrenaud, went practically unnoticed, it would mark a significant moment in her life. Her character has a sister—and Catherine Dorléac, who had not seriously considered a career in acting, took the role, appearing with Françoise under their mother's maiden name, Deneuve.

At the same time, the sisters, whose parents entrusted them with great freedom, were frequenting the trendiest nightclubs in Paris, where Dorléac loved to dance, uninhibited—a characteristic that directors would incorporate into her roles—while Deneuve, more reserved, looked on. This was where Deneuve, at seventeen, met Roger Vadim and moved in with him shortly after, earning her more attention and greater access to the film world. Dorléac, meanwhile, experienced difficulty with commitment in her love life but

showed an openness to desire. Her melancholy and extreme sensitivity meant that she fell in love easily but never for very long (one exception being her relationship with actor Jean-Pierre Cassel). She confessed she was "always in love, not with one man but with a lot of men. Because each has something that I like that the other doesn't have."[3] In the end, her independence or dissatisfaction left a trail of broken hearts, a trait often mirrored in her film roles.

In Philippe de Broca's *L'Homme de Rio* (*That Man from Rio*, 1964), Dorléac's presence permeated the role of Agnès. After her boyfriend Adrien (Belmondo) unexpectedly ends up on a plane to Rio de Janeiro to rescue her from kidnappers, he describes Agnès in a way that is almost indistinguishable from Dorléac. As she sleeps at a little boy's house in a favela, he says to Adrien, "She's pretty!" "But high-maintenance, believe me!" Adrien counters. "She always wants something we don't have. She's dreamy, always off-the-wall. . . . A woman, Sir Winston, is someone who's waiting for you at home, someone who's tender and understanding. You come home, she opens the door. She plays piano or the harp. You're home. This one can't even boil me an egg, but I follow her across the world." Dorléac, herself and in the roles she played, projected independence and a carefree spirit that made her elusive, motivating men all the more to fall in love with her. François Truffaut would be no exception.

A MODERN MISTRESS IN A LOST MAN'S FANTASY: *LA PEAU DOUCE*

In 1964's *La Peau douce*, Dorléac played a flight attendant with a grounded outlook and independent spirit, a role that valorized her beauty, style, and personality. This *film d'auteur* from the Nouvelle Vague, also validated her as an actress. In a press release about *La Peau douce*, Truffaut described it as being about love. Anticipating negative reviews, Truffaut ironically protested with a preemptive defense, "What? Another film about love? Another film about love? French people only make films about love! After making *Jules et Jim*, about two men and one woman, you can't find anything else to offer us besides *La Peau douce*, about two women and a man?"[4] But love and a new love triangle was not what Truffaut found himself defending. "Yes, I made a film on adul-

Catherine Deneuve and Françoise Dorléac in Jacques Demy's *Les Demoiselles de Rochefort* (*The Young Girls of Rochefort*), 1967

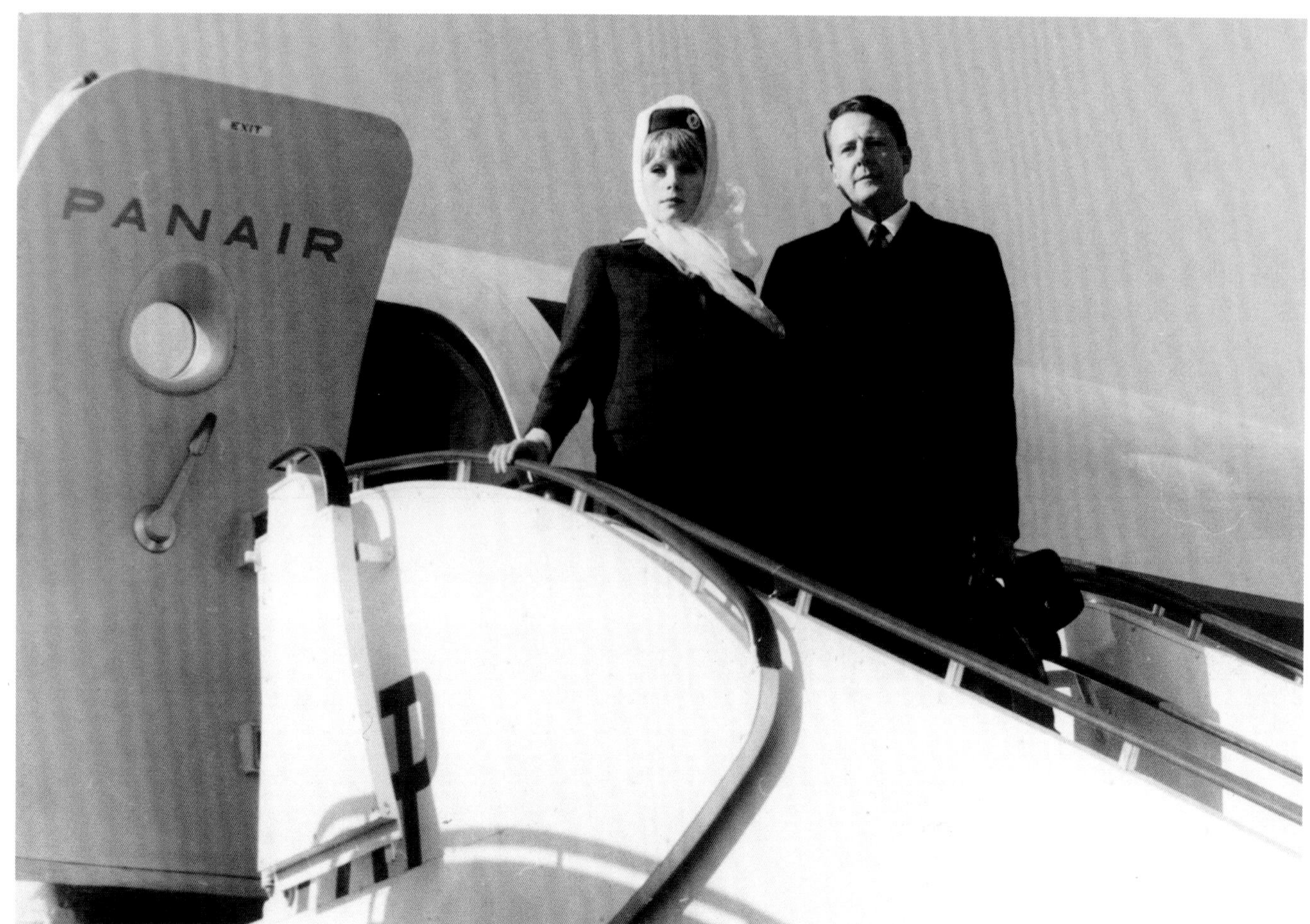

tery," he responded in an interview at the time of the film's release, "but making sure only to shoot scenes that aren't usually shown. Coincidences, the spaces in between. What I liked was to start a scene by the cliché and go beyond it."[5]

Making a film about love or adultery at a time when values from an old order had already been radically questioned seemed to puzzle critics. Even the word *adultery* itself sounded old in 1964, which might be why Truffaut tried to divert attention from it or defend his slant on it. There was no denying, however, that this outdated topos—the husband, the wife, and the lover—was at the heart of the film. Truffaut explained that he wanted to break stereotypes of the wife and mistress, to "contradict [them], in the sense that I made the wife very sensual and the mistress lively, funny, sweet,"[6] also describing the wife as "violent, beautiful, attractive," and the mistress as "not at all a tease." Claiming the film

was "part of a somewhat utopic idea," Truffaut stated, "We were talking about relationships between men and women, about adultery, and we wanted to make a film where the wife, the husband, and the mistress were all equal." Despite his intention, the center of *La Peau douce* resides undeniably in Françoise Dorléac.

Truffaut met Dorléac at a French cinema festival in Tel Aviv at the beginning of 1963. Though they were somewhat annoyed by each other at first, they found common ground through their love of literature. Dorléac quickly consumed the books Truffaut lent her from his suitcase, and upon returning home, they continued their discussion of literature in letters—an indirect act of seduction. In his letters, Truffaut gave her the nickname *Framboise* (meaning "raspberry" and rhyming with *Françoise*) from a Boby Lapointe song. The two met once in Paris before Dorléac left for Rio to make de Bro-

Top and right: Françoise Dorléac (Nicole) and Jean Desailly (Jean) in François Truffaut's *La Peau douce* (*The Soft Skin*), 1964

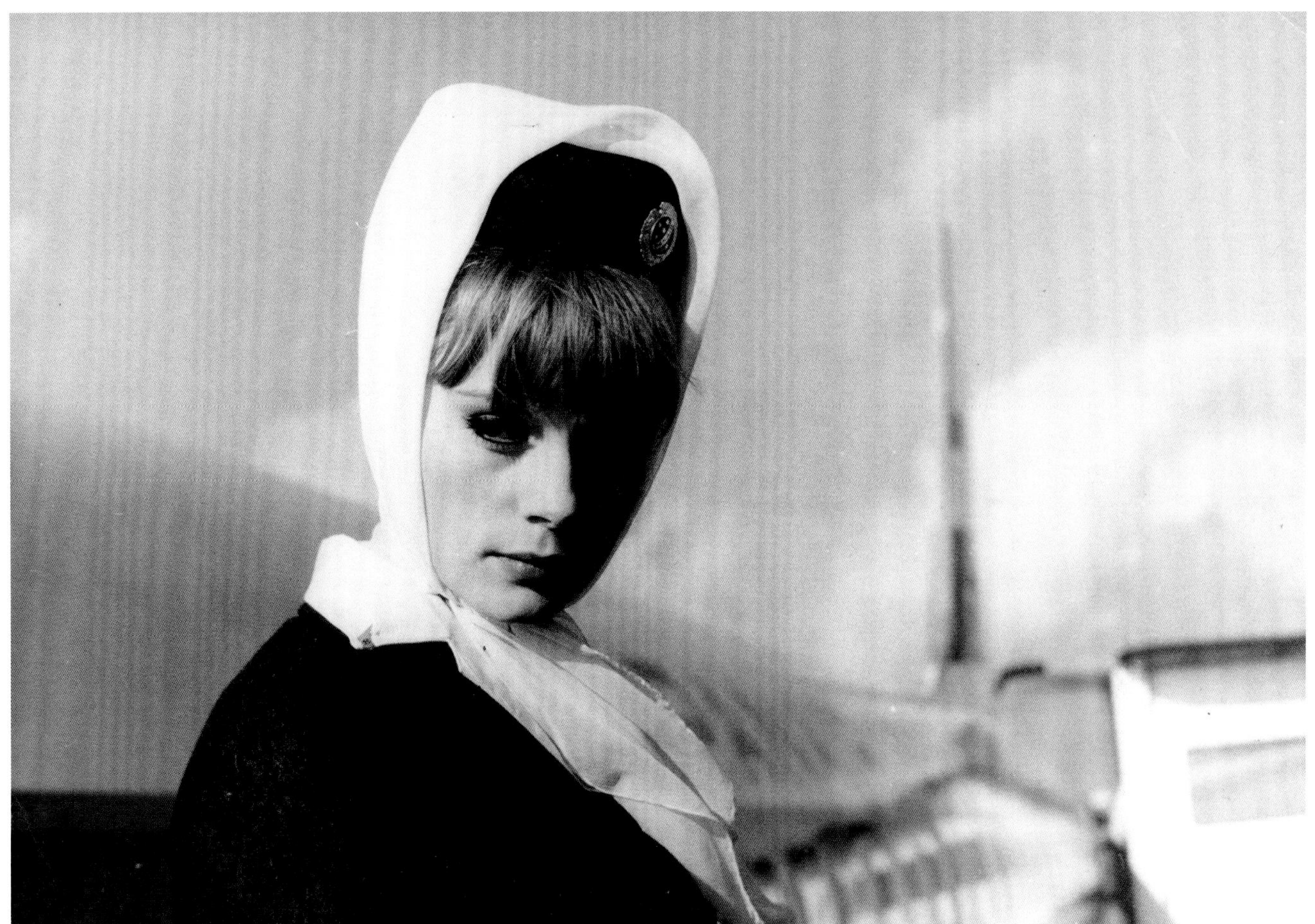

ca's film. Upon her return, she found the script for *La Peau douce* waiting. Her character, Nicole, seemed too harsh to Dorléac, so she asked Truffaut to soften her. As they met to transform the role, real life started mirroring the script. "Françoise nourishes the heroine with her own experiences, her memories that she transposes and modifies, and there will be, of course, a dance scene," wrote Aurélien Ferenczi in *Framboise*, his book about Dorléac, elements that make her character "independent and lucid" like the actress herself.[7]

In 1964, a time when the New Wave had begun to slow down, this film above all illustrated the tensions that remained between men and women and their roles in love, marriage, and society in general. As women slowly emerged from literary and cinematic tropes and into real life, actresses had real power to shape their roles on and off screen. Nicole incarnates the ultimate male fantasy—a young, attrac-

tive flight attendant—but her independent spirit is formed by Dorléac. In creating Nicole, Truffaut drew from interviews he conducted with three flight attendants, and he credited Dorléac for adding complexity to the role. "Nicole's character became much better in the course of the shoot thanks to Dorléac,"[8] he said. When Truffaut felt that Nicole escaped him or became too mysterious, he asked Dorléac's advice, then adjusted her dialogue on the set.[9]

Nicole crosses paths with the protagonist, Pierre Lachenay (Jean Desailly), a married, middle-aged literature professor—a bourgeois in the image of the man Truffaut had become. These characters in a *mise en abyme* also tell the story of Dorléac and Truffaut that was taking place behind the scenes.

A victim of his milieu, Lachenay is trapped in a cage where his desires can exist only as fantasy. The film opens with him running home to his bourgeois apartment, taking the cage-like elevator to get his suitcase and tell his wife and child goodbye before leaving for a conference in Lisbon. In the next sequence, resembling *L'Homme de Rio* when Belmondo's character races to the airport and boards a flight to try to rescue Dorléac, *La Peau douce* shows the protagonist rushing to Orly with Hitchcockian urgency. While in de Broca's film, a series of obstacles keep him from his goal, in Truffaut's *mise en scène*, the plane sequence serves to construct the image of Nicole as a fantasy figure.

Escaping his reality in Paris, Lachenay meets her for the first time on the flight. In this initial scene, her still-undefined character waits at the door of the plane, which is preparing to take off, when Lachenay arrives, running late. The camera films her from a low angle as she stands at the top of the stairs. In their first encounter on the plane, Truffaut depicts an immediate *coup de foudre* on the part of Lachenay for the flight attendant. He conveys the protagonist's desire with shots of him noticing Nicole across the aisle a few rows ahead of him and peering at her changing her shoes beneath the galley curtain. When the plane lands, Lachenay's celebrity is established by paparazzi who ask to take his picture with the flight attendant, who is still unknown to him. In the photo, published in the next day's paper, Nicole, with her fine features and glacial expression, resembles a statue, reminiscent of Jeanne Moreau's sculptural shots in *Jules et Jim*. For Truffaut, both women incarnate mystery and the eternal feminine.

At the hotel, Lachenay's image on a poster announces the conference on his book, *Balzac et l'argent* (Balzac and money). "It's an unusual topic," a journalist states during an interview with Lachenay, asking him why he chose it. "It's simple, I like Balzac a lot and I don't despise money," he answers jokingly (also mirroring the tastes of the director). Crossing paths again with Nicole in the elevator, Lachenay memorizes the room number on her key and calls her at 1:00 a.m. to invite her for a drink, which conveys his stereotypical view of her as a flight attendant who would be open to his advances. Meeting instead the next evening, they talk late into the night at a restaurant before going back to Lachenay's room, where he realizes his fantasy. When they separate, his desire

returns in his imagination as Truffaut uses his trademark superimposition of images: Their kiss is overlaid on an image of the airplane, suggesting Lachenay's freedom.

Nicole and Lachenay meet again between her flights. At a restaurant, Dorléac's sensual dance scene showcases her modernity, while Lachenay sits rigidly in his chair, hypnotized and out of date. Nicole joins him again at another conference in the country. A modern woman, Nicole is wearing jeans, but Lachenay tells her he prefers her in dresses. Again fulfilling his fantasy, when he stops at a gas station, she changes into a skirt.

Truffaut juxtaposed these scenes of passion with a bleak image of reality with the protagonist's wife. In contrast with the spontaneity and adventure in scenes with Nicole, those with his wife, Franca (Nelly Benedetti), project frustration and boredom. "Here we are in the everyday, in the most raw realism, but I think I avoided the sordid,"[10] Truffaut stated about the scenes with Lachenay's wife. Critic Georges Sadoul noted at the time that Truffaut's film had certain elements in common with Godard's *Le Mépris*: Both addressed infidelity in marriage, "tender in form, leaning toward a sort of 'neoclassicism' that does not exclude a 'neoromanticism' in the content."[11]

Calling his film "the autopsy of a couple's life," Truffaut also claimed it was not "sentimental enough,"[12] and described it as "a very realistic story of adultery that will give an antipoetic image of love, the opposite in a way of *Jules et Jim*, like a polemic response."[13] Truffaut's male protagonist, however, echoes Flaubert's *Madame Bovary*: Lachenay, trapped in a lackluster marriage, becomes trapped in a fantasy with Nicole, trying to live out romantic scenarios with her. Insisting on realism in his *mise en scène*, Truffaut masks any identification with his blindly romantic protagonist. When Truffaut presented the film to the Fédération française des ciné-clubs in 1964, he again emphasized that the film is a response to the "image of idealized love" in *Jules et Jim*, noting that "on the realistic level, love is more *La Peau douce*."[14]

The realistic love that he spoke about reflects an especially bourgeois vision of adultery in the context of married life. His protagonist/alter ego belongs to this world: he is a literature professor and family man who lives in a posh neighborhood in Paris. Truffaut used Lachenay to criticize this lifestyle (in line with Malle and Rivette in their films), but he also portrayed him as a victim. The protagonist's conflict translates an aspect of the director's own internal tension. For his conception of the script, Truffaut invented a formula that he explained in his commentary on the film: "I work a lot with real material, but it is 20 percent autobiographical, 20 percent from newspapers, 20 percent from the lives of people I know, and 40 percent pure fiction."[15] Without taking his statement too seriously, this mix of hybrid elements allows the film in a way to escape cliché. Though Truffaut admitted to including only a small percentage of autobiographical inspiration, he chose to shoot the family scenes in his own apartment in the sixteenth arrondissement of Paris. The very intimate scenes—not typical adultery scenes, as he specified—may also have been inspired by personal experiences. While filming this story of adultery, Truffaut had an affair with his actress, as he had done with other actresses on other film shoots. Lachenay's experience with Nicole in the hotel scene outside Paris, as Ferenczi noted, Truffaut had more or less lived after *Les Quatre cents coups* with the young actress Liliane David.

Truffaut tried his best to conceal the film's autobiographical elements. The day before the shoot he wrote to Helen Scott, "I'm asking you now not to talk about an 'autobiographical' film, like *Quatre cents coups*," adding that "Madeleine and I are separating. . . . Because of the script, I saw with horror the hypocrisy of married life."[16] Critic Henry Chapier wrote at the film's release that "Like Hitchcock, Truffaut serves us a film that is eminently personal in spite of its apparent banality."[17]

PIERRE LACHENAY: THE LOVE TRIANGLE'S BOURGEOIS PRISONER

Lachenay, attached to a vision of romantic love but a prisoner of the constraints of his bourgeois life, is confronted with a realistic vision of a young woman who embodies freedom. The modern aspect of Dorléac's character interacting with the uptight protagonist mirrors the director's own relationship with the actress as much as it reflects the evolving idea of what it meant to be a couple in 1960s France, a social construction undergoing profound transformations. The characters' pairing offers a new representation of romantic conventions. Nicole's more evolved ideas and attitudes about life and love highlight Lachenay's outdated, unrealistic view of her as his romantic ideal. With the two in opposition, the bourgeois protagonist looks out of touch, trapped in romanticism like Emma Bovary. With rational responses, Nicole will constantly pierce the dreams that Lachenay projects onto her, dismantling stereotypes in the process.

Nicole's character develops on two parallel paths and double visions: one, through the eyes of the protagonist and according to his romantic criteria; the other, through the *mise en scène* (and eyes of the audience) as a realistic, modern woman who contradicts his view. In Lachenay's romantic vision, the ideal woman is distant, and her inaccessibility adds to her value. In his world (and in the real one), her status as a flight attendant makes her the perfect object of desire. Lachenay's attempts to seduce her, however, reveal his fear and put him at risk of ridicule. Although the two share nights together (represented first in shadow and ellipses in Truffaut's modest *mise en scène*), Lachenay's every attempt to realize his romantic dreams fail in an uncooperative reality. When Nicole is absent, Lachenay composes a telegram that reads, "Nicole. Stop. Since I met you I am another man and this man cannot envision living without you. Stop. I love you. Pierre." But as soon as she returns, he loses confidence and throws the message away.

Caught in a Hitchcockian spiral within a Chaplinesque dark comedy, Lachenay is surrounded by the women in his triangle, who are both capable of unmasking his weaknesses and exposing the truth. He is a prisoner—of others, of situations, and even of himself. In these ways, Truffaut's protagonist also reflects a stage of his own life and his career in the midst of his failing marriage and five years after *Les Quatre cents coups*.

Going from one woman to the other, Lachenay is incapable of defining himself except through work. He also assumes different identities with his wife and his mistress: When he

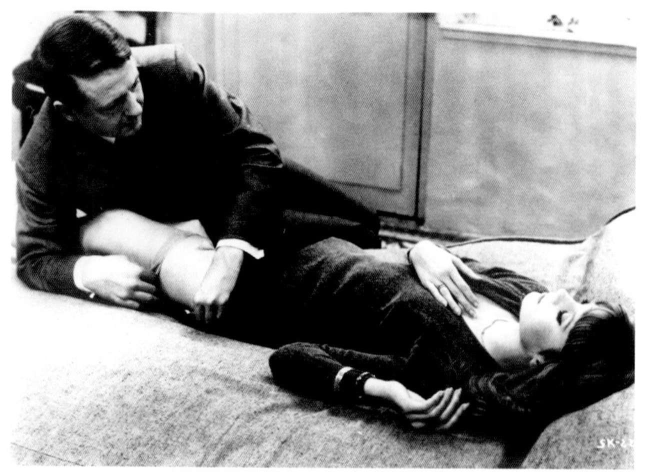

is with his wife, for example, she drives the car, but with his mistress, he takes the wheel. When Nicole breaks the fantasy by objecting to his desires, however, he relives with her experiences he has had with his wife, confusing the roles. Remaining perplexed and powerless in relation to both women, he causes them to suffer as well.

Truffaut's hero (or antihero) is a solitary man who resembles a child, lost in a world of books and women. Splitting his desire between wife and mistress, Lachenay reveals his incapacity to experience love and sexuality with one woman, another example of the Madonna-whore complex. Going further, like in Godard's *Une femme mariée*, he also breaks down the female body into multiple, fragmented pieces. Reflecting his fragility, Lachenay is unable to comprehend a woman's physical reality as a whole.[18] In a somewhat disturbing scene during their escapade at a provincial hotel, Lachenay inspects Nicole as she sleeps: The camera slowly scrutinizes Nicole's very fragmented and passive body, examining it from head to toe, as she becomes his pure object of desire. His inspection recalls Roland Barthes's idea of a lover who is looking at the body of his beloved as if it were a "strange insect," where suddenly the lover realizes "I am no longer afraid."[19] The *mise en scène* focuses on the visual aspect of Lachenay's desire. There is no dialogue; only music expresses his anxiety and desire in the presence of the silent and immobile woman. Her passivity triggers his fetishism as she becomes a (safe) object. Similarly, when Lachenay watches uncomfortably as Nicole dances, he can only look at her when he is unseen, with stolen glances, which con-

veys his fear. This moment of contemplation that suspends the narrative recalls Bardot's dance in *Et Dieu créa la femme* as men look on, hypnotized. In notable contrast, Dorléac's character in *L'Homme de Rio* also becomes immobilized in front of her lover after being drugged, but instead of taking advantage of her passivity, Belmondo's character desperately tries to awaken her.

FROM OBJECT TO SUBJECT: THE MISTRESS GAINS A VOICE

Truffaut judged his protagonist severely, confessing that Desailly's part "is a disgraceful role in the end," and even mocked him: "I had a sort of almost unhealthy jubilation making the film, showing a character blocked to that extent and by his fault. There was something sadistic in the film."[20] He admitted that the audience too might find Lachenay unsympathetic. Even the name he bestowed on his character implies cowardice: *Lâche* is French for "coward." (Desailly actually blamed the role for wrecking his career.[21]) The women's points of view in the film, however, are strong. Both mistress and wife possess real voices. Linked by similar situations despite their differing positions, ages, and social statuses, their voices tear them away from expected stereotypes. By speaking, they also both gain status as subjects, and at the same time dismantle the mechanisms that attempt to idealize or categorize them.

Fighting the flight attendant stereotype, Nicole constantly works to escape being defined as a male fantasy. After their night at the hotel where Lachenay observed Nicole's body, she regains her subjectivity by telling a story that in turn snaps him out of his fantasizing. Lachenay becomes ill at ease as the woman of his dreams becomes real, and this reality hardly seems to attract him. Their dialogue underlines the incongruity of their visions: his, locked in the fantasy he creates of her, and hers, one that is real and direct. She talks openly about her experiences with other men in a natural way that seems to shock Lachenay, even though he asked her the questions:

Nicole: In Bordeaux I thought I was in love with a boy. It wasn't going well at all. My parents wanted me to

Jean Desailly (Pierre) and Françoise Dorléac (Nicole) in the hotel scene in Truffaut's *La Peau douce* (*The Soft Skin*) 1964.

change my mind.

Pierre: But was that the first one you were with?

Nicole: Not really, the first was in London.

Pierre: Was he English?

Nicole: No, no, he was French.

Pierre: And were you in love with him?

Nicole: No, it was stupid. It didn't last very long.

Pierre: And after him?

Nicole: Two or three times, but it wasn't a big deal. I didn't really realize. I was too young, I don't know why. It's strange; the first time that it counted for me physically was just last year, with a guy I didn't want.

Noticing his uncomfortable reaction, Nicole asks, "Does it bother you that I talk about that?" In just a few lines, the film illustrates the hypocrisy of the conventional bourgeoisie in response to the *libération sexuelle* and breaks the fantasy that Lachenay has built of Nicole in his mind.

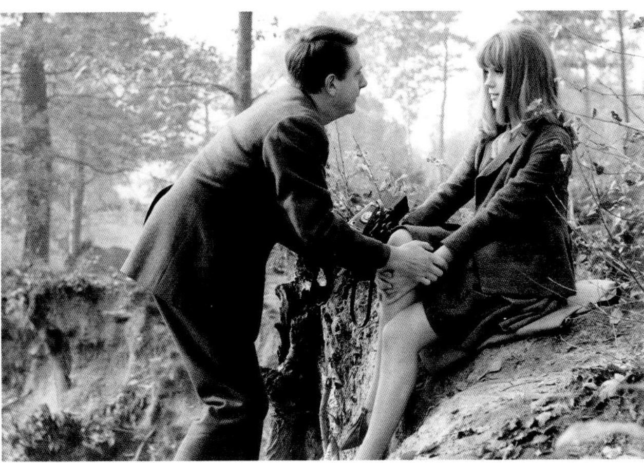

In another scene, Lachenay wants to take photographs of Nicole during their trip, seeking to document his romantic vision of their relationship (which contrasts with her more casual conception of it). Controlling her movements like a director with an actress, he places her legs in certain positions for his photo shoot. After acquiescing at first, she grows impatient with him for making her pose for long takes. Protesting that she has had enough, she tries to snap him out of his fixation, but he ignores her complaints and continues. Ironically, it is these very images that will drive Lachenay's wife to kill him.

Jean Desailly (Pierre) and Françoise Dorléac (Nicole) in the photo shoot scene in Truffaut's *La Peau douce*, 1964

Deconstructing Lachenay's *mise en scène* with her discourse, Nicole shatters his dream of a future with her. During their last encounter, Nicole clearly illustrates Lachenay's double vision. Lachenay asks Nicole to meet to show her a new apartment he wants to buy to share with her, in hopes of realizing his romantic dream of a new life and erasing his monotonous married one. As they tour the apartment, he narrates the story of their life to come, pointing to the white walls, a new page where he can dream and reconstruct. Nicole, in close-up, with the Parisian sky in the background, takes back her freedom and pierces Lachenay's out-of-touch, romantic bubble with her incisive words:

So, you want to marry me! If I say yes, you'll go find my father in Bordeaux and ask him for my hand, is that it? Listen, Pierre, for a while now, I've noticed that life isn't at all what I thought. There was a big misunderstanding between us. When you wanted to see me again in Paris, I was very touched because I thought that you judged me badly! It all happened so fast in Lisbon. When you brought me here, I suspected what it was, and if you had told me about the apartment, I would've told you what I thought right away. Look, you were right to speed things up, to go too fast. Because, in the end, we would've kept going a little longer. All that to arrive at the same point. It was useless. Think about yesterday evening at the restaurant, if you think I didn't notice how much I was getting on your nerves, how uncomfortable you were! And I could even say that for five minutes, you hated me. Yes, that's right! You know, when you are forced to tolerate each other, it's not the time to make plans for the future. Oh! I'm sure that it's hard for you, but you know, it is for me too. If you want—in any case, I would like it—we could see each other from time to time, have dinner together.

This refusal to comply with his fantasized role is precisely what makes Nicole modern. Far from the stereotype of the mistress who dreams of her lover leaving his wife to marry her, Nicole's free vision gives her a lucid, rational, and mature side that the much older Lachenay still lacks. Nicole makes him see clearly. He puts on his glasses and watches her descend from the pedestal he built for her in his mind and into the street where she finally becomes real to him and disappears from his life. The fantasy is over, but it has already ruined Lachenay's reality: His wife, having discovered the photos he took of Nicole, seeks him out at a restaurant and shoots him. (The scene was inspired by a true story.) Dorléac left Truffaut after the film shoot, and Truffaut separated from his wife, Madeleine Morgenstern, during its editing; they divorced two years later.

Lachenay's disconnection with reality is represented in images that reflect the fragmentation of many of Truffaut's masculine protagonists and their incapacity to understand or accept the needs and desires of the women in their lives, according to film scholar Anne Gillain.[22] Often extremely sensitive dreamers like Antoine Doinel, his protagonists lack the courage to deal with reality. In *La Peau douce*, as in many of Truffaut's films, it is the women who are more in touch with reality, who see clearly, and who act. Truffaut's camera, seeking to capture the elusive and show the truth of the actresses, leans on them to accomplish this. By humanizing the fantasy of the mistress, Dorléac created a modern, free, and relatable portrait of a woman in 1964, just like herself.

Though her strong presence on screen carries the weight of the film, off screen, Dorléac harbored deep insecurities that imbued her acting with a sense of reserve and complexity. She spoke candidly about these anxieties to *Elle* magazine shortly after the film's release: "I'm afraid of wrecking my career. I'm afraid of wrecking my happiness. I'm afraid of being sick, of being old, of being ugly. I'm afraid people won't love me, or won't love me anymore. I'm afraid of being alone. I'm afraid of the crowd. I'm afraid to die. I'm afraid to live."[23]

La Peau douce flopped at the Cannes Film Festival in 1964. Her sister's film, *Les Parapluies de Cherbourg*, won the Palme d'Or.[24, 25] As Deneuve went on to become a French icon, Dorléac ventured abroad, starring in two English-language films–Val Guest's *Where the Spies Are* (1965) and Roman Polanski's *Cul-de-sac* (1966)–which secured her position as a rising star. The sisters also starred together in Jacques Demy's 1967 technicolor classic *Les Demoiselles de Rochefort*, where they appeared equal and complementary, erasing any sense of rivalry. Tragically, just as she was becoming

recognized in the industry, Dorléac's life was cut short in a fiery car crash in the south of France when she was only twenty-five years old. Forever associated with the frenetic movement of the 1960s, Dorléac remains alive through her cinematic roles. The image of her dancing reflects her spirit, in the poetic words of Ferenczi, "a vivacious young woman in perpetual movement, drunk on the moment, forgetting herself finally."[26]

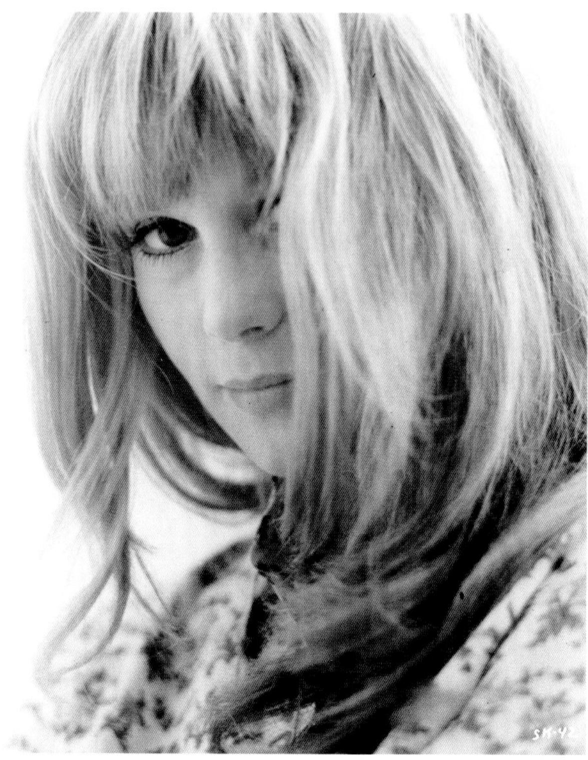

(DIS)ILLUSIONS: MODERN WOMEN SPEAK IN TRUFFAUT'S DOINEL SERIES

"I am not an apparition, I am a woman." In 1968's *Baisers volés*, Delphine Seyrig, playing the elegant older woman and love interest of Antoine Doinel, asserts her subjectivity with these words, shattering the protagonist's illusion much like Nicole does in *La Peau douce*. This is a common thread throughout Truffaut's work, in which the men are often eternal adolescents or romantics, locked in their own dream worlds, where women are either idealized, distanced fantasies or maternal figures relegated to everyday life. In a stereotype reversal, it is the men who cling to romanticism while the (modern)

Françoise Dorléac (Nicole) in François Truffaut's *La Peau douce* (*The Soft Skin*) 1964 women exist in reality and pierce the men's fantasies simply by speaking the truth rationally.

This dynamic is apparent in Truffaut's depiction of teenaged Antoine and his first crush in *Antoine et Colette* in 1962. In this second part of the Doinel series, Jean-Pierre Léaud's resilient and endearing portrayal of Truffaut's alter ego in *Les Quatre cents coups* morphs into a young and naïve romantic. Substituting his love of movies for a love of music, Antoine works in a record factory and attends classical music concerts. It is fitting then that Antoine falls under the spell of a girl he spots in the crowd at the famous concert hall Salle Pleyel during a performance of Hector Berlioz's *Symphonie fantastique*. Truffaut's *mise en scène* conveys Antoine's love at first sight cinematically, a *coup de foudre* set to music. Spotting her first as part of the crowd, depicted in a wide shot, Antoine is struck by the beauty of the unknown young woman seated across the aisle a few rows ahead of him (anticipating the scene on the plane in *La Peau douce*). As Antoine is overcome with emotion, the diegetic music of the orchestra accelerates and crescendos, and the camera closes in on her, paralleling his sudden fascination. Zeroing in on her in close-up, Colette (Marie-France Pisier) is the perfect target of his idealization.

Truffaut's script specifies a series of forty shot/reverse shots, each lasting approximately three seconds, with progressively closer framing. It also notes that Colette senses she is being watched. Crossing and uncrossing her legs, she fiddles with her necklace, finally turning around to look at Antoine. This is followed by a sudden wide shot, emphasizing the subjectivity of Antoine's experience. To him, his *coup de foudre* is reciprocated.

Carefully orchestrating the sequence, Truffaut conveys that Antoine was already *seeking* this experience, by showing him scanning the packed auditorium. Pisier suggested the autobiographical significance from the director's life when she recalled shooting what she described as a very important scene: "We had to do a series of gestures with insane precision, imposed by François, probably because they resonated with him personally."[27] The idealized vision of Colette is constructed by Truffaut's camera with subjective shots from Antoine's point of view. The scene also sets up the divide between Truffaut's hopeless romantic protagonist and the character's realistic, modern love interest. Mesmerized by Colette before they have even met, Antoine describes to his friend René the power of his experience in the concert hall, and repeats his story twice more:

> I saw her three times this week. I haven't spoken to her yet, but I made her notice me. The first time, it was Tuesday, during the *Symphonie fantastique*. I was sitting just behind her, a bit to her right. One time, she took off her scarf. The whole night, I looked at her hair and her neck; I couldn't stop looking at her. That night, I decided to talk to her, I pushed through the crowd to get to where she was, only she met with up a girlfriend. I followed them five minutes, then I went home and went to bed.

Following the obsessive encounter in his mind, their real encounter is more direct. Making small talk, Colette treats him more as a friend and does not appear to reciprocate his romantic feelings. Antoine persists, however, locked in his dream of her. He goes as far as moving to the hotel across the street from the apartment where she lives with her family. Because of his timidity, he decides to declare his love to Colette in a letter. Her reception is again realistic and dismissive. Responding with a letter that arrives suddenly under Antoine's door, Colette attempts to awaken him from his romantic delusions: "My dear Antoine, your declaration of love is very well written. It shows you have experience. I'm going to listen to Maurice Leroux tonight. Will you be there? Thanks for the books. Oh, and I forgot, my mother thought you looked romantic, probably because of your long hair. See you tonight, my friend. Colette." Unlike Antoine, Colette is direct, uninhibited, and nondramatic. After his *coup de foudre*, she demystifies the ideal image that he has constructed of her. When he meets her for dinner at her parents' house, for example, Colette is natural and relaxed, the opposite of the jittery Antoine.

For the part, Truffaut was looking for a cultivated, articulate, and easygoing young woman who could embody the differences between Colette and Antoine. "Jean-Pierre Léaud's partner must be a real young lady, not a Lolita, not a biker type, nor a little woman. She must be fresh and cheerful. Not too sexy," Truffaut told a casting director, who found the perfect incarnation of these qualities in Marie-France Pisier. Elegant and quick-witted, the actress later obtained a law degree and became known as a political activist, feminist, author, and director. Adding vitality and intelligence to the role, the independent, outspoken, and poised Pisier transformed the stereotypically undefined character of "girlfriend" into a modern young woman with agency.

For Antoine, it is a different story. After his lack of success with his fantasy of Colette, he goes on to claim that she is not his type: "Normally, I shouldn't be in love with her. She talks like a boy, she treats me like a friend. Every time I speak to her seriously, she laughs."[28] Still in denial, however, he continues to pursue her even though she does not correspond to the image he had constructed of her. Though Doinel is endearing, through Colette's eyes, the audience sees him as an immature dreamer. Through Truffaut's, we see him as an eternal adolescent who becomes more and more comical, almost Chaplinesque, and progressively humiliated as the series continues.

"I AM NOT AN APPARITION": TRUFFAUT'S SELF-TAUGHT LESSON IN *BAISERS VOLÉS*

We laugh at Antoine Doinel in love, but for Truffaut, love was dead serious. In his youth, the director often went through very dark stretches when his relationships ended. After his first breakup, Truffaut cut his arm twenty-five times with a razor blade. Finding him passed out, the young woman he desperately desired saved his life, a similar but less dramatic scenario mirrored in *Antoine et Colette*. Truffaut's fictional double served as a screen in front of a too-violent reality.

"I have a great propensity for talking about myself and a great repugnance of doing it directly," Truffaut stated. "For this reason, I have the impression of being more intimate and more sincere through borrowed subjects than through the Doinel series, where I constantly dreaded the identification between Jean-Pierre Léaud and myself," Truffaut admitted.[29] This seemingly paradoxical declaration shows Truf-

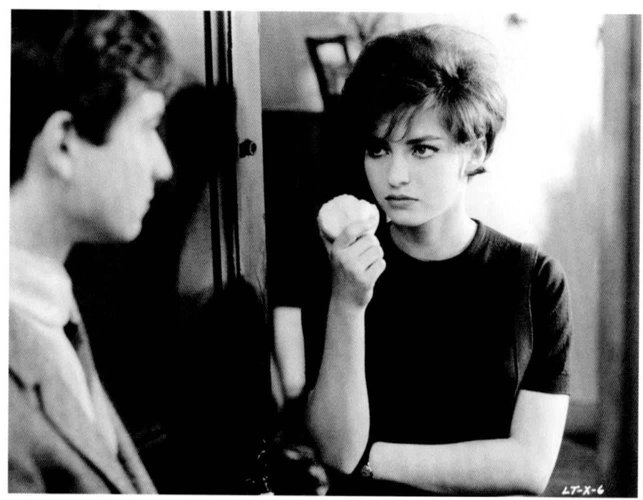

faut's desire to speak about himself and his anxiety about creating a character too close (or not close enough) to him.

The Doinel series can be seen as mirror films, reflecting Truffaut who is looking at himself through his protagonist. He went as far as transcribing phrases from his diary word for word and putting them in the mouth of Antoine Doinel. More than a spokesperson, Truffaut's character is almost a marionette, one that articulates a fundamental question that Antoine has in common with other male protagonists in Truffaut's oeuvre: *How do I please women?*

In Truffaut's world, masculine authority is either absent or ridiculous, and his male characters are childlike, standing in awe of an ideal woman. Like the nineteenth-century heroes of Stendhal (author of *Le Rouge et le Noir* and *De l'amour*), stuck in adoration before the closed doors of feminine eroticism,[30] Antoine assumes a position of inferiority in relation to women. Throughout the series, after *Les Quatre cents coups*, he is also in a position of humiliation through his failure in love, marriage, and work. Truffaut admitted that the story of Antoine Doinel was perhaps a story of failure. Could humiliating his double (one he created) serve to help manage the director's own internal conflicts?[31]

Antoine is anachronistic, not a modern man of his time. He is the one who is out of sync, who could be ridiculed. Like a cartoon character, his comic persona, according to Truffaut, allowed more serious questions to be addressed in a light-

Jean-Pierre Léaud (Antoine Doinel) and Marie-France Pisier (Colette) in François Truffaut's *Antoine et Colette*, segment in *L'Amour à vingt ans* (*Love at Twenty*), 1962

hearted way.[32] De-virilized by women, Antoine is, in essence, inconsequential. Truffaut's female characters, however, are never humiliated. On the contrary, they enjoy a privileged place, even a superior one, to men. Regarding *Baisers volés*, one critic exclaimed spontaneously, "It's crazy how Truffaut gives women the best role [*le beau rôle*]!"[33]

At the heart of Truffaut's cinema, women are numerous and appear in steady progression. After the mother in *Les Quatre cents coups* comes Colette, the unattainable woman; then Christine Darbon, the good-girl-next-door who becomes Antoine's fiancée in *Baisers volés* and his wife in *Domicile conjugal*; Seyrig's Fabienne Tabard, the older ideal woman; Kyoko, the exotic Japanese mistress; Liliane, Christine's friend. Finally, in *L'Amour en fuite* (*Love on the Run*, 1979), there is Sabine. After finding a fragmented photograph of her and gluing it back together, Antoine tracks her down and falls in love with her—just like Jules and Jim with their statue. To this long list of real and ideal women, we can add prostitutes, who appear in many films and incarnate a multitude of fantasies. Throughout the series, women are divided into binary systems: natural versus masked, and real women versus fantasies, for example. This duality reflects Antoine's compartmentalized perception that Truffaut constantly juxtaposed in his *mise en scène*, comparing, separating, but also fusing opposite types as Antoine searches for his own identity through them.

Baisers volés reveals this trend most clearly as Antoine is torn between the natural and real Christine Darbon (Claude Jade) and the idealized fantasy of Fabienne Tabard. He is lost, hunting for his sense of self in these women, illustrated in the famous scene where he obsessively repeats both their names along with his own in front of his bathroom mirror: *Christine Darbon, Fabienne Tabard, Antoine Doinel.*

Christine, his girlfriend, exists in his life without artifice. With a classic style and very little makeup, she is nonthreatening. Madame Tabard, the antithesis of Christine, represents the ultimate image of sophistication as represented by Seyrig, the star of Resnais's *L'Année dernière à Marienbad*, who maintains the same allure in *Baisers volés* with her affected and sultry voice, doubly idealized when she speaks English. First appearing as a caricature—or as an "apparition," in Antoine's

words—in a dreamlike sequence, Fabienne Tabard exhibits traits that feed his idealized image of her. In sophisticated clothes—a Chanel suit, long white boa, golden belt, jewelry, and makeup—she wears a mask of elegance that sets her apart from Christine. She is also the wife of his boss, adding to the transgressive element of his desire. Before Antoine lays eyes on Fabienne in her husband's shoe store, the non-diegetic sound of celestial sirens (in Antoine's head?) announce her presence. Framed first in a long shot, with one bare foot, Fabienne walks through the display case in the window of the store and tries on shoes. Stepping out of a fairy tale (but in the comical setting of the shoe store), her posture also recalls an iconic scene in *Marienbad* where the heroine sits with an array of shoes at her feet in her hotel room.

Like with Colette, Antoine falls under Fabienne's spell more and more, and after several comedic run-ins, he sits down to write her a letter declaring his love. After receiving it via pneumatic post, Fabienne decides to put a stop to his obsession. Showing up unannounced at his tiny *chambre de bonne* apartment where he is still in bed, she knocks at his door and enters his room as if in his dream. She offers Antoine a contract: Spending a few hours together in exchange for him never seeing her again. Antoine quickly acquiesces, smiling with a shy nod.

In this sequence, Fabienne becomes an avatar of the literary initiator—an older woman who teaches the young man the ways of the world—frequently found in French literature. The figure appears in Flaubert's *L'Éducation sentimentale* (*Sentimental Education,* 1869), for example, and notably in Balzac's *Le Lys dans la vallée* (*The Lily of the Valley,* 1835), which Fabienne cites in her response to Antoine. Again, the director's autobiography resonates. Robert Lachenay, the director's childhood friend, noted in an interview that when they were young, Truffaut talked to him "about the kiss on Madame de Mortsauf's shoulder" in the novel, which "was something that deeply moved him."[34] Echoing that character, Fabienne references the book as she realizes Antoine's literary fantasy.

Before sealing the contract, however, she attempts to deconstruct the fantasy he has made of her in his mind. Filmed

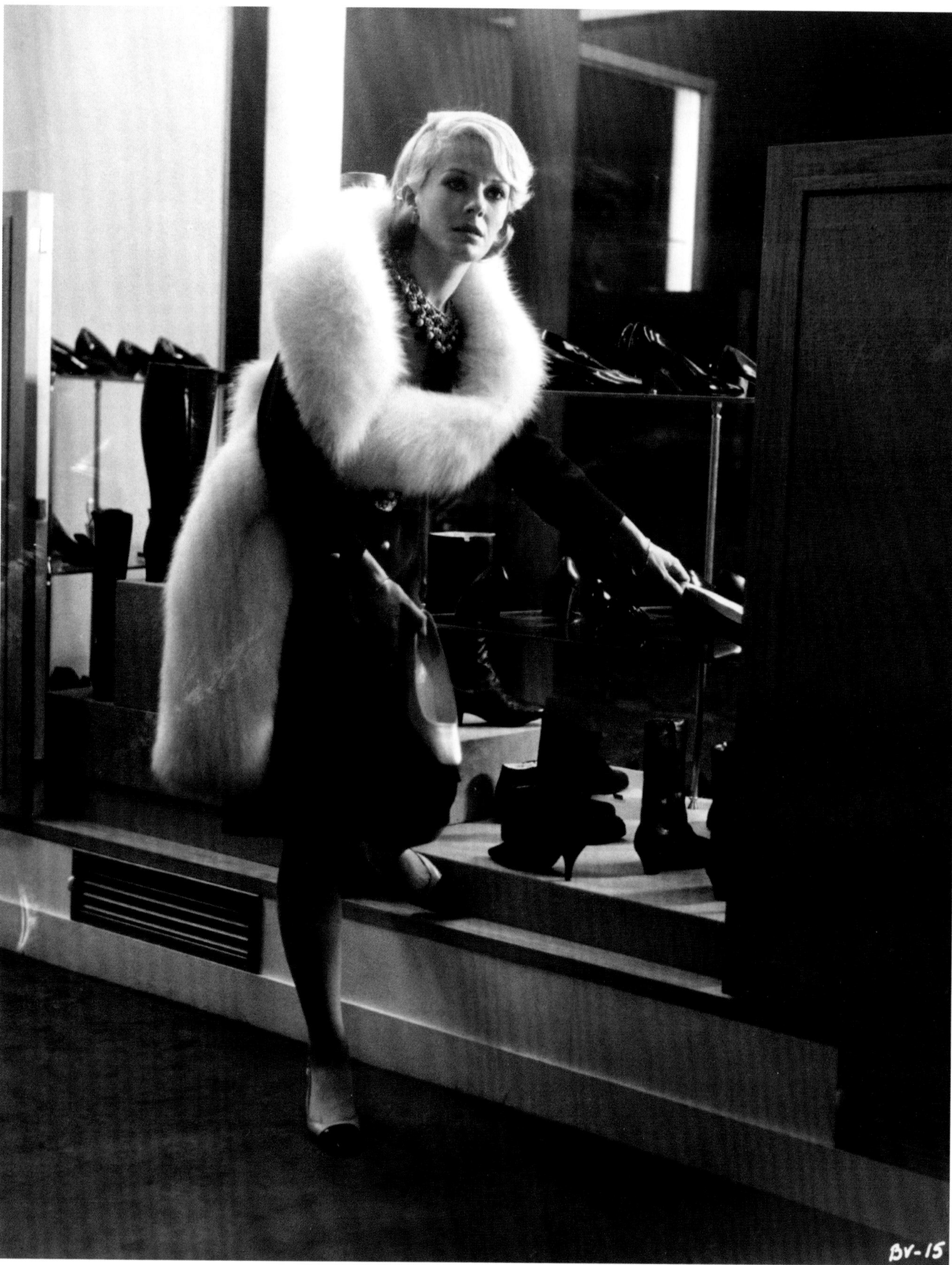
BV-15

in low angle and in close-up—a similar shot used to film Antoine's mother as she offers him a contract in *Les Quatre cents coups*—Fabienne states bluntly, "I am not an apparition. I am a woman."

Unveiling her own masquerade, Fabienne explains, "For example, this morning, before coming here, I put on makeup. I powdered my nose. I did my eyes." Extending the revelation to all women, she says, "In crossing Paris on the way over, I noticed that all women did the same thing, for pleasure or to be polite." Becoming authentic, Fabienne tries to break Antoine's illusion to make him see her as a real woman, so that he will recognize her true value as well as his own. Her message to him is clear: "We are all unique and irreplaceable."

EXALTED WIFE, ABSURD HUSBAND: MARRIAGE IN *DOMICILE CONJUGAL*

In the next installment of the story, *Domicile conjugal*, we might imagine that Antoine has learned this lesson as he and Christine begin their newlywed life. But as Christine assumes a maternal role when she has a baby, Antoine continues to go through life with a childlike innocence that sometimes exasperates her. And in her new role as mother, with all it holds in the imagination (from a psychoanalytic perspective in terms of desire in alignment with the Madonna-whore complex), Antoine's fantasy directs itself elsewhere. This configuration reflects then-recent events in Truffaut's personal life, with his separation and eventual divorce from Morgenstern in 1965: His alter ego takes a mistress and eventually separates from and divorces his wife in the film.

Domicile conjugal followed the logic of the bourgeois model of marriage, but in evoking divorce, which was more accepted but still somewhat taboo in 1970, it was not as rigid. While being modern was not a top priority for Truffaut, who favored good storytelling over experimentation, his approach in the film dedramatized infidelity. In the burlesque style of his (anti)hero, more intimate and personal scenes appear alongside domestic quarrels that contain moments of truth, revealing a sensitivity and a certain gravity that hint

at autobiographical elements, or at least ones that reflect Truffaut's sensibility.

The film opens with Christine's pride in her new station as wife. As the camera focuses on her legs in the first shot, implying desire, we also see a grocery bag dangling next to them in the frame, illustrating her association with domesticity, but also a violin case, implying some agency since she gives music lessons. Passing in front of vendors and neighbors who all greet her with "Bonjour, Mademoiselle," she proudly corrects them, emphasizing her new married status: "Not Mademoiselle, Madame!" While the position of wife is valorized through Christine, that of the husband is derided through Antoine, who is maladapted to his role.

Unable to tolerate the responsibilities of prosaic domestic life, Antoine again escapes into fantasy. Women here are divided into three types: wife, mistress, and prostitute, with the camera alternating between them. Along with the multitude of prostitutes, each dressed to represent a different fantasy, Doinel takes up with a heavily stereotyped Japanese woman who becomes his mistress, Kyoko. Appearing first in a *mise en scène* that echoes Antoine's past visions of Colette and Fabienne Tabard, Kyoko incarnates pure fantasy and remains there until her last lines. Her legs, framed in a similar way to Christine's with the grocery bag in the opening shot, here signal desirability.

Dreaming of ideal love, Antoine cannot function in the reality of married life and becomes a parody. It is especially apparent as he maneuvers awkwardly in Kyoko's Jap-

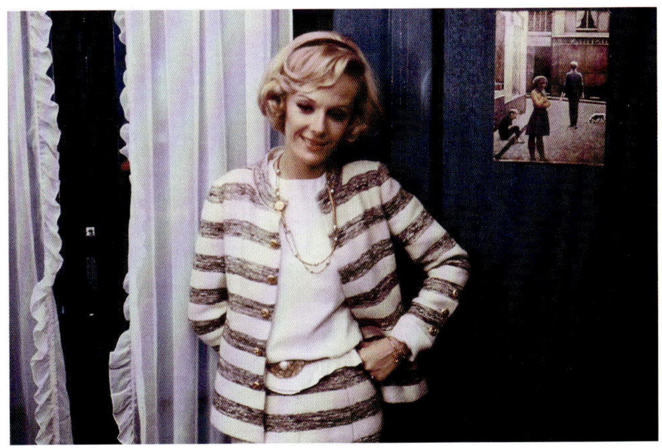

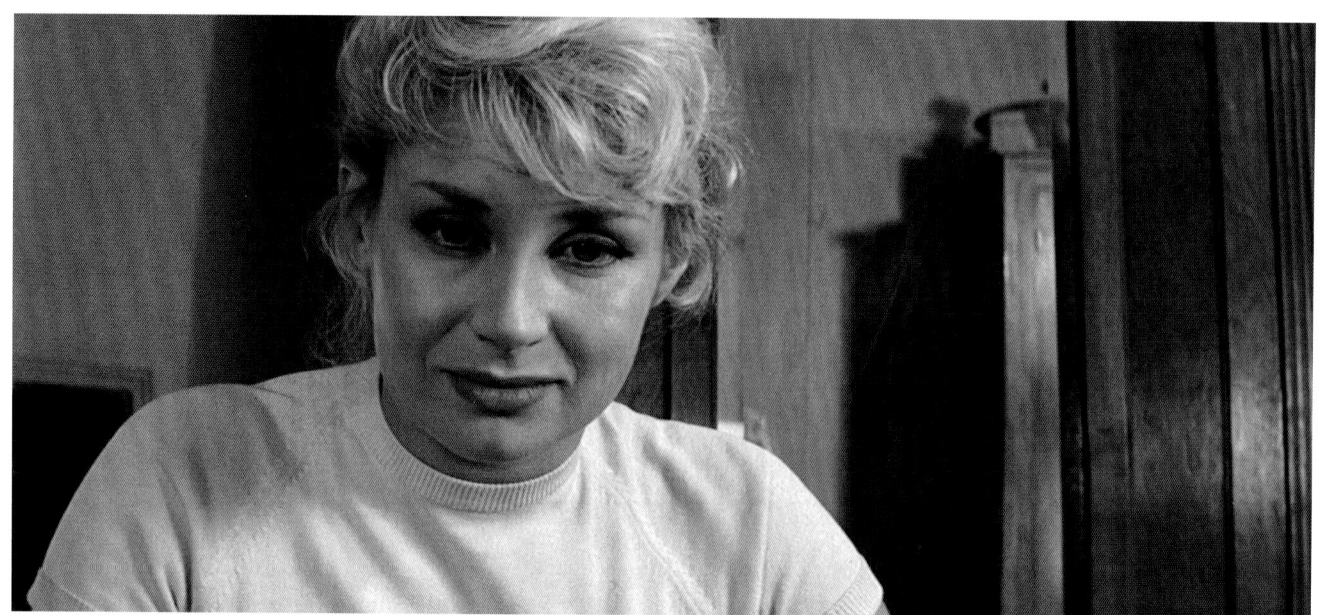

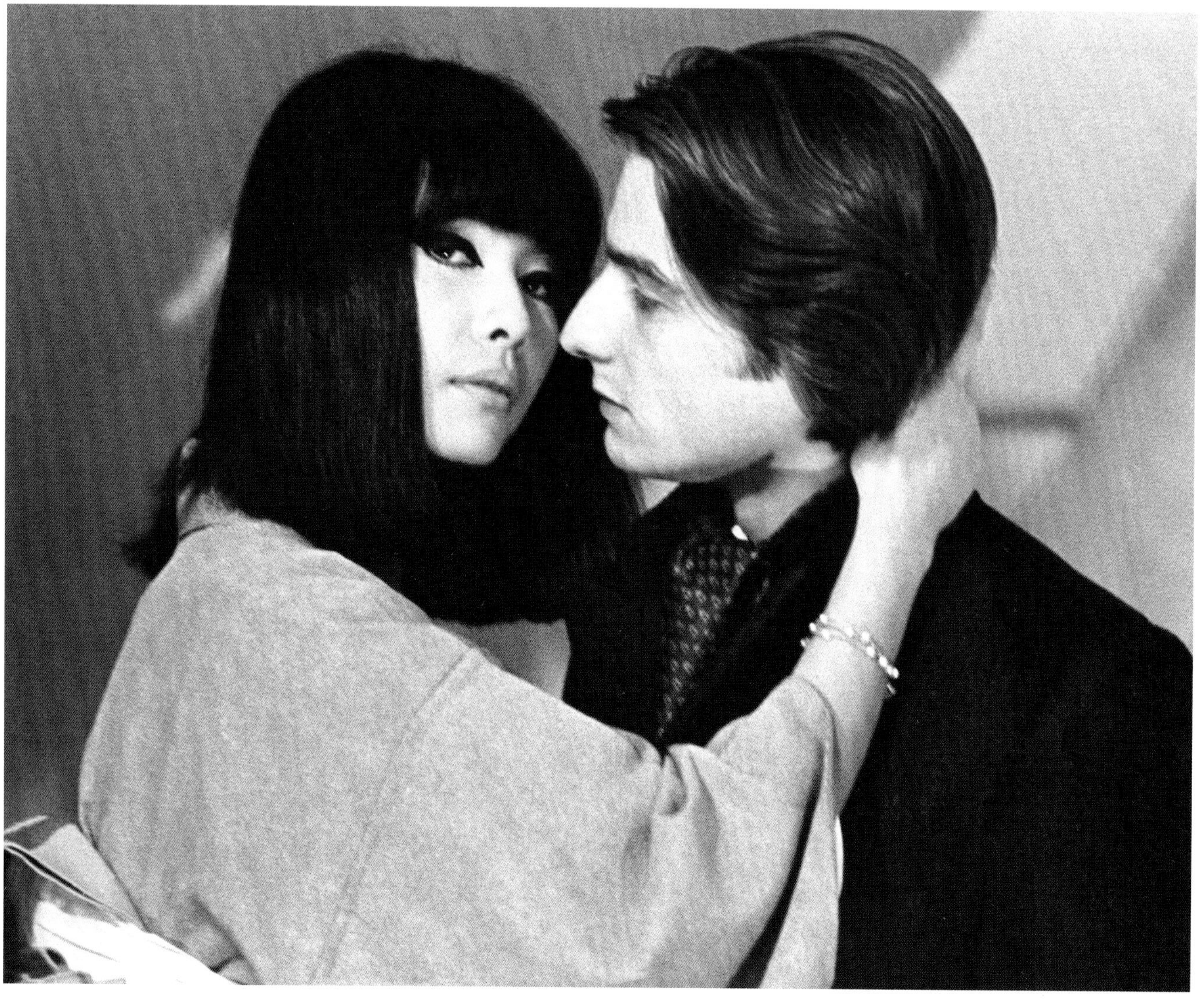

anese-style apartment, his performance resembling the physical comedy of Buster Keaton. But this comedy also functions to distance what is too serious: infidelity, marital disputes, and divorce. Upon discovering the affair, Christine vacates the bourgeois wife stereotype by dressing up as Kyoko—her husband's fantasy—an act that reinforces his confusion between his desired dream and reality.

Antoine's marriage does not survive, but the couple does not conform to the stereotype of a power struggle as seen in films such as Vadim's *Les Liaisons dangereuses*. As Antoine and Christine separate, brief moments of humor and truth convey authenticity and modernize the film. When Antoine tries to convince Christine to let him spend the night with her at their apartment, she rebels. No longer the docile wife, she tells him, "Listen, I'm not like you. I don't like what is unclear, I don't like what is vague. I don't like what is misleading. I don't like what is ambiguous. I like what is clear." When he insists, she lays down a boundary: "No, don't come closer to me, don't touch me. There's nothing left between us anymore." It is almost impossible not to hear the real-life inspiration behind her words.

In searching for his identity through women, Antoine finds nothing. Childish and unable to communicate with Kyoko, Antoine is also inept at assuming the role of lover, and the love triangle becomes a comedy. Passionate scenes between lovers in films like Malle and Moreau's *Les Amants* here become more like *The Pink Panther* (1963). Kyoko as the mistress also remains undeveloped and locked in a racial stereotype that, while weakening the film, perhaps reinforces Antoine's self-absorbed and naïve lack of tact and perception. As Antoine tires of his relationship with his mistress, he unexpectedly falls back in love with his wife.

While he dines with Kyoko in a restaurant, he gets up to phone Christine to try to reconcile with her. When he returns from his long telephone call, Kyoko has left, but her voice is finally heard in a simple but resounding note she put in a fortune cookie: "Va te faire foûtre" ("Screw you"). Many other fantasy women have tried to get through to

Truffaut's protagonists, but here, Kyoko simply gives up and saves herself.

In Antoine's world, women are strong and superior characters with power and authority. Pisier noted that "the favorite characters in [Truffaut's] films all have in common something a bit 'masculine.' They are almost all tall, strong-willed, and mysterious."[35] The women incarnating these roles are all strong as well, on and off screen: Marie-France Pisier, Françoise Dorléac, Delphine Seyrig, *nouvelles femmes* who helped Truffaut, grappling with the idea of women as illusions and fantasies, make New Wave films real and modern.

Top left: Claire Maurier (Gilberte, Antoine Doinel's mother) in François Truffaut's *Les Quatre cents coups* (*The 400 Blows*), 1959. **Bottom left:** Hiroko Matsumoto Berghauer (Kyoko) and Jean-Pierre Léaud (Antoine Doinel) in François Truffaut's *Domicile conjugal* (*Bed and Board*), 1970

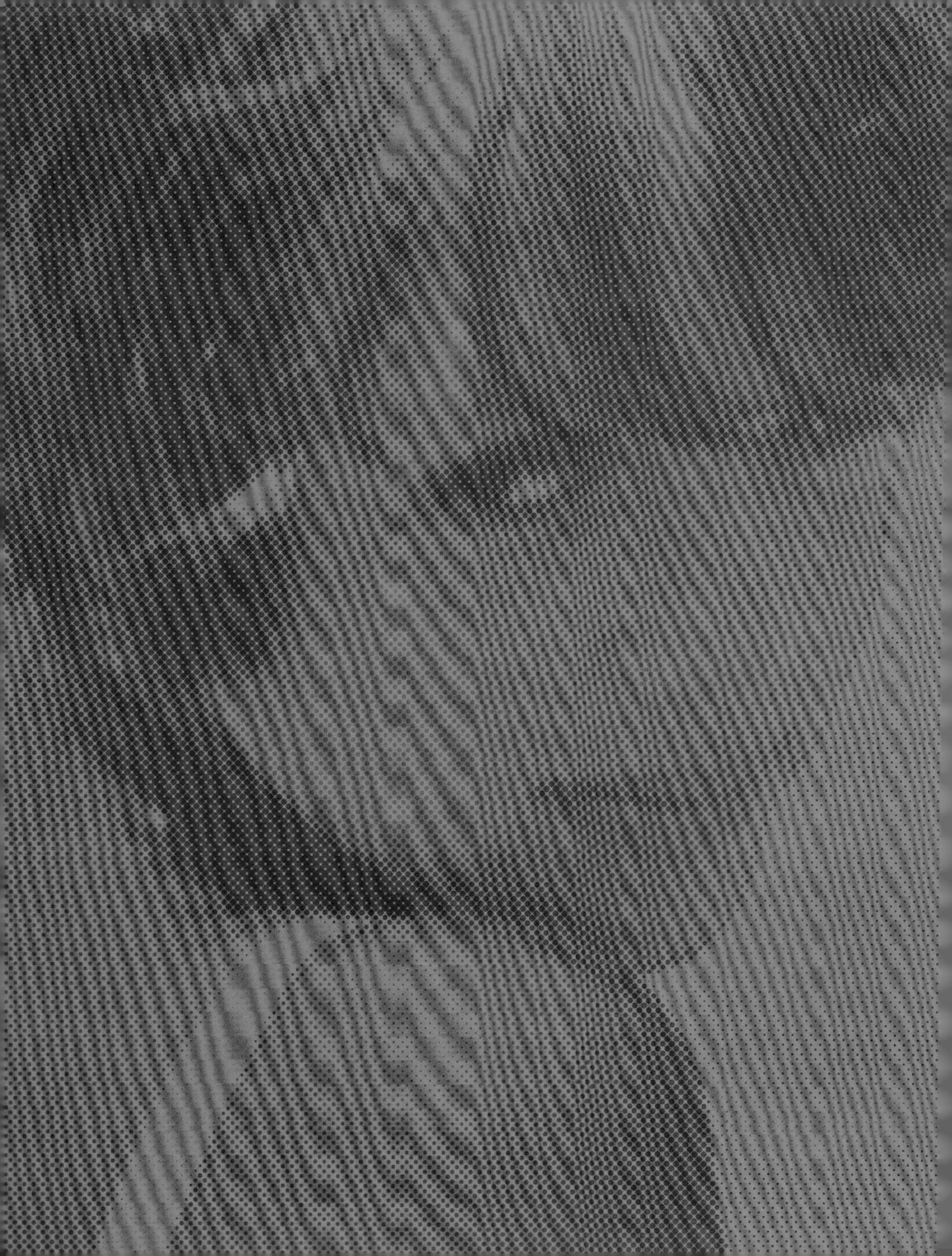

NEW WAVE *BLASONS*: POETRY OR FETISHISM?

In the mid-sixteenth century, Clément Marot popularized a new type of poem: the *blason*, or blazon, which celebrated the beauty of the female body by detailing it part by part—hair, forehead, eyes, mouth, heart, hand, thigh, knee, eyebrow—even including "hidden ones, objects of the lovers' desire," as Marot himself put it.[1] This tendency to depict the fragmented body poetically, motivated by the poet's desire, endured throughout French literary history and into the New Wave. Given their very strong literary backgrounds, it is unsurprising that the Rive droite directors especially would produce similar representations. The features of the lyrical portraits also lend themselves well to visual representations in cinema, with the directors framing each detail of the body, especially the face, in the aim of showcasing beauty while idealizing it. In this respect, the directors could be considered modern versions of the medieval poets, writing cinematic *blasons* with their cameras, often working with other elements, such as dialogue, voice-over, or artworks meant to mirror the woman we see on screen, like the Aristide Maillol sculptures resembling Méril in *Une femme mariée* or the famous statue resembling Catherine in *Jules et Jim.*

Like the anatomical poems conveying the poets' desires, however, these scenes may also reflect the desires of the filmmakers, emerging from male fantasy. The phenomenon during the New Wave period consisted of male directors who created roles played by actresses they often were in love with or admired. This stereotyped distribution can be traced throughout art history in romantic scenarios found in impressionist and postimpressionist work, carried over into photography in the twentieth century, and into cinema with directors and their stars. Are the New Wave directors then just scopophilic fetishists in line with Mulvey's theory about the male gaze? Are they heirs to the medieval poets? Or are they both?

Answers to these questions become more complex when we consider the role of the women themselves in the creative process. When a woman—character, actress, muse—detaches herself from an objectified position in art or life, she gains subjectivity.[2] In a male-dominated industry like cinema at the time, we can see how a tendency to maintain women in passive positions, as beautiful objects or objects of affection, could arise: A female character (or actress) who is elusive or assumes an active role, escaping the protagonist as well as social norms and constraints, complicates the narrative. The fact that this scenario plays out over and over in New Wave films suggests that it reflects personal conflicts as well as larger social ones.

THE ELUSIVE WOMEN OF ÉRIC ROHMER'S MORAL TALES

In Éric Rohmer's cinema, women of all types occupy a central place as the director obsessively analyzes their ineffable qualities and explores their nuances with his camera and through his male protagonists. A variety of these female characters can be seen in his *Six contes moraux* (*Six Moral Tales*), a series of films based on short stories Rohmer (then still known as Maurice Schérer) had written in his youth. The films, from 1963's *La Boulangère de Monceau* to 1972's *L'Amour l'après-midi*, are all variations on a theme. "Actually, I realized that only after they'd all been written," the director claimed. "I saw they had the same theme: while pursuing one girl, a boy meets another girl and spends time with her, the time of the film, and at the end, he returns to the first girl, realizing she was the one he was searching for and who interested

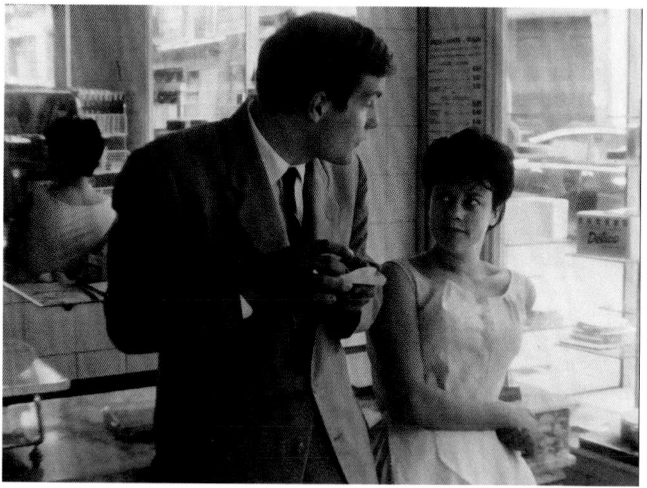

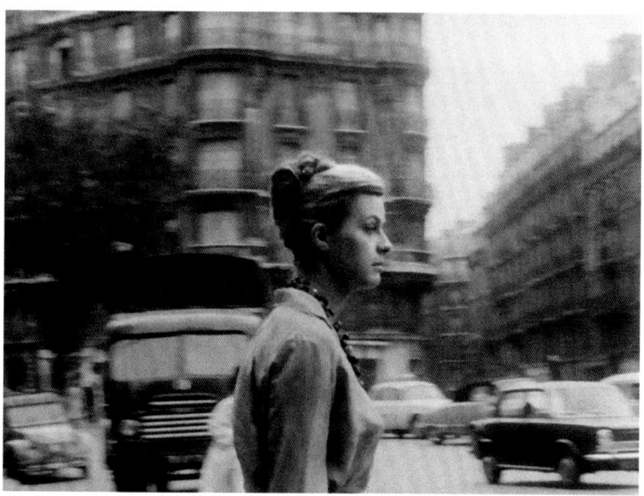

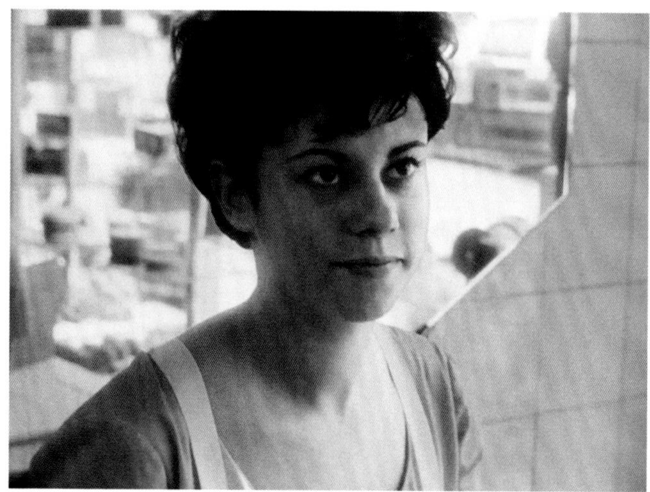

Top: Barbet Schroeder (narrator) with Claudine Soubrier (Jacqueline) **Middle:** Michèle Girardon (Sylvie) **Bottom:** Claudine Soubrier in Éric Rohmer's *La Boulangère de Monceau* (*The Bakery Girl of Monceau*), 1963

him." The audience, however, is more interested in the girl who is abandoned in the end than the one he chooses. For Rohmer, this was a way to make the narrative more intriguing, more modern: "From the start, the audience is against the narrator, and it is this tension that I find interesting."[3]

Through male protagonists who separate women into categories according to how they correspond to their ideal, Rohmer laid bare the cultural constructs influencing his characters' judgments. In *La Boulangère de Monceau*, Sylvie, a blonde student, and Jacqueline, a brunette bakery girl, are separated not only by hair color but by class, education, beauty, and sensuality–criteria that determine the narrator's choice. While Sylvie, the elegant bourgeoise, is elusive, working-class Jacqueline can always be found in the narrator's neighborhood boulangerie. The portrait of Sylvie, conforming to the protagonist's parameters for a suitable girlfriend, is already constructed in his mind by social and cultural messages (and by hundreds of years of literary influence).

One scene depicting the narrator's encounter with his blonde ideal carries traces of Charles Baudelaire's "À une passante" ("To a Passerby," 1857), a poem addressing alienation in modern society (at the time of Georges-Eugène Haussmann's renovation of Paris under Napoleon III's rule) through a chance encounter and the idea of what might have been. The male narrator is struck with desire and longing as he describes the beauty of a female stranger on the street: her "glittering hand," her leg "like a statue's," her eyes "pale sky where tempests germinate."[4] The two exchange glances as they pass by each other, leaving the narrator to lament the loss of this fleeting love at first sight. Unlike Baudelaire's protagonist, Rohmer's narrator, who has chosen the unattainable Sylvie as his love object even before meeting her, orchestrates running into her in the street to achieve an introduction. After she disappears again, he finds himself annoyingly attracted to the young bakery girl, Jacqueline, who is too available and beneath his standards in terms of beauty and social class. Though the narrator lies to himself in an attempt to disown his desire for Jacqueline, he still pursues her as a distraction while he waits for Sylvie. When Sylvie does reappear, he immediately drops Jacqueline as the cruel voice-over justifies his choice: "I could have put Sylvie off a day and kept my date with my bakery girl. But my choice had been, above all, a moral one. Having found Sylvie again, seeing the bakery girl would be a vice, an aberration. One was my truth, the other, the error, or so I told myself then."

Rohmer's interest in portraying a certain type of woman as testing the moral resolve of the male protagonist is reflected in the title of his November 1949 narrative "Chantal, ou l'épreuve" (meaning "Chantal, or the Test").[5] This became the source material for *La Collectionneuse*, his fourth *conte moral* (though shot out of order before *Ma nuit chez Maud*), in which two dandies spend their vacation in the south of France, forced to share a villa with a young woman they had never met. Haydée (Haydée Politoff), possessing "an angelic face" and "schoolgirl-like ways,"[6] as described by Rohmer's story, shatters the mold of the temptress in the film. The protagonist Adrien's (Patrick Bauchau) ideal woman, the equivalent of Sylvie in *La Boulangère*, also only appears in one sequence at the beginning of the film and does not occupy nearly as much space in the narrative as Sylvie does, nor does she have the same hold on the protagonist. Here, he is already in a committed relationship with her (played by Mijanou Bardot, his real-life wife and Brigitte Bardot's younger sister). As she exits the screen, the goal that the narrator claims to be seeking on his Côte d'Azur vacation–*faire le vide*, clearing his head–is suddenly filled by a new woman.

But before we see Haydée through his eyes, we are introduced to her in a prologue that exists outside the narrative and outside time as pure cinematic contemplation. Rohmer's camera focuses on Haydée as she walks along the beach, detailing her body in different frames–in motion and in stills–like the literary *blasons*. It also portrays her as a sort of enigma while transmitting a sense of freedom and authenticity in her character. The camera starts with wide shots of Haydée strolling at the edge of the sea, then it frames her legs in tighter shots. Like an artist's model, Haydée pauses and holds the pose a moment while the camera films her in close-up before she changes direction. When she stops again, the camera captures her face that is immobile, resembling a statue. The camera then pans down her body, framing her torso, then her back, followed by shots of her legs from behind, and then of her knees, before the camera pans

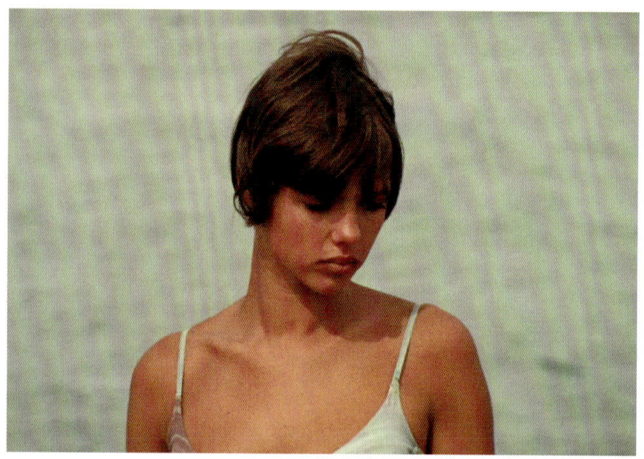

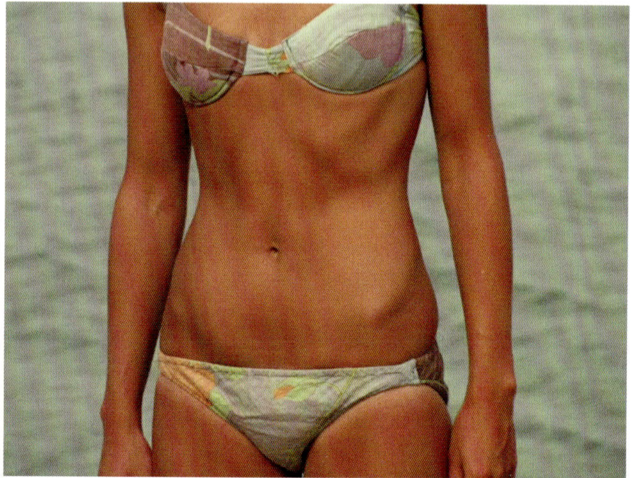

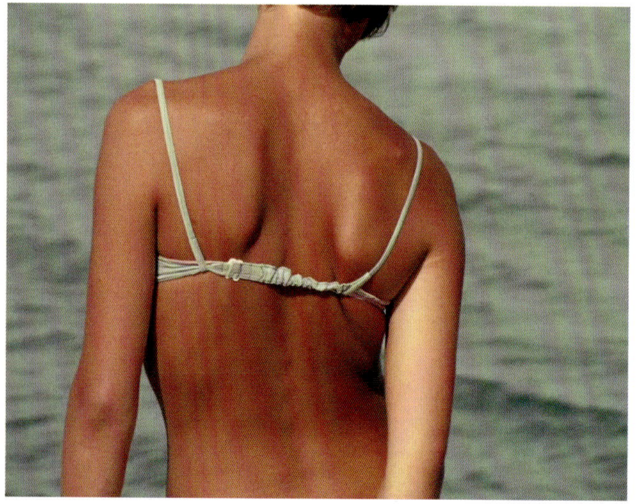

Haydée Politoff (Haydée) in Éric Rohmer's *La Collectionneuse* (*The Collector*), 1967

back up to frame her face in profile, ending with a close-up of her neck and collarbone.

These shots dissecting the body recall those of Bardot in the opening of *Le Mépris*. Here, they are static fragments without words, a solely visual inventory. The only character in the sequence, Haydée is offered to the viewer objectively and without explicitly erotic connotations, conveying the beauty of her body like photographs of a sculpture, Rohmer's own visual *blason*—a translation of his own desire or a way of capturing the elusive feminine. The sequence also recalls the origins of the cinematic medium, capable of deconstructing and reconstructing movement, capturing life itself naturally and authentically. Rohmer indirectly drew this parallel in describing Jean Renoir's *mise en scène*, a clear influence on his own: "That the grain of the skin, captured by the unfiltered lens with the aperture opened to the extreme, replaces the fake luster of makeup under screened projectors, does not matter. . . . There will always be a way in which the camera will proclaim its existence. Thanks to this profession of faith, it will give a more or less noble *blason* to everything it captures."[7] Rohmer's portrait of Haydée links her to nature and the feminine, and it defines her in terms of her body, escaping the realm of words, as opposed to the prologues of the male protagonists that include cerebral notions and dialogue.

Adrien first encounters Haydée during his own prologue when he is casually walking through the villa, examining decorative statuettes of women. He seems intrigued, as if he is searching for an answer to a mystery that the figurines could reveal. The first he observes without touching it, the camera showing its details in close-up. The second statue he takes in his hands and inspects from different angles, turning it around, fascinated, giving the impression that he is looking for something beyond it. Suddenly, from an adjacent room, he hears sounds that interrupt his contemplation: It is Haydée, in bed with an unknown man. Haydée in this instant becomes real and active, beyond Adrien's or the camera's control. She is neither the statuette Adrien holds nor the sculpture the camera framed her as in her prologue.

Fleeing the scene, Adrien sees Haydée from then on as a sort of intruder who is distracting him from his existential goal of the summer. But much like Jacqueline, the bakery girl in *La Boulangère*, Haydée annoys the narrator precisely because he is attracted to her. In other words, he is annoyed by his attraction to someone he deems beneath him—or perhaps even more irritated that she eludes him. This is not the same kind of elusive appeal that Sylvie represents in *La Boulangère*. Haydée does not correspond to Adrien's ideal. Nevertheless, she has a hold on him throughout their time together in the villa and beyond.

Adrien's thoughts are almost solely focused on Haydée and on analyzing his own reaction to her. He is constantly searching for reasons not to succumb to his disavowed desire for her. Unlike the bakery girl, Haydée is not potential young prey. She is neither naïve nor a victim of the narrator's game. If she plays along, she is aware of what she is doing. As Roger Ebert wrote in his review of the film almost fifty years after its release, both Adrien and Daniel claim they do not desire Haydée, but they enter "an undeclared contest to see which will be the first to succumb." But as the critic perceptively pointed out, "This assumes that Haydée can be had for the taking, which is by no means the case."[8]

It is precisely this freedom that makes Haydée so alluring, so modern. Despite the constant harassment by her summertime housemates, she lives in the moment, bringing home various men of her own volition. When she tires of a given visitor, she makes him leave, as illustrated by the outcast in the magenta sunglasses played by Dennis Berry. Perhaps it

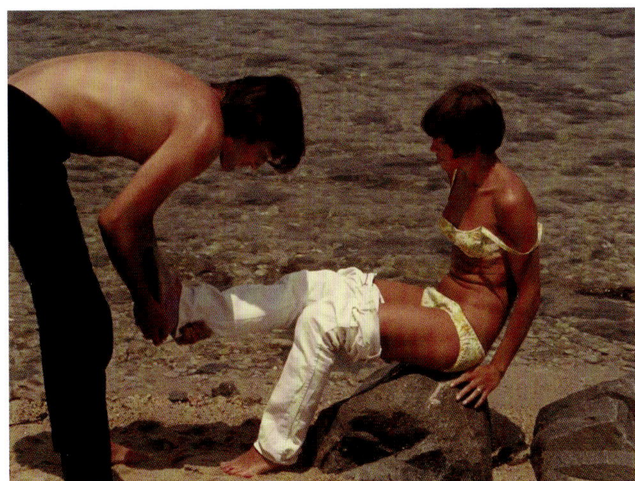

Haydée Politoff with Patrick Bauchau (Adrien) in Éric Rohmer's *La Collectionneuse*, 1967.

is this agency that annoys the male protagonists, knowing that she is not impressionable or manipulatable. Haydée is casually self-assured, bearing no sign of the nervous insecurity that her male counterparts try to conceal in themselves and that characterizes many of her young contemporaries.

She does not seem affected by the power imbalance between men and women in social contexts, and if she is at all bothered by Adrien and Daniel's barrage of bullying, she does not show it. Instead, she exudes nonchalance, sometimes flashing an ambiguous smile in lieu of a verbal response, as she does when Adrien leaves her overnight with Sam, the lecherous older American collector. When she breaks the Song vase (a scene inspired by the second version of Rohmer's short story, "Le Vase brisé," meaning "the broken vase"[9]) that Sam has just purchased for an exorbitant amount of money, she laughs. She does not appear to be concerned with expectations of conventional behavior or norms of any kind. And in the end, when Adrien thinks he has finally conquered her, she escapes again to follow what catches her attention in the moment. Haydée remains elusive but free.

HAYDÉE, OFF SCREEN: REALITY MEETS FICTION

Shot in the summer of 1966, a full two years before May '68, *La Collectionneuse* symbolizes the "end of the disillusioned postwar generation," in the words of de Baecque, who noted that the men in the film are blasé, already having transgressed every taboo. Haydée, on the other hand, articulates that she is "searching." The film depicts three modern characters "as free in their morality as [Rohmer] is puritanical, as cynical as he is idealistic," per de Baecque.[10] The characters represent, then, a sort of decadence, an artistic impasse that Rohmer implicitly illustrates through them. By using them, observing them, filming them in their entirety, "taken in the midst of their existence and the immorality of their biography," as de Baecque put it, Rohmer became more a documentarist and less a director of fiction.[11] The actors (and nonactors) in the film almost play themselves. Barbet Schroeder, the film's producer, related in an interview that Rohmer would have never done a casting call; he always went through personal contacts to cast his films, which is essentially how he found Haydée Politoff.

The director met her one evening in Pontoise at the home of Paul Gégauff (screenwriter, actor, and notorious New Wave *mauvais garçon*). The villa reportedly looked similar to the one at the beginning of *La Collectionneuse*. Though Politoff worked in real estate, which did not exactly correspond to Rohmer's ideal type of woman, she bore, in his view, a striking physical resemblance to Chantal, the heroine from his original 1949 story.[12] Her own touch of androgyny with her short haircut made her perfect for the part. Jackie Raynal, the editor of the film, related the director's enthusiastic epiphany upon meeting Haydée: "One day, Rohmer comes up to me and says, 'I found her!' He shows me a photo that she left him, because he told her that he was a director." According to Raynal, Rohmer placed the postage stamp–sized image on the reel and used it as inspiration to pen the script to *La Collectionneuse*.[13]

Yet again, the importance of the encounter is key in shaping the characters. Rohmer maintained the structure from his earlier draft of the narrative but based the characters on the actors who played them. "I used the actors I had on hand. They were friends of Barbet Schroeder and whose personalities I found really interesting," Rohmer said, "and I thought I could make them fit into the story."[14] He implemented this idea on a spectrum. For Adrien (a type of alter ego of Rohmer), Bauchau had little input in the text because Rohmer had already created the character and written his dialogue. Daniel's part, however, was less defined; Daniel Pommereulle could almost play himself. "He could say

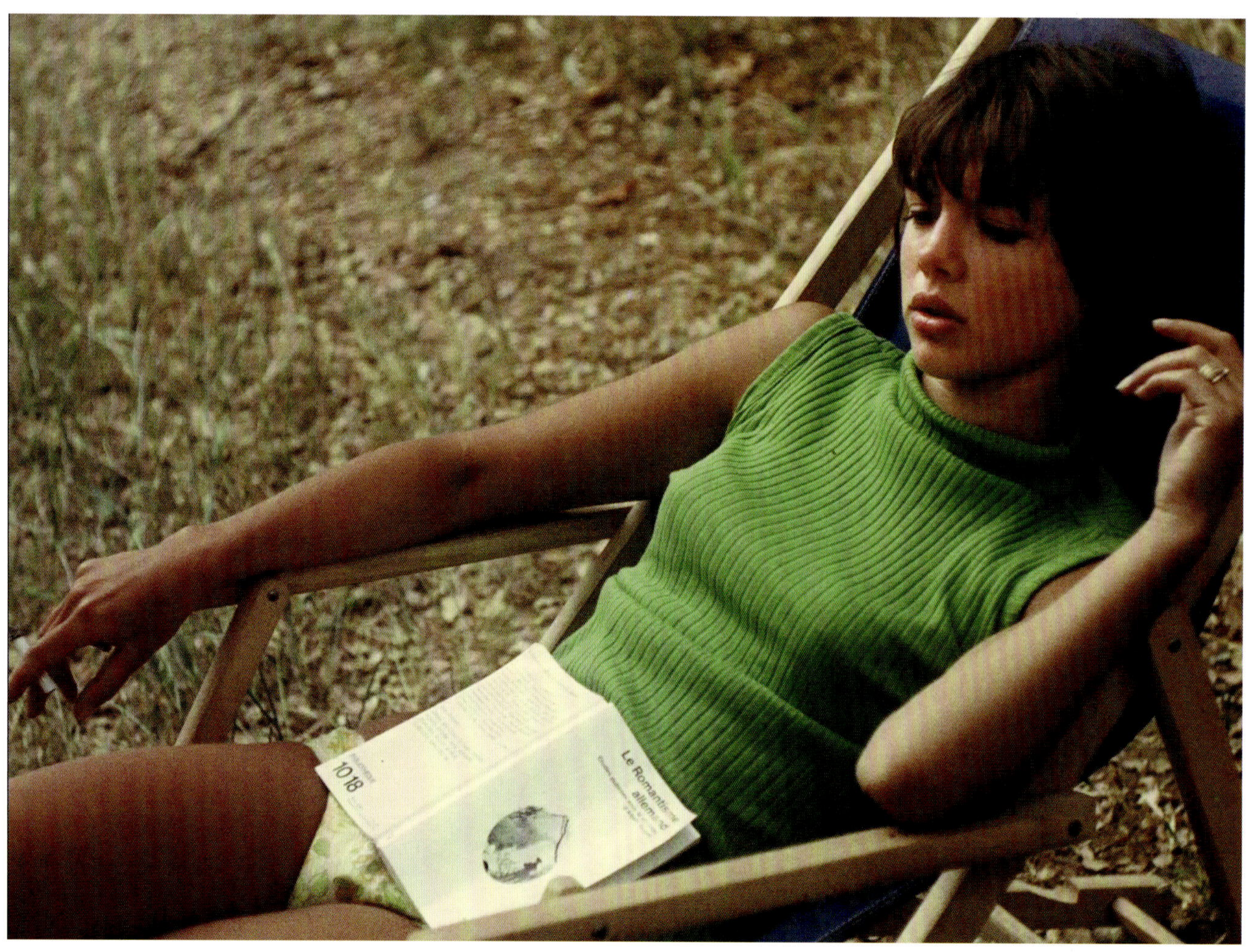

Haydée Politoff in Éric Rohmer's *La Collectionneuse*, 1967

things that he actually said in real life. His dialogue about painting, about women, are his own words," Rohmer explained. "It was true *cinéma vérité*."[15]

In creating his heroine, Politoff was highly influential, but her personality was harder to fit into the story. "Her character was more complex," Rohmer said. In preparing the film, however, he listened to her. "[Politoff] always denies being a 'collector,'" the director recounted, "but that's what was amusing because in the film she denies it too! We talked a lot, and her words and expressions became part of the film. I based the way the characters speak on the actors."[16] In effect, Rohmer never actually wrote *La Collectionneuse*. Instead, he specified the situations and left room to see what would evolve. From there, the film was written with a tape recorder. "For hours, he recorded the remarks of his actors, invited to speak freely about their passions, their loves," de Baecque explained, "always in relation to the imagined film."

Rohmer welcomed the actors' contributions in creating dialogue in a seemingly similar way Richard Linklater later worked with Julie Delpy and Ethan Hawke in the *Before* series. On the day of the shoot, Rohmer gave the actors their dialogue that was greatly inspired by their own "expressions, their tics of language, their ways of being."[17] Rohmer described one factor that motivated him to work in this way throughout his *contes moraux*: Having different characters talk with different styles was very difficult to write. To him, the "best solution" was to "make a collage" from the actors' words. "That allowed me to obtain a language which was quite esoteric . . . In fact, it's a language I don't always understand. There are words and references that I don't know. But they were people who were very picky about the words they used. They wouldn't allow substitutions. They'd absolutely refuse." *La Collectionneuse*'s actors continued to invent the text during long rehearsals before shooting each scene. Recordings of their dialogue were sent to Schroeder's young assistant Pierre Cottrell (who became a notable producer), who recalled that "the dialogue was not improvised but developed and polished on the spot, on the basis of a theme Rohmer had set, with their own vocabulary that was rather exotic for him. Given new rushes, my mission was to write a script from these cassettes" to secure subsidies from the government.[18]

Financial constraints imposed by the very small budget encouraged meticulous rehearsals: Each scene was shot only one time so as not to waste film. But this also brought about a camaraderie among the unpaid actors and crew who were all lodged in the same villa outside Saint-Tropez where the film was shot. Before some scenes, they would spend a couple hours cleaning litter from the beach, which built bonds among the actors while also feeding tensions that Rohmer used in the film, adding to its authentic feel. Some of Adrien and Daniel's cruel remarks to Haydée, for example, were inspired by the actors' off-screen comments.[19] As the characters and the actors blurred together throughout the shoot, Rohmer became almost a spy with his camera.

Rohmer became known for his meticulous attention to capturing authentic ambient sounds. According to Raynal, for *La Collectionneuse*, he noted all the noises in and around the house, from crickets to airplanes, an entire year ahead of time. The lighting was authentic, too, frugally done due to budget constraints: Cinematographer Nestor Almendros shot on 35mm film, using only five mini-projectors and sunlight that reflected off the walls and ceilings.[20]

Despite the small budget, or because of it, the film captures qualities of the actors that transcend the script. In this respect, the art of Rohmer lies in welcoming into his film what is exterior to his own personal world, observing it and interacting with it in order to create something beyond a preconceived idea typically associated with an auteur. With his genuine attentiveness to detail and open mind toward collaboration, the alchemy between director and actors brought a modern feel to his film. The process is especially evident in Politoff's own personality and presence.

CASTING OFF CONSTRAINTS AT THE CUSP OF FREEDOM

Haydée, the actress and the character, moves about on the edge of freedom, remaining elusive enough not to attack her male counterparts' egos directly but representing a threat to them nonetheless. Striking a balance between owning her own sensuality and pushing the limits of moral freedom, her character possesses traits that society was still struggling to accept in women at the time. The proof is in the film's title, implying that she is a collector of men, and in the male characters' labeling her a *petite salope* (little slut). That she does not correspond to their definition in the film, however, was new for cinema. And Rohmer, through his nonjudgmental *mise en scène*, instead shows her agency and integrity, which largely stemmed from Politoff herself.

Although she was only twenty years old when the film was made, Politoff exudes a remarkable self-confidence. In 1966, women were in a powerful time of transformation that enabled them to take more control of their identity and their freedom. Though the pill was not legalized until over a year after the film was made, Haydée's character is a role model of moral freedom with her nonchalant attitude, dedramatizing her many amorous encounters. And although the male characters in the film punish her for it, the film, more importantly, does not.

La Collectionneuse caused its own scandal, however, much like the films considered scandalous in the previous decade that also did not contain explicit scenes. Capitalizing on its content that flirted with sexual liberation, Schroeder organized a projection for Georges de Beauregard to try to obtain the money necessary to finish the film. After thirty minutes, sensing Beauregard's boredom, Pierre Rissient (an assistant director on *À bout de souffle* who had been called to help) whispered to him, "Look out! The mental orgy is about to begin."[21] His attention renewed, Beauregard au-

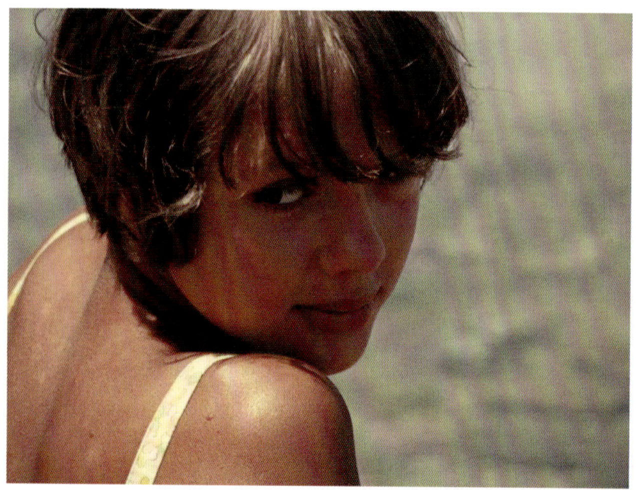

Haydée Politoff in Éric Rohmer's *La Collectionneuse*, 1967

thorized the money necessary for the film's postsynchronization. The film was also marketed from a lascivious angle, "not very far from Roger Vadim and his trompe l'oeil audacity," in de Baecque's words. The trailer assembled excerpts of what could be construed as the raciest moments, and the poster showed a woman's hand caressing a man's legs, which was far from the true spirit of Rohmer's film. Ebert, who titled his 2012 review "Let's Talk about Sex," emphasized this double characteristic of the film and the rest of Rohmer's *contes moraux*, writing, "The moral tales studied tricky questions of romance, and there was little or no sex in them but much discussion about it. He found actors of undeniable physical appeal, and his camera caressed them as they spoke, and spoke, about the possibility of caressing each other."[22]

Despite the lack of explicit scenes, the film at its release was forbidden for audiences under eighteen years old. Again, like *Les Amants* and *La Religieuse*, this only piqued the audience's interest, and the film drew a large crowd for its 1967 premiere at the newly opened and trendy movie theater Studio Git-le-Coeur in Paris's Latin Quarter. In attendance were the esteemed *nouveau roman* writers Alain Robbe-Grillet and Marguerite Duras, along with Catherine Deneuve and Brigitte Bardot (wearing a brown wig), there to support her sister, Mijanou.[23]

The film was a great success, remaining several months exclusively at Studio Git-le-Coeur and selling up to 70,000 tickets, "remarkable for a film in just one theater," according to Rohmer.[24] As the director pointed out, the audience loved it and loved Politoff: "It's the only film I made that followed the era's fashion, a little ahead of the style. Audiences loved the new fashions, the long hair, the blue jeans. Then there was Haydée Politoff, whom audiences adored. Marcel Carné signed her right after." When a journalist described her as having "a certain boldness," Rohmer confirmed, "Yes, audiences loved that."[25] Many young women copied Politoff's boyish haircut, and men, the polaroid sunglasses of Dennis Berry (future husband of Jean Seberg and of Anna Karina). Critics also loved Politoff, "a round-faced girl with an upturned nose with eloquent eyes who is everything great," as Michel Duran, a usually blasé critic, enthusiasti-

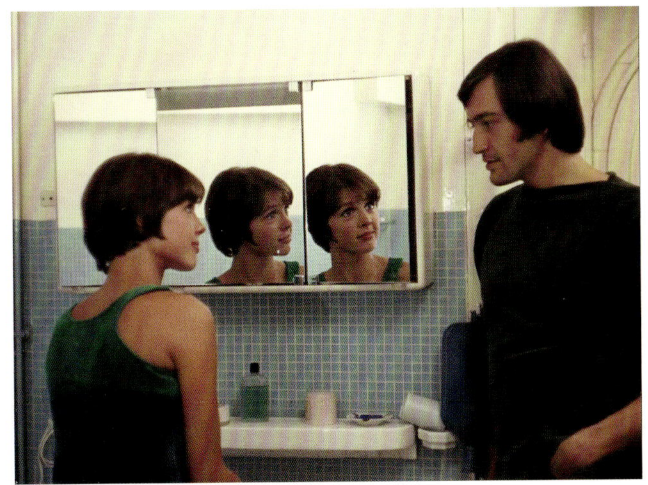

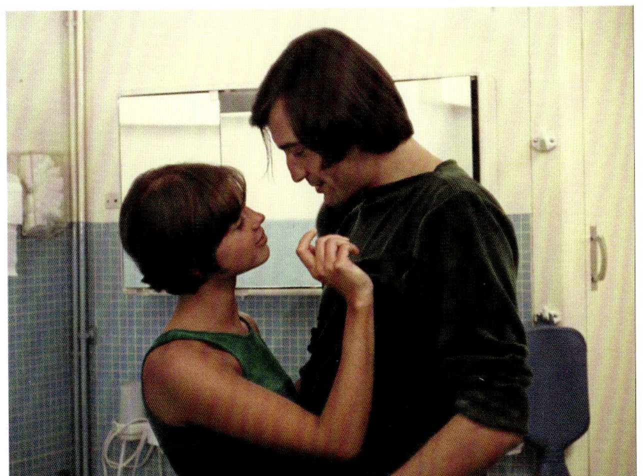

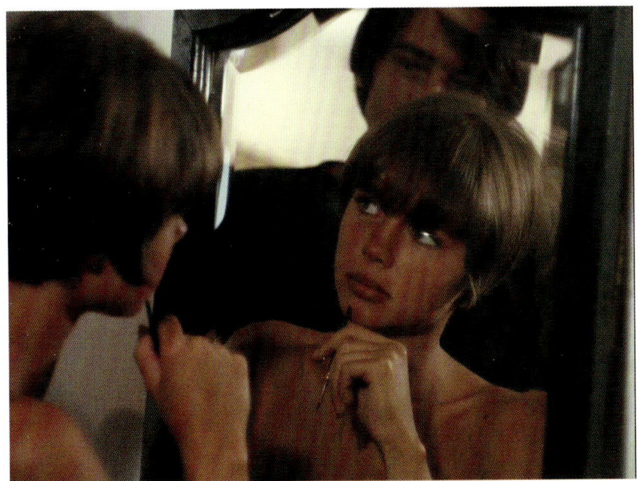

Hadyée Politoff and Patrick Bauchau (Adrien) in Éric Rohmer's *La Collectionneuse*, 1967

cally described her in the satirical newspaper *Le Canard enchaîné*.[26]

Besides being an imitable model in terms of style with her cropped haircut and androgynous ensembles, equally alluring in jeans and colorful sweaters as in her bikini and daring miniskirts, Politoff herself appears timeless in her attitude, transcending the '60s and transmitting a contemporary air. In Rohmer's evolving cinema, this moral tale gives more space to the heroine's experience compared to *La Boulangère* and *La Carrière de Suzanne* (*Suzanne's Career*, 1963). In *La Collectionneuse,* Rohmer capitalized on real-life tensions among the trio in the villa like a documentarist, showing how badly Haydée is treated not only by her male cohorts but, implicitly and by extension, also by an unequal society. She functions as a reminder of the obstacles young women faced in their search for freedom, even as France approached May '68.

Haydée's answer, and perhaps her lesson for us, is that she quietly seizes her agency without struggle, always remaining seemingly unperturbed by the comments of Daniel, Adrien, or Sam. They are never able to provoke her. Unlike the reactive men, she is even-keeled. In this way, she silently retains her freedom in an unpleasant and unfair environment. At a time when women had not yet acquired enough power to speak out freely, perhaps this was the only way, or a compromise, to achieving freedom.

Haydée's confidence and security in her sense of self go beyond that of many role models in media today, which may explain why audiences still love her. A decade before *La Collectionneuse*, modern heroines like Moreau in *Ascenseur* and Bardot in *Et Dieu créa la femme* were still condemned at the end of the narrative for their lack of morality. In 1967, Haydée Politoff as filmed by Rohmer (ironically, one of the most puritanical directors) provided a new female role model of freedom in the sensual *garçonne*, rebelling against the conventional constraints on women. In this moral tale, French cinema itself opens to a shifting society, breaking, if ever so subtly, toward an idea of freedom for women on the brink of their quest for equality.

JULES ET JIM: CATHERINE ESCAPES HER STATUE

Haydée's tacit refusal to remain someone else's static *blason* finds its counterpart in a character that predated her by half a decade: Jeanne Moreau's Catherine in *Jules et Jim*. She, too, is presented and juxtaposed with art, but Truffaut takes it further by having his male protagonists fall in love with her expressly because of her resemblance to a certain statue.

Before meeting Catherine, Jules and Jim view slides of sculptures of female figures taken by their friend Albert, who is described as "the friend of painters and sculptors." Through this projection, the film makes us aware of the medium and reminds us of cinema's double function in creating images of ideal feminine beauty and then realizing the fantasies based off them. Albert's commentary on the first three statues sets the scene for the contrast with the fourth: "This one is more exotic. She looks a bit like an Incan statue. This one's more Romanesque. It's badly weathered because I found it in the garden. This one's very touching. Reminds you of a decaying face." With the fourth image, Albert focuses on the statue's features: "This one, I like a lot. The lips are very beautiful, a bit disdainful. The eyes are very beautiful also." The reverse shot translates the reaction of Jules and Jim, attesting to the power of the image, the per-suasion of the commentary, and the statue's sudden hold over them. As the slideshow continues, Jim asks Albert to go back to the one of the beautiful statue. Transfixed, they contemplate its details in close-up, and a particularly extreme close-up of the statue's mouth illustrates a sensual point of desire.

The narrator's voice-over describes, in lyrical terms, the power of the work of art: "This slide showed a crudely sculpted woman's face whose tranquil smile mesmerized them." Mobilized by the desire of an ideal feminine beauty, Jules and Jim set off immediately to find the statue, as the voice-over narrates, "in an outdoor museum on an island in the Adriatic." Hinting at a melancholy fantasy linked to the forever lost (love) object, "the recently exhumed statue" comes to the surface and into their lives, further binding them together in an "enchanted" encounter. Pronounced in rapid, staccato phrasing, the narrator describes the scene: "They stayed an hour with the statue. It exceeded their expectations. They walked very rapidly around it in silence. They didn't speak about it again until the next day. Had they ever encountered such a smile? Never. What would they do if they ever did? They would follow it. Jules and Jim went back home, full of this revelation." In short, they are already in love with the idea of this woman before they meet her. And when they cross paths with Catherine, recognizing in her "the smile of the statue on the island," as the narrator says, "It started like a dream."

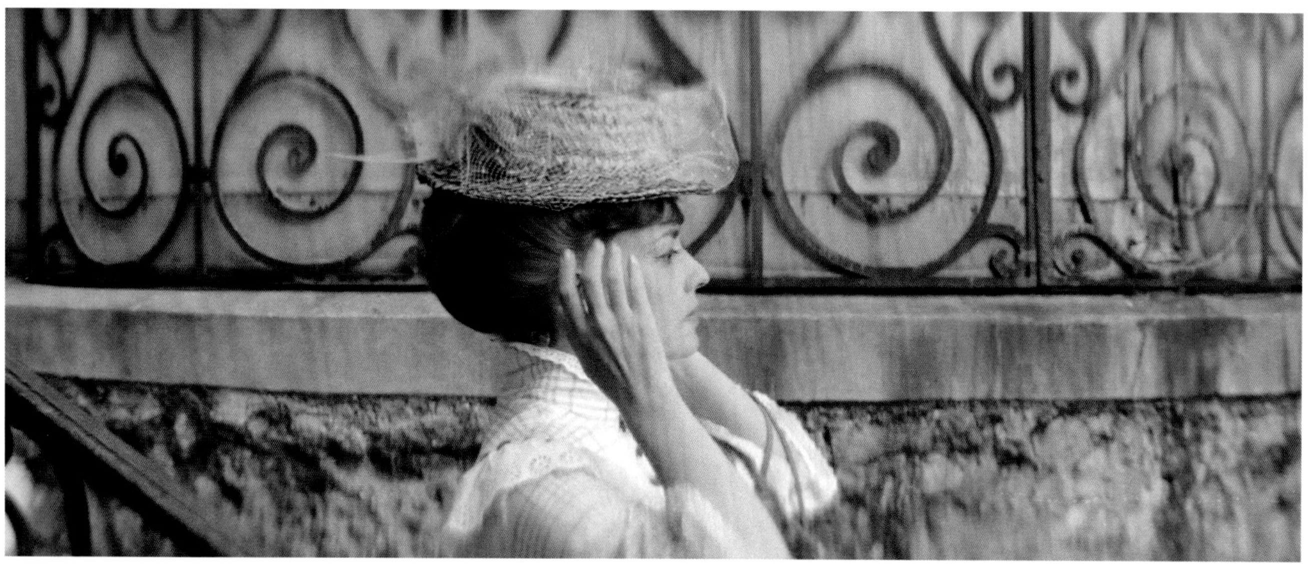

Jeanne Moreau (Catherine) in Truffaut's *Jules et Jim*, 1962

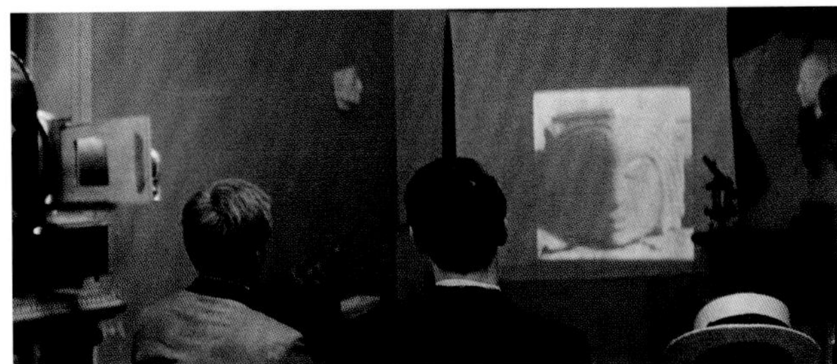

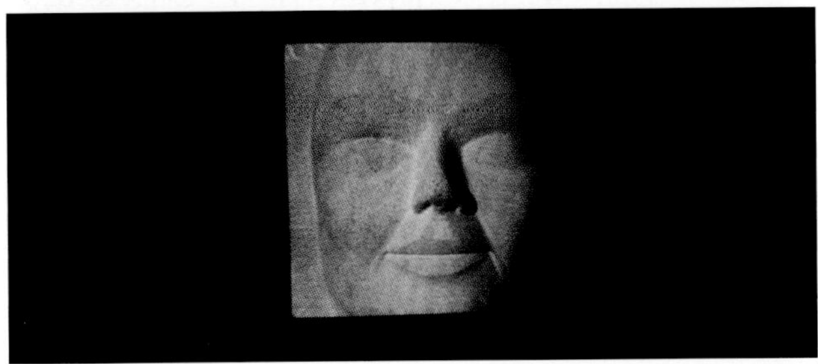

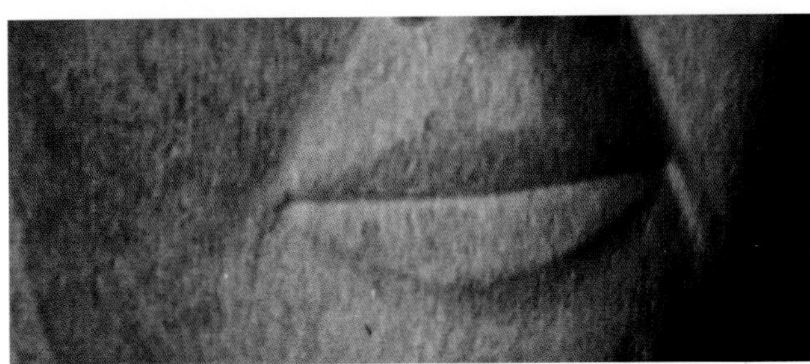

"harmony of the face." Also likening her to a statue, Hugo defines her as "sculptural and exquisite; that was Fantine; and underneath this material a statue, and in the statue, a soul."[27]

Confusing Catherine with the idea of a woman, Jules and Jim overlook her reality even though they claim she is the incarnation of a "real woman." When Jules asks Jim if he should marry her, Jim's response further distances her from reality, relegating her to an otherworldly domain: "Is she cut out to be a wife and mother? I'm afraid she'll never be happy on this earth. She's a vision for all, perhaps not meant for any one man alone." In a later scene, she is seen from an inverse perspective as Other and diabolized. Breaking the harmony of the trio, Jules and Jim walk with Catherine along the Seine after attending a play. The sequence also highlights the dual nature in which women were represented in French literature. Along with the idealized images, they were also demonized. When Jules asks who wrote that "Woman is natural, therefore abominable," Jim replies, "It's Baudelaire but he was describing a certain milieu, a particular society." Jules disagrees, saying that he was referring to women in general. He praises the poet's description of *la jeune fille*: "Horror, monster, assassin of the arts, little fool, little slut, the greatest idiocy combined with the greatest depravity," and cites another idea by the poet he admires: "I'm always astonished that they allow women inside churches. What could they possibly have to say to God?"

Catherine is a composite of Kathe and Lucie, two characters from Henri-Pierre Roché's novel of the same name, adapted by Truffaut and his co-screenwriter Jean Gruault. It is Kathe who has the statue's smile, but Lucie whose detailed description was borrowed for the film. We hear parts of it recounted in voice-over against stills of Moreau's face: "Her nose, her mouth, her chin, and her forehead bore the nobility of a province that she personifed as a child in a religious celebration." The camera completes the visual *blason* (also evoking the statue), with numerous close-ups of Moreau from the front and in profile.

The pervasive influence of this literary device is confirmed by the striking similarities between Catherine's portrait and Victor Hugo's description of Fantine in *Les Misérables*: "Dazzling from the front, delicate in profile," Hugo wrote, describing her eyes, eyelids, feet, wrists, skin, cheeks, neck, shoulders, and "her forehead, her nose, her chin," resulting in a

Rejecting the insulting portrayals, Catherine calls them "two idiots" and protests by jumping into the Seine, foreshadowing her drive off the bridge at the end of the film. Unlike the statue, Catherine can and does rebel, escaping the protagonists' control.[28] Alongside this display of liberation, however, the portrait of Catherine is not exactly a flattering one. She is seen as unstable and capricious, and her threat of power over the men turns her into a real femme fatale as Jules watches her drive Jim to his death in the penultimate scene. But with Jeanne Moreau in the role, an actress by then well known for strength and independence on and off screen, it is more difficult to demonize Catherine completely.[29] In the end, Truffaut presents a character searching to live her life, for better or worse, by her own rules, while struggling both with internal conflicts and social constraints.

Slideshow for Jules and Jim by Albert of statues of women, this one with the intriguing smile, in Truffaut's *Jules et Jim*, 1962

Next page: The statue on the island in the Adriatic that Jules and Jim travel to see; Jeanne Moreau (Catherine) in Truffaut's *Jules et Jim*, 1962

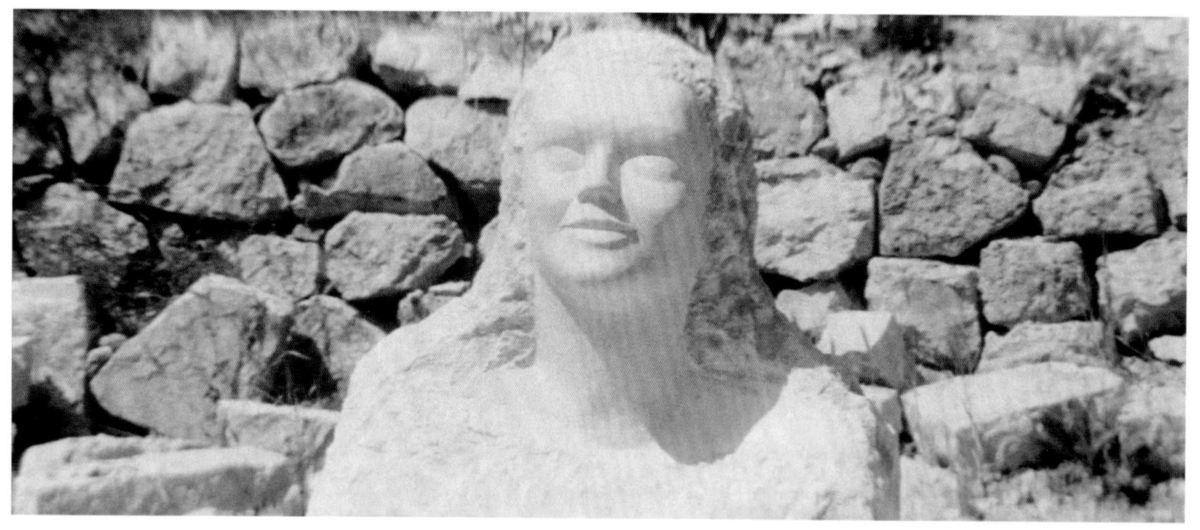

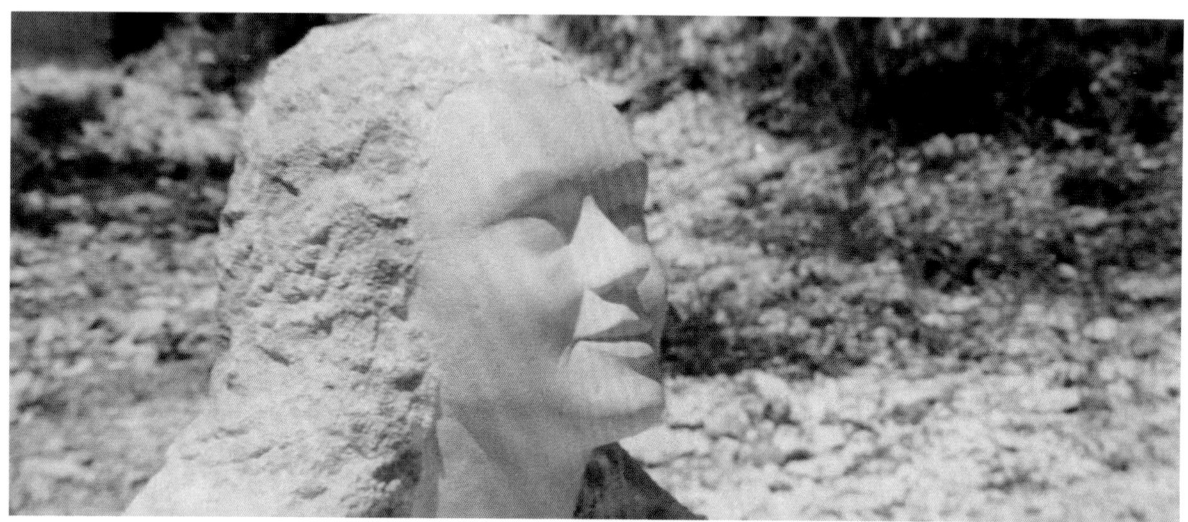

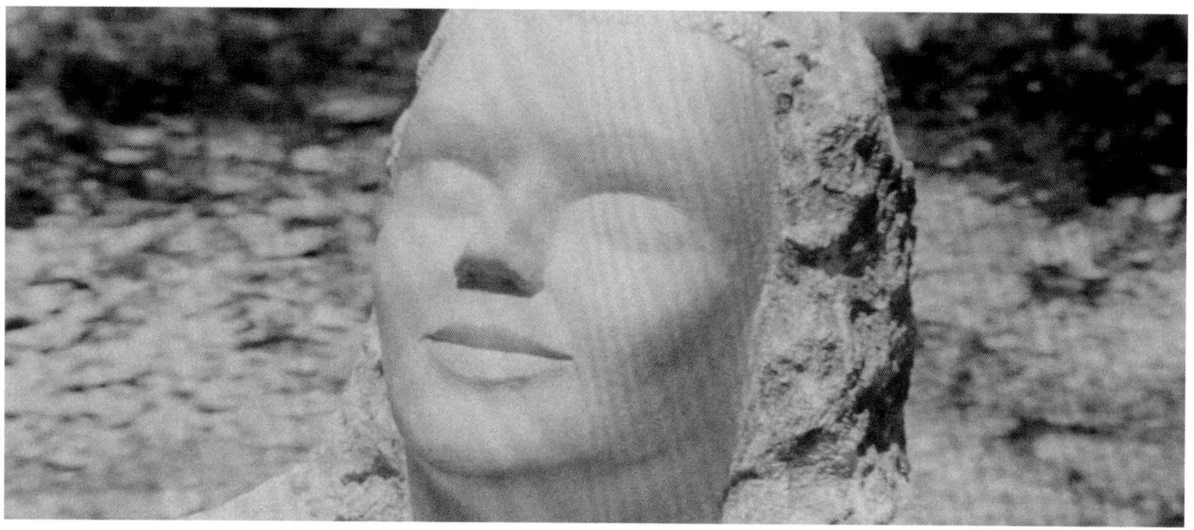

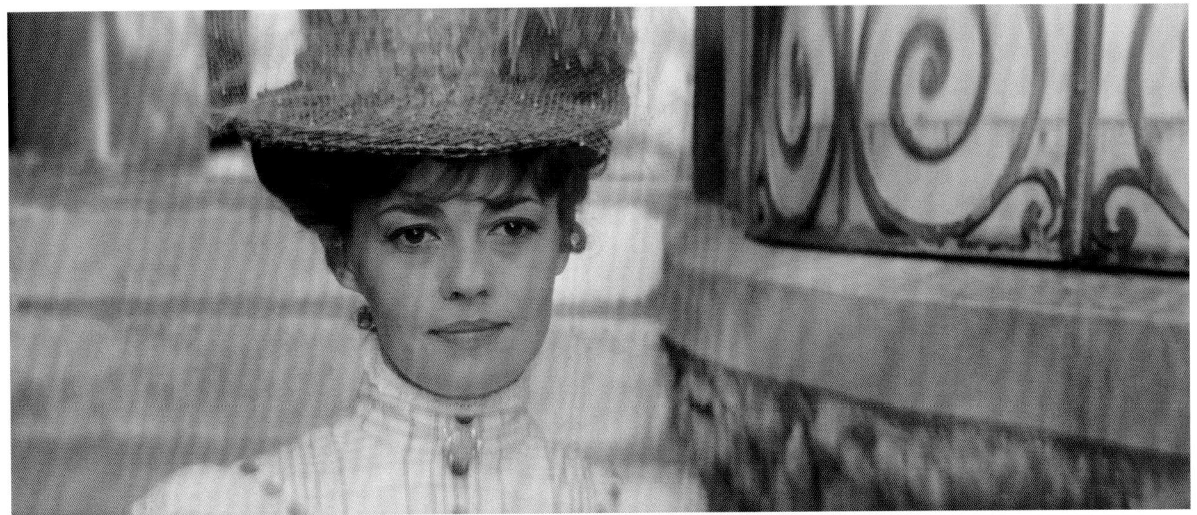

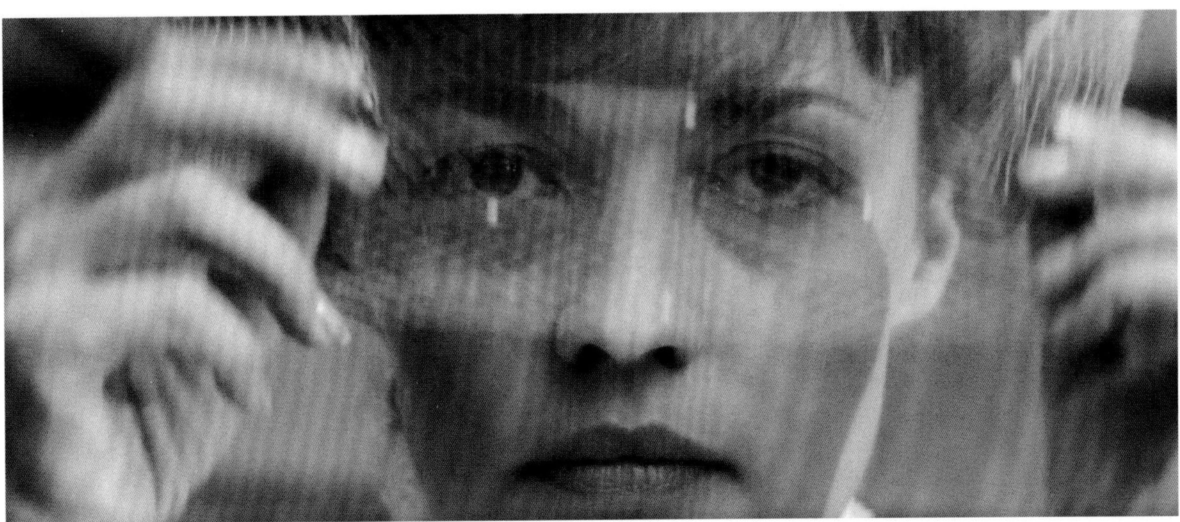

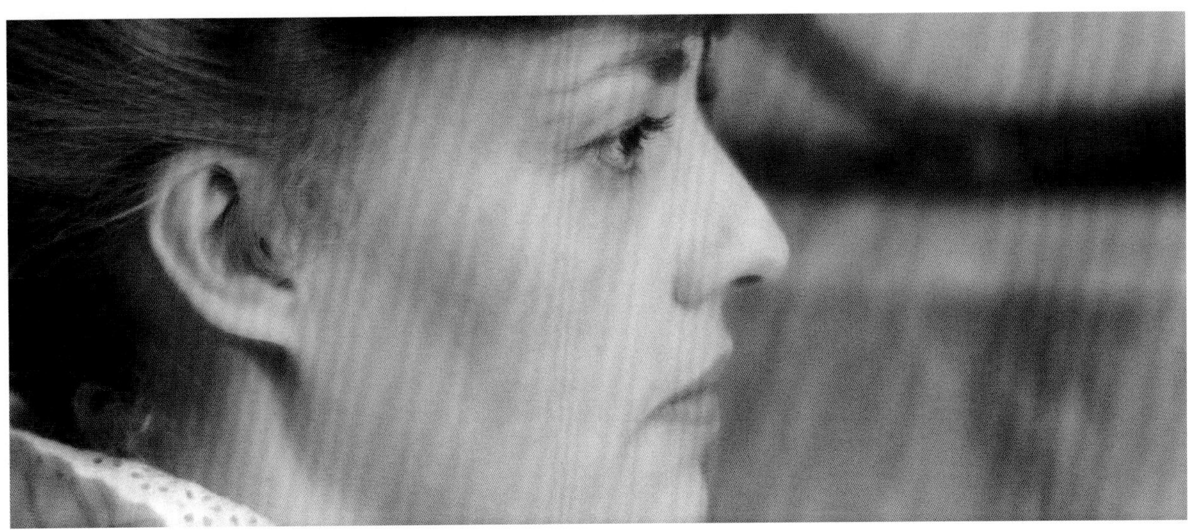

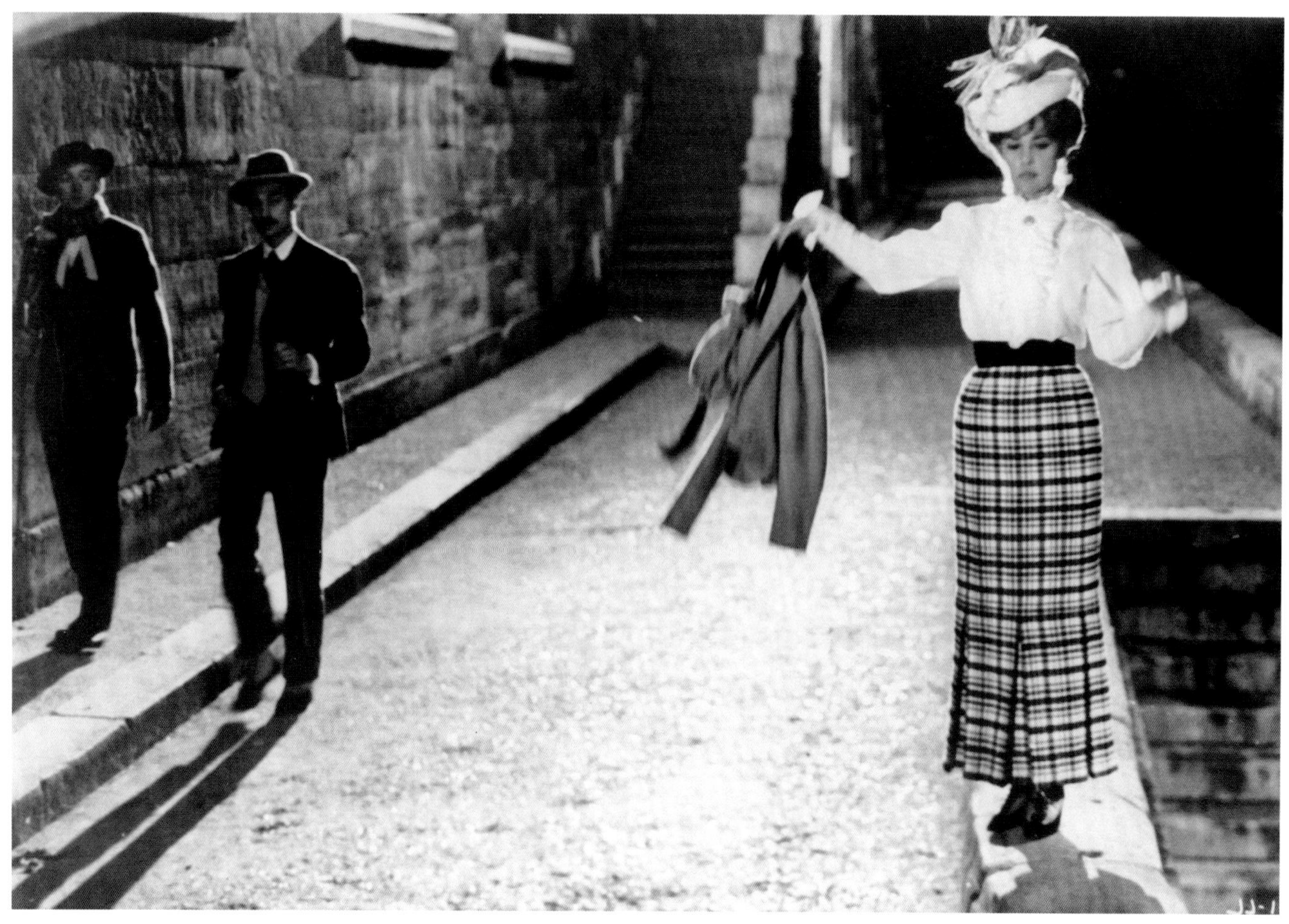

DESIRE, INFATUATION, AND FEAR FROM TRUFFAUT TO CHABROL

Truffaut also endeavored to capture Catherine's (and Moreau's) spirit–to reproduce an impression of life–as Godard did through Bruno with Karina's Véronica in *Le Petit soldat*'s photo-shoot scene. Truffaut's camera shows Catherine in freeze frames, seizing her in motion, depicting her flickering expressions and moods. If the earlier *blasons* reflect Roché's portrait of Catherine, these freer shots of Moreau seem to reflect Truffaut's own desire for the actress, resembling the medieval poets in their desire for *la femme*. Though Godard must have understood how desire for the actress could propel the desire to create, sharing the trait of creating art with Karina, he would later condemn Truffaut for not acknowledging it directly in his film about moviemaking, *La Nuit américaine* (*Day for Night*, 1973). (Truf-

faut, playing a director in the film, shows the intrigues of his actors behind the scenes, but he does not portray his own character's involvement with the actress [Jacqueline Bisset] while Truffaut himself was known to be involved with the women in his films.)[30] In this sense, desire in the creative process was a very serious element (to Godard at least), a necessary driving force in filmmaking as a collective art.

Truffaut was deeply infatuated with Moreau while filming *Jules et Jim*. "The relationship between us was very, very, very strong," Moreau admitted.[31] Though rumored to have been romantically involved, Moreau denied it, saying, "Luckily, we were not lovers." She acknowledged the role of attraction in the creative process, however. "Passion distorts things," she said. "There was a very powerful attraction, but it was an exchange of fascination and curiosity."[32] According

Oskar Werner (Jules), Henri Serre (Jim), Jeanne Moreau (Catherine) on the verge of jumping in the Seine in Truffaut's *Jules et Jim*, 1962

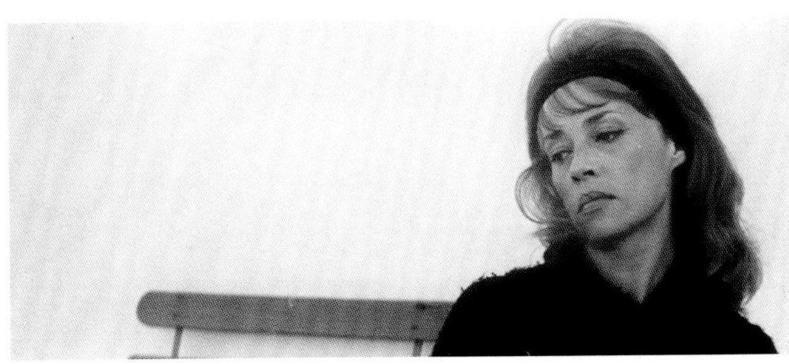

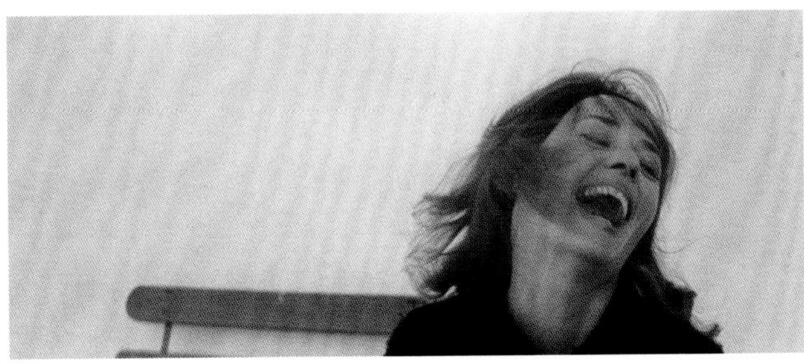

to film scholar Richard Neupert, "Apparently, there was some tension on the set. Almost all the men were just so obsessed with her," which "added a real and personal level to the film." Moreau also worked behind the scenes with Truffaut, contributing to the script with dialogue and characterization.[33]

Undoubtedly mixing his desire to create with his desire for his actress, Truffaut admitted his passion for Moreau, however, to Helen Scott in a letter: "We spent a few days at her house in the South and it was perfect happiness, which explains the sadness of coming back and the beginning of this film that separates us. I can only talk about it to you because, in Paris, I can't confide in anyone about Jeanne . . . . As always, I have the same problem, to fight or not to fight, to wait or push the events, pessimism or optimism, to live for the future or for the instant, to want or not, etc. Everything isn't rosy and I have moments of solitude but I find an intensity of feelings again like the time between Chicago-New York that you witnessed but more real, more reciprocal, less 'made up' by me. Naturally, this materializes in Jeanne and in me, in a great desire to work together as soon as possible, which explains my interest in the novel *The Bride Wore Black*."[34]

Known to fall in love with the actresses playing the leading roles in his films, Truffaut was not far from his male protagonists. According to Moreau, "Clearly he dealt with his ob-

sessions—his films and the women he was fascinated with: Fanny Ardant, Deneuve, Isabelle Adjani, Françoise Dorléac, Marie Dubois, Bernadette Lafont. Women were very, very important. And cinema. He's the one who said life in films was better than in real life."[35]

He was not afraid of profusely expressing romantic sensibility through his alter egos. Enamored by Deneuve while filming *La Sirène du Mississipi*, Truffaut appears to have used Belmondo's character, Louis, as a mouthpiece to confess his fascination with her (in addition to fixating on her face with his camera). Suspending the narrative for a scene detailing the beauty of her face, the film shows Louis composing a lyrical description of Julie (Deneuve), portraying her as a pure object of his desire.

Illustrating the relationship of a woman to a work of art in his idealized portrait, Louis says directly, "I am going to try to describe you as if you were a photo or a painting." When Julie tries to answer, he stops her. "No, be quiet," he says, as the camera remains still. His literary description, full of metaphors, details her face while the camera provides a fixed portrait: "Your face is a landscape; and two eyes, two small brown lakes. Your forehead is a prairie; your nose, a little mountain. Your mouth, a volcano." He pauses, telling her to open her mouth so he can see her teeth, directing her like an actress: "No, not too much. Okay, like that." In these lines, we can almost hear Truffaut directing Deneuve in the film. Continuing with the portrait, the protagonist hints at a more intimate relationship with Julie, like Truffaut had with the actress: "Let's talk a bit about your smile now. No, not that one. That's the one you

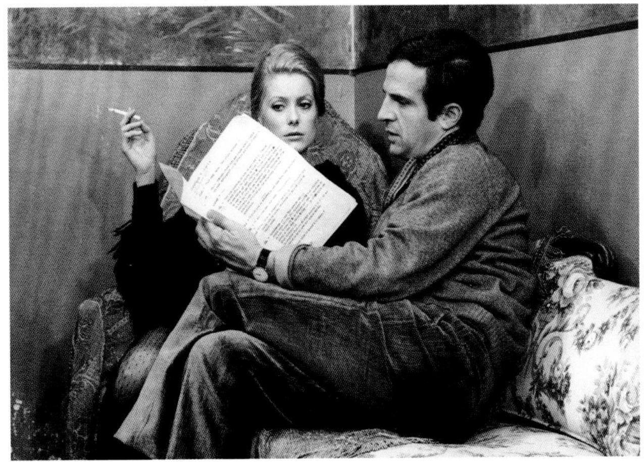

Freeze frames of Jeanne Moreau (Catherine) in Truffaut's *Jules et Jim*, 1962

Catherine Deneuve and François Truffaut discussing *La Sirène du Mississippi* (*Mississippi Mermaid*), May 1, 1968

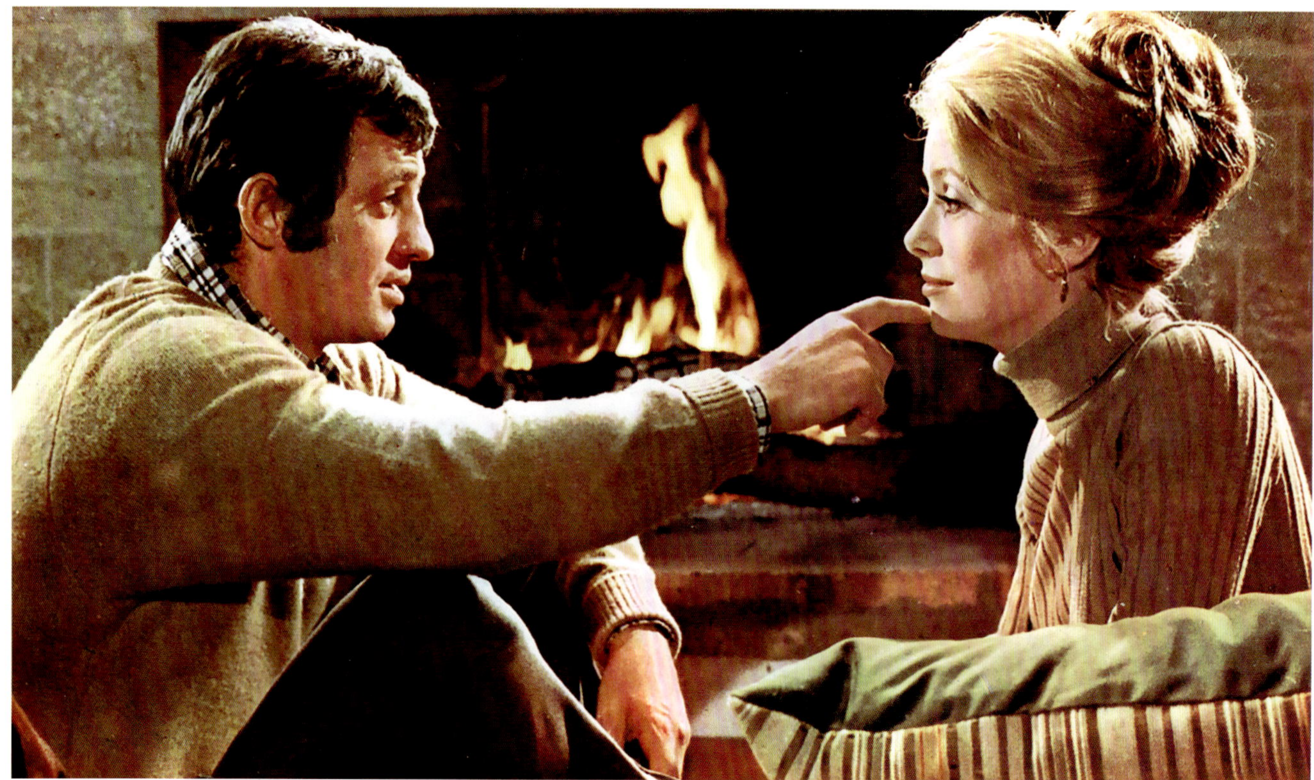

show in the street and to shopkeepers. No, give me the other one, the real one, the one of happiness." Somewhat disturbing by today's standards, this dynamic—in which the woman is coaxed into assuming a completely passive role under the direction of her lover—provides a window into the romantic male fantasy as expressed by Truffaut. With her glacial beauty and blonde chignon, Deneuve in front of the fire resonates with Hitchcock's femmes fatales more than with Jeanne Moreau's free-spirited portrayal of Catherine in *Jules et Jim*.

In another Hitchcockian portrait, Claude Chabrol's thriller *Les Bonnes femmes* (1960) depicts a romantic heroine, Jacqueline (Clotilde Joano), who is ironically punished for her belief in true love. One scene focuses on a vulnerable part of the heroine's body through the male character's fixation. "I adore your neck," whispers her future murderer as they dine together at a restaurant, "because it is long and thin and you tilt it in a way I like." Mulvey's idea of masculine anxiety in relation to the desired female body applies here in its assertion that a choice must be made between fetishistic scopophilia (that augments the beauty of the object), and

voyeurism (that includes a sadistic component). Chabrol's heroine clearly concretizes the desire and fear of the killer. With her naïve, romantic beliefs, she is the perfect prey, echoing Giulietta Masina's romantic prostitute in Fellini's *Le notti di Cabiria*. Under the predator's active gaze, the passive heroine incarnates the object of his fantasies (as in erotic spectacles of the striptease or pinup) as well as his fear. No longer strictly reduced to pure instruments of eroticism, the new more modern women in New Wave cinema may have gained some ground, but the relics that linger remain chilling as some heroines are demonized or punished by death for the threat they embody.

BARDOT'S OWN *BLASON*: VOYEURISM TO ROMANTICISM

Different from the images of other cinematic *blasons*, the opening shots of Brigitte Bardot in Godard's *Le Mépris* are an invitation to question our gaze as voyeuristic. But the famous opening sequence of Bardot's body, now synonymous with the film, originated as a way to satisfy the de-

Jean-Paul Belmondo (Louis) and Catherine Deneuve (Julie) in François Truffaut's *La Sirène du Mississippi* (*Mississippi Mermaid*), 1969

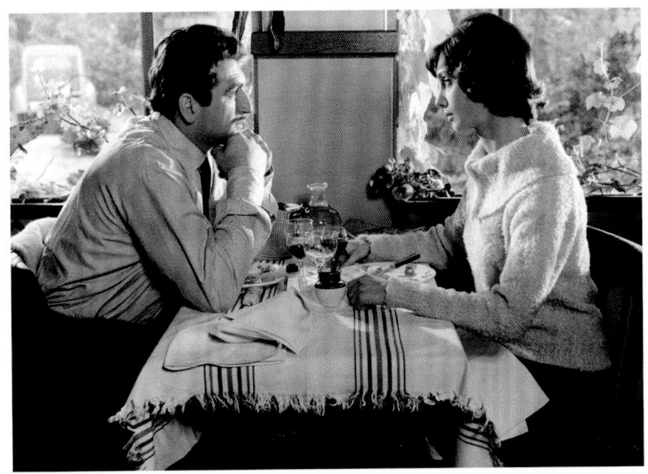

mands of producers' commercial objectives. Obligated to add three "sexy" scenes at the beginning and in the middle of the film, showing the actress in shots associated with the "spectacular" nude scenes in *Et Dieu créa la femme*, Godard acquiesced to their demands but not to their intentions. Turning in a precise description of the three scenes to the producers, the director specified that the first be made to show the deep physical and sentimental connection between the two characters played by Bardot and Piccoli in the leading roles.[36] Transforming the erotic poses into a romantic love scene, Godard undermined the producers' directives, almost parodying the famous nude postures Bardot was known for in Vadim's first film.

With the shot of Raoul Coutard's camera in the opening scenes of the film, Godard points to the presence of the camera as the mechanism that makes Bardot's body an object (pointing out the position of the spectator as voyeur through its eye). The shot illustrates, ironically, the capacity of the camera (and of the men behind it) to objectify a woman's body or to reveal her beauty, just as the sixteenth-century poets did with their pens.

In the first scene with Bardot's Camille, her questions offer a new take on the *blason*; this time her character details the parts of her own body while searching for validation of her beauty from her husband. It was not the first time that this motif, voiced by a female protagonist, appeared in Godard's cinema. In *À bout de souffle*, Patricia (Seberg) asks Michel (Belmondo), "Do you like my eyes, my mouth, or my shoulders

better? If you had to choose?" Michel ignores the question while getting dressed, then touches her on the shoulder. In a similar way, Camille in *Le Mépris*, actively creating her portrait (along with the camera), makes us aware of her position as object. As she takes inventory of her own body, she invites us to observe each part instead of passively consuming her body visually, and thereby exposing our place as voyeurs.

In the first part of the sequence, as she lies face down on the bed, propped up on her elbows, she talks to her husband about daily life ("I think I'll go see my mother tomorrow, but after, I don't know"), constrasting with the spectacle of her nude body shown in low red lighting. Camille then asks her husband (while simultaneously interpolating the viewer), "You see my feet in the mirror? Do you think they're pretty? And my ankles, do you like them?" The camera moves in while Camille's words create the effect of a slow panorama as she details each part of her body—her knees, thighs, bottom, breasts, and shoulders—for her husband and the viewer. Certain phrases (body parts) are inaudible. Whether by modesty or provocation, Godard leaves them to the viewer's imagination. By speaking and naming the parts of her body, Bardot complicates the passive configuration of the *blason*, appropriating the device while simultaneously offering her body to us as spectacle, complicitly with Godard's camera.

The lighting becomes slightly brighter and she asks, "And my shoulders? I don't think they're round enough." The scene culminates with her whole body illuminated while a tracking shot moves to her feet, then pans back up to her head. As she finishes her spoken inventory, the camera pauses. Camille asks, "And my face?" Paul has validated his love for every part of her body, and ends with her face. Now seen through a blue filter, Camille once again seeks reassurance, "Everything? My mouth, my eyes, my nose, my ears?" As Paul confirms that he loves "everything," Camille concludes that he loves her "completely."

At the end of the sequence, the couple looks at each other face to face. Paul replies, "Yes, I love you completely, tenderly, tragically." We cannot help but hear Godard behind these words as his love story unravels with Anna Karina off screen. "I do too, Paul," Camille replies, fulfilling the romantic dream.

Mario David (André) and Clotilde Joano (Jacqueline) in Claude Chabrol's *Les Bonnes femmes* (*The Good Time Girls*), 1960

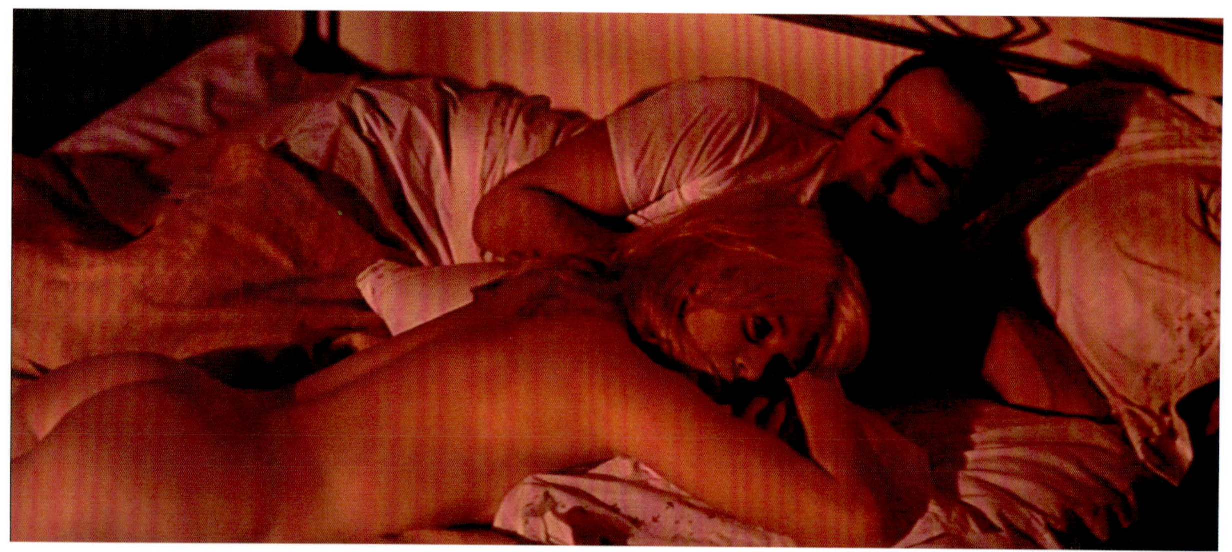

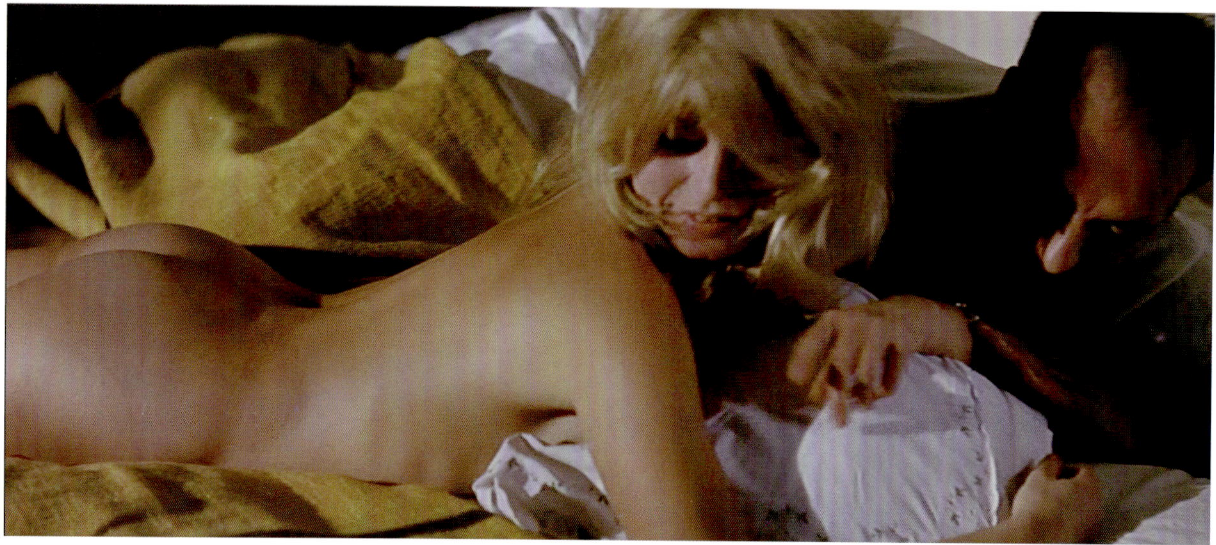

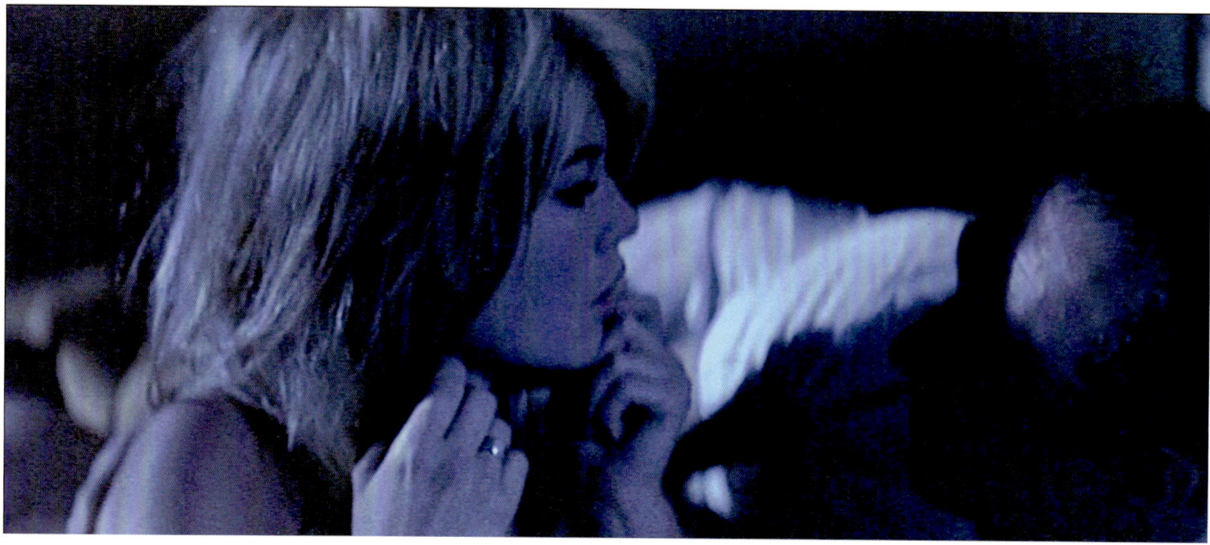

With the dramatic music of Georges Delerue, the changes in lighting, and the long duration of the scene, the dialogue de-emphasizes the erotic that was so present in *Et Dieu créa la femme*,[37] turning it into a scene about love instead of a love scene. Playing on the stereotypes of spectacle and exhibitionism, Godard creates a poetic *blason* by deconstructing it with Bardot herself. The scene that should have been, then, one with a purely erotic and commercial goal, becomes one of the most romantic love scenes of the New Wave, while implicitly questioning the commercialization of women's bodies and of Bardot as an actress. The scene also displays, however, the same paradoxical qualities signaled in *Une femme mariée*, with Godard denouncing the fetishizing of the heroine's body while doing just that.

The types of poetic descriptions found in the *blasons* and in the films make their way into real life as well, attesting to the extent to which they are embedded in the French sensibility. The tendency to capture women through art and of art idealizing female beauty permeates the cultural landscape. In Vadim's memoirs, for example, he describes Bardot appearing in Cannes in 1953 in terms that fragment and idealize her body in much the same way:

> First they saw her tresses floating on the surface of the water; then her face, streaming with drops of water, glistening in the sun like so many diamonds. Her innocent, sensual mouth and perfect oval eyes, her delicate nose, her cheeks as round as a child's, were made for pleasure and laughter. Two hands with aristocratic wrists . . . a delicate neck, a thin waist that a man could encircle with two hands; a round, provocative and tender derrière that would have been the envy of Adonis and Aphrodite; perfectly curved hips, long, firm thighs, charming ankles, and the arched feet of a dancer.[38]

Brigitte Bardot (Camille) with Michel Piccoli (Paul) in Godard's *Le Mépris* (*Contempt*), 1963

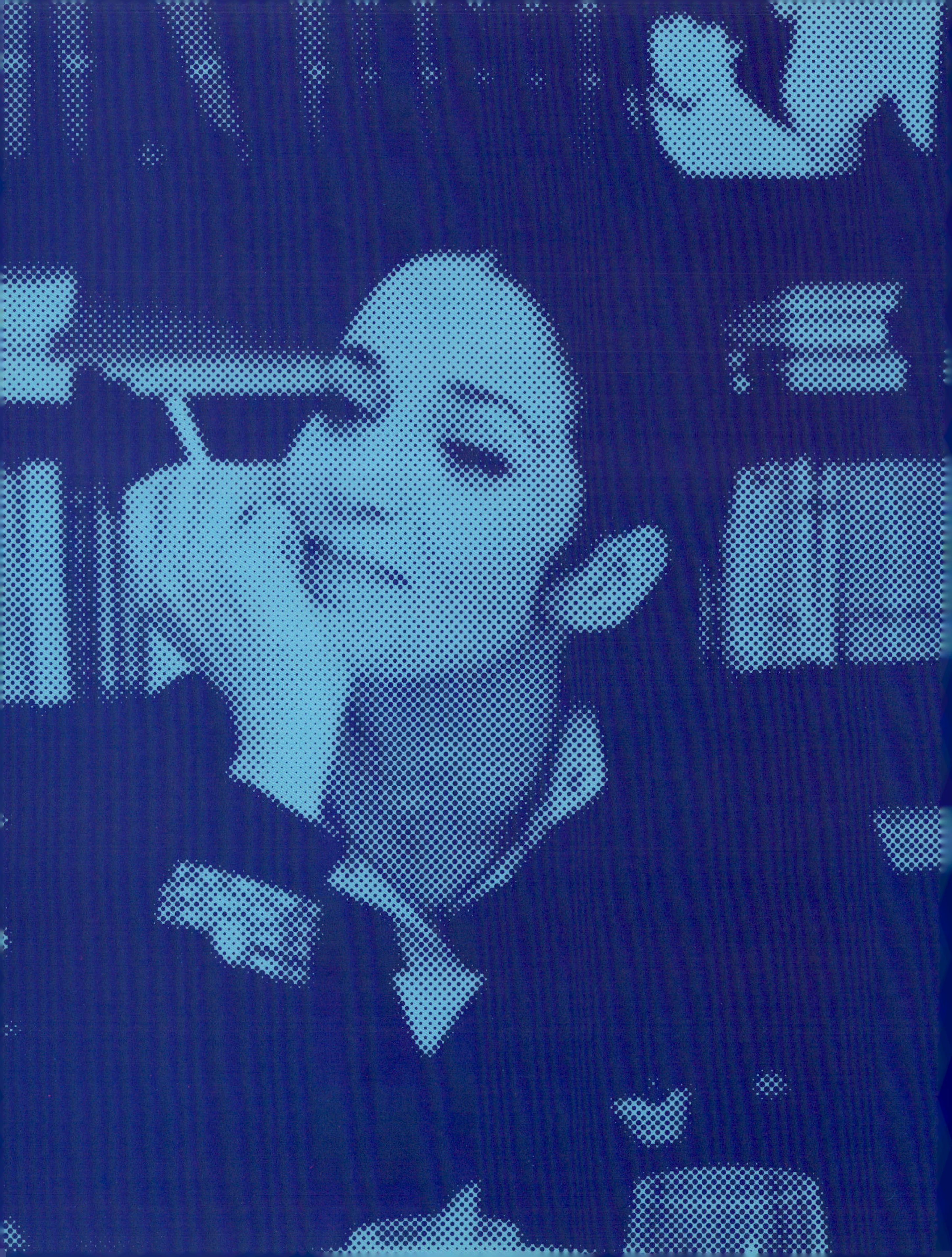

françoise fabian 11

la femme libérée | *the liberated woman*

FRANÇOISE FABIAN'S ROAD TO *MAUD*

After the modern portrait of Haydée, avatar of *la jeune fille libre* in 1967's *La Collectionneuse,* a striking evolution appears in Rohmer's next *conte moral* with 1969's *Ma nuit chez Maud* (though considered third in the series). While *La Collectionneuse* subtly anticipated the cataclysmic transformations in May '68 that brought women more rights, *Maud* grapples with what to do with an independent woman in a society that is still in many ways traditional. While May '68 stands as an emblematic date and solid reference point regarding change, the slow and steady shifts leading up to it disrupted conventions and roles that had previously been well defined. Women had greater access to higher education and more options to work outside the home. Married women no longer needed their husband's consent to hold a job. The Neuwirth Law legalized birth control in 1967 and gave women more choices regarding motherhood. Also emerging after May '68 in line with these sociocultural shifts, the MLF (the French Women's Liberation Movement) sought more freedom for women and raised awareness for women's rights.

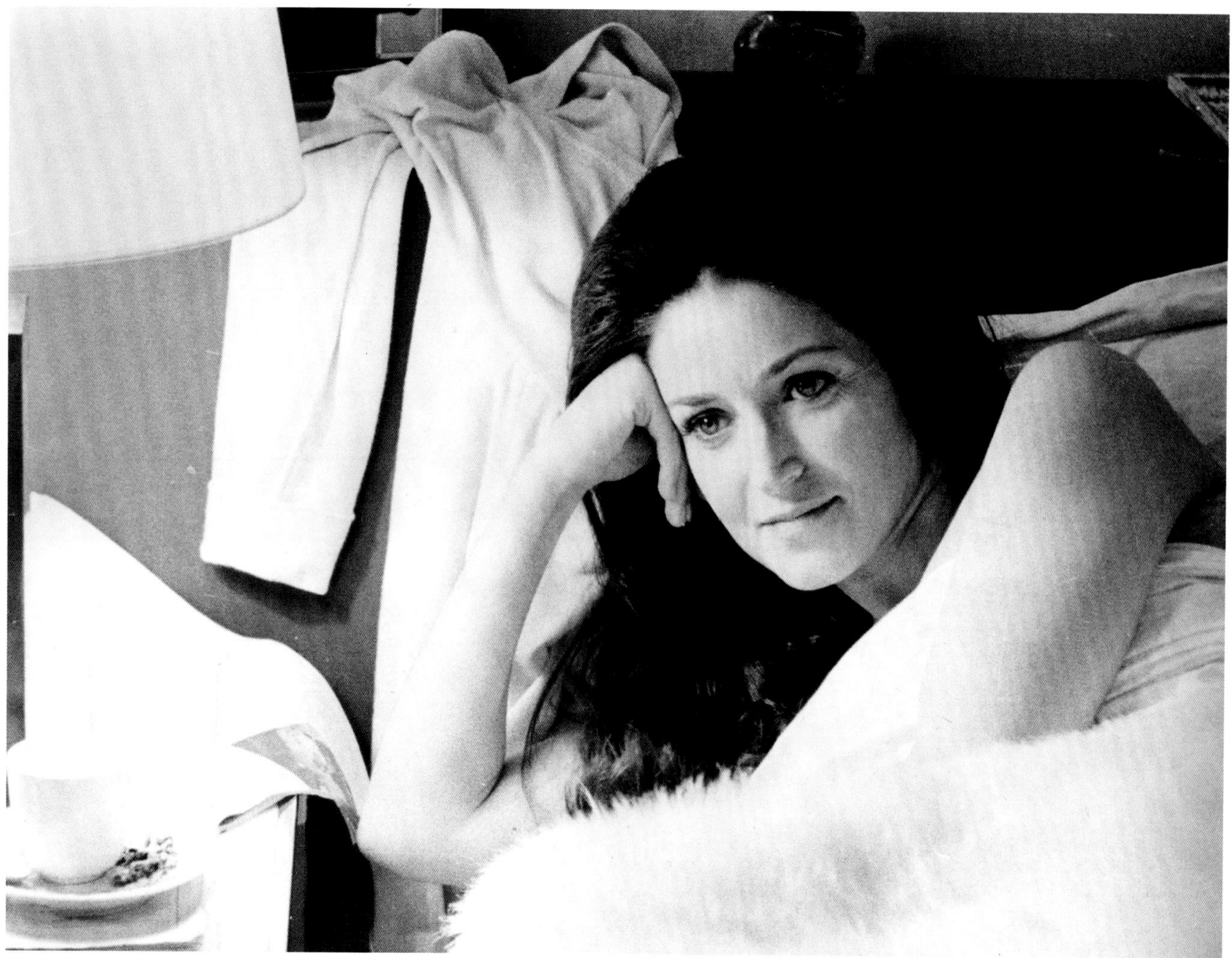

The context of *Ma nuit chez Maud* was therefore a very different one from that of the beginning of the New Wave. It is perhaps no surprise then that one of its strongest female roles came about in such a climate. More surprising, perhaps, is that it appeared in the filmography of one of the most conservative directors. This independent woman not only occupies a central place in the film's title and narrative, she appears in a work by a (male) director known for his traditional Catholic views, even if his *mise en scène* was recognized for its modernity.

Rohmer, the former French literature professor and avowed Catholic, wrote his *Six contes moraux*, we recall, first as literary texts that he claimed were always meant to be adapted to the screen. The heroines of the series evolved as the films progressed. Suzanne in his first as well as Sylvie and Jacqueline in *La Boulangère* are teenagers, still undefined. Though the next two films were made out of order, Haydée, a young modern woman finding her way, has more agency, while Maud, a thirtysomething divorcée from the haute bourgeoisie, is fully independent. Working as a pediatrician in Clermont-Ferrand, Maud is also a mother raising an eight-year-old daughter. This liberated heroine allows Rohmer to explore the many tensions in French society in 1969: the shifting role of Catholicism, marriage, and women's autonomy.

Though he wrote the initial text long before meeting Françoise Fabian, Rohmer claimed that when he was ready to make the film, he wrote the role with only her in mind.

Françoise Fabian (Maud) in Éric Rohmer's *Ma Nuit chez Maud* (*My Night at Maud's*), 1969

In fact, according to Fabian, after seeing her perform on stage, Rohmer approached her, put the script of *Ma nuit chez Maud* on her makeup table, and declared, "I'm making this film next year. I wrote it for you. If you don't do it, I'm not going to make it."[1] Truffaut had already alerted Fabian about Rohmer's intentions while driving her home after her performance in the play *La Puce a l'oreille*. "There's a director who wrote a film for you called *Ma nuit chez Maud*," she recalled him saying, "you absolutely have to do it, Françoise, it's extraordinary and he's a very important director!" Known for refusing more projects than she accepted, after reading the script, she agreed. Her agent warned her against it: "What a crazy idea to do a film in black and white on Pascal's wager, you're completely nuts." Like the character she would portray, Fabian was strong-willed. "I'm doing it," she insisted, later explaining, "because it's so intelligent, so particular, personal, deep, and it wasn't like anything else."[2]

The strange script, she recalled, began with "pages of math, of Pascal, and [Catholic] Masses." Since Fabian was unfamiliar with his work, Rohmer held a private screening of *La Collectionneuse* for the two of them. Fabian was overjoyed. They started filming *Maud* at its end, shooting the epilogue sequence on the beach first. While waiting to shoot the rest of the film that winter, Rohmer summoned Fabian to his small movie theater and showed her the edited ending, saying, as she recalled, "You see? Maud is you. I have nothing more to tell you. Maud belongs to you."[3]

Rohmer's intuition held true. Françoise Fabian fused with Maud to make her one of the most unforgettable heroines of the New Wave. Strong and charming like her character, Fabian was also fiercely independent and determined even as a young woman. "I was never afraid of anything," she related in a 2018 interview, looking back on her career. "I was wrong but I was never really afraid of life and what it could offer me."[4]

During her early life in Algiers, Fabian studied piano at a conservatory but attended a drama course one day with her first boyfriend. In spite of her horrible stage fright, she read a poem by Baudelaire, and the drama teacher thought she had talent. "It's thanks to Baudelaire that I'm here," Fabian once remarked. The teacher gave her drama lessons and later asked Fabian's father if he would allow his daughter to go to Paris so that she could audition for the Conservatoire. Fabian gave credit to her "marvelous parents" for letting her go, "even if my mother cried a whole year at the thought of her daughter being all alone in Paris."

There she found freedom and pursued her passion. "I liked the bistros and smoked my first cigarettes and walked around in the streets," she recalled. Although she was part of the "Bande du conservatoire," (the "Conservatoire Gang") that included Belmondo, Jean-Pierre Marielle, Claude Rich, Bruno Crémer, and Annie Girardot, Fabian described the period as joyous but very lonely. "I was very poor and very alone. . . . I went home to a *chambre de bonne* and crummy hotels. I worked a lot and understood what being alone was. I discovered Paris and life."[5] As a perk of belonging to the Conservatoire, Fabian was able to attend plays at the Comédie-Française and the Théâtre national populaire (TNP) for free, where she saw the renowned director Jean Vilar directing Jeanne Moreau, Gérard Philipe, and Philippe Noiret, and heard the music of Maurice Jarre.

After the Conservatoire, she worked in the theater. Thanks to her first play, directed by Raymond Castans, Fabian made contacts with the cinema world. "All of *Paris Match* came to see the play, including Roger Vadim," who worked at the popular magazine, Fabian related. One night, after the show, a photographer from *France-Soir* suggested Fabian go see Pierre Lazareff, the head of the newspaper. Displaying tremendous courage, the young Fabian called his secretary and landed a meeting with him, one of the most powerful men of Paris. When they met, she was even bolder, telling him, "I'm a student at the Conservatoire and I'd like to do theater, but I'm unknown. My mother said in order to do theater, you have to be known, so I wanted you to talk about me." Lazareff appreciated her nerve. After going to see her in the play, he gave her publicity in his newspaper. "Then it began," she explained, "a chain of events, photos, cinema." Vadim recommended her for a supporting role in a film for which he wrote the script, *Cette sacrée gamine* (*Naughty Girl*, 1956), directed by Michel Boisrond and starring Brigitte Bardot.

During her next chapter, Fabian married the director of *Casque d'or* and *Touchez pas au grisbi*, Jacques Becker, twenty-five years her senior and part of the older generation of filmmakers (but much revered by the New Wave). Though they had many projects planned together, none of them were realized because of Becker's premature death only three years after their marriage. Fabian, however, persevered. Dreaming of working with Buñuel, she managed to land the small role of a prostitute in *Belle de Jour* (1967)—even if the director did not think she fit the part. Fabian was determined. She gained nine kilos (twenty pounds) for the role and secured fifteen days' worth of work. "It's the first time I insisted with a director for a role," she explained. Her persistence paid off and that role opened another door. "[It] was in this film that Rohmer saw me and he told me: 'When I saw you, I said to myself, that is Maud.'"[6] Five years later, Buñuel also offered her a part in *Le Charme discret de la bourgeoisie*—"a great role," she said, but she turned it down because producer Serge Silberman refused to pay her.

Like her character in *Maud*, Fabian enjoyed friendships with intelligent and cultivated men, among them André Bazin, Erich von Stroheim, and later Éric Rohmer. Before shooting *Maud*, Fabian and Rohmer developed a deep friendship as they met and held long discussions similar to those of the characters in the film. "We had a lot of fun," Fabian said. "We went at least once a month to Lipp [the famous Parisian brasserie] to have lunch. We were there until closing, and we talked about everything. We didn't talk about the film. We talked about religion, love, women, life, cinema, everything, so that when we started the film, our conversation continued."[7]

It is easy to see why Rohmer wanted Fabian for the role of Maud, one that he wrote and imagined as an established and alluring adult woman—rare in the filmography of the director known for his portrayals of *jeunes filles*. Here, Fabian plays a woman who is, in her words, "comfortable with her solitude," and one who asserts her desire—another rare trait in Rohmer's heroines. At the time of its release, Fabian stated that she considered this her first cinematic role: "It's the first time I've been given the chance to play a character like that who is tailored for me, because I never had the physical features of a young girl. I always looked sort of like a woman. . . . For the first time, I was given a role of a woman . . . She's a woman who's completely exposed with her problems, and on top of that, it's an important role."[8]

DEFYING ARCHETYPES IN *MA NUIT CHEZ MAUD*

Against the blonde ideal of Françoise (Marie-Christine Barrault), Maud appears as the dark-haired temptress. Before even meeting Françoise, the narrator (Jean-Louis Trintignant) has already declared (to himself), at first sight, that he will marry her. Maud then is liable to make him stray from his path of conviction (and convention). As in all Rohmer's *contes*, the core of *Ma nuit chez Maud* consists of a male protagonist who must choose between two women who represent two types: the elusive, cerebral blonde and the sensual, available brunette (like Sylvie and Jacqueline in *La Boulangère*). In the other *contes*, the brunettes were usually also of a lower social class and considered inferior in the eyes of the narrator. In *Maud*, according to Rohmer's *mise en scène*, it is quite the opposite.

Unlike the women in the temptress category from the other films, Maud is more ambiguous, not fitting in the clearly defined black-and-white model. The narrator's long-lost friend, Vidal, a philosophy professor at the university, paints a portrait that builds her up and creates intrigue before she appears on screen: "Maud is a remarkable woman, as you'll see. There aren't many like her. You'll love her—and she you! . . . She lives a rather secluded life since her divorce, maybe because she doesn't feel at ease in her own crowd. She's a doctor, a pediatrician. So was her husband, in fact—a professor at the university who's transferred down south to Montpellier. Maud—Maud's a *very* beautiful woman."[9] She is also from a higher social class, and from one of the "biggest families of free-thinkers in central France," according to Vidal. She has a respectable position as a doctor, appears extremely cultivated and mature, and is independent—a single mother raising her young child (Fabian's own daughter) alone. In sum, she is much more interesting than the narrator's vision of his blonde ideal (who is as yet undeveloped). Rohmer, therefore, unmasks his protagonist's own construc-

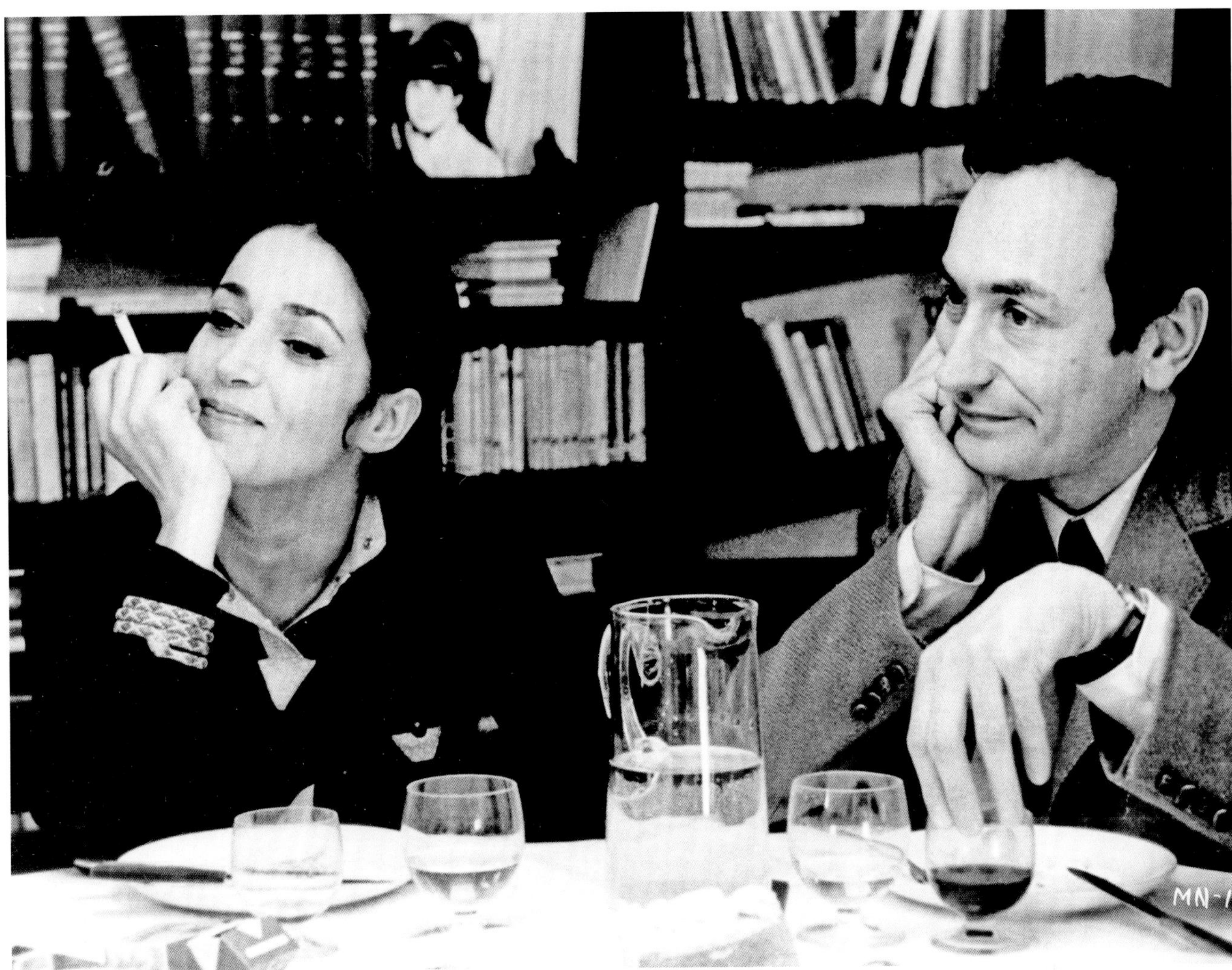

Françoise Fabian (Maud) and Antoine Vitez (Vidal) discuss Pascal's wager in Éric Rohmer's *Ma Nuit chez Maud* (*My Night at Maud's*), 1969

tions of women, as Maud is intriguing, appealing, respected . . . and, perhaps, a threat. Divorced and an atheist, she does not correspond to his self-imposed category of women suitable for marriage. The woman he claims to love is a pure prefabricated image in his mind. He even states several times in the film that "elle n'existe pas" ("she doesn't exist"). In alignment with courtly love, she is the idea of the distant, unattainable *dame*, embedded in French culture since the troubadours. The unknown woman he spots at church incarnates her perfectly. Young, blonde, and Catholic, Françoise is his ideal before they have even met.

The context of the encounter is key. When the narrator finally meets Maud, it is at her bourgeois apartment. He and Vidal are greeted at the door by Maud's maid, which already signals the hostess's high social class. Making her entrance through a door leading into the living room, as if on a theater stage, Maud is the center of attention, showcased through multiple framed "portraits," shot by cinematographer Nestor Almendros (whom Fabian also greatly admired). From their interactions before dinner, Maud establishes herself as a free-thinker before her "friend" Vidal explicitly states it. We learn that they were lovers while not romantically entangled, like the libertines of centuries past. Maud smokes cigarettes and lounges on the chair next to Vidal as they assume postures similar to those of other libertine figures in Rohmer's collection, like Adrien and Daniel of *La Collectionneuse*. Maud and Vidal act almost as reference points from which the narrator seeks to distinguish himself as a devout Catholic (even if the identity is more aspirational than accurate). During dinner, the three debate ideas that lead to a discussion of seventeenth-century philosopher Blaise Pascal and his famous wager—the concept of betting on the existence of God in order to gain eternal life as opposed to denying it and losing everything. Their discussion sets up the plot within the film. The narrator applies Pascal's wager to love, betting everything on Françoise, his ideal, while resisting the temptation to pursue a relationship with Maud, a free-thinker who, in his mind, will lead him astray.

The relaxed intellectual discussions in Maud's apartment recall a time in France when women of a certain social class enjoyed a rare moment of power. As Maud moves to change into her nightclothes before settling into her sheepskin-covered bed in the middle of her living room, she invites the men to stay so they can continue their conversation, "like the Précieuses who held salons in the seventeenth century," she says with a sly smile. When Vidal leaves, the narrator's "test" begins. Although Maud insists that he stay, under the pretext of avoiding the icy roads, the narrator hesitates. His obvious attraction to Maud creates a conflict in his already made-up mind: He is betting everything on marrying the unknown blonde, like in Pascal's wager. In order to protect himself from his own desire, and, in his mind, from the tempting Maud (who has already shed her nightgown, preferring to sleep in the nude), the narrator wraps himself in a fur cover.

In the discreetly comical scene, the narrator, bound in animal skins, prepares to spend the night in the armchair next to Maud's bed. Uncomfortable, he finally moves to the bed where he remains on top of the covers until the warmth of her bedspread beckons him. The iconic image of Maud and the narrator lying side by side during their chaste night directly signals, as we saw, the story of Tristan and Isolde, where the two mythical lovers spend the night separated by Tristan's sword. Our narrator, however, must face his own inner conflict, his own ambivalence. Though he gets into bed with Maud, he pushes her away when she starts to reciprocate. She gets up, and he runs after her, provoking her to end his indecisive (dishonest?) behavior: "I like people who know what they want," she says firmly as she pushes him

away. As he leaves her apartment, the film's title suddenly becomes ironic.

FRANÇOISE FABIAN'S ENDURING PORTRAIT OF INDEPENDENCE

The narrator continues to delude himself. After resisting temptation during their night together, he claims he is not in love with Maud. His *mauvaise foi*, or bad faith, is clearly reflected in the *mise en scène*. After spending the day with her, sharing an obvious rapport, the narrator tells Maud, "It's crazy how well we get along," adding that he feels comfortable and "at home" with her. And yet, he still claims that they do not go together. It is this double vision that sets Rohmer apart from more mainstream directors; he reveals the narrator's bad faith on screen by showing the gap between the protagonist's actions and words. Rohmer's camera reveals the truth while his narrator lies to himself. In *La Boulangère*, the narrator walked the streets incessantly, looking for Sylvie to appear suddenly at every street corner, trying to provoke fate. In *Maud*, he stalks the elusive Françoise in his car, and, when she appears, he wants to believe it is destiny.

Rohmer, a step removed from his protagonist, exposes perhaps deeper tensions at work in French society as it grapples with women's emerging power. The film's narrator is torn between the idea of a woman he wants to marry, influenced by his strict Catholic principles, and his repressed desire for a more complex, *real* woman. In *Maud*, Rohmer diverges from the more disparate categories of ideal versus real found in his other *contes* (the bourgeois chosen one against the working-class temptress). Here, the portrait of Maud emphasizes her intelligence and upper-class background, while that of Françoise is more realistic, complex and flawed beneath her perfect image. The *mise en scène* exposes what the narrator wants to hide from himself: Françoise, the Catholic good girl who does not smoke or drink, confesses she had a lover, who was also a married man. She says she was "crazy for him." The narrator, trying to find a justification, says that he respects her even more for her honesty. He confesses that he too has been with many women and had just spent the night with "someone" (who turns out to be Maud) the day he met her. They both choose to preserve the surface image of convention, making a pact never to speak of all this again.

In the epilogue, five years later, Maud, the narrator, and his now-wife Françoise, accompanied by their child, run into each other at the beach by chance. Taken aback, the narrator tells Françoise about his night at Maud's, calling it his "dernière escapade," his last fling, after realizing that Françoise's married lover was in fact Maud's husband. With Rohmer's *mise en scène* unveiling to the narrator in the end that both women are equally complex, the categories implode to reveal two *real* women. In the powerful open ending, Rohmer shows how an entire life can be constructed on a convenient lie, ignoring the truth that would call into question the idealized image of his (bourgeois Catholic) marriage. The viewer also witnesses, through their exchanged look, a silent acknowledgement of a certain truth—about their night together, about Françoise, about the narrator's failings and repressed regret? Perhaps. Through Maud's unspoken nod and half smile, we can imagine her view of a man who could not let himself be free. In the end, Maud is fine. She is the last man standing, so to speak, in Rohmer's hall of mirrors and one of his strongest, most fascinating heroines.

When asked in a recent interview if she had stage fright while making her entrance in the first scene as this important character, Fabian replied, "No, because Rohmer gave me such confidence in myself, presenting the end of the film to me, saying, 'I have nothing more to tell you. Maud is yours.' You can't give a gift like that to an actress. It's extremely rare. So, I was at home. It was easy, natural. It was like in life."[10] If we think of Preminger's notorious ill treatment of Jean Seberg, we can see here the benefit of a good director/actor relationship—and its result on screen. Fabian described her fellow actors' pleasure in playing together: "It was a delight and we felt loved. We weren't risking anything."[11]

Rohmer's desire for control over the actors' dialogue and delivery, however, was unquestionable. "He wanted the text to be known with razor-sharp precision. He'd even marked the breaths," Fabian stated. True to her nature, Fabian protested; she wanted to breathe where she wanted! Rohmer agreed: "He was very understanding. We had a marvelous man with us." True to the New Wave philosophy, the film was shot in bare-basics conditions, on a shoestring budget, with everyone contributing: "It's funny because there was no money. We were shooting in a little studio, rue du Sabot, that wasn't finished and the concrete was still wet. We had to paint a little. There were four of five of us: [Emmanuel] Machuel at the camera, Almendros, two assistants, the director and us, that's it. It was very meager." Enjoying a rare close relationship with the reserved Rohmer, Fabian revealed a hidden side to the director: "When we were at the beach, for example—he was champion of France in the eight-hundred-meter [race]—I didn't know. He was so discreet he never talked about it. He was in shorts. But we'd place the camera and he'd run eight hundred meters on the beach and come back. I said, 'You have legs like a dancer at the Lido.' He turned beet red. And in Brittany, we went to a club and danced rock 'n' roll."

Rohmer's intuition about Fabian held true, and the actress's bet on this low-budget film with an unconventional story paid off. Françoise Fabian was Maud, and her performance meant that afterward she would be taken seriously and noticed all over the world. Although the film was booed at the Cannes Film Festival at its release in 1969—"a catastrophe," the actress recalled—it went on to receive numerous awards and much attention. Stanley Kubrick and Sydney Pollack watched the film over and over, the actress reported. According to Fabian, however, her role in another film particularly struck the American director: "Every time I see Pollack, he tells me: 'I remember you less in *Ma nuit chez Maud* than in *La Bonne année*.'"[12]

Inspired by her performance in *Maud*, Claude Lelouch asked Fabian to be in his next film, *La Bonne année* (*Happy New Year*, 1973), before he had even written the script.[13] After his success with *Un homme et une femme*, where Anouk Aimée played a woman struggling to overcome her grief after her husband's death to start a new life, Lelouch imagined Fabian in a similar role. She is "a woman who has a lot of scars who doesn't believe in anything anymore," the director declared.[14] Fabian would play an elegant bourgeoise who has "an unexpected love story with a man she doesn't know," the actress described. "Because her culture didn't predispose her to meeting this type of man," Lelouch explained, it is "an encounter between two universes that weren't predisposed to meeting."[15] In effect, much like the encounter between Moreau's sophisticated married woman and her working-class lover in *Les Amants*, Lelouch pairs Fabian's character with a charismatic gangster played by Lino Ventura.

Though her character was inspired by her role in *Maud*, that of an independent, mature woman, some scenes in *La Bonne année* seemed to parody Rohmer's film. A dinner scene, for example, in which the characters talk about philosophy after coming from church, portrays her intellectual friends as annoying, reflecting most likely Lelouch's own disdain for the intelligentsia. At its core, however, is the portrait of a strong, beautiful adult woman, the kind Lelouch does best, reflecting the mainstream's desire to see women in these roles. According to Fabian, it conveyed a positive message: to keep living. "That was rather modern," she explained, "that is to say that women too could have a life and keep living while their husband wasn't there. It's an intelligent, modern, revolutionary woman . . . that's what I liked about it too."[16]

LA MAMAN ET LA PUTAIN: AFTER THE DREAM OF MAY '68

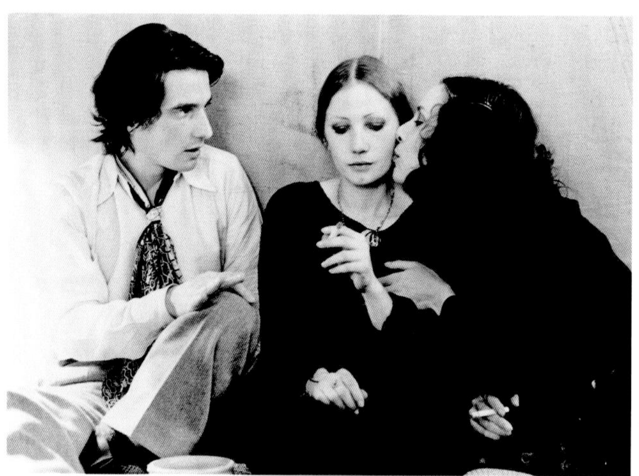

Jean-Pierre Léaud (Alexandre), Françoise Lebrun (Véronika), and Bernadette Lafont (Marie) in Jean Eustache's *La Maman et la putain* (*The Mother and the Whore*), 1973

Like the New Wave movement itself, May '68 in France represented a desire for change and a dream of new beginnings—a break with the old ways of filming in 1959, a rupture with outdated social norms a decade later. After the steady shifts in society and cinema in the years leading up to the seismic explosion of May '68, relationships between women and men were further destabilized. With emerging feminism, society grappled with new roles and new rights for women. While women slowly gained agency, men struggled with women's new demands. What began as a utopian dream brought disillusionment. There was no quick fix.

In the years after, cinema dealt with the fallout. In 1973, Jean Eustache, a direct descendent of the New Wave directors, produced the monumental *La Maman et la putain* (*The Mother and the Whore*). In the autobiographical epic, lasting over three hours and forty minutes, we wander through the streets and bedrooms of Paris in the aftershock of May '68 with characters that hold traces of cinema's New Wave dream and ones that reflect France's new reality.

The ambiance feels like the calm *after* the storm. An almost-thirty-year-old Jean-Pierre Léaud as Alexandre awakens in a dark bedroom surrounded by records—from Charles Trenet to *Don Giovanni*. When his alarm rings, he wakes up suddenly and looks at the clock, "as if while sleeping, he hadn't stopped thinking of his alarm," the script specifies. To a viewer in 1973, Léaud still holds traces of Antoine Doinel, who woke up to adulthood in *Antoine et Colette* in a similar scene, and of an edgier character in Godard's *Masculin féminin* (*Masculine Feminine*, 1966) who is caught in a similar scenario between two women and spends his time frequenting Parisian bistros and discussing politics. Here, Léaud is a mix of the two. Next to him in bed is Bernadette Lafont, who inaugurated the New Wave as a young woman on a bicycle in Truffaut's *Les Mistons*, a femme fatale in Chabrol's *Le Beau Serge*, and shop girl dreaming of a more fulfilling life in *Les Bonnes femmes*. Together, the couple incarnates French New Wave cinema from its beginnings, waking up to a new reality.

Alexandre gets out of bed quietly, trying not to awaken Marie (Lafont) before he goes out. Lafont reappears on screen this time as an older woman, playing Alexandre's "mother"/lover. Once outside in the street, the protagonist sees the young woman he was waiting for, his recent ex-girlfriend Gilberte (Isabelle Weingarten, who herself holds traces of Robert Bresson's cinema, having appeared in his 1971 film *Quatre nuits d'un rêveur*, or *Four Nights of a Dreamer*). Alexandre tells her he is there to sit in on one of her classes. She refuses, saying it bothers her: "It's the first week of class. I'm not very sure of myself." Gilberte as a young professor represents experiences of women in this new era, on their way to empowerment but still a bit insecure in the role. Alexandre is lost in his heartbreak after losing her. Trying in vain to get her back, he talks at her incessantly with no room to hear her rebuttal or her thoughts. Again, traces of Godard and Rohmer's early comical short *Tous les garçons s'appellent Patrick* come to mind, with Brialy's Patrick assailing the girl in Luxembourg Garden with a barrage of questions, trying to persuade her to go out with him. Alexandre's discourse is filled with sensual *blason*-type descriptions of her: "I love your skin. One forgets. I love your neck. In the years we spent together, I progressively forgot your face, the impression that you made on me the first time. You just had to leave for me to find it again inside me, intact, just like the first day." We are no longer in the excitement of beginnings, but in nostalgia for what once was, in society as in cinema. His words are that of mourning: "It's funny. I haven't stopped suffering. I didn't hang on to you but to my suffering. I tried to hold on to it to keep you near me. To keep us. The day that I get over it, as you say, that I no longer suffer, I will be another person. And I don't want to become another person because that day, we will not be able to get back together."[17]

After returning home, Alexandre hears Marie coming in from buying groceries. Instead of the cliché love triangle, compartmentalizing wife and lover, the couple represents a new open attitude in defining relationships. Besides her maternal role in her lover's life, Marie also provides a paycheck (she owns a dress shop) and affords him the freedom to pursue other women. When she asks him if he met anyone while he was out, he tells her, "Yes, I flirted with a girl this afternoon. I decided not to tell you, to keep something to myself. It's funny, I can't hide anything from you."

Marie: Did it work? Is she pretty? What did you do?
Alexandre: Nothing. I just asked her for her number.
Marie: You didn't even have a drink?
Alexandre: No, nothing. It lasted twenty seconds.
Marie: Are you going to call her?
Alexandre: Yes. Unless I change my mind.
Marie: Tell me, will you introduce me to her?
Alexandre: Yes, if she's worth it.

Marie goes back into the kitchen. When Alexandre asks her what she is doing, she replies, "I'm doing the dishes that you don't do." After addressing this inequality, Marie kisses him, excusing him of his duties: "I love you, you know, *vieux con* [you old bastard]." The aftershock of May '68 shows up here as a mix of free love and traditional roles for women in terms of domestic responsibilities that did not budge. When they look to see what is showing at the movies, however, Alexandre asks if she wants to see Elio Petri's *La classe operaia va in paradiso* (*The Working Class Goes to Heaven*, 1971), a political Italian film denouncing the servitude of the working-class condition and implying the cause's demise.

FREE LOVE, EMPTINESS, AND VÉRONIKA'S FINAL CONFESSION

The aftermath also shows up in Alexandre's discourse. With Gilberte, he addresses it directly, linking May '68 with the outcome of their breakup: "You started living again without anxiety gripping you. You're at peace. You think you're getting back on your feet while in reality, little by little, you're getting used to mediocrity. After crises you have to forget everything quickly, erase it. Like France after the occupation, like France after May '68. You're getting back on your feet like France after '68, my love. Do you remember? We said that we'd barely escaped, that we'd been lucky to have a childhood and we weren't sure that our children would have one in this new world where seventeen-year-olds are old men."

When he runs into a friend in a café who tells him of her suicide attempt, he speaks to her of relationships and death, linking personal loss and betrayal with world events: "Every time a girl lives with a guy, she drops everything. She probably feels like it's a renaissance, a new beginning. Giving yourself to only one man, you steal from all the others, and I'm not just talking about sexual things. I'm persuaded that what's happened in the world these past years is totally directed against me. There was the cultural revolution, May '68, the Rolling Stones, long hair, the Black Panthers, the Palestinians, not one film, nothing, nothing in style. Pop music became religious. And I only like popular music, Mozart, the Stones, Édith Piaf. Speaking of, I have some good news. You know Ferrand, the guy I hated. He died. Just like that—in his prime. [Laughs.] He did me wrong. And then he married the girl who'd gone out with me. I noticed that people who'd done me wrong, it never brought them luck."[18]

With Véronika (Françoise Lebrun, Eustache's former girlfriend whom Gilberte represented in the film), he speaks of women: "You know in general I like people, women, for external reasons mainly, reasons that have nothing to do with them, placed on them like a bathrobe, a coat that could be put on another woman. I like a woman, for example, because she played in a Bresson film [a reference to Weingarten], or because a man I admire is in love with her. What greater homage can we make to a man we admire than to take his wife?" After his rambling, he tells Véronika that if what he is saying bothers her, they can talk about something else, "small talk or the MLF." When she asks what that is, Alexandre replies, "You don't know? It's the Women's Liberation Movement. It's women who are tired of bringing their husbands breakfast in bed. So, they revolt. They have a slogan: 'We don't need men anymore under our quilts,' or something like that." Véronika replies that it is sad: "When I love someone, I like bringing them breakfast in bed,"[19] blurring the message of the women's movement.

Complicating the characters even more, Lebrun plays the part of Eustache's real-life lover/mistress, Véronika, *la putain*, a label assigned with a note of implied irony. Settling the score, when Alexandre tells Véronika the story of his genuine suffering after his rupture with Gilberte, it is Eustache's own story with Lebrun. Alexandre's desperate account in this scene translates deep emotion that confuses reality and fiction. He tells Véronika that he had been violent with Gilberte and describes blood on the walls and bandages on her face. Shattered after learning she had aborted their child, he tells Véronika that he would have preferred that she had killed herself, with an addendum articulating his reactionary views on the act itself: "And if you consider abortion a crime, I know dozens, a hundred assassins. And their accomplices."[20]

Véronika, a free-thinker and a proponent of free love, expresses openly that she has had many lovers. She also becomes friends with Marie, forming a new type of trio with Alexandre, recalling the *amour à trois* at the beginning of Truffaut's depiction of Jules, Jim, and Catherine. The threesome, however, is not free from feminine rivalry since Alexandre refuses to choose between them—a situation that recalls Varda's *Le Bonheur*—illustrating here the failure of the free love experiment. Unlike the wife in Varda's film, who silently tolerates her husband's love for another and then drowns in a lake, Marie voices, *exposes*, her suffering. She swallows pills in front of Alexandre and Véronika who then save her by making her throw up. We empathize with Marie and her feeling of loss after her lover's abandonment.

The devastating display of suffering all around in *La Maman et la putain* reaches its apogee in Véronika's lengthy final monologue in the penultimate scene, expelling all the tensions of the past decades. Extracting feminine desire from a long history of repression, she spews out her thoughts in graphic language, while also exposing the complexity of her experience of wanting freedom and wanting a child. Though her speech has been judged as reactionary, it is also revolutionary in its expression of stifled conflicts, with focused attention given to representing a woman's uncensored point of view on the matter. In close-up, with the camera focused on her face, Françoise Lebrun delivers one of the most transgressive discourses on screen with a visceral performance, and we witness the power of Véronika's emotions as she addresses Marie, Alexandre, and the audience.

"If people could understand once and for all that fucking is shit. That there's only one thing that's beautiful: It's fucking because we love each other so much that we'd want a child that looks like us and that otherwise, it's something sordid. You should only fuck when you love, really love each other,"

Véronika declares through tears. Claiming that she is telling Marie this because she "likes her a lot," she goes on to describe how many men desired her "because I had a big ass that is potentially desirable. I have very beautiful breasts that are very desirable. My mouth isn't bad either. When my eyes are made up, they're okay, too." Echoes of Bardot in *Le Mépris* resound in her lines, powerfully appropriating (and subverting) the cinematic *blason* in her discourse. "And lots of men desired me like that, you know, *dans le vide* [in emptiness]. And they often fucked me in emptiness," she continues. "They fucked me like a whore. But you know, I think that one day, a man will come who'll love me and make a baby with me, because he will love me. And love is only valid when you want to have a child together." Commenting on free love and their open relationship, she tells Marie and Alexandre that she is not reprimanding them for it: "My sadness is not a reproach, you know. It's an old sadness that has been dragging on for five years. You don't give a damn. Look at you two, you'll be great. How happy you'll be together."[21]

The scene ends suddenly on this dramatic note, suggesting that Véronika plans to leave the threesome. In the final sequence, however, after Alexandre drives Véronika home, she reveals that she may be pregnant with his child, and Alexandre, though his initial reaction is to make for his car, returns to her residence and proposes marriage. After answering yes, Véronika tells him: "I'm sick. I feel like throwing up. I'm going to throw up. Pass me a bucket, if you want to marry me, make yourself useful." After Alexandre gets it for her, she tells him to turn away, "I don't like it when people watch when I throw up." The film's final shot shows Alexandre sitting on the floor of her room seemingly in a state of resignation (or perhaps mere shock) while we hear Véronika vomiting incessantly just off screen—adding still more depth to her impassioned monologue and leaving the questions that May '68 posed for society unresolved.

Despite its surface misogyny in Alexandre's views against feminism, *La Maman et la putain* gave voice to four complex individuals, already a step forward even in the context of disappointment in the reality after the revolution. The dream of New Wave cinema, however, remained intact, expressing the most painful, personal story through its characters who held autobiographical and cinematic traces of the past. *La Maman et la putain* reached the epitome of an authenticity that cuts to the bone and pierces the soul, a testament to the power behind relationships that produce the greatest art.

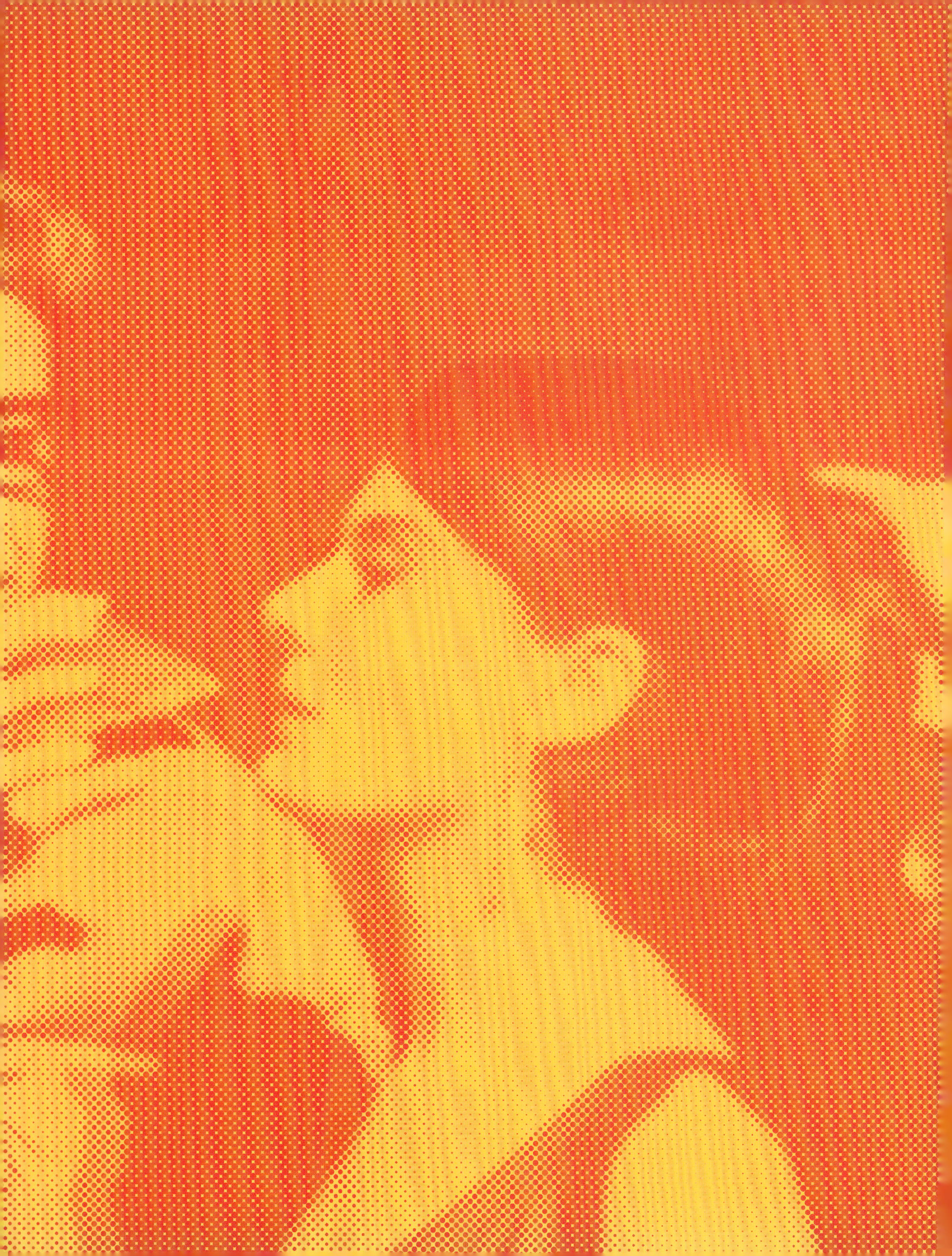

delphine seyrig 12

la femme en évolution | *the evolving woman*

BEIRUT, NEW YORK, PARIS: DELPHINE SEYRIG'S EARLY AWAKENING

Tracing Delphine Seyrig's trajectory from her iconic role in Resnais's *L'Année dernière à Marienbad* to her embodiment of Chantal Akerman's Jeanne Dielman and up through her feminism and work as a director illustrates, in parallel, a more general evolution of women in film.

In a 1976 *New York Times* article titled "She Looked Good Being Passive, but . . . ," Judith Weinraub interviewed Seyrig at a period in her career when, as a woman, she made her voice heard, expressing self-awareness, in stark contrast to the passive heroine she played in *Marienbad*. Seyrig told the journalist, "I have a heavy past, having been an actress. It was way of seducing, of proving to myself that I could be accepted. But actresses are a commercial product. They represent the whole male-female problem seen with a microscope. They are agents of the male optic."[1] Her words indicate a growing awareness of the male gaze, which Mulvey had detailed just a year prior, and of the power dynamics within the director-actress relationship.[2]

Seyrig's story, chronicled in Mireille Brangé's comprehensive biography,[3] illustrates, perhaps more than any other, the transformative power of the encounter, and in her case, one leading to self-actualization. It also reflects Seyrig's own openness to new people, cultures, and art that in turn shaped her and allowed her to grow and find herself. This tendency most likely came naturally, having parents who were adventurous, rebellious, searching. Her father, Henri Seyrig—born in France to a high-society Protestant family who had hidden the German origin of their family name, Saurich—grew up in search of an identity. After serving in Greece during World War I, Henri came back a changed man, refusing to take over the family's textile business and instead enrolling at the Sorbonne. He then returned to Greece, obtaining a spot at L'École française d'Athènes and eventually a position as an archaeologist there. Hermine de Saussure, Delphine's mother, descended from a prestigious Protestant family as well; her uncle, Ferdinand de Saussure, was one of the founders of modern linguistics. An exceptionally free woman, Hermine, nicknamed "Miette," learned to sail and set off for Greece with a friend at age twenty-two. There she met Henri, who immediately fell in love with her. Though they stayed in contact, Miette continued her adventures, notably having a child out of wedlock with a Greek sailor. When she met Henri again, he proposed marriage (which would legitimize her son), and Hermine accepted under the condition that she retain "total freedom."[4]

From their union came Delphine Seyrig, born in 1932 in Beirut, where her father was director general of antiquities for Syria and Lebanon (both under French mandate). Seyrig rarely spoke of her first ten years in Lebanon, often evoking Beirut's "light" without mentioning specific events. One friend described her as being bored in the huge house with parents who were often absent and unaffectionate. With strict Protestant values, her father loved her but could not show it. Her mother was cold to her, favoring Delphine's brother Francis. "As a child, I became a prostitute—for affection," Seyrig stated. "At two and a half years old, girls have understood everything: what valorizes them in people's eyes and what depreciates them. So, they have to choose. Choose to be likable, gracious, attractive, thus loved. Or to rebel, . . . grow up turned inward and suffer horribly." Seyrig chose to fawn: "I realized right away I had to please and what you had to do to please."[5]

The mysterious smile—"that damned smile" as Akerman later called it—Seyrig often used in lieu of a verbal response surely originated from that early desire to please, keeping her feelings to herself. Defined by her Protestant education, her childhood was also marked by a year-long separation from her parents that she spent in a boarding school in France from 1939 to 1940. Her father relocated the family to New York City for work when Seyrig was ten, sending her to various East Coast boarding schools. It was at Miss Gill's School in New Jersey that she discovered theater, announcing to her mother that she wanted to be an actress. She started collecting photographs of her idols—Greta Garbo, Marlene Dietrich, Louise Brooks, Katharine Hepburn—studying their poses, makeup, and lighting as she weathered insecurity about her own looks, including her face and her hair, as well as her voice. Upon the family's return to Beirut in 1946 (so Henri could head the French Institute of Archaeology), Seyrig's perspective on the world changed, with a sudden awareness of economic and gender inequality. Repulsed by the looks boys started giving her, and traumatized by an incident in a theater with one of them that she could not speak about, she shut down and lost trust in everyone. At fifteen, she was given permission to study in France, after agreeing to follow her parents' wishes that she dedicate herself to art.

Already, we can see how these early experiences directed the rest of her life and forged her character. "I think all women are feminists from the day they are born," Seyrig once said. "But we each have different ways of surviving. Women are deeply insecure. Saying you're not a feminist doesn't mean you aren't one. You may be afraid of saying so because you're afraid of losing ground."[6] At boarding school far from Paris in Le Chambon-sur-Lignon (whose residents were Huguenots and Protestants like the Seyrigs), she was, in her words, "desirable and desired, . . . prettier, stranger than the others, [someone] who thought that was enough to conquer a place in the sun, and who refused all work, at school or elsewhere, . . . who thought that only two destinies awaited women: dishes or prostitution."[7]

Though she expressed that being an artist would allow her to escape the kind of bourgeois marriage that had taken many of her friends' freedom, she did not know which art to choose. At sixteen, she considered writing more than acting. "I thought: 'I'm going to be able to express myself and say everything I feel.' In fact, I was doubly fooled . . . I didn't even know what I felt and, instead of being myself, I only repeated like a parrot what other writers said."[8] Stendhal, Balzac, Proust, Hemingway, and Faulkner were those Seyrig read then, but joining her brother in Paris the next year, she also discovered de Beauvoir's *Le Deuxième sexe*. No longer wearing the Huguenot cross, she was defining her views but still in search of her vocation. She admired her brother's fiancée Nicole Ladmiral, who was studying acting and would go on to work with Robert Bresson on *Journal d'un cure de campagne* (*Diary of a Country Priest*, 1951) the next year, while Seyrig worked as an extra in a play.

In January 1950, she decided to devote herself to the theater. Among her first decisive encounters was with the actor Pierre Bertin, whom she met through the Compagnie Renaud-Barrault. Bertin saw something in the seventeen-year-old Seyrig (despite her bad reading of a scene by Molière). Working with her diligently and orienting her toward modern roles, Bertin also introduced her to Jean-Louis Barrault (renowned actor and cofounder of the troupe) and also an agent, saying, "She *has* to become a star, I'm sure of it."[9] Entry into Jean Vilar's TNP became Seyrig's ultimate goal, and she enrolled in the EPJD (L'Éducation Par le Jeu Dramatique), a drama school known to feed the TNP. Roger Blin, a professor there, noticed her immediately and worked with her on Chekhov's *The Seagull*, telling her, "You have nothing to fear: You are a seagull."[10] She returned the favor in 1952 by donating an inheritance she received from her uncle to save Blin's production of Samuel Beckett's *En attendant Godot*, a gesture Beckett would not forget.

Besides theater, Seyrig's personal life was significantly influenced by her mutual *coup de foudre* with American aspiring artist Jack Youngerman in the spring of 1950. By the summer they were married, and the two embarked on a life together pursuing their art. Seyrig attended Vilar's Festival d'Avignon, where Gérard Philipe's performances in *Le Cid* and *Le Prince*

de Hombourg (that Varda famously photographed) left her mesmerized. Through no lack of determination, the next ten years would be marked by constant struggle for Seyrig as well as her husband. She accepted work where she could get it, including at the provincial theater near Lyon in La Comédie de Saint-Étienne while her husband stayed in Paris. Still she struggled. Hurt by a remark during an audition that she "didn't speak loudly enough," she became more insecure about her voice. Unable to secure a spot in the TNP or to find work in Paris, she went a year without acting before going back to Saint-Étienne. She finally booked work in two plays in Paris—one postponed, the other a flop—and then landed roles in French productions of Oscar Wilde's *An Ideal Husband* and *Lady Windermere's Fan*, which Parisian critics found a bit dated but pleased the crowds nonetheless. Now pregnant, Seyrig continued auditioning and acting at night, wrapping her torso to conceal her condition. Responding to her friend Claudine Hermann's concern, she said, "Well, Coco, what do you want me to do? I'm playing the role of an ingénue."[11]

Acclimating to motherhood introduced more challenges, among them a permanent sense of guilt and responsibility. "It's a shock to bring up a child, it's a trauma, you know, it's traumatic," Seyrig expressed almost thirty years later. "I didn't know how to take care of him, I didn't know how to hold him, I had to learn all those things. The first day I came home with the baby, I remember hitting my head against the window because the baby was crying and cold and I didn't remember how to put a diaper on him. . . . And I cried, and I remember having gone to the window and hitting myself like that, thinking, 'He is too delicate, I can't touch this baby, I love him, but . . .' That was the first day." Six months after their son Duncan's birth, Seyrig and Youngerman traveled with him to New York City to start over. There, Seyrig attended Strasberg's Actors Studio as an auditor and hired James Dean's agent, Jane Deacy.

Despite this progress, Seyrig could not get roles, and she sank into a depression. She passed the time knitting items for her and Duncan, eventually accepting work as a switchboard operator and then as a fashion model. Though the Actors Studio had rejected her as a student twice, she made her film debut in the 1959 cult classic *Pull My Daisy*, a short based on Jack Kerouac's play *Beat Generation*. For her, the shoot was a nightmare, with the atmosphere on the set pushing her into a nervous breakdown.

But her luck soon changed. On a trip to New York City in November 1959, Alain Resnais, who had once crossed paths with Seyrig and Youngerman in Paris, went to see the actress perform in Henrik Ibsen's *An Enemy of the People*.[12] He had a new project in mind, *Harry Dickson*, and was considering her for a role. According to Seyrig, "he took pictures of me and then he went back to France."[13] But there would be more to the story. The two kept in touch through letters, and when Seyrig visited Paris in the spring of 1960, he asked if she could play a middle-aged woman in a script written by Jean Cayrol (a project that became *Muriel ou le temps d'un retour*). In the meantime, he began to develop the idea for the film that would become *Marienbad* with *nouveau roman* writer Alain Robbe-Grillet, who would later describe it as a "documentary of a statue." To Resnais, it was the story of an *amour fou* (a crazy love) and "a documentary on the mechanism of fascination"[14]—coinciding with his encounter with Seyrig, which, though it would long remain a secret, had also become romantic.

During Seyrig's time in Paris, Resnais had her do a screen-test for *Marienbad*. "[He] simply observed me," the actress described.[15] "[H]e was playing with a new instrument and didn't know all the notes. I sat down, lay down, got up, walked. . . . Leaving me totally free, he made me go further than I thought I could go in the end."[16] When Youngerman joined her in Paris, he found her transformed, and when she left for Los Angeles to fulfill part of a television contract, Resnais wrote to her every day about the film. The renowned lawyer Robert Badinter got her out of her television contract, and she joined Resnais to make *Marienbad*.

THE EXPERIMENTAL GENIUS OF SEYRIG AND RESNAIS

Resnais, who was trained in editing (and had worked with Varda on *La Pointe Courte*), had already experimented with short films, among them *Nuit et brouillard*, the respected documentary about memory and Nazi concentration camps. He

had become noteworthy for his first feature, *Hiroshima, mon amour*, whose aesthetic breakthroughs would soon earn him the title of father of cinematic modernity. In Europe, a new kind of cinema was confronting the dominant classic cinema: Godard, Bergman, Antonioni, and Resnais were experimenting with narrative form, creating new types of characters, and challenging cinematic time with innovative editing.

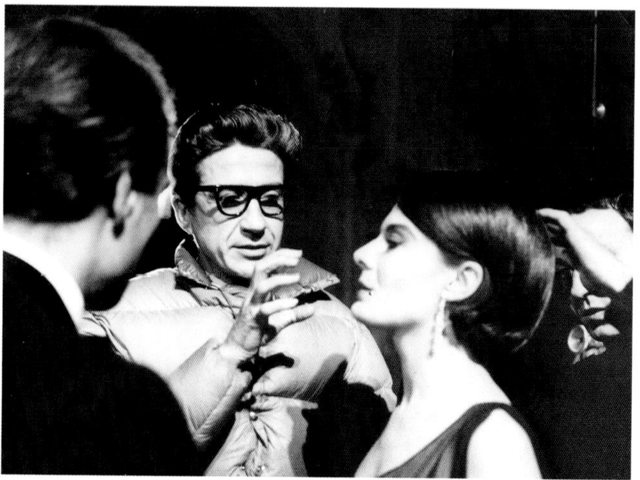

With Robbe-Grillet, Resnais continued on the path he began with Duras on *Hiroshima* but working in a very different way. Resnais and Robbe-Grillet worked separately. Confirming their same vision for the film beforehand, Robbe-Grillet wrote a meticulous, literary screenplay in which he described the scenes and shots, a "storyboard, not just script," as he called it. When Robbe-Grillet finished in mid-July 1960,[17] Resnais took the script and went to work making it into a film. With detached characters who seem to be made of stone, Resnais's second feature would center on a man's pursuit of a woman, driven by love to unearth human emotion in her, his elusive fantasy. Both trapped in a beautiful yet oppressive baroque château with other lifeless guests, the man differentiates himself from the others as being the only one with a point of view, consciousness, memory, and feeling. Trying to save the heroine and himself from social convention and a dehumanized world, the narrator seeks to awaken the woman from her internalized automatic gestures, remind her of their love story, and persuade her to escape the empty world in the static haute bourgeois prison where the story seems to begin again and again.

Alain Resnais and Delphine Seyrig on the set of *L'Année dernière à Marienbad* (*Last Year in Marienbad*), 1961

In August, back in France, Seyrig had changed; even her son noticed. Resnais and Seyrig spent a month preparing her character in the most minute detail, watching films together of Garbo and G.W. Pabst. Seyrig transformed herself: "It was a role for Grace Kelly, not for me," she declared. "I couldn't pretend to be A [her unnamed character]. . . . I was a person who had practically never set foot in a hair salon, never dressed elegantly, and . . . when I had to play that, I told myself: I have to transform from head to toe. . . . I really sought from the tip of my toe to the top of my head to be a *dame*, [a lady]."[18] Like Godard would later envision Karina in *Vivre sa vie*, Resnais wanted Seyrig to resemble Louise Brooks as Lulu in Pabst's *Die Büchse der Pandora* (*Pandora's Box*, 1929) in appearance and behavior.[19] He hired Coco Chanel to design her clothing, and "completely constructed this *femme rêvée* [dream woman] from her shoes to her coiffure on up to her makeup," Brangé described.[20] And yet, Seyrig did more than incarnate a dream woman. At the film's release, critic Raymonde Carasco acknowledged the actress's contribution, writing that Seyrig was in a sense "the third author" of the film.[21]

Like Riva's description of her work with Resnais, Seyrig said that *Marienbad* was very much a collaboration: "I didn't know what I was doing when I did *Marienbad*. It was a question of finding [it] together . . . It was not a question of explaining." For weeks before shooting, Seyrig and Resnais developed A together: "the shoes, the movements, the physical aspect and the psychology of the character." She based her style of movement on 1920s and '30s films, in which gestures "were made in a much more complete way," Seyrig explained. "If an actress had to turn around, she would go all the way around, look, and turn back." Her ideas helped give Resnais a direction: "He likes the actor to give him a choice and then he says, 'Ah, this is better, this is interesting.'"[22]

Robbe-Grillet recounted that his recorded voice guided the actors in their delivery of dialogue. "As he did for *Hiroshima*, Resnais recorded the voice of the writer. He recorded all the dialogue with my voice. I can recognize that voice in all the men," he stated, "but not in Seyrig." Robbe-Grillet confirmed that Resnais had the male actors listen to the re-cordings, but with Seyrig, "[h]e directed her personally and didn't make her listen to my voice. Although he scrupulously respected my writing while directing the film, Seyrig's character *is* Resnais."[23]

In her first serious film role,[24] Seyrig's appearance in a fixed pose, like a statue, at the beginning of *Marienbad* is also an interesting point of departure in terms of her cinematic evolution. She is imposing yet passive, an elegant automaton, frozen like the other figures in the society around her who repeat the same phrases and gestures without will. The narrator X (Giorgio Albertazzi) claims he had an affair with the unknown woman (Seyrig's character, A) in a place like Marienbad, though she denies (or cannot remember) that it ever took place. Another character, M, who may or may not be A's husband, is constantly laying out matchsticks to play what is portrayed as a mysterious mathematical game (Nim) in which he—fate, God, society's rules—always wins, though in the end, the woman leaves with the narrator, "losing herself, forever, in the peaceful night, alone with [him]."[25] The narrative blends memory, fantasy, and dreams to convey an experience of reality that the viewer can never decipher—though it continues to provoke an avalanche of interpretations.

To film *Marienbad*, Seyrig disappeared to Germany, leaving no notice for her husband. She would go on to separate from him, and the couple would later divorce. The shoot lasted fifty-nine days, from September to November, taking place in cold Bavarian palaces—Nymphenburg, Schleissheim, Amalienburg and Munich's Residenz—then completed in a Paris studio. But when it was finished, the experimental film was so disconcerting that it was not released. The film's fragmented narrative presented a strange new aesthetic. From the opening scene, audiences were taken aback by cinematographer Sacha Vierny's tracking shots of long corridors, halls, and ceilings of the baroque palace with a voice-over of the narrator whispering obsessive, *nouveau roman*-style descriptions of the décor.[26] Seyrig in *Marienbad* was also at the exact opposite end of the spectrum of Brigitte Bardot's free-spirited spontaneity and Jean Seberg's nonchalant and independent gamine. Seyrig appeared as the ultimate image of chic elegance dressed in Chanel.[27]

Resnais and Robbe-Grillet organized private screenings for influential people in hopes it would be selected at Cannes. Sartre, Alberto Giacometti, Antonioni, and Cocteau were among them. Surrealist André Breton, to whom the film was originally dedicated, was the only one who disliked it. Finally, *Marienbad* was released in Paris in June and was selected at the last minute for the Venice Film Festival in September 1961. Fiercely applauded, it won the Golden Lion for best picture. Resnais stated that at least half of the award belonged to Seyrig. The film signaled the "mort du cinéma de papa" that Robbe-Grillet had called for.[28] After receiving this award, *Marienbad* became a must-see.

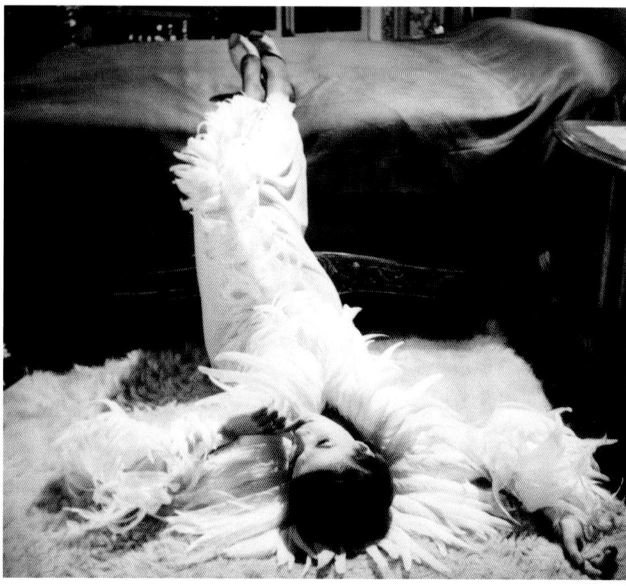

More than a critique of bourgeois society, the film's intentionally ambiguous open ending engendered many theories about its meaning. Some saw it as a fable of the nuclear age, similar to those of Bergman, Antonioni, and Godard, addressing anxieties caused by the threat of a nuclear bomb.[29] To feminist scholars, the reluctance of A to go along with X's version of the story and her denial illustrate the repression of a traumatic event (rape and sexual violence). According to this reading, her refusal to accept his story along with sudden flashes of memory as she goes near the bedroom show that she cannot openly acknowledge the trauma.

Interestingly, according to Seyrig, there was supposed to be an actual rape scene that both she and Resnais did not want to

do—"the one thing on which [Resnais and Robbe-Grillet] didn't agree."[30] By replacing it with flashes of white, Resnais wove in ambiguity, leaving the scene more open to interpretation.

Robbe-Grillet explained in an interview that it is the story of a persuasion, how X is trying to persuade A to escape the constraints of a bourgeois prison through love. The film should be approached, according to the scenarist, through affect and emotion instead of trying to analyze or interpret it. The idea of a man seeking to rescue—awaken—his love interest is not new. It is the basis of many fairy tales, notably *Sleeping Beauty*. In *Marienbad*, the narrator's goal of unearthing emotion—saving her through love—also anticipates Godard's *Alphaville*, with Lemmy Caution trying to rescue Karina's Natacha von Braun from an alienated society that has erased free thought, emotion, poetry, and love. In the first part of *Marienbad*, the story is told from the narrator's point of view, but in the second, a shift occurs that includes the woman's perspective. Like at the end of *Alphaville*, the heroine's façade starts to crack as her humanity is awakened. Though *Marienbad* is more subtle in form, with Seyrig's character at last leaving the hotel—and in doing so, choosing humanity—we are not far from Pygmalion or from *Alphaville*, which ends with Natacha pronouncing the words: "Je vous aime" ("I love you").

Marienbad's second assistant director Volker Schlöndorff described the film as a cold but real love story, *un travail d'amour* (a labor of love), and a "great declaration of love from Alain Resnais to Delphine Seyrig, and from all of us to the cinema. Never were we so lost on a shoot, and never were we so enthusiastic because we had the impression that we were reinventing cinema."[31] Seyrig later described the film's personal significance in practical terms: "*Marienbad* was very important for me because afterwards I could work and before I couldn't find any work."[32] Like her character in the film, Seyrig had also started to awaken.

Though the role redeemed her as an actress, Seyrig will forever be associated with her sophisticated image in *Marienbad*. With her affected presence in the film, she risked being locked into the role. She returned to the stage, starring opposite Antoine Bourseiller (the father of Varda's daughter, Rosalie, and costar of *Cléo de 5 à 7*) in Sacha Pitoëff's successful

Delphine Seyrig (A) in Alain Resnais's *L'Année dernière à Marienbad* (*Last Year in Marienbad*), 1961

production of *The Seagull*. She broke further away from the image she had made famous in her next collaboration with Resnais, the one he spoke to her about when they first met: *Muriel ou le temps d'un retour*, a challenging film about the Algerian War. Appearing again in the lead, this time as a middle-aged widow and a "half-hearted antiques dealer," in her words, Seyrig's character, Hélène Aughain, is the polar opposite of her elegant previous role. Like in *Marienbad*, however, the heroine is imprisoned by the quotidian, here, wanting to escape the monotony of her life in a provincial town. When her lost love comes back into her life many years later, the encounter, here too, could save her, providing her with the possibility of happiness. Instead, he destroys her hope.

"It was a bit the opposite of *Marienbad*," Seyrig pointed out in an interview.[33] *Muriel* was stylistically different, with many short takes where the actors are moving while the camera remained relatively still. Seyrig's character is constantly busy—handling cigarettes and ashtrays, wrapping packages, selling furniture. *Marienbad*'s long takes, by contrast, feature a languorous opulence. "We don't drink; we don't smoke; we walk around like in Racine's tragedies . . . without having anything to do," Seyrig said of her first film with Resnais. Hélène, on the other hand, like Jeanne Dielman, "does concrete things which helps a lot. . . . It's harder to do but it's easier to concentrate." Seyrig, who was just over thirty at the time, was made to look older. "I had to find that weariness and fatigue and the maturity, the weariness and restlessness of this woman who hadn't made a success of her life, romantically or otherwise, as she had wanted. She is struggling with life which is alright at twenty but not at forty," the actress said, describing her character as "a woman who you can sense is trying to keep her feelings in check."[34] Seyrig also kept her feelings to herself, hiding her private life and her love story with Resnais, which was confirmed fifty years later by Schlöndorff.

Like *Marienbad*, *Muriel* was a study of time and memory, intermingling the past and present, the personal and political with memories of love and war. Evoking the war in Algeria that ended the same year as its release, the film and Seyrig's role in it were daring. The script was written by Jean Cayrol, the famous poet of the Resistance who survived a German concentration camp during the war and who also narrated Resnais's *Nuit et brouillard*. Like Varda's Cléo, Resnais's Hélène is at the center of a narrative seen from her point of view. Here, Seyrig's tired and disillusioned heroine, inspired by the humanitarian nun Suzanne Aubert, reflects the reality of the war and does not enjoy Cléo's optimistic ending.

Again, Resnais was eager to collaborate in creating the character. "How would you like to do it?" Seyrig remembered him asking her. "We can do different versions and then we'll see which is better and choose that one," the director suggested. Resnais, said Seyrig, put her on the same creative plane as him, "which makes you feel comfortable."[35] The collaboration was a critical success though the film was not appreciated by moviegoers, preferring an escape rather than the reminder of a dismal reality. Seyrig won the Volpi Cup for Best Actress in *Muriel* at the Venice Film Festival in 1963. When asked about the role a decade later, she explained, "It was a question of age in *Muriel*. The woman was older than I was so I had to find someone who reminded me of this woman and I found it very easily. . . . I'm able to understand it more now, to analyze it."[36] The model, it was revealed later, was Seyrig's mother, Miette, a woman still longing for her lost love and resentful of the lost happiness and freedom of her youth. Seyrig would not let that be her fate.

THE RELENTLESS, REVOLUTIONARY MONOTONY OF JEANNE DIELMAN

Emerging from a projection of the narrator's desire in *Marienbad* and a mix of fantasy and emptiness, Seyrig worked with Marguerite Duras on the writer's first film, *La Musica* (*The Music*, 1967). Though Duras imagined Anouk Aimée in the role, the producer's insistence on Seyrig turned out to be a blessing in disguise for both director and actress. Seyrig helped Duras weather the obstacles the writer faced as she tried to direct her first feature. According to Seyrig, producers assigned Duras a male codirector to make up for her lack of experience, and Seyrig soon realized that his camerawork was steering the film away from Duras's desired goal of making it solely "about dialogue and faces." When the actress talked to her about it, Duras said she could not see behind the camera and "did not dare ask" her codirector for access.[37]

In her youth, Seyrig had envisioned becoming a nurse to help the weak as a way for her to feel strong, an instinct she evoked when encouraging Duras to stand up for herself.[38] Duras took her advice, though Seyrig posited that the clash between the directors, and the producers' general distrust of Duras as a woman behind the camera, prevented the film from excelling. "I think if she had directed it completely, the way she has now proved that she can direct all by herself . . . if she had this independence with *La Musica*, it would be a very different film," Seyrig said. "She understood very quickly and she knows exactly what she wants to make a film, what she wants to see and to hear, better than many directors." Seyrig's prescient views about Duras could also later be applied to her own experience directing.

Before arriving at that point, however, *Marienbad* continued to follow Seyrig. Her role in *Baisers volés* was not the only reference Truffaut made to *Marienbad* in the Doinel series. In *Domicile conjugal*, Antoine watches a comic's routine on TV that derides Seyrig's role in *Marienbad*—illustrating the impact and notoriety of her character throughout the New Wave.

Seyrig also played the same type of elegant woman a decade after working with Resnais in Buñuel's *Le Charme discret de la bourgeoisie*, another film in which she is a prisoner in a gilded cage of haute bourgeois convention. In Duras's *India Song* (1975), she played an equally elegant and mysterious woman. Though the films of Resnais and Duras are very different, the actress was asked if there was a connection between the two roles. She replied: "*Marienbad* is a male fantasy and *India Song* is a female fantasy," but both women "have no way of expressing themselves," adding, "that is the main link between the two."[39]

Her character in *India Song* is Anne-Marie Stretter, an ambassador's wife living in a decadent embassy in the 1930s, who occupies herself with numerous love affairs and eventually goes mad.[40] "I think I'm able to understand Marguerite's imagining a woman whom she doesn't know anything about

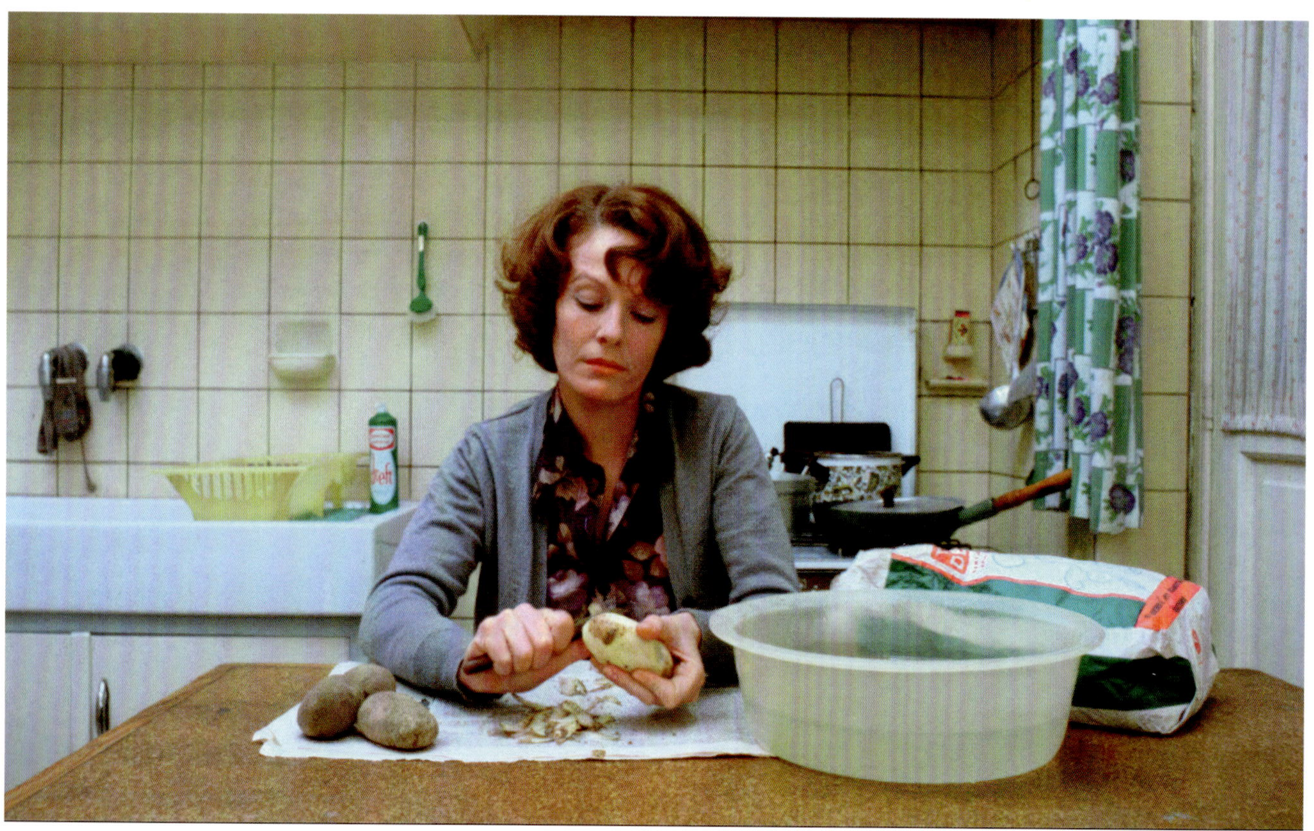

Delphine Seyrig (Jeanne Dielman) in Chantal Akerman's *Jeanne Dielman, 23 Quai du Commerce, 1080 Bruxelles*, 1975

except things that you hear, that she was able to put her own insecurity about everything that was going on around her in this woman, a mother figure and an idea, wisdom that you incarnate, that you put in a woman, this impossibility to reconcile two cultures, I think this is all in *India Song*,"[41] Seyrig related. Acting again as Anne-Marie Stretter in Duras's *Son nom de Venise dans Calcutta désert* (*Her Venetian Name in Deserted Calcutta*, 1976) and as the "unknown woman" in *Baxter, Vera Baxter* (1977), Seyrig's memorable association with Duras's experimental films was solidified on screen, with a parallel solidarity off screen. Duras considered her friendship with Seyrig *de fer*, iron-clad.[42]

The trajectory of Seyrig's most memorable roles—the sophisticated yet passive heroine in *Marienbad*, the woman imprisoned by the past in *Muriel*, and then the woman imprisoned by her present in *India Song*—led to her portrayal of a woman's suffocating in the daily existence of her socially defined womanhood in Akerman's *Jeanne Dielman, 23 quai du Commerce, 1080 Bruxelles* (1975). Seyrig's role is the epitome of unglamorous: a working-class widow and mother who supports herself and her son through prostitution, mundanely conducted at home between her other household chores. "It's rare to be offered a film whose subject has never been addressed before," Seyrig said. "It's about a housewife and what she does at home each day, her daily tasks and what matters most to her. There are one and a half or two billion women living like her. I consider it fascinating that we're finally looking at it, and also perplexing."[43]

In an interview with Michel Drucker to promote the film, the actress addressed the invisibility of the average married woman's existence: "There are men who spend their time at work and have no idea what happens at home during the day." Akerman's film rectifies that: "It observes the woman in a loving and generous way, doing the things she has to do every day—the way she cooks, the way she stands over a sink." Seyrig emphasized the importance of the film's long duration (three hours and twenty minutes). "It has turned out to be quite unbearable to watch," she stated. "Nobody has really had to watch three and a half hours of housewifing before."[44] But nearly fifty years later, *Sight and Sound* would label it the greatest film of all time.[45]

The principles of Seyrig's feminism show through her reflections about the role, which she had no trouble identifying with: "Any little girl has seen her mother wash the tub and break the eggs and cook and wash the dishes and make the bed. Any child has seen that. I saw that, so I know intimately everything this woman does in Chantal's film. What this woman does in the film I know so well that my whole life has been spent trying not to do those things," she explained. "The work of my life is to try not to do these things. I have to do them, I have to wash my tub, but I hate it. It was very interesting to me to try to be the woman that I tried to avoid."[46]

In likening it to marriage, Seyrig also found common ground with her character's experience in prostitution, "because she's not the myth of the prostitute that is generally shown, generally made by men."[47] Akerman's display of prostitution, Seyrig explained, "is very close to the sexual life of many married women . . . where the husband puts money on the table in the morning for her to buy food." The absence of a husband qualifies Jeanne Dielman's sexual life as prostitution, Seyrig said, "but that's the only difference." Seyrig even sympathized with Jeanne for murdering a man: "I've never killed anyone but I understand the aggression that she feels, and I think a lot of women who are trapped in the convention of marriage, which is very much for a lot of women a sort of prostitution because their bodies are not involved. I think they know. I think all women at one moment in their life, knew what this woman was feeling."[48]

Not only was the film important for viewers, Seyrig described it as showing her explicitly the life and expected role for women that she refused: "For me, the film touched me in very concrete ways because first of all, I rejected this type of lifestyle. In the film, I had to make coffee, something I never do. . . . It was a very concrete act. What I'm trying to say is that we accept that these things are done by certain people, predominantly women when it shouldn't just be accepted. Women do that every day because they must believe that everyone thinks it's natural for them to do it when it's not natural at all in fact. I don't live that way because I rejected it. I admit it. Because I had the means to reject it, and yes, of course most women don't. Then we could go into a big debate—you could say that women get married because they don't have the means to do differently."[49]

The activism inherent in Seyrig's reaction to the role is a testament to the film's power of simply revealing women as they are. "I felt that Chantal wanted to show what she'd seen the women around her do all her life. It's neither championing nor attacking women. It's about what touched her," the actress stated. Akerman herself described the film as based on her childhood memories, "seeing women from behind who were bent over, carrying bags." "The difference is," she went on, "I don't think a man would've made this film because from birth, men are taught different values. A woman washing dishes isn't an art. It wasn't a conscious challenge, I just told a story that interested me and this is the result."[50]

"Fifteen years ago, Delphine Seyrig was an international symbol of haute bourgeois chic. She glided through *Last Year at Marienbad*, her first major film, as an indifferent elegant presence. But inside she was seething," Weinraub wrote in 1976. Becoming a "radical feminist," per Weinraub, Seyrig's "sleek, feline sexual woman" in her roles with Resnais, Truffaut, and Buñuel had "virtually disappeared" by then. Seyrig's appearance in the stage production of Rainer Werner Fassbinder's *Bitter Tears of Petra von Kant* in a small London theater in 1976 aligned with the actress's thinking at the time with its themes of "power, passion, and the way people try to control one another," according to Weinraub. "Passion is a subject people don't dare speak of in a completely direct way now," Seyrig told Weinraub. "Authors are afraid of talking about it." Seyrig did not evoke her own passion either. After their long collaboration and discreet love story, Resnais unexpectedly left Seyrig. Though devastated, she remained unbroken. "I had always been in a rage," Seyrig said. "I had been very angry since childhood. But what man would want an angry woman? The rage came out as charm."[51]

DELPHINE SEYRIG: *FEMINISTE À LA FRANÇAISE*

Though her characters may often have been without a voice, Seyrig developed her own, continuing to act as she became an activist. "I can't give it up," she told Weinraub. "It's the way I earn my living. All I can do is try to get my own personal points across."

Between *Marienbad* and *Jeanne Dielman*, Seyrig became a major feminist figure in France. Gone was the sophisticated stereotype of her early roles, as was the staid provincialism of Jeanne Dielman with her hair fixed in an "old-fashioned set," as Seyrig described it. "We went very far with the details of the character," she added. "I hate to feel ugly, and I did feel ugly. She was so trapped. It was like being in jail." In real life, Seyrig was finally seen as herself: a divorced, independent, and successful *femme bohème* whose loose, comfortable clothing and untamed red curly hair evoked the freedom of 1970s feminists. "Women who refuse the whole concept of femininity are lucid much earlier but they suffer more," Seyrig confided to Weinraub. "Many women strive for femininity as a way of getting by. There are lots of things I wouldn't do any more."[52]

Seyrig, however, was able to do many things because of her determination. In 1964, after gaining credibility as an actress, she finally worked with Strasberg at the Actors Studio, this time not as just an auditor. Beckett, remembering her contribution to *Godot*, chose her for his 1966 short film *Comédie* with Michael Lonsdale and made her the go-to actress for his French productions. She starred in Joseph Losey's *Accident* (1967) and his 1973 adaptation of Ibsen's *A Doll's House* with Jane Fonda.

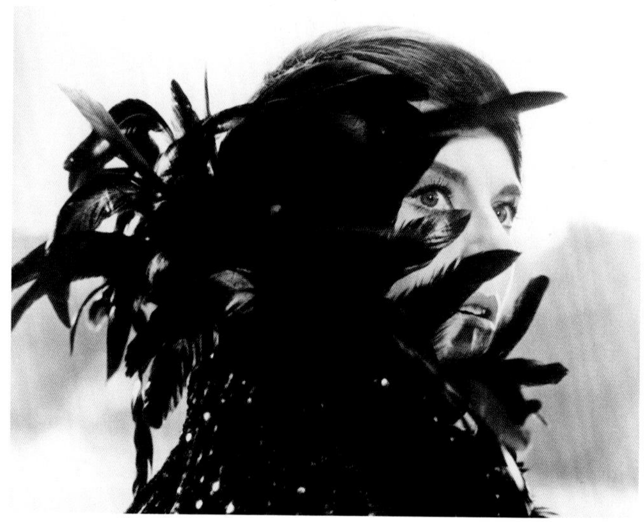

Delphine Seyrig in Alain Resnais's *L'Année dernière à Marienbad* (*Last Year in Marienbad*) 1961

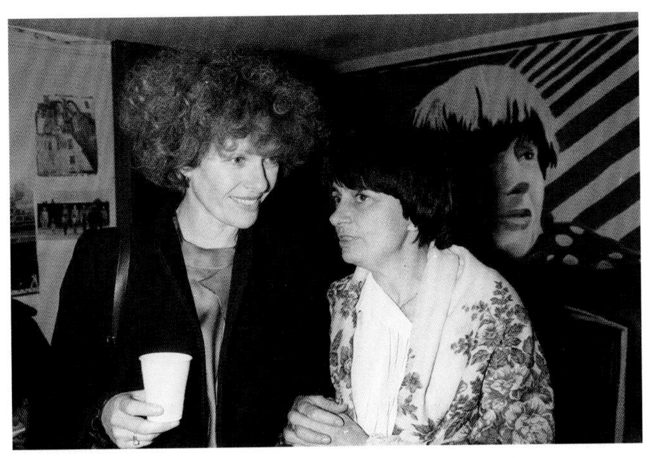

Like Fonda, Seyrig voiced her opinions outspokenly in many interviews as well as in the films she directed. She formed the feminist video collective Les Insoumuses (which roughly translates as "the defiant muses") with activist and videographer Carole Roussopoulos and Seyrig's childhood friend, translator Ioana Wieder. Together, they produced a series of videos on women in the media and workforce, and on women's reproductive rights, including *Sois belle et tais-toi*, *SCUM Manifesto* (1976), and *Maso et Miso vont en bateau* (*Maso and Miso Go Boating*, 1976). The latter parodies a 1975 TV broadcast in which host Bernard Pivot and Françoise Giroud—then the secretary of state for the feminine condition, a position Les Insoumuses found condescending—discuss "L'Année de la femme," the year of the woman (*Miso* being short for what they saw as misogyny in Pivot's statements and *Maso* for Giroud's masochism in going along with it).[53] "Video is my independence from men," Seyrig told Weinraub. "It's my feminist thing. I can express things with video that I can't with films or plays. I like being able to fiddle with the camera, and the whole editing process."[54]

In *Sois belle*, Seyrig spoke with French and American actresses—including Fonda, Shirley MacLaine, Maria Schneider, Juliet Berto, Jill Clayburgh, Ellen Burstyn, and Anne Wiazemsky—on the sexism they endured working in the film industry, anticipating #MeToo. Once she crossed over the threshold, stepping behind the camera, Seyrig used her voice to help other women be heard. In 1980, having discovered letters that American frontierswoman Calamity Jane (Martha Jane Canary) sent her daughter between 1877 and 1903, Seyrig

was so touched that she began thinking of a project about her. In 1983, she approached Babette Mangolte, whom she had known since working together on *Jeanne Dielman*, to be the director of photography on the film. Though Seyrig did not live to see the film come to fruition, Mangolte used Seyrig's footage to create 2019's *Calamity Jane & Delphine Seyrig: A Story*[55] in conjunction with Giovanna Zapperi, who worked at the Centre audiovisual Simone de Beauvoir, which Seyrig cofounded.[56] The film blends Calamity Jane, Seyrig, and Mangolte herself, who reflected on its long road to existence. "Not giving up is what the film had to be about, as it was Delphine's greatest strength," Mangolte said.[57]

Behind the scenes, Seyrig worked to promote women's rights, joining her fellow New Wave actresses and other prominent figures in signing the "Le Manifeste des 343 salopes" (its name likely a play on "Le Manifeste des 121," a 1960 document denouncing France's tactics in the Algerian War that Resnais and Robbe-Grillet both signed). Among the hundreds of signers attesting to their illegal abortions were Duras, de Beauvoir, Moreau, Varda, Deneuve, Fabian, and Lafont, as well as Françoise Arnoul, Stéphane Audran, Geneviève Cluny, Antoinette Fouque, Ariane Mnouchkine, Bulle Ogier, Marie-France Pisier, Micheline Presle, Christiane Rochefort, Françoise Sagan, Alexandra Stewart, Nadine Trintignant, Marina Vlady, Anne Wiazemsky, and Monique Wittig.

Over forty years before #MeToo, Seyrig worked to bring the government's attention to the issue of rape and articulated the imbalance of power between men and women that sometimes led to violence. "Nothing can be expected of men unless women start becoming aware of the manipulation which men do to them. Once a woman becomes aware, the solution doesn't come either, but at least the struggle begins. A little oxygen is getting in," she stated. Though Seyrig's roles provided new representations of women that raised awareness on this front, she also acknowledged that "the theater and films are very far from women's consciousness about themselves." Female solidarity within the industry could help bridge the disconnect, which Seyrig worked toward by collaborating with directors like Duras and Akerman. "Somehow," she said, "we must sense each other."[58]

Delphine Seyrig and Agnès Varda at the premiere of Varda's *Mur murs* in 1982, photograph by Patrick Robert

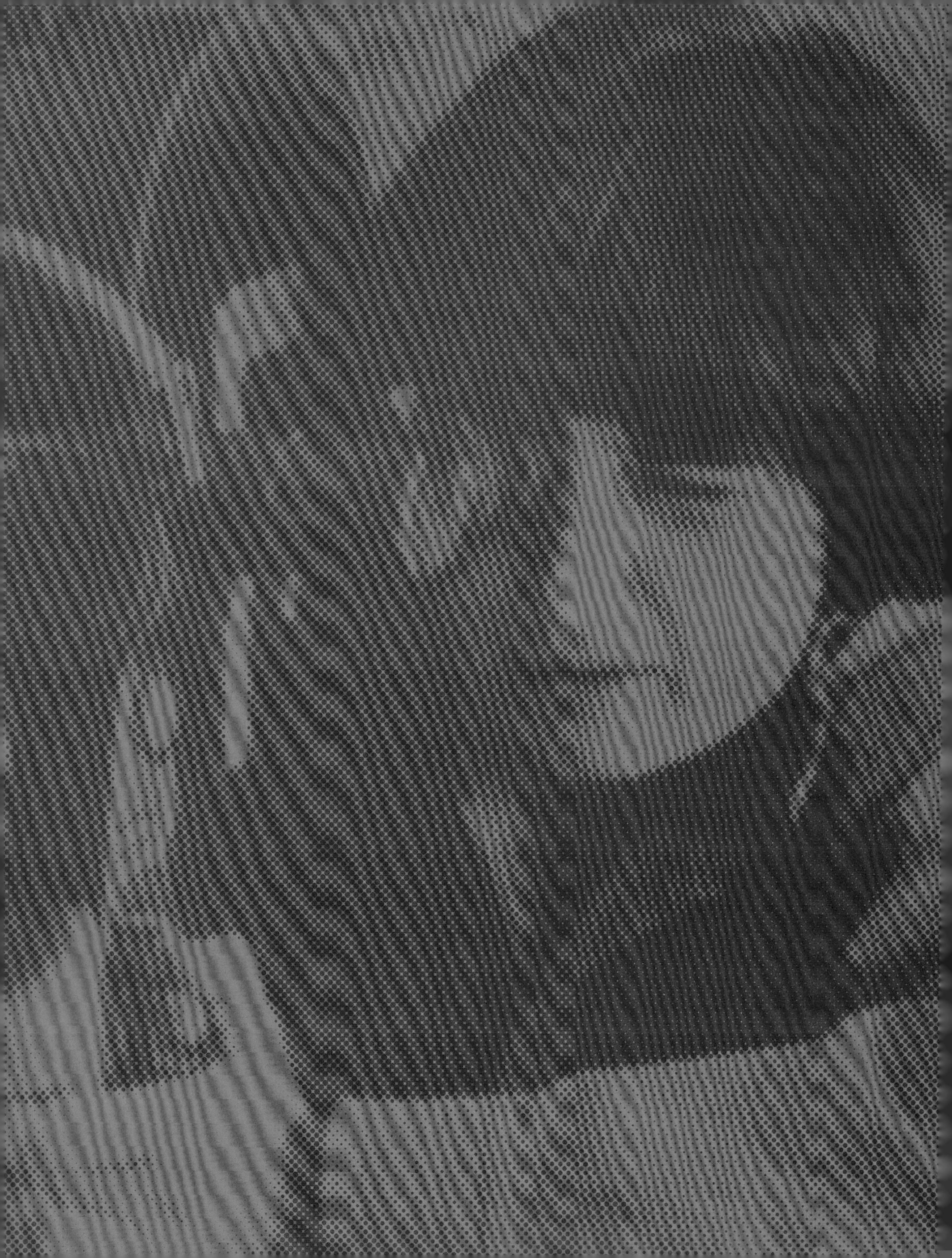

la réalisatrice | *the director*

ARLETTE TO AGNÈS: VARDA'S EARLY ART

Agnès Varda's comments about her protagonist in *Cléo de 5 à 7* illustrate her belief in the power of transformation. But as the New Wave brought profound change to society and cinema, films centered on a female perspective were still slow to appear—and even slower, women behind the camera. Working her way into the profession of *réalisatrice*, a female director on an unpaved road, Varda would prove revolutionary not only as a pioneer of the New Wave but also as a visual artist, theoretician, and documentarist of a metamorphic era in France and beyond.

"She's a woman who begins to look . . . I consider this a feminist approach. I wanted it to be a woman who defines herself only through how others see her, and at a certain point, because she starts to look at herself, she changes. In fact, she's going to redefine herself on her own."[1]

—**agnès varda** on the protagonist of *Cléo de 5 à 7*

Arlette Varda, born in Brussels in 1928 to a Greek father and a French mother, was persuaded at a young age by her mother to become an artist, but claimed, "I am unknown to myself,"[2] as Laure Adler related in her biography. When the Germans occupied Belgium, Varda moved with her large family to her mother's hometown of Sète, a fishing village in the south of France's *zone libre*. At the end of the war, she left for Paris where she developed a new lifestyle and look. Her style resembled that of an androgynous sailor, she frequented the bohemian art scene and took art classes at the famous École du Louvre. Her life was marked with decisive encounters that transformed her as an artist and as a woman. One of the most influential was with Valentine Schlegel, known as "Linou," also from Sète, who had arrived in Paris before Varda to hone her skills as a sculptor and ceramist. She taught Varda about art, encouraging her work and sharing her own contacts. Through Linou, Varda got a job as the babysitter for the children of TNP director Jean Vilar. Through him, she learned about literature and philosophy, developing a predilection for Baudelaire, Friedrich Nietzsche, Guillaume Apollinaire, and Louis Aragon.

Reflecting her lifelong penchant for redefining herself, at eighteen, Arlette officially changed her name to Agnès. "I don't like names with 'ette,'" she later explained. "You know, it looks like a little girl's name. Jumping, charming and jumping. I didn't feel like being like this."[3] Influenced by philosopher Gaston Bachelard's seminars at the Sorbonne, Varda's contemplative solitude led to feelings of isolation, prompting her to suddenly set off for Corsica with only a backpack—and without telling anyone, not even her family. For three months, she lived with fishermen, assisting them using skills she had acquired in Sète. During her trip, Varda discovered freedom and independence, and according to Adler, returned to Paris "physically and mentally transformed."

Back in Paris, Linou became one of the greatest loves of Varda's life. "Linou saved me from the combined effects of the war and my family," she stated. They lived together starting in 1951 in Varda's studio on rue Daguerre, and Varda was greatly influenced by Linou's way of seeing the world: "finding a sarcophagus in the Louvre as beautiful as graffiti on the wall of the *banlieue*,"[4] as Adler noted. With a secondhand Rolleiflex camera that her mother bought her, Varda began taking photographs, encouraged by Linou who believed in her talent. Documenting Linou's artistic production as well as everyday life in Paris "like an ethnologist," Adler wrote, Varda established her own style. She installed a lab to develop photos in her studio and soon earned professional credentials by taking night classes in photography at L'École de Vaugirard.

After a stint as a photographer for the French electric company EDF, Varda worked at a department store taking photos of children in front of the Christmas tree. Her big break came when Vilar, in the spirit of the community-oriented TNP, hired her to assist with the new Festival d'Avignon. The title-less gig involved a bit of everything, including taking photographs of the décor, sets, and eventually rehearsals. Innovating ways of photographing actors—changing the lights, shooting from the roof, a ladder, or in close-up—she impressed Vilar with her talent and pursuit of authenticity. At a time when women rarely had access to theater sets, Varda's photos of Gérard Philipe earned her recognition. "Magnifying his romanticism, sublimating his beauty and unveiling his heroic and erotic dimension" in his role as the Prince of Homburg, according to Adler, Varda's photos renewed Philipe's image and created a "media boom." Varda also adopted the TNP's values, believing that art was for everyone, that it should open people's minds and break with the social order. Other encounters continued to shape her path: With the famous photographer Brassaï, her neighbor in Paris, Varda learned the importance of point of view; with Guy Bourdin, she learned photography could be an "aesthetic and philosophical" way of questioning, per Adler. Through Bourdin, she met Fouli Elia, artistic director of *Elle* magazine. In 1954, during one of their frequent trips to photograph landscapes, Varda had Bourdin and Elia pose nude for what became two well-known shots, *Nus dans les ruines* with both men and *Ulysse* with Elia. Varda continued to mix commercial and artistic work, photographing weddings along with reports for prestigious magazines like *Réalités*, where she continued to develop her style.

Though identified as an art lover rather than a cinephile, Varda's appreciation of the TNP's actors and William Faulkner's

The Wild Palms inspired her to make a film, *La Pointe Courte*, following the unconventional structure of the latter. While women were not exactly welcome in the profession dominated by the older established directors in 1954, Varda made her way into it regardless. She simply ignored the laws requiring enrollment in the CNC (Centre national de la cinématographie) and shot her film with a very small crew and actors who, strongly believing in her, worked for free. The challenges did not abate after the shoot. Alain Resnais, suggested by a friend, initially refused when she asked him to edit the film, claiming that their styles were too similar. Varda insisted, and he finally accepted after she proved her determination by fulfilling his request of numbering the sequences—ten thousand meters of film—by hand. Resnais and Varda discovered their common artistic taste and mutual attraction while working on the film and carried on a secret relationship—confirmed by Varda's daughter decades later—that ended in 1957 when Varda took up with Antoine Bourseiller. Varda left Bourseiller while she was pregnant with their daughter Rosalie but maintained a friendship with him as well as with Resnais.

In *La Pointe Courte*, Varda interwove an intimate story of a Parisian couple in crisis with documentary footage she shot on location in Sète—a fusion of reality and fiction that lay the groundwork for the New Wave. In much the same way the Italian neorealists added authenticity to their fictional stories by using nonprofessional actors, Varda featured inhabitants of the fishing village, preserving their accents in the dialogue. Intermingling them with stage actors Silvia Monfort and Philippe Noiret, the film portrays the characters in a shared landscape that is itself a sort of character in the film. With the eye of a seasoned photographer, Varda captured the fishermen's nets and boats, the white sheets drying on the lines between buildings, and the village cats (that later became a signature in her work). With her skill at composition, the director placed her protagonists in poses that anticipated the famous shots in Bergman's *Persona* (1966), with the faces of Monfort and Noiret like those of Bibi Andersson and Liv Ullmann, blended into interlocking puzzle pieces. The structure of the narrative is equally abstract, juxtaposing the story of the villagers with that of the Parisian couple in the same way *The Wild Palms* vacillates from one story to the other by chapter.

Screened at the Cannes Film Festival (out of competition) in 1955, *La Pointe Courte* gained Varda recognition from critics, notably André Bazin, as a talented filmmaker. She spent the next several years making commissioned short films as well as artistic ones like 1958's *L'Opéra-Mouffe*. Without dialogue, but with music by Georges Delerue and cinematography by Sacha Vierny, the film consists of anonymous faces passing in front of Varda's 16mm-film camera on the rue Mouffetard: men and women of all ages, some homeless, some lost in alcohol or in their own misfortune. It also includes many older women who, according to Varda, stood as projections of her own future. Varda, then pregnant with Rosalie, captured the footage by standing on a chair.

Pregnancy and motherhood informed the film, as we saw earlier in the opening scene with the shot of a nude pregnant torso juxtaposed with a squash; it ends with a sequence showing a just-hatched chick. Throughout, Varda weaves together disparate scenes such as a forlorn woman laden with heavy bags, and graphic images of animals in a butcher shop. In the final scene, the same woman eats the flowers from a bouquet. Shots of women either in conversation or reflected in cracked mirrors anticipate the heroine of *Cléo de 5 à 7* fixating on her own fractured reflection. Another link to *Cléo* on the rue Mouffetard is Dorothée Blanck. In the vignette within the film called "Les Amoureux" (meaning "the lovers"), we see her walking nude among white sheets hanging in her courtyard, appearing (like the character she will interpret in *Cléo*) free and comfortable with her body. Varda's camera films her here with her lovers in sensual, sculptural close-ups, predating the iconic opening scenes of Resnais's *Hiroshima, mon amour*.

Speaking to Blanck years later, Varda recalled, "I shot on the rue Mouffetard with you and José Varela, and another guy named [Jean] Tasso. You had two lovers." Blanck displayed her uninhibited attitude in her reply: "Yes, may as well!" Varda continued: "With Varela, we saw you in bed. Some said it was shocking. It seemed innocent to me. You caressed his feet." Blanck responded nonchalantly: "I continued [to do that] with other lovers in my life!" Discussing another scene in which Blanck poses nude on an iron bed in a courtyard, Varda asked, "You had experience as a model. What about acting in the film?" Blanck confirmed the role matched her own personality: "It didn't require any transition. I acted in the film as I did in life."[5]

It was also in 1958 that Varda encountered another love of her life: Jacques Demy, whom she met at the short-film festival in Tours. "To Jacques, I was a teenaged-mother, and that was right up his alley. You just have to watch his films!"[6] Varda declared. After their mutual *coup de foudre*, Demy moved in at rue Daguerre and they began their personal adventure together, while preserving their individual artistic lives.

Excited by the profitable streak of the Nouvelle Vague with Demy and Godard's first features, Georges de Beauregard was interested in producing more films by young directors. When he asked Demy if he could recommend "another guy who would make an inexpensive film in black and white," the director replied, "No, but I know a girl."[7] Beauregard was willing to finance Varda's film, but with a budget that made her rethink her original idea. Like Demy's *Lola*, Varda's ambitious dream for *Cléo*—in color, shot in Venice and in the south of France—was transformed by financial constraints. Varda decided to make the film in one city in one day: Paris, shot in black and white in ninety minutes of real time.[8] Like its heroine, the idea for the film underwent a transformation from the sophisticated to the authentic. Varda's story of Cléo would go down in history as one of the greatest films of all time, as described by the 2023 issue of *Sight and Sound*.[9]

CLÉO DE 5 À 7: VARDA'S OVAL PORTRAIT REVERSAL

Cléo is about "a woman who goes from being seen to being able to see," Varda stated. It depicts how a woman is viewed as an object both by society and by herself. Cléo is a glamorous singer with a fabricated image of socially defined ideals of feminine beauty, making her self-centered. Opening with a fortune teller's ominous tarot reading, the film sees Cléo encounter the reality of her own mortality exacerbated by her superstition after a medical visit with a doctor who holds her fate in his hands. Colored by her pessimistic outlook as she awaits the results of a biopsy, Cléo's day is dark, and her fear makes the passage of time excruciating. In an in-

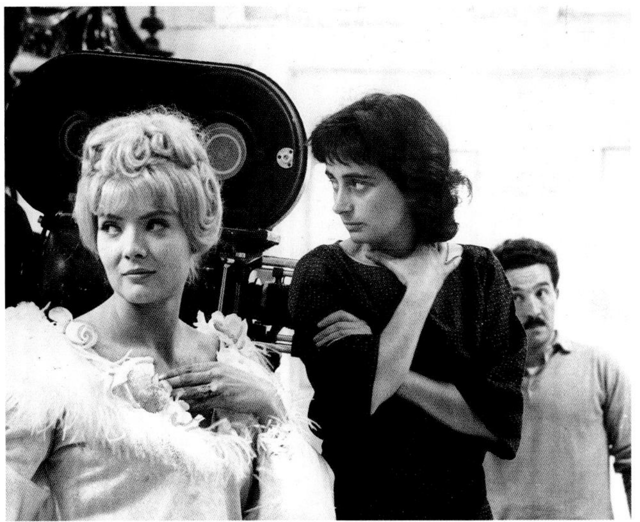

stant, she has gone from a beautiful yet superficial singer to a vulnerable woman in crisis and in search of meaning. Varda herself believed "in the power of fate, in fortune tellers, in tarot readings," according to Adler. She was "superstitious," saw "signs and symbols everywhere," and battled with anxiety. Her "somber side" and a preoccupation with death runs in parallel with the whimsical joy throughout her cinema, creating depth.[10]

"Naturally, it's a fiction," Varda said, "a fiction in color that draws us into the rest of the film. To reality." This time the reality is more than the documentary-style images of *La Pointe Courte*'s fishing village; it is the reality of a woman's life. Cléo's desperate search for answers has led her to the fortune teller, who lays out Cléo's future in cards. These death-themed images function like a storyboard of Cléo's fate that the protagonist does, but does not, want to see. Reassuring her with ambiguous messages, the fortune teller sets up the film's emphasis on perspective: "This card is not necessarily death—but it's the transformation of your entire being." Cléo concentrates on the hanged man and the skeleton cards, images that color the rest of the black-and-white film. Cléo's shock, hit by the threat of death, Varda explained, follows her through the next hour and a half while she tries to go about her day wrought with anxiety. When the film switches to black and white after this first sequence, the director clarified, it passes from fiction into "ninety minutes of reality."[11]

Top: Corrine Marchand and Agnès Varda on the set of *Cléo de 5 à 7* (*Cléo from 5 to 7*), 1962 **Next pages:** Dorothée Blanck in Agnès Varda's *L'Opéra-Mouffe* (*Diary of a Pregnant Woman*), 1958

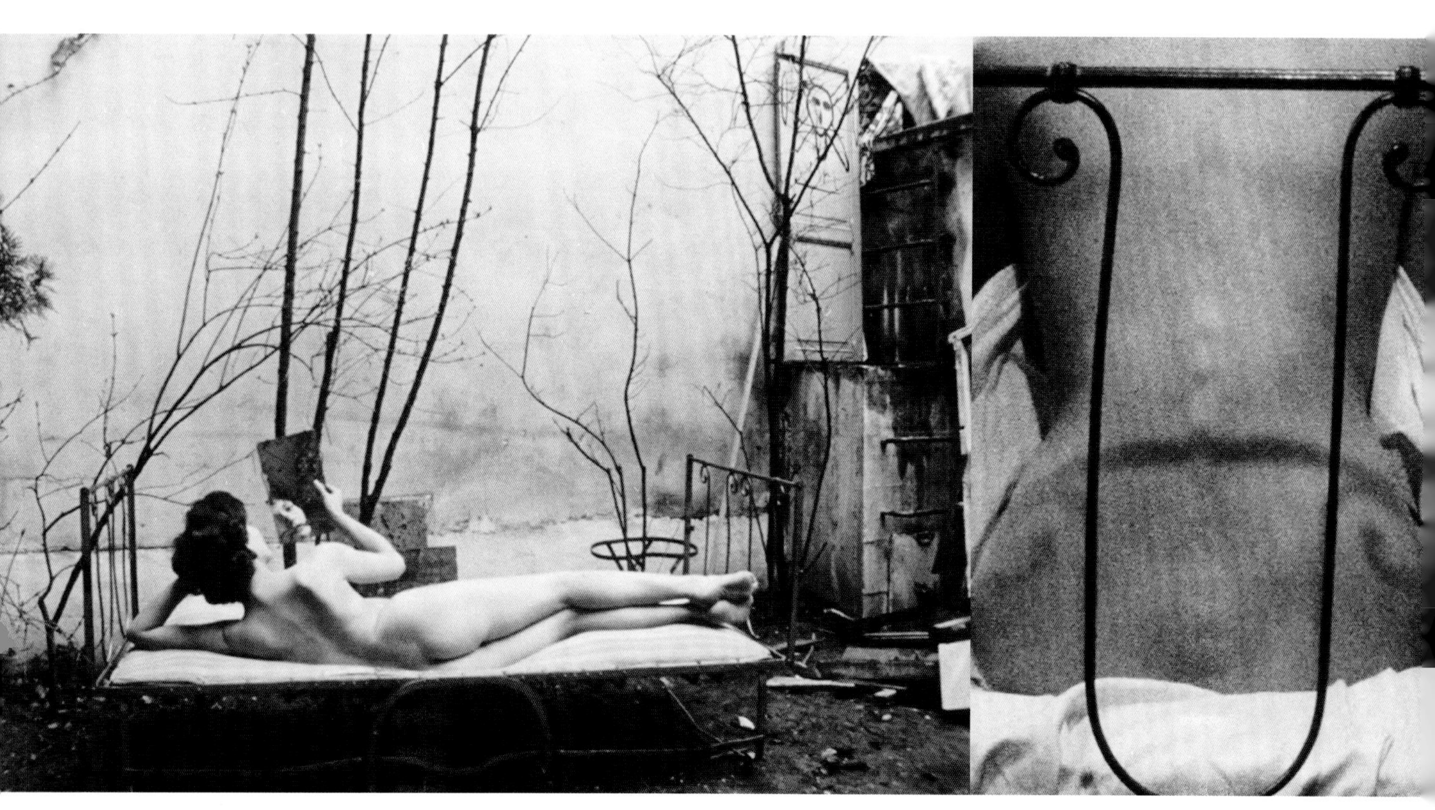

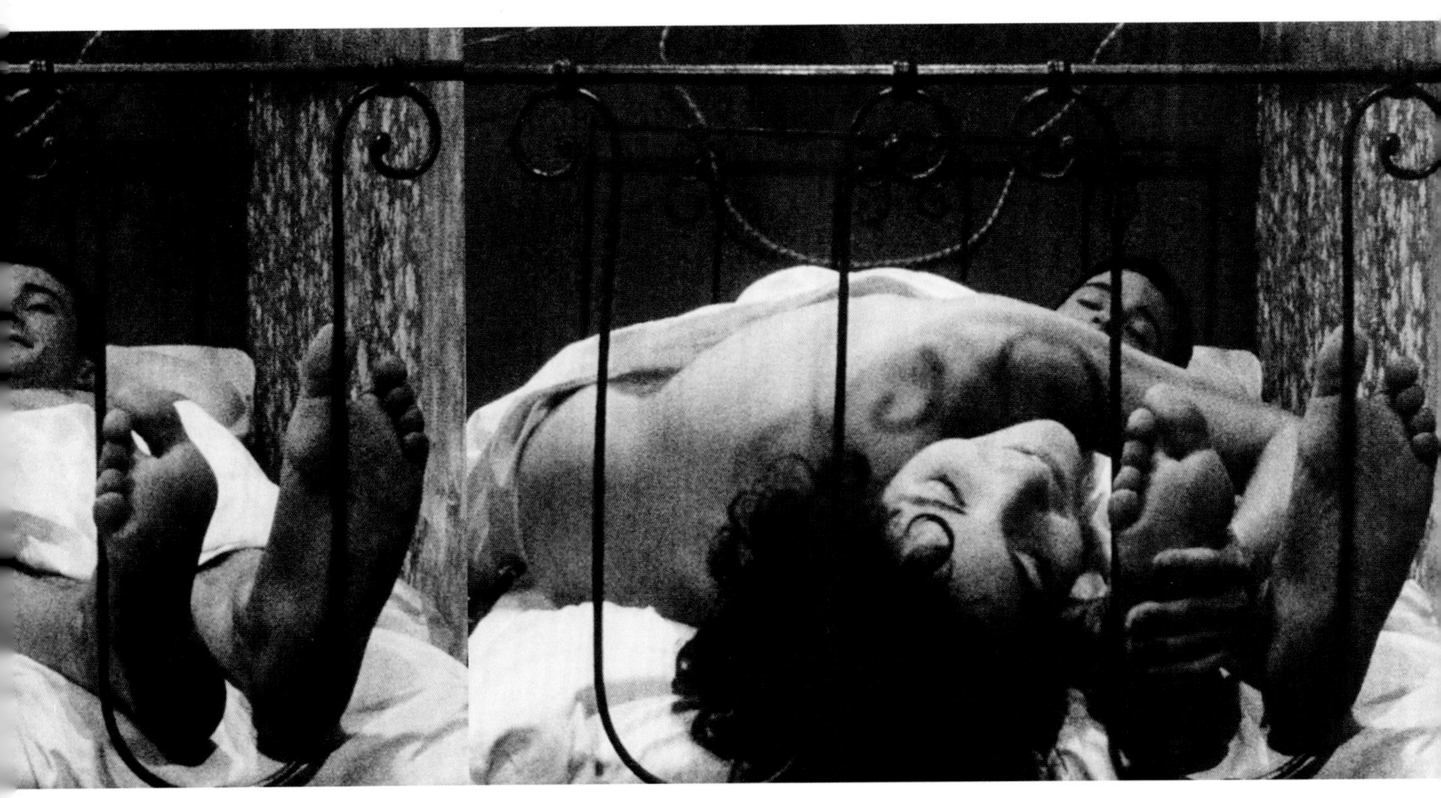

Varda decided to make the film in one city in one day: Paris, shot in black and white in ninety minutes of real time.[1] Like its heroine, the idea for the film underwent a transformation from the sophisticated to the authentic. Varda's story of Cléo would go down in history as one of the greatest films of all time, as described by the 2023 issue of *Sight and Sound*.

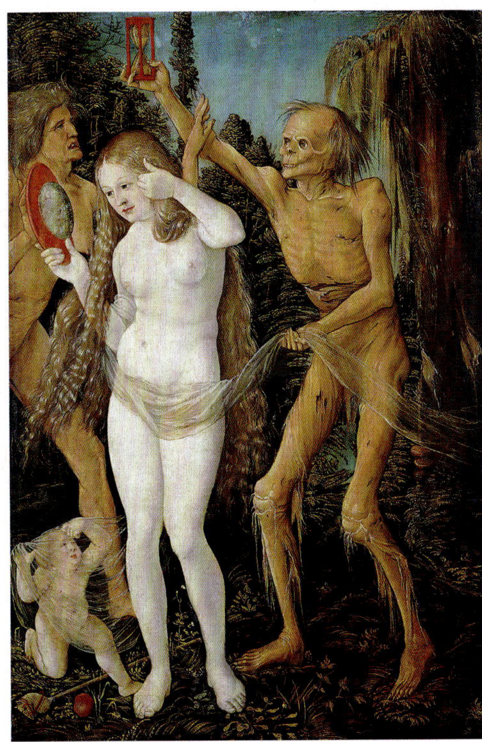

It is not just any reality, however. It is the reality of a woman, imagined and made by a female director. As Corinne Marchand, who played Cléo, said, "It's a major role. It's rare to have such a rich character at one's disposal, and for an actress, it's wonderful." All the more rare at the time was "a multilayered persona" who evolves, as Varda explained, moving "from vanity to anxiety, fear to curiosity."[12] Besides the complexity of the character, the film emphasizes her transformation from object to subject as her self-image changes.

The images that inspired the film, sixteenth-century paintings by German artist Hans Baldung Grien, are as haunting as the menacing tarot cards. Varda described Cléo's tarot reading as "exactly like this magnificent woman" who shows up in Grien's works, as "a skeleton whispers something she doesn't want to hear, or pulls her hair." Grien's paintings illustrate the theme she wanted to explore in the film, "beauty and death," and she wrote the scenario and dialogue with that in mind.[13] His work was "a huge mental reference at the center of [the] project,"[14] and she even tacked some of the images on the walls of the set. Embodying the paintings depicting a beautiful exterior eaten away by death, Cléo

suffers a crisis both physical and existential. "[S]uddenly her beauty and good health come face to face with a notion of Death who attacks her body and penetrates her entire being,"[15] Varda explained.

In an interesting twist on the idea of the Oval Portrait syndrome, with the artist/director vampirizing the model/actress to create a work of art, Marchand as Varda's "model" underwent a striking physical transformation in the film, strongly identifying with the character. Instead of being depleted by the part, however, the actress worked in the same direction as the director, giving herself to the role in a constructive way. Bernard Toublanc-Michel, one of the film's assistant directors, commented on Marchand's portrayal of Cléo: "Corinne in this role represented someone in good health on the surface, which is contrary to her character. It was a good thing, that she didn't appear to be suffering and frail. [She was] the picture of health." Speaking to Varda years later, Marchand recalled how one of Grien's paintings helped convey the director's vision: "I understood well, through that image, what you were aiming for. And as we shot from the beginning in chronological order, by the end of the film, I was exhausted by this idea and I seem to remember that at the end of the film, I was very tired compared to the first images." Varda offered more insight into the actress's transformation, confessing what she demanded of her: "More than tired! I asked you to lose weight. You lost seven kilos [over fifteen pounds] in seven weeks!" Marchand agreed: "Yes, because I really identified with the role. I thought about it a lot. I believed in it. And I truly lived it, profoundly."[16]

Varda developed the role of Cléo specifically for Corinne Marchand after having seen her on stage in the operetta *Pacifico*[17] and in Demy's *Lola*. "You wore an opera hat when I discovered you during the shoot of *Lola*," Varda recalled. Marchand added another connection to the role: "I sang a little bit already so I had a notion of how it worked." As Varda explained, "I wrote the role of Cléo for her because I believe in creating roles for specific actors. Without modifying the major lines of a film, you should nevertheless choose certain characteristic details, certain speech patterns in harmony with the personality of the actress who will play the part, gestures and words that belong to her in real life."[18]

Hans Baldung Grien's *An Allegory of Death and Beauty*, 1509

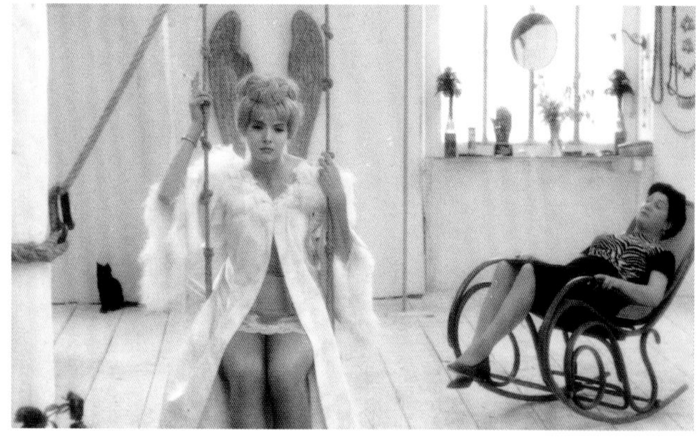

Like other New Wave directors who used their own clothing to dress their male protagonists, transforming them into alter egos, Varda lent some of her own possessions to Cléo for the film: "Cleo is wearing one of my necklaces. I had brought her my entire collection. The wings also were mine as well as the rocking chair."[19]

Varda also designed Cléo's organdy polka dot dress. "It was a sheath dress with an interior lining," recalled assistant director Marin Karmitz, which gave Marchand "an airy effect that was lovely." The director agreed: "It added a lightness in the way she walked."[20] Varda's investment in every aspect of the film, including her heroine's wardrobe, exemplifies her attention to the *mise en scène* in line with her status as an auteur. Another dress—the "little black one with darts," Varda noted—reflects the juxtaposition of light and dark compared to Cléo's white negligee, details that further illustrate the black-and-white perspectives in the film. Varda's personal touch also included the image on the film's poster: "I took this shot. Cléo's face. Luc Fournol had her hair and makeup done for a photo in the same style, and as beautiful as Brigitte Bardot and Liz Taylor, Grace Kelly and Marlene Dietrich."[21]

Different from the other examples of the Oval Portrait syndrome where the actress's life force nourishes the film while the off-screen relationship with the director might be problematic, here, Varda breathes life into her model. Instead of working out conflicts that deplete or destroy the actress, in *Cléo*, Varda works through those that empower and eventually transform her. With Marchand, Varda created a character who conveys tensions and an overlooked point of view—that

of being a woman in 1960s France, attaining more power but still highly objectified.

In Cléo's case, this status is heightened by her profession in the spotlight, where being seen is part of her job. But it is also a privileged situation: Her ability to act, to take action, is inherent in her occupation, allowing her to gain agency through performing. In this way, the role distills women's general position, seeking to acquire as much freedom as society allowed within the confines of ongoing objectification. Placing her heroine in the spotlight to illustrate this experience testifies to Varda's keen sense of awareness and her own struggle to gain equal footing in a male-dominated profession. Her Oval Portrait of Cléo works to nourish the character and actress, and her implicit commentary on social constraints also provides an inspirational path for women.

Interestingly, the couple most emblematic of the Oval Portrait syndrome brings some levity to Cléo's story. Anna Karina and Jean-Luc Godard (newlywed at the time) appear in the short film within the film, *Les Fiancés du pont Macdonald*. "When I wrote *Cléo*, I was afraid viewers would get bored," Varda stated. "I mean I wanted them to feel close to Cléo, that they worry with her, living every minute intensely, but I was afraid it would drag. So at the beginning of the fourth part, where all films lag a bit, I thought I'd try something a bit more entertaining. I imagined that Dorothée's boyfriend was a projectionist in a movie theater. They'd deliver a print to him, and he'd show them a short film. So I imagined a little silent burlesque film."

The short film further illustrates the power of perspectives: "My true motivation for making this film," Varda confessed, "was that I'd had enough of Jean-Luc's dark, very dark sunglasses that always hid his eyes. And I knew he had beautiful eyes so I made up a silly story about a guy whose dark glasses make everything dark. . . . Then suddenly, he takes off his glasses, and sees life differently."[22] Its comedic and optimistic message on perspective—seeing things darkly as Godard does with his sunglasses versus optimistically without them—represents a lighthearted version of Cléo's dramatic shift in point of view and mindset within the narrative.

Corinne Marchand (Cléo) and Dominique Davray (Angèle) in Varda's *Cléo de 5 à 7*, 1962

FROM LOOKED AT TO LOOKING OUT: CLÉO'S TRANSFORMATION

Much has been written about Cléo's transformation from object to subject. From a feminist perspective, Varda's story of a woman gaining agency in a man's world has been widely celebrated. Film scholar Ginette Vincendeau rightly cited Varda's heroines, starting with Cléo and continuing in *Le Bonheur* (1965) and *Les Créatures* (*The Creatures*, 1966), as "among the '60s' most original and penetrating cinematic portraits of women," embodying the filmmaker's quest to show how "a woman would look for her own image, her own truth." Vincendeau applauded Varda's focus on "women's experiences and their roles in relationships with men, and attention to the female body."[23] Along with these elements, dissecting "feminine myths" and promoting the female gaze set Varda apart from her contemporaries. Women in her films are "no longer the fascinating objects of the gazes of the male characters/spectator/director but autonomous, desiring subjects in their own right."[24] Vincendeau also noted that female subjectivity is especially significant in Cléo, "where Varda projected her heroine's gaze onto others,"[25] a strategy the director would continue to use in her later works. Varda described her protagonist's inner evolution as almost an awakening. It is the encounter with her true self.

In the first part of the film, a self-absorbed Cléo benefits from the privilege of power she has as a beautiful singer. Defined solely by her image and by others' views of her, she is obsessed with her own reflection. While she possesses a semblance of control in this way, she is not truly seen. Out of touch with her authentic self, she feels powerless, often behaving more like a child than an adult. In her search for identity, she is transfixed by every mirror and reflection she encounters, each sending her back a different, fragmented image of herself.

As Varda explained, "Cléo likes mirrors a lot. During the first part of the film, Cléo is described and defined by those who see her: her assistant, the hat saleswoman, her lover, the musicians, and the mirrors."[26] Cléo is seen, but as an object. From the mirrors she gazes into, the reflections from store windows as well as those in other people's eyes, Cléo's im-

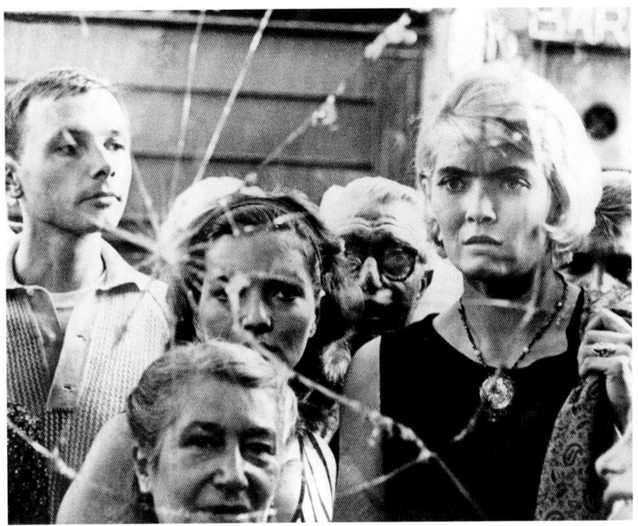

pression of herself is solely what the outside reflects back to her. Varda's cinematic articulation of this concept showcases her meticulous attention to the *mise en scène*.

After the ambiguous but ominous tarot card reading, for example, predicting "change" along with "suffering,"[27] the camera shows Cléo's face and also what she sees. As she leaves, dejected, people in the waiting room look up at her and then away. As she continues down into the entryway of the building, a mirror reflects her image back to her multiple times and "reassures her,"[28] as the script specifies. In voice-over, Cléo's internal voice states, "Being ugly is death. As long as I'm beautiful, I'm alive, and ten times more than others"—the reflection of her beauty gives her a feeling of superiority. Walking down the rue de Rivoli in her polka-dot dress, Cléo is noticed. Salesmen call out to her and people turn around to look. "As soon as she is looked at, she forgets her fear," the script indicates.[29]

When Cléo meets her assistant, Angèle, in a café and confides that the tarot cards said she is ill, she asks Angèle if it shows on her face. When Angèle tells her she is imagining things, Cléo replies, "If so, I will kill myself! Might as well say that I am dead already." Getting up from the table, she "searches for her image," as noted in the script, in the reflection of two adjoining mirrors, but the image is deformed and split. She bursts into tears.[30] Without clarity or a strong definition of herself, Cléo is lost. Angèle says to herself in

Dorothée Blanck (Dorothée) and Corinne Marchand (Cléo) in Varda's *Cléo de 5 à 7*, 1961

voice-over, "She and her hysterics—when she has everything to be happy. She needs to be looked after. She's a child."

When they go shopping to buy Cléo a hat, they pass in front of Rivoli Deuil (Rivoli Mourning), a gravestone shop, which relates more ominous messages through the *mise en scène*. As Cléo tries on hats, passersby notice her through the big store windows, "a dreamlike creature that moves as if in an aquarium," as described in the script.[31] "Everything looks great on me," Cléo says to herself as she looks in the mirror. Feeling confident again, she momentarily loses her anxiety. Angèle's influence only reinforces the power of superstition, however, and its capacity to shape perspective. When Cléo wants to wear the hat out of the store, Angèle will not allow it, reminding her that "you should never wear anything new on a Tuesday!" This portrait of Cléo shows a woman with everything but agency, imprisoned by others, by irrational beliefs, and by her own reflection.

Juxtaposing Cléo's *coquetterie* (her concern with her appearance and desire to please) with the confidence and self-assuredness of the female taxi driver in a later scene, Varda captures the atmosphere of this transitional moment for women as they gained access to new professions, breaking stereotypes. The taxi driver says to Cléo and Angèle, "It's a tough job for a woman. Dangerous sometimes, too, but I like it." As some women venture into new roles, others, like Cléo, are still caught in old constructs and constraints, confined to their image and expected behavior. At home, Cléo smiles at her reflection in the mirror before her lover arrives. His neglect, despite his declarations, adds to her insecurity. She starts to realize the imbalance of power: "I'm so kind to him. Always free when he wants me, always made up pretty."

The final blow arrives with the musicians, who tease her affectionately but condescendingly, in a way that discounts her talent. Cléo's breaking point comes after they propose new words to a tune that she was fond of the first time she heard it. Plumitif's lyrics (written by Varda herself and set to music by Michel Legrand, who plays the pianist, Bob) make Cléo articulate what she fears. As she performs the song, "Sans toi" (meaning "without you"), the *mise en scène* depicts Cléo's awakening, reinforced by Marchand's emotional

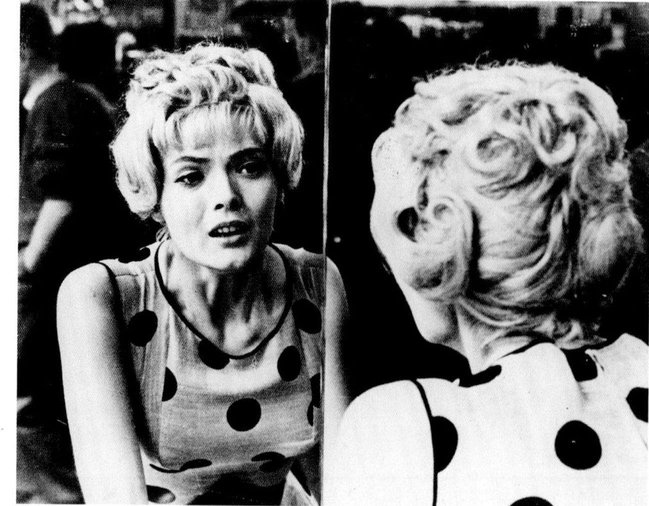

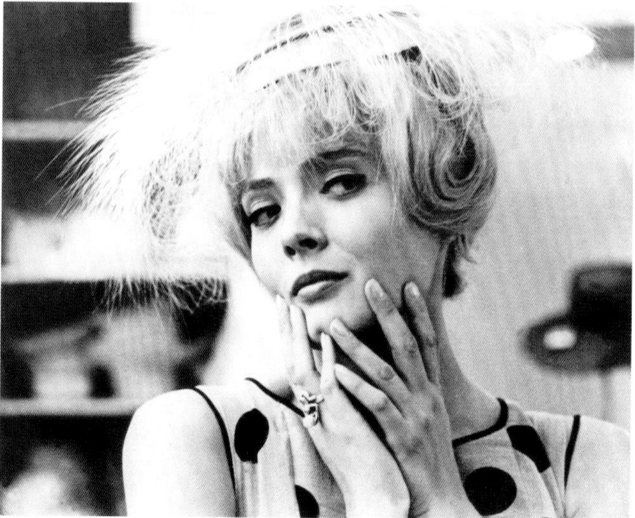

delivery. Varda expressed her appreciation of the performance and the importance of using the actress's voice instead of dubbing it, rare at the time: "When Corinne sang her own playback, we were all moved."[32]

The sequence starts with diegetic sound: Bob's piano and Cléo's vocals. Both are in the frame. As Cléo sings, the words start to resonate in her mind: "Beauty wasted. Cold and naked, my body's an empty shell without you." The camera slowly focuses on Cléo's face in close-up against a black curtain as she stares straight ahead, almost at the viewer, but lost in the lyrics. As she continues to sing the haunting words, "Alone, ugly, and ashen, without you," the accompaniment becomes extra-diegetic with strings, brass, and

Corinne Marchand (Cléo) in Varda's *Cléo de 5 à 7*, 1962

percussion reflecting Cléo's augmented emotion, what she hears in her mind.

Translated in sound and image, Cléo's experience vocalizing her deepest fears ultimately causes her to break down, sparking the beginning of her transformation. The song is filmed in one long take—"the circular movement isolating Cléo will be like a big wave that will take her away," the script indicates. As the music stops, the camera moves out to bring her back into the frame with Bob, back to reality.

"If we were going to feel the shock, I had to do a film in two parts," Varda explained, "one where she is beautiful, *coquette*, admired by others, described by her mirror and everybody who looks at her and all of a sudden because she sings a song . . . [she] has such a strong fear of death."[33] At the end of the song, Cléo accuses the musicians of exploiting her, of never believing in her or in her talent. Before disappearing behind a black curtain, she reveals her deeper truth: "Everyone spoils me, no one loves me, no one."[34] Varda described wanting "a clean cut, a real change. Forty-five minutes into the film, the beautiful Cléo feels it all crumbling: the baby doll, the blonde starlet, everything cracks. She rips off her negligee, her wig. She leaves."[35]

The dialogue further illustrates her crisis and desperate desire to find her true identity as she says, ripping off her wig, "If only I could rip my head off, too."[36] Varda noted that "she tears off her wig as if it were a mask,"[37] adding, "the entire dynamic of the film centers on the moment this woman refuses to be this cliché, on the moment when she no longer wants to be looked at, but wants instead to look at others and becomes the looking subject."[38]

As Cléo reemerges from behind the curtain in the little black dress, it is clear she is on her way to redefining her image. Grabbing her jinxed black hat before going out the door, she places it on her head as the first sign of taking control, now impervious to superstition and others' opinions. This time, when Angèle reminds her, "Cléo, remember, it's Tuesday!" she responds, "To hell with Tuesday. I'll do what I want." Descending the staircase, she enters the courtyard where a little boy is playing a toy piano. The melody again

becomes embellished by pizzicato strings followed by more instruments in the extra-diegetic soundtrack—an instrumental version of "Sans toi" we can assume plays in Cléo's head, accompanying her thoughts. As she crosses the boulevard Raspail, pigeons fly up from the sidewalk. She pauses to look at herself in another mirror outside a restaurant, and her inner voice already comments on the transformation taking place before her eyes: "This doll's face that's always the same. And this ridiculous hat. I can't even see my own fears. I always think that everyone is looking at me, and I don't look at anyone but myself. It's tiresome."[39]

In this scene, Varda is showing a woman discovering not only herself but a new worldview. "She thought she was the center of the world," Varda explained, "and suddenly she's lost her footing. It's a well-known story: the discovery of solitude and the need for others. This hidden malady makes her feel suddenly open, cut off from all her familiar ways of doing things and from then on, she becomes progressively naked, stripped of everything. She takes leave of herself, and gradually tears away her masks. So it's this kind of detachment (literally!), this discovery of herself that seemed to me so exciting to portray. And also this new way of seeing the world."[40] As an object becomes a subject and a self-absorbed woman becomes human, we also see Cléo breaking out of the prison of what Guy Debord labeled at the time "la société du spectacle," an alienated performer finding her authentic self.

CLÉO'S PART II: FINDING HER TRUE SELF THROUGH LOOKING AT OTHERS

In what Varda described as Part II of the film, the narrative shifts to emphasize the importance of encounters with the outside world, of looking at others. Cléo is destabilized: "Suddenly she begins to look, to really see the people she passes in the street, the state of things around her, a guy eating frogs, the art students in the studio. The more she enters into the life of the people around her, the more she finds herself at a loss," Varda explained.[41] With her discovery of the outside world, the film documents, through Varda's choice of images, overlooked people and scenes of Parisians' daily life: "For me, there's no fiction without its documentary side, no film without an aesthetic intent. But I wanted the film's aesthetic side to be entirely at the service of the natural emotions present."[42] Real customers appear along with a few extras in the cafés, capturing a natural and spontaneous *mise en scène* of real life.

Cléo puts on dark glasses when she plays her record on the jukebox at the café, but she is humbled to realize no one is really paying attention. As she looks at the people at the Café du Dôme, "her curiosity," says Varda, "gives importance to others."[43] In turn, we see them through her eyes—Varda's subjective camera.

Taking off her glasses as she leaves the café (like Godard did in the short film), Cléo looks at the people she passes for the first time. "From this moment on," Varda explained, "her anguish leads her to discover others and the people she discovers mirror back the image of her anguish."[44] Again, Varda conveys this notion aesthetically in the *mise en scène*: As Cléo walks down the sidewalk, a subjective camera lets us see what she sees. Recalling *L'Opéra-Mouffe*, Varda included faces of unknown older women who look back at Cléo in this scene. They are the faces that usually go unseen, perhaps projections of Cléo's future. The faces of the people in the present on the street mix with photograph-like shots, flashes of her entourage from earlier in the day who also look into the camera, at her: Angèle, her lover, the fortune teller, Bob, along with images of the ticking clock and her wig hanging from the mirror. The editing of all these shots creates a dynamic *mise en scène* of Cléo's thoughts in real time.

Varda also mixes a variation of "Sans toi," which we can understand to be Cléo's inner soundtrack, with the diegetic sound of the heroine's heels marking the passage of time, like a metronome, as the director metaphorically described it. After a funeral procession briefly impedes Cléo's path, she runs across the street to witness another sideshow of a man piercing his biceps with a thin spike. Repulsed, she runs away again and enters a building to find her friend Dorothée, who is posing as a model for a sculpture class.

After these transitional sequences, the film gives a glimpse into a relationship rarely depicted on screen at the time, that of female friendship. Dorothée (Blanck) is one of the freest characters of the era, and she proves to be a positive influence on the protagonist. Through Cléo's eyes, the camera winds through the studio as the artists work and reveals a model posing nude. The artists concentrate more on their sculptures than on the model, some briefly looking up at Cléo as she enters. Varda recalled the scene more than forty years later, telling Blanck, "I remember I asked the sculptors not to look at you, to look through you, and not at you. We see an idea through their eyes."[45] When Dorothée sees Cléo, she turns her head and looks into the camera, breaking out of her passive role as model to acknowledge her friend.

Pairing Cléo with Dorothée also highlights a difference in perspective and approach to life. The idea of nudity, for example, defines the two characters figuratively as well. While Dorothée appears natural, moving through life without artifice (or neurosis), Cléo is fearful and anxious. Cléo will confess to the soldier near the end of the film, "For me, nudity is indiscretion. It's night and sickness." But as she slowly sheds her sophisticated, superficial exterior, she becomes more vulnerable, more authentic, more naked.

Varda stated that Cléo discovered "Dorothée's simplicity as a model as she posed." When the director asked Blanck what she felt during this scene, the actress replied, "I felt freedom. In other professions, people ask you to behave this way or that way. When you pose, you're nothing. I mean, you're yourself, but nobody asks you how you're feeling. So you breathe and you think about things in your head. The painter isn't your problem. So that's what I mean, it's freedom."[46]

The role of Dorothée was strongly inspired by Dorothée Blanck herself, a perfect example of a real-life encounter bringing to life a cinematic character. While Dorothée the character moved through life without complexes, Varda described Cléo as a bit "uptight and anxious." Marchand agreed, also pointing to similarities between her own personality and that of her character: "Cléo was more uptight. She probably would've never posed nude, nor would I have for that matter."[47]

Cléo's moments with Dorothée are some of the most joyous in the film, from their adventure driving Dorothée's clunky old 2CV convertible in the streets of Paris to their visit to the projectionist's booth to their final taxi ride. Dorothée's natural, even-keeled approach to life is a lesson to Cléo, helping her further overcome her superstition. When Dorothée drops her purse and breaks a mirror, for example, Cléo panics. "It's a sign of death," she exclaims. Dorothée simply laughs and picks up the pieces, responding, "You shouldn't believe things like that. Breaking a mirror is just like breaking a plate, it's nothing." As they ride together in the taxi to Parc Montsouris, Dorothée admires Cléo's black hat, and Cléo, starting to shed the darkness of her old identity, gives it to her friend. As Dorothée exits the cab and runs carefree up the stairs on the rue des Artistes, she bids goodbye to Cléo, waving the black hat in her hand, emphasizing this transformative encounter.

Cléo suddenly seems lighter as she asks the cabdriver to drive more slowly and looks out the window at the people in the street. The soundtrack plays a sunnier instrumental ver-sion of "Sans toi" with piano, followed by violins and a full orchestra, as she converses with the cab driver, a key moment in her new view of the world. In a scene reminiscent of Rossellini's *Viaggio in Italia* (*Journey to Italy*, 1954), we see through Cléo's eyes, like Ingrid Bergman's, the promise and beauty of life. Cléo's new perspective, again like Bergman's, is defined by life instead of death, illustrated by shots of children playing. Surrounded by nature, she enters the park where a new encounter awaits.

"IT'S NOT A LOVE STORY": CLÉO AND THE SOLDIER

Walking through the park "like a sleepwalker," according to the script, Cléo symbolically crosses a bridge and starts whistling one of the happier songs from her rehearsal, "La Belle P." Her joie de vivre springs out unexpectedly in a scene recalling Marchand's role in *Lola*: "[Varda] had me descend these steps, as if I were on stage at the Casino de Paris," the actress recalled. "It's always the dream of a singer. . . . That dream came true here."

As Cléo becomes lighter, another encounter will further transform her. "At this time, she'll meet a soldier from the Algerian War who is afraid of death too," Varda explained. "It's not a love story. It's two fears that meet each other, and they'll be together for the time of a stroll in the park."[48] When Cléo meets Antoine, he baptizes her "Flore" and speaks of the summer solstice taking place on that day. Played by Bourseiller, the father of Varda's daughter, his character is an element of nature in which Cléo takes refuge, the director explained. The natural quality of their encounter is paralleled in Varda's direction of the scene: "filmed in one take, like a deep breath."[49] Varda described how she created this special mood on screen: "As we shot in black and white, this lush green lawn was filmed with a green filter lens, and in the black and white image, it created a white almost snow-like effect which suited this special encounter between a soldier and a frightened girl. I wanted it to be soft, somewhat unreal, even if we talk about reality that is fear."[50]

Like other New Wave heroines (notably Haydée in *La Collectionneuse* and Patricia in *À bout de souffle*), Cléo is search-

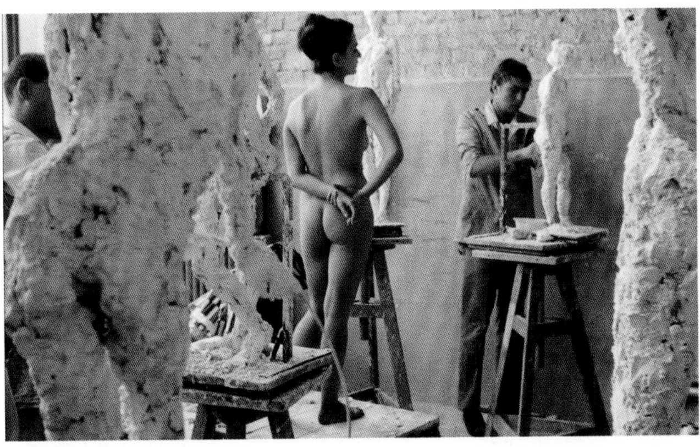

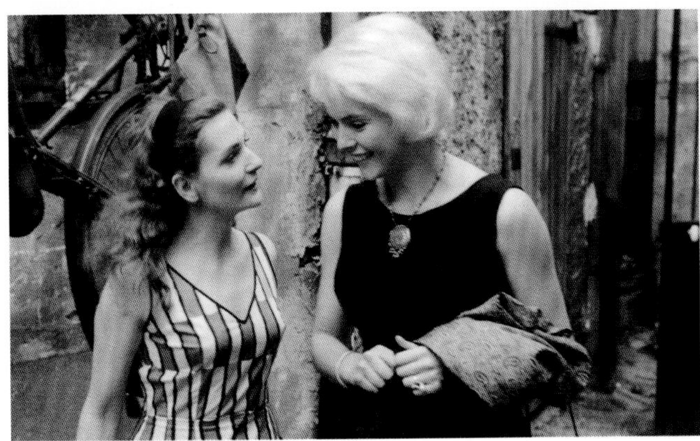

Dorothée Blanck (Dorothée) and Corinne Marchand (Cléo) in Varda's *Cléo de 5 à 7*, 1962

Next page: Ingrid Bergman in Roberto Rossellini's *Viaggio in Italia* (*Trip to Italy*); Corinne Marchand (Cléo) in Varda's *Cléo de 5 à 7*, 1962

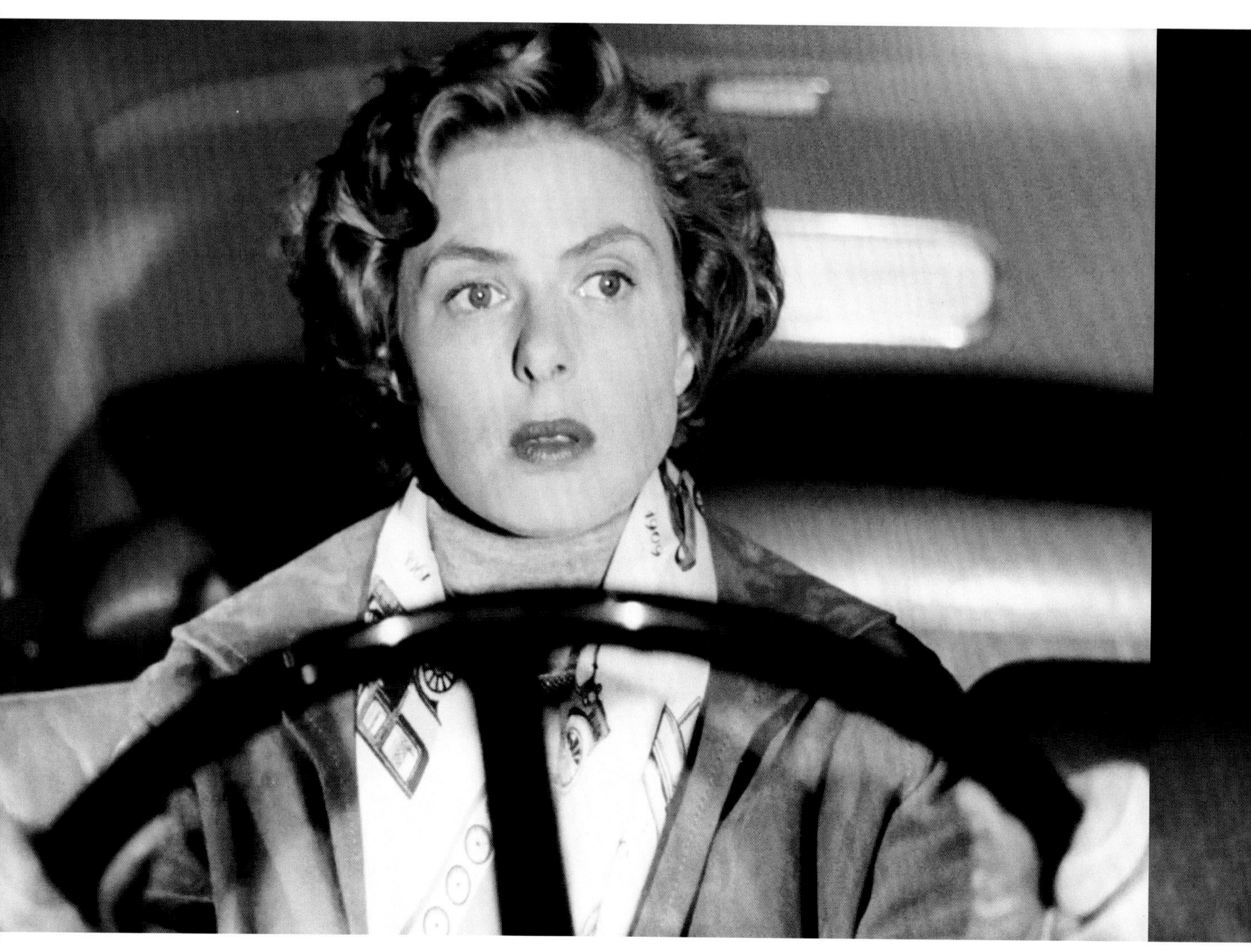

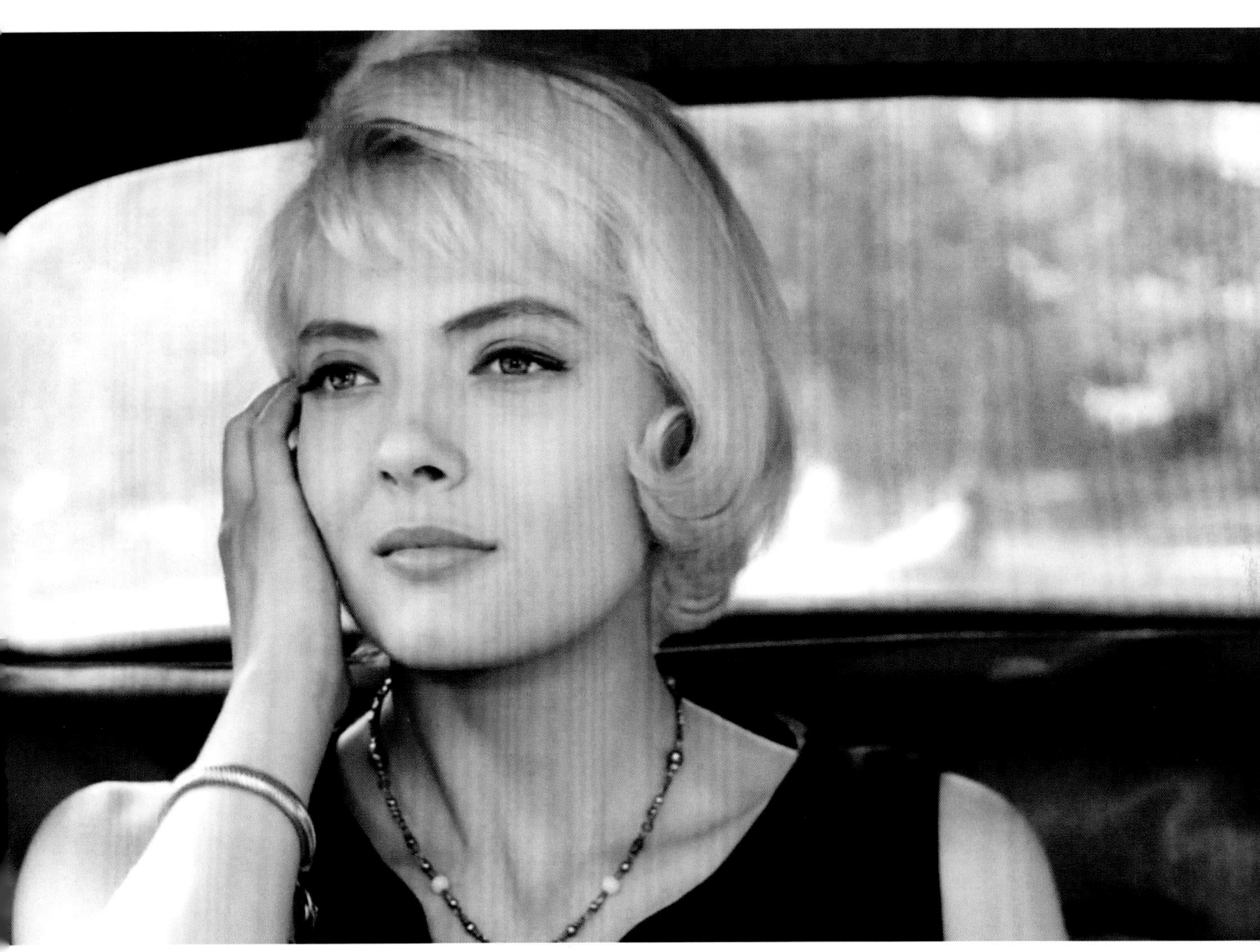

ing. According to Varda, "She's looking for an answer. And the answer comes in the person of the young solider she meets."[51] Antoine does not wear a watch; he is outside time and its constraints. Cléo remarks that he seems "so calm." When she confides in him about her fear while waiting for her test results, she confesses, "I'm afraid of everything: birds, storms, elevators, needles, and now this enormous fear of dying." Antoine's reply puts her fear into perspective: "If you were with me in Algeria, you'd be scared all the time." Daring to address the Algerian War, Varda implicitly demonstrated her political engagement elsewhere in the film as well—news of the war plays over the radio in the taxi scene.

Despite Varda's insistence that the film was not a love story, the characters' discussion about love sheds light on the complexity of human relationships after the trauma of war. Along with its feminine perspective, Varda also conveys a male point of view. When Cléo asks Antoine if he has ever been in love, he replies, "Yes, many times, but never as much as I would have wanted, because of girls, you know how they are. They fall in love, and then actually, they love being loved. They are afraid of everything, of giving themselves deeply, to be damaged, to get bruised. They only love halfway, they keep some in reserve. Their body is like a toy, it isn't their life. So I stop and disengage." Cléo agrees with him: "Yes, it's like what you say; I am always afraid of being taken advantage of, and now, what use is it?" Antoine lightens the mood, but empathizes: "The two of us are in a bubble. Do you feel better?" In this bubble, the two spend the rest of their time "being together," as Varda described it, in the beauty of the Parisian landscape.

Through this encounter, Cléo also discovers authenticity and empathy. Antoine talks to her "like no one had ever talked to her probably; he says whatever is on his mind; he is with her," Varda explained. Their complicity, being together without artifice, allows Cléo to reveal herself to Antoine along with her real name: "Florence." Called "Cléopatra" by her musicians, Antoine (her version of Mark Antony?) says he prefers her real name to "Cléo." As she takes off the mask and shares her real self with him, the theme of nudity reappears in the narrative. "When we are naked, it's easy," Antoine explains. "Love, birth, water, sun, the beach, all of

it." Many of these elements traverse Varda's filmography, a cinema known for this same kind of nudity, revealing with simplicity the true essence of all her subjects.

Varda guides her characters in the final sequence with this simplicity. As they go together to the hospital, Antoine's presence has also helped transform Cléo in terms of her fear and notion of time. Now, fully in the present, Cléo says she will call the doctor later, choosing to spend the moment with Antoine. As they sit on the bench, the doctor happens to drive past them in his car. He relays the results that ambiguously confirm her fears, but proposes a treatment plan, a perspective of hope. Antoine confesses that he is sad to leave, adding that he would like to be with Cléo. "You are," she tells him, confidently, now living in the present. "I feel like I am no longer afraid," she says, "I feel I am happy." With these lines, the director leaves us at peace along with her protagonist in a final scene that communicates the magic and healing power of authentic human relationships.

Speaking to Bourseiller and Marchand years later, Varda implied that the depth of the scene lies in their own encounter, the emotion conveyed through their acting. "I marvel at your relationship," she said, "by something extremely subtle between you, by a gentle complicity you shared, that's what I call being together. It's not about being in love. It's something you can feel in exceptional circumstances." Marchand concurred: "We were in a bubble at that time. I seemed to express it through my eyes." "Antoine, you had tears in your eyes," Varda added. When Bourseiller asked if the audience felt it, Varda reassured him: "Yes, it's there. I can only express my gratitude."[52]

After shooting this final sequence, the director discovered a flaw in the shot: a poorly placed track that appeared blurred between the two characters in the frame. Convincing Beauregard to authorize a reshoot, Varda had the actors return to film it again. They "say the same thing, look at each other, no tracks in the shot, but something is not working," she recounted. "We do it again, take two, three. For me, it's no good, they're not there." In the end, she used the footage from the first shoot, with the blurry rail. The anecdote illustrates perfectly the elusive quality of encounters that produce on-screen magic when they are right. As Varda explained, "But that taught me something, a real lesson: It's very difficult to reconstruct and recreate the magic of a moment in which everyone was in accord. The impulse, the director's desire in the *mise en scène*, the actors' emotions, everything was good. You can't just try to recapture something so ephemeral and miraculous. What a lesson!"[53]

Sacrificing perfection for authenticity is one key to Varda's films and others that express deeper truths. Another is simplicity. As Varda noted, "I wasn't out to make an ambitious film, just the meeting of two people at a moment of acute crisis."[54] Another fundamental notion at the heart of Varda's cinema is also what defines the films of the French New Wave: "It's the story of being together. Can we help each other understand each other?"[55] These are the films that remain so relevant throughout generations. As society evolves, the sensitivity and artistry of directors like Varda give us new models, like those in *Cléo*, like Varda herself, that help us weather the changes.

THROUGH HER OWN LENS: AGNÈS VARDA, AUTEUR

"It's often said you're 'up against the wall' when you have to perform, show your guts and true face—as if most of the time we had a fake face and hidden guts, an extra head to hide behind, an appropriate face," Varda declares in voice-over at the beginning of *Documenteur* (1981). "Me, all I see is that—

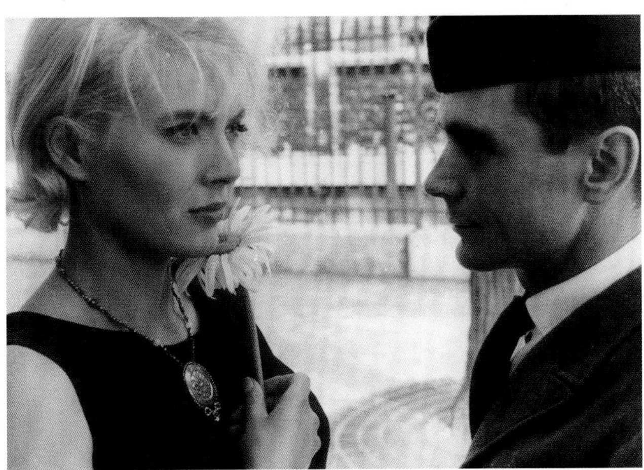

Corinne Marchand (Cléo) and Antoine Bourseiller (Antoine) in Varda's *Cléo de 5 à 7*, 1962

faces. And I find them real, more real than conversations." As she speaks, we see an array of distinctive faces on screen—of faces painted on murals and of real people recorded by her camera. Throughout her career—from *L'Opéra-Mouffe* and *Cléo* to *Daguerréotypes* (1975), *Sans toit ni loi* (*Vagabond*, 1985), and the aptly titled *Visages villages* (*Faces Places*, 2017)—Varda was mesmerized by anonymous faces. In investigating their mystery, she valorized all kinds of people with her lens.

Considering the context of 1950s France, with the many obstacles that female directors faced, it is easy to see what made Varda a true pioneer. Although *La Pointe Courte* anticipated the New Wave movement by almost five years, her films also escaped a generalized label. Each had its own identity, just like the countless faces she celebrated in them. Espousing ideals of social justice, women's rights and relationships, and environmental awareness, Varda's activism seamlessly flowed through her camera in her works of fiction and documentary. Her approach to filmmaking adhered to the idea of the auteur with great integrity. In writing, producing, directing, and editing, her pursuit of telling her own stories required relentless determination and grit. Demanding the right to the final cut of her films illustrated her full commitment to her vision, and her choice to protect her creativity over financial gain.

Faces to Varda seemed "real, more real than what's conveyed by words." In *Documenteur*, she described being lost "in everything around words, everything around faces. Where I am, there's nothing but words and faces." In a sense, this illustrated Varda's idea of *cinécriture*, a term she coined combining *cinema* and *writing* that recalls Alexandre Astruc's *caméra-stylo*. Practicing her own camera-writing through her carefully composed shots and meticulously crafted editing, she focused her attention on the unconventional and the overlooked, whether it be people or landscapes, then finding a theme or unifying motif that she translated through words and images.

As Varda claimed to see herself in the people she met, her succession of portraits of anonymous people also acts as a type of self-portrait mosaic as well as a way of searching for

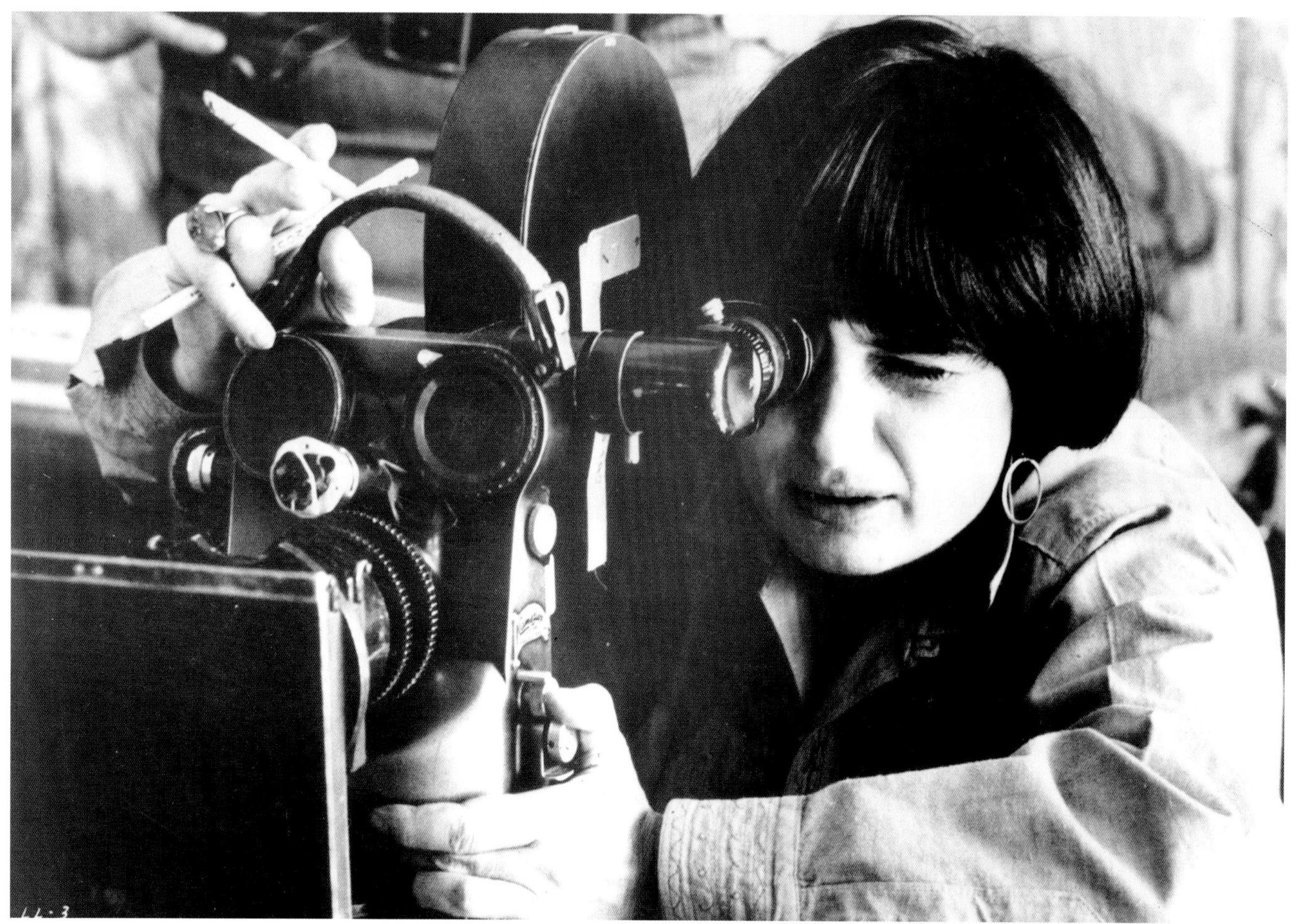

herself. With the camera settling on a close-up of one wom-an's face in *Documenteur*, for example, Varda's commentary in voice-over explains, "This woman, with her face without laughter and her lost expression, she is probably me, real, but I don't recognize myself in her. Nothing meets her eyes but faces, lonely faces, lists of faces, groups of faces, men's faces." Acting as a stand-in for Varda, the woman on screen, encountering other anonymous faces, mirrors the director's own experience in filming them. "There's the word *face* for all the faces that are nameless for her," Varda continues in voice-over, "each one like a voyage. She passes by and ob-serves but she knows nothing about them except that they all close their eyes when they sleep."

In *Visages villages*, Varda teamed with photographer JR to celebrate unknown, everyday people they encountered on their itinerary through the French countryside. The camera takes its time, showcasing different landscapes and pausing to interview and photograph individuals. The director and photographer enlarge the photographs to billboard-sized dimensions and paste them on silos, trains, and buildings, elevating the farmer, waitress, and miner to a status usual-ly reserved for celebrities or models used to sell products. The well-chosen English title, *Faces Places*, illustrates the importance of both in Varda's universe that always sought to level the playing field of social class, wealth, gender, and appearance, and always lingered to contemplate the beau-ty of landscapes and the individuality of every face, every tree.

Mixing fiction and reality through environment and every-day people permeates Varda's vast filmography in varying

Agnès Varda on the set of *Lions Love (and Lies)*, 1969

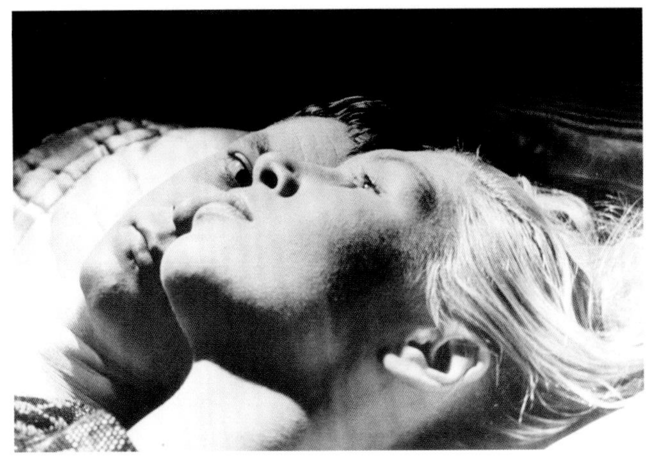

degrees. In 1975's *Daguerréotypes*, she recreated the playbook of *L'Opéra-Mouffe* by focusing on the people from her own longtime neighborhood, on her street, the famous rue Daguerre. It begins with a magician introducing the film and explaining the significance of the street named for Louis Daguerre—the nineteenth-century inventor of daguerreotypes, the first publicly available photography process. Through his innovation, people produced images of still life, city streets, and a great number of portraits featuring both famous and regular citizens. Paying homage to Daguerre, Varda captured a series of cinematic portraits of shopkeepers on her street, from the perfumery Au Chardon Bleu to the butcher shop and boulangerie. As an observer and resident, Varda recorded the lives of those she encountered daily through her *cinécriture* made of image and commentary, while also making room for their own voices. Her poetic commentary recalled the prose of Marguerite Duras, and the way she sees others in her vignettes resembles cinematic versions of those found in Nobel Prize winner Annie Ernaux's *Journal du dehors* (*Exteriors*, 1993). Both Varda and Ernaux portray quotidian exchanges at the butcher shop or in the metro, with minute attention to the unspoken, both outside observers and participants in the lives of the observed.

Varda also examined different aspects of women's station in society throughout her career. Seeking to make a film about clichés, "but those experienced by people in a sensual way," according to Varda, *Le Bonheur* addresses the idea that women are not replaceable (but are treated as such) through

the story of an ostensibly happily married father "perfectly at ease" between his wife and mistress, "two unique but replaceable women." It is also about "society's stereotypes," she explained: "family, family meals . . . motherly love, death, as well as professional and domestic routines, social behaviors and how we can probe these everyday rituals which are social and political even more than personal."[56]

In the opening shot, focusing on sunflowers in a field with a soundtrack of Mozart, the blurry image of a family of four in the distance becomes more defined as they approach the camera. With its beautiful colors in an ideal setting, the image recalls the fairy-tale films of Varda's husband, Demy. The film's narrative, however, will slay this image with an indirect, acerbic, feminist message. "In a world of prefabricated images of happiness sent to us by the media," Varda later stated, "it's interesting to take apart the clichés," anticipating the omnipresence of these types of images today. She described how an image of perfection is not always what it seems: "I imagined a summer peach with its perfect colors, and inside, there's a worm. I thought of the impressionist paintings with their air of melancholy though they depicted scenes of everyday happiness." Like in *Cléo*, Varda intermingled death with a seemingly ideal couple in a bucolic setting: "I listened to Mozart and thought of how death is in the middle of everything."[57]

Groundbreaking in its unspoken feminism—giving the betrayed heroine a voice ironically by drowning her—the film shined a bright light on the husband's impossible demand of asking his wife to accept his relationship with another woman. Scandalous at the time, *Le Bonheur* went even further than *Cléo* in conveying a woman's point of view on multiple levels, showing pressures on a woman to be a perfect wife and a seductive lover, while the two roles remain disconnected and the women interchangeable.

In *Les Créatures*, the power imbalance between another ideal wife and her unreasonable husband is even more explicit. The film opens with Catherine Deneuve smiling in close-up next to Michel Piccoli at the wheel of a convertible. After she pleads with him to drive more slowly, the film

Philippe Noiret (Lui) and Silvia Monfort (Elle) in Agnès Varda's *La Pointe Courte*, 1955

273

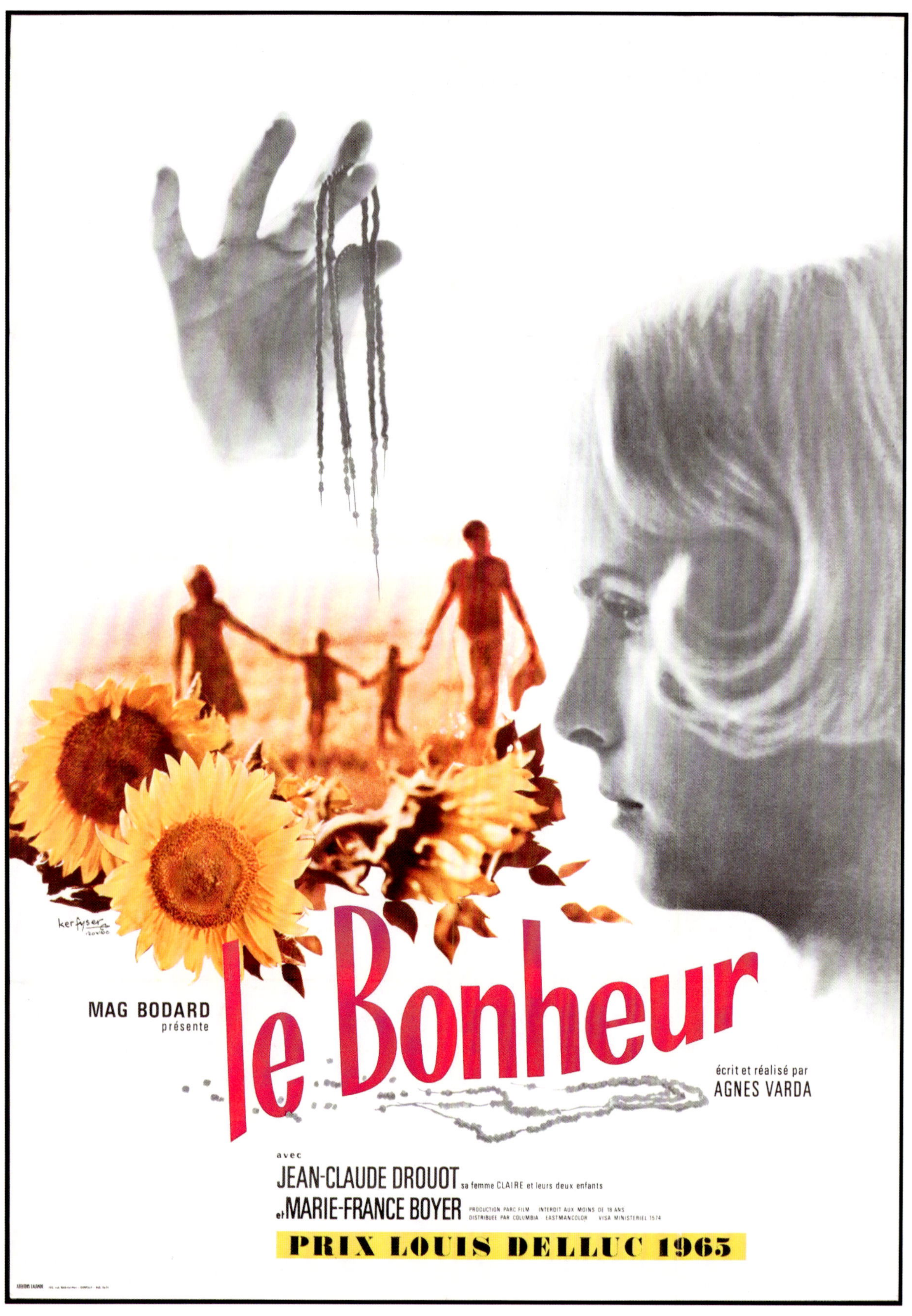

MAG BODARD
présente
le Bonheur
écrit et réalisé par
AGNES VARDA
avec
JEAN-CLAUDE DROUOT sa femme CLAIRE et leurs deux enfants
et MARIE-FRANCE BOYER
PRODUCTION PARC FILM   INTERDIT AUX MOINS DE 18 ANS
DISTRIBUEE PAR COLUMBIA   EASTMANCOLOR   VISA MINISTERIEL 1574
PRIX LOUIS DELLUC 1965

turns dark when the predictable car accident renders her unable to speak. After their dialogue in this opening scene, the wife has no voice, literally. In another Demy-esque fairy-tale setting, Varda implicitly comments on the fabricated image of marriage by showing the couple inhabiting a castle, complete with a tower and moat. Dressed often as a princess, or playing the part of the perfect housewife in an apron, Mylène (Deneuve) prepares food for her husband, Edgar, and serves him with a smile. Unlike the heroine of *La Pointe Courte*, she never talks back, literally or figuratively. Communicating only by writing on an erasable tablet, the wife serves as silent muse and maid to her husband, who is busy writing his novel. Piccoli in the role of a writer who neglects his beautiful housewife recalls, of course, Godard's *Le Mépris*. Unlike the contempt Bardot's Camille shows her husband, Varda's version exaggerates the false-happy present.

Emphasizing the idea that writing is power, her narrator, Edgar, is omnipotent, with complete control over his characters. Writing his observations of the inhabitants in the surrounding village, he is lost in his work, playing chess and a card game with the characters' faces on them, illustrating the power of the author. Soon, he is also lost in the darkness of his characters and in his own rage. An exception in Varda's oeuvre, the film goes further than others in focusing on darkness, embodied in a curious, evil object that instills hatred and violence in whomever it encounters—much like Rohmer's magical device that gives the protagonist the power to seduce in *L'Amour l'après-midi*. Produced by Mag Bodard, who took a chance on the film after producing Demy's *Parapluies de Cherbourg*, *Les Créatures* did not enjoy success at the box office. But it displays Varda's experimental approach in revealing socially accepted stereotypes, implicitly criticizing the imbalance of power between husband and wife, as well as providing a discourse on the creative process and the power of writing—and by extension, directing.

In the 1966 short *Elsa la rose*, about the famous literary couple Elsa Triolet and Louis Aragon, Varda also comments on the creative process and dynamic between husband and wife, writer and muse. Filmed at the writers' home, it shows multiple faces of a couple with shifting roles, addressing the double function of Triolet as Aragon's wife and muse. Describing her own life and their love story, Triolet through Varda's lens appears as a real woman. Through Aragon's poems, she is seen as a muse. The intermingling roles recall Karina and Godard—and Varda's own relationship with Demy, a couple on equal footing as directors. Varda shows, however, the shift in Triolet's identity in relation to her husband as she goes from muse to subject in his eyes. "When she becomes Elsa Triolet," Aragon's commentary states, his wife becomes "the Elsa Triolet of today, author of some seventeen books, no longer only the woman I imagine, but the woman who imagines, who has given life to dreams, and characters I have lived among for a quarter-century, watching them be born, I myself being one of them—a long story that I'll tell you another time. But for now, be content with this fairy tale where everything seems falsely resolved. They married and lived happily ever after—as in every fairy tale."

Like the legendary literary couple, Varda loved Demy deeply. Of all the faces in her films, Demy's in particular was extra special to her. In *Jacquot de Nantes* (1991), her love letter to Demy, Varda includes many extreme close-ups of every detail of his face as a landscape in the present (while he was dying of complications from AIDS) that punctuate her story of his childhood and how he became a director. Though separated for most of the 1980s,[58] Varda remained profoundly attached to Demy throughout her life and honored him with multiple film and media projects after his death. Of all the French New Wave's cinematic couples, Demy and Varda were a model of equality, both parties encouraging each other while pursuing their own art.

Behind the camera, Varda captured the complexities of humanity—rage and cheerfulness, despair and *bonheur*, truth and hypocrisy—through her fictions and through the many faces that appeared in front of her lens, presented with respect but neutrality. The mosaic of faces and landscapes that make up her oeuvre allow us to pay more attention as well, taking time to contemplate the value of what is often overlooked, and hear the voices often unheard.

THE SUBTLE, SWEEPING ACTIVISM OF AGNÈS VARDA

Agnès Varda's *Le Bonheur* (*Happiness*), 1965, original poster

It is almost impossible to distinguish Varda's filmmaking from her activism. Her very being as a director in the earliest days and as a photographer before that makes her an incarnation of feminism, though she would not confine herself to that label. She arduously broke ground for those who came after her with aspirations of directing their own films, and her commitment to social justice behind the scenes comes through as the foundation for her artistic endeavors. From racial and gender inequality to fascism, from poverty and homelessness to ecology, Varda's films shed light on a multitude of issues often before the rest of the world gained awareness of them.

For example, in reference to *Sans toit ni loi*, Varda said that "no one talked about the homeless back in 1984. The French acronym, SDF [*sans domicile fixe*], meaning 'homeless,' was still just police jargon."[59] Her 2000 documentary *Les Glaneurs et la glaneuse* (*The Gleaners and I*) anticipated greater awareness of environmental concerns. Whether in fiction or documentary, she always presented these causes poetically, with her own personal Varda-touch that made them into works of art. Among the names on the Manifeste des 343, Varda's demonstrated her engagement in women's rights, though it did not need to be proven: She had showcased women in her art from the beginning.

But Varda once clarified that she was "not a specialist of films about women."[60] She platformed marginalized groups of all kinds throughout her films, a form of activism every bit as loud as demanding rights with cries of protest in the street. Told in an objective, poetic style all her own, her films had a powerful capacity for persuasion. "We made a feminist film, but it's not aggressive," said Thérèse Liotard who played Suzanne in *L'Une chante, l'autre pas* (*One Sings, the Other Doesn't*, 1977). "I like men," she added. "It wasn't a film with just women. The crew included as many men as women. There were also male roles. I like that a lot, that diversity."[61] Decades before inclusion and diversity entered our daily vocabulary, Varda had applied the ideas in her filmmaking without ostentation.

"Opportunity makes the documentary filmmaker," Varda declared. She accepted an invitation to visit Cuba in 1962, when Cuban culture captivated Parisians and many left-leaning French people were fascinated by this "unique revolution," the director explained. Taking hundreds of photographs in the aim of preparing a shoot, she instead used the stills to compose a documentary short, *Salut les Cubains* (*Hello Cubans*, 1963), adding voice-over about Cuban culture with special attention to revolutionaries Che Guevara and Raúl and Fidel Castro. Echoing the enthusiasm of the Cuban people, Varda's time capsule documented this moment in history when many were excited about the agrarian and educational reforms. As Varda explained in her introduction forty years later, it must be placed in its context: "Now, illusions are lost and we revolt against the behavior of a government that bears all the hallmarks of a left-wing dictatorship."[62] When she was there, "enthusiasm, the courage the work, the political convictions were all very strong," and her "joyous film," as she described it, bears witness to that.

In another documentary short, *Black Panthers* (1968), her camera bears witness to protests surrounding the trial of Black Panther Party leader Huey P. Newton, likening the events to the May '68 riots in Paris. "Beginning in 1968 in France," she said, "demands and hopes are expressed with violence." Unlike Jean Seberg, who became personally involved in the movement, Varda used her platform as a documentarist simply to observe and preserve what she described as a "brief, specific moment in the tormented history of Black Americans."[63]

Varda and her crew met with Newton in prison and went to Los Angeles to film meetings and marches. Exclaiming "French television!" with a smile (and a nice French accent, she joked), she walked among the protesters, shooting with a 16mm-film camera loaned to her by activists at the University of California, Berkeley. Mixing this footage with the Newton interview and activists Bobby Seale's and Eldridge Cleaver's speeches at the gathering, Varda again captured history and the atmosphere, as well as a message of pride and determination. With footage of children dancing to the chants of "We gotta free Huey," she showed people touting Mao's little red book (in color), recalling Godard's *La Chinoise* that featured French youth adhering to Mao's teachings.

Varda gave the microphone to the people to voice their demands for education, fair trials, exemption from military service, and peace. The women, too, "expressed their desire to take action and make decisions and their pride in being Black," Varda explained. Kathleen Cleaver spoke of a new awareness and message that Black women were beautiful, pointing to her hair and the new trend of wearing it natural. "[I]t gives me more pride," Cleaver explained, denouncing women of color straightening their hair to correspond to a white ideal, a practice she wanted to change. Transforming from a fabricated image to an authentic one echoes Cléo in a striking way.

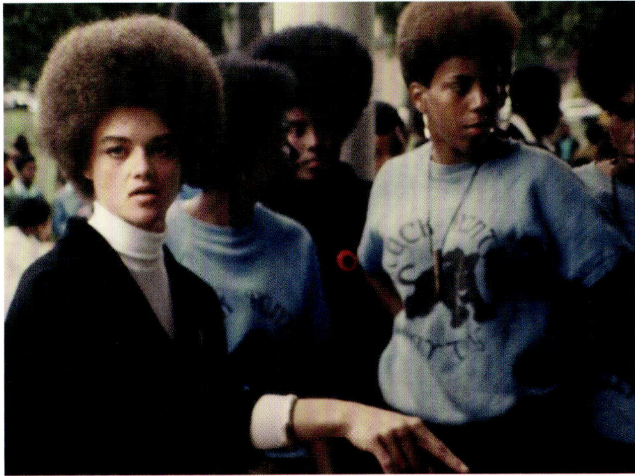

Kathleen Cleaver in Agnès Varda's *Black Panthers*, 1968

Cléo's ideas on freedom and nudity also come back in 1969's *Lions Love (. . . and Lies)*—the title referring to the three actors with wild hair (lions), the love triangle (love), and television and news (lies). "My film is an imaginary news report, a utopian fiction, what came out of my trip to Hollywood, a collage Varda-style," she explained.[64] James Rado and Gerome Ragni, the film's "hippie heroes," in her words, had written and performed in the 1967 musical *Hair*. Viva, the female member of the trio, was one of Andy Warhol's muses. All three, who regularly performed nude in films or plays, chronicled for Varda "this new generation who sought utopia and success without having to put out the effort of work." In a film also about cinema and television, Varda denounced the media's omnipresence in our lives and its bombardment of "contradictory information." Calling out television's "constant mélange of true and false,"[65] the film indeed appeared to be years ahead of its time.

In another vein, *Nausicaa* (1971) illustrates the real and perceived power of film in politics. Made in response to the 1967 military coup in Greece—and though Varda had been authorized to shoot it, the film was confiscated and had to be reconstituted through a working copy of the negative. It opens with an interview of an actor-turned-writer speaking directly into the camera after six months of incarceration and torture: "I escaped the prison called Greece with one purpose, to bear witness." He describes his experience of being "foreign" in France, which Varda parallels with that of her father—who, at twenty, had arrived to Montpellier from Smyrna, Greece (now part of Turkey), joined the foreign legion during World War I, and obtained a French passport. Bearing witness to France's trauma, she also shares her own World War II memories of raising the flag to sing "Maréchal, nous voilà!" ("Marshal [Pétain], here we are!") at school and of a visit from Pétain himself. Revealing some of her background, she discusses her father leaving the Orthodox Church after departing Greece and becoming a *libre-penseur*, a free-thinker—a trait that Varda certainly inherited.

When UNESCO declared 1975 the "Year of the Woman," French television produced *F comme femme* (*W for Woman*), asking seven female filmmakers to respond in seven minutes to the question: "Qu'est-ce qu'être femme?" ("What does it mean to be a woman?").[66]

Focusing on "our body, our sex," Varda's answer was *Réponse de femmes*, which opens with a shot of a nude baby girl, a lighthearted provocation. Through the words of women of all ages and appearances, her film addresses such topics as whether to have children, thinking as a woman, nudity, and using women's bodies to sell products. "We're told, 'Show your legs, customers like it.' I don't like my body being used and displayed like that. I don't like my body being used to boost sales," one woman says. "'Give us sons, soldiers, workers, scientists. Give us daughters, cooks, workers, mothers,' says society," a man declares in voice-over, adding, "A woman who has never known motherhood isn't a real woman." A woman's voice retaliates: "Come on! And a man who hasn't known fatherhood is less of a man?" The irony is illustrated by the names of Einstein, Balzac, and Mozart. The women express what they will no longer tolerate, for example, negative labels ("nuisances, frivolous gossips, bitches, sluts"). "Starting now, things are going to change," they say, revolting. "I won't put up with being loved by misogynists any longer. I'm unique, okay, but I'm every woman."

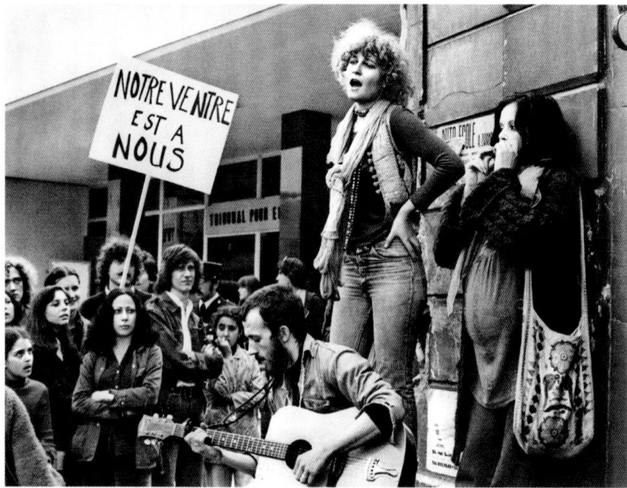

L'Une chante, l'autre pas and *Sans toit ni loi* also center on women, the first chronicling the friendship of two women, the second a homeless woman on the road. On the set of the former, Thérèse Liotard articulated the rarity of these types of women's roles at the time: "Eighty percent of roles in France are for men. With Agnès, we were lucky that the two best roles are women." Her costar Valérie Mairesse added: "And old cinema also tends to be about the male world and male problems, not so much about women's problems. Here for once, we're really talking about those,"[67] explaining that "in men's films, a woman is kind of an object. She's often there just for her body and that's all." Liotard agreed: "Sois belle et tais-toi" ("Be pretty and shut up"). "You don't always get the chance to break out and play something other than an airhead or a nymphomaniac," added Mairesse.

The film addresses feminism through the lives of two advocates for women's rights. It is "a film that tries to illustrate very naturally this beautiful line by Simone de Beauvoir," Varda explained: "On ne naît pas femme, on le devient" ("We are not born a woman, we become one"). She also pointed out the importance of images in shaping our definition and ideas about women. "[It is] a film on women and their images," she said, "on society's stereotypes and the new images

that women are establishing slowly."[68] Varda proved her tenacity to get this kind of film made by producing it entirely herself. "I don't have money personally so it means finding government funding, French coproducers, whether governmental or private, and selling the film in advance." This mode of financing allowed her to make films her way. "I'm the last one who gets paid," she added. "I take all the risk."

With *Sans toit ni loi*, Varda had originally intended to make a film about homeless people. When a policeman told her about finding a young man under an apple tree who had died of cold, she was touched. Starting from this tragic end, Varda set out to reconstruct an imagined trajectory of what happens in the lives of people like him. Inspired by two cypress trees on a hilltop in the south of France for the landscape, Varda began her background research for the film: into the lives of homeless people as well as those of the trees. She visited shelters, blood banks, and railway stations to investigate the places vagrants frequented, and she crisscrossed France to scout locations to film. "To 'feel' the road like female drifters, who provoke, destruct, or reject, I walked too, though without a backpack," she said. "The poor, the homeless, the dirty and rebellious who take drugs and drink," she explained, "they moved me deeply."[69]

Varda centered the narrative around one drifter, Mona (Sandrine Bonnaire) and the diverse characters she encounters on her path, like those Varda and JR would capture in *Visages villages*. The fictional heroine here acts as Varda's proxy as an embodiment of total freedom from convention and expectations. Bonnaire said that when Varda offered her the role, the director told her, "[Mona] stinks, she's contemptuous, and she never says thank you." While shaping the actress to fit the role, Varda described as essential the part Bonnaire contributed to it: "A character is made from a strong idea and an actor's personality. I asked Sandrine, who I think is great, she's talented and rebellious." Varda admired Bonnaire's acting in the film "providing a presence and an intensity in every moment." She wondered how the actress managed to express "such rage and violence" at seventeen and a half years old—admiring perhaps her demonstration of the rage Varda was unable to express fully in her fiction, as in *Les Créatures*. Confessing that she did not flatter Bonnaire's

Valérie Maresse (Pomme) and Thérèse Liotard (Suzanne) in Agnès Varda's *L'Une chante, l'autre pas* (*One Sings, the Other Doesn't*), 1977 appearance with her *mise en scène*, Varda complimented on her "playing the game and accepting the conditions."[70] The actress abstained from washing her hair for two months while filming. Worried about being typecast, however, Bonnaire insisted she was not like Mona: "It's not me at all. I'm a pretty gentle, cheerful person."[71]

But Mona does share a certain steely vigor with Varda. "Whatever happens to Mona, she is not a victim," the director asserted. "She likes freedom for freedom's sake, not to annoy her parents or society. She has no ideology. She wants to be left alone." While pursuing others with her camera in a quest to pierce their mystery, Varda loved her own freedom. Perhaps the camera acted as a medium and a filter for the director, allowing her to approach people while also keeping her distance, preserving her autonomy.

"I think Mona is really a girl of our times, by which I mean vagrants have been around since the Middle Ages, but women on the road on their own are a relatively recent phenomenon. They impress me even more than guys. . . . They don't grumble or act miserable." Varda's motivation for the film resonates with her own Corsican adventure as a young woman. "I wanted to film the meaning of freedom and dirt," she explained. "Our society rejects dirt even more than poverty."[72]

Dirt and poverty come back in *Les Glaneurs et la glaneuse*, raising environmental awareness while shedding light on her filmmaking philosophy. Showing rejected potatoes after harvests in the provinces and leftover produce on the streets in Parisian markets, the film also gives visibility to marginalized or forgotten people. Besides peasants, landowners, and farmers, Varda interviewed artists and lawyers to convey the process of gleaning. A poignant vignette at the end of the film shows an articulate graduate student, Alain, scavenging through the leftover produce at the market for his meal, while astutely explaining the vitamin content in each of his choices. We find out later that he is a volunteer at a shelter, teaching newly arrived immigrants to read and speak French. Comparing the process of gleaning with her filmmaking, Varda explains how she too is a gleaner, traveling around in search of encounters, images, and faces. She honors the imperfections of that undertaking—just like she marvels at the age spots on her hands—by including would-be discarded footage in her final cut.

Varda's work reflects her sensitivity to beauty in the imperfect, embodied by the heart-shaped potato in *Les Glaneurs* that graces the poster of the film. Invited by the Venice Biennale to create an installation, on the floor she scattered hundreds of imperfect potatoes accompanied by a tryptic of screens, titled *Patatutopia* (2003), displaying potatoes at different stages and in different forms.[73] Wandering around the room was sometimes Varda herself, dressed as a potato from which her recorded voice recited the many different potato varieties in French. The whimsical project illustrates the heart of Varda's documentaries and fiction: the respect and value of each person as a unique individual. Through her nonjudgmental, poetic style, Varda showed in her films that we are all valuable and all connected, with nature and with each other, and all deserving of respect—creating in the process a transformative oeuvre and legacy.

Sandrine Bonnaire (Mona) in Agnès Varda's *Sans toit ni loi* (*Vagabond*), 1985

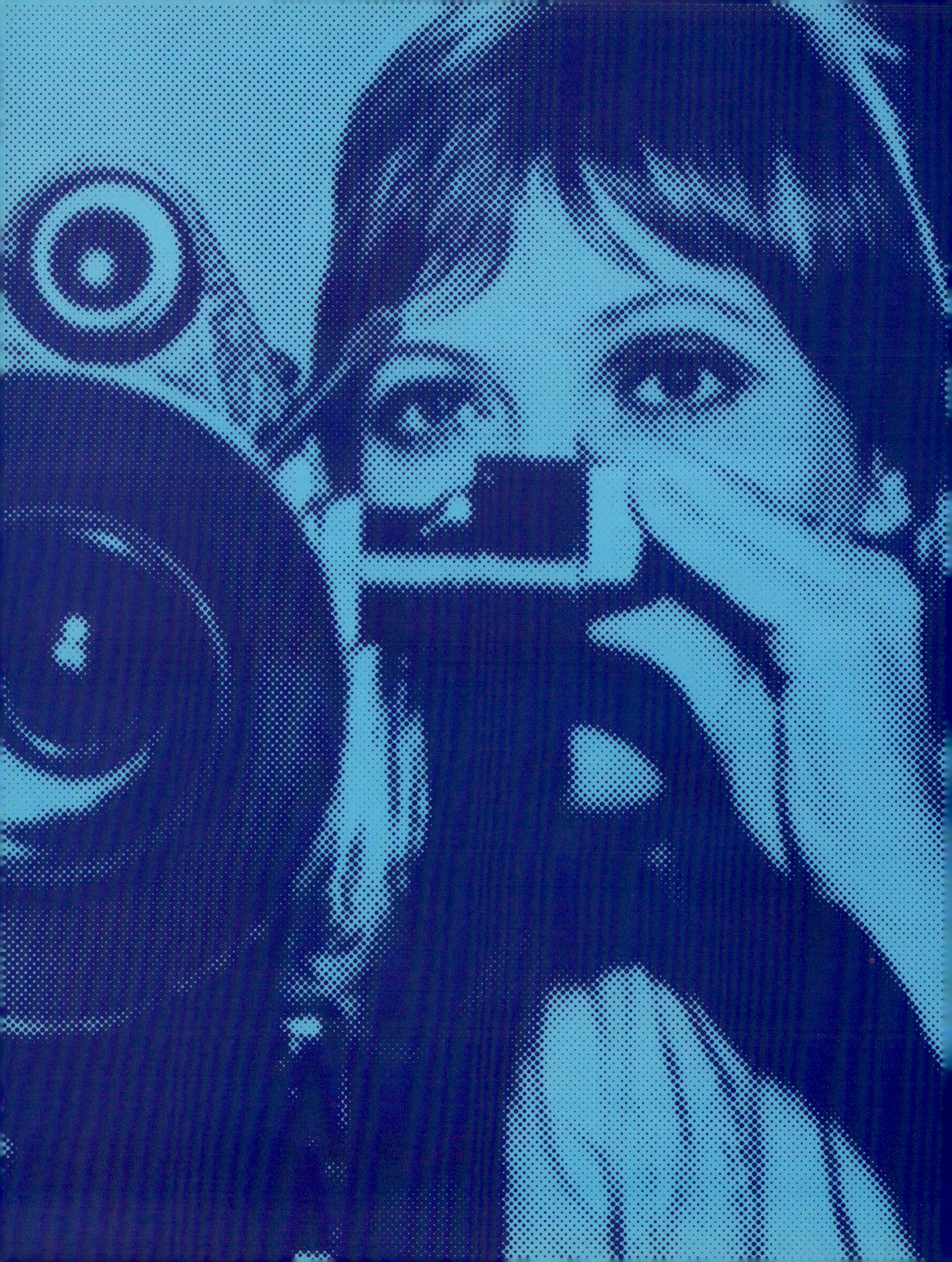

nouvelles femmes, 14
nouvelles voix

new women, new voices

After their revolutionary cinematic work in the French New Wave, many of the actresses and women associated with the movement furthered their careers on screen and off. Some became authors, directors, or activists—many did all three. Vast in scope and influence, the New Wave also employed countless competent and dedicated women too often unrecognized for their contributions to the success of an enterprise. Honoring every work by every woman who made the movement what it was—and carried its spirit into the future of cinema—can never be accomplished in a single book. With that in mind, this chapter is a celebration of some of the endeavors of women who were a part of this exceptional moment in film history, the French New Wave.

HELEN SCOTT, *AMIE AMÉRICAINE*

Behind the scenes, Helen Scott was largely responsible for the New Wave's success in the United States. A New Yorker, she became fluent in French during a childhood stint in Paris with her mother and brothers while her father—a journalist, lawyer, and diplomat originally from Ukraine—worked as a foreign correspondent in Moscow. In 1959, after a storied early career in politics and activism halted suddenly by her McCarthy-era blacklisting, Scott began working for the US office of Unifrance, an agency promoting French films abroad. It was she who welcomed François Truffaut on his first visit to the US following the success of *Les Quatre cents coups* in Cannes.

Scott transcended her role as interpreter during interviews for Truffaut, who did not speak English. She introduced him to her vast network of influential journalists and critics, establishing his credibility and expressing her own enthusiasm for his work. Upon Truffaut's return to France, the two actively corresponded, Truffaut keeping her abreast of the New Wave's most promising films and directors, and Scott reporting back on their progress (and her own efforts to promote them) in American markets. The pair continued their friendship and collaboration. Scott encouraged Truffaut to shoot *Bonnie and Clyde* (though he never did) after being the first reader of the script; and she helped him through the turmoil of filming his 1966 adaptation of Ray Bradbury's *Fahrenheit 451* in English, even contributing dialogue to the film.

Helen Scott is perhaps best known, however, for her contribution to the monumental book, *Hitchcock* by Truffaut, published in 1966. In August 1962, when Truffaut convened with the master of suspense for a week's worth of detailed interviews about Hitchcock's filmmaking process, between them was Scott—who not only served as interpreter but also transcribed the interviews and translated them for French and English editions of the corresponding book. It was Scott who convinced Truffaut to gear the book toward a wider audience, rather than just Hitchcock's fans at *Cahiers du cinéma* and

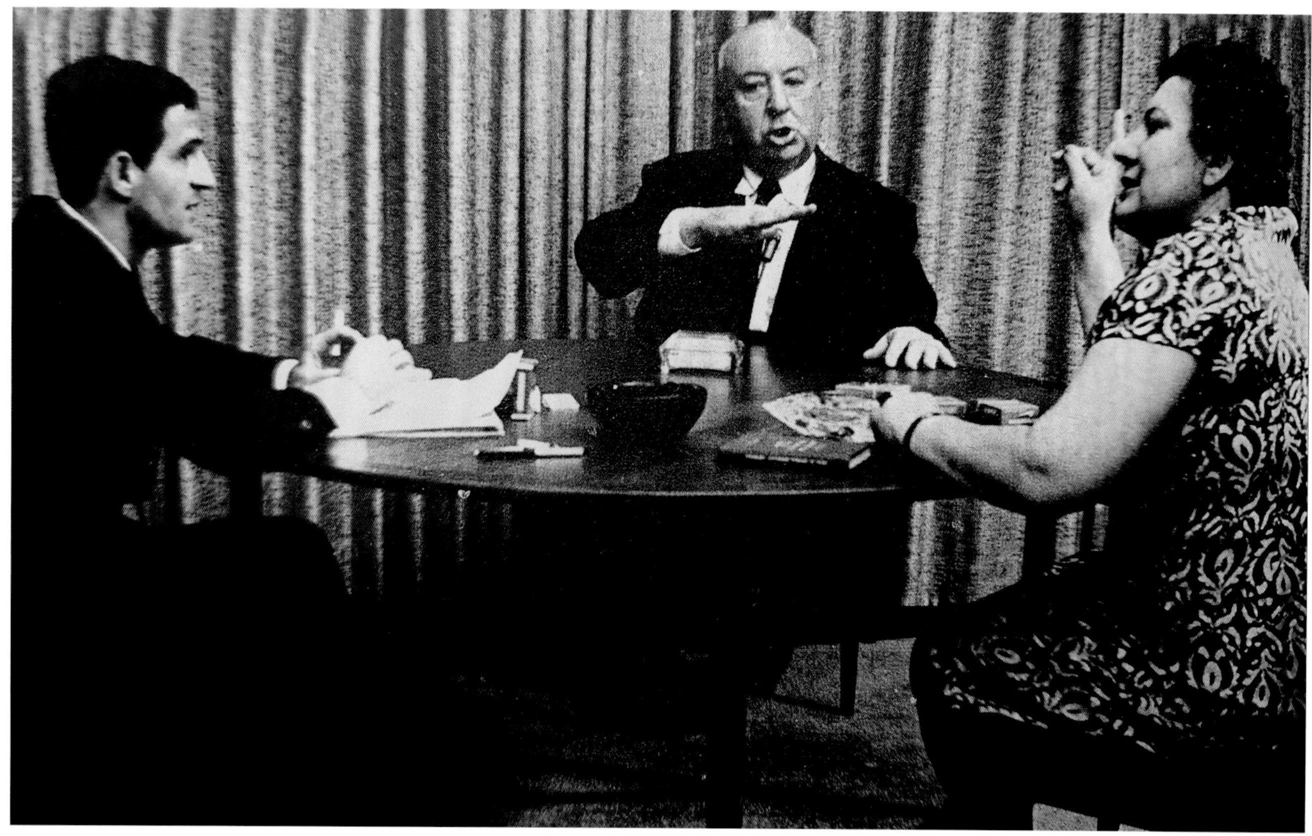

François Truffaut and Alfred Hitchcock with Helen Scott interpreting, Hollywood, 1962 during the interviews for the book *Hitchcock/Truffaut*, 1966

esoteric cinephiles. The book has since become iconic and has been reedited and translated into numerous languages.

Moving to Paris in 1966, Scott remained close friends with Truffaut until his death in 1984. More than thirty years after her own death in 1987, film critic Serge Toubiana published her early correspondence with Truffaut, revealing for the first time the full extent of Scott's role in bringing the French New Wave to the US. "[I]f François Truffaut is so famous in America, nearly forty years after his death," Toubiana wrote, "he owes it in part to Helen Scott."[1]

ANNA KARINA, AUTEUR

"Things have changed," Anna Karina said in a 2016 interview. "But at the time, if you were a woman, you didn't really have a voice. If you were a woman it was just, 'Be beautiful and shut up.'"[2] Karina refused to heed the command. Writing, she once explained, had been part of her life from a young age: "I've been writing short stories since I was a little girl. I left school when I was fourteen, but I always liked to write."[3]

The lack of support for actresses trying to branch out to pursue writing or directing was so strong during the '60s and early '70s that when Karina wrote her first script, she submitted it to the CNC under the pseudonyms "Jean Dagordy" and "Michel Wally." She also presented it to her friends anonymously, under the guise of asking them whether she should accept the leading role. Encouraged by their enthusiasm for her script, she decided to find a director.

While visiting the United States, she saw people filming in 16mm, inspiring her to take on the challenge herself. She did not stop there. Because "no one else really believed in" the film, Karina explained, in 1972 she founded her own production company in order to make it—Raska Productions, a portmanteau of the first syllables of her then-partner Jean-Pierre Rassam's surname and her own. "I put a lot of money into it myself—not a lot, because it's not a very expensive pic-

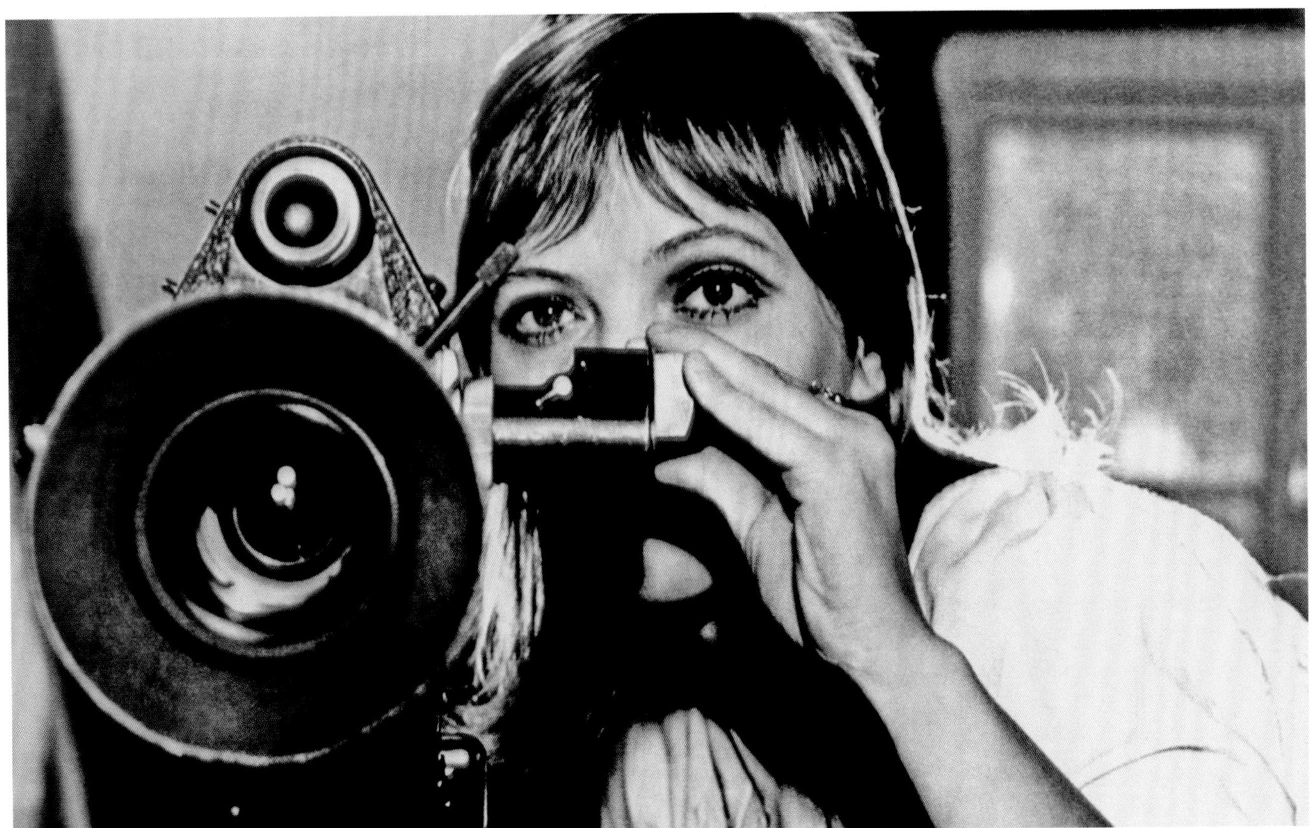

Anna Karina behind the camera for her film *Vivre ensemble* (*Living Together*), 1973

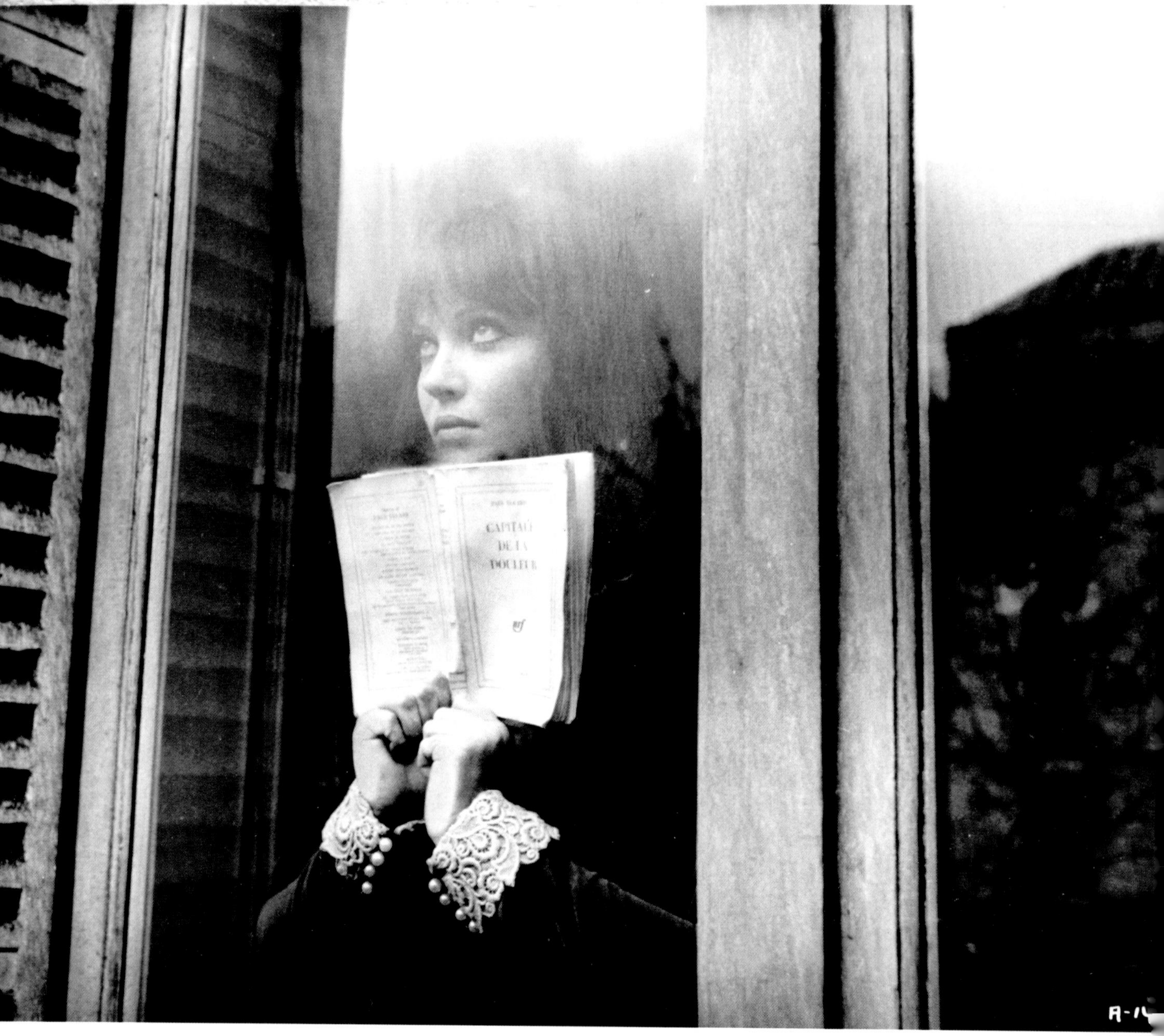

Capitale
de la
Douleur
nrf

ture, but a lot for me," she said.[4] Then, to appease the distributor with a star they could sell (and since her name held no cachet as director), she cast herself in the lead.

In true New Wave fashion, Karina oversaw every aspect of production, from scheduling to costuming, with occasional help from her industry connections. Truffaut's production manager, for example, helped her create a budget, and her friends worked for free in one scene as background actors. "I gave them a big meal and they were very happy," Karina recalled.[5] With such a small budget and crew, filling in the gaps for what they could not afford mostly fell to Karina. She used her own apartment in the Latin Quarter as a set, and she even cut the actor's hair herself. "I had to shoot backwards, starting with the end of the film, because of the male character with his beard and haircut that I had to cut little by little," she said. Shooting on location in New York City (which they did without authorization) presented more obstacles: While filming one scene in Harlem, someone attacked director of photography Claude Agostini with a knife.

It did not take long for Karina to earn the attention and respect of her male crew. "The first day was difficult because they were all watching. 'What is she going to do? Does she know where to put the camera?'" she said. "I was talking normally, saying, 'Put the camera over there' and 'Do this like that,' and they were not really listening, so I talked a little louder, and they were half-listening. Then suddenly I would scream, which is something actors do, I would scream very loudly, and everybody would stop. There would be a silence. And then I would talk very softly again. That was the first day, and then afterwards, no problem. Actually, I don't think I had a lot of trouble. I didn't have more trouble than anybody else would have had. It's not because I'm a woman. Maybe people were laughing behind my back but that I can't say."[6] Actor Michel Lancelot, who played Karina's love interest in the film, described her as "a woman and, at the same time, she's a guy. I wouldn't say a man. She's a guy."[7] Taking an active role in the editing process gave Karina the opportunity to work with women also, as most editors at the time were women. "It's funny because when I did the picture, I was only working with men and when we were cutting, we were only women. They used to be Jean-Luc's assistants, so I knew them for a long time."[8]

The product of all her labor was *Vivre ensemble* (*Living Together*, 1973), which follows the relationship between a stuffy professor (Lancelot) and a free-spirited bohemian (Karina). She based the story off a friend's real-life experience[9] and divided it into seven tableaux (recalling those in *Vivre sa vie*) to reflect her idea of there being different chapters in life. The tableaux inserts—which Karina explained as "a nod to silent film and also because we had no money"—were handwritten by Jean Aurel (with whom she made two films).[10]

Like in the New Wave films, she incorporated spontaneous documentary-type footage into the fiction she had written. In the New York City park scenes, for example, the characters walk among actual political demonstrations—less a political statement on Karina's part than a commitment to authenticity. "I feel they should be in the picture because it's part of life and it's really what was going on in New York at the time," she explained. But in Paris, she included a poster of May '68, not as an homage to the revolution that took place five years earlier but "to show that people really don't care very much about what they say about things. They forget so quickly." The scene was inspired by her own memories of having lived next to the Sorbonne during the student protests. "I saw a lot of people not being very honest about many things. Actually, May '68, I don't think it was really that important," she said skeptically. "It didn't change at all, nothing." If her view of politics seemed pessimistic, she nonetheless gave her heroine a better outcome than the ones she played in many Godard films. Though her film can be seen as feminist in this way, she claimed that it was not linked to the women's liberation movement. Hesitant to adhere to the practices of the MLF, she maintained her own point of view in that regard: "There are a lot of points I would go for, but I don't agree with the way they're doing it. I don't think you should make war against men."[11]

Choosing positivity over antagonism, Karina redeems her heroine in *Vivre ensemble*, illustrating the arc of a woman, Julie, who goes from being free but lost to gaining independence and agency: She begins the film living day by day and

Anna Karina (Natacha) in Jean-Luc Godard's *Alphaville*, 1965 ends it as a woman who supports herself financially while embracing motherhood at the same time. Taking down the photographs of the men previously on the wall above her bed, her many conquests, Julie replaces them with images of her baby, her partner, and herself—the picture of a new kind of family in which the mother earns the living, going to work and leaving the baby with his father. Intentional or not, this role reversal sheds light on the inequality of the situation, showing the frustration of the one home alone all day with the baby, in this case, Alain, the father. Losing his status of professor, Alain slowly occupies a weaker position, resorting to giving private lessons to ten-year-olds in their small apartment. Unfulfilled, he becomes depressed and resorts to drinking, the opposite trajectory of Karina's character, who finds equilibrium in her new identity.

In making the film, Karina too entered a new chapter of her life, seizing her agency, finding her voice, and creating art of her own. "I wanted to do something by myself. When you've been working with directors, suddenly you feel like doing something by yourself," she said when the film was released. Karina presented her film in Cannes where it was selected as part of the Semaine de la critique (Critics' Week), which she found extremely gratifying. "Since it was a time when women didn't yet make films, it had a little bit of success but not much," she said. "What makes me happy is that it is still here. It's my child anyway."[12]

Besides directing her best-known film, Karina sang, wrote songs, and continued to act. For Pierre Koralnik's *Anna* (1967), she recorded seven songs written by Serge Gainsbourg and realized her lifelong dream of starring in a musical comedy. She also wrote the 1983 novel *Golden City* "just for fun,"[13] Karina said, and then "wrote a second one, and then a third one, and some musicals and songs too." Her passion to create continued throughout her whole life. In 2008, she wrote, directed, and starred in *Victoria*, a musical road movie: "It's about an amnesiac woman who travels in Canada. She doesn't know who she is anymore, she forgot all her memories."[14] If Karina's heroine was searching for her identity, the books and films she wrote, starred in, and directed preserve the memories of her own many

chapters, illustrating how many rich lives she lived in just one—fulfilling her character's wish in *Pierrot le fou*: "I want to live!"

JEANNE MOREAU IN HER OWN WORDS

"Being an actress allowed me to meet people and live differently. And it also made me want to do something else," Jeanne Moreau explained in a 1972 interview. "Maybe I'll write. I've been writing for a long time. It's a good way to chat with oneself. You can't always say things aloud. I feel like writing a book, but it'll take me many years. I like to keep busy. Because I'm still too active, I want to keep moving. I'm saving things for the end, for later. . . . It will be the story of a passion, my passion for life."[15]

In the mid-'70s, Moreau started this autobiographical project, which she called *Mon livre* (my book), by dictating anecdotes and observations to herself on tape. Though the work obsessed her, she could not let herself complete it. Expressing herself with such a high degree of sincerity also meant accepting extreme vulnerability. In 2001, on the occasion of her induction into the Académie des beaux-arts—and as the first woman to receive such an honor—Moreau gave a speech that offered a glimpse at her long-awaited autobiography. In it, she evoked her childhood in Vichy and in the countryside, when she was still called "Jeannette."

Though the book remained unfinished, parts of it were published posthumously in 2023 by the French publisher Gallimard as *Jeanne par Jeanne Moreau*. Besides the excerpts from *Mon livre*, this collection of ephemera also included an alphabet book (with childhood memories under the letter *A*: *Absence, Ancêtres, Antigone, Armée, Avril . . .),* personal correspondence (with many letters to Roger Nimier), and various reflections, such as thoughts on her mother and her own experience of motherhood. She also shares cinematic memories as a young girl who did not want to dress like Shirley Temple, who witnessed passion and violence in Renoir's *La Bête humaine* (*The Human Beast*, 1938). We learn of her crush on Pierre Fresnay (illustrious actor of

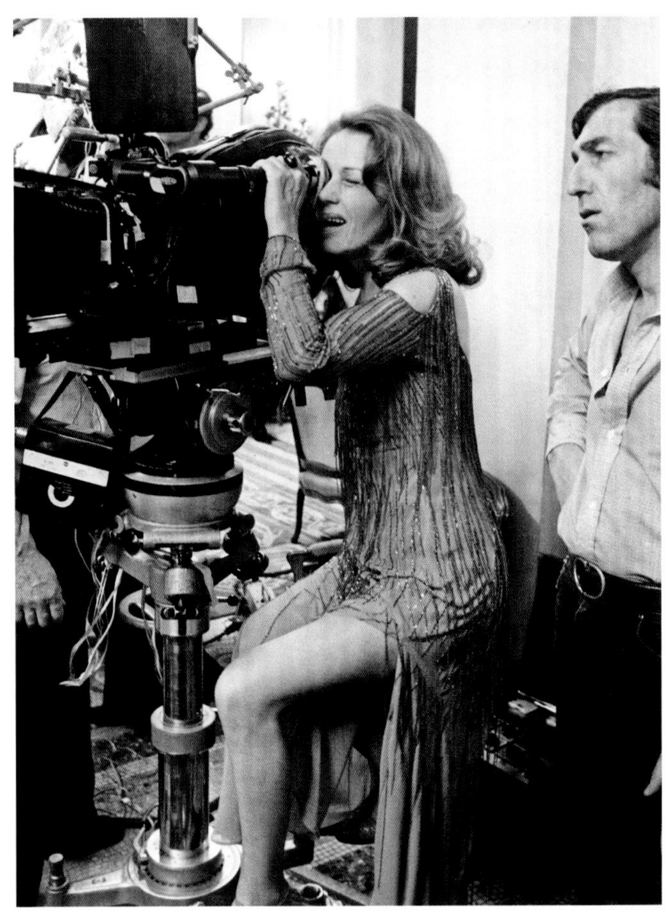

private life fed her creativity, Moreau answered, "Precisely. We're like bees."

In her mid-forties, Moreau was asked what she would do if directors no longer offered her roles in five or six years. Her response: "That's not the way things will happen. I don't have time to tell myself that in five or six years I'll have no more film offers. . . . But I'll make movies—as a director."[17] Moreau's incisive self-reflection is also preserved in *Lumière* (1976), a celebration of female friendship which she wrote, directed, and starred in as a famous actress in the middle of her career. In the opening scene, she and three other actress characters reexamine events from the year earlier and share stories of their first experiences with boys. The scenario illustrates her mood in 1972 when she stated, "There's certainly a time in life, at about thirty-five or thirty-six, when we suddenly stop and think. And we're more inclined to have these periods of introspection at that age than before. And it's not caused by an external event, a heartache, or whatever else. Not at all. It's a moment when we feel overwhelmed. Time goes by. Life is a road we travel until we reach a point where we look back and ask ourselves, what's up ahead?"[18] In a 2017 review, *New Yorker* critic Richard Brody praised the film as "a calm, lyrical melodrama with an air of lightness and grace, a survivor's story."[19]

stage and screen) and her wonder over the impertinence and elegance of Danielle Darrieux. She describes trips to the Gaumont-Palace to see Charlie Chaplin, Fred Astaire, and Ginger Rogers.

Moreau's honest writing conveys her experiences as she evolved into a young woman, discovering theater, love, friendship, and the directors who changed her life, personally and professionally. Of *Ascenseur pour l'échafaud*, she wrote, "For the first time, I was associated with people who worked all together on the creation of a film . . . and with whom I felt equal." Living her own version of *Jules et Jim* with Louis Malle and Roger Nimier, the actress described the intermingling of cinema and real life in *Ascenseur*: "There were real affective relationships. It was really a love story. I was in love with the film, I was in love with Louis, I was fascinated by Roger Nimier."[16] Asked in an interview if her

Moreau would go on to direct *L'Adolescente* (*The Adolescent*) in 1979, a film she cowrote and narrates in voice-over. It follows a twelve-year-old girl who leaves Paris on Bastille day in 1939 and comes of age during the war. The heroine's wise and loving grandmother is played by Simone Signoret. In 1983, Moreau paid homage to another great actress in her television documentary *Lillian Gish*. Interviewing Gish in English, Moreau's portrait also emphasizes the power of the actress's face and the truth of her acting. Like Gish in the silent era, as an actress Moreau was a reference point for the women of her era through the parts she chose. In 2001, at seventy-four, she starred as Marguerite Duras, her close friend, in Josée Dayan's *Cet amour-là*. Moreau once stated that the only activity that she held higher than acting was writing. An homage to both professions, Moreau's portrayal of Duras synthesized their two voices and illustrated the need for women to appear in diverse and complex roles at all ages.

Jeanne Moreau on the set of her film *Lumière* (*Light*), 1975

EMMANUELLE RIVA, LIFELONG POET

As a very young girl, Emmanuelle Riva liked reciting poems in public. "I liked saying them in front of others. I couldn't keep them only for myself. I had to make the author's word heard, like a pleasure of sharing," she explained. "I wanted to speak all of these writings. To share them! I told myself that it was impossible not to make that my life's work. I was stuck in the provinces. I didn't know what to do," she said of her time as a young stage actress in the Vosges region of France. Recalling her first audition in Paris, she stated over fifty years later, "if I hadn't succeeded, I would be dead."[20]

Along with her many respected roles, Riva published four books of poetry. "I think it helps me a lot to be able to write. It's an equilibrium, a calm, something that is accomplished, an act," she said in an early interview. "Action is very necessary," she went on to explain, "because in the beginning I wasn't active. I was someone who was dreaming, who let herself go with the flow, and I became aware that it wasn't ideal. One day I felt the urge to write, to speak with others because I was shy in the beginning." Describing her process, she explained, "I write whenever it strikes me. I don't do it intentionally, at all. The pencil almost writes by itself. It imposes itself. It's often a joy to write, a delight. It's seldom a suffering. . . . It's a communication."[21]

Riva practiced another medium of communication while filming *Hiroshima, mon amour*. While French critic Jean Domarchi described *Hiroshima* as "a documentary on Emmanuelle Riva," the actress was documenting what she saw around her in photographs she took of daily life in Hiroshima, a city struggling to restore itself after its destruction during the war. A collection of her images[22] was published in *Hiroshima 1958* (2009).[23]

MACHA MÉRIL, RENAISSANCE WRITER

From lighthearted to serious, Macha Méril's numerous books reflect her rich personality, and her writing is as multifaceted as the roles she played. Much of her work contains echoes of her own history. Méril was born Princess Maria-Magdalena Vladimirovna Gagarina to Russian aristocrats who im-

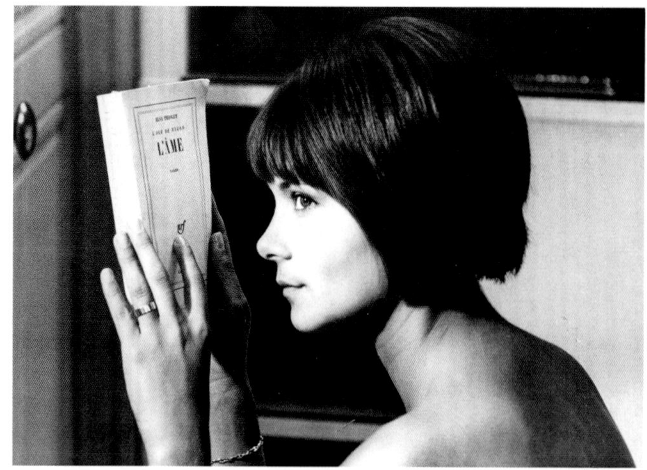

migrated to France during the 1917 October Revolution. In her 2020 novel *Vania, Vassia et la fille de Vassia*, Méril wrote of Russian refugees living in France after the 1917 Revolution who grapple with their political and cultural identities in the wake of World War II. Other novels draw on Méril's experiences in entertainment, as in 1982's *La Star*, about a forty-year-old actress who is wondering whether she is still beautiful, whether she has been a good wife and mother.

Méril does not shy away from subjects that are personal or ignore seemingly frivolous ones. In her 2001 book, *Patati, patata, trois petits tours et puis ça va*, she shares her thoughts on everything from rain, high heels, and short skirts to global warming and the desire to please others, and she has even written cookbooks. In one, she proposes psychological and sensual recipes centered on playful themes like how to charm a man, how to separate from one, and how to reconcile quarreling friends. In *Michel et moi*, she recounts her great late-in-life love story with composer Michel Legrand, whom she first fell in love with in 1964 and reconnected with some fifty years later when she was in her mid-seventies and he in his mid-eighties. "I often told you about my freedoms and my prisons. Of my suns and my shadows. Of my prides and my doubts. Of what animates and what hinders the life of a woman of my generation. After all these years, a dazzling sensation seizes me: the discovery of love. It has a name: Michel Legrand."

Other works explore the lives of strong, liberated women like herself. After having incarnated Colette in a 1985 television

Macha Méril (Charlotte) in Jean-Luc Godard's *Une femme mariée* (*A Married Woman*), 1964

"We need to write today.
We have to start writing."

—marie dubois

Marie Dubois (actress from *Tirez
sur le pianiste* and *Jules et Jim*)
in Seyrig's *Sois belle et tais-toi,*
calling on other women, other
actresses to express themselves.

miniseries, Méril teamed with Philippe Lorin on *Sur les pas de Colette*, chronicling this story of a woman "too talented, surely too free" for her day and who suffered a bad reputation because of it. In the same vein, Méril valorized often overlooked feminine wit in the anthology *L'Esprit au féminin* (2012) and presented a history of feminine humor in *L'Humour au féminin en 700 citations* (2015) that includes quotations from women ranging from the marquise de Sévigné to Arletty to Françoise Sagan. In 2020, Méril, the actress, appeared alone on stage in *Sorcière*, in which she recited texts by Marguerite Duras.[24]

Despite her prolific career as a writer, Meril said in 2020 that her "writer passport" wasn't given to her until she appeared on the French literary television show *La Grande librairie* that year. "I was finally recognized as a writer. That's France. When you have a label, you have it forever. I really think that my place as a writer is more important than my place as an actress because I have a lot of things to say."[25]

Méril expressed the same sentiment in her 2024 interview on French radio (RTL), in which she described a benefit of the #MeToo movement as *la libération de la parole*—freedom of speech. Méril has always encouraged radical openness and solidarity among women by exercising it herself. When France inscribed abortion in its constitution as a guaranteed right in 2024, she spoke about her experience with infertility caused by the unsafe conditions of an abortion performed before it was legal. "I don't think I know a woman my age who didn't undergo an abortion at one point or another. And it was extremely dangerous. We went abroad, to Switzerland or Belgium. We were butchered, or in France there were the *faiseuses d'ange* [literally "angel-makers," illegal abortionists] who trafficked women. Frankly, it was unbearable, intolerable. It had to change," she said. For Méril, May '68 in France was "a feminine movement," born with women's legal access to the pill. "All of a sudden, women became aware that, all together, what was the fate of only a few would be everyone's fate: We were going to liberate ourselves."

ANNE WIAZEMSKY, AUTO-NOVELIST

In her youth, Anne Wiazemsky's identity was largely inseparable from that of Nobel Prize-winning writer François

Mauriac, her grandfather (and author of *Thérèse Desqueyroux*). Though she would later attain her own authorial acclaim, Wiazemsky at seventeen, and with no formal training, first gained recognition for her role in Robert Bresson's *Au hasard Balthazar* (*Balthazar*, 1966), an unconventional and moving film about a girl and her donkey. Wiazemsky became one of Bresson's cinematic muses, or "models" as he called them, and the target of his romantic feelings. "I'm inventing you just as you are," Bresson told her about her role in the film.[26]

It is no wonder that Wiazemsky, linked to both Mauriac and Bresson, caught the attention of Jean-Luc Godard, who revered these *maîtres* of literature and cinema. He and Wiazemsky first crossed paths on the set of *Balthazar*, and Godard spotted her again reading Jean Genet's *Journal d'un voleur* (*The Thief's Journal*, 1949) in a café. Their third encounter at a television studio involved Godard physically running into her in the staircase—recalling the famous incident between Sylvie and the narrator in Rohmer's *La Boulangère de Monceau*. While these meetings were not enough to ignite a spark for Wiazemsky, she discovered Godard's sensitivity through his films. After seeing *Masculin féminin*, she wrote him a letter explaining that she had perceived it as "a sort of message that was addressed to [her]," though acknowledging that her interpretation was "totally irrational." To her surprise, Godard confessed that he had been in love with her since their first meeting.[27] She married him the following year while shooting *La Chinoise* in 1967, Godard's film anticipating May '68.[28]

The story of how they met, Wiazemsky wrote in intimate, cinematic detail in her book *Une année studieuse* (*A Studious Year*, 2012). We also witness her boldness through other anecdotes in the novel—about approaching, for example, the renowned political philosopher Francis Jeanson (who later appeared with her in *La Chinoise*) at a cocktail party to ask for private philosophy lessons as she was studying for her *baccalauréat*. As a philosophy student at the Université Paris Nanterre, Wiazemsky strongly influenced the story of *La Chinoise*, shot in the apartment she shared with Godard. Chronicling her time with the director and the events leading to their personal and cinematic union, her novel sheds light on

Godard's influence on her life and her own relationship with literature, an interest they shared. Along with her next book, *Un an après* (*One Year Later*, 2014), *Une année studieuse* formed the basis for Michel Hazanavicius's *Le Redoutable* (*Godard Mon Amour*, 2017) about her time with Godard.

Wiazemsky was an avowed feminist, signing the Manifeste des 343 in 1971. She published numerous books drawing heavily from her experiences as an actress and as a woman, including 1993's *Canines* and 2007's *Jeune fille* about her relationship with Bresson. Through her singular blend of novel and memoir, she became a sort of literary chronicler of the New Wave era.

JEAN SEBERG'S SPIRITED EXPERIMENT

In 1974, aspiring actor Jean-François Ferriol approached Jean Seberg with the idea of making a movie about Billy the Kid. The project became *Ballad for Billy the Kid*, a short film about cult figures who faded into has-beens, with Seberg cowriting (with her then-husband Dennis Berry and Ferriol), directing, starring in, and editing. Though she had always dreamed of being a writer, she had assumed the role of auteur in cinema more as an experiment. "I haven't been burning to direct for years, or anything like that," she told *Films Illustrated*. "It scared me a lot: I keep thinking of that precise French audience who know what they want. I would like to do more."[29]

The film, which Seberg described as not "that much different from a home movie," was shot in just a week with an extremely small budget and crew. But her fame garnered attention for it, and the press noted her energy and efficiency in doing the work—qualities that shone through in a letter to her parents: "I've been all day every day shut up in an airless, dark room doing the cutting of my little film. It looks pretty good—at least I like it!"[30]

Seberg found the experience gratifying despite the film's lack of box-office success. Dissatisfied with the risqué nature of the roles being offered her, she resolved to devote more time to writing. "I have to do something. I couldn't just be a housewife. So I have entered my literary phase. I can write as

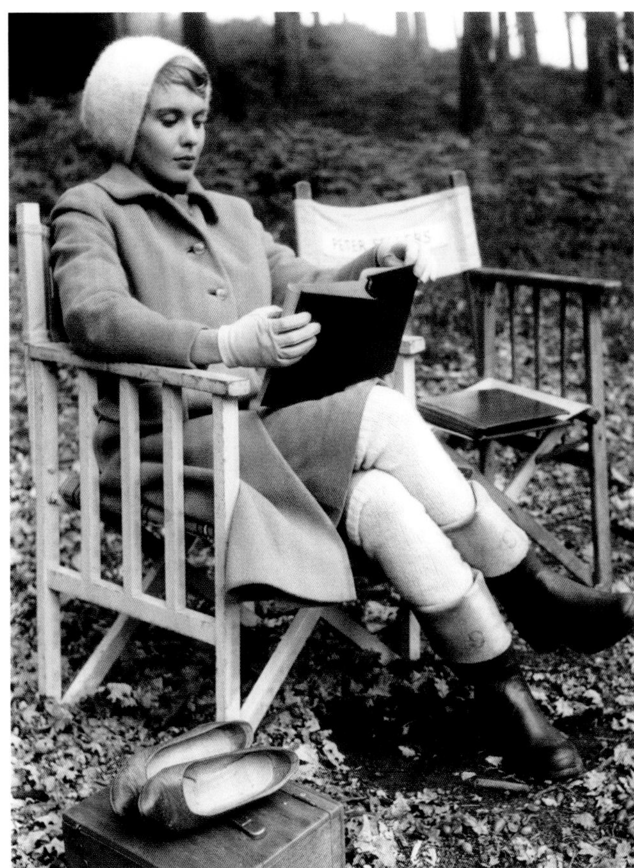

easily in French as in English. Perhaps I'll give up the movies altogether someday. I've never programmed my life. It's always been impulsive, instinctive. Things have happened to me—some good, some bad. Luck counts for so much, but I don't know if I believe in fate. What I find interesting now are the people who ask themselves questions."[31]

Though little of Seberg's written work remains, friends attested to her talent as a writer, and her father-in-law, blacklisted Hollywood director John Berry, called her "a hellava poet." "She could write. She had everything going for her, but then she'd have that negative moral judgement of herself that I certainly never had [of her],"[32] the director said.

MARIE-FRANCE PISIER'S UNAPOLOGETIC FEMINISM

"A lot of actresses have a feminist façade. They pass themselves off as Simone de Beauvoir, but once you go a little deeper,

Jean Seberg on the set of Jack Arnold's *The Mouse that Roared*, 1959

behind it, there is nothing. Marie-France was the opposite," recalled director Stéphane Giusti. "Marie-France could get on your nerves with her convictions. She didn't care."[33]

Born in Indochina (now Vietnam), Pisier moved to France after her parents' divorce with her sisters and mother, a strong figure in their life who demanded her daughters further their education. Pisier started her acting career while obtaining university degrees in law and political science. In 1964, she and her sister Évelyne, like-minded in their moral progressivism and political engagement, traveled to Cuba with politician Bernard Kouchner, who dated Pisier before eventually marrying Évelyne. Described by author Marie Lebey as "brilliant and powerful," in 1968, the sisters participated in student protests alongside Daniel Cohn-Bendit (with whom the actress was also romantically linked).[34]

In the late 1960s, a journalist asked Pisier, an outspoken feminist from a young age, if "the image we have of you of very nice with your little white dress and your big hair corresponds to what you are." "What I am?" the actress replied with slight indignation. "I wonder why it's always girls who are asked to play this sort of game. I reveal my internal self with tact and intelligence. It would be more fun if you did that with boys."[35] In a May 1970 interview, Pisier expressed that "from puberty until a few years ago," she "very strongly, violently" wished she had been born a boy. "Now, it has completely calmed down," she said. "I feel that we are going through a very disturbing time. It's become common to say that misogyny doesn't exist anymore in the same way racism no longer exists. I feel it's completely the contrary. Before, at least misogyny hid itself behind laws that were anti-egalitarian between men and women at their core. And now that there is no longer as great a distance between the way men and women are treated in society, even if there are unbelievable injustices, . . . misogyny takes a different allure. It is very worrisome and to me, very dangerous because most of the time it looks like paternalism."[36] The following year, Pisier, a strong defender of women's reproductive rights, joined her fellow actresses in signing the Manifeste des 343.[37]

When Pisier was asked if intelligence was a disadvantage in cinema, she replied candidly, "There's a form of lucidity that can be bothersome at first, an *esprit critique* and withdrawal into yourself."[38] She would not let this kind of immobilizing self-awareness hinder her output: In a film career spanning fifty years, Pisier starred in dozens of films, won two César Awards, wrote screenplays, and directed two films—including 1990's *Le Bal du gouverneur* (*The Governor's Party*), which she adapted from one of her own novels.[39]

But even these successes could not fully capture Pisier's boundless potential. Comparing her to Seyrig, Guisti described Pisier as too intelligent and well-rounded to carve out a career up to her level.[40]

BRIGITTE BARDOT, PARADOX OF FREEDOM

The same freedom and rebellion that defined Bardot as a young woman held true after her disappearance from the screen. Turning down roles opposite Frank Sinatra, Steve McQueen, and Marlon Brando, Bardot chose to live her life out of the spotlight. "I was really sick of it," she said. "Good thing I stopped, because what happened to Marilyn Monroe and Romy Schneider would have happened to me."[41] In its place, Bardot chose another pursuit. Early in her film career, Bardot was known for her soft spot for animals. Often rescuing strays, she would sometimes even keep them in her hotel room on location during a shoot. Devoting herself to the cause, she later established the Brigitte Bardot Foundation for the Welfare and Protection of Animals.

With the same nonchalance as she had in her early days, Bardot has expressed views on immigration, however, that were condemned for "inciting racial hatred" and opinions on #MeToo considered misogynistic.[42] Disregarding societal norms or rules, for better and for worse, Bardot does not concern herself with the judgment of others: "I live only for my cause," she stated.[43]

NADINE TRINTIGNANT AND NELLY KAPLAN BEHIND THE CAMERA

Varda was not the only woman who made a career behind the camera, though she was one of the few for most of the

New Wave era. In the late '60s and early '70s, other female directors started to emerge. After starting as an assistant editor in 1955, Nadine Trintignant released her first short film, *Fragilité, ton nom est femme*, which translates as "Fragility, your name is woman," in 1965. Like the New Wave directors, the subjects she addressed were personal, often inspired by her life. Two years later, with her then-husband Jean-Louis Trintignant, she made her first feature, *Mon amour, mon amour* (*My Love, My Love*, 1967), about an architect's mistress who does not dare tell him she is pregnant. Like Méril, Trintignant also highlighted the life of Colette in 2004's *Colette, une femme libre*, a television miniseries she wrote and directed (and which starred Marie Trintignant, her daughter with Jean-Louis).

Nelly Kaplan brought back New Wave favorite Bernadette Lafont for the now-famous feminist feature *La Fiancée du pirate* (*A Very Curious Girl*, 1969). Incarnating the exploited, socially disadvantaged, and disliked Marie, Lafont dismantles the dynamics of her patriarchal and capitalist provincial town by selling herself to the townspeople, exposing their hypocrisy by recording her encounters with dignitaries and playing the tape in church.[44] Largely known for this film in particular, Kaplan has gained more attention in recent years.

Echoing many of the stories of the New Wave actresses, Kaplan found success through determination and a decisive encounter. Born in Buenos Aires to a Russian Jewish family, seventeen-year-old Kaplan left Argentina for France in January 1953 with very little money. Through a letter from the Argentine Cinémathèque, she was introduced to Henri Langlois, cofounder of the Cinémathèque française.

There, she met film pioneer Abel Gance, a *coup de foudre* that helped her break into cinema and also "brought him back to life," in Kaplan's words. Collaborating with Gance starting on *La Tour de Nesle* (*Tower of Lust*, 1955), she was his "right-hand man," taking care of everything that went wrong behind the scenes (and sometimes appearing on screen). Assisting with his film *Cyrano et d'Artagnan* (1964) in Italy under grueling conditions, she even directed some difficult scenes."[45]

Kaplan, who was close with Françoise Sagan and many surrealist artists in Paris, directed her own shorts in the early 1960s about various artists as well as a documentary feature on Picasso in 1967—*Le Regard Picasso* (*The Picasso Look*). Her 1976 film *Néa* (*A Young Emmanuelle*), adapted from a story by Emmanuelle Arsan, was considered a flop, though some now view it as having been ahead of its time. Kaplan herself was perhaps ahead of her time. Though she did not participate in the feminist marches of the 1970s or sign the Manifeste des 343, she indirectly blazed a feminist trail through her films. As Joan Dupont wrote in *Film Quarterly*, "Kaplan's originality and her success were remarkable, but in those days of revolutions and revelations, she was perhaps overshadowed by the contemporaneous creative talents of Chantal Akerman with *Jeanne Dielman . . .* and Marguerite Duras with *India Song*."[46]

MARCELINE LORIDAN-IVENS, ACTIVE WITNESS TO HISTORY

As we saw in Rouch and Morin's 1961 documentary *Chronique d'un été*, Marceline Loridan-Ivens alluded to the problem of antisemitism by reflecting on her past. Midway through the film, she exposes her personal history as a Holocaust survivor, displaying the numbers on her arm during a political discussion with others involved in the film, including an African student who has no idea what the numbers mean. The trauma from the war was fresh but hidden. Though during the first part of the film Loridan-Ivens walks almost blank-faced in the streets of Paris, she does not speak of her experience. As she fulfills her assignment in the scope of the film's *cinéma-vérité* experiment, she appears joyful, extending her microphone to ask passersby about their lives. Her question, "Êtes-vous heureux?" ("Are you happy?") is one of her most memorable moments in the film. The answers of the older people sometimes reflect hardship of a personal nature while the youth exude naïve excitement. No one mentions war. It was as if France had repressed the experience of past wars and looked away from the one in the present. The viewer tends to forget also that the horrors of World War II occurred only fifteen years prior to the film's release, until Loridan-Ivens, still a young woman, evokes her experience during the discussion.

Over forty years later, Loridan-Ivens at seventy-five confronted her past directly in her film *La Petite prairie aux bouleaux* (*The Birch-Tree Meadow*, 2003), in which Anouk Aimée appears as a survivor of Auschwitz-Birkenau who visits the site as an adult. The setting of the film provides structural evidence of the atrocities of the concentration camp, where over one million Jews were murdered, and where Loridan-Ivens herself was imprisoned as a young teenager. Writing the script with Jean-Pierre Sergent and Elisabeth D. Prasetyo, along with with contributions by Jeanne Moreau, the director constructed a film that serves as a personal testimony and a reminder of the tragedy France had started to forget or never really worked through at all. It also conveys the scope of what was lost through the specificity of one woman's story. As scholar Sandy Flitterman-Lewis explains, the film was Loridan-Ivens's way "of transmitting the unutterable," and quotes the filmmaker as saying:

> Hidden from everyone is the fact that each deportee was an individual, with her own experience, her own life, her own feelings and personality. Today each survivor has memories, grief, of this period that marked her in her flesh and her soul. They all share with the other survivors having lived the same tragedy, but each of us, as a function of what she was and what she became, has personal feelings that escape general group classification, feelings that can't be uttered. It was important for me to transmit through cinema, because that's my profession, what can't actually be spoken.[47]

Like Loridan-Ivens herself, her message, however, was hopeful. "Even in the most unbearable situations, she made us laugh," said fellow Holocaust survivor Simone Veil, who met Loridan-Ivens in Auschwitz-Birkenau and became her lifelong friend, noted Flitterman-Lewis. Aimée, as the film's protagonist, looking over a long-deserted concentration camp, cries out from above, "Je suis vivante!" ("I am alive!").

Loridan-Ivens continued to examine her trauma through film and writing, including a memoir in 2016, *But You Did Not Come Back*, written in letter form to her father who died in the camps. Her broad commitment to social justice manifested in films tackling diverse political conflicts. Documenting Algerian independence at its start in the 1962 short, *Algérie, année zero*, codirected with Jean-Pierre Sergent, she did not shy away from controversial topics, including the Vietnam War. Many of these works were in collaboration with husband Joris Ivens, whom Loridan-Ivens called "irreplaceable." Describing their relationship, she wrote, "Our reciprocal confidence was total . . . working intensely, together against the odds."[48]

As French rabbi Delphine Horvilleur put it, Loridan-Ivens reminded us "what it means to remember and choose life, to know that what happened to you doesn't say everything about you. Because there's always something else you can be, change, create."[49]

—

With these *nouvelles femmes* expressing themselves, voicing their experiences through poetry, novels, scripts, photographs, films, and the roles they chose as actresses, they began gaining greater access to the power to create, as artists, as directors, as auteurs, realizing their own versions of Astruc's *caméra-stylo*, of Varda's *cinécriture*. No longer silenced, a dialogue could begin, a step toward greater understanding. "If women started writing, things would change a lot," Marie Dubois affirmed.

With these *nouvelles femmes* expressing themselves, voicing their experiences through poetry, novels, scripts, photographs, films, and the roles they chose as actresses, they began gaining greater access to the power to create, as auteurs, artists, and directors, realizing their own versions of Astruc's *caméra-stylo*, of Varda's *cinécriture*. No longer silenced, a dialogue could begin, a step toward greater understanding. "If women started writing, things would change a lot," Marie Dubois affirmed.

"I felt like I was sort of a
revolutionary to be there, to
participate in a march toward
freedom, toward new forms of
society, toward new forms of
relationships between men and
women . . . Women of the New
Wave . . . were women of change,
those who all of a sudden had
different physiques, we weren't
all very pretty, we were real. We
were closer to real women, normal
women. We weren't blow-up
dolls. We weren't stars, we weren't
'actresses.' I felt that very strongly,
and I felt it every instant."

—macha méril

conclusion

looking back, moving forward

In times of significant change, with new generations dreaming of a utopian future or processing traumatic events of the past, it is difficult to assess the magnitude of societal shifts or their consequences. Evolution becomes clear in hindsight. With a distance of almost seventy years after the slogan "La Nouvelle Vague arrive!" appeared in the press, we can now see how the New Wave changed cinema as well as society, offering new models for living and relating, including greater possibilities for *nouvelles femmes*.

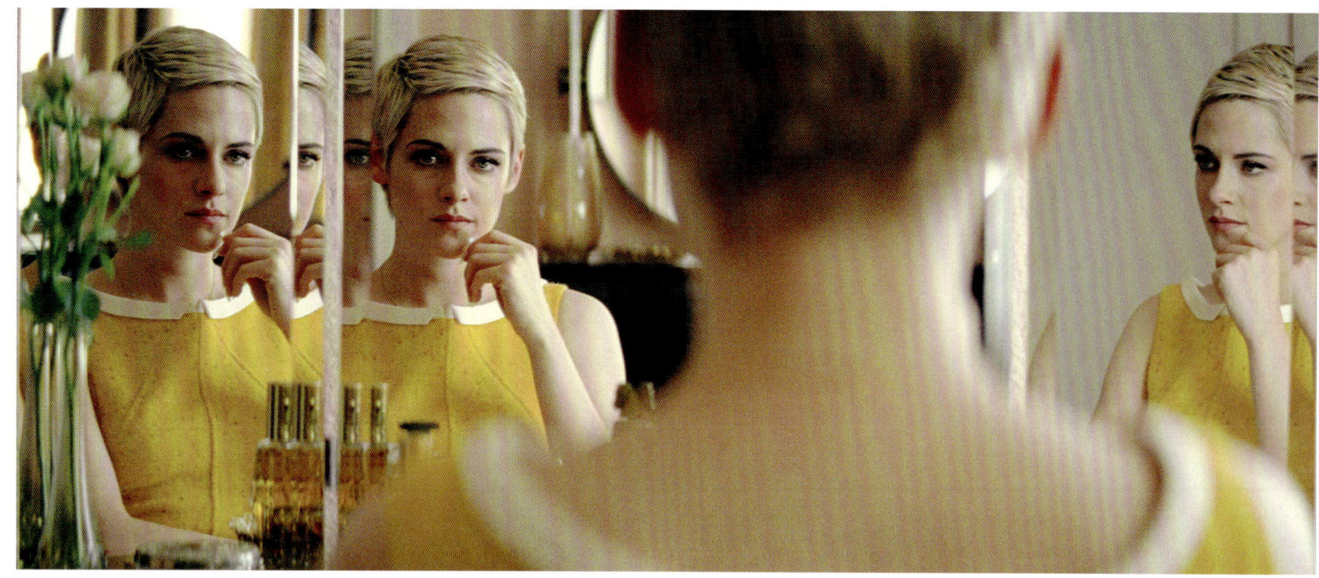

Yet the stereotypes are more easily recognizable, too—the ingénue, the bourgeois wife, the idealized prostitute—and the injustices stand out even more: the lack of reproductive rights, the power imbalances between directors and actresses, the scandal of free women on screen. The list goes on.

Our current progress toward equality is harder to assess—recalling the well-known metaphor of the patriarchy as the water a fish does not know it is swimming in. Looking to the past helps us evaluate how far we have come, but also how much we still have in common with the New Wave generation—how much we have left to do, especially for women. As feminist and philosopher Elisabeth Badinter pointed out in her book *Messieurs, encore un effort . . .* (2024), society must dismantle the unspoken expectations of women that still persist in order to attain true equality.

Reframing the women of the French New Wave shines a light on these concerns and provides a measuring stick for steps forward as well as steps back. We can appreciate the new voices brought to the screen by Anouk Aimée, Brigitte Bardot, Françoise Dorléac, Françoise Fabian, Anna Karina, Macha Méril, Jeanne Moreau, Emmanuelle Riva, Jean Seberg, Haydée Politoff, Delphine Seyrig, and Agnès Varda, as well as others like Bulle Ogier, Jane Birkin, Romy Schneider, and their contemporaries. We remember the actresses' encounters with directors who helped create more authentic images of them. Their films changed the ways women could see themselves off screen as well, with the promise of more agency.

Breaking the mold for women in French cinema, these New Wave women and directors shook up the cinematic landscape worldwide. In the 1970s, new images of women also appeared in American cinema that had up until then been strictly patrolled by the Hays Code. Jane Fonda, after Vadim's cult fantasy *Barbarella* (1968), contributed a modern and nuanced image of the call girl in *Klute* (1971). Diane Keaton at the center of *Looking for Mr. Goodbar* (1977) was an independent, liberated woman in New York City. Known for refusing offers for mainstream films that she deemed too commercial, like *Bonnie and Clyde* (1967), Tuesday Weld followed her own path with roles in *Pretty Poison* (1968) and *Play It as It Lays* (1972). Karen Black, an advocate of LGBTQ rights, caused a stir with her performance as a transgender woman in *Come Back to the Five and Dime, Jimmy Dean, Jimmy Dean* (1982), but she continued to choose eclectic roles in independent films. Years later, Tilda Swinton, Juliette Lewis, Parker Posey, and Laura Dern, among others, all did the same.

Gena Rowlands with John Cassavetes, much like Karina and Godard, mixed real life and cinema in their authentically intense films together, like in the iconic *Faces* (1968)

Kristen Stewart as Jean Seberg in Benedict Andrews's *Seberg*, 2019

and *A Woman under the Influence* (1974). Later, Uma Thurman incarnated strong women with independent directors like Quentin Tarantino in the *Kill Bill* series. Kristen Stewart's wide-ranging roles have taken her from blockbusters to auteur films, including her collaborations with Olivier Assayas and her appearance in *Seberg* (2019), which illustrates cinema's political power and shows us a Jean Seberg who remains upsettingly relevant.

In France, modern actresses like Isabelle Huppert, directly descending from the New Wave, and Juliette Binoche are joined by Marion Cotillard, who has embodied complex women through her work with eclectic directors since her first leading role (opposite Anna Karina) with Dennis Berry,[1] followed by Olivier Dahan, Jacques Audiard, the Dardenne brothers, Leos Carax, Mona Achache, and Ellen Kuras. The New Wave also opened doors for actresses like Adèle Haenel, Charlotte Gainsbourg, Bérénice Bejo, Léa Seydoux, Adèle Exarchopoulos, Virginie Efira, and many more.

Agnès Varda succeeded not only in a man's world but later in an industry that had lost its enthusiasm for independent cinema in its quest for profits. "The difficulty of making movies is huge for an auteur, not just a female auteur, any auteur of independent cinema," Varda expressed in an interview in 1977. Always ahead of the game, Varda described the "post–New Wave era" even then as "the return of the star system in France, the return of big commercial productions and also the invasion of pornography which has captured a huge share of the potential market"—a further obstacle for small productions. "So, the free independent feminist cinema I want to make is very difficult to produce," she explained. "There's no doubt about it, so difficult that I have to produce it myself. I can't find anyone willing to take the risks and make the effort it takes to produce these films."[2]

With Varda as the exception during the New Wave, the sparse number of female directors illustrated the continued struggle for women to express themselves in film. Duras, Kaplan, Trintignant, Akerman, and the New Wave actresses who went on to direct succeeded against unimaginable odds, opening the door to future generations of female directors. Seyrig's *Sois belle et tais-toi* anticipated the need for more women's voices in cinema. "Because men write, produce, and direct movies according to their fantasies, it would take a cinema made by women . . . to bring about changes in the work experience of actresses and in the movies in which they appear," *The New Yorker*'s Richard Brody wrote in 2021,[3] describing the plight of actresses as portrayed in Seyrig's film.

French director Mia Hansen-Løve, however, challenged the practice of categorizing female directors by their gender in a 2024 piece for *Cahiers du cinéma*: "Do people incessantly ask men how it is to be a male director, and make films while raising children? I admit: I hate the idea that male directors talk about cinema when we have to keep commenting on our gender and reporting on our feminism. At the same time, I accept this moment while hoping that we can soon move beyond it, and that female directors can be considered as artists in their own right, and not as a homogenous group."[4] Her words echo the sentiments of Varda herself, who addressed women's rights in her cinema without ever defining or promoting it in terms of gender.

Though we have yet to reach parity, countless directors—who just so happen to be women—are telling new stories. We can now appreciate the many new (female) voices in contemporary cinema, contributing diverse perspectives that shatter the homogenous label in the singular *la femme* into the plural *des femmes*. Duras, Seyrig, and director Liliane de Kermadec envisioned this shattering during a televised conversation back in 1975, emphasizing the importance of funding female directors to explore beyond the bounds established by male directors. "I think that women's cinema is part of a 'different cinema.' Different cinema is by definition a political cinema," Duras said. "The amount of money we have available makes the film political. I was never paid for any film. For eight years, my salary wasn't even that of a second assistant. That is also political. 'Different cinema,' women's cinema is thus a political cinema. Whether we like it or not, it's a different cinema."[5] "The question is," Seyrig posited, "Are we going to give money to women directors to film things that don't have pistols, cars, women's backsides? Maybe we don't feel like showing that."

"I think that one day, there will be works by women that will not only be films but cities, ones that escape this idea that a work by a woman is something restrictive," Kermadec added. Seyrig agreed, "We don't know what kinds of films we will make, but we know what films we will not make." "Works by women that aren't knitting," Kermadec answered facetiously. "Forget this idea that women's work is knitting."[6]

The metaphor recalls the activist women during the French Revolution, *les tricoteuses*, or the knitters. On October 5, 1789, working-class women from the Paris markets famously marched to the Palace of Versailles protesting high food prices and shortages. Achieving their objective, the women became heroines of the revolution. Veterans of the march and others began sitting in the gallery at the Convention nationale to support left-wing politicians. After the *Déclaration des droits de l'homme et du citoyen de 1789* (*Declaration of the Rights of Man and of the Citizen*), the political activist and playwright Olympe de Gouges drafted her famous *Déclaration des droits de la femme et de la citoyenne* (*Declaration of the Rights of Woman and of the Female Citizen*) in 1791, demanding women's right to vote and participate in politics.[7]

In 1793, during the Reign of Terror, de Gouges was executed for her political beliefs, and the Convention nationale banned women from the gallery. Deprived of active participation in politics, the women became *les tricoteuses*, gathering at the guillotine in the Place de la Révolution and knitting as the executions took place. Though their voices were silenced, their knitting stood as an act of defiance. This historical detour leads to the image atop the steps of the red carpet at the 2024 Cannes Film Festival, where women covered their mouths in protest of the silencing of actresses who suffered abuse in the film industry, resonating with France's revolutionary past.

The reckoning has reverberated across French cinema in recent years. During the 2024 César Awards (the French equivalent of the Oscars), actress Judith Godrèche gave a speech that sent shockwaves through the French film industry: "For a while now, speech is being liberated, the image of our idealized fathers is being scratched, power seems almost balanced. Would it be possible for us to be able to look truth in the face? Take our responsibilities? Be the actors, actresses of a universe that questions itself?"Méril too pointed to the importance of "reexamining history to see how men who were untouchable used their impunity," adding, "It's not over."[8]

Godrèche looked to cinema's past to "dream of a possible revolution," citing Rivette's heroines of *Céline et Julie vont en bateau* (*Céline and Julie Go Boating*, 1974) and calling on today's women to speak out. "We travel with our films. We are lucky to be in a country where it seems that freedom exists," she said. "Let us have the courage to say aloud what we know deep down. Let us not incarnate heroines on screen to find ourselves hidden in the forest in real life."[9] Some bastions of the New Wave have lived to see this new generation of women continue the struggle for power and agency that they themselves fomented.[10] "A new world is being created with a very new way of living," Méril noted, "still under construction—it's fascinating."[11]

"It's a strange journey," Godrèche continued. "I do believe that I've been in many ways for my entire life as an actress a muse. I've been reduced to silence in so many ways," she said, explaining, "I never allowed myself to completely embrace that I was allowed to create my world, to write my own movies." Just as Moreau pointed out in her own case, life has a direct influence on cinema. After kickstarting a new #MeToo wave in French cinema, Godrèche made her own short film, *Moi aussi* (meaning "me too"), which debuted at Cannes the same year. "It's a wonderful thing that women are now speaking out," actress Léa Seydoux said on the day of its premiere. "Things are clearly changing, and it was high time [they] did."[12]

The evolution we see today had in fact been brewing for many years. Today's women in cinema owe a great deal to the New Wave pioneers whose unique voices resounded through their art and whose activism started to move the needle for women's rights. The films give us insight into what it was like to be women in the 1960s, and the actresses themselves expressed their difficulties and frustrations off screen. In *Sois belle et tais-toi*, Maidie Norman discussed being relegated to playing maids due to her race. The parts offered to Luce Guilbeault were always "prostitutes or alcoholics, wasted women, abandoned women," and Patti D'Arbanville resented having to infantilize herself for roles when she was well into her adulthood.[13] In general, women's solidarity on screen was a scarcity.[14]

Since then, women's roles in film and in society have become broader, richer, and more complex. After Chantal Akerman continued along the path paved by Varda, French filmmakers like Claire Denis and Catherine Breillat followed suit, gaining acclaim with their distinguished filmographies as auteurs. Céline Sciamma has given voice to often overlooked communities, from women of color in the underprivileged banlieues of Paris to members of the LGBTQ community searching for identity. Actress turned director, Hanson-Løve has cited Rohmer as an influence in her intimate films about family and relationships, often inspired by her own life in the spirit of the New Wave. Julie Delpy, known for her contributions to her character Céline in Richard Linklater's *Before* series, has written, directed, produced, and starred in her own films. Playing on cultural differences in her comedies, she addresses the pressure on women to maintain youth in films like *The Countess* (2009), anticipating Coralie Fargeat's *The Substance* (2024) with Demi Moore that denounces the criteria of youth and beauty as defining women's value. Like Delpy, Agnès Jaoui has refused to be confined to one specialty and has established herself with an award-winning career as a screenwriter, director, actress, and singer.

Greta Gerwig addressed societal pressures on women in the blockbuster, *Barbie* (2023), giving center stage to America Ferrera's now famous monologue that harks back to Varda's 1975 *Réponse de femmes* in terms of the contradictory messages women receive. "You have to be a boss, but you can't be mean," Ferrera's character says.[15] "You're supposed to love being a mother, but don't talk about your kids all the damn time. . . . You're supposed to stay pretty for men, but not so pretty that you tempt them too much. . . . You have to never get old, never be rude, never show off, never be selfish, never fall down, never fail, never show fear, never get out of line. It's too hard!"[16] Surpassing these restrictive messages, Gerwig and *Barbie*'s many actresses are mainstream

models of agency. The leading Barbie, Margot Robbie, has produced and starred in a number of other female-centered films, and Gerwig added female perspectives to the cinematic landscape in *Lady Bird* (2017) and *Little Women* (2019). Sofia Coppola's entire filmography has focused on young women's stories, from *The Virgin Suicides* in 1999 and *Marie Antoinette* in 2006, both with Kirsten Dunst, to *Priscilla* in 2023–the latter two reexamining famous figures with a redemptive modern lens. Jane Campion has proven her prowess as a director for decades from *The Piano* (1993) to *The Power of the Dog* (2021).

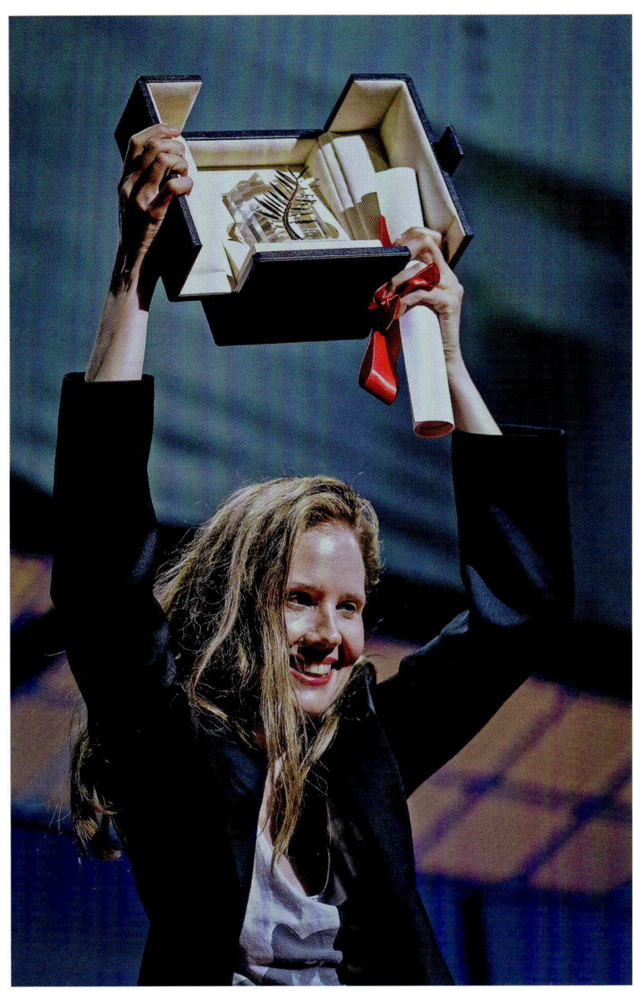

Justine Triet illustrates how far things have evolved, having cowritten and directed the internationally acclaimed *Anatomie d'une chute* (*Anatomy of a Fall*, 2023). Coming full circle back to Otto Preminger, the film pays homage to his 1959

Justine Triet receiving the Palme d'Or for *Anatomie d'une chute* (*Anatomy of a Fall*) at the Cannes Film Festival, May 27, 2023

classic *Anatomy of a Murder*, reimagining the story from a woman's perspective (portrayed in a commanding performance by Sandra Hüller). The contempt in Samuel and Sandra's marriage in *Anatomie* recalls that of Bardot and Piccoli's characters in *Le Mépris*, and as both films show, contempt shuts down the words that could heal—when there is no longer dialogue, it turns love into silent resentment. Varda wrote the silence explicitly into *Les Créatures*, illustrating the inequality in the couple's dynamic. Written by Triet and her partner, writer/director Arthur Harari, *Anatomie* addresses these unspoken struggles for power and love in a relationship through a quest for truth in a court of law, their cowriting providing multiple points of view.[17] Triet's multifaceted camera analyzes the story and the couple from every angle, while the truth remains elusive.

This same type of mystery haunts the plot of Alice Diop's *Saint Omer* (2022), in which a Senegalese immigrant with a doctoral degree in philosophy stands trial for infanticide and defends her own worth and identity regarding motherhood, social class, and Frenchness in a postcolonial world. Audrey Diwan's *L'Événement* (*Happening*, 2021), adapted from Annie Ernaux's eponymous memoir (2000), also follows a brilliant university student from a modest background who becomes pregnant in 1963 France, when contraception and abortion were still illegal. Both films address the cost of motherhood for women in terms of education and autonomy. Both are based on true stories.[18]

New voices in cinema open a dialogue of understanding, a mosaic of people telling their stories that can help us learn how to live together—*vivre ensemble*, as Karina titled her film. Julia Ducournau, Rebecca Zlotowski, Maïwenn, Mati Diop, Alice Winocour, Virginie Despentes, Claire Burger, Valérie Donzelli, Aïssa Maïga, Valérie Lemercier, Valeria Bruni Tedeschi, and their contemporaries have all added their voices to the conversation.

At the end of her Césars speech, Godrèche reminded us of cinema's fundamental goal, one that lies at the core of the New Wave, defining its films, its directors, its actors, and its viewers. "Cinema is made of our desire for truth," she said.

"Films look at us as much as we look at them. They are equally made from our need for humanity, aren't they?"

In *Réponse de femmes*, Agnès Varda's final dialogue between women and men calls for that humanity to help reimagine views and behaviors in a changing society, a message we can adopt and adapt to include new voices in our own evolving world. I leave the last word to Varda:

Une femme: We women are taking charge of our evolution, and if you still need women and love, it's you who must change your habits and some of your tastes.
Une femme: I am a woman. Women must be reinvented.
Un homme: Then love must be reinvented.
Les femmes ensemble: D'accord. [Okay.]
Varda (in voice-over): In that case, to be continued . . .

Une femme: I am a woman.
Women must be reinvented.
Un homme: Then love must be
reinvented.
Les femmes ensemble: D'accord.
[Okay.]
Varda (in voice-over): In that case,
to be continued . . .

—agnès varda

author's note

Considering the context of the French New Wave led me to certain choices in my approach that merit clarification. For a book infused with French culture, including certain French terms seemed essential. You will find phrases like *mise en scène* or *cinéma de papa* in the aim of contributing that flavor to the book. I also refer to films using their original French titles (and include their English titles at the first mention). Other choices were daunting. Selecting terms that reflected the era while honoring the strides made toward more equality was more complicated. I refer to female actors, for example, as "actresses" as much for clarity's sake as for a desire to align with the French term *actrice*. This choice also illustrates a cultural difference: While in the US, the term *actor* is now used for everyone, in France, the term *actrice* persists. Similarly, the feminine version of *auteur*, *autrice* (or *auteure*), has now been adopted for female authors and directors. I chose a hybrid approach for this book, adhering in this case to the English idea of the auteur for all but maintaining the distinction between actress and actor.

Being aware that society has greatly evolved since the 1960s, thankfully becoming much more inclusive, the films remain time capsules of an era defined by heteronormative parameters. My text therefore aligns with those (obsolete) norms that have since been surpassed. In the context of the New Wave era, women suffered oppression while slowly gaining power. It is through a lens that tracks their evolution that I approached the films, one that I hope can be applied to other groups that have been marginalized by a patriarchal society as we now strive for equality for all.

Finally, while this book is by no means exhaustive, my focus on these particular actresses and directors does not intend to ignore the contributions of the numerous other women—stars as well as those in smaller roles and those behind the scenes—who contributed to the French New Wave. Nor does it mean to disregard the enormous influence and talent of the male actors and directors, who have often been acknowledged but also deserve credit here for revolutionizing cinema along with the many talented women who crossed their paths, creating art from transformative encounters.

*Please note that unless otherwise indicated, translations from French to English are the author's.

acknowledgments

As I researched this book, I became more and more aware of the importance of encounters in realizing a project, not only in cinema, a collective art, but also on a personal level. We can trace the trajectory of a film or of actresses and directors where decisive encounters changed the course of their careers or led to aesthetic breakthroughs. The same holds true for this book that came about through pivotal encounters that shaped it and brought it to fruition.

First and foremost, I want to express my deep gratitude to Chris Navratil, whose initial idea for the book inspired me to rethink the French New Wave from a new angle. His belief in this project, unwavering encouragement, and guidance has been invaluable from start to finish.

I would equally like to thank Gloria Fowler and Steve Crist at Chronicle Chroma, whose enthusiastic support, flexibility, and patience were instrumental in bringing to life an in-depth look at these *nouvelles femmes* and their contributions to cinema.

Very special thanks go to Ellen Gutoskey, whose fresh vision changed the course of the book and helped me imagine each woman's story in new ways. I am grateful for her keen eye, style, and thoughtful suggestions that have elevated this work beyond what I could have imagined. I would also like to thank Leah Jenness for her support in managing the project and contributing to the editing through the initial stages, and Sandra Katz for her edits and comments at the end.

Alex Camlin's early designs acted as a vision board throughout my writing. I would like to thank him for the cover and Chronicle Chroma's Alexandria Martinez for giving the book its flair.

My sincere thanks go to Chronicle's production team, publicist, and sales and marketing team for their significant work in bringing this book into the world.

I would also like to thank Derek Davidson at Photofest for his dedication and endless patience behind the scenes on the selected images, as well as Julie Tesser for her organization and perseverance in tracking down prized outliers.

I am grateful for the many meaningful encounters I have made in academia that nurtured my thought as a scholar and writer. In particular, I would like to extend my profound gratitude to Laurence Schifano for her guidance, support, and precious insight during my doctoral studies at Université Paris Ouest Nanterre. Her direction of *De l'amour, des femmes et de la Nouvelle Vague: Reconfigurations culturelles et création d'une modernité filmique française* (2011) deeply shaped my thought and approach to the New Wave and provided the foundation for this book. I would also like to thank my dissertation committee: Antoine de Baecque, Giorgio De Vincenti, and Gilles Mouëllic for their valuable insight and suggestions.

Francis Vanoye's work on artists and models, and on directors and alter egos greatly influenced my exploration of actresses and directors. Jenene J. Allison's research on eighteenth-century French women also inspired my approach in this book.

I would like to thank the following authors in particular for their research and insight into the lives of New Wave actresses and directors that contributed significantly to my chapters: Aurélien Ferenczi on Françoise Dorléac, Garry McGee on Jean Seberg, Mireille Brangé on Delphine Seyrig, Laure Adler on Agnès Varda, Serge Toubiana on François Truffaut, Noël Herpe on Éric Rohmer, and Antoine de Baecque on Truffaut, Rohmer, and Jean-Luc Godard.

Thank you to Antonio Di Trapani and Gabriele Anaclerio for their stimulating and in-depth collaborative work at Università Roma Tre on the documentary *La Nouvelle Vague*.

I wish to express my deep gratitude to Stacey Katz Bourns for her support of my class on the French New Wave at Harvard University. This opportunity allowed for many years of meaningful engagement with my students whose new reactions to the films and insight in class discussions inspired many ideas in the book and led to other important encounters.

I would equally like to thank Virginie Greene and the faculty and staff at Harvard who worked with me to bring Anna Karina and Dennis Berry to campus in 2018. Thank you to Angela Hartwick and Daryl Visscher for their valuable collaboration on the event as well as for allowing me to be part of the pursuit of documenting the story of Berry and Karina throughout the years.

The students in my class on the French New Wave at Stanford Continuing Studies and the Ciné-club group also deserve special recognition for their contributions through our discussions and debates that have all enriched this work immensely.

To my colleagues, fellow researchers, and students at Northeastern University, I have benefitted greatly from collaborations and discussions that have indirectly and directly influenced the book.

I am especially grateful to David Campos for his intellectual companionship and constant support that were crucial to this project and beyond. I cherish my friendship and passionate discussions with Kriengsak Silakong on cinema, and with Monique Delvallée on psychoanalysis.

Finally, thank you to my mother, Wanda Knudson, for her strength, patience, and unending support throughout the entire project, and to my family and friends for their understanding and encouragement that have sustained me through all the setbacks and steps forward along the way.

Each of you has left an enduring mark on this book and on my life. It is my hope that *Nouvelles Femmes* will, in turn, spark new conversations, leading to more meaningful encounters with cinema and to greater understanding among everyone who identifies with the complex stories the films portray.

With deep appreciation,

Ericka Knudson

ENDNOTES

Introduction: *A Generational Shift in Society and Cinema*

i. Raganelli, Katja and Konrad Wickler. *Les Femmes sont de nature créative: Agnès Varda* [*Women are Naturally Creative: Agnès Varda*]. 1977.

Chapter One: *Avant La Vague*, Before the Wave

1. Williams, Tony. "Le Quai des brumes." *Senses of Cinema*, no. 69, Dec. 2013, www.sensesofcinema.com/2013/cteq/le-quai-des-brumes/.
2. "Origins of Poetic Realism." *Cinema Waves: Movements in Film*, cinemawavesblog.com/about/.
3-4. Jeancolas, Jean-Pierre. *Histoire du cinéma français*. Paris, Nathan, 1995.
5. "Realism and the War Years." *French and Francophone Film, Research Guide*, Library of Congress, guides.loc.gov/french-and-francophone-film/movements-and-genres/realism-and-war-years/.
6. Mills, Ted. "Jean-Luc Godard's Breathless: How World War II Changed Cinema & Helped Create the French New Wave." *Film History*, 21 Mar. 2021, www.openculture.com/2021/03/jean-luc-godards-breathless-how-world-war-ii-changed-cinema.html#google_vignette.
7. "1948 French Films." *The New York Times*, 6 Feb. 1998, www.nytimes.com/1998/02/06/opinion/IHT-1948-french-films-in-our-pages100-75-and-50-years-ago.html.
8. "Realism and the War Years." *French and Francophone Film, Research Guide*.
9. "Cinéma du Look." *French and Francophone Film, Research Guide*, Library of Congress, guides.loc.gov/french-and-francophone-film/movements-and-genres/cinema-du-look.
10-11. Gimello-Mesplomb, Frédéric. "The economy of 1950s popular French cinema." *Studies in French Cinema*, vol. 6, no. 2, 2006, pp. 141-150. halshs-01808380.
12. Varda, Agnès. "Trois Pièces sur cour: la serre du bonheur, à deux mains et l'arbre de nini." Gardeners Court Galleries, Domaine de Chaumont-sur-Loire, 2019, https://domaine-chaumont.fr/en/centre-arts-and-nature/2019-art-season/agnes-varda.
13-15. Marie, Michel. *La Nouvelle Vague: Une école artistique*. Paris, Nathan, 1998. For an English translation of Truffaut's article, "A Certain Tendency in French Film" see: learning.hccs.edu/faculty/selena.anderson/engl2342/readings/a-certain-tendency-in-french-film-by-francois-truffaut/view/.
16. Truffaut, François. "Vous êtes tous témoins dans ce procès: Le Cinéma crève sous ses fausses légendes." *Arts*, no. 619, 15 May 1957, p. 1.
17. "Realism and the War Years." *French and Francophone Film, Research Guide*.
18. Marie. *La Nouvelle Vague*.
19. "Danielle Darrieux obituary: from pre-war modernity to the epitome of Parisian chic." *Sight and Sound*, 10 Aug. 2020, www2.bfi.org.uk/news-opinion/sight-sound-magazine/comment/obituaries/danielle-darrieux-epitome-parisian-chic.
20. "Maria Casarès." OFPRA, www.ofpra.gouv.fr/en/images-gallery/famous-refugees/maria-casares-actress.
21. Bergan, Ronald. "Michèle Morgan Obituary." *The Guardian*, 21 Dec. 2016, www.theguardian.com/film/2016/dec/21/michele-morgan-obituary.
22. Scovell, Adam. "Simone Signoret: remembering a French screen legend on her centenary." *British Film Institute*, 21 Mar. 2021, www.bfi.org.uk/features/simone-signoret-centenary.
23. Astruc, Alexandre. "Naissance d'une nouvelle avant-garde: la caméra-stylo." *L'Écran français*, no. 144, 30 Mar. 1948.
24. Rauger, Jean-François. "Jean-Luc Godard's paradoxical and provocative film criticism." *Le Monde*, 13 Sept. 2022, www.lemonde.fr/en/obituaries/article/2022/09/13/jean-luc-godard-s-paradoxical-and-provocative-film-criticism_5996810_15.html.
25. "Louis Malle on *Elevator to the Gallows*." *Parlons cinéma*, 1975, www.criterionchannel.com/videos/louis-malle-1975.
26. Truhler, Kimberly. "The Style Essentials--'Hitchcock Style' Star Grace Kelly in 1954's *Rear Window*." *GlamAmor*, 10 Feb. 2010, www.glamamor.com/2010/02/rear-window.html.
27. "Bechdel Test." *Merriam-Webster*, www.merriam-webster.com/dictionary/Bechdel%20Test.
28-29. Mulvey, Laura. "Visual Pleasure and Narrative Cinema." *Screen*, vol. 16, no. 3, 1 Oct. 1975, p. 6-18, doi:10.1093/screen/16.3.6.
30. Truffaut, François, *Hitchcock by François Truffaut, With the Collaboration of Helen G. Scott*. Simon & Schuster, 1985.
31. Mulvey. "Visual Pleasure and Narrative Cinema."
32. On the occasion of the screening of the restored version of *Vertigo* at the Chicago Film Festival in 1996.
33. Truffaut. *Hitchcock by François Truffaut*.
34. "Un peu d'histoire, Françoise Giroud ou l'invention d'un slogan." Directed by Julien Diaz, l'INA, 1973, www.ina.fr/ina-eclaire-actu/video/vdd10007791/l-invention-d-un-slogan.
35-36. "Louis Malle on *Elevator to the Gallows*." *Parlons cinéma*.
37. Rozier, Jacques. Q&A post-screening talk. Cinéma Action, Paris, 28 Sept. 2005.
38. Truffaut. "Le Cinéma français crève sous les fausses legends." ["The film of tomorrow appears to me as even more personal than an individual and autobiographical novel, like a confession or a diary… The film of tomorrow will be an act of love."]
39. "Louis Malle on *Elevator to the Gallows*." *Parlons cinéma*.
40. As told to Fonda by Joshua Logan, her godfather and director of the film.
41. Actresses Juliet Berto, Jane Fonda, Maria Schneider, Ellen Burstyn in *Sois belle et tais-toi* (*Be Pretty and Shut Up*) by Delphine Seyrig, 1981.
42. Describing a gaze constructed by patriarchal society viewing women as objects and passive in relation to men as active.
43. "Breaking Free from the Male Gaze." University of Westminster, www.westminster.ac.uk/about-us/our-university/outreach-for-schools-and-colleges/extended-project-qualification-epq-support/breaking-free-from-the-male-gaze.
44. For statistics on women's enrollment in colleges, see: https://www.npr.org/2024/06/13/g-s1-4038/women-outnumber-men-colleges-earnings#:~:text=That%20slow%20progress%20comes%20despite,the%20U.S.%20Department%20of%20Education.
45. Raganelli and Wickler. *Les Femmes sont de nature créative: Agnès Varda*.
46-47. Varda, Agnès. *Réponse de femmes*. 1975.
48. Karina, Anna. Personal interview with the author. Boston, 10 April, 2018.
49. Olszynko-Gryn, Jesse, and Caroline Rusterholz. "Reproductive Politics in Twentieth-Century France and Britain." Cambridge University Press, 26 Mar. 2019, www.ncbi.nlm.nih.gov/pmc/articles/PMC6434651/. [A manifesto by 331 doctors in support of abortion was consequently released in 1973. The Veil Act (named after Simone Veil, the Minister of Health at the time) legalized contraception and abortion in 1975.]
50. Raganelli, Katja and Konrad Wickler. "Portrait of Actress Delphine Seyrig." 1977.
51. "Macha Méril est l'invitée de RTL." *Droits des femmes*, RTL [French Radio], 8 Mar. 2024, www.dailymotion.com/video/x8u37b2.
52. Linhart, Virginie. *Jeanne Moreau, l'affranchie*. Arte.fr, 2017.
53. Duras, Marguerite. *Hiroshima mon amour*. Translated by Richard Seaver, Grove Press, 1962.
54. Rouch, Jean, and Edgar Morin. *Chronique d'un été*. Éditions Montparnasse, 2011, https://journals.openedition.org/lectures/7825?lang=es.
55. "Jeanne Moreau on *Elevator to the Gallows*." The Criterion Collection, 2006, www.criterionchannel.com/videos/jeanne-moreau-on-elevator-to-the-gallows.
56. "Macha Méril est l'invitée de RTL." *Droits des femmes*.

Chapter Two: *Brigitte Bardot: La Femme Naturelle,*
The Natural Woman

1. Bardot, Brigitte. *Initiales B.B.: Mémoires*. Paris, Grasset, 1996.
2-3. Vadim, Roger. *Bardot, Deneuve, Fonda: My Life with the Three Most Beautiful Women in the World*. Simon & Schuster, 1986.
4. Sragow, Michael. "Vadim & Bardot's Creative Marriage." The Criterion Channel, 21 Dec. 2016, www.criterionchannel.com/roger-vadim-brigitte-bardot/season:1/videos/roger-vadim-brigitte-bardot.
5-6. Vadim. *Bardot, Deneuve, Fonda*.
7-8. Pulleine, Tim. "Roger Vadim." *The Guardian*, 11 Feb. 2000, www.theguardian.com/news/2000/feb/12/guardianobituaries.timpulleine.
9. Czarkowska-Krupa, Agnieszka. "Brigitte Bardot & Roger Vadim – Love of The Twenties." *Old Camera*, 4 Feb. 2023, oldcamera.pl/en/brigitte-

10. Soares, Andre. "Simone Simon: La Bête Humaine 1938 Femme Fatale." *Thinking Film*, 2014, www.altfg.com/film/la-bete-humaine-1938-simone-simon/.

11. Vadim. *Bardot, Deneuve, Fonda.*

12. Bardot. *Initiales B.B.*

13. Vadim. *Bardot, Deneuve, Fonda.*

14. Bardot. *Initiales B.B.*

15-16. Vadim. *Bardot, Deneuve, Fonda.*

17-19. Bardot. *Initiales B.B.*

20-23. Vadim. *Bardot, Deneuve, Fonda.*

24. Sragow. "Vadim & Bardot's Creative Marriage."

25. Bardot. *Initiales B.B.*

26 Truffaut, François. *Les Films de ma vie.* Paris, Flammarion, 1975, p. 328.

27. Godard, Jean-Luc. "Bergmanorama." *Cahiers du cinéma,* no. 85, July 1958. In Godard, Jean-Luc. *Godard par Godard: Les années Cahiers,* Paris, Flammarion, 1989.

28.-29. de Baecque, Antoine. *Godard, biographie.* Paris, Grasset, 2010.

30. "Brigitte Bardot and the Scandal that Made Saint-Tropez Famous." Iconic Riviera, iconicriviera.com/brigitte-bardot-the-scandal-that-made-st-tropez-famous/.

31. Vincendeau, Ginette. "La Vérité: Women on Trial." The Criterion Collection, 12 Feb. 2019, www.criterion.com/current/posts/6195-la-verite-women-on-trial.

32. Bazin, André. *Le cinéma français de la Libération à la Nouvelle Vague (1945-1958).* Jean Narboni, ed., Paris, Petite bibliothèque des Cahiers du cinéma, 1998.

33. de Baecque. *Godard.*

34. Truffaut. *Les Films de ma vie,* p. 329.

35. Vadim. *Bardot, Deneuve, Fonda.*

36. Bardot, Brigitte. Interview. "B.B. en chansons." Jean-Luc Prévost, *Film Office,* 1992.

37. Bardot. *Initiales B.B.*

38. Bazin, André. "Et Dieu créa la femme. En effeuillant la mariée." *Le Parisien libéré,* 4 Dec. 1956.

39. Truffaut. *Les Films de ma vie.*

40. Barthes, Roland. *Mythologies.* Paris, Seuil, 1957.

41. Pulleine. "Roger Vadim."

42. Vadim. *Bardot, Deneuve, Fonda.*

43. Bazin, André. *France-Observateur,* 24 Apr. 1958. *Le Cinéma français de la Liberation à la Nouvelle Vague: 1945 – 1958.*

44. Bergman, Ingrid and Alan Burgess. *Ingrid Bergman: My Story.* Dell, 1981.

45. Saada, Philippe. "Riz Amer, Camarades." Studio Canal, 2003.

46. Vadim. *Bardot, Deneuve, Fonda.*

47. Robinson, Jeffrey. *Bardot: An Intimate Portrait.* Dutton, 1996.

48. Sragow. "Vadim & Bardot's Creative Marriage."

49. Blumenfeld, Samuel. "Bardot, une vie confisquée." *Le Monde,* 11 Aug. 2021, www.lemonde.fr/series-d-ete/article/2021/08/11/bardot-une-vie-confisquee_6091203_3451060.html.

50-51. "Brigitte Bardot and the Scandal that Made Saint-Tropez Famous." Iconic Riviera.

52. Bazin. *France-Observateur,* 24 Apr. 1958.

53. Vincendeau. "La Vérité: Women on Trial."

54. Robinson. *Bardot: An Intimate Portrait.*

55. Vadim. *Bardot, Deneuve, Fonda.*

56. Czarkowska-Krupa. "Brigitte Bardot & Roger Vadim – Love of The Twenties."; see also Robinson. *Bardot: An Intimate Portrait.*

57. Bardot in Vincendeau. "La Vérité: Women on Trial."

58. Servat, Henry-Jean. "The Temptress of St. Tropez." *Vanity Fair,* 17 Feb. 2012, www.vanityfair.com/hollywood/2012/03/bardot-201203.

Chapter Three: *Jeanne Moreau: La Femme Passionnée,* **The Passionate Woman**

1. Cowie, Peter. "Talking Welles with the Great Jeanne Moreau." 24 Aug. 2016, The Criterion Collection, www.criterion.com/current/posts/4195-talking-welles-with-the-great-jeanne-moreau.

2-4. "Jeanne Moreau, 1972." Interview by France Roche. *Tête d'affiche.* Raoul Sangla, dir., 30 Jan. 1972, L'INA, 1975, www.criterionchannel.com/videos/jeanne-moreau-interview.

5. Cowie. "Talking Welles with the Great Jeanne Moreau."

6. About Moreau being "unphotogenic," see Steinbach, Alice. *Without Reservations: The Travels of an Independent Woman.* Random House, 2002, p. 44.

7. "Jeanne Moreau, 1972." *Tête d'affiche.*

8. "Jeanne Moreau et Louis Malle." *Le Cercle de minuit,* 18 May 1993. L'INA, www.ina.fr/ina-eclaire-actu/video/i12032324/jeanne-moreau-et-louis-malle.

9. Linhart. *Jeanne Moreau, l'affranchie.*

10. "Jeanne Moreau on *Elevator to the Gallows.*" Interview recorded at the Brasserie La Lorraine, Paris, 2005. The Criterion Collection, 2006, www.criterionchannel.com/videos/jeanne-moreau-on-elevator-to-the-gallows.

11. "Malle and Moreau Cannes 1993." *Le Cercle de minuit,* Michel Field, L'INA. The Criterion Collection, www.criterionchannel.com/videos/malle-and-moreau-at-cannes-1993.

12. "Jeanne Moreau on *Elevator to the Gallows.*"

13.-17. "Malle and Moreau Cannes 1993."

18. "Jeanne Moreau on *Elevator to the Gallows.*"

19. Linhart. *Jeanne Moreau, l'affranchie.*

20. "Malle and Moreau Cannes 1993."

21. "Jeanne Moreau on *Elevator to the Gallows.*"

22-23. "Malle and Moreau Cannes 1993."

24-25. "Jeanne Moreau on *Elevator to the Gallows.*"

26. "Jacques Rivette." *La Nouvelle Vague, 50 ans après,* Julien Diaz. L'INA, www.ina.fr/ina-eclaire-actu/video/vdd10007786/jacques-rivette.

27. de Givray, Claude. "Le Coup du berger de Jacques Rivette." *Cahiers du cinéma,* no. 77, Dec. 1957. In *La Nouvelle Vague,* Antoine de Baecque and Charles Tesson, ed., Paris, Cahiers du cinéma, 1999.

28. *Paris nous appartient (Le Coup du berger).* DVD cover, MK2, 2007.

29. Billard, Pierre. *Louis Malle: le rebelle solitaire.* Paris, Plon, 2003.

30. "Jeanne Moreau on *The Lovers,* 1958." Le journal télévisé, aired 4 Nov. 1958, www.criterionchannel.com/videos/jeanne-moreau-on-the-lovers-1958.

31. "Jeanne Moreau on *The Lovers,* 1972." *Tête d'affiche.* Interview directed by Jacques Nahum and Raoul Sangla, aired 30 Jan. 1971. https://www.criterionchannel.com/videos/jeanne-moreau-on-the-lovers-1972

32. "Jeanne Moreau on *Elevator to the Gallows.*"

33-34. Billard. *Louis Malle: le rebelle solitaire.*

35. Moreau, Jeanne. "Mon amour pour Louis Malle." L'INA, Arditube, www.youtube.com/watch?v=pHQCRBvMqgg.

36. Chochard-Le Goff, Chloé. *Jeanne, de l'attachement à l'indifférence, dans Les Amants de Louis Malle.* 2010. Université Paris Ouest Nanterre, Master 1 thesis.

37. Doniol-Valcroze, Jacques. "Le pouvoir de la nuit." *Cahiers du cinéma,* no. 89, Nov. 1958, p. 43.

38. "Louis Malle interviewed by Jean Desailly explains his choice of classical composer Johannes Brahms for his film *Les Amants.*" 3 July 1959, mediaclip.ina.fr/en/i19239855-louis-malle-on-the-music-of-his-film-les-amants.html.

39. Chochard-Le Goff. *Jeanne, de l'attachement à l'indifférence.*

40. Callahan, Dan. "Jeanne Moreau 1928-2017." Rogererbert.com, 31 July 2017, www.rogerebert.com/features/jeanne-moreau-1928-2017.

41. Linhart. *Jeanne Moreau, l'affranchie.*

42. "Jeanne Moreau on *The Lovers,* 1958."

43. In Billard. *Louis Malle: le rebelle solitaire.*

44. Sellier, Geneviève. "Jeanne Moreau: star de la Nouvelle Vague." *Le Genre et l'écran,* 1 Aug. 2017, www.genre-ecran.net/?Jeanne-Moreau-star-de-la-Nouvelle-vague.

45. de Vilmorin, Louise. "Louis Malle, un homme qui m'est inconnu." *L'Avant-Scène,* no. 2, Mar. 1961.

46. Callahan. "Jeanne Moreau 1928-2017."; Amengual, Barthélémy. "Le réalisme des Amants ou les papiers collés du Tendre." *Etudes Cinématographiques,* no. 4, Winter 1960.

47. *La Croix* (1880-1940 ; 1945), Jean Rochereau and Henri Rabine; *La France catholique* (1906) in Geneviève Sellier. *La Nouvelle Vague: un cinéma au masculin singulier.* Paris, CNRS, 2005.

48. On the Supreme Court ruling: "The Lovers." *The File Room,* www.thefileroom.org/documents/dyn/DisplayCase.cfm/id/247.

49. Billard. *Louis Malle: le rebelle solitaire.*

50. Sellier. "Jeanne Moreau: star de la Nouvelle Vague."

51. Linhart. *Jeanne Moreau, l'affranchie.*

52-53. "Jeanne Moreau on *The Lovers*, 1972."
54. Linhart. *Jeanne Moreau, l'affranchie*.
55-59. "Jeanne Moreau, 1972." *Tête d'affiche*.
60. Linhart. "Jeanne Moreau, l'affranchie."
61. "Jeanne Moreau, 1972." *Tête d'affiche*.
62-63. Linhart. *Jeanne Moreau, l'affranchie*.
64. "Jeanne Moreau, 1972." *Tête d'affiche*.
65-66. Linhart. *Jeanne Moreau, l'affranchie*.
67. "Bardot était chiante, Moreau chez Thierry Ardisson." L'INA Arditube, 14 Dec. 1991, www.youtube.com/watch?v=wz9pQa2Ppnc.
68. "Locarno Film Festival Welles Retrospective." Wellesnet, wellesnet.com/phpbb2/viewtopic.php?t=201&start=165.
69. "Cinépanorama: Jeanne Moreau, 1962." Interview on the set of *La Baie des anges*. The Criterion Channel, www.criterionchannel.com/videos/cinepanorama-jeanne-moreau-1962.
70-71. Callahan. "Jeanne Moreau 1928-2017."
72. "Brigitte Bardot et Jeanne Moreau: Les Girls in Mexico." *Life*, Apr. 1965,
73. Linhart. *Jeanne Moreau, l'affranchie*.
74. "Jeanne Moreau on *Elevator to the Gallows*."

Chapter Four: *Emmanuelle Riva: La Femme Mûre*, The Mature Woman

1-2. "Emmanuelle Riva on *Hiroshima mon amour* 1." Interview François Chalais, 1959 Cannes Film Festival, L'INA, www.criterionchannel.com/videos/emmanuelle-riva-on-hiroshima-mon-amour.
3. Germanaz, Axelle. "Hiroshima mon amour (1959)." Lexicon of Global Melodrama, 2022, www.transcript-open.de/pdf_chapter/bis%205999/9783839459737/9783839459737-025.pdf.
4. As told to *The Hollywood Reporter* in February 2013.
5. Mai-Duc, Christine. "Emmanuelle Riva, revered French actress who broke an Oscar age barrier, dies at 89." *Los Angeles Times*, 28 Jan. 2017, www.latimes.com/local/obituaries/la-me-emmanuelle-riva-snap-story.html.
6. "Emmanuelle Riva on *Hiroshima mon amour* 2." Interview The Criterion Channel, 2003, www.criterionchannel.com/videos/emmanuelle-riva-on-hiroshima-mon-amour-1.
7. "Hiroshima, mon amour by Marguerite Duras [dir. Alain Resnais]." Chunking Books, chunkingbooks.com/product/hiroshima-mon-amour/.
8. Duras, Marguerite. "Marguerite Duras on Writing the Screenplay on Alain Resnais's *Hiroshima mon amour*." Translated by Nicholas Elliott, *Literary Hub*, 22 Aug. 2022, lithub.com/marguerite-duras-on-writing-the-screenplay-for-alain-resnaiss-hiroshima-mon-amour/.
9. "Hiroshima, mon amour by Marguerite Duras [dir. Alain Resnais]." Chunking Books.
10. Duras. *Hiroshima mon amour*. Translated by Richard Seaver.
11-13. "Emmanuelle Riva on *Hiroshima mon amour* 2."
14. "Marguerite Duras on Writing the Screenplay on Alain Resnais's *Hiroshima mon amour*."
15-16. "Emmanuelle Riva on *Hiroshima mon amour* 2."
17. Shoard, Catherine. "Emmanuelle Riva, French icon who starred in Amour, dies aged 89." *The Guardian*, 28 Jan. 2017, www.theguardian.com/film/2017/jan/28/emmanuelle-riva-french-icon-who-starred-in-amour-dies-aged-89.
18. "Emmanuelle Riva on *Hiroshima mon amour* 1."
19. Mai-Duc. "Emmanuelle Riva, revered French actress who broke an Oscar age barrier, dies at 89."
20. "Emmanuelle Riva on *Hiroshima mon amour* 1."
21. As noted by Laurent Kretzschmar who translated Serge Daney's article. Serge Daney. "The Tracking Shot in Kapò." [first appearing in *Trafic* No. 4, P.O.L. Editions, 1992] for *Senses of Cinema*, Feb. 2004, www.sensesofcinema.com/2004/feature-articles/kapo_daney/.
22. "Emmanuelle Riva obituary: an actor formidable in love and loss." *Sight and Sound*, 18 Dec. 2019, www2.bfi.org.uk/news-opinion/sight-sound-magazine/comment/obituaries/emmanuelle-riva-actor-formidable-love-loss.
23. Petit, Susan. "The Worlds of Beatrix Beck." *Simone de Beauvoir Studies*, vol. 12, 1995, pp. 140-7. JSTOR, www.jstor.org/stable/45186671.
24. "Jean-Paul Belmondo et Jean-Pierre Melville 'Léon Morin prêtre.'" Archive L'INA, www.youtube.com/watch?v=2duOmaron5E.
25.-26. "Emmanuelle Riva est Thérèse Desqueyroux." *Dimanche en France*, 1962, L'INA, www.ina.fr/ina-eclaire-actu/video/i13044002/emmanuelle-riva-est-therese-desqueyroux.
27-31. Mai-Duc. "Emmanuelle Riva, revered French actress who broke an Oscar age barrier, dies at 89."

Chapter Five: *Anna Karina: La Femme du Portrait Ovale*, The Woman in the Oval Portrait

1-2. Berry, Dennis. *Anna Karina, Souviens-toi*. Arte, 2017.
3. Talu, Yonca. "Interview: Anna Karina." *Film Comment*, 31 May 2016, www.filmcomment.com/blog/interview-anna-karina/.
4. Golenda, Gabrielle. "Vivre sa vie." cargocollective.com/vivresavie/dreyer-s-joan-of-arc.
5. Anna Karina interview with Emmanuelle Sterpin. Vagenende brasserie, bd. St Germain, 2017. SND M6 video, Gump.tv, Maxime Bonneau [*Vivre ensemble* DVD bonus].
6. Berry. *Anna Karina, Souviens-toi*.
7-8. Diatkine, Anne. "Anna Karina, libre comme l'ère." *Libération*, 15 Dec. 2019, www.liberation.fr/cinema/2019/12/15/anna-karina-libre-comme-l-ere_1769432/.
9. "Anna Karina on Meeting Jean-Luc Godard." The Criterion Collection, www.youtube.com/watch?v=7vt_VU-98wM.
10. Anna Karina interview with Emmanuelle Sterpin.
11-12. Berry. *Anna Karina, Souviens-toi*.
13. Anna Karina interview with Emmanuelle Sterpin.
14. "M. et Mme Godard tournent ensemble." *La Presse*, edition provincial, 3 June 1961, numerique.banq.qc.ca/patrimoine/details/52327/2756483.
15-16. Berry. *Anna Karina, Souviens-toi*.
17. "An Interview with Anna Karina." YouTube, www.youtube.com/watch?v=75WyOWr-9wE.
18. Berry. *Anna Karina, Souviens-toi*.
19. Anna Karina interview with Emmanuelle Sterpin.
20. Berry. *Anna Karina, Souviens-toi*.
21-22. Anna Karina interview with Emmanuelle Sterpin.
23. Sragow, Micheal. "Creative Marriages: Godard & Karina." The Criterion Channel, www.criterionchannel.com/creative-marriages-godard-karina/season:1/videos/creative-marriage-godard-karina.
24. "Anna Karina on Meeting Jean-Luc Godard."
25. "M. et Mme Godard tournent ensemble."
26. "Anna Karina on Meeting Jean-Luc Godard."
27. "An Interview with Anna Karina."
28. "Anna Karina on Meeting Jean-Luc Godard."
29. "An Interview with Anna Karina."
30. "Exile Paradise." *The New Yorker*, 20 Nov. 2000, www.newyorker.com/magazine/profiles/2000/11/20/exile-paradise.
31. "An Interview with Anna Karina."
32. "Quand Anna Karina retrouvait Godard 20 ans après et quittait le plateau les larmes aux yeux." *Les Inrockuptibles*, 15 Dec. 2019, www.lesinrocks.com/cinema/quand-anna-karina-retrouvait-godard-20-ans-apres-et-quittait-le-plateau-les-larmes-aux-yeux-325956-15-12-2019/.
33. Mintzer, Jordan. "Anna Karina, Radiant Actress, Jean-Luc Godard's Muse Dies at 79." *The Hollywood Reporter*, 15 Dec. 2019, www.hollywoodreporter.com/news/general-news/anna-karina-dead-radiant-actress-jean-luc-godard-muse-was-79-1203437/.
34. "Entretien avec Anna Karina (2001)." Cinémathèque Française, 16 Dec. 2019, www.cinematheque.fr/article/1502.html.
35. "Jean-Luc Godard et Anna Karina, vingt ans après." *Bains de Minuit*, 25 Dec. 1987.
36. Vanoye, Francis. *L'Emprise du cinéma*. Paris, Aléas, 2005, p. 191.
37. "Entretien avec Anna Karina (2001)." Cinémathèque Française.
38-40. de Baecque. *Godard*.
41. Berry. Anna Karina, *Souviens-toi*.
42. Godard, Jean-Luc. *Introduction à une veritable histoire du cinéma*. Paris, Albatros, 1980, p. 33.
43. "Entretien avec Anna Karina (2001)." Cinémathèque Française.
44. "M. et Mme Godard tournent ensemble."
45. In de Baecque. *Godard*, p. 170.
46-47. "An Interview with Anna Karina."
48. "M. et Mme Godard tournent ensemble."
49. "Entretien avec Anna Karina (2001)." Cinémathèque Française,
50. " An Interview with Anna Karina."
51. Sragow. "Creative Marriages: Godard & Karina."
52. Michel Séméniako interview with Guy Jollivet and Ericka Knudson, 18 Apr. 2006, Paris.
53. de Baecque. *Godard*, pp. 161-2.

54.   Collet, Jean, et al. Interview conducted by Jean Collet, Michel Delahaye, Jean-AndréFieschi, André S. Labarthe and Bertrand Tavernier. *Cahiers du cinéma*, no. 138, Dec. 1962 in *Godard par Godard, les années Karina, (1960 – 1967)*, Paris, Flammarion, 2007.

55-56.   de Baecque. *Godard*, p. 113.

57.   Godard, Jean-Luc. *Godard par Godard: Les années Cahiers*. Paris, Flammarion, 1989.

58.   de Baecque. *Godard*, p. 210.

59.   Talu. "Interview: Anna Karina."

60.   Schifano, Laurence. "Le portrait ovale, syndrome filmique?" *L'Empire du récit: mélanges offerts à Francis Vanoye*, Claude Leroy and Schifano, ed. Paris, Non Lieu, 2007, pp. 73-86. Schifano notes "a tragic shared link between the artistic and vital spheres" in this topos, underlining its persistence in literature and cinema, citing Jean Epstein who notes what she calls "the oval portrait syndrome": "the progressive elimination of real life to the passionate transfer effectuated from the beloved to the oeuvre—his tomb."

61.   Poe, Edgar Allan. "The Oval Portrait." *Edgar Allan Poe: Poetry and Tales*, Patrick Quinn, ed. Library of America, storyoftheweek.loa. org/2021/10/the-oval-portrait.html.

62.   "Entretien avec Anna Karina (2001)." Cinémathèque Française.; Whyte, Alistair. "Anna Karina Interview 1973." YouTube, www.youtube.com/watch?v=OIbpzyUtrUw.

63.   Anna Karina interview with Emmanuelle Sterpin.

64-68.   de Baecque. *Godard*, pp. 230, 237-8.

69.   Talu. "Interview: Anna Karina."

70.   Brooks, Xan. "Anna Karina on Love, Cinema, and Being Godard's Muse: 'I didn't want to be alive any more'." *The Guardian*, 21 Jan. 2016, www.theguardian.com/film/2016/jan/21/anna-karina-on-love-cinema-and-being-jean-luc-godards-muse-i-didnt-want-to-be-alive-anymore.

71.   Talu. "Interview: Anna Karina."

72.   Brooks. "Anna Karina on Love, Cinema, and Being Godard's Muse."

73-74.   Talu. "Interview: Anna Karina."

74.   de Baecque. *Godard*, note 199, p. 257.

76.   Sragow. "Creative Marriages: Godard & Karina.".

77.   Talu. "Interview: Anna Karina."

78.   In de Baecque. *Godard*, note 125, p. 257.

79.   "Journey to the End of the Beach: Godard, Karina and Pierrot le fou." *Sight and Sound*, 16 Dec. 2019, www2.bfi.org.uk/news-opinion/sight-sound-magazine/features/pierrot-le-fou-jean-luc-godard-anna-karina-end-affair-marriage-story.

80.   The lines: "must the other pursue. My life is a fault at last, I fear:" and "[It seems too much like a fate], Indeed!" are cut from the original Browning poem

81.   Karina, Anna. Presentation and Q&A of *Pierrot le fou*. Harvard University, 12 Apr. 2018.

82.   Bergala, Alain. *Godard au travail: les années 60*. Paris, Cahiers du cinéma, 2006.

83.   The idea of a life of contemplation vs. a life of action also haunted Godard's works.

84.   Talu. "Interview: Anna Karina."

85.   Brooks. "Anna Karina on Love, Cinema, and Being Godard's Muse."

86.   Sragow. "Creative Marriages: Godard & Karina.".

87.   Monaco, James. *The New Wave: Truffaut, Godard, Chabrol, Rohmer, Rivette*. Oxford University Press, 1976.

88.   Godard. *Introduction à une veritable histoire du cinéma*, p. 63.

89.   Brooks. "Anna Karina on Love, Cinema, and Being Godard's Muse."

90.   As described by the theoretician Jean-Pierre Esquénazi.

91.   Godard. *Introduction à une veritable histoire du cinéma*, p. 63.

92.   In de Baecque. *Godard*, p. 179.

93-94.   Whyte. "Anna Karina Interview 1973."

95.   "Entretien avec Anna Karina (2001)." *Cinémathèque Française*.

96.   Berry. *Anna Karina, Souviens-toi*.

97.   "Anna Karina and Jean-Luc Godard: Fiction and Friction." Aenigma Images, 2019, www.aenigma-images.com/2019/04/anna-karina-and-jean-luc-godard-fiction-and-friction/;"Anna Karina." *New Wave Film*, www.newwavefilm.com/french-new-wave-encyclopedia/anna-karina.shtml.

Chapter Six: *Anouk Aimée: La Prostituée Romantique,*
The Romantic Prostitute

1.   "Anouk Aimée." *Le Chronique de Dominique Besnehard*, Radio France, 19 May 2019, www.radiofrance.fr/franceinter/podcasts/la-chronique-de-dominique-besnehard/anouk-aimee-8223903.

2-3.   Darley, Mathilde, Marion David, Lilian Mathieu, Gwénaëlle Mainsant, and Véronique Guienne. "Prostitution Policies in France." Assessing Prostitution Policies in Europe, 2018, halshs-02407699.

4.   Hollier, Denis, and R. Howard Bloc. *A New History of French Literature*. Harvard University Press, 1994.

5.-7.   Varda, Agnès. *L'Univers de Jacques Demy* [*The World of Jacques Demy*]. 1995, www.criterionchannel.com/videos/the-world-of-jacques-demy-1.

8.   Mathieu, Clément. "Dans les archives de Match: Agnès Varda et Jacques Demy, un amour éternel." *Paris Match*, 29 Mar. 2019, www.parismatch.com/culture/cinema/agnes-varda-jacques-demy-histoire-amour-1615797#18.

9-11.   "Interview with Anouk Aimée by Agnès Varda." In *L'Univers de Jacques Demy*, www.criterionchannel.com/videos/anouk-aimee-on-lola.

12-14.   Varda. *L'Univers de Jacques Demy*.

15.   French, Philip. "Lola." *The Guardian*, 18 Sept. 2010, www.theguardian.com/film/2010/sep/19/lola-dvd-review-phillip-french.

16.   "What Is the Madonna-Whore Complex?" *CXO Media*, July 2022, www.cxomedia.id/human-stories/20220721154651-74-175649/what-is-the-madonna-whore-dichotomy.

17.   Bareket, O., et al. "The Madonna-Whore Dichotomy: Men Who Perceive Women's Nurturance and Sexuality as Mutually Exclusive Endorse Patriarchy and Show Lower Relationship Satisfaction." *Sex Roles: A Journal of Research*, vol. 79, no. 9-10, 2018, pp. 519-532, doi:10.1007/s11199-018-0895-7.

18.   "Interview with Anouk Aimée by Agnès Varda." In *L'Univers de Jacques Demy*.

19.   Varda. *L'Univers de Jacques Demy*.

20.   Vincendeau, Ginette. "Lola: Demy's Paradise Found." The Criterion Collection, 21 July 2014, www.criterion.com/current/posts/3231-lola-demy-s-paradise-found.

21.   "Anouk Aimée." *Le Chronique de Dominique Besnehard*.

22.   Balle, Catherine. "Dominique Besnehard sur la mort d'Anouk Aimée: 'C'était une rêveuse angoissée'." *Le Parisien*, 18 June 2024, www.leparisien.fr/culture-loisirs/cinema/dominique-besnehard-sur-la-mort-danouk-aimee-cetait-une-reveuse-angoissee-18-06-2024-TRZJAPG7QBEHXEVON5IFM2IEMU.php.

23.   "Zoom." Vol. I, in collaboration with Jean-Pierre Thomas, 25 Oct. 1966.

24.   Hollier and Bloc. *A New History of French Literature*, p. 783.

25.   Beauvoir, Simone de. *Le Deuxième sexe* II. Paris, Gallimard, 1976 [1949], p. 453.

26.   de Baecque. *Godard*.

27.   Douchet, Jean. *Nouvelle Vague*. Cinémathèque française, Paris, Hazan, 1998.

28-29.   In Bergala. *Godard au travail: les années 60*, p. 104, note 5.

30-32.   de Baecque. *Godard*.

33.   Godard. *Introduction à une veritable histoire du cinéma*, p. 69.

34.   How, Desson. "Truffaut & Life's Auteur Edge." *The Washington Post*, 25 July 1999, www.washingtonpost.com/archive/lifestyle/style/1999/07/25/truffaut-38/a9ec5401-d932-4d79-8ea5-426469ab-b4c7/.

35.   Sellier. *La Nouvelle Vague: un cinéma au masculin singulier*.

Chapter Seven: *Macha Méril: La Femme Censurée,*
The Censored Woman

1.   MacCabe, Colin. *Godard: A Portrait of the Artist at Seventy*. Farrar, Straus and Giroux, 2003.

2-4.   "JLB/MM." Interview with Macha Méril. *Une femme mariée*, Criterion Collection, DVD, 2010.

5.   Godard. *Introduction à une véritable histoire du cinéma*.

6.   "Regarding the Film Censorship Commission." JSTOR, www.jstor.org/stable/42773510; CNC, www.cnc.fr/a-propos-du-cnc/les-dates-cles-du-cnc_1242898.

7.   "JLB/MM." Interview with Macha Méril.

8.   *L'Avant-scène*, no. 461, Mar. 1965.

9.   "JLB/MM." Interview with Macha Méril.

10.   *L'Avant-scène*, no. 461.

11.   "Une femme mariée (ex- 'La femme mariée')." *L'Avant-scène*, no. 461.

12.   "JLB/MM." Interview with Macha Méril.

13.   Chapier, Henry. "Une femme mariée de Jean-Luc Godard: Une

14. comédie insolente et farfelue des mœurs contemporaines…" *Combat*, 7 Dec. 1964.

14. Debord, Guy. *La Société du spectacle*. Paris, Gallimard, 1992.

15. MacCabe. *Godard: A Portrait of the Artist at Seventy*.

16. "JLG/ADB." Interview with Antoine de Baecque. *Une femme mariée*, Criterion Collection, DVD, 2010.

17. "JLB/MM." Interview with Macha Méril.

18. Vanier, Alain. "Jean-Luc Godard: Une vision fragmentée du monde." *Les Lettres Françaises*, 17 Sept. 1964.

19. "JLB/MM." Interview with Macha Méril.

20. Thevoz, Michel. "Collages : Une femme mariée (ex-La femme mariée)." *Cahiers du cinéma*, no. 163, Feb. 1965, p. 80.

21. "JLB/MM." Interview with Macha Méril.

22. *L'Avant-scène*, no. 461.

23. "JLB/MM." Interview with Macha Méril.

24. "Jacques Rivette parle de son film 'La Religieuse'." L'INA, 9 May 1966, fresques.ina.fr/festival-de-cannes-fr/fiche-media/Cannes00411/jacques-rivette-parle-de-son-film-la-religieuse.html.

25. Nort, Antoinette. "Les 'Religieuses' de Diderot et Rivette." *Diderot et le temps*, Stéphane Lojkine and Adrien Paschoud, ed. Aix-en-Provence, Presses universitaires de Provence, 2016.https://doi.org/10.4000/books.pup.10698.

26-27. Talu. "Interview with Anna Karina."

28. Karina, Anna. "An Evening with Anna Karina." Moderated by Melissa Anderson, 11 May 2016, Brooklyn, BAM Rose Cinemas, www.youtube.com/watch?v=3cAGQpBWil8.

29. Frappat, Hélène. *Jacques Rivette, secret compris*. Paris, Cahiers du cinéma, 2001.

30. Talu. "Interview with Anna Karina."

31-32. Macheret, Mathieu. "Reprise : 'La Religieuse,' quand Jacques Rivette créait un scandale d'Etat." *Le Monde*, 19 Sept. 2018, www.lemonde.fr/cinema/article/2018/09/19/reprise-la-religieuse-quand-jacques-rivette-creait-un-scandale-d-etat_5357095_3476.html.

33. Karina. "An Evening with Anna Karina." Moderated by Melissa Anderson.

34. Frappat. *Jacques Rivette, secret compris*.

35. Macheret. "Reprise : 'La Religieuse,' quand Jacques Rivette créait un scandale d'Etat."

36. "Jacques Rivette parle de son film 'La Religieuse'."

37. de Gaulmyn, Isabelle. "French Catholicism and the rupture of Vatican II." La Croix International, 9 Feb. 2018, international.la-croix.com/news/religion/french-catholicism-and-the-rupture-of-vatican-ii/6899.

38-39. Teicher, Jordan G. "Why is Vatican II So Important?" NPR, 10 Oct. 2012, www.npr.org/2012/10/10/162573716/why-is-vatican-ii-so-important.

40. "Vatican II Aggiornamento." Carroll College, www.carroll.edu/about/history/catholic-history-heritage/vatican-ii#:~:text=Saint%20John%20XXIII%20stated%20that,to%20date%E2%80%9D%20in%20Italian).

41. Pepino, John. "Anatomist of the Catholic collapse in France and beyond." *The Catholic World Report*, 13 Sept. 2022, www.catholicworldreport.com/2022/09/13/anatomist-of-the-catholic-collapse-in-france-and-beyond/.

42. Karina. "An Evening with Anna Karina." Moderated by Melissa Anderson.

43. Truffaut, François and Helen Scott. *"Mon petit Truffe, ma grande Scottie": Correspondance 1960-1965*. Serge Toubiana, ed. and comments, Paris, Denoël, 2023.

44. de Baecque, Antoine and Serge Toubiana. *François Truffaut*. Paris, Gallimard, 1996, pp. 351-2.

45-46. Truffaut and Scott. *"Mon petit Truffe, ma grande Scottie."*

47. Lelouch, Claude. *A Man and a Woman: 37 Years Later*. DVD, 1994.

48. Pillet, Elie. "'Toutes les secondes de sa vie, elle les a consacrées au mot amour,' pluie d'hommages pour Anouk Aimée." *Le Figaro*, 18 June 2024, www.lefigaro.fr/cinema/toutes-les-secondes-de-sa-vie-elle-les-a-consacrees-au-mot-amour-pluie-d-hommages-pour-anouk-aimee-20240618.

49. Simon, Alex. "Claude Lelouch." *The Hollywood Interview*, Apr. 2008.

50-51. Pillet. "'Toutes les secondes de sa vie, elle les a consacrées au mot amour,' pluie d'hommages pour Anouk Aimée."

52. Lelouch, Claude. *Ma vie pour un film*. Interviews with Yonnick Flot, Paris, Lherminier, 1986, p. 109.

53. Lelouch, Claude. "37 ans plus tard avec Claude Lelouch." *Les Films 13*, DVD, 2003.

54. Lelouch. *Ma vie pour un film*, pp. 19-20.

55. Lelouch, Claude. "Le cinéma de Claude Lelouch en 13 vidéos." L'INA, 26 Oct. 2017, "Passeurs d'histoires: vidéo '2011 - Lycée : la section cinéma reçoit Claude Lelouch'." [Lelouch stated: "My mother hid me in movie theaters when I was little. We were hunted by the Gestapo…I think that cinema started by saving my life."]

Chapter Eight: *Jean Seberg: L'Américaine à Paris*, **The American in Paris**

1-6. McGee, Garry. *Jean Seberg Breathless: Her True Story*. Bear Manor Media, 2007.

7. Willoughby, Christopher. *Bob Willoughby: A Cinematic Life*. Chronicle Chroma, 2022.

8. McGee. *Jean Seberg Breathless*.

9. Willoughby. *Bob Willoughby: A Cinematic Life*.

10-11. McGee. *Jean Seberg Breathless*.

12. Willoughby. *Bob Willoughby: A Cinematic Life*.

13-15. McGee. *Jean Seberg Breathless*.

16. Truffaut, François. "Otto Preminger, *Bonjour tristesse*," 1958 in Truffaut, *The Films in My Life*, translated by Leonard Mayhew, Simon & Schuster, 1978 [1975 Paris, Flammarion].

17-18. McGee. *Jean Seberg Breathless*.

19. Fotiade, Ramona. *A bout de souffle: French Film Guide*. Bloomsbury, 2013.

20. Andrew, Dudley, ed. *Breathless: Jean-Luc Godard, director*, Rutgers University Press, 1988.

21. McGee. *Jean Seberg Breathless*.

22. Godard, Jean-Luc, in Emmanuel Laurent, *Deux de la Vague*, DVD, 2010.

23. Fotiade. *A bout de souffle: French Film Guide*.

24. Laurent. *Deux de la Vague* [*Two in the Wave*], trailer, 2010, Unifrance, www.youtube.com/watch?v=aljJS8YltdE.

25-33. McGee. *Jean Seberg Breathless*.

34-35. Cavett, Dick and Jean-Luc Godard, "Jean-Luc Godard : Part I," dir. Richard Romagnola, *The Dick Cavett Show* (1975-1982). CBS, 1980.

36. McGee. *Jean Seberg Breathless*.

37. "One can see what possibilities of error exist in an art composed of disrespect, where reticence, as it were, is unable to hide its secrets; the most religious of arts, since it values man above the essence of things a reveals the soul within the body: in the cinema, in other words." Godard, Jean-Luc. *Godard on Godard*, Jean Narboni and Tom Milne, ed. Da Capo Press, 1972.

38. McGee. *Jean Seberg Breathless*.

39. Andrew, ed. *Breathless: Jean-Luc Godard*.

40. "Françoise Giroud à propos de la nouvelle vague Grand Ecran," 15 Feb. 1973. L'INA.

41-43. McGee. *Jean Seberg Breathless*.

44. Laurent, *Deux de la vague*, trailer.

45-48. McGee. *Jean Seberg Breathless*.

49. Melville, Herman. "The Confidence-Man: His Masquerade." Online Literature, www.online-literature.com/melville/confidence-man/1/.

50-61. McGee. *Jean Seberg Breathless*.

Chapter Nine: *Françoise Dorléac: La Femme Réelle*, **The Real Woman**

1. "Claude Berthod écoute Françoise Dorléac." *Elle*, 10 July 1964. Bibliothèque du Film Archives: François Truffaut collection 006 B005.

2-3. Ferenczi, Aurélien. *Framboise: Quelques hypothèses sur Françoise Dorléac*, Lyon, Institut Lumière, 2024.

4. Press conference Unifrance – Archives from the Bibliothèque du Film, Fonds François Truffaut 006 B005.

5. Manceau, Michèle. "La Peau douce, François Truffaut." *L'Express*, 14 May 1964.

6. "François Truffaut commente quelques scènes du film." *La Peau douce*, MK2, DVD, Feb. 2002.

7. Ferenczi. *Framboise*.

8. Letter January 1, 1964, Films du Carrosse archives, "Helen Scott" dossier in de Baecque and Toubiana. *François Truffaut*.

9. Ferenczi. *Framboise*.

10-11. Sadoul, Georges. "La Peau douce." *Lettres françaises*, 4 May 1964.

12. "François Truffaut commente quelques scènes du film." *La Peau douce*.

13. Interview with Raymond Bellour and Jean Michaud. "'La peau douce'

donnera de l'amour une image anti-poétique." *Lettres françaises*, 30 Oct. 1963.

14. Fabre, Claude. "Quelques instants avec F. Truffaut." *Liberté-Lille*, 13 Sept. 1964.
15. "François Truffaut commente quelques scènes du film." *La Peau douce*.
16. Gillain, Anne. *François Truffaut, le secret perdu*. Paris, Hatier, 1991.
17. Chapier, Henry. "Les films de Cannes à Paris." Combat, 23 May 1964.
18. Gillain. *François Truffaut, le secret perdu*.
19. Barthes, Roland. *Fragments d'un discours amoureux*. Paris, Seuil, 1977.
20. "François Truffaut commente quelques scènes du film." *La Peau douce*.
21. "Tough Love… *The Soft Skin* (*La Peau douce*) 1964." I Thank You Arthur, 29 May 2022, ithankyouarthur.blogspot.com/2022/05/tough-love-soft-skin-la-peau-douce-1964.html.
22. Gillain. *François Truffaut, le secret perdu*.
23. "Claude Berthod écoute Françoise Dorléac." *Elle*.
24-25. Harper, Dan. "La Peau douce." *Senses of Cinema*, no. 86, May 2018, www.sensesofcinema.com/2018/cteq/la-peau-douce/.
26. Ferenczi. *Framboise*.
27. *Le Roman de François Truffaut*. Special edition of *Cahiers du cinéma*, Dec. 1984.
28. Truffaut, François. *Les Aventures d'Antoine Doinel*. Paris, Ramsay, 1987, p. 143; and phrases from the diary of Truffaut, 6 June 1950, in de Baecque and Toubiana. *François Truffaut*, p. 106.
29. "François Truffaut, entretien avec Yvonne Baby." *Le Monde*, no. 8356, 25 Nov. 1971.
30. Kristeva, Julia. *Histoires d'amour*. Paris, Denoël, 1983.
31. Vanoye, Francis. "Ford, Fonda, Wayne." Conference, "L'autobiographie en procès", Colloque Nanterre (18 oct. 1996) 1997, no 14, RITM. Recherches interdisciplinaires sur les textes modernes, Université de Paris X, Centre de recherches interdisciplinaires sur les textes modernes, Nanterre, p. 120.
32. Truffaut's description of Doinel.
33. Toubiana, Serge. Commentary, *Baisers volés*, MK2, DVD.
34. Lachenay, Robert. Testimony in *Le Roman de François Truffaut*, p. 15, *Cahiers du cinéma*, special edition, Dec. 1984. In de Baecque and Toubiana, *François Truffaut*, p. 48.
35. *Cahiers du cinéma*, special edition, Dec. 1984. In de Baecque and Toubiana, *François Truffaut*, p. 96.

Chapter Ten: *Haydée Politoff: Le Blason Moderne*,
The Modern Blazon

1. *Blasons anatomiques du corps féminin*, E. Sansot & Cie., Paris 1907 [published from the 1550 edition] with preface, notes and a glossary by the bibliophile AD**B***.
2. See Francis Vanoye, *L'Emprise du cinéma*. Lyon, Aléas, 2005. Vanoye notes the relationship between creation and the artist's desire that "nourishes his creation from what he sees and what he desires…The model offers itself, sacrifices itself on the altar of pictoral creation. See also Laurence Schifano. "Le Portrait ovale, syndrome filmique?" pp. 73-85.
3. "Parlons cinema, Éric Rohmer," 1977 [French television] https://www.youtube.com/watch?v=SrmFEzBKvLU
4. Baudelaire, Charles. "A une passante," *Fleurs du mal*. https://fleurs-dumal.org/poem/224
5. de Baecque, Antoine and Noël Herpe, *Éric Rohmer, biographie*, Paris, Stock , 2014.
6. In de Baecque and Herpe, *Éric Rohmer*.
7. Rohmer, Eric. "Jeunesse de Jean Renoir," *Cahiers du cinéma*, no. 102, December 1959, in Eric Rohmer, *Goût de la Beauté*, Paris, Flammarion, 1989, p. 265.
8. Ebert, Roger. "Let's Talk about Sex," RogerEbert.com, May 14, 2012, https://www.rogerebert.com/reviews/great-movie-la-collectionneuse-1967
9-12. de Baecque and Herpe, *Éric Rohmer*.
13. Interview with Jackie Raynal. 16 March 2011. In de Baecque and Herpe, *Éric Rohmer*.
14-16. "Parlons cinema, Éric Rohmer," 1977.
17. de Baecque and Herpe, *Éric Rohmer*; "Parlons cinema, Éric Rohmer," 1977.
18. In de Baecque and Herpe, *Éric Rohmer*.
19-21. de Baecque and Herpe, *Éric Rohmer*.

22. Ebert. "Let's Talk about Sex."
23. de Baecque and Herpe, *Éric Rohmer*.
24-25. "Parlons cinema, Éric Rohmer," 1977.
26. de Baecque and Herpe, *Éric Rohmer*.
27. Hugo, Victor. *Les Misérables* Vol. I, book 3, 1817, III: Quatre à quatre.
28. Murphy, Kathleen, "La Belle Dame Sans Merci," *Film Comment*, vol. 28, no. 6, Nov.-Dec. 1992.
29. Wakeman, Gregory. "Jules and Jim: The Relationship That's Still Taboo," BBC.com, January 25, 2022. https://www.bbc.com/culture/article/20220124-jules-and-jim-the-relationship-thats-still-taboo
30-32. How, Desson. "Truffaut & Life's Auteur Edge," *The Washington Post*, 25 July, 1999. https://www.washingtonpost.com/archive/lifestyle/style/1999/07/25/truffaut-38/a9ec5401-d932-4d79-8ea5-426469ab-b4c7/
33. Wakeman. "Jules and Jim: The Relationship That's Still Taboo."
34. Truffaut and Scott. *"Mon petit Truffe, ma grande Scottie."*
35. How. "Truffaut & Life's Auteur Edge."
36-37. de Baecque and Herpe, *Éric Rohmer*.
38. Vadim. *Bardot, Deneuve, Fonda*.

Chapter Eleven: *Françoise Fabian: La Femme Libérée*,
The Liberated Woman

1-5. Dialogue with Françoise Fabian and Frédéric Bonnaud. Cinémathèque Française, 30 July 2018, Paris [From the retrospective Françoise Fabian 2-9 July 2018]. Vimeo, https://vimeo.com/282267424.
6. "Françoise Fabian à propos du film Ma nuit chez Maud." *Pour le cinéma*, Pierre Mignot, dir., Frédéric Rossif and Robert Chazal, prod., 1969. L'INA, https://www.ina.fr/ina-eclaire-actu/video/i00006620/francoise-fabian-a-propos-du-film-ma-nuit-chez-maud.
7. Dialogue with Françoise Fabian and Frédéric Bonnaud. Cinémathèque Française.
8. "Françoise Fabian à propos du film Ma nuit chez Maud." *Pour le cinéma*.
9. Rohmer, Éric. *Six Moral Tales*. The Criterion Collection.
10-13. Dialogue with Françoise Fabian and Frédéric Bonnaud. Cinémathèque Française.
14-15. "*La bonne année* [making-of] with Claude Lelouch, Françoise Fabian." L'INA, https://www.youtube.com/watch?v=gpm41OVNC5Q.
16. Dialogue with Françoise Fabian and Frédéric Bonnaud. Cinémathèque Française.
17-21. Eustache, Jean. *La Maman et la putain*. [script] Paris, Cahiers du cinéma, 1986.

Chapter Twelve: *Delphine Seyrig: La Femme en Évolution*,
The Evolving Woman

1. Weinraub, Judith. "She Looked Good Being Passive, but…" *The New York Times*, 31 July 1976.
2. Mulvey. "Visual Pleasure and Narrative Cinema."
3-5. Brangé, Mireille. *Delphine Seyrig: Une vie*. Paris, Nouveau Monde, 2018.
6. Weinraub. "She Looked Good Being Passive, but…"
7-11. Brangé. *Delphine Seyrig*, notes 65, 80, 107, 199.
12. Raganelli and Wickler. "Portrait of Actress Delphine Seyrig," 1977.
13. Seyrig, Delphine. "Delphine Seyrig on Last Year at Marienbad." Berkeley Art Museum and Pacific Film Archive, 1977, bampfa.org/news/audio-archive-delphine-seyrig.
14. Brangé. *Delphine Seyrig*, note 253.
15. Seyrig. "Delphine Seyrig on Last Year at Marienbad."
16. Brangé. *Delphine Seyrig*.
17. Lagier, Luc. "Dans le labyrinth de Marienbad." Studio Canal Image, PdJ Production, 2005. YouTube, www.youtube.com/watch?v=xVt-6K5Nk6Os.
18-21. Brangé. *Delphine Seyrig*. notes 270 and 263.
22. Raganelli and Wickler. "Portrait of Actress Delphine Seyrig."
23-24. Lagier. "Dans le labyrinth de Marienbad."
25. Brangé. *Delphine Seyrig*.
26. Raganelli and Wickler. "Portrait of Actress Delphine Seyrig.".
27. Seyrig. "Delphine Seyrig on Last Year at Marienbad."
28. In Brangé. *Delphine Seyrig*.
29. Vincendeau, Ginette. "Ginette Vincendeau on Last Year in Marienbad." The Criterion Collection, 2009, www.criterionchannel.com/videos/ginette-vincendeau-on-last-year-at-marienbad.

30.   Seyrig. "Delphine Seyrig on Last Year at Marienbad."
31.   In Brangé. *Delphine Seyrig*, note 280.
32.   Raganelli and Wickler. "Portrait of Actress Delphine Seyrig.".
33-34.   "L'invité du Dimanche: Delphine Seyrig on *Muriel*." 1969. The Criterion Channel. https://www.criterionchannel.com/videos/l-invite-du-dimance-delphine-seyrig-on-muriel
35.   Seyrig. "Delphine Seyrig on Last Year at Marienbad."
36-37.   Raganelli and Wickler. "Portrait of Actress Delphine Seyrig.".
38.   Brangé. *Delphine Seyrig*.
39.   Seyrig, Delphine. "Delphine Seyrig on Last Year at Marienbad."
40.   On Marguerite Duras's *India Song*. The Criterion Collection, www.criterion.com/films/31904-india-song.
41.   Raganelli and Wickler. "Portrait of Actress Delphine Seyrig."
42.   In Brangé. *Delphine Seyrig*.
43.   "Chantal Akerman and Delphine Seyrig on Jeanne Dielman." *Les Rendez-vous du Dimanche*, Chantal Akerman and Delphine Seyrig with Michel Drucker, 16 Feb. 1976. The Criterion Channel, www.criterionchannel.com/videos/chantal-akerman-and-delphine-seyrig.
44.   Weinraub. "She Looked Good Being Passive, but…"
45.   Mulvey, Laura. "The Greatest Film of All Time: *Jeanne Dielman, 23 quai du Commerce, 1080 Bruxelles*." *Sight and Sound,* 1 Dec. 2022, www.bfi.org.uk/sight-and-sound/features/greatest-film-all-time-jeanne-dielman-23-quai-du-commerce-1080-bruxelles.
46-48.   Raganelli and Wickler. "Portrait of Actress Delphine Seyrig.".
49-50.   "Chantal Akerman and Delphine Seyrig on Jeanne Dielman." *Les Rendez-vous du Dimanche*.
51-52.   Weinraub. "She Looked Good Being Passive, but…"
53.   Murray, Ros. "The Practice of Disobedience." *Another Screen*, www.another-screen.com/the-practice-of-disobedience.
54.   Weinraub. "She Looked Good Being Passive, but…"
55.   Mangolte, Babette. *Calamity Jane & Delphine Seyrig: A Story*, 2019. Metrograph, metrograph.com/film/?vista_film_id=9999003414.
56-57.   Grasset, Mathilde. "Babette Mangolte à l'ombre des sequoias." *Cahiers du cinéma*, 19 Apr. 2024, www.cahiersducinema.com/actu-alites/babette-mangolte-a-lombre-des-sequoias/.
58.   Weinraub. "She Looked Good Being Passive, but…"

Chapter Thirteen: *Agnès Varda: La Réalisatrice*, The Director

1.   Varda, Agnès. "Cléo from 5 to 7: Remembrances." 2005. The Criterion Channel, www.criterionchannel.com/videos/cleo-from-5-to-7-re-membrances.
2.   Adler, Laure. *Agnès Varda*. Paris, Gallimard, 2023.
3.   Myers, Owen. "Agnes Varda: 'I Fought for Radical Cinema All My Life'." *The Guardian*, 29 Mar. 2019, www.theguardian.com/film/2019/mar/29/agnes-varda-last-interview-i-fought-for-radical-cinema-all-my-life.
4.   Adler. *Agnès Varda*.
5.   Varda. "Cléo from 5 to 7: Remembrances."
6.   Adler. *Agnès Varda*.
7.   Kline, T. Jefferson, ed. "Introduction." *Agnès Varda Interviews*. University Press of Mississippi, 2014.
8.   Koresky, Michael. "Cléo de 5 à 7." [program notes]. *The Complete Films of Agnès Varda*, The Criterion Collection, p. 29.
9.   "Sight & Sound Greatest Films of All Time Poll, 2022." 1 Dec. 2022, *Sight and Sound*, www.bfi.org.uk/news/revealed-results-2022-sight-sound-greatest-films-all-time-poll.
10.   Adler. *Agnès Varda*.
11-12.   Varda, Agnès. "Cléo from 5 to 7: Remembrances."
13.   "Academy Visual History with Agnès Varda." Interview by Manouchka Kelly Labouba, 9 Nov. 2017, Academy Museum of Motion Pictures, www.youtube.com/watch?v=_RR1361-7nw.
14.   Varda. "Cléo from 5 to 7: Remembrances."
15.   Capdenac, Michel. "Agnès Varda: The Hour of Truth." *Les Lettres françaises*, no. 922, 12-18 Apr. 1962. Translated by T. Jefferson Kline. In *Agnès Varda Interviews*.
16.   Varda. "Cléo from 5 to 7: Remembrances."
17.   Nana says that she performed at the Châtelet theatre in *Pacifico*. This operetta opened at the Porte Saint-Martin in November 1958. It also featured Corinne Marchand. "Vivre sa vie: A to Z." *Senses of Cinema*, 2008, www.sensesofcinema.com/2008/before-the-revolution/vivre-sa-vie-a-to-z/.
18.   Capdenac, Michel. "Agnès Varda: The Hour of Truth." *Les Lettres françaises*, no. 922, 12-18 Apr. 1962. Translated by T. Jefferson Kline in *Agnès Varda Interviews*.

19-22.   Varda. "Cléo from 5 to 7: Remembrances."
23-25.   Vincendeau, Ginette. "A Woman's Truth." *The Complete Films of Agnès Varda*, The Criterion Collection, 2020.
26.   Varda. "Cléo from 5 to 7: Remembrances."
27-31.   Varda, Agnès. *Cléo de 5 à 7* [script]. Audrey Diwan and Véronique Le Bris, prefaces. Paris, Gallimard, 2023.
32.   Varda. "Cléo from 5 to 7: Remembrances."
33.   "Academy Visual History with Agnès Varda." Interview conducted by Manouchka Kelly Labouba.
34.   Varda. *Cléo de 5 à 7* [script].
35.   Varda. "Cléo from 5 to 7: Remembrances."
36.   Varda. *Cléo de 5 à 7* [script].
37-38.   Kline. "Introduction." *Agnès Varda Interviews*; Capdenac. "Agnès Varda: The Hour of Truth."
39.   Varda. *Cléo de 5 à 7* [script].
40-42.   Capdenac. "Agnès Varda: The Hour of Truth."
43.   Varda. *Cléo de 5 à 7* [script].
44.   Capdenac. "Agnès Varda: The Hour of Truth."
45-47.   Varda. "Cléo from 5 to 7: Remembrances."
48.   "Academy Visual History with Agnès Varda." Interview by Manouchka Kelly Labouba.
49.   Varda. *Cléo de 5 à 7* [script].
50.   Varda. "Cléo from 5 to 7: Remembrances."
51.   Capdenac. "Agnès Varda: The Hour of Truth."
52.-53. Varda. "Cléo from 5 to 7: Remembrances."
54.   Capdenac. "Agnès Varda: The Hour of Truth."
55.   "Academy Visual History with Agnès Varda." Interview by Manouchka Kelly Labouba.
56-57.   Raganelli and Wickler. *Les Femmes sont de nature creative: Agnès Varda*.
58.   Hattenstone, Simon. "Agnès Varda: 'I Am Still Alive, I Am Still Curious, I Am Not a Piece of Rotting Flesh'." *The Guardian*, 21 Sept. 2018, www.theguardian.com/film/2018/sep/21/agnes-varda-i-am-still-alive-i-am-still-curious-i-am-not-a-piece-of-rotting-flesh.
59.   Varda, Agnès. "*Sans toit ni loi*: Souvenirs, entretiens, notes et commentaires 18 ans après la sortie du film." 2002. Criterion Collection, DVD.
60-61.   Raganelli and Wickler. *Les Femmes sont de nature creatives*.
62.   Varda, Agnès. "*Salut les Cubains* Introduction." Criterion Collection, DVD.
63.   Varda, Agnès. "*Black Panthers* Introduction". Criterion Collection, DVD.
64.-65. Varda, Agnès. "*Lions Love and Lies* Introduction." 2014. Criterion Collection, DVD,
66.   Varda, Agnès. "*Réponse de femmes* Introduction." 2017. Criterion Collection, DVD.
67-68.   Raganelli and Wickler. *Les Femmes sont de nature creatives*.
69-72.   Varda,. "*Sans toit ni loi*: Souvenirs, entretiens, notes et commentaires 18 ans après la sortie du film."
73.   For the Patatutopia exhibit, see: https://www.nathalieobadia.com/artists/62-agnes-varda/works/9924-agnes-varda-patatutopia-2003/

Chapter Fourteen: *Nouvelles Femmes, Nouvelles Voix*, New Women, New Voices

1.   Truffaut and Scott. "*Mon petit Truffe, ma grande Scottie*."
2.   Mintzer. "Anna Karina, Radiant Actress, Jean-Luc Godard's Muse Dies at 79."
3.   Talu. "Interview: Anna Karina."
4.   Anna Karina interview with Emmanuelle Sterpin.
5-6.   Whyte. "Anna Karina Interview 1973."
7.   Karina, Anna. *Vivre ensemble*. 1973. Laurent Bourdon, DVD booklet.
8-11.   Whyte. "Anna Karina Interview 1973."
12.   Anna Karina interview with Emmanuelle Sterpin.
13-14.   Talu. "Interview: Anna Karina."
15.   "Jeanne Moreau, 1972." *Tête d'affiche*.
16.   Moreau, Jeanne. *Jeanne par Jeanne Moreau*. Paris, Gallimard, 2023.
17-18.   "Jeanne Moreau, 1972." *Tête d'affiche*.
19.   Hudson, David. "New Wave Muses Behind the Camera." *The Daily*, 1 Aug. 2022, www.criterion.com/current/posts/7886-new-wave-muses-behind-the-camera.
20-21.   "Emmanuelle Riva récite ses poèmes." *Discorama*. ORTF, 1969, www.ina.fr/ina-eclaire-actu/video/i13044998/emmanuelle-riva-re-cite-des-poemes.

22. "Photos of Hiroshima by *Hiroshima mon amour* Star Emmanuelle Riva (1958)." Open Culture, 14 Oct. 2014, www.openculture.com/2014/10/photos-of-hiroshima-by-hiroshima-mon-amour-star-emmanuelle-riva.html.

23. *Hiroshima 1958*. Shashasha, www.shashasha.co/en/book/hiroshima-1958.

24. "Macha Méril: Livres, bibliographie." Book Node, booknode.com/auteur/macha-meril/livres.

25. "Macha Méril, comédienne et écrivain, défend son oeuvre à l'occasion des Belles pages de Guéthary." France 3- Nouvelle-Aquitaine, 28 Aug. 2020, www.youtube.com/watch?v=hws7qG0QiLl.

26. Williams, James S. "Anne Wiazemsky Obituary." *The Guardian*, 10 Oct. 2017, www.theguardian.com/film/2017/oct/10/anne-wiazemsky-obituary.

27. Wiazemsky, Anne. *Une année studieuse*. Paris, Gallimard Folio, 2012.

28. Hudson, David. "Anne Wiazemsky 1947-2017." The Criterion Collection, 5 Oct. 2017, www.criterion.com/current/posts/5006-the-daily-anne-wiazemsky-1947-2017.

29-32. McGee. *Jean Seberg Breathless*.

33-34. Castro, Catherine. "À la recherche de Marie-France Pisier." *Marie Claire*, www.marieclaire.fr/marie-france-pisier,1373895.asp.

35. Pisier, Marie-France. "La misogynie prend le visage du paternalisme." ORTF, 22 May 1970, www.youtube.com/watch?v=Ebg8KarhA3E.

36. "Marie-France Pisier à propos de la misogynie." *Le petit cinéma de Georges de Caunes*, 22 May 1970, www.ina.fr/ina-eclaire-actu/video/i21103012/marie-france-pisier-a-propos-de-la-misogynie.

37. Castro. "À la recherche de Marie-France Pisier."

38. Bergan, Ronald. "Marie-France Pisier obituary." *The Guardian*, 25 Apr. 2021, www.theguardian.com/film/2011/apr/25/marie-france-pisier-obituary.

39. Pisier, Marie-France. *Le Bal du gouverneur*. Paris, Grasset, 1990.

40. Castro. "À la recherche de Marie-France Pisier."

41. Servat. "The Temptress of St. Tropez."

42. Goldsztajn, Iris. "How Do You Solve a Problem like Brigitte Bardot?" *Vogue*, 21 June 2023, www.vogue.com/article/how-do-you-solve-a-problem-like-brigitte-bardot.

43. Servat. "The Temptress of St. Tropez."

44.-46. Dupont, Joan. "Searching for Nelly Kaplan." *Film Quarterly*, vol. 71, no. 4, Summer 2018, filmquarterly.org/2018/06/08/searching-for-nelly-kaplan/.

47-49. Flitterman-Lewis, Sandy. "Of Marceline Loridan Ivens." *Another Gaze*, 30 Dec. 2018, www.anothergaze.com/marceline-loridan-ivens/.

Conclusion: *Looking Back, Moving Forward*

1. Berry, Dennis. Chloé. 1996. [The New Yorker, www.newyorker.com/magazine/2015/06/08/saint-joan.]

2. Raganelli and Wickler. *Les Femmes sont de nature creatives*.

3. Brody, Richard. "In 'Be Pretty and Shut Up!,' Actresses Challenge the Male-Run Movie Business." *The New Yorker*, 23 June 2021, www.newyorker.com/culture/the-front-row/in-be-pretty-and-shut-up-actresses-challenge-the-male-run-movie-business.

4. Hansen-Løve, Mia. *Cahiers du cinéma*, no. 806, Feb. 2024, pp. 66-7.

5-6. "Delphine Seyrig and Marguerite Duras on Women's Cinema." ORTF, 19 Apr. 1975, mediaclip.ina.fr/en/i23131509-delphine-seyrig-and-marguerite-duras-on-women-s-cinema.html.

7. Denoël, Charlotte. "Les Tricoteuses pendant la Révolution française." *L'Histoire par l'Image*, Dec. 2008, histoire-image.org/etudes/tricoteuses-revolution-francaise.

8. "Macha Méril est l'invitée de RTL." *Droits des femmes*.

9. Godrèche, Judith. Speech at 2024 César Awards. *L'Obs*. 24 Feb. 2024, www.nouvelobs.com/cinema/20240224.OBS84877/cesar-2024-le-discours-de-judith-godreche-contre-les-violences-sexuelles-dans-le-cinema.html.

10-11. "Macha Méril est l'invitée de RTL." *Droits des femmes*.

12. Coyle, Jake. "#MeToo Struggled to Find Traction in France Then Judith Godrèche Came Forward." AP News, 15 May 2024, apnews.com/article/metoo-cannes-judith-godreche-8015d6dc14efd-6c00912f8dd824f9985.

13-14. Brody. "In 'Be Pretty and Shut Up!,' Actresses Challenge the Male-Run Movie Business."

15. Ford, Rebecca. "America Ferrera Did That Epic Barbie Monologue '30 to 50 Times'." *Vanity Fair*, 24 June 2023, www.vanityfair.com/hollywood/2023/07/america-ferrera-barbie-monologue-30-to-50-times.

16. Burack, Emily. "Read America Ferrera's Powerful Monologue in Barbie." *Town & Country*, 5 Aug. 2023, www.townandcountrymag.com/leisure/arts-and-culture/a44725030/america-ferrera-barbie-full-monologue-transcript/.

17. Triet, Justine. "Anatomie d'une chute." Viennale, www.viennale.at/en/film/anatomie-dune-chute.

18. Wehrli, Elodie. "L'Événement: une experience du reel." *Pages de gauche*, 6 Oct. 2022, pagesdegauche.ch/levenement-une-experience-du-reel.

SELECTIVE FILMOGRAPHIES

INTRODUCTION

Bernadette Lafont

1957 *Les Mistons* (*The Mischief Makers/The Brats*) (short film) - François Truffaut

1958 *Le Beau Serge* (*Handsome Serge*) - Claude Chabrol

1960 *Les Bonnes Femmes* (*The Good Time Girls*) with Stéphane Audran, Clotilde Joano, Lucile Saint-Simon - Claude Chabrol

1961 *Les Godelureaux* (*Wise Guys*) with Stéphane Audran - Claude Chabrol

1972 *Une belle fille comme moi* (*A Gorgeous Girl Like Me*) - François Truffaut

1973 *La Maman et la Putain* (*The Mother and the Whore*) with Francoise Lebrun and Isabelle Weingarten - Jean Eustache

Claire Maurier

1959 *Les Quatre Cents Coups* (*The 400 Blows*) - François Truffaut (Part 1 in the Doinel Series)

Stefania Sabatini and Yveline Céry

1962 *Adieu Philippine* (*Goodbye Philippine*) - Jacques Rozier

Virginie Vitry and Anne Doat

1956 *Le Coup du Berger* (*Fool's Mate*) (short film) - Jacques Rivette

Juliette Mayniel

1959 *Les Cousins* (*The Cousins*) - Claude Chabrol

1960 *Les Yeux sans visage* (*Eyes without a Face*) with Alida Valli - Georges Franju

Anne Colette

1957 *Tous les garçons s'appellent Patrick* (*All Boys Are Called Patrick*) (short film) with Nicole Berger - Jean-Luc Godard

1958 *Charlotte et son Jules* (*Charlotte and Her Boyfriend*) (short film) - Jean-Luc Godard

Nathalie Baye

1977 *L'Homme qui aimait les femmes* (*The Man Who Loved Women*) - François Truffaut

Stéphane Audran

1960 *Les Bonnes Femmes* (*The Good Time Girls*) - Claude Chabrol

1962 *L'Oeil du malin* (*The Third Lover*) - Claude Chabrol

1968 *Les Biches* (*The Does*) - Claude Chabrol

1969 *La Femme infidèle* (*The Unfaithful Wife*) - Claude Chabrol

Isabelle Huppert

1988 *Une affaire de femmes* (*Story of Women*) - Claude Chabrol

BRIGITTE BARDOT

1952 *Le Trou normand* (*Crazy for Love*) - Jean Boyer

1952 *Manina, la fille sans voiles* (*Manina, the Girl in the Bikini*) - Willy Rozier

1953 *Si Versailles m'était conté* (*Royal Affairs in Versailles*) - Sacha Guitry

1954 *Le Fils de Caroline, chérie* (*Caroline and the Rebels*) - Jean-Devaivre

1955 *Futures vedettes* (*School for Love*) - Marc Allégret (Roger Vadim, screenwriter)

1955 *Les Grandes Manoeuvres* (*The Grand Maneuver*) - René Clair

1955 *Cette sacrée gamine* (*Naughty Girl*) - Michel Boisrond (Roger Vadim, screenwriter)

1956 *En effeuillant la marguerite* (*Plucking the Daisy*) - Marc Allégret (Roger Vadim, screenwriter)

1956 *Et Dieu créa la femme* (*And God Created Woman*) - Roger Vadim

1958 *En cas de Malheur* (*Love is My Profession*) - Claude Autant-Lara

1960 *La Vérité* (*The Truth*) - Henri-Georges Clouzot

1962 *Vie privée* (*A Very Private Affair*) - Louis Malle

1962 *Le Repos du guerrier* (*Love on a Pillow*) - Roger Vadim

1963 *Paparazzi* - Jacques Rozier

1963 *Le Mépris* (*Contempt*) - Jean-Luc Godard

1965 *Viva María!* - Louis Malle

1969 *Les Femmes* (*Women*) - Jean Aurel

1973 *Don Juan 73* (*If Don Juan Were a Woman*) - Roger Vadim

JEANNE MOREAU

1954 *Touchez pas au Grisbi* (*Hands Off the Loot!*) - Jacques Becker

1958 *Ascenseur pour l'échafaud* (*Elevator to the Gallows*) - Louis Malle

1958 *Les Amants* (*The Lovers*) - Louis Malle

1959 *Les Liaisons dangereueses 1960* (*Dangerous Liaisons*) - Roger Vadim

1960 *Moderato cantabile* (adapted from the novel by Marguerite Duras) - Peter Brook

1962 *Jules et Jim* (*Jules and Jim*) - François Truffaut

1963 *La Baie des Anges* (*Bay of Angels*) - Jacques Demy

1965 *Viva María!* with Brigitte Bardot - Louis Malle

1968 *La Mariée était en noir* (*The Bride Wore Black*) - François Truffaut

As director:

1976 *Lumière* (*Light*)

1979 *L'Adolescente* (*The Adolescent*)

1983 *Lilian Gish*

EMMANUELLE RIVA

1959 *Hiroshima mon amour* (*Hiroshima Mon Amour*) - Alain Resnais

1961 *Léon Morin, prêtre* (*Léon Morin, Priest*) - Jean-Pierre Melville

1962 *Thérèse Desqueyroux* (*Therese*) - Georges Franju

ANNA KARINA

1960/1963 *Le Petit Soldat* (*The Little Soldier*) - Jean-Luc Godard

1961 *Ce soir ou jamais* (*Tonight or Never*) – Michel Deville

1961 *Une femme est une femme* (*A Woman Is a Woman*) - Jean-Luc Godard

1962 *Vivre sa vie* (*My Life to Live*) - Jean-Luc Godard

1964 *Bande à part* (*Band of Outsiders*) - Jean-Luc Godard

1964 *Le Voleur du Tibidabo* (*The Thief of Tibidabo*) – Maurice Ronet

1964 *De l'amour* (*All about Loving*) - Jean Aurel

1965 *Alphaville, une étranage aventure de Lemmy Caution* (*Alphaville*) - Jean-Luc Godard

1965 *Pierrot le fou* - Jean-Luc Godard

1966 *Made in U.S.A.* - Jean-Luc Godard

1966 *La Religieuse* (*The Nun*) - Jacques Rivette

1967 *L'Étranger* (*The Stranger*) – Luchino Visconti

1967 *Anna* – Pierre Koralnik

As director:

1973 *Vivre ensemble* (*Living Together*)

2008 *Victoria*

ANOUK AIMÉE

1953 *Le Rideau cramoisi* (*The Crimson Curtain*) - Alexandre Astruc

1961 *Lola* - Jacques Demy

1966 *Un homme et une femme* (*A Man and a Woman*) - Claude Lelouch

1969 *Model Shop* - Jacques Demy

2003 *La Petite prairie aux bouleaux* (*The Birch-Tree Meadow*) - Marceline Loridans-Ivens

Catherine Deneuve

1964 *Les Parapluies de Cherbourg* (*The Umbrellas of Cherbourg*) - Jacques Demy

1967 *Les Demoiselles de Rochefort* (*The Young Girls of Rochefort*) - Jacques Demy

1967 *Belle de jour* - Luis Buñuel

1968 *Manon 70* - Jean Aurel

1969 *La Sirène du Mississippi* (*Mississippi Mermaid*) - François Truffaut

1970 *Peau d'Âne* (*Donkey Skin*) - Jacques Demy

1980 *Le Dernier métro* (*The Last Metro*) - François Truffaut

Marina Vlady

1967 *2 ou 3 choses que je sais d'elle* (*2 or 3 Things I Know About Her*) - Jean-Luc Godard

MACHA MÉRIL

1964 *Une femme mariée* (*A Married Woman*) - Jean-Luc Godard

1967 *Belle de jour* - Luis Buñuel

Laurence de Monaghan, Béatrice Romand, Aurora Cornu

1970 *Le Genou de Claire* (*Claire's Knee*) - Eric Rohmer

Zouzou, Françoise Verley

1972 *L'Amour l'après-midi* (*Love in the Afternoon/Chloe in the Afternoon*) - Eric Rohmer

JEAN SEBERG

1957 *Saint Joan* - Otto Preminger

1958 *Bonjour tristesse* - Otto Preminger

1960 *À bout de souffle* (*Breathless*) - Jean-Luc Godard

1964 *Le Grand escroc* (*The Big Swindler*) segment in episodic film *Les Plus belles escroqueries du monde* (*The World's Most Beautiful Swindlers*) - Jean-Luc Godard

1964 *Lilith* - Robert Rossen

As Director:

1974 *Ballad for Billy the Kid* (short film)

FRANÇOISE DORLÉAC

1964 *L'Homme de Rio* (*That Man from Rio*) - Philippe de Broca

1964 *La Peau douce* (*The Soft Skin*) - François Truffaut

1967 *Les Demoiselles de Rochefort* (*The Young Girls of Rochefort*) - Jacques Demy

Marie-France Pisier

1962 *Antoine et Colette* (*Antoine and Colette*) segment in *L'Amour à vingt ans* (*Love at Twenty*) (Part 2 in the Doinel Series) - François Truffaut

1974 *Céline et Julie vont en bateau* (*Céline and Julie Go Boating*) and cowriter

1979 *L'Amour en fuite* (*Love on the Run*) and cowriter

As director:

1990 *Le Bal du gouverneur* (*The Governor's Party*)

2002 *Comme un avion* (*Like an Airplane*)

Claude Jade

1968 *Baisers volés* (*Stolen Kisses*) (Part 3 in the Doinel Series) - François Truffaut

1970 *Domicile conjugal* (*Bed and Board*) (Part 4 in the Doinel Series) with Delphine Seyrig and Hiroko Matsumoto Berghauer - François Truffaut

1979 *L'Amour en fuite* (*Love on the Run*) (Part 5 in the Doinel Series) with Dorothée with Dani, Marie-France Pisier - François Truffaut

HAYDÉE POLITOFF

1967 *La Collectionneuse* (*The Collector*) (no. 4 in the series) - Éric Rohmer

Catherine Sée

1963 *La Carrière de Suzanne* (*Suzanne's Career*) (short film) - Éric Rohmer

Michelle Girardon and Claudine Soubrier

1963 *La Boulangère de Monceau* (*The Bakery Girl of Monceau*) (short film) - Éric Rohmer

Jacqueline Bisset

1973 *La Nuit américaine* (*Day for Night*) - François Truffaut

FRANÇOISE FABIAN

1967 *Belle de jour* with Catherine Deneuve - Luis Buñuel

1969 *Ma nuit chez Maud* (*My Night at Maud's*) - Éric Rohmer

1973 *La Bonne année* (*Happy New Year*) - Claude Lelouch

Chantal Goya

1966 *Masculin féminin* (*Masculine Feminine*) - Jean-Luc Godard

Francoise Lebrun

1973 *La Maman et la Putain* (*The Mother and the Whore*) with Bernadette Lafont and Isabelle Weingarten - Jean Eustache

DELPHINE SEYRIG

1961 *L'Année dernière à Marienbad* (*Last Year at Marienbad*) - Alain Resnais

1963 *Muriel ou Le Temps d'un retour* (*Muriel, or The Time of Return*) - Alain Resnais

1970 *Peau d'Âne* (*Donkey Skin*) - Jacques Demy

1972 *Le Charme discret de la bourgeoisie* (*The Discreet Charm of the Bourgeoisie*) - Luis Buñuel

As Director:

1974 *Les Trois Portugaises* (*The Three Portuguese Women*) codirected with Carole Roussopoulos and Ioana Wieder

1976 *SCUM Manifesto* codirected with Carole Roussopoulos

1976 *Miso et maso vont en bateau* (*Miso and Maso Go Boating*) codirected with Carole Roussopoulos

1976 *Où est-ce qu'on se "mai"?* codirected with Carole Roussopoulos

1977 *Il ne fait pas chaud* (*It's Not Hot*) codirected with Carole Roussopoulos

1979 *Pour mémoire* (*For Memory*) codirected with Carole Roussopoulos and Ioana Wieder

1981 *Sois belle et tais-toi* (*Be Pretty and Shut Up*)

2019 *Calamity Jane and Delphine Seyrig: A Story* with Babette Mangolte, director

Marguerite Duras (Director)

1967 *La Musica* (*The Music*) codirected with Paul Seban

1969 *Détruire, dit-elle* (*Destroy, She Said*)

1971 *Jaune le soleil* (*The Sun in Yellow*)

1972 *Nathalie Granger*

1974 *La Femme du Gange* (*The Woman of the Ganges*)

1975 *India Song*

1976 *Son nom de Venise dans Calcutta désert* (*Her Venetian Name in Deserted Calcutta*)

1976 *Des journées entières dans les arbres* (*Whole Days in the Trees*)

1977 *Baxter, Vera Baxter*

1977 *Le Camion* (*The Truck*)

1981 *Agatha et les lectures illimitées* (*Agatha and the Unlimited Readings*)

1985 *Les Enfants* (*The Children*)

Chantal Akerman (Director)

1968 *Saute ma ville* (*Blow Up My Town*)

1971 *L'Enfant aimé ou Je joue à être une femme mariée* (*The Beloved Child or I Play at Being a Married Woman*)

1972 *Hotel Monterey*

1972 *La Chambre* (*The Room*)

1974 *Je, tu, il, elle* (*I, You, He, She*)

1975 *Jeanne Dielman, 23, quai du commerce, 1080 Bruxelles*

1977 *News from Home* (*Les Nouvelles d'Amérique*)

1978 *Les Rendez-vous d'Anna* (*The Meetings of Anna*)

AGNÈS VARDA (DIRECTOR)

1955 *La Pointe Courte*

1958 *Ô saisons, ô châteaux* (*O Seasons, O Châteaux*) (short film)

1958 *Du côté de la côte* (*Along the Coast*) (short film)

1958 *L'Opéra-Mouffe* (*Diary of a Pregnant Woman*) (short film)

1961 *Les Fiancés du pont MacDonald* (*The Fiancés of the MacDonald Bridge*)

1962 *Cléo de 5 à 7* (*Cleo from 5 to 7*)

1963 *Salut les Cubains* (*Hello Cubans*) (short film)

1965 *Le Bonheur* (*Happiness*)

1966 *Les Créatures* (*The Creatures*)

1966 *Elsa la Rose* (short film)

1968 *Black Panthers* (short film)

1969 *Lions Love (...and Lies)*

1970 *Nausicaa* (short film)

1975 *Daguerréotypes*

1975 *Réponse de femmes* (*Women Reply*) (short film)

1977 *L'Une chante, l'autre pas* (*One Sings, the Other Doesn't*)

1981 *Mur Murs*

1981 *Documenteur*

1982 *Ulysse* (short film)

1984 *Les Dites Cariatides* (*The So-Called Caryatids*) (short film)

1985 *Sans toit ni loi* (*Vagabond*)

1988 *Jane B. par Agnès V.* (*Jane B. for Agnes V.*)

1991 *Jacquot de Nantes*

1995 *L'Univers de Jacques Demy* (*The World of Jacques Demy*)

2000 *Les Glaneurs et la glaneuse* (*The Gleaners and I*)

2008 *Les Plages d'Agnès* (*The Beaches of Agnes*)

2017 *Visages, Villages* (*Faces Places*)

2019 *Varda par Agnès* (*Varda by Agnes*)

NOUVELLES FEMMES, NOUVELLES VOIX

Marie Dubois

1960 *Tirez sur le pianiste* (*Shoot the Piano Player*) - François Truffaut

1962 *Jules et Jim* (*Jules and Jim*) - François Truffaut

Nadine Trintignant (Director)

1967 *Mon amour, mon amour* (*My Love, My Love*)

1969 *Il est difficile de tuer quelqu'un, même un lundi* (*It's Hard to Kill Someone, Even on Monday*)

1971 *Ça n'arrive qu'aux autres* (*It Only Happens to Others*)

1973 *Défense de savoir* (*Defense of Knowing*)

1976 *Le Voyage de noces* (*The Honeymoon Trip*)

1980 *Premier voyage* (*First Journey*)

Nelly Kaplan (Director)

1961 *Gustave Moreau* (short film)

1963 *Abel Gance, hier et demain* (*Abel Gance, Yesterday and Tomorrow*) (short film)

1967 *Le Regard Picasso* (*Picasso's Eye*)

1969 *La Fiancée du pirate* (*A Very Curious Girl*)

1971 *Papa les petits bateaux* (*Papa the Little Boats*)

1976 *Néa* (*Nea: A Young Emmanuel*)

1979 *Charles et Lucie* (*Charles and Lucie*)

1983 *Abel Gance et son Napoléon* (*Abel Gance and his Napoleon*)

Anne Wiazemski

1967 *La Chinoise* (*The Chinese Girl*) - Jean-Luc Godard

Marceline Loridans-Ivens

1961 *Chronique d'un été* (*Chronicle of a Summer*) - Jean Rouch and Edgar Morin

As director:

1962 *Algérie, année zero*, codirected with Jean-Pierre Sergent

1968 *Le 17ème parallèle* codirected with Joris Ivens

1976 *Comment Yukong déplaça lse montagnes* series codirected with Joris Ivens

1976 *Une histoire de ballon, lycée no. 31 Pékin* series codirected with Joris Ivens

1977 *Les Kazaks* codirected with Joris Ivens

1977 *Les Ouigours* codirected with Joris Ivens

1988 *Une histoire de vent* codirected with Joris Ivens,

2003 *La Petite prairie aux bouleaux* (*The Birch-Tree Meadow*)

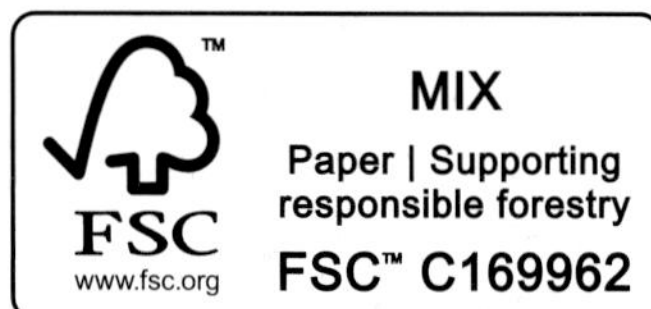

CHRONICLE CHROMA
Chronicle Chroma is an imprint of Chronicle Books.
Los Angeles, California

Follow us on Instagram @chroniclechroma

chroniclechroma.com

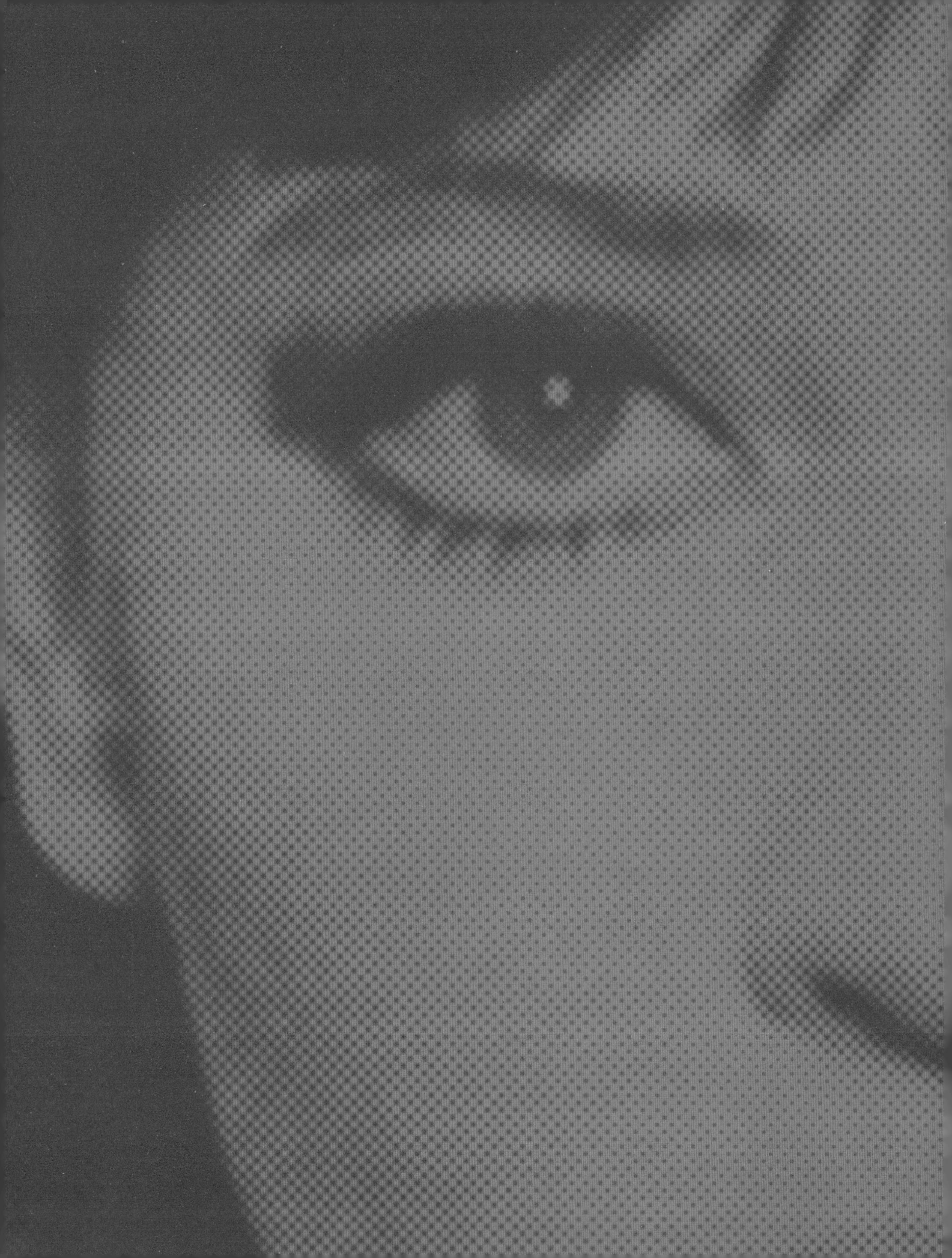